A Companion to American Fiction 1780–1865

Blackwell Companions to Literature and Culture

This series offers comprehensive, newly written surveys of key periods and movements and certain major authors in literary culture and history. Extensive volumes provide new perspectives and positions on contexts and on canonical and post-canonical texts, orientating the beginning student in new fields of study and providing the experienced undergraduate and new graduate with current and new directions, as pioneered and developed by leading scholars in the field.

Published

1	A Companion to Romanticism	*Edited by Duncan Wu*
2	A Companion to Victorian Literature and Culture	*Edited by Herbert F. Tucker*
3	A Companion to Shakespeare	*Edited by David Scott Kastan*
4	A Companion to the Gothic	*Edited by David Punter*
5	A Feminist Companion to Shakespeare	*Edited by Dympna Callaghan*
6	A Companion to Chaucer	*Edited by Peter Brown*
7	A Companion to Literature from Milton to Blake	*Edited by David Womersley*
8	A Companion to English Renaissance Literature and Culture	*Edited by Michael Hattaway*
9	A Companion to Milton	*Edited by Thomas N. Corns*
10	A Companion to Twentieth-Century Poetry	*Edited by Neil Roberts*
11	A Companion to Anglo-Saxon Literature	*Edited by Phillip Pulsiano and Elaine Treharne*
12	A Companion to Restoration Drama	*Edited by Susan J. Owen*
13	A Companion to Early Modern Women's Writing	*Edited by Anita Pacheco*
14	A Companion to English Renaissance Drama	*Edited by Arthur F. Kinney*
15	A Companion to Victorian Poetry	*Edited by Richard Cronin, Antony H. Harrison and Alison Chapman*
16	A Companion to the Victorian Novel	*Edited by Patrick Brantlinger and William B. Thesing*

A Companion to Shakespeare's Works

17	A Companion to Shakespeare's Works, Volume I: The Tragedies	*Edited by Richard Dutton and Jean E. Howard*
18	A Companion to Shakespeare's Works, Volume II: The Histories	*Edited by Richard Dutton and Jean E. Howard*
19	A Companion to Shakespeare's Works, Volume III: The Comedies	*Edited by Richard Dutton and Jean E. Howard*
20	A Companion to Shakespeare's Works, Volume IV: The Poems, Problem Comedies, Late Plays	*Edited by Richard Dutton and Jean E. Howard*

21	A Companion to the Regional Literatures of America	*Edited by Charles L. Crow*
22	A Companion to Rhetoric and Rhetorical Criticism	*Edited by Walter Jost and Wendy Olmsted*
23	A Companion to the Literature and Culture of the American South	*Edited by Richard Gray and Owen Robinson*
24	A Companion to American Fiction 1780–1865	*Edited by Shirley Samuels*
25	A Companion to American Fiction 1865–1914	*Edited by G. R. Thompson and Robert Paul Lamb*

A COMPANION TO

AMERICAN FICTION

1780–1865

EDITED BY **SHIRLEY SAMUELS**

Blackwell
Publishing

BLACKWELL PUBLISHING
350 Main Street, Malden, MA 02148-5020, USA
108 Cowley Road, Oxford OX4 1JF, UK
550 Swanston Street, Carlton, Victoria 3053, Australia

First published 2004 by Blackwell Publishing Ltd

Library of Congress Cataloging-in-Publication Data

A companion to American fiction, 1780–1865 / edited by Shirley Samuels.
p. cm. – (Blackwell companions to literature and culture)
Includes bibliographical references and index.
ISBN 0-631-23422-5 (alk. paper)
1. American fiction–19th century–History and criticism–Handbooks, manuals, etc. 2. American
fiction–18th century–History and criticism–Handbooks, manuals, etc.
I. Samuels, Shirley. II. Title. III. Series.

PS377.C66 2004
813'.209–dc22
2003026891

A catalogue record for this title is available from the British Library.

Set in 11/13 pt Garamond 3
by Kolam Information Services Pvt. Ltd, Pondicherry, India
Printed and bound in the United Kingdom
by TJ International Ltd, Padstow, Cornwall

The publisher's policy is to use permanent paper from mills that operate a sustainable forestry policy, and
which has been manufactured from pulp processed using acid-free and elementary chlorine-free practices.
Furthermore, the publisher ensures that the text paper and cover board used have met acceptable
environmental accreditation standards.

For further information on
Blackwell Publishing, visit our website:
www.blackwellpublishing.com

Contents

List of Illustrations   viii
Notes on Contributors   ix
Acknowledgments   xvi

Introduction   1
Shirley Samuels

PART I   *Historical and Cultural Contexts*   5

1   National Narrative and the Problem of American Nationhood   7
    J. Gerald Kennedy

2   Fiction and Democracy   20
    Paul Downes

3   Democratic Fictions   31
    Sandra M. Gustafson

4   Engendering American Fictions   40
    Martha J. Cutter and Caroline F. Levander

5   Race and Ethnicity   52
    Robert S. Levine

6   Class   64
    Philip Gould

7   Sexualities   75
    Valerie Rohy

8   Religion   87
    Paul Gutjahr

9   Education and Polemic   97
     Stephanie Foote

10   Marriage and Contract   108
     Naomi Morgenstern

11   Transatlantic Ventures   119
     Wil Verhoeven and Stephen Shapiro

12   Other Languages, Other Americas   131
     Kirsten Silva Gruesz

PART II   *Forms of Fiction*   **145**

13   Literary Histories   147
     Michael Drexler and Ed White

14   Breeding and Reading: Chesterfieldian Civility in the Early Republic   158
     Christopher Lukasik

15   The American Gothic   168
     Marianne Noble

16   Sensational Fiction   179
     Shelley Streeby

17   Melodrama and American Fiction   191
     Lori Merish

18   Delicate Boundaries: Passing and Other "Crossings"
     in Fictionalized Slave Narratives   204
     Cherene Sherrard-Johnson

19   Doctors, Bodies, and Fiction   216
     Stephanie P. Browner

20   Law and the American Novel   228
     Laura H. Korobkin

21   Labor and Fiction   239
     Cindy Weinstein

22   Words for Children   249
     Carol J. Singley

23   Dime Novels   262
     Colin T. Ramsey and Kathryn Zabelle Derounian-Stodola

24   Reform and Antebellum Fiction   274
     Chris Castiglia

PART III   *Authors, Locations, Purposes*   285

25   The Problem of the City   287
     Heather Roberts

26   New Landscapes   301
     Timothy Sweet

27   The Gothic Meets Sensation: Charles Brockden Brown,
     Edgar Allan Poe, George Lippard, and E. D. E. N. Southworth   314
     Dana Luciano

28   Retold Legends: Washington Irving, James Kirke
     Paulding, and John Pendleton Kennedy   330
     Philip Barnard

29   Captivity and Freedom: Ann Eliza Bleecker,
     Harriet Prescott Spofford, and Washington Irving's "Rip Van Winkle"   342
     Eric Gary Anderson

30   New England Tales: Catharine Sedgwick, Catherine Brown, and the
     Dislocations of Indian Land   353
     Bethany Schneider

31   Harriet Beecher Stowe, Caroline Lee Hentz, Herman
     Melville, and American Racialist Exceptionalism   365
     Katherine Adams

32   Fictions of the South: Southern Portraits of Slavery   378
     Nancy Buffington

33   The West   388
     Edward Watts

34   The Old Southwest: Mike Fink, Augustus
     Baldwin Longstreet, Johnson Jones Hooper,
     and George Washington Harris   400
     David Rachels

35   James Fenimore Cooper and the Invention of the American Novel   411
     Wayne Franklin

36   The Sea: Herman Melville and *Moby-Dick*   425
     Stephanie A. Smith

37   National Narrative and National History   434
     Russ Castronovo

Index   445

Illustrations

1.1 "Uniola Cottage: Mrs. Gilman's Summer Residence Sullivan's Island"   17

4.1 Illustration from *The Token; or, Affection's Gift*   44

5.1 Frontispiece from *Further Disclosures by Maria Monk*   58

7.1 Title illustration for Ik Marvel, *Reveries of a Bachelor*   82

16.1 "The Widow's Hope"   182

18.1 Runaway slave   209

22.1 Title-page for Clara Arnold (ed.), *The Juvenile Keepsake*   253

23.1 Title-page of Ann Stephens' *Malaeska; The Indian Wife of the White Hunter*   263

24.1 "Huzza for the Rummies! That's the ticket!"   280

25.1 "The Little Pauper"   294

26.1 Title-page from Mrs. C. M. Kirkland, *A Book for the Home Circle*   308

30.1 "Indians Dream of Heaven"   359

31.1 "Life in Philadelphia"   374

33.1 "The Struggle"   391

35.1 "The Expected Canoe"   420

Notes on Contributors

Katherine Adams is Assistant Professor of English at the University of Tulsa, where she teaches courses in nineteenth-century American literature, African American literature, and women's studies. She is the author of several articles on race, gender, and nationalism in American literature. Her current project is a book about the trope of privacy as it operates within various mid-nineteenth-century publics.

Eric Gary Anderson is an Associate Professor of English at Oklahoma State University, where he teaches American, American Indian, and Southern literatures. He is the author of *American Indian Literature and the Southwest: Contexts and Dispositions* (University of Texas, 1999) as well as of numerous essays in books such as *Speak to Me Words: Essays on Contemporary American Indian Poetry* (University of Arizona, 2003) and *South to a New Place: Region, Literature, Culture* (Louisiana State University, 2002). Currently he is working on two research projects, one on early southeastern captivity narratives and one on William Faulkner's environmental imagination.

Philip Barnard teaches in the Department of English at the University of Kansas. He writes on American literature and cultural theory, and has translated and edited fiction and theory by figures including Victor Séjour, Jean-Luc Nancy, and Philippe Lacoue-Labarthe. He is co-editor of *Revising Charles Brockden Brown: Culture, Politics, and Sexuality in the Early Republic* (University of Tennessee Press, 2004).

Stephanie P. Browner is the Dean of the Faculty at Berea College and an Associate Professor in the Department of English, Theatre, and Speech Communication. She is author of a book on literature and the internet, and her book *Profound Science and Elegant Literature: Imagining Doctors in Nineteenth-Century America* (University of Pennsylvania) will be available in 2004.

Nancy Buffington is an Assistant Professor of English at the University of Delaware. She has published essays on Robert Montgomery Bird, the history of African Americans in Delaware, the construction of whiteness, and writing pedagogy. She is co-editor of the composition reader *Living Languages: Contexts for Reading and Writing* (Prentice-Hall, 1997).

Chris Castiglia is Associate Professor of English and Women's Studies at Loyola University, Chicago. He is the author of *Bound and Determined: Captivity, Culture-Crossing, and White Womanhood from Mary Rowlandson to Patty Hearst* (Chicago University Press, 1996) and of *Interior States: The Romance of Reform and the Inner Life of a Nation* (forthcoming from Duke University Press). He is editing, with Glenn Hendler, a critical edition of Walt Whitman's *Franklin Evans* (also forthcoming from Duke), and, with Russ Castronovo, a special issue of *American Literature* on esthetics and American cultural studies.

Russ Castronovo is Jean Wall Bennett Professor of English and American Studies at the University of Wisconsin-Madison. He is the author of *Fathering the Nation: American Genealogies of Slavery and Freedom* (University of California Press, 1995) and *Necro Citizenship: Death, Eroticism, and the Public Sphere in the Nineteenth-Century United States* (Duke University Press, 2001). He is also co-editor (with Dana Nelson) of *Materializing Democracy: Towards a Revitalized Cultural Politics* (Duke University Press, 2002).

Martha J. Cutter is an Associate Professor of English at Kent State University, where she teaches classes on multiethnic literature of the United States, women's literature, and African American writing. Her first book is *Unruly Tongue: Language and Identity in American Women's Fiction, 1850–1930* (University Press of Mississippi, 1999), and she is currently completing a book on contemporary multiethnic American literature. She has published articles in journals such as *American Literature*, *African American Review*, *American Literary Realism*, *MELUS*, *Women's Studies*, *Legacy*, *Criticism*, and *Callaloo*.

Kathryn Zabelle Derounian-Stodola is Professor of English at the University of Arkansas at Little Rock and President of the Society of Early Americanists. She has published widely on the Indian captivity narrative form and on early and nineteenth-century American women's writings. Her most recent book is an edited collection, *Women's Indian Captivity Narratives* (Penguin, 1998). She is currently working on a book-length study of the captivity narratives by whites and Dakotas about the US–Dakota Conflict, entitled *The War in Words: Reading the US–Dakota Conflict of 1862 through the Captivity Literature*.

Paul Downes teaches at the University of Toronto and is the author of *Democracy, Revolution and Monarchism in Early American Literature* (Cambridge University Press, 2002). He is currently working on critical human rights theory and nineteenth-century American literature.

Michael Drexler is an Assistant Professor of English at Bucknell University. His most recent article, "Brigands and Nuns: The Vernacular Sociology of Collectivity after the Haitian Revolution," appeared in *Messy Beginnings: Postcoloniality and Early*

American Studies, edited by Malini Schueller and Edward Watts (Rutgers University Press, 2003).

Stephanie Foote teaches at the University of Illinois at Urbana-Champaign. She is the author of *Regional Fictions* (University of Wisconsin Press, 2001), and is currently at work on two book-length projects. The first, *Impossible People*, is a study of the parvenu and class mobility in the nineteenth century, and the second, *Circulating Women*, is a study of the rise of a queer field of literary production in the twentieth-century United States.

Wayne Franklin is Davis Distinguished Professor of American Literature at Northeastern University. Author of *Discoverers, Explorers, Settlers* (University of Chicago Press, 1979), *The New World of James Fenimore Cooper* (University of Chicago Press, 1982), and *A Rural Carpenter's World* (University of Iowa Press, 1990), he is founding editor of the "American Land and Life" series published by the University of Iowa Press. He also co-edited *Mapping American Culture* (University of Iowa Press, 1993) with Michael Steiner and edited *American Voices, American Lives* (Norton, 1995), and serves as editor for the "Literature to 1700" section of the *Norton Anthology of American Literature*. At present he is finishing work on the first biography of James Fenimore Cooper written since the novelist's papers became available to scholars in 1990.

Philip Gould is Professor of English at Brown University. His most recent work is *Barbaric Traffic: Commerce and Antislavery in the Eighteenth-Century Atlantic World* (Harvard University Press, 2003).

Kirsten Silva Gruesz teaches nineteenth- and twentieth-century literature of the Americas at the University of California, Santa Cruz. Her book *Ambassadors of Culture: The Transamerican Origins of Latino Writing* was published by Princeton University Press in 2002. She has published articles on topics from Spanish print culture in the US borderlands to sentimental poetry to contemporary Central American fiction, and is currently at work on a book about the history of Spanish–English bilingualism in the US.

Sandra M. Gustafson is an Associate Professor of English at the University of Notre Dame. She is currently at work on a book on culture and democracy in the antebellum United States. Her publications include *Eloquence is Power: Oratory and Performance in Early America* (University of Notre Dame Press, 2000) and numerous essays, notably on William Apess, James Fenimore Cooper, Jonathan Edwards, Margaret Fuller, and Deborah Sampson Gannett.

Paul Gutjahr is an Associate Professor of English, American Studies, and Religious Studies at Indiana University. He is the author of *An American Bible: A History of the Good Book in the United States, 1770–1880* (Stanford University Press, 1999), the co-editor of *Illuminating Letters: Essays on Typography and Literary Interpretation* (University of Massachusetts Press, 2001), and the editor of an anthology entitled *Popular*

American Literature of the Nineteenth Century (Oxford University Press, 2001). He has also written numerous articles and book reviews.

J. Gerald Kennedy is William A. Read Professor of English at Louisiana State University. He is the author of *Poe, Death, and the Life of Writing* (Yale University Press, 1987) and *Imagining Paris: Exile, Writing, and American Identity* (Yale University Press, 1993). He recently edited *A Historical Guide to Edgar Allan Poe* (Oxford University Press, 2001) and is co-editor of *Romancing the Shadow: Poe and Race* (Oxford University Press, 2001). He is currently writing a book on literary nationalism, multicultural counter-narratives, and the invention of the American nation, 1820–50.

Laura H. Korobkin, a former lawyer and litigator, is an Associate Professor of English at Boston University. Her publications include *Criminal Conversations: Sentimentality and the Nineteenth-Century Legal Stories of Adultery* (Columbia University Press, 1998), as well as law and literature analyses of *The Scarlet Letter*, *Wieland*, and *Their Eyes Were Watching God*.

Caroline F. Levander is an Associate Professor of English at Rice University. The author of *Voices of the Nation: Women and Public Speech in Nineteenth-Century Literature and Culture* (Cambridge University Press, 1998) and co-editor of *The American Child: A Cultural Studies Reader* (Rutgers University Press, 2003), she has published articles in *American Literature, American Literary History, The Henry James Review,* and *Prospects: An Annual of American Cultural Studies*. She is currently writing a book tentatively entitled "Cradling Liberty: The Child, Race, and Nation Making in North America."

Robert S. Levine is a Professor in the Department of English at the University of Maryland, College Park. He is the author of *Conspiracy and Romance* (Cambridge University Press, 1989) and *Martin Delany, Frederick Douglass, and the Politics of Representative Identity* (University of North Carolina Press, 1997), and has edited a number of volumes, including *The Cambridge Companion to Herman Melville* (Cambridge University Press, 1998), a Bedford Cultural Edition of William Wells Brown's *Clotel* (Bedford Books, 2000), and *Martin R. Delany: A Documentary Reader* (University of North Carolina Press, 2003).

Dana Luciano is an Assistant Professor in the English Department at Georgetown University, where she teaches sex and gender studies and nineteenth-century US literature. She has published essays on Charles Brockden Brown, Catherine Maria Sedgwick, Herman Melville, Henry James, and Pauline E. Hopkins, and has completed a book entitled *Configurations of Mourning: Embodiment, Loss and the Longing for Form in Nineteenth-Century America*. Her current research focuses on the temporality of dissident sexualities.

Christopher Lukasik is an Assistant Professor of English and American Studies at Boston University. He is completing a book entitled *Discerning Characters: Social Distinction and the Face in American Literary and Visual Culture, 1780–1850*.

Lori Merish teaches in the English Department at Georgetown University. The author of *Sentimental Materialism: Gender, Commodity Culture, and Nineteenth-Century American Literature* (Duke University Press, 2000), she is currently completing a book-length study of literature by and about antebellum working-class women, *Laboring Women and the Languages of Class: Sex, Race and US Working-Class Women's Cultures, 1830–1860*.

Naomi Morgenstern is an Assistant Professor in the Department of English at the University of Toronto, where she teaches American literature and critical theory. Her essays have appeared in such journals as *differences*, *Novel*, *Genders*, and *Studies in the Novel*. She is currently completing a manuscript on contract theory and American literature.

Marianne Noble is an Associate Professor of Literature at American University, Washington DC. She is the author of *The Masochistic Pleasures of Sentimental Literature* (Princeton University Press, 2000) and of numerous articles on gothic and sentimental literature. She is currently working on a manuscript on the moral and epistemological limits of sympathy in such authors as Melville, Twain, Dickinson, Alcott, and Whitman.

David Rachels teaches at the Virginia Military Institute. His publications include *Augustus Baldwin Longstreet's Georgia Scenes Completed: A Scholarly Text* (University of Georgia Press, 1998) and *The First West: Writings from the American Frontier, 1776–1860*, co-edited with Edward Watts (Oxford University Press, 2002).

Colin T. Ramsey is an Assistant Professor of American Literature at Appalachian State University in Boone, North Carolina. Along with the early history of dime novels, his research interests include Benjamin Franklin's early career and Indian captivity narratives.

Heather Roberts teaches in the English Department at Clark University.

Valerie Rohy is Assistant Professor of English at the University of Vermont. She is the author of *Impossible Women: Lesbian Figures and American Literature* (Cornell University Press, 2000) and the co-editor of *American Local Color Writing, 1880–1920* (Penguin, 1998). She has also published essays on James Baldwin, Mary Wilkins Freeman, María Cristina Mena, and Pauline Hopkins. Her current book project addresses sexuality, race, and discourses of regression in American literature.

Shirley Samuels is a Professor of English and American Studies at Cornell University. Her most recent book is *Facing America: Iconography and the Civil War* (Oxford Univesity Press, 2004). She is also currently the section editor of "American Literature before 1865" for the Blackwell online project literature-compass.com.

Bethany Schneider is Assistant Professor of English at Bryn Mawr College. She is working on a book entitled *From Place to Populace: State Proliferation and Indian Removal in American Literature, 1820–1840*.

Stephen Shapiro teaches in the Department of English and Comparative Literature at the University of Warwick. A co-editor of *Revising Charles Brockden Brown: Culture, Politics, and Sexuality in the Early Republic* (University of Tennessee Press, 2004), he writes on American literature and cultural materialism, and is preparing a book-length study on Brown, ideology, and the Atlantic world-system.

Cherene Sherrard-Johnson is an Assistant Professor of English at the University of Wisconsin-Madison. She is currently at work on a book that analyzes the artistic exchange between writers and visual artists during the Harlem Renaissance (1917–35).

Carol J. Singley is Associate Professor of English and a Fellow in the Center for Childhood Studies at Rutgers University, Camden, where she co-directs the American Studies program. She is the author of *Edith Wharton: Matters of Mind and Spirit* (Cambridge University Press, 1995), editor of books on Wharton, and co-editor of three volumes of critical essays, including *The American Child: A Cultural Studies Reader* (Rutgers University Press, 2003). She is currently writing a book about adoption narratives in American literature and culture.

Stephanie A. Smith is Associate Professor of English at the University of Florida. She took her Ph.D. from the University of California at Berkeley in 1990, and prior to teaching at Florida she freelanced as a writer and editor. She is co-editor with N. Katherine Hayles of the "Science and Literature" series at Michigan. A novelist, she is the author of *Other Nature* (1995), *The-Boy-Who-Was-Thrown-Away* (1987), and *Snow-Eyes* (1985). Her critical essays appear in *differences*, *Criticism*, *Genders*, and *American Literature*. She also wrote *Conceived by Liberty: Maternal Figures and Nineteenth-Century American Literature* (Cornell University Press, 1995). Recent excerpts from her new book on language and democracy appear in *Body Politics and the Fictional Double* (Indiana University Press, 2000) and *The Cambridge Companion to Women's Writing* (Cambridge University Press, 2001).

Shelley Streeby teaches US cultural studies at the University of California, San Diego. She is the author of *American Sensations: Class, Empire, and the Production of Popular Culture* (University of California Press, 2002) and has also published essays in *American Literary History*, *boundary 2*, and *Criticism*.

Timothy Sweet is Professor of English at West Virginia University. He is author of *Traces of War: Poetry, Photography and the Crisis of the Union* (Johns Hopkins University Press, 1990) and *American Georgics: Economy and Environment in Early American Literature* (University of Pennsylvania Press, 2002).

Wil Verhoeven is Professor of American Culture and Cultural Theory at the University of Groningen, the Netherlands. He is co-editor of the Charles Brockden Brown Electronic Archive and Scholarly Edition (UVA and KSUP) and general editor of a series of ten "Anti-Jacobin Novels" as well as *The Collected Works of Thomas Holcroft* (both for Pickering & Chatto). The author of numerous essays on American literature and culture, he also edited *Revolutionary Histories: Transatlantic Cultural Nationalism, 1775–1815* (Macmillan, 2002) and is currently completing a monograph, *American Arcadia: English Radicals and American Land-Speculators, 1789–1800*.

Edward Watts is Professor of Writing, Rhetoric, and American Cultures at Michigan State University. He is author of *Writing and Postcolonialism in the Early Republic* (University of Virginia Press, 1998) and *An American Colony: Regionalism and the Roots of Midwestern Culture* (Ohio University Press, 2002). He co-edited with Malini Johar Schueller *Messy Beginnings: Postcoloniality and Early American Studies* (Rutgers University Press, 2003) and, with David Rachels, *The First West: Writing from the American Frontier* (Oxford University Press, 2002).

Cindy Weinstein is Associate Professor of Literature at Caltech. She is the author of *The Literature of Labor and the Labors of Literature: Allegory in Nineteenth-Century American Fiction* (Cambridge University Press, 1995) and *Family, Kinship, and Sympathy in Nineteenth-Century American Literature* (Cambridge University Press, 2004), and the editor of *The Cambridge Companion to Harriet Beecher Stowe* (Cambridge University Press, 2004).

Ed White teaches in the English Department at Louisiana State University and is the author of "Early America as Imagined Community" (*American Quarterly*, 2004) and *The Backcountry and the City: Feelings of Structure in Early America* (University of Minnesota Press, forthcoming).

Acknowledgments

My warm thanks to the contributors, whose prompt and engaged responses to the topics were a fabulous learning experience for me. My gratitude to the two graduate students at Cornell who helped with the nitty-gritty of putting out letters and putting together details: Hilary Emmett and Jen Dunnaway. Among the encouraging voices from Blackwell, I'd like to single out Gillian Somerscales as a wonderful copy-editor. And on the home front, always, I save my hugs for John Briggs Seltzer and Ruth Ayoka Samuels.

Shirley Samuels

Introduction

Shirley Samuels

What does American fiction look like in the foundational period of the early republic, from the earliest declarations of nationhood until secession and civil war? This collection of essays sets out to present the current state of criticism in an area that is at once extremely familiar and just beginning to be studied. During the academy's earlier appraisals, critics assumed that nineteenth-century American literature needed time to mature from its dependency on English and European models. Even before such landmark studies as those by F. O. Matthiessen (*American Renaissance*), Richard Chase (*The American Novel and its Tradition*), and Leslie Fiedler (*Love and Death in the American Novel*) in the mid-twentieth century, which defined the terms in which the field was thereafter discussed, the period assumed for such maturation was about two generations past the American Revolution. The notorious coincidence of the deaths of Thomas Jefferson and John Adams on the same day (July 4, 1826) marked the close of the first generation. The next generation reached its writerly potential, as this argument has it, during the 1850s, in a lull before the terrible sectional crisis known as the American Civil War put literary appreciation in the shadow of national violence.

Twentieth-century assessments of early nineteenth-century American literature stressed the dependence on English traditions even as the thematics of nationalism, new landscapes, and new racial and ethnic interchanges produced a form of American exceptionalism. The relation between dependency and exceptionalism still included the assumption that fiction needed to evolve. It scarcely needs saying that this volume stresses neither dependence nor exceptionalism. At the same time, we notice the current critical preoccupation with pointing out the problematics of applying the adjective "American" – more appropriately used of a hemisphere – to literature produced within the boundaries of the United States.

Since the 1970s, as literary critics have joined their enterprises with those of cultural historians, they have found different ways of comprehending the literary productions of the 1780s and following decades. Without reprising the tendentious arguments about American exceptionalism, such critics have described literature in the United States as an enterprise bound up in formative ways with the social, political, and cultural structures of the new nation. In responding to such challenges, this collection includes contributions by critics who present a number of salient approaches to the period. Crucially, they analyze not only fiction but also historical and political crises. These crises place fiction in a context that makes it comprehensible not only as a document of its own time but also as a testament to the shaping power of enterprises like nationalism, class distinctions, gender formation, and the places and displacements associated with race and ethnicity.

Studies of American fiction have been pouring out in recent years, challenging terms set by earlier studies and rendering newly apparent the visibility of fiction in the cultural life of the new nation. Such studies have emphasized, for example, how variant social and sexual formations affected the young men and women who formed associations with each other with purposes ranging from benevolence to social reform. These associations were often described in fictional treatments. Sometimes the fictional treatments were designed to further the purposes of the association, such as the novels published under the auspices of the temperance movement; other, more sensationalized treatments – such as the exposés of George Lippard, the Philadelphia crusader against vice – were published with different ends in view.

The purpose of this new *Companion to American Fiction* is to situate the work of the newest generation of critics who interpret American literature in relation to each other and to earlier critics. The contributions are organized under three broad headings. The first section is designed to orient the reader to the large categories, such as landscape, race, and ethnicity, within which writers produced their works. The second section explains categories of fictional production. Even though some generic treatments overlap with each other and with the third section, which focuses more specifically on individual authors, critical examinations of styles of literary writing in the period are crucial to the overall project of tracing literary forms and purposes. The third section emphasizes more local details such as the way in which James Fenimore Cooper transformed a Revolutionary War anecdote, the engagement of Catharine Sedgwick with Native American land claims, and how Herman Melville imagined himself into the whaling trade.

How are we to account for the persistence of certain authors and the surprising surges into view of others? Persistence can be perplexing, even as critics such as Jane Tompkins have attempted to comprehend it as a quiet form of conspiracy. That Nathaniel Hawthorne, whose now canonical novel *The Scarlet Letter* had a limited readership at publication, has become standard fare for students would have surprised most professors in the New England colleges of his day. Still, Hawthorne had influential friends. Tompkins finds them represented by men like Ralph Waldo Emerson, who walked Hawthorne's casket to its Concord resting place, and she argues that these friends ensured his continuation in the canon. That Susan B. Warner, widely renowned in her lifetime for the intensely private universe of *The Wide, Wide World*, had disappeared from view by the mid-twentieth century would also have surprised nineteenth-century American readers. But the virtues she celebrated, virtues closely allied with Protestant prayer tactics, had become separated from a concept of great literature relying on concepts of esthetic value now understood to be divorced from polemic, let alone religious conversion.

On this view, the separation of value from polemic, as well as the concept of influential friendships, might seem to have promoted Hawthorne's ambiguity over the moral certainty of Warner. Yet, in a thorough reading of Hawthorne's sketches and novels, a reader finds that an obsessive reiteration of moral values pervades his writing. So the question of persistence versus vanishing remains in many ways generational. Readers of the late twentieth century, influenced by a variety of excellent criticism that provided new strategies for understanding value such as Marxism, feminism, race theories, and psychoanalysis, began to study a plethora of texts. Some forms of criticism were clearly canonical: readings of Melville and Hawthorne continue to be popular. Some were antithetical to the canon: many critics represented in this volume have published books on popular culture. As a measure of representative selection now, exactly as many critics in this volume write about Susan B. Warner's *The Wide, Wide World* as write about Nathaniel Hawthorne's *The Scarlet Letter*.

The volume also considers historical, political, and cultural contexts in detail. To study the literature and culture of the early United States must involve at once celebration and shame. The national government celebrated as democratic endorsed what we now see as horrifying practices. These practices included most obviously slavery, but also the abuse and murder of immigrants whose beliefs differed from the norm (such as Irish Catholics), the exploitation of women and children, and the forcible removal of populations whose bodies and concepts of land use stood in the way of an evolving policy of Manifest Destiny. The most famous target of such measures was the Cherokee people, but just as destructively murderous policies were enacted against other Native American tribes and resistant Mexicans. To find in the literature of resistance to such removals qualities of esthetic value to study and even to celebrate may seem distasteful in the face of the historical horrors such literature annotates. Yet the dynamic interchange between historical context and the beauty of an engaged written response can also bear witness to the value of current critical approaches.

In this collection, critics from many backgrounds and diverse regions of the Anglo-European world consider what concepts of value emerge from such interchange. The preparation of an index to track which authors emerge from their vision presents a significant challenge to understanding what it means to make claims on behalf of American fiction before 1865. There seems to be a wonderful persistence of interest in Herman Melville, whose *Moby-Dick* has served for a long while as an avatar of American culture. Here Melville's ambiguous account of the slave trade, "Benito Cereno," attracts more critics. A vivid resurgence of interest in authors who absorbed nineteenth-century audiences, notably Harriet Beecher Stowe, results in an extraordinary number of citations of *Uncle Tom's Cabin*. More surprising, perhaps, is the attention given to the challenging author Charles Brockden Brown, who shows up in several essays as a key author for, variously, accounts of race, gender, sexuality, class, immigration, legal questions, and environmental anxieties.

Over the course of compiling this volume the works of Charles Brockden Brown and Harriet Beecher Stowe have come to stand out as compass points around which a study of American literature to 1865 can be oriented. Indeed, as Ed White and Michael Drexler have argued in their contribution on literary history, Brown's work and its historical reception can be used as a barometer of the state of the field in general. Little appreciated in the years following his death, Brown enjoyed a popular resurgence in the late twentieth century largely owing to Leslie Fiedler's identification of his works as seminal texts of the American incestuous gothic (see chapter 7 by Rohy). Moreover, through their extraordinary allegorical diversity, Brown's novels provide us with a detailed sense of the anxieties plaguing the founders of the fledgling American republic. Such concerns include the frailty of human reason, the threat of the polluting other, whether racial, ethnic, or propertyless, and an anxiety regarding the often violent westward expansion into Indian territory.

For example, Brown's gothic family saga *Wieland* appears here as an allegory of a nation haunted by the potential volatility of democracy. Marianne Noble argues that in this work Brown explores the corruptibility of human reason and the threat to the fundamental democratic ideal of government by the people. Noble sets the stage for Stephanie Browner's discussion of *Arthur Mervyn*, in which she suggests that Brown's depiction of the plague that hit Philadelphia in the 1790s may be read as a medical allegory of national disease and disorder. As Dana Luciano notes, the culpability for this disease and disorder was laid at the door of the ethnically other: the Irish Clithero, the enigmatic Carwin; Robert Levine and Philip Gould extend such identifications of the other to include the racial other, whether African or Native American, and the propertyless, rootless other. In contrast to the certain lack of sympathy for the Native American implied by Levine's reading stands Timothy Sweet's piece on "New Landscapes," in which he argues that the bloody *Edgar Huntly* is a satirical take on Benjamin Rush's account of (and endorsement of) westward settlement. Sweet's essay, then, would seem to show Brown in a more liberal light than do the other contributors, a depiction that is supported by Naomi Morgenstern's piece on Brown's rendering of marriage and contract at the end of the eighteenth century.

Above all, we mean for this volume to serve as an invitation. That invitation most explicitly encourages readers to find in the words of deeply engaged critics a place to engage with fascinating authors. These authors can provide windows on new worlds as well as retelling stories that might have seemed familiar. And as they tell these stories they form the language, the manners, the politics, and the culture of the strange and familiar early republic, the formative world of the early United States.

PART I
Historical and Cultural Contexts

1

National Narrative and the Problem of American Nationhood

J. Gerald Kennedy

In circumstances singular in the history of modern nationalism, the American colonies of the Atlantic seaboard achieved political sovereignty decades before they approached national solidarity. Most subsequent national revolutions in Europe involved the overthrow of dynastic aristocracies by common people already unified by history and tradition. The incongruous beginnings of the United States, however, complicated and indeed obstructed the development of national identity. Geographic- ally far-flung and demographically as well as religiously diverse, the states were "united" (as Jefferson asserted) mainly by their opposition to royal tyranny, and after the British surrender at Yorktown the inherently disunited states confronted a myriad of difficulties on the level of practical governance that long occluded the problem of nation-building. Jefferson had in a sense invented an American nation in the Declaration's sweeping first sentence, which invokes "the laws of nature and of nature's God" to justify the separation of "one people" from another (Jefferson 1984: 19). Yet "the people" rhetorically reified by the pronoun "we" were hardly "one"; the putative nation that transcended the individual states existed nowhere except in Jefferson's eloquent fiction of self-creation. The former colonies could be organized constitutionally into a republic taking its place "among the powers of the earth," but the United States were not a nation in 1776 or in 1787 or even in 1800.

Unlike France, Greece, Germany, or Italy – all of which underwent national revolutions in the wake of the American Revolution – the several states lacked a language uniquely their own, a shared legendary past, or a binding traditional culture. About their want of a metropolitan center James Fenimore Cooper remarked in 1837: "It is not easy for any but close observers, to estimate the influence of such places as London or Paris. They contribute, essentially, to national identity, and national tone, and national policy; in short, to nationality – a merit in which we are almost entirely wanting" (Cooper 1982: 264).

Unlike the emerging nations of Latin America that likewise overcame colonial origins, the United States possessed no dominant religion and its European population was decidedly less homogenous, composed (as Crèvecœur observed) of a "promiscuous breed" of "English, Scotch, Irish, French, Dutch, Germans, and Swedes" (Crèvecœur 1981: 68). In 1790, 40 percent of the white population was non-English, and within a few decades arriving Irish immigrants faced nativist hostility. Spread across disparate states stretching 1,500 miles from north to south and often 300 miles inland, the populace additionally included vast numbers of non-citizens – the folk dismissively termed "merciless Indian savages" in the Declaration, as well as many thousands of black slaves whose very presence could not be acknowledged in that document's final draft. In sum, Jefferson's imagined nation comprised only a portion of the domestic population. Eleven years later, the Constitution's opening phrase ("We, the people of the United States") again begged the question: Who belonged to this problematic "people" aspiring to nationhood?

The issue of national belonging presumed a more basic question, however: the one later posed by Ernest Renan in his lecture "What is a Nation?" Demonstrating by examples from Europe and the Middle East that neither race, language, religion, nor geography – alone or in combination – sufficed to explain the kinship inherent in national belonging, Renan suggested that the nation is ultimately "a spiritual principle" drawn from "a rich legacy of memories" and manifesting itself in a "present-day consent, the desire to live together" (Renan 1990: 19) Yet the assent to communal life, to what Benedict Anderson has called the "imagined community" of the nation, depends not only upon memory but also, as Renan concluded, upon its suppression:

> Forgetting, I would even go so far as to say historical error, is a crucial factor in the creation of a nation, which is why progress in historical studies often constitutes a danger for [the principle of] nationality. Indeed, historical enquiry brings to light deeds of violence which took place at the origin of all political formations, even of those whose consequences have been altogether beneficial. Unity is always effected by means of brutality. (Renan 1990: 11)

Individuals live within national communities precisely because "they have forgotten many things" (Renan 1990: 11) that constitute sources of potential resentment and division. Yet the imperative to reconstruct a national past, to venerate what Anthony D. Smith calls "the myths and memories of the nation" (Smith 1999: 104), ensures that remembering and forgetting will always be locked in a reciprocity fraught with cultural danger and charged by the politics of belonging. And so the nation proves ultimately to be a provisional collectivity, a "daily plebiscite" in Renan's formulation (1990: 19), a virtual community differently conceived by different internal groups, its operative sense of connection depending on a precarious historical consensus secured by forgetfulness, on an official story always threatened by indignant recollection.

Renan's claim that nations arise from "brutality" possesses obvious implications for the singular formation of the American nation – the colonists' wresting of land from a Native population, their subjugation of African Americans, and their simultaneous, contradictory appeal in the Declaration to universal principles of liberty and equality as well as to an exclusionary vision of citizenship. The ethnic heterogeneity, geographical dispersion, religious diversity, and systematic racial oppression (in slavery and Indian removal) that defined the young republic also deeply complicated the forgetting crucial to national unity. Those who produced the images, emblems, songs, and stories of American nationhood found themselves obliged not only to rewrite the past, effacing all that was shameful, but also to ignore or dismiss continuing indignities within the would-be nation. Others, marginalized by national mythology, refused to forget past injustices, instead stirring memory and conscience.

Arguably, nation-building – the multiform, self-conscious construction of ideas and images of nationhood – did not become a general project until the formation of an American mass culture around 1820. And by then the social factors that belied the notion of "one people" made it anything but a unified undertaking. Correcting the view that American literary nationalism was mostly a reaction to British condescension, Robert S. Levine has examined sectional tensions over slavery exposed by the Missouri Compromise of 1820, and he underscores "the crucial role of internal conflict in the formation of the new nation's literatures" (Levine 1998: 225). Regional attachments and varying moral convictions disposed mainstream writers to different degrees of historical candor. Contested from the outset, the vast effort to articulate the identity of an American nation engaged individuals of all regions, classes, and positions. For several decades it absorbed the first generation of native-born professional writers, many of whom labored to create a national literature in the absence of a perceptible nation. The campaign also generated principled opposition: among others, Poe decried the "misapplied patriotism" that cajoled readers into "liking a stupid book the better, because, sure enough, its stupidity is American" (Poe 1984: 506). Literary nationalism likewise inspired counter-narratives by Native American and African American memoirists, insistent upon claiming a place in the nation or challenging the official, self-justifying narratives of the dominant culture.

Nation-building, or what Eric Hobsbawm has wryly called "the invention of tradition," encompassed an array of cultural activities. It encouraged the formation of an education system to inculcate an American ideology; the creation of ceremonies and celebrations to glorify national history; and the erection of monuments to commemorate a heroic past. It hastened the adoption of "America" as the common name of the nation after the popular and poetic "Columbia" had been claimed by a South American nation in 1819. It inspired the compilation of Noah Webster's dictionary of American English (1828) and generated early biographies by Mason Locke Weems, John Marshall, and Jared Sparks that apotheosized George Washington as the nation's savior. It promoted the study of American geography, history, science (native flora and fauna), and archeology. It determined the iconography of the Capitol rotunda in the 1820s and motivated the composition of songs such as Frances Scott

Key's "Defence of Fort McHenry" (1814) and Samuel Francis Smith's national hymn, "America" (1831), defiantly set to the tune of "God Save the King" while extolling the "pilgrims' pride" in a "sweet land of liberty." Within the literary sphere, nation-building also fostered the creation of poems, tales, memoirs, and novels that collect-ively contributed to an overarching national narrative, whose loosely connected elements made up a popular fable representing the struggle for land and freedom by motley Euro-American settlers, even as it obscured their oppression of non-European peoples and masked rifts along lines of region, religion, and ethnicity.

Launched after the War of 1812 by such organs as *The North American Review* in Boston, the call for literary nationalism acknowledged the weight of British cultural authority and the relative immaturity of American culture, but insisted on the worth of native subjects and the imperative to convert them into distinctive works of literature. In an 1820 essay on "National Literature" James Kirke Paulding remarked:

> It has been often observed by such as have attempted to account for the scarcity of romantic fiction among our native writers, that the history of the country affords few materials for such works, and offers little in its traditionary lore to warm the heart or elevate the imagination . . . , though it seems to be without the shadow of a foundation. (Paulding 1976: 132)

By then, unfortunately, American cultural achievement had become a matter of jest; British reviewer Sydney Smith provoked a furor when he asked, "In the four quarters of the globe, who reads an American book? or goes to an American play? or looks at an American picture or statue?" He concluded a series of derisive questions by demanding, "under which of the old tyrannical governments of Europe is every sixth man a Slave, whom his fellow creatures may buy and sell and torture?" (Smith 1976: 157). To assuage self-doubt and proclaim the distinctiveness of their own culture, Euro-Americans turned to literature and the arts in the 1820s to affirm a civic faith in liberty, equality, and opportunity. They underscored the nation's difference from Europe by centering their culture not in metropolitan capitals but rather in relation to the natural wilderness; America was (as Perry Miller observed) "nature's nation." Yet efforts by American novelists to construct stories of national identity often exposed an insistence upon racial superiority as a "chosen people" of Anglo-Saxon origin, especially in stories of early struggle with Indian tribes. A closer examination of a few such works will illustrate the unresolved contradictions that beset other versions of the American national narrative.

Irving's *The Sketch-book* (1819–20; see Irving 1983) offers a prologue. Conceived to reaffirm Anglo-American kinship, the volume flatters British readers with apprecia-tive views of English scenes as it incorporates a handful of pieces suggesting the worth of American materials. Two well-known humorous tales, "Rip Van Winkle" and "The Legend of Sleepy Hollow," project the rise of a Euro-American nation from the storied Hudson valley landscape associated with Irving's Diedrich Knickerbocker. In contrast, however, the Indian sketches "Traits of Indian Character" and "Philip of Pokanoket" raise unsettling questions about the fundamental nature of that nation. Susan Scheckel has observed that, for white Americans of the early nineteenth century, "Indians provided a crucial site of reflection on national identity" (Scheckel 1998: 12), and though Irving does not explicitly ponder American nationhood, the subject haunts his meditations on Indian life. He inserts these sketches (reprinted from the *Analectic Magazine*) into a volume that, in an act of unconscious exclusion, celebrates England as "the land of our forefathers" (Irving 1983: 791), and Irving's own rhetoric inadvertently exposes his racial bias. Although he insists in "Traits" that "the unfortunate aborigines of America" have been "doubly wronged" by white settlers who have called Native people "savage and pagan" (p. 1002) in order to demonize and dispossess them, Irving himself cannot refrain from references to the "savages." Noting that in *The Sketch-book* the Indian pieces follow a description of "Stratford-on-Avon," William L. Hedges has suggested that Irving intended them "to do in some way for his own country what he felt Shakespeare had done for his" (Hedges 1965: 114), to invest the national past with memorable imaginative appeal. But if so, Irving adopted a peculiar strategy: he represents King Philip, or Metacomet, as a proto-national hero, "a patriot attached to his native soil" (Irving 1983: 1028), and Native Americans generally as both courageous and aggrieved, thus implicitly rebuking English and American readers, whose common ancestors perpetrated unspeakable injustices. Insofar as Irving evokes his country's past, he outlines a narrative of persecution too scandalous to be written. He concludes "Traits" by suggesting that should the American poet

> venture upon the dark story of their wrongs and wretchedness; should he tell how they were invaded, corrupted, despoiled; driven from their native abodes and the sepulchres of their fathers; hunted like wild beasts about the earth; and sent down with violence and butchery to the grave; posterity will either turn with horror and incredulity from the tale, or blush with indignation at the inhumanity of their forefathers. (Irving 1983: 1012)

Here Irving identifies the ethical dilemma between shameful remembrance and stubborn denial faced by Euro-American writers of his generation. Compared to his genial sketches of English life, the Indian memorials thus mark a puzzling gesture. If Irving meant to appease nationalists at home and to show British readers the rich material available to American writers, he simultaneously raised troubling questions about the emerging nation and its patently disunited people.

In the decades that followed, a plethora of writers nevertheless took up the challenge of producing tales and novels to articulate a larger narrative that would explain the nation to itself and the world. Homi K. Bhabha insists that the "strange forgetting" observed by Renan "constitutes the *beginning* of the nation's narrative" (Bhabha 1990: 310); if so, the Indian stories of this generation often revealed symptoms of occupational amnesia. The conscientious Hawthorne could publish "Roger Malvin's Burial" (1832), for example, only by "casting certain circumstances judicially into the shade" (Hawthorne 1982: 88), suppressing the bloody details of a preceding militia raid on a local tribe. Cooper, Catharine M. Sedgwick, and Lydia M. Child were among the earliest to produce Indian novels conceived as national stories.

Cooper was the first to embrace fully the challenge of national narrative, and his novels of frontier struggle, beginning with *The Pioneers* (1823), adapted the historical romance popularized by Sir Walter Scott to the vast, complex subject of frontier settlement – the relentless incursion of Euro-Americans into a wilderness inhabited by Native tribes. Inevitably Cooper told the story from the perspective of the dominant culture, yet he decried what was euphemistically called the "disappearance" of the Indian, and his backwoods hero Natty Bumppo (nicknamed Hawk-Eye or Leatherstocking) preferred the company of Chingachgook, his Indian companion, to life in the settlements. As in *The Pioneers* when he denounces the wanton slaughter of passenger pigeons, Natty repeatedly voices Cooper's scorn for the ravages of so-called "civilization." The scout emerged from a minor role in that novel to become the central figure in four subsequent Leatherstocking novels that display his sagacity and self-reliance as they transform him into a distinctive national hero. From *The Last of the Mohicans* (1826) and *The Prairie* (1827) to *The Pathfinder* (1840) and *The Deerslayer* (1841), Cooper portrayed different historical phases in the westward advance of Euro-American settlers, capturing as well particular epochs in their hostilities with Native Americans. Revealingly, his heroic frontier scout suffers from both indignation at the decimation of Native tribes and fits of racial pride in which he rails against Indian savagery while boasting of his Anglo-Saxon bloodlines. From such unrecognized contradictions the narrative of the nation began to emerge.

Motivated by Cooper's example, Child launched her literary career with the 1824 novel *Hobomok*. Reared in Massachusetts, where Daniel Webster and others were extolling the Puritans not simply as New England's founders but also as the fathers of the nation, Child felt obliged to honor their "persevering fortitude" (Child 1986: 6) in a historical narrative that nevertheless exposed, in the person of Mr. Conant, the patriarchal harshness of their theology. Deriving her plotline from *Yamoyden*, a narrative poem about King Philip's war, she tells the story of Mary Conant, a free-thinking Puritan daughter who becomes an outcast, marrying an Indian named Hobomok after Charles Brown, her banished Anglican lover, has been reportedly lost at sea. Child casts Hobomok as a "good" Indian who warns the Puritans of impending attacks by local tribes; as Carolyn L. Karcher explains, the author "had not yet begun to contest the Puritan chroniclers' version of the wars that decimated the Indians, as she would five years later in a book aimed at arousing opposition to the U.S. government's 'crooked and narrow-minded policy' toward Indians: *The First Settlers of New-England* (1829)" (Karcher 1994: 22).

The unexpected reappearance of Brown, however, produces a turn reflective of the buried racial politics of literary nationalism. Deferring to Brown's prior claim on Mary's heart, Hobomok privately arranges an Indian divorce and abandons his wife (and their infant son) to disappear into the wilderness, leaving Brown and Mary free to wed. As critics have noted, Hobomok thus personifies the vanishing American, and young Charles Hobomok Conant, as Brown's adopted son, meanwhile matriculates at Harvard (and an English university), drops his Indian name, and rarely mentions his father, concealing his mixed blood in acts of forgetfulness that signify his repudiation of Native American ethnicity and his identification with an ostensibly superior Anglo-Saxon culture.

Two years later in *The Last of the Mohicans* Cooper revisited many of the same problems. Nina Baym argues that the novel challenges the representation of "gender relations" in *Hobomok* and aims to correct Child's "dangerously mistaken view of female generic power" as it relates to interracial relationships (Baym 1992: 22, 25). In Cooper's tale, set in New York during the French and Indian War, Cora and Alice Munro, the daughters of the British commanding officer at Fort William Henry, create most of the plot's narrative complications by traversing dangerous terrain and exposing themselves to capture by Indians. Around a bloody historical event, the massacre of surrendering British troops by vengeful Huron Indians, Cooper weaves a harrowing tale of capture, disguise, and rescue. Significantly, the budding romance between fair Alice and a Southern colonist, Major Duncan Heyward, projects the incipient formation of a Euro-American people. Conversely, the attraction of the Huron chief Magua to dark-haired Cora poses the national threat of miscegenation, and though Cooper also hints that the heroic and worthy Uncas, son of Chingachgook, secretly loves Cora, he disposes of the problem of interracial marriage by staging the deaths of all three characters in the novel's climactic struggle. As if to explain the attraction of two Indians to Cora, the author reveals that Colonel Munro's elder daughter was the product of his first marriage in the West Indies to a woman of mixed (white and African) blood. Thus, despite the fact that Cooper (through Munro) laments slavery and (through Magua) recites manifold injustices heaped upon Native people by Euro-Americans, he still refuses to envision a future American nation – the progeny of Cora and Uncas – uniting European, Native American, and African blood. In fact, he has Natty Bumppo repeatedly proclaiming himself "a man without a cross" (mixed blood) to valorize the principle of racial purity for an emerging American people. Published just after Congress approved the policy of Indian removal, *The Last of the Mohicans* overtly mourns the disappearance of Native people and covertly rationalizes their elimination.

Responding to both Child and Cooper, Sedgwick conceived a somewhat more liberal vision of a multicultural nation in her 1827 novel, *Hope Leslie*. Set in New England at the time of the Pequod massacre by the Puritans, the narrative graphically recounts that atrocity to explain the attack on the Fletcher household where two young Pequod captives, Oneco and his sister Magawisca, have been informally adopted. In the assault, which claims the lives of Mrs. Fletcher and an infant child, Chief Mononotto reclaims his two children and takes young Everell Fletcher captive, intending to sacrifice him. The novel's defining symbolic moment occurs when the heroic Magawisca saves her beloved Everell from a violent death but loses her arm in the process. Her mutilation signifies both her devotion and the contaminating influence of Anglo culture. In a scene reminiscent of Hobomok's renunciation, she later blesses Everell's union with Hope Leslie, the plucky English lass who rescues her from prison, and withdraws into the forest, concluding that "the Indian and the white man can no more mingle, and become one, than day and night" (Sedgwick 1998: 349). Yet the destiny of Hope's sister Faith (or Mary) somewhat qualifies this gloomy augury of national disunity. Taken captive in the raid that ended Mrs. Fletcher's life, Faith weds Oneco and embraces Native American life so completely that she even forgets the English language. Sedgwick (like Child) thus uses interracial marriage to challenge the notion of Anglo-Saxon cultural superiority and to suggest a viable bond between white women and Indians, both victims of patriarchal Puritan authority. Like Cooper, however, she cannot conceive of a multicultural nation, and her Indians at last vanish into the wilderness. Yet her tale of early America balances respect for certain Puritan figures (notably John Winthrop and John Eliot) with a frank revelation of the dominant culture's misdeeds as well as a poignant representation of American history from an Indian perspective.

Child, Cooper, and Sedgwick responded to the call for national narratives with works that located in the complicated, often bloody relations between white settlers and Indians a defining story that helped to explain what made the proto-national American culture of the 1820s different from English culture. So too did William Gilmore Simms, whose 1835 novel *The Yemassee* portrayed the destruction of a South Carolina tribe by English colonists as a solemnly tragic event. Others, however, conceived of the Indian novel in a more zealously nationalistic (that is, ethnocentric) fashion. Robert Montgomery Bird's *Nick of the Woods* (1837) demonizes Native Americans while revealing the genocidal terrorism of the aptly named Nathan Slaughter, who passes as a non-violent Quaker but proves to be the murderous "Nick of the Woods," a legendary Indian hater. The real menace of the novel, according to Joshua David Bellin, is an "interculturalism" that "defies racial, cultural, and even individual purity and integrity" (Bellin 2001: 27); Bird sees extermination as the final solution to threatened admixture.

The Cherokee controversy of 1829 (which inspired Child's *First Settlers*) and Andrew Jackson's implementation of Indian removal in 1830 seemed literally and figuratively to deny Native Americans a place in the emerging nation and thus raised the stakes of literary nationalism. Although few Indians had access to formal education or literacy, Native voices entered the debate that hinged on whether America was to be a civic nation, defined by equal constitutional rights, or an ethnic nation, rooted in a Eurocentric idea of cultural identity. One early Native participant in this conversation was David Cusick (Tuscarora), whose *Sketches of Ancient History of the Six Nations* (1827) traced the development of the Iroquois Confederacy as a significant example of representative government, refuting white stereotypes about Indian lawlessness. Another arresting intervention was James Seaver's 1824 biography of Mary Jemison, a white woman who (like her fictional counterparts, Mary Conant and Faith Leslie) had renounced Euro-American "civilization" for a Native American life and identity. Even more important for the construction of a national narrative were the writings of William Apess, a Pequod Indian of mixed blood who traced his ancestry to

King Philip. Apess's *A Son of the Forest* (1829) presents an autobiographical memoir of American self-making that highlights the author's service during the War of 1812 (in the face of the government's denial to "Natives" of "the right of citizenship") and his subsequent conversion to Christianity (Apess 1992: 31). As Cheryl Walker notes, Apess's own deeply conflicted writing depends on "irony and mimicry," and his "Eulogy on King Philip" (1836) occupies a crucial place in Native American counter-narratives of the nation, for there, perhaps taking a cue from Irving's "Philip of Pokanoket," Apess compares King Philip to George Washington, extolling the chief as "a personification not only of Indian America but of the nation America should aspire to become, a nation of justice for both whites and peoples of color" (Walker 1997: 167). While the US army waged war in the 1830s and 1840s on such tribes as the Sac, Fox, and Seminoles, Native Americans such as Black Hawk and George Copway also published personal narratives that in different ways challenged exclusionary national fables.

The campaign to construct a national literature produced many narratives concerned with other aspects of American history and cultural development. Cooper's first important novel, *The Spy* (1821), unfolding the story of the mysterious double agent Harvey Birch, ushered in a vogue for historical romances set during the American Revolution. Eliza Cushing and John Neal both soon contributed narratives evoking the national rebellion that profoundly divided the American people into rebels and Tories. Cushing's *Ticonderoga* (1824) underscores these internal divisions: though a "lover of freedom," Captain Courtland feels bound to serve the King, while his daughter Catherine ardently supports the American cause; she finally weds the brave American officer Captain Grahame, who saves her father from the hatchet of Ohmeina, a Mohawk fighting with the Americans. On the eve of America's golden jubilee, Cooper's *Lionel Lincoln* (1825) looks back exactly fifty years, as does Child's pre-revolutionary historical romance, *The Rebels*. Like *The Spy*, Sedgwick's *The Linwoods* (1835) incorporates the larger-than-life figure of George Washington; the plot illustrates the way such novels tended, in Shirley Samuels's view, to project the Revolution as a family conflict fusing "politics and domesticity" (Samuels 1996: 62). The subject of the American Revolution also attracted John Pendleton Kennedy, the author of *Horse-Shoe Robinson* (1835), and prompted a spate of novels by Simms, which included *The Partisan* (1835) and *The Kinsmen* (1841). Novels of the Revolution served several cultural purposes: they evoked the nation's founders at a time when the last survivors of the "heroic generation" were passing from the scene; they permitted the fictional differentiation of American national character from that of England; and at the same time they paradoxically reminded many Americans of their blood kinship with the Anglo-Saxon English.

Kennedy and Simms also helped to articulate a version of the national story especially concerned with the history of the American South and its "peculiar institution," slavery. Conceived in response to the rise of abolitionism, Kennedy's *Swallow Barn* (1832) exemplifies the plantation novel, idealizing the Virginia estate of Frank Meriwether as a scene of "feudal munificence" (Kennedy 1986: 71). There, gracious repasts and genteel diversions advance the halting courtship of Bel Tracy and Ned Hazard. A late chapter connects the putatively chivalric world of the plantation with the beginnings of the nation through the figure of Captain John Smith, dubbed "the True Knight of the Old Dominion" (p. 500). Kennedy represents Meriwether's slaves as "happy under his dominion" (p. 34), and while the master later concedes that slavery is "theoretically and mortally wrong" (p. 455), he paternalistically deems it necessary to the ultimate welfare of his servants. Beverley Tucker's *George Balcombe* (1836) and Caroline Gilman's *Recollections of a Southern Matron* (1838) both project similar visions of gentility and comfort, contingent upon slave labor. Many of Simms's novels also express, as Mary Ann Wimsatt observes, "the ideals of the ruling class" (Wimsatt 1989: 38). In response to Stowe's anti-slavery novel, *Uncle Tom's Cabin* (1852), Simms revived a popular figure from his early work, Captain Porgy, to produce, in the 1850s, a handful of comic Revolutionary War novels, such as *Woodcraft* (1854), which extract humor from the vociferous, doglike loyalty of Porgy's faithful slave, Tom. The plantation novel tacitly appealed to Jefferson's notion of the yeoman farmer as the quintessential American democrat; the freedom and autonomy enjoyed by the plantation owner seemed, in the Southern narrative, a realization of the Declaration's promises. Northern, abolitionist versions of plantation life painted a different picture.

Slave memoirists and autobiographers likewise challenged the pastoral ideal with jarring counter-narratives of bondage, cruelty, and humiliation. As we see in William Grimes's 1825 narrative, former slaves often played upon the rhetoric of American nationalism to underline the monstrous irony of their unfree condition. In closing his account, Grimes mordantly remarks:

> If it were not for the stripes on my back which were made while I was a slave, I would in my will, leave my skin a legacy to the government, desiring that it might be taken off and made into parchment, and then bind the constitution of glorious happy *and free* America. Let the skin of an American slave bind the charter of American Liberty. (Grimes 1999: 232)

Moses Roper concludes his 1838 narrative by insisting that whatever cruelties he has experienced, he loves the free institutions of the nation and hopes that America will "soon be indeed the land of the free" (Roper 1999: 520). The most famous of all slave memoirs, the 1845 narrative by Frederick Douglass, recounts a tale of Franklinesque self-education and Emersonian self-reliance, thus consciously Americanizing his transformation from a degraded slave to a free man. Douglass would later pen a novella, "The Heroic Slave" (1853), which boldly conjures the legacy of the Revolution in the slave rebellion led by Madison Washington, whose very name recalls Virginia's tradition of patriotism. Through such rhetorical moves, African American writers attempted to insert their own story of struggle within a larger national narrative.

Figure 1.1 "Uniola Cottage: Mrs. Gilman's Summer Residence, Sullivan's Island." Frontispiece from Caroline Gilman, *Recollections of a Southern Matron and a New England Bride* (Philadelphia: J. W. Bradley, 1860). Collection of Shirley Samuels.

The clamorous project of American nation-building reached a crescendo during the presidential election of 1844, when James K. Polk scored an improbable victory by campaigning for the annexation of Texas and territorial expansion. The following year, John L. O'Sullivan popularized the belief that America had a "Manifest Destiny" to occupy the continent, and the subsequent Mexican War confirmed US imperial ambitions. But nationalistic fervor did not produce national unity; Thoreau and Douglass were among many writers who opposed the war. In "Some Words with a Mummy," Poe satirized the arrogance of a nation that imagined itself the epitome of progress and cultural superiority, slyly alluding to the disconcerting election of Polk. The Compromise of 1850, a last maneuver in the attempt to save the Union, marked a historical turning point and heralded a brief, spectacular flood of national narratives – Hawthorne's *The Scarlet Letter* (1850) and *The House of the Seven Gables* (1851); Melville's *Moby-Dick* (1851); Stowe's *Uncle Tom's Cabin*; William Wells Brown's *Clotel* (1853); Thoreau's *Walden* (1854); and John Rollin Ridge's *The Life and Adventures of Joaquín Murieta* (1854), among others. In diverse ways all construct quintessentially American stories to articulate judgments about the underlying nature of the inchoate nation – some, perforce, from the perspective of minority exclusion. In retrospect, the implicit narrative of Whitman's poem "Song of Myself" (1855) marks the first compelling evocation of a democratic, multiracial America. Soon eclipsed by the spectacle of civil war, Whitman's precarious vision of national unity resolved the conflicts and contradictions that had from the outset bedeviled novelists, haunted literary nation-building, and thwarted the achievement of American nationhood. Whether the multicultural population of the United States could finally achieve the oneness of its motto (*E pluribus unum*) by rectifying those past injustices that impeded forgetfulness would be the test of the modern era and the burden of all subsequent narratives of the American nation.

REFERENCES AND FURTHER READING

Anderson, Benedict (1991). *Imagined Communities: Reflections on the Origin and Spread of Nationalism*, rev. edn. New York and London: Verso.

Apess, William (1992). *A Son of the Forest* (first publ. 1829). In *On Our Own Ground: The Complete Writings of William Apess, A Pequot*, ed. Barry O'Connell. Amherst: University of Massachusetts Press.

Baym, Nina (1992). "Putting Women in their Place: *The Last of the Mohicans* and other Indian Stories." In Nina Baym, *Feminism and American Literary History: Essays*. New Brunswick: Rutgers University Press.

Bellin, Joshua David (2001). *The Demon of the Continent: Indians and the Shaping of American Literature*. Philadelphia: University of Pennsylvania Press.

Bhabha, Homi K. (1990). "DissemiNation." In Homi K. Bhabha, ed., *Nation and Narration*. London: Routledge.

Child, Lydia Maria (1986). *Hobomok and other Writings of Indians*. New Brunswick, NJ: Rutgers University Press. (First publ. 1824.)

Cooper, James Fenimore (1982). *Gleanings in Europe: England*, ed. Donald A. Ringe, Kenneth W. Staggs, James P. Elliott, and R. D. Madison. Albany: State University of New York Press. (First publ. 1837.)

Crèvecœur, J. Hector St. John de (1981). *Letters from an American Farmer*, ed. Albert E. Stone. New York: Penguin. (First publ. 1782.)

Grimes, William (1999). *Life of William Grimes, the Runaway Slave* (first publ. 1825). In *I Was Born a Slave: An Anthology of Classic Slave Narratives*, ed. Yuval Taylor. Chicago: Lawrence Hill.

Hawthorne, Nathaniel (1982). *Tales and Sketches*, ed. Roy Harvey Pearce. New York: Library of America.

Hedges, William L. (1965). *Washington Irving: An American Study, 1802–1832*. Baltimore: Johns Hopkins University Press.

Hobsbawm, Eric, and Ranger, Terence, eds. (1983). *The Invention of Tradition*. Cambridge: Cambridge University Press.

Irving, Washington (1983). *The Sketch-book of Geoffrey Crayon, Gent.* (first publ. 1819–20). In *History, Tales and Sketches*, ed. James W. Tuttleton. New York: Library of America.

Jefferson, Thomas (1984). "A Declaration by the Representatives of the United States of America, in General Congress Assembled" (first publ. 1776). In *Writings*, ed. Merrill D. Peterson. New York: Library of America.

Karcher, Carolyn L. (1994). *The First Woman in the Republic: A Cultural Biography of Lydia Maria Child*. Durham, NC: Duke University Press.

Kennedy, John Pendleton (1986). *Swallow Barn: or, A Sojourn in the Old Dominion*. Baton Rouge: Louisiana State University Press. (First publ. 1832.)

Levine, Robert S. (1998). "Section and Nation: The Missouri Compromise and the Rise of 'American' Literature." *REAL: Yearbook of Research in English and American Literature* 14, 223–40.

Miller, Perry (1967). *Nature's Nation*. Cambridge, Mass.: Belknap/Harvard University Press.

Paulding, James Kirke (1976). "National Literature" (first publ. 1820). In Richard Ruland (ed.), *The Native Muse: Theories of American Literature*, vol. 1. New York: E. P. Dutton.

Poe, Edgar Allan (1984). Review of Drake and Halleck (first publ. 1836). In *Essays and Reviews*, ed. G. R. Thompson. New York: Library of America.

Renan, Ernest (1990). "What is a Nation?" (first publ. 1882). In Homi K. Bhabha (ed.), *Nation and Narration*. London: Routledge.

Roper, Moses (1999). *A Narrative of the Adventures and Escape of Moses Roper from American Slavery* (first publ. 1838). In *I Was Born a Slave: An Anthology of Classic Slave Narratives*, ed. Yuval Taylor. Chicago: Lawrence Hill.

Samuels, Shirley (1996). *Romances of the Republic: Women, the Family and Violence in the Literature of the Early American Nation*. New York: Oxford University Press.

Scheckel, Susan (1998). *The Insistence of the Indian: Race and Nationalism in Nineteenth-Century American Literature*. Princeton: Princeton University Press.

Sedgwick, Catharine Maria (1998). *Hope Leslie; or, Early Times in the Massachusetts*, ed. Carolyn L. Karcher. New York: Penguin. (First publ. 1827.)

Smith, Anthony D. (1999). *Myths and Memories of the Nation*. New York: Oxford University Press.

Smith, Sydney (1976). Review of Seybert's *Statistical Annals of the United States* (first publ. 1820). In Richard Ruland (ed.), *The Native Muse: Theories of American Literature*, vol 1. New York: E. P. Dutton.

Walker, Cheryl (1997). *Indian Nation: Native American Literature and Nineteenth-Century Nationalism*. Durham, NC: Duke University Press.

Wimsatt, Mary Ann (1989). *The Major Fiction of William Gilmore Simms: Cultural Traditions and Literary Form*. Baton Rouge: Louisiana State University Press.

2
Fiction and Democracy

Paul Downes

Pausing in the *Autobiography* to recall his early delight in reading, Franklin pays tribute to John Bunyan, the author of *The Pilgrim's Progress* (1678):

> Honest John was the first that I know of who mix'd Narration and Dialogue, a Method of Writing very engaging to the Reader, who in the most interesting parts finds himself as it were brought into the Company, & present at the Discourse. De foe in his Cruso, his Moll Flanders, Religious Courtship, Family Instructor, and other Pieces, has imitated it with Success. And Richardson has done the same in his Pamela, &c. – (Franklin 1987: 1326)

Fiction, in Franklin's brief account, is a uniquely inviting genre – a genre that distinguishes itself by its attempt to represent the spoken voice and by its capacity to generate an appealing sensation of presence. Fiction, Franklin suggests, opens its doors to the reader and speaks to him or her in what feels like the present tense. In other words, there is something *democratic* about the method of writing that Franklin associates with Bunyan, Defoe, and Richardson. These prototypical novels do not confront the reader with the impermeable visage and authoritative voice of an absolute monarch; their very success depends upon participation, and, from an economic perspective if no other, upon as wide a participation as possible.

Fiction breaks down conceptual barriers, then; but it also, as Franklin's words remind us, performs another kind of magic. The reader of Bunyan, Defoe, Richardson, or, for that matter, Susanna Rowson, "finds himself *as it were* brought into the Company, & present at the Discourse." The presence that fiction offers, in other words, does not come about without a passage through that curious "as it were." For all the openness of its borders (fiction sometimes behaves as if, and is perceived as if, there were no police at its borders, no customs and immigration control, no passports required), fiction nevertheless alters whoever or whatever steps behind its "parchment barriers." The effects of fiction in which Franklin so delighted are, we continually have to remind ourselves, special effects. Fiction's voices and fiction's "present" are equivocal, and Franklin's reader experiences this equivocation with pleasure (he or she is "engaged") but also with a little bewilderment: the reader "finds himself" being brought into this company, a formulation that conveys the momentary disruption of autonomy and self-certainty that accompanies the engaged consumption of fiction. Franklin, moreover, noting that Defoe and Richardson had very successfully imitated Bunyan, knew that imitation was not only one of fiction's internal formal skills – it was also something that fiction encouraged as a mode of participating in and exercising power in a democratic society. Fiction's door might be an open door, but it was also, always, a stage door.

Franklin's remarks anticipated more recent academic attempts to think through the relationship between fiction and democracy in the late eighteenth- and early nineteenth-century United States. For the most part, these attempts have noted the correlation between the rise of the novel and the spread of democracy, even if the post-revolutionary escalation in the consumption and production of novels actually coincided with a well-documented series of attempts to limit the extension of the franchise. A more nuanced approach to the politics of the genre, however, has taken into account the novel's dual relationship to voice and print. The American Revolution and the proliferating genre of narrative fiction gave "voice" to more "ordinary people"; but both phenomena also exploited the range and effects of print reproduction in such a way as to give greater cultural force to various forms of anonymous utterance. And anonymity, as Franklin well knew, was as effective at provoking popular suspicion as it was at achieving democratic transformation.

Franklin had himself been the first to publish a novel in America (Richardson's *Pamela* in 1744), but it was not until the final decades of the century that the market for these books took off in earnest. By 1803 the Revd. Samuel Miller was complaining that "all classes of persons in society from the dignified professional character to the lowest grades of laboring indigence, seek and devour novels" (1803: 171–2). Cathy Davidson, in her landmark study of the early American novel, notes that while the number of social libraries in the American colonies (open to members who bought shares and paid an annual fee) grew by 376 between 1731 and 1800, most of those new libraries, 266 of them, opened in the final decade of the century (1986: 27). And Robert Winans' research into the titles checked out of the New York Society Library lends some support to Miller's lament about the kinds of books people were choosing to read. "Fiction accounted for less than ten percent of the entries in the *Catalogue* of the New York Society Library," writes Winans, "but the loan records of the library for 1789–90 prove that fiction constituted thirty-five percent of the borrowings from the library, twice the percentage of the next largest category" (1975: 271).

Indeed, there is much to suggest that late eighteenth-century cultural critics saw the rise of the novel and the spread of democracy as related phenomena. For "Federalist men of letters," Lewis Simpson writes, there existed "an analogy between the threat of democracy to the political order and the danger of democracy to the organization and control of literature" (1960: 253). "In the department of *belles-lettres*," wrote a contributor to the *Columbian Phoenix* (Boston) in 1800, "some fatality seems to impose insurmountable obstacles to our excellence, and threatens an eternal democracy instead of a well-organized republic of letters, and almost in defiance of nature, a perpetual equality of fame" (quoted in Simpson 1960: 259). "This is a novel reading age," wrote the editor of the *New York Magazine* in 1797, and, as Nina Baym suggests, "it was an unprecedented cultural event for the masses to be determining the shape of culture" (1984, 27, 27–8).

Most criticism of the novel in the late-eighteenth century United States, however, focused not on its remarkable ability to invite readers of all ages and classes to become "present at the Discourse," as Franklin had put it (this capacity was taken for granted and is, indeed, the only reason these laments feel forced to appear at all), but on the novel's tendency to invite all manner of characters and situations into its pages, without regard for traditional notions of what ought to be granted the privilege of esthetic representation. Noah Webster voiced a familiar concern when he warned that novels introduce young readers to "the vicious part of mankind" (1790: 29). "The free access which many young people have to romances, novels and plays," declared the typically self-exonerating preface to one such novel, "has poisoned the mind and corrupted the morals of many a promising youth" (Enos Hitchcock's *Memoirs of the Bloomgrove Family*, quoted in Orians 1937: 205).

Concern over who or what was allowed to enter the pages of fiction paralleled the widespread fear, in the aftermath of the Revolution, that what George Washington called an excess of democracy had encouraged many vulgar and unqualified individuals to enter into political life. While a spokesman for democracy writing in the *Gazette of the State of Georgia* in 1789 called for the election of "a class of citizens [from] a humbler walk in life," a New Englander writing in Boston's *American Herald* in 1786 claimed such promotion of the "popular spirit" would only ensure that more "blustering, ignorant men" would seek election. This populist democracy (figured, for example, by "Rip Van Winkle"'s "lean bilious looking fellow, with his pockets full of handbills . . . haranguing vehemently about rights of citizens") was not what many leading American revolutionaries had anticipated, and hence (though it can still come as a surprise to our ears) a signatory of the Declaration of Independence like Elbridge Gerry could even be heard referring to democracy as "the worst of all political evils" (quoted in Shoemaker 1966: 83). The novel and democracy demonstrated a lack of discrimination, then, and this was the source of both their appeal and their danger.

Lack of discrimination, of course, could be seen as either the achievement of democracy and fiction or as the source of their depravity and disorder. Moreover, this lack of discrimination seemed to be coupled, in both instances, with a fantastic ontological transformation. The "as it were" of fiction threatened to activate a potential representability in everyone who passed through its open borders. Anyone who could read – or even listen to – a novel thereby had access to something analogous to the absolute monarch's two bodies (the monarch's "body politic" threatened to return as the reader's "body fictional"). "Present at the discourse," while physically removed, the reader of novels participated in an excessive experience that called to mind the very excesses of monarchic extravagance that the Enlightenment revolutionaries had hoped to dispel. Novel-reading, suggested Thomas Jefferson in 1818, was apt to produce "a bloated imagination, sickly judgement, and disgust towards all the real business of life" (1904–5: vol. 5, 91). Hegemonic republicanism, in other words, conflated class prejudice and monarchophobia in attacks on fiction which in their own incoherent way tell us a great deal about the anxieties generated in this period by the whole notion of political and literary representation.

Just as the novel's participants (its characters, its author and its reader) become "present at the discourse" only by entering into the "as it were" of representation, so the democratic citizen or the democratic politician exercises his or her political power only by "finding himself [or herself]" present elsewhere – by becoming re-presentable. The radically expanded notion of representation enshrined in the American Constitution (from 1789 on government would consist entirely – in theory – of representatives of "the people") meant that representation was no longer something that *some* would have to seek in order to exercise control over those who held power. Rather, the only power remaining in this modern democracy would be, the architects of the Constitution argued, *represented* power. No one would hold political power in such a democracy without simultaneously becoming a representative of "the people." "The proposed government," wrote Federalist John Jay, "is to be the government of the people – all its offices are to be their offices, and to exercise no rights but such as the people commit to them" (quoted in Wood 1972: 546). In Gordon Wood's memorable formulation, "it was this disembodiment of government from society that ultimately made possible the conception of modern politics" (p. 608). We are inclined, for example, to equate democracy with the "giving of a voice" to the ordinary man or woman. But it is precisely the modern democratic revolution that instituted (once and for all, it would seem) the end of *viva voce* political election. Opening up the ballot box to "the people," democracy closed every voting booth to sight. Democracy and the novel, that is to say, brought a new sense of freedom and enfranchisement *and* new possibilities for concealment and self-difference.

If democracy was founded on representation – no citizen could appear on the stage of political power except in the "costume" of representation – how would one begin to define the particular dangers of fiction? William Hill Brown's *The Power of Sympathy* (1789) economically dramatizes these issues by reproducing anxious conversations about the consumption of fiction in the midst of a story about a peculiarly democratic affection. The dangers of excessive novel-reading and excessive democracy cannot be disentangled from the horrors of a disrupted kinship structure in a novel that has, nevertheless, been judged by many readers to be merely one more example of post-revolutionary conservative paranoia.

William Hill Brown's *The Power of Sympathy* (Brown 1996) seems, at first glance, to belong to the genre of the seduction novel (that is both how it describes itself in its preface and how it has been received by recent readers). But insofar as it has a particular story to tell, Brown's novel tells the story of a *reformed* seducer and of a couple (Harrington and Harriot) who fall hopelessly in love. The lovers are refused entry into the legitimate world of marriage, however, not because of a villain's desire to avoid the bonds of matrimony, but because what Harrington calls "tyrant custom" won't allow it (p. 92). The scandal that animates this novel – and gives it any force of originality to which it might lay claim – is the scandal of incest: sibling incest. The central pair of lovers share the same father, the villainous Mr. Harrington, and it is his seduction of a lower-class serving girl, Maria Fawcett (an event that takes place before the events of the novel unfold), that precipitates the novel's central crisis.

The Power of Sympathy, in other words, is a post-seduction novel. Seduction stories are stories of tyranny, wickedness, and the deployment of social superiority in the service of degrading one (a young woman) who has come to depend upon another (a powerful man). Seduction stories are stories of innocence spoiled, of naïve trust in the outward signs of civility and sincerity, of the sacrifice of independent judgment. Seduction stories, that is to say, are eminently colonial, or revolutionary, in their sensibility. They are products of a revolutionary imaginary, peopled by arbitrary tyrants and dependent victims, obsessed with the image of the socially superior but morally repugnant victimizer. As such, the seduction story finds one of its most important political counterparts in the Declaration of Independence with its depiction of the "present king of Great Britain" and his "long train of abuses and usurpations."

With its focus on the next generation – the children of the seduction – *The Power of Sympathy* concerns itself with the dilemmas of a post-seduction society. Its preoccupations – with the relation of one generation to its predecessors, the place of the past, of blood and of the family name – are those of an incipient democracy. Patriarchal seduction accounts for the tyranny in Brown's novel, but it is to the figuration of "incestuous" sibling love and the legal resistance it generates that we must turn to understand how *The Power of Sympathy* theorizes the transformative operations of constitutional democracy.

As Julia Stern has recently remarked, *The Power of Sympathy*'s doomed love affair coincides with a political transformation: Harrington's affection for Harriot coincides with what Stern calls "a nascent egalitarian sensibility" (1997: 26). At first, the idea of marriage to Harriot meets only with ridicule from Harrington. "I am not so much of a republican," Harrington tells his friend at an early point in his courtship, "as formally to wed any person of this class" (Brown 1996: 11). Once he finds himself in love, however, Harrington shows a different face. Hearing a "mechanic's daughter" snubbed at a party held in his and Harriot's honor, Harrington delivers a democratic outburst: "Inequality among mankind is a foe to our happiness," he tells his friend; "one order of men lords it over another. Upon what grounds its right is founded I could never yet be satisfied" (p. 34). "For this reason," Harrington continues, "I like a democratic government better than any other kind of government; and, were I a Lycurgus, no distinction of rank should be found in my commonwealth" (p. 34).

All this might seem rather unremarkable, however, were it not for the revelation – a revelation for which the attentive reader has been prepared – that the lovers are in fact siblings, the legitimate son and illegitimate daughter of a villainous father. With this sensational turn, the novel appears, at first, to participate in a post-revolutionary backlash against democracy (of the kind descried by Elbridge Gerry): The excesses of democracy, according to this line of thought, can be polemically figured by the eruption of unnatural and uncontrollable desire. "I am not ignorant that *licentiousness* too often assumes the sacred name of liberty," wrote Judith Sargent Murray (as "The Gleaner") in 1794, "[But] between liberty and licentiousness we cannot trace the smallest analogy." Murray, at once a significant early feminist and an exemplary republican, perfectly articulates the lines that connect democratic licentiousness with aristocratic depravity. "Liberty has been compared to an informed, elevated, and well regulated mind," she continues; "her movements are authorized by reason . . . Licentiousness is said to resemble the unbridled and tumultuous career of him, who, intoxicated by the inebriating draught, and having renounced his understanding, would invert the order of nature; eager to pour the inundation which shall level every virtue, and annihilate every distinction" (Murray 1995: 56–7).

In *The Power of Sympathy* it is sibling love that threatens to "invert the order of nature" and "annihilate every distinction" by challenging the distinctions of kinship and marriage law. Indeed, excessively worried post-revolutionary Americans might even have sensed something horrifyingly French in the first American novel. In his *Philosophy in the Bedroom* (1795) the Marquis de Sade writes (in the guise of a found pamphlet entitled "Yet Another Effort, Frenchmen, if You Would Become Republicans"): "[Incest] loosens family ties and the citizen has that much more love to lavish on his country; . . . I would venture, in a word, that incest ought to be every government's law – every government whose basis is fraternity" (1965: 324).[1]

The links Sade sets up between radical republicanism and a radical rethinking of the relationshp between kinship and the associations set up by democratic citizenship are precisely those which threaten the world of *The Power of Sympathy* in the form of Harrington and Harriot's love. De Sade's provocation reminds us that the political revolutions of the late eighteenth century often proceeded by encouraging individuals to break with generational, familial, or blood-based models of deference or obligation. Thus it is not difficult, as I have suggested, to read *The Power of Sympathy* as a novel that thematizes an "excess of democracy" in the form of the sibling–lovers' resistance to all the restrictions and patternings of a kinship system that limits their individual freedom.

Complicating matters, however, is the fact that the history of monarchical power, as all good revolutionaries knew in the late eighteenth century, is also a history of significant inter- and intrafamilial marriage among the royal houses of Europe. Writing to John Langdon, Thomas Jefferson held forth on this aspect of monarchism:

> The practice of kings marrying only in families of kings has been that of Europe for some centuries. Now, take any race of animals, confine them in idleness and inaction, whether in a sty, a stable, or a stateroom, pamper them with high diet, gratify all their sexual appetites, immerse them in sensualities, nourish their passions, let everything bend before them, and banish whatever might lead them to think, and in a few

generations they become all body and no mind; and this, too, by a law of nature, by that very law by which we are in the constant practice of changing the characters and propensities of the animals we raise for our own purposes. Such is the regimen in raising kings, and in this way they have gone on for centuries. (January 11, 1789, in Jefferson 1904–5: vol. 5, 441–3)

Jefferson thus considered the reform of rules of descent and abolition of primogeniture as central to a "system by which every fibre would be eradicated of antient or future aristocracy; and a foundation laid for a government truly republican" (Cunningham 1987: 58). Monarchism, in the revolutionary imagination of Thomas Jefferson (and many others), was itself the pre-eminent form of incestuous political power, everywhere invested in maintaining wealth and authority within carefully preserved family lines. The American Revolution would, according to this line of thought, liberate individuals from blood tyranny. (That this blood tyranny constituted not only a politics but also an erotics is evident from Jefferson's simultaneous preoccupation with monarchism's sexual appetites. Intrafamilial sexual relationship almost seems to bear the burden, in Jefferson's monarchophobic assessment, of all sexual appetite: kings marry "only in families of kings" and "gratify all their sexual appetites.")

The extent to which sibling love bears the traces of a despised monarchic contamination is evident, I would suggest, in the persistent refusal (even today) to think past the gothic disgust such love generates. Sibling love, in *The Power of Sympathy*, comes to figure that which "imperial" patriarchal tyranny leaves in its wake (the detritus of a despot) *even as* its inscription in this novel can be shown to re-mark the force of a revolutionary break with monarchism. As the central "event" of this novel, the sibling love of Harriot and Harrington registers something undecidable in the structure of the revolutionary moment: Is revolution, this novel asks, the unfortunate result of tyranny or the vehicle of democracy? Is the love between Harrington and Harriot the last insult of patriarchy (in the novel's final letter Harrington is referred to as the "sacrifice of seduction" [Brown 1996: 102]) or the novel's figuration of radical republicanism? Is their relationship a colonial leftover, the trailing end of patriarchal tyranny, or the beginning of a new order, the figuration of democracy's break with the past?

Crucially, the novel's two central characters are not as horrified by their blood relationship as we might expect them to be. Rather than abandon their class-crossing relationship (warned, by incest, of the dangers of excessive republicanism), the lovers cling to the legitimacy of their affection and the justice of their claim on marriage. Their blood relationship is the legacy of patriarchal tyranny; but, rather than simply accepting the unfortunate consequences, the lovers, doomed though they are, momentarily represent the possibility of a new way of figuring the relationship between the law, the heart and the father's name. "I have seen her," writes Harrington, after the revelation has been made; "I pressed her to my heart – I called her my love – my *sister*." Harrington's first impulse is to challenge the criminality of their affection: "How am I guilty?" he asks; "How is this transport a crime?" (Brown 1996: 80).

In fact, then, it is the deconstruction of the mutually exclusive discourses of the natural and the juridical, the familial and the political, that is figured by Harrington and Harriot's scandalous desire. Harrington and Harriot's love undermines an anxious determination (expressed by the law, but also by those characters and readers who express horror at the near-calamity) to distinguish the order of the natural from that of the political precisely in order to command the power of their conflation in the moment of political intervention. Reining in the revolution means, according to this reading, limiting access to that very conflation of the natural and the political that gave the Declaration of Independence its felicitous force (the Declaration's "it becomes necessary...in the course of human events"). The lovers yearn to celebrate the formalization of a relationship that, for them, is contingent first and essential, or natural, only within a politics or discourse that Harriot refers to as the "already written" ("I curse the idea of a brother – my hand refuses to trace the word; and yet – *The name appears Already written; blot it out, my tears!*": Brown 1996: 87).

Harriet and Harrington's story, then, is the story of two young Americans who find themselves on the border.[2] What begins to emerge is the curious possibility that a radical assertion of independence from the past and a break with the politico-juridical discourse of blood relations coincides – in the figure of the incestuous siblings – with a claim (to the right of siblings to marry) that some post-revolutionaries can experience only as the intolerable trace of monarchical depravity or monarchical blood-politics. The excesses of democracy and the traces of monarchic depravity coincide here in the fantastic figure of the sibling–lover. I would contend, moreover, that it is a version of this coincidence that anxious cultural commentators detected in the popular fiction of the late eighteenth and early nineteenth centuries. Fiction's broad license (everything and everyone could, in principle, enter its domain) drew attention to the dangers as well as the possibilities opened up by a radicalization of representability; and the conflation of democratic equality with the forbidden eroticism of sibling incest effectively suggests the thrill that fiction's suspense – and democracy's promise – offers so promiscuously.

Not surprisingly, then, *The Power of Sympathy*'s guardians of the marriage law also play a policing role with regard to the reading of fiction. Thus an extended section of the epistolary action is devoted to a discussion of fiction and its dangers, a discussion that echoes the justification with which Brown prefaces his novel. This novel, we are told, is more "advantageous" than most: "the dangerous consequences of seduction are exposed, and the advantages of female education set forth and recommended" (Brown 1996: 7). This quite stereotypical appeal to seduction and female vulnerability gets replayed in the novel's scene of critical literary judgment. "As much depends on the choice of books," Worthy tells Miss Bourn's concerned mother, "care should be taken not to put those in the way of young persons, which might leave on their minds any disagreeable prejudices, or which has a tendency to corrupt their morals" (p. 20). Novels, democratic politics, and incestuous love share a threatening potential in *The Power of Sympathy* even as they provide the novel with its form, its narrative, and its thrill.

The Power of Sympathy's familiar discussion of the novel, however, finally serves only to emphasize the ambivalence of the sentimental critique of fiction. It feels compelled to, yet is repeatedly unable to distinguish books that are corrupting from books that are about corruption. The ambiguous reciprocal relationship between the novel and the world ("I will not dispute," concludes Mr. Holmes, "whether the novel makes the woman, or the woman makes the novel . . . I believe the result will show they depend, in some measure, upon each other" [Brown 1996: 29]) names another example of a *transport* that requires careful regulation. Summed up in Harrington's tortured address, "my love – my sister" (p. 80), the sibling–lovers' "criminal transport" threatens social convention not simply because it breaks a rule, but because it displays an insistent uncertainty that is at once the source of much of this novel's figurative fascination and the site of its sympathetic appeal. In both cases – that of the genre's uncertain referentiality and that of the lovers' uncertain relationship – *The Power of Sympathy* argues against the refusal to engage with this suspense. By combining a narrative of seduction and incest with a discourse on fiction and its effects, Brown's novel encourages a recognition of the crucial interrelationship of literary and political anxieties in the post-revolutionary period.

Further investigation into the relationship between democracy and kinship in early American fiction will surely be informed by work underway on the political philosophy of fraternalism and kinship (Derrida, Butler), and the efforts of various post-Marxists to articulate a theory of the relationship between equality and liberty in democratic theory and practice (Balibar, Lefort). Questions of blood, the body, and the very corporeality of the subject of democracy and of human rights have also come to the forefront of recent work on the politics of human rights (Agamben 2000). From a strictly literary perspective, however, there is still much to be said about the politics (and the implicit political theory) of, for example, Fenimore Cooper's narratives of Anglo-American and white–Native union or non-union (What should the blood of democracy look like? Who are democracy's ideal parents?), or about a more focused and penetrating study of kinship and the American Revolution such as Hawthorne's "My Kinsman Major Molineux" ("If you prefer to remain with us," the revolutionary tells the innocent at the end of the story, "perhaps . . . you may rise in the world, without the help of your kinsman"). Certainly, one would want to look at *The Power of Sympathy's* sprawling and magnificent progeny, Herman Melville's *Pierre*, in which the incestuous relationship between Pierre and Isabel is rarely disentangled from the young man's confused political fantasies: "As they hurried on," we read near the close of the novel, "Pierre was silent; but wild thoughts were hurrying and shouting in his heart. The most tremendous displacing and revolutionizing thoughts were upheaving in him, with reference to Isabel; nor – though at the time he was hardly conscious of such a thing – were these thoughts wholly unwelcome to him" (Melville 1971: 353). Undecidably artificial himself (Are we to take Pierre seriously? Or is he just a fabulous caricature?) and "upheaved" and "displaced" by the crossings of blood, desire, and political justice, Pierre is Melville's wild incarnation of the American novel's still-vital affinity with democracy.

Notes

1 In Sarah Sayward Wood's *Julia, and the Illuminated Baron* (1800), unwitting incest is represented as arising from the rapacious advances of a free-thinking French revolutionary, an "infidel" who belongs to the secret order of the Illuminati. Wood's preface suggests how we should read her cursed lover: "This volume, to the reader's eye displays Th' infernal conduct of abandon'd man; When French philosophy infects his ways... Reversing order, truth, and ev'ry good, And whelming worlds, with ruin's awful flood." Incest, in Wood's gothic novel, is merely one more horrifying possibility associated with revolutionary (French) philosophy.

2 See the John Sayles movie *Lone Star* (1996) for an intriguing recent version of this story.

References and Further Reading

Agamben, Giorgio (2000). *Means without End: Notes on Politics*, trans. Vincenzo Binetti and Cesare Casarino. Minneapolis: University of Minnesota Press.

Balibar, Etienne (1994). *Masses, Classes, Ideas: Studies on Politics and Philosophy before and after Marx*, trans. James Swenson. New York: Routledge.

Barnes, Elizabeth (1997). *States of Sympathy: Seduction and Democracy in the American Novel*. New York: Columbia University Press.

Baym, Nina (1984). *Novels, Readers and Reviewers: Responses to Fiction in Antebellum America*. Ithaca, NY: Cornell University Press.

Brown, William Hill (1996). *The Power of Sympathy*. New York: Penguin. (First publ. 1789.)

Butler, Judith (2000). *Antigone's Claim: Kinship between Life and Death*. New York: Columbia University Press.

Cunningham, Noble E., Jr. (1987). *In Pursuit of Reason: The Life of Thomas Jefferson*. New York: Ballantine.

Davidson, Cathy N. (1986). *Revolution and the Word: The Rise of the Novel in America*. New York: Oxford University Press.

Derrida, Jacques (1997). *The Politics of Friendship*, trans. George Collins. London: Verso.

Fliegelman, Jay (1982). *Prodigals and Pilgrims: The American Revolution against Patriarchal Authority 1750–1800*. Cambridge, UK: Cambridge University Press.

Franklin, Benjamin (1987). *Writings*. New York: Library of America.

Hawthorne, Nathaniel (1987). *Tales*. New York: Norton.

Jefferson, Thomas (1904–5). *Works*, 12 vols., ed. Paul Leicester Ford. New York: Putnam's.

Lefort, Claude (1988). *Democracy and Political Theory*, trans. David Macey. Minneapolis: University of Minnesota Press.

Looby, Christopher (1996). *Voicing America: Language, Literary Form, and the Origins of the United States*. Chicago: University of Chicago Press.

Melville, Herman (1971). *Pierre; or, The Ambiguities*. Evanston, Ill., and Chicago: Northwestern University Press/Newberry Library. (First publ. 1852.)

Miller, Samuel (1803). *A Brief Retrospect of the Eighteenth Century*, 2 vols. New York: T. & J. Swords.

Mulford, Carla (1996). "Introduction." In *William Hill Brown's* The Power of Sympathy *and Hannah Webster Foster's* The Coquette, ed. Carla Mulford. New York: Penguin.

Murray, Judith Sargent (1995). "Sketch of the Present Situation of America, 1794." In *Selected Writings of Judith Sargent Murray*, ed. Sharon M. Harris. New York: Oxford University Press.

Orians, G. Harrison (1937). "Censure of Fiction in American Romances and Magazines: 1789–1810." *PMLA* 52: 1 (March), 195–214.

Ruttenburg, Nancy (1998). *Democratic Personality: Popular Voice and the Trial of American Authorship*. Stanford: Stanford University Press.

Sade, Marquis de (1965). *The Complete Justine, Philosophy in the Bedroom and other Writings*, trans. Richard Seaver and Austryn Wainhouse. New York: Grove.

Shoemaker, Robert (1966). "'Democracy' and 'Republic' as Understood in Late Eighteenth-Century America." *American Speech* 41, 83–95.

Simpson, Lewis P. (1960). "Federalism and the Crisis of Literary Order." *American Literature* 32: 3, 254–66.

Stern, Julia A. (1997). *The Plight of Feeling: Sympathy and Dissent in the Early American Novel.* Chicago: University of Chicago Press.

Warner, Michael (1990). *The Letters of the Republic: Publication and the Public Sphere in Eighteenth-Century America.* Cambridge, Mass.: Harvard University Press.

Webster, Noah (1790). *A Collection of Essays and Fugitive Writings on Moral, Historical, Political,* *and Literary Subjects.* Boston: I. Thomas & E. T. Andrews.

Winans, Robert (1975). "The Growth of a Novel Reading Public in Late-Eighteenth Century America." *Early American Literature* 9, 268–75.

Wood, Gordon S. (1972). *The Creation of the American Republic, 1776–1787.* New York: Norton.

Wood, Sarah Sayward (1800). *Julia, and The Illuminated Baron. A Novel: Founded on recent Facts Which have Transpired in the Course of the Late revolution of Moral Principles in France.* Portsmouth, NH: Charles Peirce.

Ziff, Larzer (1991). *Writing in the New Nation: Prose, Print, and Politics in the Early United States.* New Haven: Yale University Press.

3
Democratic Fictions

Sandra M. Gustafson

What could a novel called *Democracy* be about? Our answers to this question depend upon the meanings we attach to its two key terms, "democracy" and "novel." Pronounced self-evident by Thomas Jefferson in 1776 ("all men are created equal"), "democracy" is anything but transparent, as we can see from the numerous ways in which the word is used today. In the most general terms it refers broadly to a version of government by the people, an ideal of social equality, or both. The variety of meanings encompassed under these two ideals sometimes complement one another, but as often contradict each other.[1] Compared to "democracy," "the novel" is relatively easy to define. As a genre the novel characteristically focuses on contexts and relationships – the individual in society, the one in relation to the many. In contrast to more limiting forms such as the sonnet or the drama, the capacious novel has few formal requirements beyond the development of characters, the description of a setting, and the unfolding of a plot. Historically the novel has often been identified as a "democratic" form because of this generic flexibility, as well as its relative accessibility to readers. To write a novel about democracy, then, would be to depict characters whose surroundings and relationships are defined by "democracy" in some or all of its many senses. Their stories would proceed in a world permeated by the abstract ideas of popular governance and equality embodied in particular institutions, relationships, and actions. Readers could anticipate that the tension between the abstract ideal and the particular embodiments of that ideal would contribute important themes and plot devices to a novel called *Democracy*.

In his 1880 novel *Democracy* Henry Adams portrays a corrupt and opaque political order (complete with early lobbyists) absorbed in its own rituals and needs, without reference to the implications for the citizens it claims to represent. His focus is on the social and governing elites, his plot a failed romance. Adams's heroine is a young widow named Madeline Lightfoot Lee who worships beauty and craves power. She moves to Washington DC after the death of her husband and child to fill her emotional void with a view of "the interests of forty millions of people and a whole continent, centering at Washington . . . the tremendous forces of government, and the machinery of society, at work" (Adams 1983: 18). Lee imagines the US government as a vast machine that she experiences as both fearfully powerful and esthetically compelling.

Lee is drawn to a superficially idealistic but ambitious and morally corrupt party leader, Senator Silas Ratcliffe. The United States uniquely represented democracy on the world stage during the nineteenth century, and Lee identifies Ratcliffe with the best possibilities of the nation. "I must know whether America is right or wrong," she exclaims, referring to democratic government. "I really want to know whether to believe in Mr. Ratcliffe" (Adams 1983: 49–50). Lee sees the best of Ratcliffe, not in his overblown Senate speeches, but at a dinner party where he sets out to impress her with his display of entertaining table talk. Ratcliffe's dialect stories and "sharp little sketches of amusing political experiences" (p. 41) shape political life into recognizable and appealing esthetic forms. Well-crafted narrative is central to politics, as it is to fiction. When Ratcliffe later belittles George Washington ("A fair military officer, who made many blunders . . . A respectable, painstaking President . . . This government can show today a dozen men of equal abilities" [p. 78]), he earns Madeline's disapproval and opens the door to doubts about his character. She longs for heroic leadership, but she finds banal corruption. She hankers for Power, pure and uncontaminated, but finds instead personal interest and ethical ambiguity. Ratcliffe's major moral lapses occur when he fails to distinguish his personal good from the good of his party or the country. His courtship of Madeline is a political scheme to win the White House, not an expression of love. Contemplating their failed union, Madeline persists in identifying Ratcliffe with American democracy but now in a tone of despair, lamenting that "Democracy has shaken my nerves to pieces." Her desire to travel to Egypt "to live in the Great Pyramid and look out for ever at the pole star" (p. 189) portrays the Orient as a place of beauty and solace for the burdens of a modernity troubled by a dual transformation of power: through democratic politics, which transformed monarchical and aristocratic political and social power; and through technological change, which altered the modes and uses of physical power.

Adams wrote in the aftermath of the Civil War, during the waning years of Reconstruction, at a time of great cynicism and despair about popular government as well as fear of the tremendous industrial expansion that the United States was undergoing. European immigrants were surging into the country to fill the new factories at the same time as the experiment in interracial democracy that followed the granting of full citizenship rights to African American men was coming to a sordid end, with resurgent hierarchies of class and race trumping democratic ideals. Adams's choice of form reflects those realities. His *Democracy* is a novel of manners set in Washington high society. The action takes place at salons and dinner parties and soirées, on outings and excursions populated by political and social elites from around the United States and Europe. There are no major African American characters. The only European immigrants are diplomats and fortune-hunting aristocrats. For Adams, the deliberate irony of choosing this title for a novel with this form points to the gap between the abstract ideal of "democracy," in both its political and social senses, and the actual circumstances of democracy's implementation.[2]

Adams turned to the novel of manners as a means to portray the failure of the democratic political and esthetic ideals articulated by an earlier generation of American novelists.[3] At least since British poets William Wordsworth and Samuel Taylor Coleridge published their preface to the *Lyrical Ballads* in 1798, articulating the spirit of the age of democratic revolution in esthetic terms (blank verse that has the ring of "man talking to men," everyday scenes and characters), writers with progressive political sympathies sought to embody their democratic ideals in new literary forms.[4] The creation of a self-consciously democratic literature in the United States paralleled the emergence there of a distinctive and nearly unique body of democratic political and social thought.[5]

For novelists, the primary means for making literary representation mirror political representation are three: character, style, and plot. Character offers perhaps the simplest and most readily visible strategy of democratic fiction. Authors create "common" or "lowly" characters, inviting readers to identify with them and learn about their lives in a bid to win sympathy for them. Philosopher Martha Nussbaum writes that novels "construct and speak to an implicit reader who shares with the characters certain hopes, fears, and general human concerns, and who for that reason is able to form bonds of identification and sympathy with them, but who is also situated elsewhere and needs to be informed about the concrete situation of characters." Nussbaum goes on to explain that a reader who identifies with a character can have his or her political views altered, in that the novel can make its readers aware of "how the mutable features of society and circumstances bear on the realization of shared hopes and dreams." In a democracy, where ordinary people possess tools to alter "the mutable features of society," reading about and identifying with the struggles and ambitions of those outside one's realm of experience can change one's ideas about a political issue (Nussbaum 1995: 7).[6]

One new type of character to emerge in nineteenth-century American fiction was the democratic hero, a figure which until that time had largely been considered a contradiction in terms. Previously heroes were nobles as well as being noble. The "mob" was made up of gross, grasping, vicious, or humorous types. Even the new type of heroine portrayed in such novels as Samuel Richardson's *Pamela* elicited traditional prejudices when the maid-turned-gentry wife was widely criticized for manipulating her husband into marrying her. Beginning in the 1820s – the decade of suffrage expansion, the framing of more inclusively representative state constitutions, Andrew Jackson's presidency, and the rise of the Democrats as the first modern political party – James Fenimore Cooper created the first monumental American hero in the Leatherstocking tales, a series of five novels (1823–41) featuring the illiterate frontiersman Natty Bumppo. In important ways Natty resembled the popular image of Jackson. His lowly origins, superior wilderness skills, and identification with supposedly "vanishing" Native Americans represent the first stage in the mastery of a continent, an imperialist Manifest Destiny propounded by Democratic leaders who saw the American land as the material basis of an egalitarian society. Cooper felt ambivalent toward his greatest character and the heroic democracy that he represented, as we can see from the fact that Natty never marries or reproduces. The frontiersman type of the common man will vanish as civilization progresses, Cooper suggests, to be replaced in leadership roles by "natural" elites. Regardless of the aversion to American democracy that Cooper developed in his later years, Natty Bumppo profoundly influenced later democratic fictions. Most notably he was a model for the lowly hero of Mark Twain's *Huckleberry Finn* (1884), who represents the pre-political, natural innocence and camaraderie of Americans reclaimed from the anti-democratic corruptions of slavery.

Like Huck Finn, Natty Bumppo is a natural democrat, a "common" man untouched by social hierarchies, rather than a democrat in the political sense. The figure of the common-man-as-political-democrat is best exemplified by Holgrave, the hero of Nathaniel Hawthorne's *House of the Seven Gables* (1851). Holgrave's humble origins, aversion to established traditions and institutions, multiple talents, self-reliance, and willingness to reinvent himself typify the social ideals of the "Young America" wing of the Democratic Party that Hawthorne embraced. Hawthorne's depiction of Holgrave is not without a gentle mockery. Still, his portrait of the young photographer whose truthful artistic representations use nature's own sunshine as a medium, offering an artistic analogue to the democratic ideal of governmental naturalness and transparency, is as hopeful as anything in Hawthorne's works. Hawthorne ends *House of the Seven Gables* with Holgrave's marriage to the capable and unpretentious Phoebe Pyncheon, scion of the Puritan elites who had persecuted and stolen from Holgrave's ancestors two centuries earlier. In this way he symbolically resolves class conflict in the United States.

While Cooper and Hawthorne embodied democratic values in specific characters, Harriet Beecher Stowe took a different approach to democratic characterization. *Uncle Tom's Cabin* (1852) has two heroes: the noble and self-sacrificing enslaved African American Uncle Tom, and Eva St. Clair, the angelic young daughter of a wealthy slave-owning family from New Orleans. Both heroes are "lowly" in different senses – Eva because of her youth and Tom because of his race and enslavement. By creating a "double hero," Stowe implies a more egalitarian ideal than a single dominant hero can convey. Stowe surrounds her heroes with a diverse and boisterous American society that does not stand upon formalities or respect hierarchies. Her depiction of a Kentucky bar-room offers one of the most exuberant depictions of egalitarian society in nineteenth-century fiction. Her lengthy description of the hats worn in the room begins: "everybody in the room bore on his head this characteristic emblem of man's sovereignty; whether it were felt hat, palmleaf, greasy beaver, or fine new chapeau, there it reposed with true republican independence." She concludes her portrait with a description of democratic frontier manners, noting that the Kentuckian "is altogether the frankest, easiest, most jovial creature living" (Stowe 1998: 109–10).[7] *Uncle Tom's Cabin* explicitly calls for the egalitarian ideal depicted here to be further extended through the abolition of slavery. The mechanism that she imagines effecting this change in formal civic status is the same one that Martha Nussbaum describes: the sympathetic identification that the reader achieves by recognizing the common experience of receiving mother love that she or he shares with the characters.[8]

Sympathetic characters are Stowe's most important tool for democratic representation, but they are not her only one. The varieties of character speech that she includes in her novel contribute another democratic dimension of her text. Stowe sought to accurately represent the many varieties of American English dialect that her geographically diverse characters would use, from the antiquated "thees" and "thous" of the Quaker Hallidays to the sharp, clipped speech that gives away Aunt Ophelia's Vermont origins, the light Kentucky drawl of the Shelbys, and the more heavily accented "Black English" of the enslaved characters. (The democratic significance of dialect writing is suggested as well by the explanatory note prefacing *Huckleberry Finn*, where Mark Twain claimed to represent "the Missouri negro dialect; the extremest form of the backwoods South-Western dialect; the ordinary 'Pike-County' dialect; and four modified varieties of this last" (Twain 1985: n.p.). "Voice" and its representation have been tied to democracy since the assembly debates of ancient Athens, and they became important elements in American fiction after the Revolution, when advocates of the post-colonial United States sought to legitimate the nation's distinctive American versions of English, its democratizing political order, and its artistic products.[9] Distinctive speech encodes a particular social background and a set of personal or collective experiences whose literary representation the author may tie to political representation. As the Russian literary theorist M. M. Bakhtin observed in his influential essay "Discourse in the Novel," novelists depict social conflicts by representing the interplay of different voices on the page. The narrator's language, too, relates to the speech of the characters, providing another way for the novelist to depict tensions and hierarchies within a society.[10]

In *Moby-Dick* (1851) Herman Melville exploited the representational possibilities of voice in ways that related it directly to the main issues of democratic politics in his day. The famous first line of the novel, "Call me Ishmael," is a direct address to the reader that establishes a powerful narrative voice even as it disguises the speaker's identity (Melville 1983: 795). With this opening command Melville makes us aware that he is creating a representation of the narrator whose textual "voice" we hear telling us his story.[11] These three short words raise key themes of voice, identity, and representation that run through and tie together the novel's weighty religious, epistemological, esthetic, and political preoccupations. Ishmael's self-involved introductory monologue gradually opens up to include other people, notably in the conversations that he has with the idol-worshiping cannibal Queequeg, whose ungrammatical, repetitive, parodically "savage" English provides a childlike and humorous counterpoint to the seriousness and dark irony of schoolmaster Ishmael's educated speech.[12] Ishmael comes to embrace the rough, egalitarian democracy that he finds with Queequeg and the other "savage" crew members. The evolving dialogue between alienating, hierarchical Western civilization and fraternal, democratic non-Western savagery is abruptly derailed with the belated emergence of Captain Ahab, who in a scene of oratorical mastery on the quarterdeck dominates the crew and binds them to his illicit will. The crew's cheers of unified assent dissolve into a drunken brawl that ends with near-disaster when a squall hits the boat. Once mastered by Ahab, the crew disintegrates in his absence, for Ahab has replaced their democratic bonds to one another with a hierarchical bond to him.

Melville literally dramatizes his political themes in these chapters. Like Stowe, he uses numerous dialects to represent a heterogeneous society on board the *Pequod*, but he takes the representation of democracy a step further by incorporating different genres into the novel form. Ishmael dominates the first quarter of the novel. Everything is filtered through his eyes and related in his voice. Then, in the quarterdeck scene, Melville begins to shift from a first-person narrative to a dramatic presentation, until four chapters later he presents the squall in a fully dramatic mode. The novel briefly becomes a play modeled on Shakespearean tragedy. Melville switches genres to highlight the sudden evacuation of Ishmael's identity in the face of Ahab's dominating power, as becomes clear in the opening line of chapter 41 where Ishmael reasserts himself: "I Ishmael was one of that crew" (Melville 1983: 983). The remainder of the novel enacts a contest for control of the story between Ahab, who is monomaniacally fixated on killing the white whale, and Ishmael, whose encyclopedic effort to capture the whale as an object of knowledge is simultaneously an attempt to avoid being captured himself by Ahab's narrative compulsions, which drive the main plot. Melville intercuts chapters of "plot" and "knowledge" until Ishmael finally surrenders control to Ahab in the culminating chase scenes, disappearing as narrator only to re-emerge in the novel's play-like epilogue as the lone survivor of the voyage.

What do Melville's experiments with the novel form have to do with democracy? The *Pequod* is a symbol for the American ship of state, riven among competing democratic, hierarchical, and autocratic elements.[13] The contest for (narrative) control of the *Pequod* represents the persistent tensions within an American society that rhetorically embraced democracy without fully embodying it in an egalitarian social order. Sympathetic to the democratic ideal, and yet skeptical of the Young America movement that claimed to embody that ideal while remaining pro-slavery, Melville was the first major novelist to raise the problems of authorship and authority and to explore their implications for democracy in terms of novelistic form.

Melville anticipated Henry Adams in perceiving a dual transformation of power that tied democratic politics to technological change. The *Pequod* is an ocean-going factory where sperm whales are cut down and their fat boiled to yield the sperm oil that will fuel lamps to illuminate hours of darkness, transforming time and work. The Marxist critic C. L. R. James characterizes the *Pequod* crew as "modern industrial workers" and notes that they are "in perfect harmony" with "Nature and technology" (James 1953: 20, 31). The *Pequod* is decorated with whale teeth and bones, symbolizing an art that blends the natural with the technological. As they sail the Pacific, Ishmael describes the spectacle of the fire-lit ship: the "darkness was licked up by the fierce flames, which at intervals forked forth from the sooty flues, and illuminated every lofty rope in the rigging, as with the famed Greek fire. The burning ship drove on, as if remorselessly commissioned to some vengeful deed" (Melville 1983: 1245). Classical imagery, powerful visual description, and dramatic color make this passage a vivid one. "So it seemed to me," Ishmael flatly concludes at the end of a painterly page-long description, and with that intrusion of Ishmael's voice Melville alerts his readers to the ways in which narrative perspective shapes this and every scene. Like Madeline Lightfoot Lee and Henry Adams, Ishmael highlights the esthetic elements of the scene, investing them with greatest significance.

Melville understands esthetics as a technology, a mode of representation that produces something, analogous to the way in which representative forms (citizenship laws, elections) produce "democracy." The spontaneous, natural, participatory democracy that Melville idealizes in fleeting moments among the "savage" crew members or in the sperm-squeezing scene remains for him essentially pre-political. Technologies of political and artistic representation such as the vote or the classical allusion do not capture a reality, any more than Ishmael can fully describe or know the sperm whale. They make a picture of a reality that cannot escape distortion. The fate of the *Pequod* suggests that Melville took a tragic view of democracy in 1850, just as Henry Adams did in 1880. For both of these novelists the artistic forms of democratic representation created by Cooper, Hawthorne, and Stowe – democratic heroes, multiple voices and idioms – fail to address the fundamental problem of democratic representation: the inevitability and inadequacy of abstraction.

Notes

1 Derived from the ancient Greek *demokratia*, or rule of the people, "democracy" designates a variety of political systems that incorporate a principle of inclusiveness, ranging from representative or constitutional democracy to participatory democracy. It is also used to refer to social egalitarianism, which in turn can be (but is not necessarily) tied to economic equality. Political democracy and social democracy, though sometimes found together, are not necessarily linked. Alexis de Tocqueville's *Democracy in America* (1835–40) famously related political democracy in the United States, embodied most concretely in universal white manhood suffrage, to social egalitarianism and economic equality. Tocqueville's standard of comparison was post-feudal Europe. During the century-long "Cold War" between the United States and the Soviet Union, which began around 1890 and ended with the fall of the eastern bloc in 1989, both sides in the conflict claimed to embody "democracy." The

United States asserted its model of representative political democracy, while the Soviet Union proclaimed its social and economic programs as the truer democratic form. Two useful brief discussions of the meanings of democracy are Williams 1976, 1983: 93–8, and Eisenstadt 1999.

2 Adams's personal history of political ambivalence related more to his own failed relationship to democracy than to issues of racial justice. His commitment to reform politics was rendered ineffective at least in part by his distaste for the quality of democratic public life. *The Education of Henry Adams* (1918) offers his elegy for the lost political world of his famous ancestors, Presidents John Adams and John Quincy Adams, who famously resisted political democratization. The extension of the suffrage, he felt, had lowered the tone of American politics to the point where honorable and capable men like himself could no longer participate.

3   In 1984 Joan Didion published her own novel, *Democracy*, in explicit homage to Henry Adams as the head of a line of writers preoccupied with the tensions between democracy and technological transformation. Despite their shared literary strategies, there are substantial differences in their political visions. While Adams disparages democracy, Didion views democracy as an unfulfilled ideal.

4   In the United States, the creation of a democratic esthetics was the explicit project of the Young America movement of the 1830s and 1840s, led by journalist John O'Sullivan and attracting some of the period's most important writers, including Nathaniel Hawthorne, Herman Melville, and Walt Whitman. Edward L. Widmer discusses the movement in *Young America* (1999). "Democracy" is a frequently used, though often undertheorized and underhistoricized term in literary and cultural criticism of the United States. In his influential *American Renaissance*, for example, F. O. Matthiessen identified the "common denominator" uniting his canon of five major authors (Emerson, Thoreau, Melville, Hawthorne, and Whitman) as "their devotion to the possibilities of democracy" (1941: ix).

5   In *Athens on Trial* Jennifer Tolbert Roberts aptly observes that from the days of Plato and Aristotle Western political thought was built on hostility to democratic Athens (1994: xi–xii). Democratic ideals (however variously defined) achieved widespread acceptance in the West only after World War I. The development of a body of democratic political thought began in the age of democratic revolutions and gathered force in the United States in the 1820s. The transatlantic dialogue over democratic political and social forms during this period was a vibrant and often cantankerous one, with America's defenders, such as Frances Wright and James Fenimore Cooper, celebrating democratic politics and society while its detractors, including Frances Trollope and Charles Dickens, criticized either the idea of democracy or the imperfect embodiment of democratic ideas in the United States.

6   Building on the work of Ian Watt, Cathy N. Davidson argues for the democratizing influence of the novel in the United States in *Revolution and the Word*. Nussbaum's account of literary sympathy in *Poetic Justice*, which draws directly on the theory of sympathy articulated in Adam Smith's *Theory of Moral Sentiments* (1759), is a notably optimistic account of sympathetic identification. Many scholars – too many to name – have offered important qualifications and challenges to this view of sympathy's democratic potential.

7   The description appears at the beginning of chapter 11, "In Which Property Gets into an Improper State of Mind."

8   Along with *Huckleberry Finn*, *Uncle Tom's Cabin* is one of the most disputed novels ever written in the United States. Stowe is an imperfect spokesperson for democracy because of her beliefs about intrinsic racial differences (the idea that there are human "races" characterized by different qualities and abilities, also known as romantic racialism) and her interest in the colonization effort (the political movement to transport liberated slaves to Africa, which Stowe depicts through the characters of George and Emily Harris). For two important conflicting accounts of Stowe's literary and political values, see Baldwin 1955 and Tompkins 1985: 122–46.

9   See e.g. Looby 1996; Ruttenburg 1998.

10 Bakhtin writes: "The novel can be defined as a diversity of social speech types (sometimes even diversity of languages) and a diversity of individual voices, artistically organized. The internal stratification of any single national language into social dialects, characteristic group behavior, professional jargons, generic languages, languages of generations and age groups, tendentious languages, languages of the authorities, of various circles and of passing fashions, languages that serve the specific sociopolitical purposes of the day, even of the hour (each day has its own slogan, its own vocabulary, its own emphases) – this internal stratification present in every language at any given moment of its historical existence is the indispensable prerequisite for the novel as a genre" (1981: 262–3).

11 Melville's contemporaries would have known that the biblical Ishmael is the son of Abraham by the slave girl Hagar, of whom it is prophesied that he will be in perpetual

conflict with those around him. This prophecy is fulfilled when, at his wife Sarah's insistence, Abraham disowns Ishmael and sends him into the wilderness. They may also have known that "Ishmael" means "God hears," an assertion that becomes a question for the narrator as the novel progresses.

12 I discuss the democratic significance of "savage" speech in *Eloquence is Power* (2000), e.g. p. 139.

13 Alan Heimert offers the most comprehensive analysis of *Moby-Dick*'s political symbolism in "Moby-Dick and American Political Symbolism."

References

Adams, Henry (1983). *Democracy: An American Novel*. New York: New American Library.

Bakhtin, M. M. (1981). "Discourse in the Novel." In *The Dialogic Imagination: Four Essays by M. M. Bakhtin*, ed. Michael Holquist, 259–422. Austin: University of Texas Press.

Baldwin, James (1955). "Everybody's Protest Novel." In *Notes of a Native Son*, 13–23. Boston: Beacon.

Davidson, Cathy N. (1986). *Revolution and the Word: The Rise of the Novel in America*. New York: Oxford University Press.

Didion, Joan (1984). *Democracy*. New York: Vintage.

Eisenstadt, S. N. (1999). *Paradoxes of Democracy: Fragility, Continuity, and Change*. Baltimore: Johns Hopkins University Press.

Gustafson, Sandra M. (2000). *Eloquence is Power: Oratory and Performance in Early America* (Chapel Hill, NC: University of North Carolina Press).

Heimert, Alan (1963). "Moby-Dick and American Political Symbolism." *American Quarterly* 15 (Winter), 498–534.

James, C. L. R. (1953). *Mariners, Renegades and Castaways*. New York: University Press of New England.

Looby, Christopher (1996). *Voicing America: Language, Literary Form, and the Origins of the United States*. Chicago: University of Chicago Press.

Matthiessen, F. O. (1941). *American Renaissance: Art and Expression in the Age of Emerson and Whitman*. New York: Oxford University Press.

Melville, Herman (1983). *Redburn, White-Jacket, Moby-Dick*. New York: Library of America.

Nussbaum, Martha C. (1995). *Poetic Justice: The Literary Imagination and Public Life*. Boston: Beacon.

Roberts, Jennifer Tolbert (1994). *Athens on Trial: The Antidemocratic Tradition in Western Thought*. Princeton: Princeton University Press.

Ruttenburg, Nancy (1998). *Democratic Personality: Popular Voice and the Trial of American Authorship*. Stanford: Stanford University Press.

Stowe, Harriet Beecher (1998). *Uncle Tom's Cabin*, ed. Jean Fagan Yellin. New York: Oxford University Press.

Tompkins, Jane (1985). "Sentimental Power: *Uncle Tom's Cabin* and the Politics of Literary History." In *Sensational Designs: The Cultural Work of American Fiction, 1790–1860*, 122–46. New York: Oxford University Press.

Twain, Mark (1985). *Adventures of Huckleberry Finn*, ed. Walter Blair and Victor Fischer. Berkeley: University of California Press.

Widmer, Edward L. (1999). *Young America: The Flowering of Democracy in New York City*. New York: Oxford University Press.

Williams, Raymond (1976, 1983). *Keywords: A Vocabulary of Culture and Society*, rev. edn. New York: Oxford University Press.

4

Engendering American Fictions

Martha J. Cutter and Caroline F. Levander

During the period from 1780 to 1865 many foundational ideas about gender ideology were articulated in literary and cultural texts. Advice books to women and men, religious conduct books, and magazines created and reinforced certain ideas about gender. Literary and autobiographical texts then revamped, recreated, or (at times) completely undermined these constructions. In particular, three concepts regarding gender were promulgated, debated, and reformulated in literary and cultural texts in these years: the "self-made" man; the "true woman" or "domestic saint"; and the idea that men and women should have "separate" spheres from each other. It would seem, then, that concepts of gender roles at this time, for both men and women, were relatively fixed and distinct, with differences between the sexes being emphasized. However, closer examination of the notion of men and women having "separate" spheres in fact reveals that these gender roles were evolving and somewhat flexible. In particular, the rhetoric of sentimentality, motherhood, and religion promoted by women writers often expanded women's "private" sphere into the arena of political action. In the end, then, men and women could participate in and endorse radically different ideologies about gender and still, ideally, produce a similar result: an American (whether male or female) who is politically active and informed, yet also moral and virtuous. Of course, gender, like race, does limit an individual's ability to intervene in political or social debates and even attain public voice; but both men and women did sometimes find ways to act outside restrictive gender ideologies in order to promote their own social and political empowerment.

The Self-made Man and the True Woman

While American authors of the seventeenth and early eighteenth centuries, such as Edward Taylor, William Bradford, and Anne Bradstreet, were preoccupied with religious identity, later writers become concerned with the question, as Hector

St. John de Crèvecœur phrased it in 1782, of "What is an American?" and, more specifically, of "What is an American man?" One answer that emerges in both fiction and nonfiction in the period under study is that the American man is "self-made." Unlike his British counterpart, he does not rely on social position, family heritage, or inherited wealth; he does not even have a rich cultural tradition of literature and poetry behind him to ground his explorations of identity. But what he does have is the United States itself: a blank slate, a *tabula rasa* on which, and in which, he can inscribe his identity. As Nina Baym and others have pointed out, there were impediments to this inscription in the form of an Other (often women, but sometimes African Americans or Native Americans) that "beset" the new American Adam and attempted to prevent this inscription; but the American Adam conveniently ignored this fact, seeing in the "New World," the New Eden of America, his chance to cast off the tainting influence of an older and more corrupt civilization (England) and create himself anew.

Although other authors may have been the first to express the concept of the self-made man, the clearest formulation of this ideology appears in Benjamin Franklin's well-known *Autobiography* (1793). One of the most famous scenes depicts Franklin arriving in Philadelphia, poor, alone, with hardly a penny to his name:

> I was in my working Dress [. . .]. I was dirty from my Journey; my Pockets were stuf'd out with Shirts and Stockings; I knew no Soul, nor where to look for Lodging. I was fatigu'd with Traveling, Rowing and Want of Rest. I was very hungry, and my whole Stock of Cash consisted of a Dutch Dollar and about a Shilling in Copper.

Franklin spends some of these precious shillings on bread and is given "three great Puffy Rolls" that he must carry under his arms, having no more room left in his pockets. Thus he enters the city of Philadelphia, where he will eventually become one of the leading figures, as scholar, printer, inventor, politician, signatory of the Declaration of Independence, and ambassador to France. In this scene Franklin deliberately emphasizes how little he has and how ragged he is so that his later success and fame will be all the more astonishing, admirable, and imitable. Indeed, his autobiography as a whole is a kind of conduct manual that will instruct other men in how to achieve success.

These concepts of the self-made man and literature as instructions for life will recur in a number of other works, such as Horatio Alger's *Ragged Dick, or, Street Life in New York with the Boot Blacks* (1868), Henry David Thoreau's *Walden* (1854) and even Frederick Douglass's *Narrative of the Life of Frederick Douglass, an American Slave, Written by Himself* (1845). Alger's didactic novel *Ragged Dick* tells the exuberant story of a plucky young boy who, through hard work, industry, and a pleasant demeanor is able to transform himself from a poor, orphaned street urchin shining shoes into a wealthy businessman. In *Walden* Thoreau is more stoical and austere in his treatment of the concept of the "self-made man": enduring pain and hardship he casts off all his possessions and begins anew, to live life "deliberately." In the woods on the shore of Walden Pond, Thoreau earns food and shelter "by the labor of my hands only." Of course, like many of the Transcendental writers, Thoreau wants to connect with nature and the natural world; however, he wants to do this by using his own hands, his own labors, and his own skills. He too, in short, wants to be "self-made."

And yet, of course, there are limitations to this ideology, which become clear if we consider Nina Baym's claim in "Melodramas of Beset Manhood" (1999) that women act as the "barren land" or "impediment" that must be cleared or conquered in order to establish masculine identity. For example, in order to fit this model, Frederick Douglass, in his 1845 slave narrative, must downplay the role of his mother, relegate his wife – who actually provides the money for his escape from slavery – to a footnote, and deride "ignorant" and "superstitious" slaves who have not yet learned to believe in Anglo-American religion and in the power of standardized, American English. The contradictions in the ideology of the self-made man also become apparent in Hector St. John de Crèvecœur's *Letters from an American Farmer* (1782). In this epistolary, semi-fictional account of his life as a farmer and his travels in the United States, Crèvecœur asserts that what is unique about the American character is its autonomy, its independence of the ways and traditions of the past:

> *He* is an American, who, leaving behind him all his ancient prejudices and manners, receives new ones from the new mode of thought he has embraced, the new government he obeys, and the new rank he holds . . . Here the rewards of his industry follow with equal steps the progress of his labor . . . The American is a new man. (Letter III)

Yet later in the collection, he confronts more specifically the fact that this "new man" is not self-made, but is often quite literally "made" on the backs of others. In Letter IX, he discovers a slave who has been left to die in the woods:

> I perceived a negro, suspended in the cage, and left there to expire! I shudder when I recollect that the birds had already picked out his eyes, his cheek bones were bare; his arms had been attacked in several places, and his body seemed covered with a multitude of wounds . . . "How long have you been hanging there?" I asked him. "Two days, and me no die; the birds, the birds; aah me!"

The blood of the slave stains the earth below his cage, metaphorically suggesting that this land of America, this land of the self-made man, is stained with the countless blood of Others who have not been afforded the opportunity to be self-made. The author can draw no didactic lesson from this horrific scene, and the fissures in the ideology of the "new man," the New Adam, are no longer hidden but clear to see.

Hannah Foster's 1797 novel *The Coquette* similarly examines the limitations of the ideology by asking whether a woman can be self-made. Based loosely on actual events, *The Coquette* tells the story of Eliza Wharton, a woman who has two suitors but is dissatisfied with both. Eliza takes too much time deciding between these two men and they eventually abandon her. She then enters into an adulterous affair, becomes pregnant, and dies in childbirth. As Walter Wenska (1977–8) argues, the novel raises difficult questions about the limits and definitions of freedom in a new land theoretically dedicated to freedom itself. Wenska asserts that Eliza Wharton is a rebel who seeks a freedom not typically allotted to her sex, one who refuses to settle into the "modest freedom" of marriage. Sharon M. Harris (1995) in fact argues that Foster challenges "the 'truth' of patriarchal structures established to guide – and to control – women's lives, by satirizing the Franklinesque use of maxims [. . . and] illuminates the political ideology of excluding women from citizenship and systems of power that is fostered in the social milieu." Like the earlier works discussed, the novel is didactic, but it also raises the question of *why* Eliza cannot have the kind of freedom that Franklin, Ragged Dick, or Frederick Douglass has – the freedom to be self-made, rather than unmade or unmaid. Perhaps this question goes unanswered, but it is certainly implanted in the construction of gender in the United States at a very early moment.

If the American woman could not be self-made, what then could she be? Several critics have pointed to interrelated ideas about women's role and status in this period. Women are not to enter the public sphere, but are (rather) "domestic saints" located in the "private sphere" of the home, separate from the real world. They exercise power not through direct action or voice, but through indirect influence and moral persuasion of their sons and husbands. Historians such as Barbara Welter, Nancy Cott, and Carroll Smith-Rosenberg have demonstrated that from 1780 to 1860 Americans were preoccupied with the feminine virtues of purity, piety, submissiveness, and domesticity – a group of attributes which together made up the figure known as the domestic saint, the Angel in the House, or the "True Woman." The ministers, preachers, doctors, and other writers who promoted the cult of domesticity assumed "that women would be happy insofar as they served others and made them happy" (Cott 1977: 71). Women were "passive, submissive responders" in this paradigm, since, as Welter argues, "submission was perhaps the most feminine virtue expected of women" (1966: 158). This image also promulgated a concept of woman's voice as submissive and self-sacrificing. For example, advice manuals such as William Alcott's *The Young Wife, Or, Duties of Woman in the Marriage Relation* (1837) tell women that even when in the right, "It is better to forbear. Think twice before you speak once [. . .] 'the tongue is a fire – a world of iniquity'" (p. 211). Women were to be passive, submissive, domestic, and self-denying but also *silent*, or at least deferential in their speaking patterns.

However, as several critics have noted (see Levander 1998; Cutter 1999; Ruttenburg 1998), woman's status as a domestic saint or true woman with a submissive voice was a source of controversy in novels from this period. Furthermore, some women writers simultaneously embraced and contested the ideology of the domestic saint, of woman's "separate" sphere, and of her submissive voice. Nowhere is this controversy over woman's voice more apparent than in a novel such as Fanny Fern's (Sara Payson Willis Parton's) *Ruth Hall* (1855). When the heroine's young, articulate, and witty daughter Nettie expresses her desire to become an author, her mother's response is rather shocking; Ruth says, "God forbid . . . no happy woman ever writes" (Fern 1986:

Figure 4.1 No caption appears for this illustration, which accompanies the first publication of Nathaniel Hawthorne, "Endicott and the Red Cross," in S. G. Goodrich (ed.), *The Token; or, Affection's Gift. A Christmas and New Year's Present* (New York: Leavitt & Allen, n.d.). Collection of Shirley Samuels.

175). And yet Ruth herself is a writer, and Fern also depicts her marshaling (at times) a speaking voice that challenges masculine authority. How can this paradox be explained? Fern implies that Ruth (under the pseudonym of "Floy") writes for the benefit of her children (to support them after her husband's death): she writes to earn bread for them, she writes to make money, but she does not write out of ambition or to have a "voice." "And still 'Floy' scribbled on, thinking only of bread for her children" (p. 133). Even in her triumphant verbal duel with the nasty editor Mr. Tibbetts, Ruth is still thinking of her children: "I have two little ones dependent on my exertions, and *their* future, as well as my own, to look to" (p. 156). Ruth's assertion of a future for herself as a writer is syntactically encoded or shielded within her assertion of a future for her children; the language of domesticity is privileged and Ruth's orientation towards others is emphasized over her orientation towards self. Again and again, Fern emphasizes that Ruth has no ambition to write a book (p. 136), that she has no ambition to be an artist (p. 182), and that she writes only out of necessity. Woman's status as a "domestic saint" or a "true woman" with a submissive voice is both preserved and refigured by a text such as *Ruth Hall*. Ruth does attain power through her writing and through her tongue, but she shields the attainment of power within a rhetoric of domesticity that expands the power of the true woman without fundamentally challenging its tenets about woman's "place" and "voice."

A more radical challenge to the cult of domesticity that still does not completely undermine it is presented by Harriet Jacobs in her slave narrative, *Incidents in the Life of a Slave Girl* (1861). Jacobs argues that she should – and should not – be held to the strict moral standards of the cult of domesticity. She employs many of the conventions of the sentimental novel, such as direct addresses to her (female) readers, a rhetoric of heightened emotion, and tropes of darkness and light. Like a sentimental heroine, Jacobs attempts to protect her virtue, only to find that her efforts fail. But rather than dying (as is the fate of the fallen heroine in a sentimental novel such as *The Coquette*), Jacobs asserts that she should not be judged by the same standards as other women: "Still, in looking back, calmly, on the events of my life, I feel that the slave woman ought not to be judged by the same standard as others" (1987: 56). In other novels by African American women from this period, such as Harriet Wilson's *Our Nig; or, Sketches from the Life of a Free Black* (1859), a similar pattern is apparent. Wilson's heroine Frado is both like the (white) domestic saint, in that she is pure, pious, and domestic, but unlike her in that she is treated as a slave, abused, derided, and ridiculed. Frado retains her purity, but it is clear that for both Jacobs and Wilson these ideologies of gender are paradoxical – ways in which they attempt to attain "power" from within women's "traditional sphere," while also pointing out the limitations of this traditional (and separate) sphere for individuals who, by virtue of their race and/or class, have never been defined by the dominant culture as "ladies" or "true women." Furthermore, neither writer is comfortable portraying women as ambitious writers who have a need for voice. Jacobs writes to encourage women to help other slaves, and Wilson's persona Frado authors a novel to support her son. The notion of a voice of "self-expression" that is at once ambitious and feminine is therefore both approached and elided by these texts.

"Separate" Spheres? Rhetoric of Sentiment, Religion, and Motherhood

Not all women writers of this period subscribed to the idea of women's "separate" voice and sphere of action. Several critics recently have argued that the "separate spheres" ideology did not influence women as much as has been claimed. These critics postulate that the distinction between the "private" realm of the home and the "public" realm of history and politics is arbitrarily imposed by scholars, not a belief to which either women or men strictly adhered in this time period (see in this regard especially Baym 1995). Certain texts by women writers in fact do present more radical challenges to the ideology of the self-made man, the true woman, and men's and women's "separate" spheres of influence and action. These women writers in fact often used their status as true women and the cult of domesticity to intervene in the public sphere from which they were debarred. Through evoking an ethics of sentimentality, motherhood, and religion, many writers expanded the concept of women's "separate" sphere into the external world of politics and so gained for women a public voice.

Nowhere is this strategic challenge more apparent than in Harriet Beecher Stowe's *Uncle Tom's Cabin* (1852). Identified by Abraham Lincoln as "the little lady who wrote the book that started this big war," Stowe, as well as her novel, relied on the "moral suasion" that women wielded as a result of their domestic virtue in order to refute the popular idea that woman's proper place was outside of the political debate occurring in the public sphere. As Mrs. Bird, one of Stowe's many exemplars of true womanhood in *Uncle Tom's Cabin*, declares when Senator Bird tells her of the fugitive slave law, "It's a shameful, wicked, abominable law, and I'll break it, for one, the first time I get a chance." The ensuing debate between husband and wife clearly illustrates the political power that woman's voice wields, precisely because of its greater virtue, and therefore women's ability to influence public debate. To her husband's declaration that the fugitive slave law is "not a matter of private feeling" but rather a "great public interest" that requires all citizens to "put aside our private feeling," Mrs. Bird responds with divine law. Asserting that she does not "know anything about politics, but can read [her] Bible," Mrs. Bird successfully counters public laws created by men with God's law – a law that women's higher moral virtue enables them to wield authoritatively – in order to persuade the Senator to feel and act "right" when the fugitive slave, Eliza, asks for help. Mr. Bird, therefore, is not simply a self-made man who upholds public law, but is influenced by the true woman at his side. The best political decisions, in Stowe's view, result from this kind of collaborative exchange between public men and domestic women.

Like Mrs. Bird and other of her female characters, Stowe deployed the moral suasion accruing to the true woman in order to persuade readers to "feel right" about the slave question. In so doing, she hoped that her women readers would, in turn, use their prominent position in the private sphere to influence their husbands and sons to become politically active in the abolitionist cause. Many did become interested in the slave question. Some writers, however, were inspired to refute Stowe's abolitionist message by writing pro-slavery responses to *Uncle Tom's Cabin*. Caroline Lee Hentz's immensely popular *The Planter's Northern Bride* (1854), for example, describes how a Northern woman who marries a Southern planter gradually comes to appreciate the benefits that slavery affords to the slave as well as the slave-owner. Eulalia Moreland has the "pure, sweet, fresh womanliness" and "deep, genuine, but unobtrusive piety" (Hentz 1854: 101) requisite to the true woman. However, by the novel's end she has become a champion of slavery, the very institution of which she was initially skeptical. In the popular Southern writer Augusta J. Evans's *Macaria; or,*

Altars of Sacrifice (1864), the female protagonist Irene similarly uses her piety, purity, and moral suasion in order to convince characters and readers alike that secession offers "the only door of escape from the political bondage" in which the North desires to place the South (Evans 1992: 364). The true Southern woman featured in Evans's earlier pro-slavery novel *Beulah* (1859) became such a popular character throughout the South that camps and towns were named after Beulah, and the novel was reputed to protect Confederate soldiers from Union bullets.

The political impact that these pro- and anti-slavery novels had on the US public sphere makes explicit what much woman's writing implicitly accomplished. Whether they contributed to such overtly political periodicals at *The Slave's Friend*, wrote for Sarah Josepha Hale's *Godey's Lady's Book*, or authored domestic bestsellers like Susan Warner's *The Wide Wide World* (1851) or Maria Cummins's *The Lamplighter* (1854), women used their writing to influence crucial public debates about the nation's borders, citizens, and governance. And they did so by emphasizing the true woman's central social task – motherhood. Indeed, the emphasis that advice manuals and fiction tended to place on motherhood became a primary way of justifying women's engagement in public conversation. Considered by many to be as much a "republic of the mother" as a nation conceived and birthed by the founding fathers, the United States depended for its longevity and political success on its young citizens and the training in citizenship that they received as infants. As Noah Webster contends, "this infant empire" depended on its child citizens. The "cornerstone of national survival," these young Americans must learn to place "the welfare of the country" before their own. Such an education in public responsibility requires that mothers, beginning in the nursery, treat their offspring as "budding citizens of a free republic." In this way, women, though increasingly confined to the private sphere as the nineteenth century progressed, continued to feel that their maternal responsibilities were integral to national wellbeing. Popular advice manuals like Lydia Maria Child's *The Mother's Book* (1831) were therefore dedicated to "American mothers, on whose intelligence and discretion the safety and prosperity of our Republic so much depends" (Child 1989: 1). Advice manuals such as *The Daughter's Own Book; or, Practical Hints From a Father to his Daughter* (1834) aimed to provide this necessary maternal influence for those girls who were deprived of their own mothers by death, illness, or distance. Fiction by Lydia Maria Child, Susan Warner, Louisa May Alcott, and others consistently featured motherhood as a powerful source of emotional and moral good to child protagonists.

Religion, as much as motherhood, proved to be an increasingly important institution through which women could indirectly influence public opinion. Just as Mrs. Bird invokes the Bible to take a stand against the fugitive slave law, so too did many women find in the special piety attributed to their gender a means of contributing to political policies. As Ann Douglas has shown, the "militant, heroic, aggressive," and quintessentially masculine jeremiad tradition of early Protestant ministers gave way, by the nineteenth century, to a religious establishment in which "ministers and mothers" joined forces in order to effect social change (1977: 21). Assuming greater

leadership within religious organizations, women gradually reoriented these organizations so that, having formerly been interested only in the inner souls of their
parishioners, they took an interest also in the social conditions that tempted individuals to sin in the first place. Similarly, novels like *The Lamplighter* illustrated how
religious education could transform motherless girls like Gerty Flint from indigent
street children into true women. Selling 100,000 copies by the end of its first year,
Cummins's novel resonated with readers in part because it charted how "a child
utterly untaught in the ways of virtue" (Cummins 1854: 73) could become a powerful
public exemplar of bourgeois decorum through spiritual awakening. As an icon of
true womanhood, Gerty tells girls who ask how they can be like her that they "must
cultivate [their] *heart*" (1854: 213).

   This attention to "cultivating the heart" also motivated many women to interest
themselves in spiritually based social outreach. As Lori Ginzberg has shown, the
church-sponsored benevolent societies that proliferated during the nineteenth century
were increasingly run by women, with ministers taking a secondary and essentially
consultative role. These societies produced literature and periodicals that invoked
woman's purity in calling for changes to laws and policies on social questions ranging
from temperance, to labor reform, to women's dress reform. Caroline Dall, for
example, argued in *"Woman's Right to Labor"* (1860) that working-class women should
receive higher wages to protect their purity once they enter the workplace. Because
men's "lust is a better paymaster than the mill-owner," "the question which is at this
moment before the great body of working women," according to Dall, is "death or
dishonor" (Dall 1860: 5). Working women's pay should therefore be sufficient to keep
them from having to sell their innocence to survive.

   Men as well as women persuaded readers to adopt their political views by using the
rhetorical techniques that Ann Douglas and others have tended to associate exclusively with women writers and with the feminization of American culture. In other
words, even as many women writers used the ideals associated with true womanhood
to contribute to vital dialogue about public policies, so too did male public speakers
and writers tap the rhetorical power accruing to femininity to persuade audiences to
adopt their political positions. Glenn Hendler, Bruce Burgett, and Mary Chapman
recently have explored how the writings of self-made public men like George
Washington depended on the heightened sentiment many scholars in the past have
tended to associate with femininity. In "The Heroic Slave" (1853) Frederick Douglass
attempts to gain his readers' sympathy for the successful leader of an 1841 slave
mutiny. He therefore creates a male protagonist who, in the process of "pouring out
his thoughts and feelings, his hopes and resolutions," immediately convinces a
passerby of the correctness of his views. With "the speech of Madison" ringing
"through the chambers of his soul," Mr. Listwell is compelled to reconsider his
feelings about slavery, and he declares that "from this hour, I am an abolitionist."
Douglass relies on the same strategies as Stowe to persuade readers of the heroism of
his protagonist, Madison Washington, and to gain an empowered voice and identity
for this African American male character.

Cracks in the Façade of Gender Ideologies

The gender ideologies that became powerful markers of identity from the late eighteenth century through the mid-nineteenth century shaped US national culture, but they did not include everyone living within the nation's expanding borders. Sojourner Truth was purported to have stated in her famous 1851 Akron Convention speech: "Nobody ever helps me into carriages, or over mud-puddles, or gives me any best place! And ain't I a Woman?" She insisted that although she was a worker, illiterate, a female, black, and not a domestic saint, she still had the right to be treated with dignity. Yet it has become clear over time that Truth may not have said these words and that this radical challenge to true womanhood may have come from the white woman who compiled and edited Truth's speech twelve years after the convention, Francis Gage. The voice of a black woman who resides "outside" of gender ideologies may thus have been simultaneously created and co-opted. A work such as William Craft's *Running a Thousand Miles for Freedom* (1860) also makes clear that certain types of subjectivity are still denied, despite the expansion of women's influence. William Craft and his wife Ellen escape from slavery in the South through a very clever strategy: Ellen (who is very light-skinned) agrees to "pass" for white and male, and to have William pretend to be her slave and constant attendant. In this guise they travel from Georgia to Philadelphia. As soon as Ellen puts on her disguise, William refers to her as his "master." But then, as if threatened by this destabilization of race and gender, when they reach freedom William must reassert his own subjectivity and his mastery of Ellen:

> On leaving the station, my master – or rather my wife, as I may now say – who had borne up in a manner that much surprised us both, grasped me by the hand, and said, "Thank God, William, we are safe!" then burst into tears, leant upon me, and wept like a child. The reaction was fearful. So when we reached the house, she was in reality so weak and faint that she could scarcely stand alone. (Craft 1860: 79)

As Ellen Weinauer (1996) has argued, the text indicates that Ellen Craft can pass for male for only so long. Eventually, her "true womanhood" reasserts itself, so that she must be carried over the threshold of freedom by William, the self-made and (now) heroically free African American man. But what of Ellen Craft? Her subjectivity, freedom, and voice remain dependent on that of her husband's.

It might seem, then, that in these years gender ideologies expanded beyond the rigid ideals of the true woman and the self-made man and granted new types of subjectivity, power, and voice to new types of individuals (white women and black men), but that African American women, and men and women from other races and classes, remain disempowered and voiceless. Yet the very presence of individuals like Sojourner Truth and Ellen Craft in history and culture indicates that this picture is incomplete. The portrait of Ellen Craft's cross-dressed, cross-raced self is the first thing readers see when they open *Running a Thousand Miles for Freedom*, and in fact it was sold separately from the book to raise money to free other slaves. Within the text William Craft tries to re-place Ellen within the category of "true woman" – but a troublingly ambiguous racialized and gendered self remains as a cultural icon (Weinauer 1996: 52). Similarly, Sojourner Truth's powerful personal example of a woman known for working tirelessly and ceaselessly as a speaker and fundraiser in the abolitionist and women's rights movements remains to disrupt notions of "true womanhood." The presence of Sojourner Truth and Ellen Craft within history and culture indicate that there are cracks in the façade of gender ideologies – cracks that might one day break open these ideologies and extend subjectivity, freedom, and voice to *all* men and women, regardless of their race, class, or gender.

References and Further Reading

Alcott, William A. (1837). *The Young Wife, Or, Duties of Woman in the Marriage Relation*. Boston: George W. Light.

Baym, Nina (1995). *American Women Writers and the Work of History, 1790–1860*. New Brunswick: Rutgers University Press.

Baym, Nina (1999). "Melodramas of Beset Manhood: How Theories of American Fiction Exclude Women Authors." In *American Literature, American Culture*, compiled by Gordon Hutner, 431–42. New York: Oxford University Press.

Burgett, Bruce (1998). *Sentimental Bodies: Sex, Gender, and Citizenship in the Early Republic*. Princeton: Princeton University Press.

Child, Lydia Maria (1989). *The Mother's Book*. Cambridge, Mass.: Applewood. (First publ. 1831.)

Cott, Nancy F. (1977). *The Bonds of Womanhood: "Woman's Sphere" in New England 1780–1835*. New Haven: Yale University Press.

Craft, William (1860). *Running a Thousand Miles for Freedom; Or, the Escape of William and Ellen Craft From Slavery*. London: William Tweedie.

Crèvecœur, J. Hector St. John de (1925). *Letters from an American Farmer*. New York: Charles & Albert Boni. (First publ. 1782.)

Cummins, Maria Susana (1854). *The Lamplighter*. London: John Cassell.

Cutter, Martha J. (1999). *Unruly Tongue: Identity and Voice in American Women's Writing, 1850–1930*. Jackson: University Press of Mississippi.

Dall, Caroline (1860)."Woman's Right to Labor"; or, Low Wages and Hard Work. Boston: Walker, Wise.

The Daughter's Own Book (1834). *The Daughter's Own Book; or, Practical Hints From a Father to his Daughter*. Boston: Lilly, Wait, Colman, & Holden.

Douglas, Ann (1977). *The Feminization of American Culture*. New York: Farrar, Straus & Giroux.

Douglass, Frederick (1853). "The Heroic Slave." In *Autographs for Freedom*, ed. Julia Griffiths. Boston: Jewett.

Evans, Augusta J. (1992). *Macaria; or, Altars of Sacrifice*. Baton Rouge: Louisiana State University Press. (First publ. 1864.)

Fern, Fanny [Sara Payson Willis Parton] (1986). *Ruth Hall*. New Brunswick, NJ: Rutgers University Press. (First publ. 1855.)

Franklin, Benjamin (1793). *The Private Life of the Late Benjamin Franklin. Originally Written by Himself, and Now Translated from the French*. London: J. Parsons.

Ginzberg, Lori D. (1990). *Women and the Work of Benevolence: Morality, Politics, and Class in the Nineteenth-Century United States*. New Haven: Yale University Press.

Harris, Sharon M. (1995). "Hannah Webster Foster's *The Coquette*: Critiquing Franklin's America." In Sharon M. Harris (ed.), *Redefining the Political Novel: American Women Writers, 1797–1901*, 1–22. Knoxville: University of Tennessee Press.

Hendler, Glenn, and Chapman, Mary, eds. (1999). *Sentimental Men: Masculinity and the Politics of Affect in American Culture*. Berkeley: University of California Press.

Hentz, Caroline (1854). *The Planter's Northern Bride*. Philadelphia: T. B. Peterson & Bros.

Jacobs, Harriet A. (1987). *Incidents in the Life of a Slave Girl, Written by Herself*. Cambridge, Mass.: Harvard University Press. (First publ. 1861.)

Levander, Caroline F. (1998). *Voices of the Nation: Women and Public Speech in Nineteenth-Century Literature and Culture*. New York: Cambridge University Press.

Ruttenburg, Nancy (1998). *Democratic Personality: Popular Voice and the Trial of American Authorship*. Stanford: Stanford University Press.

Smith-Rosenberg, Carroll (1985). *Disorderly Conduct: Visions of Gender in Victorian America*. New York: Oxford University Press.

Stowe, Harriet Beecher (1852). *Uncle Tom's Cabin; or, Life among the Lowly*. London: Routledge.

Thoreau, Henry David (1962). *Walden and other Writings*, ed. Joseph Wood Krutch. New York: Bantam. (First publ. 1854.)

Webster, Noah (1790). *A Collection of Essays and Fugitive Writings on Moral, Historical, Political and Literary Subjects*. Boston: I. Thomas & E. T. Andrews.

Weinauer, Ellen M. (1996). " 'A Most Respectable Looking Gentleman': Passing, Possession, and Transgression in *Running a Thousand Miles for Freedom*." In Elaine K. Ginsberg (ed.), *Passing and the Fictions of Identity*, 37–56. Durham, NC: Duke University Press.

Welter, Barbara (1966). "The Cult of True Womanhood, 1820–1860." *American Quarterly* 18, 157–74.

Wenska, Walter P. (1977–8). "The Coquette and the American Dream of Freedom." *Early American Literature* 12: 3 (Winter), 243–55.

5

Race and Ethnicity

Robert S. Levine

Herman Melville's domestic potboiler *Pierre* (1852) is not typically thought of as a novel about race and ethnicity, but Melville's ironic use of genealogical motifs provides a useful introduction to the vexed terrain of race and ethnicity in early American fiction. Speaking in the jingoistic voice of the American literary nationalist, Melville at the outset of the novel celebrates the vitality of American genealogies, focusing initially on the well-known Randolph family of Virginia, "one of whose ancestors," Melville states, "married Pocahontas the Indian Princess, and in whose blood therefore an underived aboriginal royalty was flowing over two hundred years ago" (1971b: 10). The emphasis here is on the fluid intermixing of blood, with the ironically developed notion that the Southern nationalist Randolphs, who pride themselves on their whiteness, have bloodlines that are both miscegenated and pure. The ethnic and racial hybridity of the Randolphs, Melville suggests, is true for the novel's Glendinnings as well, despite the fact that these New Yorkers also pride themselves on their white genealogical purity. Though Mrs. Glendinning hopes to sustain that purity by marrying off her son, Pierre, to the radiantly white Lucy Tartan, Pierre finds himself attracted to the darker Isabel. As the novel develops, he becomes increasingly apprehensive that the darkly attractive Isabel may be his sister, for he learns that his father may have had a daughter out of wedlock, just as his father before him, a hero of the Revolution, may have had sexual relations with his slaves (Levine 1999). As with the ironic account of the Randolphs' blood mixture, the hintings about Isabel, Pierre, his father, and his grandfather are meant to trouble, or undercut, the Glendinnings' prideful family genealogy. In *Pierre*, racial, ethnic, and, by extension, national identities are depicted as incoherent and on the verge of collapse, for the racial and ethnic otherness "outside" the white family turns out to be lodged uneasily inside the homes of the post-revolutionary generation.

Recent critical work on race and ethnicity in early national and antebellum fiction has tended to implicate authors in what could be termed the national eugenicist project of Mrs. Glendinning. In *Master Plots: Race and the Founding of an American*

Literature, for example, Jared Gardner elaborates a literary genealogy that has a white supremacist logic of distinctly American purity at its center. The novel in particular played a crucial role in this project, he says, by "scripting stories of 'origins' that imagined white Americans as a race apart, both from the Europeans without and the blacks and Indians within the new nation" (1998: xi). But what is lost in such an insistence on fiction's participation in the creation of a white republic is the possibility that a number of America's most complex writers took race and ethnicity as a *subject*, rather than as an assumed foundation, of their fiction. As the representation of genealogy in *Pierre* makes clear, Melville, for one, mocks the notion that Americans could exist as a breed apart, and in the overall novel suggests the intermixing of American aristocratic families not only with the Indians but also with their black slaves.

Melville was hardly alone in raising questions about the nation's ethnic and racial foundations, and about white racial hierarchies. Considerations of race and ethnicity in early national and antebellum fiction were of course complicated by the fact that the nation was founded by immigrants; thus there could be no national "purity" preceding the settlers and colonizers other than that embodied by the native Americans themselves. In certain respects, then, all American fiction can be viewed as ethnic fiction – that is, fiction which thematizes or helps to develop what Thomas J. Ferraro has termed "attributive belonging" (2003: 78). Race would inevitably have a central place in such a broadly conceived notion of US ethnic literature, insofar as whiteness, in a slave culture, was part of national belonging, and blackness was explicitly excluded. But race and ethnicity overlapped during this period, in complex ways, and were not so easily separable. In the eighteenth century, for example, race and nation were linked to notions of family lineage, around the idea of the nation as a family. The emerging question that late eighteenth- and early nineteenth-century US writers had to address was the nature of that family; or, to put this differently, how does one move from belonging to one sort of family (a particular ethnic group) to another (the new American nation)? Werner Sollors, the most influential recent commentator on race and ethnicity in American culture, has conceptualized this dilemma in terms of a cultural conflict between notions of descent and consent: "Descent language emphasizes our positions as heirs, our hereditary qualities, liabilities and entitlements; consent language stresses our abilities as mature free agents and 'architects of our fates' to choose our spouses, our destinies, and our political systems" (Sollors 1986: 6). For Sollors, a central component of Americanization is the process of making choices, from within an ethnic group, about national belonging. In a slave culture, however, some groups had more choices than others.

Tensions between descent and consent inform J. Hector St. John de Crèvecœur's *Letters from an American Farmer* (1782), a text that has generally been taken as the *locus classicus* for US ethnic studies, and which, with its fictionalized persona and epistolary strategies, may be read as a proto-American novel. The narrator, James, famously declares near the outset of the narrative that America displays an ethnic pluralism in which formerly European peoples – "a mixture of English, Scotch, Irish, French,

Dutch, Germans, and Swedes" (Crèvecœur 1981: 68) – choose to surrender their ancient prejudices and "are melted into a new race of men" (p. 70). In his blending of race and ethnicity, Crèvecœur shares a vision similar to that of numerous eighteenth-century political philosophers who regarded nationality in terms of race. It is worth emphasizing, however, that even as *Letters* idealizes what would come to be celebrated in mainstream nineteenth- and twentieth-century American culture as the nation's defining values of ethnic pluralism, the text suggests that members of some ethnicities, or races, are better able than others to "melt" into Americans. Whereas the hard-working and temperate Germans will succeed in the Americanization process in nine of twelve cases, Crèvecœur writes, only four of twelve Irish will have similar success, with the vast majority succumbing to drink and violence. In his own case, James achieves a certain amount of early success, while increasingly confronting the limits of pluralism in the emergent nation. In a haunting chapter on his journey to South Carolina, for example, he confronts head-on the horrors of slavery, and at the end of the book, when he considers bringing his family to live with the Indians, he proclaims that a link between white and red would be "disagreeable no doubt to Nature's intentions" (p. 222). Such a statement raises the question of whether "Nature" would feel any less violated by a link between white and black or even German and Irish. While *Letters* begins with evocations of the biological and cultural mixing that helps to produce the new American, it is clear that Crèvecœur would like to keep black and red blood out of that mix, and that even the mix among different European peoples may, in his mind, be more metaphorical (about national belonging) than actual (about the end of race and ethnicity).

The 1790s saw an emerging consensus that the pluralistic new nation was nonetheless going to define itself as a white Protestant republic, and thus there were increasing efforts to make distinctions between Americans and non-Americans, as evidenced by the Naturalization Act of 1798 and the Federalists' repressive Alien and Sedition Acts of that same year. But how easy was it to make distinctions between the "alien" and the "American" in a culture of immigrants? This question is at the heart of the four novels written by Charles Brockden Brown during the late 1790s. In *Wieland* (1798), for example, published the year of the Alien and Sedition Acts, Brown depicts in the ventriloquist Carwin a disturbing alien who seems almost single-handedly to bring down a small domestic community in rural Pennsylvania. But is Carwin truly an alien? He is identified by various characters as perhaps a Roman Catholic, perhaps Spanish, and perhaps Irish, and it is true that his possible alien status adds to his psychological powers over the fearful group. But Brown makes clear that it is just as possible that Carwin is as American as any character in the book, and that it is a genealogy of mental illness in the Wieland family, along with a willing consent to the national paranoia exemplified by the Alien and Sedition Acts, that helps to bring about the violent events of the novel – none of which would seem to have been actually committed by Carwin. (In a later fragment published serially in one of his literary magazines, Brown in "Memoirs of Carwin" [1803–5] depicts Carwin as born and raised in Pennsylvania.) In his novels of the 1790s Brown simultaneously shares in white Protestant anxieties about ethnic and racial others even as he collapses such binaries, showing in the bloodlettings of *Edgar Huntly* (1799), for instance, that white Americans can be just as "savage" as Native Americans. As anxious and nativist as his novels might be, they are also knowing meditations on and critiques of the process of defining a nation against racial and ethnic others. Through the sheer energy of his imagination, Brown, particularly in his urban novels *Ormond* (1799) and *Arthur Mervyn* (1799–1800), actually seems to celebrate the possibilities of pluralism in American life, even as he continues to focus on the possible dangers facing the new nation from mysterious strangers. Similarly pluralistic energies can be found in Hugh Henry Brackenridge's *Modern Chivalry* (1792–1815), which both conveys the author's anxieties about an unfettered pluralistic democracy and gives a privileged place to the Irish servant Teague O'Regan.

The pluralistic ideals of Crèvecœur and other late eighteenth-century US national-ists would remain central to US literature and culture of the nineteenth century, even as concerns persisted about the threats posed by difference. Timothy Marr has noted that in the opening decades of the nineteenth century "ethnicity was simply a term of condescension used to mark the strangeness of unconverted difference" (2001: 7). In this regard, race and ethnicity would be linked by white writers to the figure of the Indian as non-national other, and thus it is not surprising that Noah Webster's 1828 dictionary presents "ethnic" and "heathen" as synonymous terms derived from heath or woods. Central to the literary nationalism of the American 1820s were fictions of the heath or woods by James Fenimore Cooper, Lydia Maria Child, and Catharine Sedgwick, who presented the nation in the fraught process of becoming a white republic. These fictions are complex and at times rather conflicted in their presenta-tion, during a time of forced Indian removal, of a progressive vision of American history that regarded as inevitable the concomitant rise of white civilization and "vanishing" of the Indian. The critic William Boelhower writes that "it was the Indian as ethnic who raised the first major challenge to the idea of a homogenous nation" (1987: 45). Child's *Hobomok* (1824) and Sedgwick's *Hope Leslie* (1827) can be viewed as posing precisely such a challenge by imagining and actually presenting the possibility of interracial romances between white and red that had the promise of producing a multicolored and multicultural US. In both novels, however, ascendant whites ultimately assume power over disappearing (conquered) Native Americans; and in *Hope Leslie* the subversive Indian woman Magawisca even proclaims her resigned acceptance of the inevitability of vengeful "savage" Indians moving westward and eventually disappearing from the nation.

James Fenimore Cooper popularized the progressive model of American history in such nationalist works as *The Pioneers* (1823), *The Last of the Mohicans* (1826), and *The Prairie* (1828). *The Pioneers* is of particular interest for the ways in which Cooper conjoins race, ethnicity, and nation in the representation of Templeton (a fictionalized Cooperstown) during the 1790s. Cooper optimistically declares at the outset of the novel that the nation is a place "where every man feels a direct interest in the prosperity of a commonwealth, of which he knows himself to form a part"

(1988: 15–16), and he underscores notions of national unity through a paralleling image of diverse and small waterways combining into one: "the numerous sources of the Susquehanna meander through the valleys, until, uniting their streams, they form one of the proudest rivers of the United States" (p. 15). But the very image of "source" begs the question of genealogy. What are the connections between these various sources and the current national formation? Where do people come from and what are the relationships between their origins and the new nation? Cooper presents numerous ethnic characters who are contributing to the commonweal at Templeton – the Frenchman Monsieur Le Quoi, the German Old Fritz, the Irish Mrs. Hollister – all of whom have "closely assimilated themselves to the Americans, in dress and appearance" (p. 124). But how "American" are they? Throughout the novel Cooper presents the ethnic characters, who may look the part of Americans, as different from the characters of English descent by emphasizing their distinctive "foreign" dialects. The novel's most problematic ethnic character is Monsieur Le Quoi, a former planter in the West Indies, who eventually chooses to return to Paris. In light of the demagogic violence that explodes at the end of the novel, Cooper seems intent on arguing for the importance of having English-speaking Protestant republicans watching over the disruptive democratic–ethnic energies that he believed were capable of bringing down the republic.

Here genealogy asserts racial and ethnic hierarchies. From the outset of *The Pioneers* Oliver Edwards is presented as an Indian who has been violated by Judge Temple's stray gunshot and, more importantly, by his appropriation of the lands that would become Templeton. Depicting Edwards in this way allows Cooper to explore the key racial and ethnic tensions related to whites' dispossession of the Native Americans. Moreover, as long as Edwards is imagined as an Indian, Cooper, like Child and Sedgwick, can hold out the possibility of a redemptive interracial marriage between the "red" Edwards and the white Elizabeth Temple, with the power of consent (Edwards's education and willingness to live in the home of his reputed enemy) winning out over what Temple refers to as "those revengeful principles, which you have inherited by descent" (Cooper 1988: 141–2). But as it turns out, descent is easily conjoined with consent when all of the parties involved are white and of English lineage: for it is revealed at the novel's conclusion that Edwards is in fact the son of Temple's deceased English friend Effingham. Genealogy in the novel thus reveals the close ties of white Anglo families to the progressive destiny of the United States, with the death of Indian John suggesting the Native Americans' anguished recognition that they will not have a role in the unfolding millennial drama. Such was the literary nationalism of the 1820s at its most orthodox and inflexible.

The literary nationalism of the 1820s helped to give rise to the Protestant evangelical nationalism of the 1830s and 1840s, decades that saw an upsurge of nativist writings, particularly in the northeast, and would culminate in a war against what was regarded as the Catholic/pagan country of Mexico. Galvanized by an upsurge of Catholic immigration to the United States during the 1830s and 1840s, Protestant church leaders deployed the vast publishing network of the American Tract

Society (founded in 1825) and related organizations to disseminate Protestant republican values. Lyman Beecher, in his widely read nativist tract *Plea for the West* (1835), conveyed concerns similar to those informing Cooper's *The Prairie* about the dangers of leaving the West vulnerable to Catholic imperial powers, and these concerns came to inform the bestselling convent-captivity novels of the period. Rebecca Theresa Reed's *Six Months in a Convent* (1835) and Maria Monk's *Awful Disclosures of the Hotel Dieu Nunnery* (1836) presented sadistic nuns and priests, violations in the confessional, and evidence of Roman Catholic conspiracies. Monk's sensational book of horrors sold upwards of 300,000 copies through 1860 and spawned numerous other convent-captivity novels, such as Charles Frothingham's *The Convent's Doom* (1854) and Josephine Bunkley's *Miss Bunkley's Book: The Testimony of an Escaped Novice from the Sisterhood of Charity* (1855). In important ways, these novels helped to disseminate nativist tropes and images in the culture, as evidenced by Edgar Allan Poe's "The Pit and the Pendulum" (1843), George Lippard's *The Monks of Monk Hall* (1844), and Melville's "Benito Cereno" (1855), all of which make use of inquisitorial imagery. But nativist imagery in antebellum fiction did not always appeal to a Protestant consensus or (as in "Benito Cereno," for example) ironically attack that consensus. Often such images conveyed Protestant attractions to the Roman Catholic other. In the Marian imagery of Harriet Beecher Stowe's *Uncle Tom's Cabin* (1852) and *Agnes of Sorrento* (1862), and in Hilda's achievement of confessional intimacy at St. Peter's in Hawthorne's *The Marble Faun* (1860), one senses that for at least these two Protestant New England writers, Roman Catholicism, with its order, consolation, and beauty, held out considerable attractions as well.

Stowe and Hawthorne conveyed their attraction to Roman Catholicism during the 1850s and early 1860s, times of increasing conflict and uncertainty in antebellum America. The Compromise of 1850 and the Kansas–Nebraska Act of 1854 raised the question of whether the nation planned to commit itself in perpetuity to upholding the institution of slavery. Concurrent with, and perhaps fueled by, Southerners' insistence on white mastery was the startling rise to power in the northeast during the mid-1850s of the Know-Nothings, who maintained that the United States was a white Anglo-Saxon nation that would best prosper if rid of threatening (i.e. non-American) racial and ethnic others. The debates on citizenship central to the controversies on slavery and nativism culminated in the Dred Scott decision of 1857, in which the Supreme Court denied to blacks the possibility of becoming US citizens. Given that the Irish, Italians, and other ethnic groups were regarded by the Know-Nothings (and white nativists more generally) as peoples of color (see Ignatiev 1995), this decision had the far-reaching effect of ratifying ideals of racial and ethnic purity as central to the continuing project of defining and upholding the nation. In many respects the Dred Scott decision was also the culmination of the racial "science" of the period, in which writers such as Josiah C. Nott and George R. Gliddon, in their popular *Types of Mankind* (1854), provided what they regarded as irrefutable scientific evidence that whites were physically and morally superior to blacks and other peoples of color.

Figure 5.1 Frontispiece from *Further Disclosures by Maria Monk, Concerning the Hotel Dieu Nunnery of Montreal* (New York: Leavitt, 1836). Photograph courtesy of the Library of Congress.

It is therefore not surprising that some of the most complex American fiction of the 1850s, such as Melville's *Pierre*, turned to genealogy to raise questions about the very ideals and possibilities of racial superiority and purity that informed the cultural debates and racist discourses of the period. Like *Pierre*, Nathaniel Hawthorne's *The House of the Seven Gables* (1851) depicts an ambiguous genealogical history of violation and deceit. In the late seventeenth century Colonel Pyncheon founded the house of the seven gables on land taken from the plebeian Maules, hoping to set "his race and future generations fixed on a stable basis" (Hawthorne 1981: 17), even as racial metaphors throughout the novel challenge the value and possibility of achieving such racial fixity. Depicted in parallel relation to the Pyncheons are Chanticleer and the other hens at the house, with the narrator commenting again and again on how Chanticleer's "race had degenerated, like many a noble race besides, in consequence of too strict a watchfulness to keep it pure" (p. 89). But is purity even possible or desirable? In his extended meditation on Governor Pyncheon's corpse near the end of the novel, the narrator initially describes the Judge's face as "singularly white" (p. 276), then as gray, then as sable, and finally as an oxymoronic "swarthy whiteness" (p. 276). The narrator's vision of racial mixing and instability is consistent with Holgrave/Maule's earlier remark on the lunacy of the Pyncheon desire for racial purity: "Human blood, in order to keep its freshness, should run in hidden streams, as the water of an aqueduct is conveyed in subterranean pipes" (p. 185). There is a suggestion, then, that the "miscegenated" marriage at the end of the novel between a Maule and a Pyncheon only makes visible the racial mixing that had come before, and a suggestion as well that Hawthorne would want some limits on that mixing – hence the characters' retreat to a country house that would keep them at a distance from the urban immigrant population, which is emblematized by the Italian organ-grinder and his money-grubbing monkey. Similar sorts of retreat, it should be pointed out, are enacted again and again in women's domestic novels of the period, for no matter how sympathetically the immigrant populations are limned, heroines in such popular novels as Maria Cummins's *The Lamplighter* (1854) and Fanny Fern's *Ruth Hall* (1855) fear joining the ranks of the urban poor, who are just about always depicted as ethnic immigrants.

Though Hawthorne does not comment explicitly on connections between the Pyncheons' genealogical history and the development of white supremacy in the United States, his genealogical romance encourages readers to distrust all "official" histories of privilege and domination, including those histories that connect racial purity to social and political forms of superiority. A similar lesson is central to the first novel published by an African American, William Wells Brown's *Clotel; or, The President's Daughter* (1853), which raises all kinds of questions about the racial categories of the period. Like Harriet Beecher Stowe in *Uncle Tom's Cabin*, Brown makes it clear that race has become increasingly difficult to distinguish in a nation in which a long history of the masters' sexual exploitation of their female slaves has helped to produce a large number of light-complected blacks. Stowe attempts to hold on to racial categories in *Uncle Tom's Cabin* by presenting all miscegenated characters as black, and by working with what the historian George Fredrickson has termed a "romantic racialist" view of blacks as especially prone toward Christianity and domesticity. In *Clotel*, however, Brown rejects romantic racialism in favor of what could be termed colorism, showing how in black and white culture respectively different shades of color bring different configurations of community and different attitudes towards race; his is a political or cultural view of race, as opposed to the mystical biologism of Stowe and other romantic racialists. But perhaps Brown's most acute intervention in the novel is to raise questions about the politics (and reality) of racial difference, given that many "blacks" are the sons and daughters of people like Thomas Jefferson, the father of Clotel. Brown is at his most arch and ironic on the issue when he describes how the darkly complected Daniel Webster, "a real live senator of the United States" (2000: 173), and one of the architects of the fugitive slave law introduced under the Compromise of 1850, could be mistaken as black by those who did not know him. In Brown's novel, then, "race" has the power of striking back against racists.

One sees similar efforts to trouble racial categories in the second novel published by an African American, Frank J. Webb's *The Garies and their Friends* (1857). The novel follows the fate of a number of black middle-class families in Philadelphia, focusing in particular on the new family in their midst, the Garies, which consists of a white slave-owner, his slave mistress (soon to become his legal wife), and their two children, Emily and Clarence, who are white to the eye but regarded as "black" by Philadelphia's white racists. Chief among those racists is George Stevens, the son of intemperate laborers, who enlists working-class Irish to help him in his plot to destroy black neighborhoods, purchase the abandoned land at low prices, and then make huge profits in the real estate market by "gentrifying" the real estate and selling it to whites at much higher prices. As Webb shows in his depiction of Stevens's plan to use the Irish to further his real estate plotting, the Irish characters are willing to help out, not only because Stevens has legal power over one of them, but also because the racist violence helps them to assert their own claims to white Americanism. In its depiction of Stevens's successful deployment of the Irish in an anti-black riot, *Garies* critiques the overlapping racial and ethnic formations that are self-destructively pushing the nation towards ruin.

In response to this crisis, Webb extends the concepts of race and ethnicity beyond genealogy in his portrayal of Emily Garie's political evolution. Though she is able to pass, Emily, who was raised as a privileged white, refuses to break from the blacks who have helped to sustain her. She declares to her brother Clarence, who had managed to pass by completely breaking off all contacts with black family and friends: "You walk on the side of the oppressor – I, thank God, am with the oppressed" (Webb 1997: 336). Though she does have "black" blood, Emily in this formulation places politics over blood, consent over descent. She defines herself as someone who wishes to battle oppression, and in doing so she *chooses* to be black. Arguably, that decision is not completely her choice, given that she is the daughter of a slave mother, but many of the "friends" of the Garies do make the choice to side with the oppressed. Choosing the oppressed over the oppressor, these characters, black and white, exemplify American revolutionary ideals and point the ways to new American genealogies that are grounded in consent over descent, and political morality over blood-lines. Even so, with its insistence on the explanatory power of Stevens's genealogical connection to intemperate parents, the novel hesitates to fully renounce the determining power of blood.

The same year that Webb published *Garies*, Melville published *The Confidence-Man*, which eschews genealogy in favor of a vision of a multiplicity of peoples whose racial and ethnic identities are achieved only through their own performances in the immediate present. Even blackness, as the Confidence Man shows in his con game as Black Guinea at the outset of the novel, is something that can be performed. Whereas Crèvecœur imagined a melting pot in which individuals from various European nations regenerated themselves into a new, modern, cohesive nation providing equal opportunities for all, Melville in *The Confidence-Man* offers a dark side of this vision, presenting a nation of whites and blacks, immigrants and Native Americans, brought together in the ship of state only to pursue their own selfish ends. Departing from *Moby-Dick*'s appealing image of the *Pequod*'s federated racial and ethnic diversity, *The Confidence-Man* in many respects is the most chilling novel of race and ethnicity ever published in the United States, in part because it evokes so powerfully the unfulfilled promises of pluralism in the country. Set on the steamship *Fidèle* as it courses down the Mississippi river to the slave markets of New Orleans, the novel unblinkingly portrays the inhumanities of slavery. But it also portrays the great racial and ethnic mix that would inspire the democratic fervor of writers such as Walt Whitman:

> [T]here was no lack of variety. Natives of all sorts, and foreigners; men of business and men of pleasure . . . Fine ladies in slippers, and moccasined squaws; Northern speculators and Eastern philosophers; English, Irish, German, Scotch, Danes; Santa Fé traders in striped blankets, and Broadway bucks in cravats of cloth of gold; fine-looking Kentucky boatmen, and Japanese-looking Mississippi cotton-planters; Quakers in full drab, and United States soldiers in full regimentals; slaves, black, mulatto, quadroon; modish young Spanish Creoles, and old-fashioned French Jews; Mormons and Papists; . . . grinning negroes, and Sioux chiefs solemn as high priests. (Melville 1971a: 6)

For the optimistic nationalist, here is the melting pot par excellence from which emerges the new individual (the American) in the new nation (the United States); for Melville in 1857, the ship of state is a "ship of fools" (p. 12), an amalgam of mysterious and greedy individuals who may or may not be who or what they seem to be. In the novel's world of "NO TRUST" (p. 6), race and ethnicity are traits that are performed by strangers in the service of greed, even as Melville makes clear, through his account of slavery and Indian hating, that race and ethnicity have a real existence in the social world and that their hierarchies are forged through violence. Paradoxically, in the primarily male world of the steamship, no one is who he seems to be even as each individual can only be what he seems to be. In the theatricality of the ship of state, Melville has anticipated the post-modern moment of the simulacrum. In the context of the 1850s, however, the centrality of biblical type to the allegory of the ship of state very pointedly links the ship to the dominant culture's reigning millennialist vision: that of the nation's white Anglo-Saxonist Manifest Destiny. But, as Melville makes clear with the apocalyptic extinguishing of the lamp at the end of his ethnic/racial dystopia, such a vision threatens to leave the nation in the dark.

REFERENCES AND FURTHER READING

Boelhower, William (1987). *Through a Glass Darkly: Ethnic Semiosis in American Literature.* New York: Oxford University Press.

Brown, William Wells (2000). *Clotel; or, The President's Daughter*, ed. Robert S. Levine. New York and Boston: Bedford/St. Martin's. (First publ. 1853.)

Cassuto, Leonard (1997). *The Inhuman Race: The Racial Grotesque in American Literature and Culture.* New York: Columbia University Press.

Cooper, James Fenimore (1988). *The Pioneers*, ed. Donald A. Ringe. New York: Penguin. (First publ. 1823.)

Crèvecœur, J. Hector St. John de (1981). *Letters from an American Farmer*, ed. Albert E. Stone. New York: Penguin. (First publ. 1782.)

Ferraro, Thomas J. (2003). "'At Long Last Love'; or, Literary History in the Key of Difference." *American Literary History* 15, 78–86.

Franchot, Jenny (1994). *Roads to Rome: The Antebellum Protestant Encounter with Catholicism.* Berkeley: University of California Press.

Fredrickson, George M. (1972). *The Black Image in the White Mind: The Debate on Afro-American Character and Destiny, 1817–1914.* New York: Harper Torchbooks.

Gardner, Jared (1998). *Master Plots: Race and the Founding of an American Literature, 1787–1845.* Baltimore: Johns Hopkins University Press.

Gossett, Thomas R. (1997). *Race: The History of an Idea in America.* New York: Oxford University Press. (First publ. 1963.)

Hawthorne, Nathaniel (1981). *The House of the Seven Gables.* New York: Penguin. (First publ. 1851.)

Horsman, Reginald (1981). *Race and Manifest Destiny: The Origins of American Racial Anglo-Saxonism.* Cambridge, Mass.: Harvard University Press.

Hudson, Nicholas (1996). "From "Nation" to "Race": The Origin of Racial Classification in Eighteenth-Century Thought." *Eighteenth-Century Studies* 29, 247–64.

Ignatiev, Noel (1995). *How the Irish Became White.* New York: Routledge.

Levine, Robert S. (1989). *Conspiracy and Romance: Studies in Brockden Brown, Cooper, Hawthorne, and Melville.* Cambridge, UK: Cambridge University Press.

Levine, Robert S. (1999). "Pierre's Blackened Hand." *Leviathan: A Journal of Melville Studies* 1, 23–44.

Lott, Eric (1993). *Love and Theft: Blackface Minstrelsy and the American Working Class.* New York: Oxford University Press.

Maddox, Lucy (1991). *Removals: Nineteenth-Century American Literature and the Politics of Indian Affairs.* New York: Oxford University Press.

Marr, Timothy (2001). "Melville's Ethnic Conscriptions." *Leviathan* 3, 5–29.

Melville, Herman (1971a). *The Confidence-Man: His Masquerade*, ed. Hershel Parker. New York: Norton. (First publ. 1857.)

Melville, Herman (1971b). *Pierre; or, The Ambiguities*, ed. Harrison Hayford, Hershel Parker, and G. Thomas Tanselle. Evanston and Chicago: Northwestern University Press and Newberry Library. (First publ. 1853.)

Nelson, Dana D. (1992). *The Word in Black and White: Reading "Race" in American Literature,*

1638–1867. New York: Oxford University Press.

Samuels, Shirley (1996). *Romances of the Republic: Women, the Family, and Violence in the Literature of the Early American Nation*. New York: Oxford University Press.

Sollors, Werner (1986). *Consent and Descent in American Culture*. New York: Oxford University Press.

Sollors, Werner (1997). *Neither Black nor White Yet Both: Thematic Explorations of Interracial Literature*. New York: Oxford University Press.

Sundquist, Eric J. (1993). *To Wake the Nations: Race in the Making of American Literature*. Cambridge, Mass.: Harvard University Press.

Webb, Frank J. (1997). *The Garies and their Friends*, ed. Robert Reid-Pharr. Baltimore: Johns Hopkins University Press. (First publ. 1857.)

6
Class

Philip Gould

Significant changes occurred in the meaning of the term "class" during the early nineteenth century, a period when numerous developments in the American economy helped to bring about the change from a society where divisions in rank and wealth exist to a modern "class society." The social theorist Anthony Giddens defines this as "one in which class relationships are of primary significance to the explanatory interpretation of large areas of social conduct" (Blumin 1989: 8). A good deal of American fiction written during the decades immediately preceding the Civil War (1820–60) registers – and helps to shape – the development of a modern class society and the new class consciousness accompanying it. This corpus of literary work especially reveals the cultural importance of the new kind of "middle-class" identity emerging in this era. The values associated with the middle class – sentimental feeling, Christian ethics, familial love, cultural refinement, individual rights, hard work, entrepreneurial initiative – came to dominate American culture and American fiction during these decades. Many prose literary forms generally upheld the ideal of an open, fluid society in which advancement was based on merit instead of inherited privilege; in this way, much of middle-class fiction either denied the reality of class conflict in the United States or imposed forms of sentimental feeling to manage it. By the 1840s and 1850s, however, new kinds of work were emerging, which challenged middle-class propriety and directly criticized the development of capitalist society.

*

Late eighteenth-century Americans did not understand the meaning of "class" as we do today. The word derived largely from scientific discourse and denoted a group, species, or category. Colonial and post-revolutionary Americans certainly assumed the inevitability of social distinctions – indeed, considered them necessary to a stable social order – but these did not actually describe what we would call today class interests or class consciousness. As the historian Gordon S. Wood has argued, American society in the 1770s was characterized by social "ranks":

> These differences of title and quality did not resemble our modern conception of "class." Although the colonists talked of "gentlemen of the first rank," people of "middling circumstances," and the "meaner sort," they did not as yet think clearly in terms of those large-scale horizontal solidarities of occupation and wealth with which we are familiar today... In the mid-eighteenth century most Americans... thought of themselves as connected vertically rather than horizontally, and were more apt to be conscious of those immediately above and below them than they were of those alongside them. (Wood 1991: 21–3)

This is not to say that eighteenth-century fiction ignores social problems; rather, that it views them in its own historical and ideological terms. The post-revolutionary period was highly aware of social tensions within the republic, and violent episodes such as Shays' Rebellion (1786–7) and the Whiskey Rebellion (1794) confirmed for many Americans the danger that the "meaner sorts" posed to liberty and property. Yet it would be misleading to see fictional treatments of sporadic episodes of social and political unrest as expressing "class" conflict. They are nothing like William Dean Howells' *A Hazard of New Fortunes* (1890) or Upton Sinclair's *The Jungle* (1906), which were written in response to episodes like the Haymarket Square Riot (1886) and the Pullman Strike (1894) – episodes that were generated by modern social and political assumptions based upon class interests.

A good example of fiction that addressed social dilemmas arising from the American Revolution is Hugh Henry Brackenridge's *Modern Chivalry* (1792–1815). This picaresque "novel" (its generic status is somewhat ambiguous) actually did incorporate the Whiskey Rebellion into its larger satirical portrait of the pitfalls and false pretenses of Jeffersonian republicanism. The adventures of Captain Farrago and his Irish servant Teague O'Regan reveal the social and political landscape of post-revolutionary America. Through a series of farcical episodes in which Teague is catapulted into positions of social and political authority, readers are forced to contemplate the chaotic disorder consequent on the Revolution's democratizing tendencies and the gradual erosion of traditional assumptions about hierarchical order. Fueled partly by Brackenridge's own frustrations with the attempt to assume political leadership on the Pennsylvania frontier, the satire still falls short of theorizing class-based solidarities. Rather, the overall effect of *Modern Chivalry* is less the condemnation of one particular social group and more the debunking of human nature itself. Even the upper crust feels its scorn. When faced, for example, with the prospect of Teague preparing for the ministry, the narrator concludes, tongue-in-cheek, "In state affairs, ignorance does very well, and why not in church? I am for having all things of a piece; ignorant statesmen, ignorant philosophers, and ignorant ecclesiastics."

The democratic effects of the Revolution, however, did concern early American writers. One might read Teague O'Regan as a comic version of those "low" characters in early American novels who actually destroy the social and political order. These characters are dangerous, first and foremost, because they lack property. In terms of late eighteenth-century ideology, property is both evidence of and the means by which the (male) individual secures moral virtue, social respectability, and political identity. The thematic cornerstone to Crèvecœur's *Letters from an American Farmer* (1782), for example, a work that combines the genres of the political essay, travel writing, and the bildungsroman, emphasizes the congruence between cultivation of the land and cultivation of the self. The characters who symbolically endanger the US republic in Charles Brockden Brown's well-known novels written in 1798–1800 lack property and the stake in the republic it implies. One immediately thinks, for example, of Carwin, the malevolent biloquist who disrupts the false utopia of *Wieland* (1798), and Clithero, the sleep-walking murderer in *Edgar Huntly* (1799). These novels debunk the agrarian vision of American virtue rooted in "middling" farmers that one finds in Crèvecœur and in Jefferson's *Notes on the State of Virginia* (1785). Figures like Carwin and Clithero are notably "outsiders" to the early American republic because of ethnic and national difference as well. Their fictional representation suggests larger national fears of immigration (particularly Irish and French immigration), which, for example, contributed to the Federalists' passage of the Alien and Sedition Acts in 1798. In these characters, then, crystallize a wide range of social and cultural anxieties, involving such questions as the probity of the lower orders, the place of difference in national culture, and the persistent tensions between "American" virtue and "Old World" influence.

The "market revolution" in early nineteenth-century America contributed significantly to the modern understanding of "class." Between the 1810s and the 1840s the development of commercial and industrial capitalism, as well as increased population growth, demographic movements, and the beginnings of urbanization, all significantly changed the social and economic landscape. The historian Joyce Appleby has emphasized the importance of economic initiative and social mobility during this era, claiming that "After 1800 a very large rent in the social fabric opened up for people who were ready to walk through it" (Appleby 2000: 134). The democratization of American politics both accompanied and propelled these changes. Beginning with Maryland in 1801, most states dropped property requirements for voting and office-holding. The apparent expansion of both economic and political opportunities reinforced the cultural value many Americans placed on the ideal of "equality." The development of commercial and industrial capitalism, however, was actually was making American society more socially stratified, so that by the Civil War more than half of the nation's wealth was held by 5 percent of the population (Lang 2003: 2). Despite rising economic inequities, however, most Americans during the opening decades of the nineteenth century "were convinced . . . that inequalities were promoted not by capitalist development, but rather by the political privileges of an aristocracy" (Appleby 2000: 254).

By the 1840s these assumptions would change dramatically. While not abandoning the ideal of equality, Americans generally became more conscious about the increasingly strident expressions of social and economic divisions, and the visibility of the poor and destitute in the expanding cities. Both reformers and working men's political parties began to view inequality through the lens of modern capitalism, a change that facilitated the development of class consciousness. Episodes like the Astor Place Riots in New York City in 1849 demonstrated the increased class consciousness of urban mechanics and wage laborers – the backbone of the Jacksonian Democratic party – who now showed outright contempt for wealthy elites and aristocratic cultural pretensions. It was during this era that Karl Marx and Friedrich Engels famously theorized the concept of social "class" according to economic realities (the "substructure") that theoretically determined all other features of culture, politics, and ideology, or belief systems (the "superstructure"). Marxist theory understands social formations in terms of three major classes – aristocracy, bourgeoisie, and proletariat – whose interests naturally differ according to their different relations to the "means of production." The bourgeoisie and the proletariat are inevitably in a war of sorts with one another because the former embraces a surplus value of labor that is meant to maximize profits by minimizing the costs of labor. Marx and Engels describe the "alienation" of labor in *The Communist Manifesto* (1848):

> The worker becomes a commodity that is all the cheaper the more commodities he creates ... What this fact expresses is merely this: the object that labour produces, its product, confronts it as an alienated being, as a power independent of the producer... In political economy this realization of labour appears as a loss of reality for the worker, objectification as a loss of the object or slavery to it, and appropriation as alienation, as externalization.

Recent theorists of class formation have criticized traditional Marxism as being too interpretively static and historically deterministic (O'Hara 1995). Generally, antebellum American reformers were not doctrinaire Marxists, though the most radical spokespersons for social change and class oppression often did speak in that language. Consider, for example, the New England reformer Orestes Brownson's analysis of "wage slavery" in "The Laboring Classes" (1840):

> We really believe that our Northern system of labor is more oppressive, and even more mischievous to morals, than the Southern ... We have no toleration for either system. We would see the slave a man, but a free man, not a mere operative at wages ... [Industrial capitalism] is the system which in name sounds honester than slavery, and in substance is more profitable to the master. It yields the wages of iniquity, without its opprobium.

Not only does such language suggest the potential for radical reform to capitalist social and economic forms during this era; it also reveals the degree to which capitalism and chattel slavery, as well as class and race, were historically entangled.

Most reform movements in antebellum America, however, were of a more utopian and sentimental cast. The kinds of socialist movement that proliferated in this era were influenced more by communitarian idealism than scientific socialism. Less inclined to Marxist views about the historical inevitability of the "dictatorship of the proletariat," utopian socialism in America was inspired by varying degrees of Christian feeling, agrarian idealism, and the theoretical models of Charles Fourier. One thinks, for example, of the Brook Farm community in the 1840s, the Fruitlands group headed by Bronson Alcott and Charles Lane, and Robert Owen's founding of New Harmony, Indiana. These experiments attempted to remedy the evolving class divisions and economic hardships of capitalist society by abolishing private property and individualized competition – the two principal foundations of nineteenth-century economic liberalism. The communitarian route to a "classless" society of perfect harmony was premised on idealistic assumptions about human capacities for selfless benevolence, which, if founded on eighteenth-century Scottish philosophical assumptions, found cultural expression in many kinds of Romantic and Transcendentalist writings of this era. Such assumptions were satirized by Hawthorne (who stayed unhappily for a while at Brook Farm) in *The Blithedale Romance* (1852).

Antebellum fiction generally reveals the conservative cultural intentions of the modern American "middle class." This certainly can be an unwieldy term for historians and literary critics alike. Not only is the very meaning of class changing in this period, but the interpretive weight "middle-class America" is required to carry is often excessive. Yet the refinements that many social theorists have brought to bear on traditional Marxist categories do provide a more flexible interpretive apparatus for thinking about middle-class formation. "A class," as Jon Elster defines it, "is a group of people who by virtue of what they possess are compelled to engage in the same activities if they want to make the best use of their endowments" (O'Hara 1995: 415; Elster 1985: 331). For the developing middle class in nineteenth-century America, as the historian Stuart Blumin influentially has argued, the distinction between manual and nonmanual forms of labor was crucial to forging a cohesive social identity. Earlier, in eighteenth-century British America, "middling folk" included artisans, farmers, and shopkeepers, all of whom generally were lumped together with the poorer elements of society. By contrast, the new, urban, white-collar types produced by an expanding commercial economy – store managers, bankers, wholesale merchants, accountants, advertisers, factors, clerks, and so forth – marked themselves off during the 1830s and 1840s from wage-earning mechanics and laborers (Blumin 1989: 107). As one cultural historian has summed up the new terms for middle-class identity: "By the 1830s, middle class no longer meant a point of equilibrium between two other fixed classes; to be middle-class was to be, in theory, without fixed social status. Members of the middle class imagined themselves [headed towards] greater wealth and prestige" (Halttunen 1982: 29).

Of course, one cannot reduce all antebellum fiction to middle-class cultural formations. Yet the two are undeniably connected. During this period imaginative works of prose fiction sometimes express, distort, mystify, and revise middle-class ideologies emphasizing economic individualism, democratic rights, Christian feeling, the normative status of Anglo-Protestantism, and national expansion. Earlier in this era, successful works like Washington Irving's *The Sketch-book* (1819–20) managed to reconcile the salient tensions in middle-class culture between republicanism and liberalism and between aristocratic manners and working-class industry. Geoffrey Crayon's status as an American "gentleman" traveling abroad expresses the desire of the middle class to adapt aristocratic traditions of cultural refinement (often associated with Britain and Europe) for their own social and cultural group. Later on in the antebellum period, major canonical novels like *Moby-Dick* (1851) and *Uncle Tom's Cabin* (1852) struggled over the ethical terms of unfettered individualism (in Melville's Ahab) in relation to sentimental and communal values (in Ishmael, or in Stowe's Halliday family).

Even anti-slavery novels by African Americans were enmeshed in cultural issues that concerned class as well as race. It is impossible, for example, to read Harriet Jacobs' *Incidents in the Life of a Slave Girl* (1861) without recognizing the anti-slavery novel/slave narrative's cultural project of forging affective bonds across racial boundaries with white, Northern, and largely middle-class readers. Jacobs achieves this by skillfully playing to their values, particularly through her fictional persona Linda Brent's familial and maternal devotion and her resourceful ingenuity in getting the best of her seducer, Dr. Flint. Anti-slavery works like Frederick Douglass's *The Heroic Slave* and William Wells Brown's *Clotel; or the President's Daughter* (both 1853) similarly legitimize themselves by appealing to sentimental virtue (in both men and women) and resourceful individualism. This does not mean that antebellum African American fiction is completely quietist, complacent in massaging middle-class mores; only that these writers are forced to some degree to appeal to white, middle-class audiences if they are to recruit them to the anti-slavery cause. Probably the best example of an important African American novel dissenting from the codes of middle-class Protestant America is Harriet Wilson's *Our Nig; or, Sketches from the Life of a Free Black* (1859), which handles the often overlapping issues of race and class in the antebellum North in such a way as to expose the inconsistencies and hypocrisies of Northern bourgeois culture.

As one recent critic of the "syntax of class" in antebellum fiction has argued, middle-class identity formation paradoxically rejected the very notion of class interests in the United States (Lang 2003: 10). One can find such an argument in a wide array of political writings about nineteenth-century American society, such as Frances Wright's *Views of Manners and Society in America* (1821) and Albert S. Bolles's *The Conflict between Labor and Capital* (1876). The early American novel similarly handles the rising and falling fortunes of its major characters with just this belief in the social fluidity of a nation premised on the values of opportunity, merit, and hard work. Thus the motif of the success story in middle-class fiction functioned largely as a cultural trope, one which upholds middle-class aspirations and ideals while simultaneously aiming to defuse class tensions. This thematic partnership between individual potential and American conditions found its consummate expression in the late eighteenth century in Benjamin Franklin's *Autobiography* (written *c.*1771–90). In mid-nineteenth-century America the closest approximation to the Franklinian success myth was Horatio Alger's *Ragged Dick; or, Street Life in New York with the Boot Blacks* (1868). In one representative passage Dick (soon to become the respectable "Richard") exhibits the virtue of rational calculation so necessary to entrepreneurial success in business:

> Ten dollars a week to him was a fortune, and three times as much as he had expected to obtain at first. Indeed he would have been glad, only the day before, to get a place at three dollars a week. He had reflected that with the stock of clothes which he had now on hand, he could save up at least half of it, and even then live better than he had been accustomed to do; so that his little fund in the savings bank, instead of being diminished, would be steadily increasing. Then he was to be advanced if he deserved it. It was indeed a bright prospect for a boy who, only a year before, could neither read nor write. (Alger 1990: 184)

Such a passage is typical of the middle-class success story's focus on the new urban capitalist hero's virtues of initiative and enterprise, which ultimately ensure his public success. Yet these virtues, tethered as they are to an overall model of rational calculation in a highly competitive market structure, also tend to make identity a capitalist commodity. Dick "is," in other words, what he owns, saves, and reinvests.

The middle-class success story is not confined to male writing or masculine gender. Antebellum American fiction generally breaks down the presumed boundaries of "separate spheres" based on stereotypes of masculine individualism and feminine feeling. Even Ragged Dick deserves economic success because he has the capacity for sentimental feeling. Both men and women were expected in antebellum culture to exhibit the "sentimental ideal of sincerity" (Halttunen 1982: xvii). What this means for literary and cultural history is that the capitalist market itself was imbued with sentimental ideals. The bestselling sentimental fiction written by women in the 1850s provides evidence of the close relation between the two. Maria Cummins' domestic novel *The Lamplighter* (1854), for example, traces the fortunes of the poor, orphaned Gerty and her loving friend (and eventual mate) Willie Sullivan. Willie's rise in capitalist society is premised on the domestic virtues learned in the home: economic triumph and sentimental virtue reciprocally animate one another. As Gerty muses,

> Who, during the many years she had known him, could have proved himself more worthy of confidence than Willy? Had he not, from his boyhood, been exemplary in every virtue, superior to every meanness and every form of vice? Had he not in his early youth forsaken all that he held most dear, to toil and labor beneath an Indian sun, that he might provide comforts and luxuries for those whose support he eagerly took upon himself?

Like Dick's progress from rags to riches, Willie's enacts the fantasy of absolute social fluidity in America – but in this case it also has imperialist overtones, since Willie's professional rise occurs while he clerks on a cotton plantation in India.

The consummate example of this genre for a *female* protagonist is Fanny Fern's semi-autobiographical account of her rise to literary fame in *Ruth Hall: A Domestic Tale of the Present Time* (1855). Fern (the pseudonym for Sarah Payson Willis Parton) carefully synthesizes the sentimental novel and the bourgeois success story. Poor, widowed, and dispossessed by every callous family member and New York editor imaginable, Ruth rises in the world through her talent, industry, and womanly virtue. Her success, however, occurs entirely within the amorphous category of the middle class – that is, even at her lowest moments, when she struggles as a writer to earn money to regain custody of one of her children, Ruth is never represented as a member of the working classes. Her virtue secures her social and moral identity, regardless of her financial state. Even as she negotiates the cold realities of the literary marketplace, her character is anchored in "timeless" values that resist the unstable contingencies of the market. This creates the thematic tension in *Ruth Hall* between sentimental and capitalist economies. Confronting one self-serving editor, for example, she wonders "whether *she* ought not to profit by it as well as himself, and whether she should not ask him to increase her pay." Ruth expands production, plays editors of competing newspapers off against one another, secures her own copyright, bests her aristocratic-ally foppish brother in the literary world, and finally realizes that "Floy" (her pen name) is a public commodity to be traded at the greatest profit. Yet the novel never severs the ideological tie that binds women's writing to sentimental virtue. In Ruth's case, she writes to secure her children and a home. "She must work harder – harder," she thinks: "And so 'Floy' scribbled on, thinking only of bread for her children, laughing and crying behind her mask, – laughing all the more when her heart was heaviest."

The companion argument to middle-class success stories emphasized the need for sympathy for the urban poor. Middle-class writing generally deploys feeling as a way of defusing social conflict rather than awakening readers, as it later would, to ineluct-able class divisions. One of the sketches from *Fern Leaves from Fanny's Port-Folio* (1853), for example, entitled "The Little Pauper," traces the lonely wanderings of a young girl through the urban landscape, highlighting the contrast between rich and poor: "Rosy little children pass her on their way to school, well-fed, well-clad and joyous, with a mother's parting kiss yet warm on their sweet lips." Yet the tale's social contrasts are not founded upon ideologies of capital, labor, and self-interest; if anything, scenes like these displace the potential for class conflict by utilizing feeling as writerly esthetic and mobilizing it as readerly response. Fern has a well-to-do matron ("Warm hearts beat sometimes under silk and velvet") embrace the young waif, so that the child is restored to hope through the workings of Christian feeling, and now is able to look for consolation to heaven instead of to its worldly alternatives threatening middle-class life: socialist organizations, brothels, or urban gangs. This is the sure-fire formula for so much of middle-class fiction about the urban poor: sentiment subsumes class differences while "reform" takes place in the heart before its effect can be felt in society. Fiction is the enabling medium of that process.

This kind of sympathy secures both intimacy and distance between bourgeois readers and dispossessed subjects. Its cultural legacy, moreover, is felt in early reform fictions about American industrial capitalism. More self-consciously than earlier writings that were meant to expose the hardships of the poor, including novels like Melville's *Redburn* (1849) and *Israel Potter* (1855), for example, or reform fiction appearing in evangelical magazines, women's periodicals, and temperance publications, the early industrial novel attempts to diagnose the new realities of labor and capital within the factory system. Works like Rebecca Harding Davis's "Life in the Iron Mills" (1861) and Elizabeth Stuart Phelps's *The Silent Partner* (1872) were more likely to acknowledge the permanence of "class" divisions and antagonisms. Yet their more realistic socio-economic analysis also relies on traditional sentimental formulas for sympathetic class relations.

For example, the opening section of Davis's work literally "frames" the observation of a well-to-do narrator who is gazing through a window at the industrial wasteland below. The anonymity of the scene, however, allows the narrator to both sympathize with the working class and preserve her social identity: "I look on the slow stream of human life creeping past, night and morning, to the great mills. Masses of men, with dull, besotted faces bent to the ground, sharpened here and there by pain or cunning." Yet the narrator also demands, "I want you to hide your disgust, take no heed to your clean clothes, and come right down with me, – here into the thickest of the fog and mud and foul effluvia." The tensions suggested here – between blindness and insight, difference and sameness, connection and disconnection – persist throughout the narrative. They also describe the nature of the aristocratic protagonist Perley Kelso's quest in *The Silent Partner* to both change the industrial order and discover her true moral self. In both works the humanitarian bonds between bourgeois and proletarian characters are at best tenuous: they tend to keep these classes separate, but wish to render them more equal.

The new urban and industrial realities of antebellum America – though only a shadow of the changes that would occur after the Civil War – produced new social "types" that became fodder for prose writing. As the traditional artisan economy gave way to a proto-industrial one, and as urbanization and immigration continued to increase, the American city became the fictional locus for larger cultural negotiations of these changes. The urban observer – in the form of the detached *flâneur* or the more engaged sentimental reformer – evolved into a narrative device with which to capture this changing American scene. Lydia Maria Child's *Letters from New York* (1843–5), for example, represents the latter form, combining fictive set-piece scenes with overt political commentary, and prefigures later exposés of the sufferings of urban immigrants in Jacob Riis' *How the Other Half Lives* (1890) and Lincoln Steffens' *The Shame of the Cities* (1904).

The urban sketch blended into the genres of short story, reform tract, and political exposé. All were premised on modern social ills, though they tended to provide entertainment as well as instruction, providing titillating glimpses into the "realities" of city life. These new social types included the city's dandies, roughs, gangs, and prostitutes; the Bowery b'hoy and Bowery g'hal; confidence men, sharpers, and mesmerists; ethnic types like "free" African Americans and Irish immigrants. Works like George Foster's *New York in Slices* (1849) and *New York by Gaslight* (1850) and Cornelius Mathews' *A Pen-and-Ink Panorama of New-York City* (1853) capitalized upon this cultural interest, while Benjamin Baker's very popular play *A Glance at New York in 1848* (1848) virtually invented the figure of the Bowery b'hoy – which became an overnight sensation – as a social type who was part rough and part dandy: the Whitmanesque American man. While canonical fictions like Melville's highly symbolic tale "Bartleby, the Scrivener: A Story of Wall Street" (1853) surely cannot be reduced to the genres of the urban sketch or reformer's exposé, the story's law office is filled with the social types of the new urban clerical and professional classes, and the story itself suggests the distinctively modern urban problems of anonymity and isolation found in the antebellum urban sketch as well.

Finally, the most acutely class-conscious fiction in antebellum America was written in what the literary critic David Reynolds calls the "subversive style." This brand of popular and melodramatic writing employed sensational plots, irrational narrative forms, and highly sexualized subject matter in order to mount radical critiques of the status quo. The genre culturally was influenced by sensationalist city newspapers (the "penny press"), popular crime narratives, and radical strains of Jacksonian ideology. The more immediate literary influence for the novel about the "mysteries and miseries" of the city was Eugène Sue's *The Mysteries of Paris* (1843). But American fiction in the subversive style also marks a tradition running from the lesser-known John Neal, through Poe, on to figures like George Lippard and George Thompson, and even, to a lesser extent, some of the sensational fiction Louisa May Alcott published anonymously. George Lippard's *The Quaker City; or, the Monks of Monk-Hall* (1845) and *New York: Its Upper Ten and Lower Million* (1853), and George Thompson's *Venus in Boston* (1849) and *City Crimes* (1849) repudiated sentimental piety in favor of erotic violence and scathing political commentary. These fictions meant to unveil the corrupt underside of human nature in general, and in particular the moral and social pretensions of ministers, politicians, wealthy businessmen, and other elite professionals. Not immune to resorting to forms of feeling that quickly exploded into melodrama, sensationalist fiction threw the class polarities of capitalist society into bold relief. These works reveal not the harmony but the extreme dissonance between the two major historical trends in nineteenth-century America: the capitalist economy and democratic politics.

REFERENCES AND FURTHER READING

Alger, Horatio (1990). *Ragged Dick; or, Street Life in New York with the Boot Blacks*, intr. Alan Trachtenberg. New York: Signet. (First publ. 1868.)

Appleby, Joyce (2000). *Inheriting the Revolution: The First Generation of Americans*. Cambridge, Mass.: Harvard University Press.

Blumin, Stuart (1989). *The Emergence of the Middle Class: Social Experience in the American City, 1760–1900*. Cambridge, UK: Cambridge University Press.

Denning, Michael (1987). *Mechanic Accents: Dime Novels and Working Class Culture in America*. New York and London: Verso.

Dimock, Wai Chi, and Gilmore, Michael T. (1994). *Rethinking Class: Literary Studies and Social Formations*. New York: Columbia University Press.

Elster, Jon (1985). *Making Sense of Marx: Studies in Marxism and Social Theory*. New York: Cambridge University Press.

Foley, Barbara (2000). "Historicizing Melville's 'Bartleby.'" *American Literature* 72, 87–116.

Foner, Eric (1996). "Free Labor and Nineteenth-Century Political Ideology." In Melvin Stokes and Stephen Conway (eds.), *The Market Revolution in America: Social, Political, and Religious Expressions, 1800–1880*, 99–127. Charlottesville: University Press of Virginia.

Greerson, Jennifer Rae (2001). "The 'Mysteries and Miseries' of North Carolina: New York, Urban Gothic Fiction, and *Incidents in the Life of a Slave Girl*." *American Literature* 73, 277–310.

Halttunen, Karen (1982). *Confidence Men and Painted Women: A Study of Middle-Class Culture in America, 1830–1870*. New Haven: Yale University Press.

Herbert, T. Walter (1993). *Dearest Beloved: The Hawthornes and the Making of the Middle Class*. Berkeley: University of California Press.

Lang, Amy Schrager (2003). *The Syntax of Class: Writing Equality in Nineteenth-Century America*. Princeton: Princeton University Press.

Lott, Eric (1993). *Love and Theft: Blackface Minstrelsy and the American Working Class*. New York: Oxford University Press.

O'Hara, Daniel (1995). "Class." In Frank Lentricchia and Thomas McLaughlin (eds.), *Critical Terms for Literary Study*, 406–28. Chicago: University of Chicago Press.

Reynolds, David S. (1988). *Beneath the American Renaissance: The Subversive Imagination in the Age of Emerson and Melville*. Cambridge, Mass., and London: Harvard University Press.

Ryan, Mary (1981). *Cradle of the Middle Class: The Family in Oneida County, New York, 1790–1865*. New York: Cambridge University Press.

Sellers, Charles (1991). *The Market Revolution: Jacksonian America, 1815–1846*. New York: Oxford University Press.

Stansell, Christine (1986). *City of Women: Sex and Class in New York, 1789–1860*. New York: Knopf.

Thompson, E. P. (1963). *The Making of the English Working Class*. London: Gollancz.

Walters, Ronald G. (1978). *American Reformers, 1815–1860*. New York: Hill & Wang.

Wilentz, Sean (1984). *Chants Democratic: New York City and the Rise of the American Working Class, 1788–1850*. New York: Oxford University Press.

Wood, Gordon S. (1991). *The Radicalism of the American Revolution*. New York: Knopf.

7
Sexualities

Valerie Rohy

In the United States, fiction was understood from the first not merely to represent sexuality, but also to engage it, incite it, enact it. Late eighteenth-century polemics accused novels of corrupting their readers – especially young and female readers – with forbidden sexual knowledge and lurid romantic fantasies. Further, anti-novel rhetoric associated the activity of reading itself with sexual perversity – with, that is, the compulsive pursuit of a solitary, unproductive, and self-gratifying pleasure. An 1802 tract bluntly entitled "Novel Reading, a Cause of Female Depravity" charged that "Without the poison instilled [by novels] into the blood, females in ordinary life would never have been so much the slaves of vice" (Davidson 1986: 45). And despite the waning of such arguments in the nineteenth century, as late as 1838 the *Knickerbocker* could maintain, its moral indignation unabated, that novels elicit "a fascination which arises from the power which a master will exercise over the volition of inferior spirits, leading them captive, and exciting them with the stimulus they love most." This literary sadomasochism, the essay suggested, could not fail to elicit a readerly response: "there are no novels so saleable as those which lead the affections step by step into a sphere of irritating tumult, fevering the blood with uncontrollable sympathies, and steeping the interior man in a sea of voluptuous sensuality" (Baym 1984: 59).

We may well doubt that any reading subject is innocent of sexuality prior to the "uncontrollable" and fevered influence of the novel. But what the *Knickerbocker*'s own rhetorical mastery elides is the way in which that reading subject is also produced *as a subject* by novels' "leading" discourses. Fiction interpellates "the interior man" as liberal subject and bestows on him his interiority and privacy. The subjectivity thus instated in turn sustains a certain notion of sexuality, replete with "affections," "sympathies," even the capacity for excitement, and understood as a knowable property of the individual.

In this process, the sexual subject born of reading is policed not only by external prohibitions but also by the invention and naturalization of what will pass as her own

intimate desires. In American culture, this internalized, discursive construction of
sexual subjectivity has its historical roots in the eighteenth century, when the
articulation and regulation of sexuality operated not only through legal codes, church
authority, and medical institutions, but also through popular texts, including fiction
and conduct books. The early republic saw an "overall decline in state regulation of
morality" in tandem with an extension of subtler, largely internalized controls
(d'Emilio and Friedman 1988: 42; see also Foucault 1990: 37; d'Emilio and Friedman
1988: 72). Changes in the juridical treatment of sexuality reflected the new nation's
aim to shed antique and despotic laws, although the results were far from permissive:
in 1779 the state of Virginia rejected Thomas Jefferson's proposal to abolish the death
penalty for crimes of rape, sodomy, bestiality, and polygamy (Katz 1976: 24). Yet
even this dubious advance marks one step of the process whereby, as scientific
understandings of sexual deviance replaced theological explanations, civil law super-
seded church doctrine as the template for sexual discipline and the decentralized,
internal regulation of sexuality in turn took over former functions of civil law
(d'Emilio and Friedman 1988: 67; Foucault 1990: 68). Where sexuality was concerned, then, the nationalist project was served less by juridical reforms than by the
explicitly heterosexual, reproductive ideology of familial nationalism – or is it
national familialism? – which, promoted in the early republic, persists today in the
United States.

Both external and internal, public and private technologies of sexual discipline
reflect evolving meanings of desire, and what could be recognized *as* desire, within a
changing American culture. Foucault argues that since the eighteenth century Western societies have seen a shift from a regulatory focus on sexual acts to a "new
specification of individuals" as subjects defined by sexual identity (1990: 42–3). In
the United States, notions of homosexuality and heterosexuality as essential sexual
identities emerged only from the 1880s. Prior to that, although acts of sodomy were
prohibited, ostensibly nonsexual same-sex relationships could enjoy considerable
intimacy without being deemed perverse. The female narrator of Rose Terry Cooke's
1858 story "My Visitation," for example, harbors a "blind, irrational, all-enduring
devotion" to another woman (1994: 26), which inspires her to refuse men's marriage
proposals but does not render her unsympathetic. Instead, Cooke places her narrator
in the tradition of female "romantic friendship," seen as an acceptable supplement or
alternative to heterosexual love through most of the nineteenth century (Faderman
1981: 160). The cultural tolerance of romantic friendship depended upon the widely
accepted notion that femininity – at least as embodied by white, bourgeois women –
naturally precluded sexual desire (Welter 1966: 154). Where sexuality was concerned,
the "cult of true womanhood" both demanded female purity and imagined that "true"
women were incapable of impurity; in a paradoxical prohibition of the impossible that
later shaped views of lesbian sexuality, female desire *both* did not exist *and* required
constant regulation.[1]

In early US fiction, such cultural constructions of sexuality inform novelistic
explorations of the marriage plot, seduction narratives, stories of miscegenation and

racist exploitation, suggestions of homosexuality and incest, and figures of "unnatural" female desire. How, then, are various forms of sexuality recognized and defined in the late eighteenth and early nineteenth centuries? What is the relation between normative and non-normative sexualities in US fiction? And what is the role of literature in contesting and sustaining sexual ideologies?

Love and Death

Although the task of reading sexuality in American fiction is as old as American fiction itself, among twentieth-century critical views Leslie Fiedler's work offers a salient point of reference. In his 1948 essay "Come Back to the Raft Ag'in, Huck Honey!" and an expanded version of this argument, *Love and Death in the American Novel* (1960), Fiedler argues that in canonical American fiction the conventional marriage plot is supplanted by gothic, morbid sexuality and by idealized, often cross-racial, male homoeroticism. *Love and Death* seeks to show "the failure of the American fictionist to deal with adult heterosexual love and his consequent obsession with death, incest, and innocent homosexuality" (Fiedler 1960: xi) – this last yielding "the archetypal image, found in our favorite books, in which a white and a colored American male flee into each other's arms" (p. x). If the incestuous gothic appears in such texts as Charles Brockden Brown's *Wieland* (1798–9), Edgar Allan Poe's "The Fall of the House of Usher" (1839), and Herman Melville's *Pierre* (1852), the idealized archetype of male bonding recurs, Fiedler suggests, in James Fenimore Cooper's *The Last of the Mohicans* (1826), Mark Twain's *Adventures of Huckleberry Finn* (1884), and Melville's *Moby-Dick* (1851), whose narrator Ishmael famously recalls how "in our hearts' honeymoon, lay I and Queequeg – a cozy, loving pair" (Melville 1967: 58).

Since 1960, scholars have raised significant objections to Fiedler's thesis, even as his claims have gained the status of critical cliché. Indeed, the responses to *Love and Death* neatly capture a half-century's changing views of sexuality and US fiction. More recent psychoanalytic theory has shifted its emphasis from diagnosis to indeterminacy and from individual to cultural formations, but the mid-twentieth-century psychoanalytic tradition reflected in Fiedler's writing valuably underscored the centrality and denaturalized the effects of sexuality in literature. In the 1970s and 1980s, however, critics informed by feminist and African American theories took Fiedler to task for his exclusion of female authors and writers of color from the American canon, pointing out the ways in which such omissions determine and constrain his conclusions. Fiedler's work, it seemed, was a white man's fantasy about white men's fantasies. Finally, the rise of historicism and queer theory in the late 1980s and 1990s led readers to question Fiedler's disregard for literature's social contexts and his rehearsal of popular and psychoanalytic notions of homosexuality as immature or regressive (Wiegman 1995: 157).

Despite its shortcomings, despite its ahistorical embeddedness in its own historical moment, Fiedler's thesis remains remarkable, both in its bold, early interrogation of race and homosexuality and in its prescient attention to the *intersections* of race and sexuality – a matter to which critics are only now returning seriously. Fiedler also invites us to consider the relation of heterosexuality to homosexuality, and of normative to non-normative sexualities, in early US fiction. In this he decisively counters what Foucault would call the repressive hypothesis (Foucault 1990: 10). Fiedler recognizes perversity as an internal and constitutive part of the American tradition, not an external threat or accidental impurity. "[H]orror is essential to our literature. It is not merely a matter of terror filling the vacuum left by the suppression of sex, of Thanatos standing in for Eros. Through these gothic images are projected certain obsessive concerns of our national life" (Fiedler 1960: xxii).

Here Fiedler describes the gothic, but he will include homosexuality in his literary "chamber of horrors" (1960: xxii). Whatever the title of *Love and Death* may suggest, for Fiedler gay love is not love at all, but another form of death or gothic "terror" – even the "pure marriage of males" (p. 345) whose boyish, unconsummated innocence he takes pains to separate from the vulgarity of adult homosexuality (Looby 1995: 538). Yet even this phobic construction valuably describes American writing as a literature, to borrow from Foucault, of "blatant and fragmented perversion" (Foucault 1990: 47). American fiction does not repress perversity but produces perversity; it does not exclude deviance but is structured by deviance; it does not avoid horror but seeks horror and speaks horror.

Along with incestuous and homoerotic themes, the perversity of canonical American literature yields the recurring images of monstrous female desire, in Fiedler's view a key site of gothic sexuality. Since in the nineteenth-century ideology of passionless "true womanhood" female sexuality could appear *only* as excessive and abnormal, female sexuality joined those other non-normative pleasures conveniently made to represent the shame, anxiety, insatiability, messiness, anarchy, and confusion that inconveniently attend all sexuality. Even a text, like Hawthorne's "Rappaccini's Daughter" (1844), that renders the woman a passive object of men's desires, projects onto her the deadly consequences of "unnatural" and "depraved" reproduction and the dangers of sexuality as such (Hawthorne 1987: 403–4). Poe's "Ligeia" (1838) is more direct, making Ligeia's will to live a bawdy pun on erotic appetite. Driven by a "gigantic volition" (63), Ligeia *is* desire. To sustain her own life, she wants Rowena's body; and she takes it in a bedroom scene structured by rhythms of excitation and exhaustion – a flush, a "tremor," a warmth, a "glow," a "pulsation" (Poe 1982: 72–3). Although we cannot call such eros – or, as Poe writes, such "unspeakable horrors" – "lesbian" prior to the invention of homosexual identity, we can be certain it is not romantic friendship (p. 73). Instead, "unnatural" female desire, whether heterosexual or homosexual, is allied with a monstrous female masculinization in American fiction. In this discourse, the non-normative is not suppressed but solicited: deviance is summoned to be repudiated, to define normative sexuality through differential relations, and to be enjoyed by a culture that will also disavow its lurid enjoyment.

Symptoms of Desire

While Fiedler recognizes the structuring presence of non-normative sexualities in American literary traditions, his explanation of this presence fails to account for the imbrication of perversity and the law. In *Love and Death* it is the "failure of love" in American fiction – which is to say, the failure of normative heterosexual love – that opens a space to be filled by gothic morbidity or male homoeroticism: "the death of love left a vacuum at the affective heart of the American novel into which there rushed the love of death" (Fiedler 1960: 126). In this reading, gothic perversities and male homosexuality are opportunistic or compensatory formations which *take the place of* normative heterosexuality. Where one is, the other cannot be: sexuality, for Fiedler, is a simple either/or proposition. But where Fiedler regards sexual normalcy and deviation as mutually exclusive and distinctly opposed, other readers, including Freud himself, see them as inextricably conjoined and complicit (Wiegman 1995: 156). Foucault writes: "Modern society is perverse, not in spite of its puritanism or as if from a backlash provoked by its hypocrisy; it is in actual fact, and directly, perverse" (1990: 47). Perversity, that is, inhabits the discourse of sexual propriety, not as an exception to the rule of law but as a mainstay of that law.

Thus Fiedler's claim that sexual corruption and backwardness arise in literature, if not in life, from an absence of normative (heterosexual, marital, procreative) sexuality goes astray by inverting the actual relation of these terms. The appearance of perversity indicates not the *failure* of the norm but its *success*. The representation of non-normative desire is not inimical but essential to normative sexual codes. Fiedler reads homosexuality as a symptom of heterosexuality (the appearance of homosexuality is *an effect of* an attenuated heterosexuality); however, we might say that heterosexuality is a symptom of homosexuality (the appearance of heterosexuality as natural and culturally validated is *an effect of* representations of homosexual and other deviance). Indeed, the sexually normative is a symptom of the non-normative, expressed in negative terms as the other of its other. This is the focus of Hawthorne's "The May-Pole of Merry Mount" (1836), which defines marriage against the priapic revelry of wild beasts and "Gothic monsters" (Hawthorne 1987: 173). Although the intervention of the Puritan "men of iron" (p. 179) ejects Hawthorne's young couple from the debauched Eden of Merry Mount into adult sexual responsibility, this fall into propriety requires the polymorphous perversity of Edgar and Edith's "former pleasures" (p. 176) and "early joys" (p. 184) as the prehistory out of which a productive and reproductive heterosexuality will emerge. *Pace* Fiedler, the normative is a compensatory formation that results from the failure of perversity; as Hawthorne suggests, it is the remainder that appears after illicit enjoyment is subtracted from the whole of sexuality.

Such texts as "May-Pole" make it difficult to see heterosexuality as wholly marginalized in American literature. Fiedler, however, is not simply mistaken. Marriage and procreation are not missing from American fiction, but they can seem to be missing. If normative heterosexuality is everywhere, what accounts for the perception that it is nowhere to be found? The normative seems both absent and ubiquitous because it is *always* and *never* represented. Seldom a primary object of fictional scrutiny, it maintains its authority precisely by seeming not to be a problem worthy of narrative attention. Sadism may demand a story, but the norm can pass itself off as nature and, even in the marriage plot, as a mere backdrop to more interesting affairs. This closeting effect does not so much occlude our view of heterosexuality as it does strategically encourage us not to look – or rather, not to see. In this structure, Paul Morrison has argued, homosexuality bears the analytic burden heterosexuality escapes: "Heterosexuality explains nothing, including the crimes committed in its name. Homosexuality explains everything in need of explanation, including the crimes committed against it in the name of compulsory heterosexuality" (2001: 9). Of course, Morrison's claim presupposes the "invention" and reification of homosexual and heterosexual identities in the late nineteenth century. Earlier in American culture, before the modern order of sexual identity made homosexuality the privileged – which is to say, uniquely cursed – avatar of deviance, the logic Morrison describes obtained more broadly: normative sexuality could remain discreetly closeted while non-normative sexual practices and desires (seduction and rape, miscegenation, homosexuality, excessive female appetites) were subject to obsessive examination.

Before the twentieth century, that is, the "strategic silence that underwrites the norm" primarily applied to monogamous, reproductive heterosexual marriage, which in the United States has been mythically epitomized by the white, bourgeois couple (Morrison 2001: 3). Foucault suggests that sexual prescriptions focused on marital relations until the beginning of "a centrifugal movement with regard to heterosexual monogamy" in the eighteenth century (1990: 38). Thereafter marriage increasingly enjoyed the privileges of discretion – privileges that in the United States have framed the sexual implications of the right to privacy. Like Poe's purloined letter (whose undivulged contents presumably betray a compromising amour), normative sexuality gets hidden in plain sight, "a little *too* self-evident," and so strangely elusive (Poe 1982: 109). The invisibility-in-visibility of sexual norms recurs in literary criticism as well, if for different reasons. Even feminist readings of the marriage plot can elide the possibility of non-heterosexual organizations of desire; and queer criticism, its search for non-normative sexuality mimicking the old sweep of the police searchlight, can omit the normative from the province of the sexual. Unmarked and unremarked, the invisible becomes the inevitable: when marriage is not recognizable as heterosexuality, it passes as the sum of sexuality, the only game in town.

Seduction to Marriage

Fiedler's claim that American writing betrays "a desperate need to avoid the facts of wooing, marriage, and child-rearing" (1960: xx) is complicated by the marriage conclusions of many popular novels by white women, by William Wells Brown's *Clotel* (1853) and Hannah Crafts' *The Bondwoman's Narrative* (*c.*1850s), and, in Fiedler's own canon, by Cooper's *The Pioneers* (1823) and Hawthorne's *The House of the Seven Gables* (1851). Although such novels' often perfunctory marriages may not be ringing endorsements of heterosexuality, the failure to promote heterosexuality successfully hardly constitutes a desperate avoidance.[2] In the late eighteenth century, the emergent heterosexual discourse of romantic love, largely disseminated by fiction, stressed the primacy of emotional ties and personal choice in marriage and reinforced the ideology of American individualism (Cott 1977: 83). The ideology of romantic love, however, coupled with the loosening of sexual standards, yielded anxieties about feminine sexual propriety which took form in a proliferation of "moral tales" and didactic stories for the heterosexual education of young female readers. At a time when anti-novel discourses accused fiction of corruption, novelists did not always disagree. In *The Power of Sympathy* (1789), William Hill Brown borrows from a newspaper account of the events on which Hannah Webster Foster would base *The Coquette* (1797), whose author blamed Elizabeth Whitman's demise on the fact that "she was a great reader of romances, and having formed her notions of happiness from that corrupt source, became vain and coquetish" (Foster 1986: x). Taking the opposite approach, other seduction novels justified indelicate subjects by touting their prophylactic power. Susanna Rowson suggested in 1794 that her *Charlotte Temple* would warn girls against repeating its heroine's mistakes: "Oh my dear girls – for to such only am I writing – listen not to the voice of love, unless sanctioned by paternal approbation" (Rowson 1991: 26). At the same time, seduction novels often criticized women's subordinate status and limited economic options, as well as sexual double standards. *The Coquette* allows Eliza Wharton to complain, not without cause, that "Marriage is the tomb of friendship," though Mrs. Richman counters that marriage offers women "safety" by "circumscribing our enjoyments" (Foster 1986: 24). Such texts defended conventional morality while recording sexual inequities, and inflamed desire while counseling caution.

After the days of the seduction novel, hugely popular sentimental women's novels changed the narrative formula: if the standard seduction plot concluded with the wayward protagonist's repentance and death, popular female authors of the mid-nineteenth century found another conventional ending in marriage. Some, like Susan Warner's *The Wide, Wide, World* (1852) and Fanny Fern's *Ruth Hall* (1854), do not supply the heroine with a husband, but many, including Catharine Maria Sedgwick's *Hope Leslie* (1827), E. D. E. N. Southworth's *The Hidden Hand* (1859), and Elizabeth Stoddard's *The Morgesons* (1862), follow the marriage convention. Yet, unlike the seduction novel, such women's fiction was not centrally concerned with either male or female sexuality. Its heroines stress the spiritual over the physical, both in deference to ideologies of "true womanhood" and female chastity, and in reaction against the seduction novels' insistence on women's sexual victimization (Baym 1993: 26). Because courtship and marriage are not the primary focus of these novels, Nina Baym suggests, their happy marriages function as "symbols of successful

Figure 7.1   Title illustration for Ik Marvel, *Reveries of a Bachelor: or A Book of the Heart* (New York: Baker & Scribner, 1851). Collection of Shirley Samuels.

accomplishment of the required task" (1993: 12), which is the heroine's progress toward maturity, self-knowledge, and self-sufficiency.

Still, one may ask, why *this* symbol? What makes marriage the privileged emblem of feminine accomplishment in such narratives? It is no small irony that the fictional reward for women's accomplishment of independence should be dependence. In the paradox of "true womanhood," white bourgeois women assume the constraints of the feminine ideal as a sign of power. Describing this double bind, Nancy Cott cites de Tocqueville, who proposed in *Democracy in America* that the American woman "has learned by the use of her independence to surrender it without a struggle and without a murmur when the time comes for making the sacrifice" (Cott 1977: 78). Popular fiction plays its role in this learning process not only by displaying virtue's rewards but also by interpellating the reader as a liberal subject whose sense of her own agency and responsibility in fact prepares her for a subordinate wifely role. As Baym elsewhere suggests, the rhetoric of female independence in midcentury women's fiction may provide merely a more subtle means of internalized control, one that, unlike the seduction novel, does not need to confront women with external threats because it persuades women "to control themselves, in an atmosphere where control by main force is less and less possible" (1984: 189).

In one sense their lack of narrative engagement with marriage may make these female-authored novels more feminist; yet in another sense it makes them less so. In *Hope Leslie*, for example, Sedgwick shows a fine skepticism, producing the righteous Esther Downing as proof that "marriage is not *essential* to the contentment, the dignity, or the happiness of woman" (1998: 371) and withholding the spectacle of Hope's wedding from her readers: "We leave it to that large, and most indulgent class of our readers, the misses in their teens, to adjust, according to their own fancy, the ceremonial of our heroine's wedding, which took place in due time" (p. 369). And yet, with the inexorable progress of "in due time," that wedding must occur, despite Hope's disregard for courtship and marriage, despite the lack of sexual attraction between herself and her destined mate Everell, and despite the ways in which marriage will socially and legally obviate the very qualities that made Hope the novel's heroine. The generic arbitrariness and merely symbolic quality of this illogical but entirely predictable conclusion reinforce its inevitability. It is as if marriage is what happens to women – virtuous women, at least – while they're busy doing other things. The heroine need not concern herself with finding a husband because she will end up married, such novels blithely assure us, *whether she wants to or not*.

Racial Fantasies

While African American authors also employed the marriage plot, sometimes sharing the sexual conventions of midcentury white women's fiction, race and racism in the antebellum United States necessarily shaped the contours and meaning of such narratives. In Hannah Crafts' *The Bondwoman's Narrative*, Crafts' narrator Hannah, a slave in North Carolina, professes no interest in marriage, yet in the last pages we find her happily united with "a fond and affectionate husband" (Crafts 2002: 268). But Hannah has more complex reasons to avoid marriage than do the heroines of such novels as *The Hidden Hand*: "Marriage like many other blessings I considered to be especially designed for the free, and something that all the victims of slavery should avoid as tending essentially to perpetuate that system" (p. 206).

The conditions of slavery – its commodification of reproduction, official nonrecognition of slaves' marriages, and lack of legal protection for slaves' families – make Hannah's marriage more overdetermined than those of white heroines. Her marriage constitutes a "symbol of successful accomplishment," but it is not an arbitrary symbol. Marriage signifies the accomplishment of freedom because slavery renders marriage impossible and, some authors suggest, fosters sexual deviance. In *Clotel*

(1853), William Wells Brown deems marriage "the first and most important institution of human existence – the foundation of all civilisation and culture – the root of
church and state" (Brown 2000: 83). Given the denial of legal marriage to slaves and
the institution's corrosive effect on white matrimony, it is in Brown's view no wonder
that "immorality and vice pervade the cities of the Southern States" (p. 84).

Nineteenth-century novels by both black and white abolitionists, like nonfictional
slave narratives, charge slavery with the "immorality and vice" of both enslaver and
enslaved, describing sexual violence, incest, homosexuality, and gender offenses such
as female masculinization. The public exposure of slavery's systematic sexual abuses,
even at the risk of scandal and impropriety, proved a powerful strategy for abolitionists: Crafts' narrator records her personal and moral repugnance when her master tries
to impose "a compulsory union with a man whom I could only hate and despise"
(2002: 206), and Harriet Beecher Stowe's *Uncle Tom's Cabin* (1852), as Freud notes,
does not hesitate to depict slave-owners' sexualized sadism. In her essay "Mama's Baby,
Papa's Maybe," Hortense Spillers offers a similar reading, charging slavery with "the
displacement of the genitalia, the female's and the male's desire that engenders future"
(Spillers 1987: 73). In this logic, slavery *means* sexual perversity, and liberation both
promises and requires the reparation of normative gender, familial, and sexual
structures. Such Manichean rhetoric, however, categorically condemns some sexual
possibilities – homosexuality and gender crossing, for example – that are not essentially coercive but merely non-normative. In so doing, the notion of slavery as
perversity, which attributes the horrors of the "peculiar institution" to sexual peculi-
arity, effectively rehabilitates the sexual norm by concealing the culpability of
normative sexual and gender ideologies.[3]

Outside abolitionist fiction, white authors most explicitly addressed race and
sexuality in late eighteenth- and early nineteenth-century novels which, with a certain
anxious fascination, considered the possibility of intermarriage between whites and
Native Americans. Fiedler suggests that American fiction may idealize interracial
same-sex friendship as "pure marriage of males," but the possibility of reproduction
and the problem of female sexuality made heterosexual miscegenation more troubling. Relationships between white and Native American men and women are often
brought forth only to be cast aside. In *The Last of the Mohicans*, as Fiedler notes, the
ritual that unites Uncas and Cora is not their wedding but their funeral (a rite that
also binds Hawkeye and Chingachgook together in tears, a handclasp, and a vow of
loyalty) (Cooper 1981: 372). Lydia Maria Child's *Hobomok* (1824) requires Hobomok
to sacrifice his own love and vanish into the forest so that Mary may wed Charles
Brown. Sedgwick is more ambivalent in *Hope Leslie*, allowing Faith and Oneco to
remain together, if childless, and questioning its heroine's racism. When Hope
protests her sister's marriage to Oneco – "God forbid!...my sister married to an
Indian!" – Magawisca reproaches her: "Think ye that your blood will be corrupted
by mingling with this stream?" (Sedgwick 1998: 196–7). Yet *Hope Leslie* forces
Magawisca to enact a more obscene version of Hobomok's renunciation. Her mutilation at the hands of her father is the cost of foreclosing miscegenation in favor of the
socially appropriate union the novel will finally celebrate. Thereafter, her sexuality

cast off and left behind, Magawisca will enjoy only Everell's fraternal love, as their youthful passion is *retroactively* deemed impossible: according to Everell, "nature had put barriers between us" (p. 224). Culture, in the guise of nature, forbids their union precisely by assigning it the place of the individual and national past – the place, that is, of the American history to which the Noble Savage is relegated and the immature pleasures from which adult sexuality must develop. In this fantasy miscegenation, like other non-normative sexualities, can have no future; such novels as *Hope Leslie* and *Last of the Mohicans* defuse the threat of a racially mixed generation by consigning it to the same graveyard as the Native Americans whose extinction Cooper regretfully predicts.

This unfeigned but murderous regret signals the profound ambivalence at the heart of white fantasies of race and sexuality—that is, the mixed longing and dread with which a perverse and racialized past is regarded. A critical commonplace holds that early US literature is a literature of lack, anticipation, futurity, youthful searching – in short, a literature of *desire*. But along with its national pursuit of progress and futurity, that literature and that desire are equally nostalgic, yearning to go back to a past that never existed – the past of prelapsarian, immature modes of desire, or, in Fiedler's words, "juvenile and regressive" pleasures (1960: 344), which become, in their supposed sterility and incipient vanishing, objects of a brutally nostalgic desire. Like other fictions, early US fiction is a space of fantasy, which is always to say, a space of sexual fantasy. But fantasy never wholly escapes the law, whose management of desire proceeds not only through prohibition but also through invention. Instead, American fiction works both to incite and to police desire; it calls into being the forms of love it purports merely to describe; and if it exerts hegemonic control over sexuality, it may also, as the *Knickerbocker* wrote in 1838, inflame the reader with "uncontrollable sympathies."

NOTES

1   The prohibition of the impossible is Lacan's formulation; on the discursive regulation of female sexuality in nineteenth-century America, see Baym 1984: 183.

2   Fiedler does persuasively suggest that male authors avoided marriage plots as a reaction against both the eighteenth-century Richardsonian novel of seduction and the rise of sentimental women's writing in the United States, where the ideology of "separate spheres" also made romantic love the business of women (1960: 57–68).

3   Harriet Wilson's *Our Nig* (1859), a novel about racism in the North, takes a more critical view of patriarchal heterosexuality, examining what sexual consent and even love mean for women, like Frado's mother and Frado herself, in the face of economic strictures (see Tate 1992: 48).

REFERENCES

Baym, Nina (1984). *Novels, Readers, and Reviewers: Responses to Fiction in Antebellum America.* Ithaca, NY: Cornell University Press.

Baym, Nina (1993). *Woman's Fiction: A Guide to Novels by and about Women in America, 1820–70,* 2nd edn. Chicago: University of Illinois Press.

Brown, William Wells (2000). *Clotel; or, The President's Daughter*, ed. Robert S. Levine. Boston: Bedford/St. Martin's. (First publ. 1853.)

Cooke, Rose Terry (1994). "My Visitation." In *Two Friends and other Nineteenth-Century Lesbian Stories by American Women Writers*, ed. Susan Koppelman, 24–42. New York: Meridian.

Cooper, James Fenimore (1981). *The Last of the Mohicans*. New York: Bantam. (First publ. 1826.)

Cott, Nancy F. (1977). *The Bonds of Womanhood: "Woman's Sphere" in New England, 1780–1835*. New Haven: Yale University Press.

Crafts, Hannah (2002). *The Bondwoman's Narrative*, ed. Henry Louis Gates, Jr. New York: Warner.

Davidson, Cathy N. (1986). *Revolution and the Word: The Rise of the Novel in America*. New York: Oxford University Press.

d'Emilio, John, and Freedman, Estelle B. (1988). *Intimate Matters: A History of Sexuality in America*. New York: Harper & Row.

Faderman, Lillian (1981). *Surpassing the Love of Men: Romantic Friendship and Love between Women from the Renaissance to the Present*. New York: William Morrow.

Fiedler, Leslie (1960). *Love and Death in the American Novel*. New York: Criterion.

Foster, Hannah Webster (1986). *The Coquette*. New York: Oxford University Press. (First publ. 1797.)

Foucault, Michel (1990). *The History of Sexuality: An Introduction*. New York: Vintage.

Hawthorne, Nathaniel (1987). *Selected Tales and Sketches*. New York: Penguin.

Katz, Jonathan (1976). *Gay American History: Lesbians and Gay Men in the USA*. New York: Meridian.

Looby, Christopher (1995). "'Innocent Homosexuality': The Fiedler Thesis in Retrospect." In Gerald Graff and James Phelan (eds.), *Adventures of Huckleberry Finn: A Case Study in Critical Controversy*, 535–51. Boston: Bedford/St. Martin's.

Melville, Herman (1967). *Moby-Dick*. New York: Bantam. (First publ. 1851.)

Morrison, Paul (2001). *The Explanation for Everything: Essays on Sexual Subjectivity*. New York: New York University Press.

Poe, Edgar Allan (1982). *The Tell-Tale Heart and other Writings*. New York: Bantam.

Rowson, Susanna (1991). *Charlotte Temple and Lucy Temple*. New York: Penguin.

Sedgwick, Catherine Maria (1998). *Hope Leslie; or, Early Times in the Massachusetts*, ed. Carolyn L. Karcher. New York: Penguin. (First publ. 1827.)

Spillers, Hortense (1987). "Mama's Baby, Papa's Maybe: An American Grammar Book." *Diacritics* 17, 65–81.

Tate, Claudia (1992). *Domestic Allegories of Political Desire: The Black Heroine's Text at the Turn of the Century*. New York: Oxford University Press.

Welter, Barbara (1966). "The Cult of True Womanhood: 1820–1860." *American Quarterly* 18, 151–74.

Wiegman, Robyn (1995). *American Anatomies: Theorizing Race and Gender*. Durham, NC: Duke University Press.

8

Religion

Paul Gutjahr

Religious printed material has a long history in North America, and between the Revolution and the Civil War religious literature of every size and description saturated the newborn country's culture. Dating back to the sixteenth century when, in 1539, the Italian Juan Pablos arrived in Mexico City to set up a printing office under the patronage of Mexico's first Catholic bishop, much of what would be printed in America would have a distinctly religious taint (Tebbel 1972: vol. 1, 1–3). A century later, the Puritans continued this linkage between religion and print in their own publishing and literacy activities. In 1639 the first printing press in Britain's American colonies appeared in the Massachusetts Bay Colony. From this press came the first book to be published in these colonies: *The Whole Booke of Psalmes* (or the "Bay Psalm Book" as it came to be popularly known), in 1640.

Propelling the American publishing industry forward in the British colonies were the unusually high literacy rates found in the Massachusetts Bay Colony. At the time, these were among the highest in the world because of the preponderance of highly educated Puritans who had migrated to the colony. These Puritans held the firm conviction that every person ought to be able to read the Bible for him- or herself. This belief in the necessity of personal Bible reading helped create the first law on education passed in the British colonies in 1642, and paved the way for decades of religious printing in the region. By the time of the Revolutionary War, there were some fifty printing presses active in the colonies, the vast majority located in New England (Thomas 1970: 7). The northeastern region of the United States, with its long history of literacy and publishing, developed in the late eighteenth and early nineteenth centuries into the epicenter of publishing in the United States, particularly in the cities of Boston, Philadelphia, and New York.

While eighteenth-century American printers published any number of items, from almanacs to copies of local government contracts, among the most popular – and thus financially lucrative – staples of printing houses were Protestant sermons. The religious scholar Harry Stout has estimated that in New England by the time of the Revolution some five million different sermons had been written and preached in the American colonies. The average weekly churchgoer of the region listened to some 7,000 sermons in a lifetime (Stout 1986: 3–4). Perhaps the most famous American printer of the eighteenth century, Philadelphia's Benjamin Franklin, made a considerable profit in printing the sermons of the era's most famous traveling evangelist, George Whitefield, who in a single year reportedly preached to 800,000 people. So popular and common was the American sermon that the antebellum educator and statesman Edward Everett would point to it as one of the great cornerstones of the country's unique literary tradition.

Just how closely wed religion and American print culture were before the Civil War becomes abundantly clear in the 1820s, a watershed decade for publishing in the United States. Whereas a print run of 2,000 copies of a book was the industry standard before 1820, a number of factors coalesced during the ensuing decade to enable publishers to print several hundred thousand copies of a title if they wished. Improvements in publishing technologies such as papermaking, power printing, and stereotyping all contributed to this change, as did key cultural shifts in American society, such as rising female literacy rates, a push by various ideologies which turned the activity of reading from a luxury into a necessity (Gilmore 1989: 1–50), and better transportation networks to help disseminate printed material. These diverse factors worked together to make the United States a society that was increasingly formed, framed, and fractured by the power of print.

Within these radical and far-reaching changes stands the fact that true mass media in the country had their origin in religious publishing. David Paul Nord has convincingly argued that it was through the impressive and unceasing efforts of the printing enterprises of two religious organizations, the American Bible Society (founded 1816) and the American Tract Society (1825), that many Americans were exposed to their first constant barrage of printed material, and it was religious in nature (Nord 1984).

Before turning to better-known literary authors, works, and genres, it is absolutely critical to understand that by the end of the 1820s the American Bible and Tract Societies had emerged as the unchallenged leaders in the area of American printing technology and national print distribution. The important innovation of stereotyping, which enabled type plates for pages to be reused rather than being set up anew for each printing of a book, found its first use in the United States with a religious catechism produced by John Watts. The American Bible and Tract Societies went on to use stereotype plates to produce bibles, tracts, books, and pamphlets in unprecedented numbers more than a decade before the famous literary firm of Harper & Brothers became the first nonreligious press to make wide use of stereotyping in the 1830s.

The Bible and Tract Societies were also the first to use power presses, adopting Daniel Treadwell's steam-powered presses near the end of the 1820s. By 1829 the American Bible Society had installed sixteen Treadwell presses, while the American Tract Society was using nine Treadwell presses (Nord 1984: 10–11). The scale of these

printing enterprises is noteworthy. These societies leaped over the 2,000-copy stand-
ard press run of the opening decades of the nineteenth century. By the late 1820s the
American Bible Society was producing 300,000 bibles a year, the American Tract
Society six million tracts a year (Gutjahr 1999: 30; Nord 1984: 22).

The distribution practices of these societies were also organized and extensive, and
their reach would be made all the more impressive by the advent of railroad travel in
the 1840s. By using both an extensive network of volunteer agents and an already
well-established network of Protestant churches and church schools across a wide
variety of denominations, these two societies combined to produce and distribute
somewhere around sixty million pieces of religious literature by the time of the Civil
War. Their ability to tap into existing networks gave these societies a greater ability
to penetrate the country, in particular the regions closer to the frontier, than other
publishers.

It should also be remembered in the midst of these statistics that the vast majority
of American trade publishers before the Civil War also had extensive catalogs of
religious titles, contributing to the absolute saturation coverage of religious printed
material in the years leading up to the Civil War. Christian books, tracts, newspapers,
journals, gift books, and even almanacs increasingly flooded the American print
marketplace in the years between the Revolution and the Civil War, guaranteeing
that the most common and accessible pieces of literature to be found throughout this
period were religious in nature.

*

Against this backdrop of a print culture absolutely crammed full of religiously
oriented material, one can to begin to understand the development of differing
forms of religious fiction in the early United States. The history of American
publishing laid the groundwork for a largely Christian print culture in the years
preceding the Civil War, but as the United States grew, other traditions added their
voices to the religious literature found in America. It is helpful first to look at the
development of the literatures in the Christian tradition, and then to take a wider
view of the contribution of different religious traditions as their print voices emerged.

The deep antipathy of American Protestants toward the novel found its roots in the
theology of the seventeenth century, when the religious, and thus often the cultural,
leaders of the Puritan movement decried any literature that distracted people from
reading the Bible and living their lives according to the truths it contained. Timothy
Dwight – poet, theologian, and president of Yale in the early decades of the
nineteenth century – captured the caution and indeed hatred many Protestants felt
toward fiction in the decades immediately following the Revolution when he stated:
"Between the Bible and novels there is a gulph fixed which few readers are willing to
pass" (Dwight 1821: vol. 1, 518). He was not alone in his condemnation of novel-
reading; a host of religious – and even non-religious – commentators condemned the
form as irredeemably corrupting (Lehuu 2000: 126–55). Such censures found wide

circulation in the United States as the American Tract Society added its voice to these condemnations by issuing a number of tracts on the dangers of novel-reading, often comparing its effects to the evils of alcohol or the ravages of debilitating and even deadly diseases. These tracts were echoed by countless newspaper articles, entries in almanacs and advice manuals, and whole chapters in the immensely popular gift books of the day warning readers about the insidious nature of fiction.

Protestants who wrote against fiction in general, and novels in particular, most often grounded their arguments in four closely intertwined lines of reasoning. Pre-eminent among these was a notion, derived from the "common sense" strand of Scottish philosophy, of the importance of basing one's life on the truth. As one critic preached in 1807, novels removed one from the truth through their tendency to "give false notions of things, to pervert the consequences of human actions, and to misrepresent the ways of divine providence" (quoted in Martin 1961: 61). Fiction was evil and dangerous simply because it was fiction and not the truth. All virtuous action, and thus any ability to lead a worthwhile life, depended on embracing what was true and avoiding even the slightest hint of dissimulation or falseness.

A second line of reasoning argued that novels, with their romantic and adventurous tales, inflamed the imagination, and thus the passions. Awakening uncontrollable animal instincts also worked at cross-purposes with ideals of virtue, which were heavily dependent on notions of hard work, discipline, and perseverance (Brown 1940: 3–51).

Arousing these instincts became particularly dangerous in light of the third line of reasoning which fueled Protestant hostility toward fiction, namely that as reading material became ever more accessible in the nineteenth century and literacy rates rose, people were reading material in an increasingly unmediated fashion. The days were disappearing when the father of a household read aloud to his family, both picking the material to be read and interpreting it as he read it. Now, young and old, male and female were increasingly reading material in isolation, and getting from that material all sorts of ideas which might send them down the wrong path (Davidson 1986: 42–3).

Finally, Protestants protested that novels were dangerous because they took time away from more worthy activities, principal among them Bible reading and other devotional practices. Even more dangerously, novels might so influence American reading tastes that the Bible would come to seem nothing more than "a wearisome book" (quoted in Gutjahr 1999: 147).

In the end, it was this concern with the Bible that fueled much of the Protestant reluctance to accept the novel form. A concern with truth (as most explicitly revealed in the Bible) was the cornerstone of American Protestantism in the late eighteenth and early nineteenth centuries. It is not surprising, then, that various theological camps which held less tightly than others to the importance of Bible reading and a biblical hermeneutic propounding the absolute historicity of the scriptures played a key role in the development of the acceptance of fiction among American Protestants. As various subsections of American Protestantism became more elastic in their understandings of biblical historicity and doctrinal orthodoxy, the novel became more accepted in their ranks.

The gradual acceptance of religious fiction among Protestants in the United States was a slow process that would reach a turning point around the 1850s and reach almost full fruition in the closing decades of the century. The eventual acceptance of fiction had its roots in several different factors. First, biblical teachings had long been presented in story form by both Protestant preachers and writers. An early genre which foregrounded the linkage between the Bible and story was the allegory. Allegories such as John Bunyan's *Pilgrim's Progress* and Edmund Botsford's *The Spiritual Voyage, Performed in the Ship Convert, under the Command of Capt. Godly Fear* enjoyed the wide support of nineteenth-century American Protestant readers because they tempered storytelling with representative – not purely human – characters and heavily didactic messages. Such allegorical stories, as well as a striking change in preaching which saw storytelling used as a means to interpret and emphasize biblical truth, helped constitute a liminal genre between the truth of the Bible and truth that could be communicated in the form of the novel (Reynolds 1980).

Another important factor contributing to a gradual readiness by Protestants to countenance fiction is found, ironically, in the work of the American Tract Society itself. For all of the Society's vociferous attacks on fiction-reading, it played a pivotal role in helping to lay the groundwork for the eventual acceptance of religious fiction in the United States. Among the most popular of the Society's tracts were a number of pieces, two to four pages in length, that can best be described as "moral tales," telling the story of an individual who had overcome some hardship or had encountered Christ in some life-changing way.

The Society's moral tales were written in such a generic manner that although they purportedly told a truthful tale, it could just as easily have been a fictional one. These stories clearly had a moral lesson, but they were not always advertised or written in a strictly historical mode. Jane Tompkins has effectively argued that readers who were exposed to these stories were likely to elide this supposedly moral nonfiction with the religious fiction which would follow (Tompkins 1985: 150–60). Thus, the American Tract Society did important work in paving the way for the acceptance of the moral fictional tales that increasingly populated the print culture landscape in the decades leading up to the Civil War.

American Protestants also became softened to the presence and potential usefulness of fiction through the growing influence of European biblical Higher Criticism. Higher Criticism questioned the historicity of the Bible and the trustworthiness of its transmission and translation. Just how reliable human language was in capturing the true nature of God and transmitting the truth of that nature over time became major areas of debate and forced various groups to develop more sophisticated ideas about the rhetorical use of imagery and symbolism. As a result, Higher Criticism slowly led to a more elastic understanding of language in certain theological circles and a greater openness to representations of history, divinity, and humankind in different forms of fiction (Gura 1981: 15–71).

The influence of Higher Criticism was felt earliest among American Universalists and Episcopalians. By the 1830s, leaders of these denominations were tempering their remarks about novel-reading and even encouraging writers within their ranks to introduce biblical characters, stories, and messages into the plots of their novels. Other denominations followed suit in the 1840s, and one of the most popular novels of the next decade, Joseph Holt Ingraham's *The Prince of the House of David* (1854), sported Jesus as a leading character. Protestant wariness of the novel form would last well into the later part of the nineteenth century, but the back of the opposition was broken before the Civil War with such bestsellers as Ingraham's work.

What is interesting, yet not surprising, to note in the rise of the religious novel of this period is the fact that theological content became of less and less importance as religious novels evolved. While Ingraham made a point of including a great deal of biblical content in his novel, with a central focus on the humanity of Jesus and the development of his life and ministry, the next bestselling life of Christ, Lew Wallace's *Ben-Hur* (1880), had no such lofty theological goals. Wallace was unabashedly interested in writing a bestseller, and in pursuit of his goal was concerned to avoid upsetting any faction among his more religious readers. Thus he avoided any overt stances on doctrine and reduced the character of Jesus to only a few cameo appearances. Wallace may have subtitled his book "A Tale of the Christ" for marketing purposes, but it was much more a tale of adventure and bloody revenge than a meditation on Christ's earthly ministry.

While American authors, many of them Protestants and former Protestants who had drifted away from the churches or relinquished their faith, were more frequently populating novels with biblical characters by the 1850s, others were less overt but just as serious about filling their fiction with religious themes. This religiously inflected writing grew substantially in both range and diversity in the first half of the nineteenth century (Buell 1986: 166–90; Reynolds 1981: 127–44). On the popular level, most noticeable in this vein were the women who composed the immensely popular sentimental fiction of the period. Most commonly these women did not place the character of Jesus explicitly in their works; instead they filled their works with Christlike characters.

Three of the most popular novels written by women prior to the Civil War included a heavy-handed emphasis on the Christlike nature of central characters. Susan Warner's *The Wide, Wide World* (1850), Harriet Beecher Stowe's *Uncle Tom's Cabin* (1852), and Maria Cummins' *The Lamplighter* (1854) all sold well over 100,000 copies in the decade preceding the conflict, and all had leading characters who were clearly set forth as representations of Jesus Christ. Stowe went even further in her *Uncle Tom's Cabin* by presenting not one, but two Christ-figures in her book: a little girl named Eva, who enacts Christ's last supper by giving away locks of her hair on her deathbed, and the character who gives the book its title, a negro slave named Tom, who suffers a martyr's death and yet forgives those responsible.

While American Protestants were seeing their religious fiction loosen its ties to theology and overt goals of edification, American Catholic writers were moving in an opposite direction in the years before the Civil War. Catholic writers up through the 1840s used fiction to offer readers strongly propounded and highly intellectual arguments for the true and lasting status of the Roman Catholic Church as the one true Christian church. By the 1850s, while the Catholic penchant for forceful doctrinal material had not disappeared, Catholic novels were increasingly taking on the sentimental and sensational nature of their Protestant counterparts at the cost of their rich and reasoned doctrinal discourse.

Even before the emergence of Catholic novels in the 1830s, there had existed in first the colonies and then the states a deep antipathy between Catholics and Protestants. The result of this hatred on the Protestant side of American fiction often took the form of vitriolic works that depicted Catholicism as a sexually perverted tradition where women were encouraged to become nuns rather than mothers and men were locked into a non-democratic system of obeying the Pope, who was nothing better than a foreign monarch (Billington 1938: 345–79).

The most widely read piece of anti-Catholic writing to circulate before the Civil War was Maria Monk's *Awful Disclosures, by Maria Monk, of the Hotel Dieu Nunnery of Montreal*, first published in 1836. *Awful Disclosures* was purportedly a true tale of a young girl who had entered a nunnery only to find it to be a place of the deepest and darkest evils. Reading through its pages exposes one to countless illicit love affairs between priests and nuns, illegitimate children born from such liaisons who are then immediately baptized and killed, and the masochistic, non-democratic nature of the Catholic Church's hierarchy. Both Monk and her book were discredited soon after the book's release, but so many American readers either refused to consider the evidence against the book or simply enjoyed reading its salacious and anti-Catholic content that by the time the Civil War broke out in 1861 *Awful Disclosures* had sold more than 300,000 copies.

American Catholics fought against such scurrilous writing in the 1830s and 1840s with novels designed to serve both as a counter to the obvious excesses of Protestant sensationalism and as a "pointed reply to the growing number of Americans who dismissed Catholics as illiterate slum dwellers enslaved by the 'Beast of Rome'" (Reynolds 1981: 145). Thus, Catholic fiction most often centered on characters who began as reasonable Protestants but through the course of the novel found just how bankrupt Protestantism was in the face of the rich tradition of Catholicism.

Early important Catholic novelists in this rational vein included Charles Constantine Pise, Hugh Quigley, Mary Hughs, and even the former Unitarian and Transcendentalist Orestes Brownson, who converted to Catholicism in 1844. All of these writers used their works to present a logical and well-reasoned case for Catholicism in an attempt to fight against the increasing waves of anti-Catholicism that were washing over antebellum American culture. The early Catholic novelists – whose ranks included a considerable number of priests – argued for the primacy and legitimacy of the Catholic Church, which stood as a unifying body in the midst of the myriad fractured Protestant denominations found in the United States. With its constant tendency to spin off new sects, American Protestantism stood as a testimony to its own directionless and hopelessly fractious nature. In their works, these novelists argued that the Catholic Church, on the other hand, could prove its religious lineage all the way back to St. Peter and was invested with the same authority Christ had bestowed upon the first apostles.

By the 1850s Catholic novelists such as Jedediah Vincent Huntington, Anna Dorsey, and George Henry Miles were taking American Catholic fiction in a new direction. Moving away from heavy Catholic doctrinal content, these writers were bent on showing the appealing nature of Catholicism by portraying the evils of Protestantism and the virtues of the Roman church without using their characters to deliver lengthy polemical orations. Instead, these authors focused on the everyday lives of Americans and the good that could be done through example rather than lecture. Miles's *The Governess*, published in 1851, is representative of this softer, more sentimental Catholic fiction. Miles tells the story of the young governess Mary, who brings about the conversion of a Protestant family not by logical persuasion but by the force of her own exemplary life. Moving away from religious allegory and nuanced theological argumentation, the works of many of these later Catholic authors eschewed matters of religious controversy and embraced an appeal to the hearts rather than the heads of their readers.

*

Aside from the rich Christian tradition of fiction to be found in the United States prior to the Civil War, it is helpful to note briefly that other religious traditions – Judaism, Islam, Hinduism, Confucianism, and Buddhism – were slowly making their way into antebellum print culture. Although the scope of their publishing activity was nowhere near the size or importance of Christian publishing in this period, the years leading up to the Civil War did see important developments in the literary presence of all these traditions inside the United States.

No one is sure when the first Jews may have migrated to the American colonies, but a turning point in Jewish community formation occurred in 1654, when a group of Jewish families fleeing Portuguese persecution in Brazil made their way to New Amsterdam, which in 1664 would become New York. This small body of Jews grew in the years to come and became one of many small Jewish communities which would dot the Atlantic seaboard of the colonies. Numbering only a few thousand at the outset of the nineteenth century, the Jewish population grew steadily throughout the century, largely as a result of the ever-increasing numbers of European Jewish immigrants making their way to American shores. It is estimated that in 1840 there were only 15,000 Jews in the United States. By the time of the Civil War, the nation's total population of thirty-one million contained a Jewish population of 150,000.

Jewish publishing in this period was in its formative stages. There were only two Jewish publishers of note prior to the Civil War. The first was a rabbi by the name of Isaac Leeser, who was the first American to translate and print the Hebrew Bible in English. By 1853 he had finished the entire work, publishing it in a version which proved extremely popular in the Jewish communities of the time.

Leeser's publishing interests were almost entirely religious, while the other Jewish publisher in the period had a slightly broader publishing agenda. This was Edward Bloch of Cincinnati, Ohio (Tebbel 1972: vol. 1, 530; Madison 1976: 74–7). Bloch, in partnership with his brother-in-law Rabbi Isaac Mayer Wise, began his forays into Jewish publishing in the 1850s and was most famous for publishing a series of prayer books known as the *Minhag America*. His interests also touched upon literature. Venturing into magazine publishing, Bloch and Wise spearheaded the production of both adult and children's Jewish magazines under three different titles: *The Israelite*, *Deborah*, and *Sabbath Visitor*.

Fiction made up only a small proportion of the content of Bloch and Wise's magazines. Wise wrote some of the earliest stories himself, seeing them as an effective tool to lure readers into his magazines while teaching them various religious principles (Madison 1976: 12). Still, efforts at Jewish fiction remained small, and it would not be until the more massive waves of Jewish immigration beginning in the 1880s that anything like a substantial American Jewish literature would appear in the United States.

Just how widespread the traditions of Islam, Hinduism, Confucianism, and Buddhism in the United States were before the Civil War it is impossible to say, but the number of their adherents was tiny in regard to the general population. Major fictional literature grounded in these three traditions would not appear until after the Civil War, but fiction writers of the antebellum period make it abundantly clear that they were aware of these traditions and even familiar with their sacred texts. Melville, for example, in *Moby-Dick* makes frequent allusions to various elements of Islam, naming one of the book's chapters after the tradition's sacred holiday of Ramadan.

Those familiar with Hinduism and Buddhism in this period tended to be the educated elite. Many Unitarians and Transcendentalists showed great interest in sacred texts of these traditions. Ralph Waldo Emerson, Henry Thoreau, Theodore Parker, and Bronson Alcott were all familiar with the *Bhagavad-Gita*, and the book became a particular favorite of Emerson's (Jackson 1981: 45–84).

The New England Transcendentalists also read, and wrote, widely on several Chinese classical works in Confucian and Buddhist thought. It may be too much to say that these figures discovered the Asian religious traditions for Americans, but they did a great deal to popularize them. It should be noted, however, that while the Transcendentalists wrote extensively, they were not much interested in writing fiction and did not produce any major novels before the end of the Civil War (Versluis 1993: 235–304). Interest in what Americans of the nineteenth century would term "orientalism" did not truly grow until after the Civil War, when fiction touching more directly on the Eastern traditions began to appear in more noticeable quantities. There was, however, a growing awareness of ancient Asian religions among Americans even in the antebellum period, an awareness that would have a significant impact in the closing decades of the nineteenth century (Jackson 1981: 141–56).

Everywhere one turned in antebellum America, one could find religious and religiously inflected fiction. Attitudes toward the propriety and uses of this fiction significantly changed during the years between the Revolution and the Civil War, but the power and presence of this literature are beyond question. To study fiction in this period is to confront continually the reality and diversity of religious belief in America. Such study makes one vitally aware that it was religion that both stood as the bedrock of much of the country's print culture and provided the fuel that powered countless forms of what would become known as "American literature."

References and Further Reading

Billington, Ray Allen (1938). *The Protestant Crusade, 1800–1860*. New York: Macmillan.

Brown, Herbert Ross (1940). *The Sentimental Novel in America 1789–1860*. Durham, NC: Duke University Press.

Buell, Lawrence (1986). *New England Literary Culture: From Revolution through Renaissance*. New York: Cambridge University Press.

Davidson, Cathy N. (1986). *Revolution and the Word: The Rise of the Novel in America*. New York: Oxford University Press.

Dwight, Timothy (1821). *Travels; in New-England and New-York*, 4 vols. New Haven: T. Dwight.

Gilmore, William J. (1989). *Reading Becomes a Necessity of Life: Material and Cultural Life in Rural New England, 1780–1835*. Knoxville: University of Tennessee Press.

Goldfarb, Russel M., and Goldfarb, Clare R. (1978). *Spiritualism and Nineteenth-Century Letters*. Madison, NJ: Fairleigh Dickinson University Press.

Gura, Philip F. (1981). *The Wisdom of Words: Language, Theology, and Literature in the New England Renaissance*. Middletown, Conn.: Wesleyan University Press.

Gutjahr, Paul (1999). *An American Bible: A History of the Good Book in the United States, 1777–1880*. Stanford: Stanford University Press.

Jackson, Carl T. (1981). *The Oriental Religions and American Thought: Nineteenth-Century Explorations*. Westport, Conn.: Greenwood.

Lehuu, Isabelle (2000). *Carnival on a Page: Popular Print Media in Antebellum America*. Chapel Hill, NC: University of North Carolina Press.

Madison, Charles A. (1976). *Jewish Publishing in America: The Impact of Jewish Writing on American Culture*. New York: Sanhedrin.

Martin, Terence (1961). *The Instructed Vision: Scottish Common Sense Philosophy and the Origins of American Fiction*. Bloomington: Indiana University Press.

Marty, Martin E.; Deedy, John G., Jr.; Silverman, David Wolf; and Lekachman, Robert (1963). *The Religious Press in America*. New York: Holt, Rinehart & Winston.

Nord, David Paul (1984). "The Evangelical Origins of Mass Media in America, 1815–1835." *Journalism Monographs* 88 (May).

Orians, G. Harrison (1937). "Censure of Fiction in American Romances and Magazines, 1789–1810." *PMLA* 52: 1 (March), 195–214.

Reynolds, David S. (1980). "From Doctrine to Narrative: The Rise of Pulpit Storytelling in America." *American Quarterly* 32: 5 (Winter), 479–98.

Reynolds, David S. (1981). *Faith in Fiction: The Emergence of Religious Literature in America*. Cambridge, Mass.: Harvard University Press.

Stout, Harry (1986). *New England Soul: Preaching and Religious Culture in Colonial New England*. New York: Oxford University Press.

Sussman, Lance J. (1995). *Isaac Leeser and the Making of American Judaism*. Detroit: Wayne State University Press.

Tebbel, John (1972). *A History of Book Publishing in the United States*, 4 vols. New York: Bowker.

Thomas, Isaiah (1970). *The History of Printing in America*, 2nd edn., ed. Marcus McCorison. New York: Weathervane.

Tompkins, Jane (1985). *Sensational Designs: The Cultural Work of American Fiction, 1790–1860*. New York: Oxford University Press.

Versluis, Arthur (1993). *American Transcendentalism and Asian Religions*. New York: Oxford University Press.

9
Education and Polemic

Stephanie Foote

I

The antebellum period in the United States, between roughly 1780 and 1860, was, in terms of the development of its institutions, anything but coherent. Although it is generally considered a time of nation-building – a phrase that indicates a progressive movement away from regional particularities and toward national uniformity – it was also a time of enormous change in the very definition of the nation and its aims. Different, often incommensurable, ideas about how to define the nation and its values can be registered by looking at some of the period's critical social, material, and ideological institutions, for they are often the most sensitive registers of the nation's internal contradictions as well as of the different factions seeking to redefine the nation and its values. Of all of these institutions, education is perhaps the most useful to examine, for "education" has traditionally been among the most prized as well as the most labile of terms in the republic: as critical to the nation's eighteenth-century architects as it was to the nineteenth-century working-men's parties of the northeast, as important to women's rights advocates as to conservative nativists, as likely to appear in the editorials of African American urban newspapers as in broadside manifestos written by white men.

The very malleability of the term "education" makes it an especially good focal point for an examination of questions of values, social norms, and cultural changes; but it also makes any serious inquiry into the meaning of the term in this period difficult. Not only did the nation itself change and expand between 1780 and 1860, its regional and national economies transformed, its involvement in international politics increased, and its capitalist economy consolidated and grew exponentially. Its infrastructure, including roads, canals, and postal offices, increased in efficiency and reach, and its population changed in size and mobility. More people moved from the country to the city, more urban inhabitants were foreign-born, and more workers began to work in mills and factories. Although the character of the nation itself can be seen to have changed, it is also worth mentioning that the statistical generalities that obtain in this period were not uniformly distributed; the sectional conflict that would lead to the Civil War, for example, testifies to the unevenness of the spread of integrated capital economies and institutions. It should be kept in mind that the kinds of generalities we can make about ideas and practices pertaining to education in this period are regional only – they more often as not apply only to the North and the Midwest rather than to the South.

Yet there *are* some broad generalities that unify the practice, if not the definition, of education in this period. In general, the most prevalent and widely attended and distributed late eighteenth-century schools provided only very basic instruction in literacy and numeracy. Most of these elementary schools were ungraded – students of all ages were instructed together in a single room. The schools were taught by a person (usually male) whose qualifications were unregulated by any official group; the instructor could be very good indeed, or he could be abysmal. He, and increasingly she as the nineteenth century wore on, made a very unsatisfactory living teaching, and boarded around with various pupils' families. School terms were not long, and attendance was not mandatory, although it was often surprisingly high in the Midwest and the northeast (attendance in the South is more difficult to ascertain). Students went in and out of school depending on the kinds of labor they needed to do at home. Girls were welcome in schools, and sometimes became teachers themselves.

By the mid-nineteenth century, schools had changed significantly. Whereas in the eighteenth century there had been only a few different kinds of school – free common schools in rural areas, free schools in urban areas, or tuition academies, usually in urban areas – there were now a multitude of different kinds. Some of the new schools embodied different schemes of paying for education – charity schools in the northeast, for example, were free and for the children whose parents could not afford to send them to an academy – and some were especially constructed to demonstrate or test out different social assumptions, such as the Transcendentalist Bronson Alcott's Temple Street School. Still others were directed at distinct portions of the population, such as the Emma Willard School in Troy, which served women only, and the system of African Free Schools, which served the growing number of free black inhabitants of the Northern states. Also by the mid-nineteenth century, schools were more likely to be graded and to follow a standard curriculum, at least within a certain location or state (a standard national curriculum had been the dream of a few of the founding fathers, but was never accomplished). By the mid-nineteenth century, there were textbooks created for use only in schools, and there were professional journals for teachers, as well as an increased number of state bureaucrats involved specifically with educational issues such as how to evaluate teachers or how to raise public monies for schools. Some of these bureaucrats were in the business of research and publicity: for example, some were charged with evaluating different educational practices like the much-respected Prussian centralized system of schools, or the value of the mandatory public high school, a fairly new innovation in the nineteenth century (Kaestle 1983: 104–29).

The differences between systems of schooling in various regions of the United States over this eighty-year period make it somewhat difficult to generalize about educational systems themselves. Even the most simple generalizations – for example, that teaching and schooling became more professionalized and uniform as time wore on – need to be balanced by noting how educational systems also became more varied and prolific. But the very multiplicity of educational endeavors makes it all the more important and interesting to step back from the idea of *schooling* to look at the more abstract issue of *education*. Schooling and education are almost always conflated in histories of education, and for good reason. The extraordinary history of the free common school in New England, for example, is directly linked to that region's high literacy rates as well as to its tradition of valuing self-governance and self-improvement. In this essay, I shall often discuss education and schooling simultaneously, although I do not use the terms interchangeably. Schooling and education might be related by seeing the former as the practice, or the embodiment, of the more theoretical and ambiguous latter. But even this is not a sufficient distinction, for schooling itself as often introduced new ideas into more generally held concepts of education as education helped to shape various schools and systems of schooling.

Thus, when we look at education, we look at an institution that had abstract ideological power as well as a lived, social form. We therefore must imagine education as an institution that could be simultaneously experienced and thought about within the national horizon (education, as we shall see, was one of the ways in which the architects of the nation believed that democracy could be ensured and reproduced) as well as the local (education could help this person do *this*, and do it here and now). We must also understand "education" as a term labile enough to mediate and focus some of the most vital and formative questions of the era. In very broad terms, using the definition of ideology formulated by the political theorist Louis Althusser as people's imaginary relationships to the real conditions of their lives, we can see that education is ideological, because it gives people a specific vocabulary in which to ask questions. In particular, education gives people a vocabulary they can use to ask specific questions about the relationship of an individual to broader structures of government and authority which range from the family to the state itself.

Education was at the center of a number of different debates in antebellum America. It was perceived to be at the core of democratic life; but implementing plans to educate the inhabitants of the new nation often relied on schemes for taxation that people democratically chose to resist. Education was also the means of social mobility, a principle so entrenched that numerous indentured servants' articles made provisions for the education of the apprentice. Education was also perceived to be a leveler – the debates over the common schools championed by such progressive men as New England school reformer Horace Mann in the early part of the nineteenth century were deeply indebted to an egalitarian logic of social equality, in which the children of the rich and the poor should be educated together, giving both an equal chance in the world. As a way to ensure democracy, as a way to ensure social mobility, and as a way to expand the opportunities of persons otherwise disenfranchised, it is possible to see education as a progressive term. But education was also, as historian Carl Kaestle has shown in his excellent study, used as a means of social control. The drive to establish common schools was not simply to mitigate perceived class and status differences but also to help ensure the socialization of immigrant populations – that is, as a mechanism by which to inculcate the values of the new nation as opposed to the values that immigrants were perceived to learn from their families. Schematizing educational philosophies as either progressive or oppressive, liberatory or controlling, is not historically useful. Every scheme for education relied on social formulas and beliefs that were at least as progressive as they were restrictive.

In the next section of this essay, I shall consider two cases – that of women and that of slaves and freed persons of color – in which education, broadly understood, was at the center of a number of different debates over what counted as and in a democracy and what kinds of social values were necessary for its survival. The cases of women and persons of color exemplify the social tension between education and democratic ideals, for they demonstrate how the democratic promise that some perceived to inhere in education was amplified by people who saw in education the means to transform the very nature of the democratic republic in which they lived. In each case, education was not just the means to participate in the shaping of a democratic nation; it was the instrument that revealed the limits of that putatively democratic nation, as well as the battleground on which new definitions of who might be considered a citizen of that democracy were tested. The cases of both women and persons of color also provide the opportunity to significantly expand what the term education encompasses. While many of the struggles of the social actors I shall discuss seem at first glance to revolve around the conflation of "schools" and "education," they were often rooted in a form of cultural literacy that was unsystematic and unregulated, yet nonetheless critical for the education of some of the very people debarred from more formal education.

II

In colonial New England, girls regularly attended school; they would have learned to read and write, they would have learned to figure; yet they would have learned far more out of school than in it. From their mothers they might have learned the household arts of embroidering, sewing, and quilting, and as they learned letters and spelling, they might have committed their lessons to embroidered pieces. By 1820 young women were encouraged to go to school to learn to read, write, and cipher, but compulsory schooling for young women was not geared toward making them equal citizens: it was designed to help them become good mothers, able to instruct their children in the moral pieties that attended civic duty and virtue. It was not until 1828 that Massachusetts' public schools, albeit hitherto more numerous than in most other states, admitted girls on an equal footing with boys (Blinderman 1975: 37).

The ideology of republican motherhood captured the contradiction inherent in women's status. Women were not really citizens of the republic: they could not vote, and their legal rights were severely abridged. Women were not supposed to participate in public debates; indeed, during this period, the ideology of gendered separate spheres was widely accepted. Women, in this ideological formulation, were designed by the Creator to be the helpmates of their husbands as well as the moral compass for the entire household. Women were supposed not to be motivated by reason or intellect, those two qualities most prized by the Enlightenment architects of the early republic, and most cultivated in the curricula of the education of young men. Rather, women were presumed to be creatures of sympathy and emotion. They were therefore best suited to the creation of the moral and spiritual world of the home. Even if some young women received an education, popular sentiment about gender suggested that it was largely wasted on them. They either had or ought to have too much heart to care for it or to excel at it.

Yet it is critical to recall that *all* women worked during this period, as during every other period of American history. Many women worked in mills in New England and as domestic laborers, and many worked in the fields alongside their husbands (it goes without saying that all women of color worked, most of them as slaves, and the small number who were free worked as well). Those few women of sufficient status who did not have to do what is usually counted as remunerated labor nonetheless worked in their own households, taking care of children, preparing meals, and performing and overseeing the various tedious and difficult housekeeping chores. Although women as an abstract category of people tended to be flat and one-dimensional in ideological terms, real historical women, then as now, did not all share the same political sentiments or the same social status. Yet all women were by and large charged with the task of raising children and establishing the values of the family. Women needed to have some schooling, then, in order to begin the important process of raising future mothers and future citizens. Not fully citizens themselves, women shaped young men who would become citizens; thus the development of "republican motherhood," which tried to reconcile the contradiction between women's real status and their abstract role in democracy.

Within the ideology of republican motherhood women were considered informal educators themselves, and by the late eighteenth and early nineteenth centuries the movement to provide young women with more complete education was well established. Women's historian Sara M. Evans argues that the ideology of republican motherhood helped to establish the very female academies that taught women serious academic subjects that far exceeded the knowledge they would need to raise children (Evans 1989: 56–7). Indeed, as early as 1790 the essayist Judith Sargent Murray had used the ideology of republican motherhood to argue for female education in "On the Equality of the Sexes." The fruit of such polemics was quick to appear. In 1821, for example, Emma Willard opened her famous Troy Female Academy in which she taught not only the housewifely arts, but math, science, and languages. Many of the young women who attended Emma Willard's Female Academy went on to become teachers, and many also went on to open their own schools.

The education provided by Willard stressed academic subjects, but advances in formal schooling for women were not always geared toward conventionally academic training. The first part of the nineteenth century saw the development of two broad systems of advanced education for women. On the one hand were the Female Academies, such as Emma Willard's; on the other were the educational enterprises attached to the ideas of Catherine Beecher. Beecher, a noted educator in her own right, believed that the housewifely arts traditionally assigned to women could be codified and systematized like a science: the running of a competent republican household depended on women's ability to understand the needs of their children and their husbands and to structure the household accordingly. Beecher therefore seized the conventional role of women and elevated it into a system that, far from being "natural" or the product of instinct, was the product of learning and reason. As one historian argues, Beecher "politicized domesticity" (Evans 1989: 71).

In the decades leading up to the Civil War, increased educational opportunities for women were intimately tied to the suffrage movement. Indeed, suffrage movement leaders argued that if women were educable and reasonable, they must be deserving of more expansive political and social rights. One of the movement's most vocal members, Lucy Stone, had attended Oberlin, one of the very few institutions in the nation which offered young women a college education, and, along with other female graduates argued that women deserved to be educated at the collegiate level as well as in the professions. Suffrage leaders often "taught" the lesson of suffrage to public gatherings of men and women as well as in newspapers and periodicals.

But most women in the early republic and the antebellum period were not graduates of Oberlin, nor were they leaders of organized suffrage groups. How then, did the majority of women obtain what we might broadly consider an education – how, in other words, did they make themselves literate in the day's political and social issues? Formal schooling beyond what we would now call elementary school was often not an option for financial reasons, yet ordinary women continued their education from available sources in their world; and one of the best sources was the novel.

The first printed texts in the new republic were not novels, but many of the earliest American books – sermons by famous divines, or the work of Benjamin Franklin, or the conduct books adapted from their English counterparts – were educational. I do not mean this in its broadest sense, for any printed artifact is educational in the sense that it transmits information. Rather, I mean that these earliest texts were educational in the sense that they explicitly took as their goal the instruction and education of their readers in a specific branch of social knowledge. Thomas Paine's manifestos sought to educate the public about the applicability of Enlightenment ideals of political freedom. The *Federalist Papers* staged debates about the kind of government best suited to the disparate colonies. These texts had a self-consciously educational mission: their contents were designed to be debated in public by men. Early fiction, on the other hand, was a different kettle of fish: it was immediately assumed to pose a threat to the morals of young women, although by the middle of the nineteenth century its gendered didactic capacity was spectacularly manifest in Harriet Beecher Stowe's *Uncle Tom's Cabin*.

Despite contemporary critics' anxieties that the very act of reading fiction would corrupt readers, especially young women readers, fiction proved to be a popular form of recreation as well as education in antebellum America. Early critics argued against the habit of reading novels, charging that novel-reading was likely to plant senti- mental and dangerous ideas into young girls' minds, making them potentially ungovernable by their families. Contemporary historians, far from simply debunking this logic, have re-examined fears about novel-reading and the kinds of education that it might impart to readers. They have argued that novels did indeed serve a popular demagogic function, and were especially suited to the needs of young women, who were on the one hand debarred from participating in public political debates or higher education, and on the other hand were often impeded from enjoying private time because of their numerous household duties. Read to oneself, in time borrowed from other responsibilities, imaginative literature gave to its readers far more than the dangerously sentimental desires critics imagined. Novels provided a space for the examination of social issues regarding marriage and desire, kinship and friendship, gender roles and expectations, race and nation, and, most especially, the extension of the rights that founded the nation: rights that were abstractly understood to be universal, but which were in practice extended to only a select few people.

Ideas about education were central to literary works. Not only did literature often directly address the value of education, it tended to argue over what actually constituted education and, in redefining it, it helped to make the case that education of various kinds was a central issue for everyone, especially those members of the polity who were most often overlooked. The centrality of ideas about education in literature is hardly coincidental, for women, so often excluded from formal education, used novels as a means of informally educating themselves about their culture. Literature, even that which was *not* about education, can therefore be seen to have had an educative function in itself; like the kinds of learning offered in more formal institutions, it transmitted skills in manipulating information, it promoted a certain kind of cultural literacy, and it mediated an individual's relationship to larger structures of social authority.

Susannah Rowson's *Charlotte Temple*, the first enduring bestseller of the new republic, exemplifies this logic. Rowson was a shrewd and successful woman who was not only a novelist and playwright but the founder of a respected girl's academy. The novel recounts the story of Charlotte Temple, seduced from her English boarding school to the American colonies and there abandoned. Charlotte's fall from virtue is the story of seduction, but, more critically, it is also the story of an incomplete or insufficient education. The school she attends is a good one of its kind – it stresses deportment and the development of obedience and womanly graces – but the impact of even a single bad educator is profound, for Mlle Rue, the seducer's broker for Charlotte's sympathies, is first a teacher, and only secondly a conspirator against

Charlotte – indeed, it is her position as the former that makes her the latter. Charlotte is an early example of how much women need to know, indeed, how dangerous it is to larger structures like family and nation when a woman is kept ignorant. The narrator of the novel is therefore invested in teaching through fiction, instructing readers not only how to read the novel, but how to use the novel to teach others.

Rowson's 1794 "Essay on Female Education" was likewise concerned with the miseducation of women in boarding schools, which, as in *Charlotte Temple*, taught women only the sentimental side of life rather than the practical. The dangers of unsupervised reading and knowledge were not portrayed only by Rowson; they were a favored topic of early novel-writers like Tabitha Tenney and Hugh Henry Brackenridge. Many novels were distinctly in favor of the education of young women. William H. Brown's 1789 *The Power of Sympathy*, for example, wished to expose "the dangerous consequences of seduction" while "the Advantages of Female Education are set forth and recommended" (Blinderman 1975: 98).

III

While providing education to white women was a matter of some controversy, white women were at the very least considered human beings. But there was another group of people in the antebellum period over whom lakes of ink were spilled, and whose status threatened the core of the republic. Slaves and slavery were a far more incendiary topic in the discourse of education than were women, for the possibility of an educated slave conjured fears of rebellion and destruction in the South. Indeed, many of the restrictions on teaching slaves to read and write in the South stemmed from a number of slave revolts led by educated slaves. The history of both slaves and freed black people in America is deeply connected to debates over education, for it was in those debates that the paradox of what white America assumed they knew about black people and what black people were assumed to know about themselves was most clearly developed.

Slaves were by definition property, not persons. Most of the black population in the United States lived in the Southern slave states, but there was a sizable population of free black persons in Northern cities. The history of education for black persons was significantly different in the North. As early as 1787 the New York Manumission Society achieved the opening of a free public school for black students (Kaestle 1983: 35–6). Similar Quaker-run schools were established in Philadelphia: one for boys in 1770, one for girls in 1787, and another for adults in 1789. Carl Kaestle reports that by the mid-nineteenth century there were African Free Schools operating in New Jersey, New York, Rhode Island, Massachusetts, and Delaware. There were also a number of fee-charging tuition schools operated by black teachers (Kaestle 1983: 38). In addition to such formal schooling there were the literary societies, whose development among the black population of the urban northeast Elizabeth McHenry has documented. Such literary societies functioned as educational enterprises. They offered a gathering place for motivated black people who wished to discuss the latest publications; they promoted the teaching of reading and writing; they encouraged members to write their own pieces for publications in the black and white press; they established libraries; and they created a network of sociability and potential upward mobility through a shared commitment to self-improvement. McHenry's fascinating research demonstrates that free black citizens not only prized education, they established informal systems to continue it and therefore to craft ways to participate in the public life of the nation.

Indeed, it is through informal networks that historians can best document the education of Southern slaves as well as Northern free blacks. Public education for slaves in the South was nonexistent, and even public education for white children in the South lagged behind that established in Northern states. The issue of slave literacy was especially charged because slave-owners were already convinced that slaves had a special form of communication, that is to say, a special form of literacy they could use to contact one another. Among the uprisings and revolts that became most fearsome and legendary were those of two highly educated slaves: Toussaint L'Ouverture, who led the establishment of an independent Haiti in 1803, and Nat Turner of Virginia, who led a rebellion in 1831. Each of these men had been literate. L'Ouverture was an Enlightenment figure, who believed in universal manhood suffrage, as well as the capacity for his people to govern themselves and treat diplomatically with other nations. Turner was a powerful minister whose charismatic interpretations of the Bible inspired his followers to the famed uprising that ended with his siege in Dismal Swamp and his eventual capture. Indeed, it was after the revolt of Nat Turner that laws against teaching slaves to read or write were made more stringent in virtually every state.

But the formal education that supporters of slavery wished to withhold demonstrated the contradiction at the heart of the institution. Slavery's proponents argued that slaves did not have higher faculties. They could not, in this argument, be taught anything, for they were closer to animals than to people, and they therefore acted on instinct. This racialist logic, though, went hand in hand with the fear that slaves could indeed learn and reason, and that, once exposed to the rudiments of an education, they could begin to argue for their own emancipation. Indeed, escaped slaves who found their way to the North relied on information supplied by others who had already escaped, as well as those white sympathizers who had been in contact with them. Perhaps the most famous of these escaped slaves was Frederick Douglass, one of the nineteenth century's greatest polemicists against slavery. Douglass is an especially good example of how formal education could be acquired by the strategic use of native wit. Relating his acquisition of letters, he describes the prohibition his master imposed on his mistress when he found her teaching him to read. But Douglass saw in education and literacy the tools to obtain emancipation, and saw too, that his master's fear of slave literacy testified to its true value. Douglass not only went on to trick white people into teaching him to read, he illegally taught his fellow slaves the rudiments of literacy before he escaped. Douglass became one of the nineteenth century's most impassioned rhetoricians, speaking not just on behalf of slaves, but of women as well at the Seneca Falls convention of 1848.

Douglass's slave narrative, although one of the most famous, was by no means singular. The antebellum period witnessed an enormous outpouring of rhetoric and writing by freed or escaped slaves, many of whom, like Douglass, or David Walker, or Sojourner Truth, argued not only for the basic humanity of black people, but for their education. Perhaps of equal importance is their modeling of various forms of what it meant to be educated, for part of the power of Douglass and Truth can be located in their assumption that white people were in desperate need of the most basic education about slaves and slavery. Slave narratives tended not only to argue for the humanity of slaves, they tended also to point out systematic shortcomings in the republic itself. That is to say, they did not draw the line at criticizing the South; they made trenchant observations about the limitations of the North. Harriet Jacobs' *Incidents in the Life of a Slave Girl*, for example, as well as Frederick Douglass's autobiography, detail prejudice against black people in the urban North. Each argued that economic competition between white and black workers is a form of racism. Their autobiographies, as well as their critique of the Northern as well as the Southern economic system, stand, along with a host of other slave narratives, as educational documents in themselves. Intended to educate white readers, and deeply invested in the idea of education itself, slave narratives became one of the most powerful polemical tools in the public campaign to recognize slaves as persons.

IV

Education in the early republic was a charged issue. For many of the architects of the nation, a democracy could survive only if its citizens were educated; but education itself provided the means for noncitizens to become disenchanted with their status in the world. Intimately tied to the belief that citizens should know how to govern themselves, and should know how to understand the world that surrounded them, the battles over education were less often about what should be taught than to whom learning should be made available. Yet it was precisely in the drive to be educated that the claims of women and slaves, for example, could be first heard in the public sphere, and it was through their efforts to educate others about their status that the shape of the republic continued to change. The history of formal schooling in the United States in the antebellum period details the way in which the definition of the educated citizen was expanded to include not only the most privileged of citizens — wealthy white men who could count on a formal education from their earliest years through university — but also working people, women, and persons of color. But within the history of education as formal schooling must be included the history of previously unrecognized forms of literacy — ways of making sense of and reading the social world — that also count as education and that also provided a basis for passionate public debate about citizenship, democracy, and political rights.

REFERENCES AND FURTHER READING

Best, John Hardin, and Sidwell, Robert T. (1966). *The American Legacy of Learning: Readings in the History of Education*. Philadelphia: Lippincott.

Blinderman, Abraham (1975). *American Writers on Education before 1865*. Boston: Twayne.

Cremin, Lawrence A. (1970). *American Education: The Colonial Experience, 1607–1783*. New York: Harper & Row.

Davidson, Cathy N. (1986). *Revolution and the Word: The Rise of the Novel in America*. New York: Oxford University Press.

Douglass, Frederick (1997). *Narrative of the Life of Frederick Douglass, an American Slave, Written by Himself*. New York: Norton. (First publ. 1845.)

Evans, Sara M. (1989). *Born for Liberty: A History of Women in America*. New York: Free Press.

Kaestle, Carl F. (1983). *Pillars of the Republic: Common Schools and American Society*. New York: Hill & Wang.

McHenry, Elizabeth (2002). *Forgotten Readers: Recovering the Lost History of African American Literary Societies*. Durham, NC: Duke University Press.

Pulliam, John D., and Van Patten, James (1995). *History of Education in America*, 6th edn. Englewood Cliffs, NJ: Prentice-Hall.

Rowson, Susannah Haswell (1987). *Charlotte Temple*. New York: Oxford University Press. (First publ. 1794.)

Stowe, Harriet Beecher (1984). *Uncle Tom's Cabin; or, Life among the Lowly*. New York: Norton. (First publ. 1852.)

Tenney, Tabitha Gilman (1992). *Female Quixotism Exhibited in the Romantic Opinions and Extravagant Adventures of Dorcasina Sheldon*, ed. Jean Nienkamp and Andrea Collins. New York: Oxford University Press. (First publ. 1801.)

10

Marriage and Contract

Naomi Morgenstern

In the wake of the American Revolution, Jay Fliegelman has suggested, "no word in the American political lexicon would be more consistently and more universally acknowledged to be sacred than 'union' ... " (1982: 126). But union, be it the union of states or the union of federally recognized American citizens, also presented difficulties. How would the union of political equals affect that other revolutionary ideal, individual freedom? This question, while it had ramifications for every subject of the new nation, bore a privileged relationship to the discourse of marital union. With its apparently simultaneous participation in both political (or contractual) forms of alliance *and* natural forms of human attachment, marriage promised to reassure Americans of the legitimacy and solidity of their new structures of association. In marriage, writes historian Jan Lewis, "'that SOCIAL UNION, which the beneficent Creator instituted for the happiness of Man,'" revolutionary Americans found "a metaphor for their ideal of social and political relationships" (1987: 689).

At the same time, however, much of the literary writing of the late eighteenth century finds in marriage a distillation of a number of difficult questions about the relationship between freedom and equality in an ostensibly post-feudal society. In narratives of incest and seduction, and in explorations of marital inequality and the right to divorce, American writers of this period help us to appreciate how anxieties about gender relations in the aftermath of independence were inextricable from anxieties about the new nation's expanding investment in the political, legal, and economic notion of contract.

While marriage in post-revolutionary America continued to be thought of as a "civil contract," historian Michael Grossberg writes, "in a vital transition the accent shifted from the first word to the second" (1985: 19). As contractually defined, marital relationships were to be consensual, intentional, reciprocal, and dissolvable. In fact, American law in this period moved in the direction of an entire deregulation of the marital state towards the notion of matrimony as a private contract. A marriage, which had once consisted of a five-step nuptial course (espousals, publication of banns, execution of the espousal contract at church, celebration, and sexual consummation), could now simply consist of a contractual agreement to marry, period. American judges thus came to endorse "common-law" marriage or the "self-solemnized" marriage even as their British counterparts sought to invalidate "irregular" forms of union. American couples could conduct a marriage in whatever way they pleased, wrote a nineteenth-century South Carolina chancellor: they could "express their agreement by parol . . . [and] signify it by whatever ceremony their whim, or their taste, or their religious belief select." "It is the agreement itself," he continued, "not the form in which it is couched which constitutes the contract" (quoted in Grossberg 1985: 79). As James Fenimore Cooper put it in his revolutionary era novel, *Lionel Lincoln*, "The laws regulating marriage in Massachusetts threw but few impediments in the way of the indissoluble connection" (Cooper 1984: 227).

According to American legal historian Milton J. Horwitz, the nineteenth-century turn to a "will-theory of contract" displaced previous investments in substantive justice:

> Only in the nineteenth century did judges and jurists finally reject the longstanding belief that the justification of contractual obligation is derived from the inherent justice or fairness of an exchange. In its place, they asserted for the first time that the source of the obligation of contract is the convergence of the wills of the contracting parties . . . Modern contract law was thus born staunchly proclaiming that all men are equal because all measures of inequality are illusory. (1977: 161)

But while nineteenth-century marital practice participated in this investment in contractual relationships, it did not do so unequivocally. Considering the period's multiple "breach of promise suits," Michael Grossberg argues that in fact "the will theory of contract was a peculiarly male concept, one that was less binding on women who entered agreements than men" (1985: 38). Women, as seduction fiction testifies, were considered not quite as capable of contracting as men, and contractual abuses and insufficiencies became predictably gendered: men were more likely to practice marital fraud, and women more likely to fall for a less-than-contractual contract: "Behold even while she is rising in beauty and dignity, like a lily of the valley, in the full blossom of her graces," we read in William Hill Brown's *The Power of Sympathy* (1789), "she is cut off suddenly by the rude hand of the Seducer . . . But did she understand the secret villainy of his intentions – would she appear thus elate and joyous? Would she assent to her ruin? . . . O! WHY is there not adequate punishment for this crime, when that of a common traitor is marked with its deserved iniquity and abhorrence!" (Brown 1996: 68).

In fact, marriage in the late eighteenth and early nineteenth centuries – and this is one of its fascinations from a historical and theoretical perspective – maintained a relationship to both feudal and modern forms of political association. The tension between its investment in contractual notions of equality and its patriarchal investment in coverture marked marriage as the concentrated site of American ambivalence about the political transformations the country was witnessing. In the pre-revolutionary American colonies, as in England, the killing of a wife by a husband was murder, but the killing of a husband by a wife was *petit treason*, analogous to regicide. Historian Linda Kerber points out that this was the only element of the old law of domestic relations that was eliminated by legislators of the early American republic. With this single exception, the entire system of legal coverture was left in place by the new constitutions that emerged out of the War of Independence. The husband and wife are "one person in law," wrote the massively influential English legal scholar William Blackstone in his *Commentaries on the Laws of England* (1979: vol. 1, 430); but that person was the husband. "No other contract," writes historian Amy Dru Stanley, "contained a rule obliterating the identity and autonomy of one party to the contract. Coverture had no parallel in commercial contracts . . . unlike any other contract, the marriage contract ordained male proprietorship and absolute female dispossession, establishing self ownership as the fundamental right of men alone" (1998: 11).

One way of approaching the peculiar inconsistencies of marriage, then, is to point out the extent to which marriage served to prevent women from gaining full access to the evolving realm of political, legal, and economic contractual autonomy. And indeed, as we might expect from an era of radical rethinking, there were some American writers at the end of the eighteenth century who were willing to address the inconsistencies in the post-revolutionary treatment of women. Judith Sargent Murray, for example, pinpointed the paradoxical status of women in relationship to contract as early as 1790. In "On the Equality of the Sexes," Murray notes that while women are poorly educated and spend their early years learning about the most superficial of things, still when it comes time for marriage "it is expected that with the other sex we should commence immediate war, and that we should triumph over the machinations of the most artful." This proves – in a backwards sort of way – that women must actually be superior: "the infamy which is consequent upon the smallest deviation in our conduct," Murray writes, with tongue in cheek, "proclaims the high idea which was formed of our native strength; and thus, indirectly at least, is the preference acknowledged to be our due" (1995: 9–10). As Murray makes clear, the marriage contract is, for women, the contract to end all contracts: It is the first and last contract a woman will make. For a brief moment, and *only* for that moment, the female subject and citizen occupies the "universal" position reserved for men.

Women's troubled relationship to contract is also broached in Hannah Foster's *The Coquette* (1797), whose heroine, Eliza Wharton, resists both particular marital choices and marriage more generally ("I do not intend to give my hand to any man at present" [Foster 1996: 144]). She makes what will turn out to be a fatal error, however, by assuming that she can enter into contracts with men other than the marital one. "I told him that I was under no obligation to give him any account of my disposition towards another," she writes of one such agreement, "and that he must remember the terms of our present association to which he had subscribed" (p. 145). One of her more disciplinary female companions, Mrs. Richman, cautions Eliza that she should consider herself "somewhat engaged" (p. 127). Eliza, she argues, has "wrong ideas" when it comes both to matrimony and to freedom. But we could just as confidently suggest that these "wrong ideas" mark the beginnings of an American critique of women's relationship to contract and conjugality.

This critique anticipates the more recent feminist argument that what nineteenth-century legal historians referred to as the shift from status to contract (see Horwitz 1977) in fact marked the ascendancy of a *fraternal* patriarchy, within which the social contract between men worked precisely by presupposing and obscuring a sexual contract between a man and a woman. Fraternal contractualism, as Carole Pateman has so influentially shown, both requires and disguises the fact that women necessarily and structurally play a paradoxical role: women must be individuals capable of consenting to the marriage contract, even as this same contract effects a signing away of their subjectivity under the law of coverture. A woman contracts, in other words, in order to preclude her right to make contracts – in order to suspend her standing as an individual.

It is thus hard not to think that the appeal of marriage – and the appeal *to* marriage ("All marriages not forbidden by God shall be encouraged," proclaimed a post-revolutionary Pennsylvania statute) – allowed Americans to mask contradictions between older and newer ways of thinking: marriage could stand for harmony and unity even as the rise of contractualism and revolutionary thought would itself make marriage literally unthinkable without the structural possibility of its dissolution. The "equal" marriage subsequently gave way under very little pressure to the kind of wifely deference exemplified in Washington Irving's sketch, "The Wife" (1819), in which the compliant spouse is simply what her husband needs her to be: radically dependent when her dependency will shore up his sense of self, and stronger than strong when her support is called for. In Irving's heaven of full-blown domestic ideology, the husband is imagined, unapologetically, as the king of his own castle, the "monarch" at home (1906: 40). And although Catharine Maria Sedgwick's historical novel about the Revolution, *The Linwoods; or, "Sixty Years Since" in America* (1835), emphasizes the crucial relationship between marital choices and political allegiances, it is noticeably reserved on the issue of women's rights. When the hero declares himself to the heroine he exclaims, "I will not leave you till you have the reasons of my love; till you admit that *I have deliberately elected the sovereign of my affections;* till you feel, yes *feel* that my devotion to you can never abate" (Sedgwick 1835: vol. 2, 223, emphasis added). This curious text reimagines loyalty (political, romantic, and sometimes even filial loyalty) as the essential revolutionary value; and this trick is managed, in large part, by exploiting gender differences: Women are depicted as educable, whereas men – men with character – must stay true. Thus Isabella Linwood's gradual adoption of a new set of political values and a new love object culminates in a first-hand experience of the struggles of the patriot soldiers (vol. 2, 259–60).

But there is another way of approaching the politics of the marriage contract. As subjects of this contract-to-end-all-contracts, post-revolutionary American women could also be thought of as exemplary subjects of any contractual agreement. The paradoxes and inconsistencies of their experience were, and are, the paradoxes and inconsistencies of the contractual fantasy. Contract ideology promises an autonomy and an equality that it cannot provide; it promises the political dream of equality without any compromise of individual sovereignty. The contract allows us to be free and equal, at once, and with no excess – no cost. This is the foundational gift of the contract whose impossibility is masked by the allegory of gender.

Nowhere in early American fiction are these issues addressed with more complexity than in the fiction of Charles Brockden Brown (1771–1809). Brown's fictional dialogue *Alcuin*, written in late 1796 and 1797 and published in 1798,[1] explores the possibility of conjugal equality, the socially constructed form of gender, and the idea that radical contractualism ought to encompass both the beginning of a marriage *and* its end (in the form of easily available divorce). In fact, this text's willingness to test the limits of feminist thought resulted in the decision to withhold its final sections from publication at a time when fear of French radicalism was generating a wave of caution in American philosophical circles. In Brown's dialogue, a schoolteacher, Alcuin, is invited to the social evenings held at the home of a physician, whose widowed sister, Mrs. Carter, articulates many of the positions on women's rights and marital politics with which Brown was familiar from his reading of the English radicals William Godwin and Mary Wollstonecraft.[2] Alcuin, whose own convictions remain difficult to pin down, agrees with Mrs. Carter that while there is a difference between the sexes, it is not a difference that matters very much: "The differences that flow from the sexual distinction are as nothing in the balance," says Mrs. Carter; "the natives of the most distant regions do not less resemble each other, than the male and female of the same tribe" (Brown 1987: 10, 19).

Between visits to Mrs. Carter's house, however, Alcuin purportedly travels to a fictional "paradise of women" and returns to tell Mrs. Carter the tale of his guided tour. In this paradise, the difference between men and women is not part of culture, or custom, Alcuin is informed, but merely concerns animal existence and physical constitution. Reproduction, Alcuin's guide suggests, constitutes the whole of what his visitor seems to imply by "marriage," an institution which the paradisical world otherwise manages to do without. While granting that there are sexes and that reproduction is necessarily sexed (as it certainly was in the 1790s!), the guide asks if culture must really be built up over such a base: "One would imagine that among you," he says to Alcuin, "one sex, had more arms, or legs or senses than the other. Among us there is no such inequality" (Brown 1987: 47). ("Nothing about political relations," echoes Carole Pateman two hundred years later, "can be read directly from the two natural bodies of humankind that must inhabit the body politic" [1988: 226].)

But Alcuin is reluctant to accept this stripped-down version of sexual difference. "Since the sexual difference is something," asks Alcuin, "and since you are not guilty of the error of treating different things as if they were the same, doubtless in your conduct towards each other, the consideration of sex is of some weight" (Brown 1987: 43). Alcuin's question, in other words, collapses the idea of a fundamental and foundational difference between the sexes into the very ability to draw any distinction at all, to know sameness from difference. And once the conceptual structure of sexual difference has been removed, it becomes harder to know how to think about the individual. "No two persons are entitled in the strictest sense, to the same treatment," says the representative of *Alcuin*'s fantastic world, "because no two can be precisely alike..." (p. 45). But do individuals differ endlessly from one another? And if democracies are made up of those who differ endlessly from one another, how are structures of representation to work at all? Would not each person require a direct representative who would have to be him- or herself? Sexual difference, Alcuin's anxious questions remind us, functions precisely to limit or contain our thinking about difference and equality.

Alcuin's final, and apparently most radical section, then, finds Mrs. Carter forced by her insistent interlocutor to explain her positions on marriage and divorce. At once demonstrating her familiarity with contemporary radicalism ("a class of reasoners... lately arisen who aim at the deepest foundation of civil society" [Brown 1987: 52]), and asserting her distance from its riskier propositions ("that detestable philosophy which scoffs at the matrimonial institution itself" [p. 54]), Mrs. Carter reaffirms her commitment to marriage. Only the calculating seducer, or a monster of sincerity, Mrs. Carter suggests (anticipating Brown's *Ormond*), one who was the dupe of his own illusions and passions, could oppose the conjugal relation. Such a man would be dangerously unreformable or pathologically incurable (p. 51). For Mrs. Carter, a world without marriage is a world of mere sensuality and not one in which free rational individuals can participate in contractually ordered relationships. "When I demand an equality of conditions among beings that equally partake of the same divine reason," Mrs. Carter asks Alcuin, "would you rashly infer that I was an enemy to the insti-tution of marriage itself?"

As a reasonable and contractually sound institution, however, marriage, for Mrs. Carter, must be accompanied by the possibility of divorce. "It is absurd," William Godwin had written in 1793, "to expect the inclinations and wishes of two human beings to coincide through any long period of time" (Godwin 1946: vol. 2, 506). Mrs. Carter is no less assured. "What reverence is due to groundless and obstinate attachments[?]," she asks, "that a man continues to associate with me contrary to his judgment and inclination is no subject of congratulation" (Brown 1987: 64).[3] Mrs. Carter makes the case for the impossible, then: for conjugality as a free bond, always, absolutely, and uncompromisingly the product of volition and spontaneity, without an instant of constraint. In a move that should be familiar to us from the 1996 Defense of Marriage Act, however, Alcuin responds by raising the stakes. Invoking "lawless appetite," he imagines a scene in which "marriages can be dissolved and contracted at pleasure . . . till the whole nation were sunk into a state of the lowest degeneracy" (p. 65). Mrs. Carter is not duped. Let us leave this flamboyant rhetoric to the "schoolboys," she declares (p. 65).[4]

Brown's willingness to explore the radical ideas of Godwin and Wollstonecraft in his fiction inevitably led him to figure the limits and aporias, as well as the progressive possibilities, of their political philosophy. In *Ormond* (1799), Brown took a young female protagonist, Constantia Dudley, educated in true radical style by her Godwinesque father, and followed her attempts to resist, defer, and question proposals of marriage. Despite the misleading – though crucial – title of the novel (which names what, or whom, it fails to contain), *Ormond* is a female bildungsroman which culminates not in marriage, but in Constantia Dudley's justified murder of her would-be husband, the same Ormond. In Brown's novel the female bildungsroman descends into gothic heterosexual terrain: "She will be to me a wife, or nothing;" says Ormond, "and I must be her husband or perish" (Brown 1999: 168).

Ormond distinguishes itself by demonstrating a restless ambivalence toward the contractual subject who came to occupy center stage in revolutionary and post-revolutionary thought. In fact, "contract" or "to contract" operates in Brown's novel as a crucial "switch word": while one can draw up a marriage contract, one can also contract a disease or a passion; and as any reader of *Ormond* knows, there is plenty of fatal disease and fatal attraction in Brown's post-revolutionary Philadelphia. Yellow fever functions in this novel as (among other things) an anxious registration of the instability and limitations of the contract-making subject, that subject who is supposed to be an impermeable individual. In the novel's climax, the inscrutable radical and outspoken opponent of marriage, Ormond, pursues Constantia to a secluded house. Having "contracted" a passion for Constantia, he is unwilling to accept the heroine's characteristic deferral of any decision that would compromise her independence. Ormond is intent on raping Constantia, but by the time the novel's ostensible narrator arrives on the scene, Ormond is dead. Constantia is his murderer, but "her act," we are told, "was prompted by motives which every scheme of jurisprudence known in the world not only exculpates, but applauds" (Brown 1999: 274). After numerous meditations on the instability and difficulties of contract, *Ormond* culminates in a scene of primitive violence and in what appears to be a rejection of its own theoretical complexity.

What is most bizarre about the end of *Ormond*, however, is that even in the midst of this gothic nightmare the villain adheres to, and makes the argument for, contract ideology. Ormond tells Constantia that killing herself to prevent rape will not work (he will rape her anyway) and, furthermore, that it is an entirely unnecessary sacrifice. Rape cannot essentially harm Constantia's virtue, he maintains, for her *will* will be left intact. Constantia will not be contaminated, Ormond insists, for she will not have consented: there will not have been a contractual moment. "Die with the guilt of suicide and the brand of cowardice upon thy memory," Ormond tells Constantia, "or live with thy claims to felicity and approbation undiminished. Choose which thou wilt. Thy decision is of moment to thyself, but of none to me. Living or dead, the prize that I have in view will be mine" (Brown 1999: 269). Instead of associating Ormond in all his mad violence with the rejection of contract (his madness as the other to Constantia's constant reasonableness), Brown ultimately makes a far more difficult and intriguing case. In the figure of Ormond madness and contract ideology (not merely its distortion or transgression) coincide.

In an anonymous review, published in 1800, of Samuel Richardson's *Clarissa*, Brown argued that Clarissa dies "not a martyr to any duty, but a victim of grief; a grief occasioned by an unreasonable value set on things of which she is deprived, *not by her own fault*, but by that of others" (Brown 1992: 101, emphasis added). It is Clarissa's own "will" and the judgment of the Deity which should be important, he argues, not "the force of unjust and tyrannical relations . . . the esteem of the mis-judging world" or, most surprisingly, "the possession of corporeal integrity" (p. 102).[5] While Brown's argument seems sound enough, we should not miss the fact that it also echoes with Ormond's perverse claim. And if one takes away the sneer of the gothic villain, and forgets for the moment that this position is articulated by the would-be rapist, Ormond's own point (not just Brown's) can be thought of as a feminist one: One cannot be held responsible for a violence to which one has not consented; or, "don't blame the victim."

This, in fact, was one of Mary Wollstonecraft's arguments when she wrote critically of the "prevailing opinion that with chastity all is lost that is respectable in woman . . . Nay the honour of a woman is not made even to depend on her will." Turning to *Clarissa*, Wollstonecraft continued: "When Richardson makes Clarissa tell Lovelace that he had robbed her of her honour, he must have had strange notions of honour and virtue. *For, miserable beyond all names of misery is the condition of a being, who could be degraded without its own consent!*" (Wollstonecraft 1992: 168, emphasis added). Wollstonecraft and Brown thus raise the stakes of the relationship between radical feminism and contract theory. Is the problem, in the aftermath of the democratic revolutions, that women are not allowed access to the (fantasy of a) disembodied subject position (the contractual subject with property in his own person), or is it precisely this fantastic and contractual account of the subject that feminism ought to disrupt? The issues raised seem stranger still if we recognize Lovelace as the source (unbeknown to her, apparently) of Wollstonecraft's opinions. Lovelace asks, "what honour is lost where the *will* is not violated and the person cannot help it?" (Richardson 1968: vol. 4, letter 154, 452). That the contractual thinking of feminists (Wollstonecraft and Brown) and rapists (Lovelace and Ormond) coincides at the end of the eighteenth century ought to remind us that the politics of the sexual contract have never been simple. It would be a long time, however, before American literature would address the politics of the sexual contract with as much anguished sophistica-tion as can be found in the fiction of Charles Brockden Brown.

Notes

1 The final part of the dialogue appeared for the first time in 1815 (five years after Brown's death). For more on the publication history of *Alcuin* see Arner 1987; Reid 1987; Davidson 1981; Kierner 1995.

2 For Brown's indebtedness to Godwin and Wollstonecraft see Fleischmann 1983: 22–40; Davidson 1981; Kierner 1995; Krause 1982: 419–26.

3 "Divorce [was] first ... legitimated by most states right after the American Revolution. New state legislators' willingness to allow divorce gave compelling evidence that the contractual ideology of the Declaration of Independence resonated through their thinking about spousal relations ... How could consent in marriage (as in government) be considered fully voluntary, if it could not be withdrawn by an injured partner?" (Cott 2000: 47). For the association between the Revolution and divorce see also Hartog 2000: 71; Salmon 1986: 58–80.

4 What Mrs. Carter calls for did not become anything like a reality in the United States until the no-fault divorce laws of the 1970s. As the historian of marriage in America Hendrik Hartog argues, "in 1790, in 1815, even yet in 1840 divorce was not conceptually part of the law of marriage." It was instead "a public remedy for a public wrong" to protect an innocent party and punish a guilty one.

5 On the connection between Clarissa and Constantia see Fiedler 1992. See also Tennenhouse, who, after asserting that "the evidence about the Richardson boom [in America in the 1790s] is indisputable," looks specifically at American versions of Richardson's novel (1998: 184).

References and Further Reading

Arner, Robert D. (1987). "Historical Essay." In Charles Brockden Brown, *Alcuin: A Dialogue*, ed. Sydney J. Krause et al., 273–312. Kent, Ohio: Kent State University Press.

Blackstone, William (1979). *Commentaries on the Laws of England 1765–1769*, 4 vols. Chicago: University of Chicago Press.

Bloch, Ruth (1987). "The Gendered Meanings of Virtue in Revolutionary America." *Signs: Journal of Women in Culture and Society* 13: 1, 37–59.

Brown, Charles Brockden (1987). *Alcuin: A Dialogue*, ed. Sydney J. Krause et al. Kent, Ohio: Kent State University Press. (First publ. 1798.)

Brown, Charles Brockden (1992). "Objections to Richardson's *Clarissa*." In Charles Brockden Brown, *Literary Essays and Reviews*, ed. Alfred Weber and Wolfgang Schäfer, 100–2. New York: Peter Lang. (First publ. 1800.)

Brown, Charles Brockden (1999). *Ormond; Or, The Secret Witness*, ed. Mary Chapman. Peterborough, Ont.: Broadview. (First publ. 1799.)

Brown, Wendy (1995). *States of Injury: Power and Freedom in Late Modernity*. Princeton: Princeton University Press.

Brown, William Hill (1996). *The Power of Sympathy*. New York: Penguin. (First publ. 1789.)

Chapman, Mary (1999). "Introduction." In Charles Brockden Brown, *Ormond; Or, The Secret Witness*, ed. Mary Chapman, 9–31. Peterborough, Ont.: Broadview.

Christophersen, Bill (1993). *The Apparition in the Glass: Charles Brockden Brown's American Gothic*. Athens, Ga.: University of Georgia Press.

Cooper, James Fenimore (1984). *Lionel Lincoln; or, The Leaguer of Boston*, ed. Donald A. and Lucy B. Ringe. Albany: State University of New York Press. (First publ. 1825.)

Cott, Nancy F. (2000). *Public Vows: A History of Marriage and the Nation*. Cambridge, Mass.: Harvard University Press.

Davidson, Cathy N. (1981). "The Matter and Manner of Charles Brockden Brown's *Alcuin*." In Bernard Rosenthal (ed.), *Critical Essays on Charles Brockden Brown*, 71–86. Boston: Hall.

Davidson, Cathy N. (1986). *Revolution and the Word: The Rise of the Novel in America*. New York: Oxford University Press.

Ferguson, Robert A. (1984). *Law and Letters in American Culture*. Cambridge, Mass.: Harvard University Press.

Fiedler, Leslie (1992). *Love and Death in the American Novel*. New York: Doubleday. (First publ. 1960.)

Fleischmann, Fritz (1983). *A Right View of the Subject: Feminism in the Works of Charles Brockden Brown and John Neal*. Erlangen: Palm & Enke.

Fliegelman, Jay (1982). *Prodigals and Pilgrims: The American Revolution against Patriarchal Authority 1750–1800*. Cambridge, UK: Cambridge University Press.

Foster, Hannah Webster (1996). *The Coquette*. New York: Penguin. (First publ. 1797.)

Godwin, William (1946). *Enquiry Concerning Political Justice and its Influence on Morals and Happiness*, 3 vols., ed. F. E. L. Priestley. Toronto: University of Toronto Press. (First publ. 1793.)

Grossberg, Michael (1985). *Governing the Hearth: Law and the Family in Nineteenth-Century America*. Chapel Hill: University of North Carolina Press.

Gunderson, Joan R. (1987). "Independence, Citizenship and the American Revolution." *Signs: Journal of Women in Culture and Society* 13: 1, 59–76.

Hartog, Hendrik (2000). *Man and Wife in America: A History*. Cambridge, Mass.: Harvard University Press.

Horwitz, Milton J. (1977). *The Transformation of American Law 1780–1860*. Cambridge, Mass.: Harvard University Press.

Irving, Washington (1906). "The Wife." In *The Sketch Book*, 39–49. New York: Maynard, Merrill & Co. (First publ. 1819–20.)

Kerber, Linda (1980). *Women of the Republic: Intellect and Ideology in Revolutionary America*. Chapel Hill: University of North Carolina Press.

Kerber, Linda (1998). *No Constitutional Right to be Ladies: Women and the Obligations of Citizenship*. New York: Hill & Wang.

Kierner, Cynthia A. (1995). "Introduction." In Charles Brockden Brown, *Alcuin: A Dialogue*, 3–37. Albany: New College and University Press.

Krause, Sydney J. (1982). "Historical Notes." In Charles Brockden Brown, *Ormond; or, The Secret Witness*, ed. Sydney J. Krause et al., 389–478. Kent, Ohio: Kent State University Press.

Krause, Sydney J. (2000). "Brockden Brown's Feminism in Fact and Fiction." In Klaus H. Schmidt and Fritz Fleischmann (eds.), *Early America Re-explored: New Readings in Colonial, Early National, and Antebellum Culture*, 349–84. New York: Peter Lang.

Lewis, Jan (1987). "The Republican Wife: Virtue and Seduction in the Early Republic." *William and Mary Quarterly* 44: 4, 689–721.

Murray, Judith Sargent (1995). "On the Equality of the Sexes" (first publ. 1790). In *Selected Writings of Judith Sargent Murray*, ed. Sharon M. Harris, 3–14. New York: Oxford University Press.

Pateman, Carole (1988). *The Sexual Contract*. Stanford: Stanford University Press.

Reid, S. W. (1987). "Textual Essay." In Charles Brockden Brown, *Alcuin: A Dialogue*, ed. Sydney J. Krause et al., 313–56. Kent, Ohio: Kent State University Press.

Richardson, Samuel (1968). *Clarissa; or, The History of a Young Lady*. New York: Everyman's Library. (First publ. 1747–8.)

Salmon, Marylynn (1986). *Women and the Law of Property in Early America*. Chapel Hill: University of North Carolina Press.

Samuels, Shirley (1985). "Plague and Politics in 1793: *Arthur Mervyn*." *Criticism* 27: 3, 225–46.

Samuels, Shirley (1996). *Romances of the Republic: Women, the Family and Violence in the Literature of the Early American Nation*. New York: Oxford University Press.

Scheik, William J. (1981). "The Problem of Origination in Brown's *Ormond*." In Bernard Rosenthal (ed.), *Critical Essays on Charles Brockden Brown*, 126–41. Boston: Hall.

Sedgwick, Catharine Maria (1835). *The Linwoods; or, "Sixty Years Since" in America*, 2 vols. New York: Harper & Bros.

Smyth, Heather (1998). "'Imperfect Disclosures': Cross-Dressing and Containment in Charles Brockden Brown's *Ormond*." In Merril D. Smith (ed.), *Sex and Sexuality in Early America*, 240–61. New York: New York University Press.

Stanley, Amy Dru (1998). *From Bondage to Contract: Wage Labor, Marriage, and the Market in the Age of Slave Emancipation*. Cambridge, UK: Cambridge University Press.

Stern, Julia A. (1997). *The Plight of Feeling: Sympathy and Dissent in the Early American Novel.* Chicago: University of Chicago Press.

Tennenhouse, Leonard (1998). "The Americanization of *Clarissa.*" *Yale Journal of Criticism* 11: 1, 177–96.

Wollstonecraft, Mary (1992). *A Vindication of the Rights of Woman,* ed. Miriam Brody. New York: Penguin. (First publ. 1792.)

Wood, Gordon S. (1991). *The Radicalism of the American Revolution.* New York: Random House.

11
Transatlantic Ventures

Wil Verhoeven and Stephen Shapiro

Part I

When the hero of Royall Tyler's *The Algerine Captive*, Updike Underhill, returned to his native country in 1795 after an absence of seven years, the first thing that struck him was "the extreme avidity, with which books of mere amusement were purchased and perused by all ranks of his countrymen – not merely in sea ports but also in inland towns and villages."[1] Underhill, or Tyler, is quite right in pointing out, as he goes on to do, that the exceptionally high literacy rate in New England – compared with both the rest of America and Europe – was a major cause of the accelerating secularization of the reading public's taste in general and of the growth of novel-reading in particular during the last three decades of the eighteenth century. Moreover, fundamental changes that took place in the marketing and dissemination of print in the same period had a significant impact on the demographics of the reading public. Booksellers began to adopt the market strategies similar to those used by present-day publishers, and thereby radically redefined the relationship between producers and consumers of print, particularly of popular fiction. Yet most significant of all was the exponential rise in the number of circulating libraries in the second half of the century, most notably in the 1790s, when the rate of circulation library establishment tripled while the growth of the population only doubled. Robert Winans has calculated that the percentage of fiction in booksellers' catalogues rose from 9 percent in the period 1754–65 to 12 percent in the period 1791–1800; at the same time, the percentage of fiction in the catalogues of circulating libraries rose from 10 percent to over 50 percent.[2] Even though no loan records for circulating libraries from this period are available, these data would support Winans' thesis that "the American reading public in the late eighteenth-century was largely a novel-reading public."[3]

But what novels did Americans read? The wrong ones, is the short answer – at least according to Updike Underhill. "While this love of literature, however frivolous, is pleasing to the man of letters," he observes, "there are two things to be deplored. The first is that, while so many books are vended, they are not of our own manufacture.... The second misfortune is that ... the English Novel ... paints the manners, customs, and habits of a strange country."[4] He therefore calls for a declaration of literary independence, urging that American authors from now on write their own novels and that they write about American manners, *not* English ones. Updike was far from alone in believing that in literary terms, America remained a colony of Britain; that, in David Simpson's words, "It was to prove more difficult to declare independence from Samuel Johnson than it had been to reject George III."[5] It is one of those ironies of decolonization, as Edward Watts has convincingly argued, that through cultural mimicry and self-marginalization, the early republic tried to "restabilize the community by recreating the only standard of legitimacy the populace had ever known: that of the colonizers."[6] Thus, for several decades after the Peace of Paris, literature produced in America would, at best, endeavor to improve on British literary models, rather than commit itself to local subjects and subjectivities. The history of the eighteenth- and early nineteenth-century novel in America is therefore by no means simply the history of American novels.

No early American author was more aware of the precarious condition of domestic literary production and consumption, and no author did more to amend the situation, than Charles Brockden Brown. A prominent member of the Friendly Club, New York's "first successful attempt to form a coterie for serious literary discussion and criticism,"[7] Brown threw himself into a frenzy of literary activity and in the three years between 1798 and 1801 produced no fewer than six romances and two epistolary novels. In addition to this, he wrote poetry, short stories, essays, and political pamphlets, and edited two magazines, which he filled with many products from his own pen. Brown's ambition was unmistakable: he wanted to help establish and institutionalize a national literature in the United States and become America's first professional man of letters. However, the ambitious American author who had defiantly dismissed earlier European models of the novel in the preface to his 1799 novel *Edgar Huntly* and who in December 1798 had sent a copy of his first novel, *Wieland*, to Vice-President Jefferson, seeking a recommendation from one of the most cultivated and widely read gentlemen in the nation, had by 1801, with the publication of his last novels, *Clara Howard* and *Jane Talbot*, abandoned all hope of declaring America's literary independence.

Not long after that date, in a review essay entitled "A Sketch of American Literature, 1806–7," published in the first issue of the *American Register*, Brown gives us a summary as well as sobering account of the state of American letters at the beginning of the nineteenth century. Although in his assessment "America is probably as great a mart for printed publications as any country in the world," Brown comes to the conclusion that, in terms of the volume of original publications, "the American states, are, in a literary view, no more than a province of the British empire," bearing in this respect "an exact resemblance to Scotland and Ireland." In the final analysis, Brown reluctantly concedes, the volume of "original publications" in America is not so much determined by the presence or absence of "original genius" as by the blunt dynamics of the marketplace: as the inhabitants of Bristol, York, Edinburgh, and Dublin get their cloths from Manchester, their hardware from Birmingham, and their books from "the great manufactory of London," so do the citizens of Baltimore, Philadelphia, New York, and Boston. Yet even more significant than America's post-colonial cultural inferiority complex was the impact of the forces of transatlantic free-market capitalism on the North American market for print in general, and fiction in particular. The rise of the novel in the eighteenth century in America cannot be understood outside the context and conditions of the contemporary American print market.

Throughout the eighteenth century the economic character of American print culture had been its key distinguishing feature. In comparison to their European colleagues, American printers had several obstacles to overcome in their struggle to survive, causing the domestic American print market to be "a primal scene of rivalry."[8] Their main disadvantage was a chronic lack of capital. Type-founding, for instance, did not gain a foothold in North America till toward the end of the century, and thus American printers remained dependent on type imported from Europe. Another bottleneck was the production of paper. Before the technique of using wood pulp was developed in 1849, paper mills depended on a constant supply of rags, ropes, and similar flax- or hemp-based material to produce paper. The shortage of type and the cost of paper (up to half the cost of printing) were not conducive to the production of relatively voluminous yet ephemeral books, such as novels, whether they were written by American or by British authors. Thus, it took Franklin two years (from 1742 to 1744) to print the first American edition of Richardson's *Pamela*. In fact, no other unabridged English novel would be reprinted in American until the Revolution – after which the war effort caused the print market for novels to all but shut down entirely. The Peace of Paris reopened the trade with Britain, and book production in America was also restarted; but type, paper, and capital remained in short supply. This shortage continued to hamper the production of books all through the 1790s and even into the early decades of the nineteenth century.

Cost and profitability tended to privilege the printing of abridgements over the complete texts of British novels, but this is no indication of the actual popularity of the full versions of the novels by Richardson, Sterne, Smollett, Fielding, Defoe, and Mackenzie, which were imported and read in America in ever-increasing numbers. Faced with the limitations of the American printing industry, American printers and booksellers had always endeavored to meet the growing demand for fiction by engaging in the large-scale import of cheaper books printed in Europe. In fact, in eighteenth-century America bookselling was synonymous with book *importing*; consequently, by far the most of the books eighteenth-century American readers read were imported books. James Raven has calculated that in the five years immediately following the Declaration of Independence "the total *annual* shipment of books to the mainland American colonies might have amounted to more than 120,000 separate volumes and printed items."[9] Irish and Scottish reprint booksellers dominated a sizable chunk of this trade. Before the Act of Union of 1801, Dublin printers were particularly well placed to produce books cheaply. Operating outside the jurisdiction of English copyright laws, they had managed to develop a lucrative piracy business. The demand in America for cheap books, especially novels, was so high that even American booksellers joined in the lucrative market of pirated books. Thus, a cut-throat competition developed among American printers in the trade in pirated English books.[10] Particularly fierce was the competition between Mathew Carey in Philadelphia and the Harper Brothers in New York, each trying to beat the other by cornering the market first. In 1822 Mathew Carey produced 1,500 pirated copies of Scott's *Quentin Durward* within twenty hours of receiving a copy of the novel; in 1836 Carey and Hart booked all the seats on the mail stage to New York in order to ship Edward Bulwer Lytton's *Rienzi, The Last of the Roman Tribunes* there before the Harpers could begin distributing their pirated edition of the novel.

Ultimately, however, even the more successful American importers were only small players in the transatlantic book trade – which after the Act of the Union was dominated even more than before by London book tycoons. In Britain, from the 1780s onwards, there had been a rise in the number of cooperative bookselling firms and partnerships. In this climate, William Lane's empire of the Minerva Press emerged as the most successful fiction-producing plant in the world. In the United States, however, such a consolidation in the market did not take place until later, notably between 1800 and 1840. As a result of this uneven competition, of the hundreds of colonial and early republican printers/publishers, only Mathew Carey survived into the nineteenth century. This meant that for much of this period American readers continued to read what the London printers printed. Even an apparent exception to this trend such as Susanna Rowson's early "American" classic *Charlotte Temple* (1791) first appeared with William Lane's Minerva Press.

But the fate of Brown's novels is even more illustrative of the dependence of the American novel market on the transatlantic trade. Despite, or perhaps because of, Brown's efforts to create the first American national tales, not one of his novels was a popular, let alone a commercial success, and not one of them was ever reprinted in America during his lifetime. Even before he had abandoned his literary vocation, Brown had expressed his frustration over his failure to foster any kind of local interest in his work in a letter to his brother: "Book-making, as you observe, is the dullest of all trades, and the utmost that any American can look for, in his native country, is to be reimbursed his unavoidable expenses."[11] His only hope, therefore, was to get a foothold in the European market: "The saleability of my works," he wrote in the same letter, "will much depend upon their popularity in England, whither Caritat has carried a considerable number of Wieland, Ormond and Mervyn."[12]

If Brown sounds gloomy about the chances of establishing an independent republic of letters in the United States, this is undoubtedly because he had just witnessed the demise of the republic of Enlightenment belles-lettres that the French entrepreneur and patron of the arts Hocquet Caritat had established in New York during the 1790s. The proprietor of the biggest contemporary circulating library in America, Caritat was one of America's first publishers in the modern sense of the word, as well as a promoter of original American literature, a wholesale book importer, and one of the earliest book *exporters*. He was also Brown's first publisher, personal supplier of books, and literary agent. Brown's short-lived career as a professional writer is mirrored in the meteoric rise and fall of Caritat's republic of letters; both are symptomatic of the fundamental changes that were being wrought in the world of print and ideas in the changing political climate in the late 1790s and early 1800s. During this period, a wave of counter-revolution and xenophobia increasingly strangled efforts to give America its own print culture both by instituting an atmosphere of Federalist censorship and intellectual intolerance, and by creating obstacles to the flow of books from Europe to America.

In all likelihood, Caritat did indeed take the sheets or the unbound volumes of three of Brown's novels with him on his trip to Europe in 1800. But there is no evidence that *Wieland* actually ever appeared with Minerva,[13] though a cheaply produced, one-volume edition of *Ormond* did appear in 1800, using the remaindered sheets of the New York Swords printing, with a new title-page and advertisements page inserted. What happened to the sheets of the Maxwell printing of *Arthur Mervyn* is not known; but the edition Lane printed in 1803 is a genuinely new edition, and so is that of *Edgar Huntly*, which appeared in the same year, also in three volumes. In 1804 came *Jane Talbot*, in two volumes, and in 1807, also in two volumes, *Clara Howard*, except now retitled in Minerva house style as *Philip Stanley; or, The Enthusiasm of Love*. Such retitling was characteristic of the business philosophy of the Minerva Press. The practice adds a sad and ironic twist to Brown's (by then) foundered literary ambitions: none of these reprints made any reference whatsoever to the earlier American editions, nor is it likely that Brown ever received any royalties from Minerva. Even though none of Brown's books was ever reprinted in America during his lifetime, for the "Godwin of America" to find his highly original work repackaged and restyled for the British mass entertainment market would have added professional insult to financial injury.[14]

Caritat's fate is eerily similar to that of Thomas Paine upon his return to the United States in the fall of 1802. Both made the mistake in thinking that in post-revolutionary American society a free press was still a basic ingredient of republican liberty. Neither saw, at least not in time, that a competitively organized market press rooted in civil society – and this included commercial circulating libraries and popular presses like Minerva, as much as newspapers – would ultimately erode competition and devour rival media. The mass opinion market was thereby monopolized by all available means, including populism and sensationalism, and hence ultimately restricted freedom of expression. Paine, who had witnessed the transformation of the sedate colonial press in America into a fierce, competitive medium of public political debate, was now crushed by the powerfully organized, market-driven Federalist press. Similarly, Caritat, who only a couple of years before had started out so ambitiously selling and circulating the Library of the Enlightenment and Progressive Thought on the North American continent, soon found himself peddling the products that came off Lane's presses into the United States, and subsequently even ended up shipping the raw literary materials of the New World to Minerva's pulp fiction reprocessing plant on Leadenhall Street. If the Caritat–Lane story tells us anything, it is that in the first decade of the nineteenth century the transatlantic circulation of commodities won the day over the circulation of intellectual content. The press's appetite may have been as indiscriminate as it was unstoppable, but its products were as predictable as they were cheap.

Wil Verhoeven

NOTES

1   Royall Tyler, *The Algerine Captive; or, The Life and Adventures of Doctor Updike Underhill – Six Years a Prisoner Among the Algerines*, ed. Caleb Crain (New York: Modern Library, 1797), 5.

2   Robert B. Winans, "The Growth of a Novel-Reading Public in Late Eighteenth-Century America," *Early American Literature* 9 (1975), 270–1.

3   Ibid., 268.

4   Ibid., 6.

5   Cited in Edward Watts, *Writing and Postcolonialism in the Early Republic* (Charlottesville and London: University Press of Virginia, 1998), 5.

6   Ibid., 13.

7   Fredrika J. Teute, "Friendly Converse between Women and Men in Late Eighteenth-Century New York," in Philip Barnard, Mark L. Kamrath, and Stephen Shapiro (eds.), *Revising Charles Brockden Brown: Culture, Politics, and Sexuality in the Early Republic* (Knoxville: University of Tennessee Press, 2004).

8   James N. Green, "English Books and Printing in the Age of Franklin," in Hugh Amory and David H. Hall (eds.), *The Colonial Book in the Atlantic World* (Cambridge, Mass.: Cambridge University Press, 2000), 253.

9   James Raven, "The Export of Books to Colonial North America," *Publishing History* 42 (1997), 21.

10 Hellmut Lehmann-Haupt, *The Book in America: A History of the Making and Selling of Books in the United States*, rev. and enlarged edn. (New York: Bowker, 1951), 111. (First publ. 1939.)

11 Quoted in William Dunlap, *The Life of Charles Brockden Brown*, 2 vols. (Philadelphia: Parke, 1815), vol. 1, 100.

12 Ibid.

13 An edition of *Wieland* appeared in London with Henry Colburn in 1811.

14 The epithet was coined by John Neal, "American Writers, No. II," *Blackwood's Edinburgh Magazine* 16: 93 (Oct. 1824), 425.

Part II

A "post-nationalist" criticism asks that cultural events within the political geography of the United States be interpreted as part of the larger world, not in isolation from it. Rather than seeing historical events, artifacts, and performances as internalizing a nation's boundary lines, a more globally oriented approach sees a region's inhabitants influenced by their location within a world-system of interrelationships. Despite utopian claims about self-sufficiency, the United States has always been shaped by a global network of commodity exchanges and movement of peoples. Because cultural interaction is by definition a process of encounter and exchange, a non-nationalist "US

Studies" considers the Atlantic as a relational unit of linkages, rather than a territorial obstacle of division and difference, and contextualizes America's place within the circumatlantic basin of Europe, Africa, the Caribbean, and the Americas. Fernand Braudel influentially argued that, rather than analyzing any particular European nation as a coherent unit formed in opposition to others (his example was early modern Spain), it made better sense to consider the Mediterranean's dense web of transportation, communication, and trade as the source of a common southern European culture that transcended any one political state's regions. Similarly, if documents and performances have recurring characteristics that cross national boundary lines, these notations of experience emerge via the contacts circulating through a land's ports of entry and transnational institutions of intellectual and social exchange.

Reading texts and cultural events as American seems commonsensical. When working in American Studies, nothing appears more obvious, than to ask how an object expresses or relates to its creator's national identity. The underlying assumption is that an essential nationality ultimately determines our personality and our most deeply held fantasies and fears. For studies of the pre-industrial era, this idea of an exceptional American self is problematic on two accounts. First, the notion of interiority as the site of authentic identity was undergoing construction throughout the eighteenth and nineteenth centuries, alongside the contemporaneous separation of public and private spheres. Earlier beliefs about selfhood recognized that individuals might have passions, but these drives were not thought to express a special, hidden truth about one's self. Many writers of the pre-industrial period considered a person's passions as unremarkable, if not an obstacle to either their participation within the Enlightenment or their communion with the divine. While one strand of proto-Romantic writers, like Rousseau, argued that an untrained self's reactions were natural and ideal, a more commonly held view believed that culture was the opposite of nature. Any claim for a document's importance because of its particularly national, or naturally American, qualities would have been seen by many pre-nine-teenth-century agents as a sign of failure to achieve secular progress or sacred grace. Over the course of the nineteenth century these evaluations began to be reversed as heartfelt expressions began to be celebrated as noteworthy markers of a better self.

Alongside the rise of interior personality came the emergence of nationality as a collective facet of one's special self. As Romantic-era aesthetics made the analogy between an interior mental space of vital imagination and a local or regional geography, it argued that culture was most vibrant when it conveyed the imagined traits of nationality. By the early nineteenth century, new canons of national literature categorized and evaluated writing according to the degree to which it displayed the peculiar spirit of each land. The rise of nationalist culture represents an attempt to resolve a tension created by modernity's division of experience between the public and private spheres, since nationality was both a public mode of defining society and a private feeling of personality.

Before the Civil War many influential modes of cultural expression, like Christian evangelicism, did not consider the nation-state as the main point of reference. The emotional identity of nationality was often considered secondary to other more pressing goals of survival and enfranchisement for marginalized groups, such as Native Americans, enslaved Africans, Europeans who came as indentured or bound laborers, subsistence hunters and farmers on the frontiers, and women of all social classes. When we consistently ask that a past cultural document reveal its nationality, we forget that these contemporary desires are constructed assumptions about the nature of identity that belong to the concerns of a specific historical period.

As humans enter a mobile circuit of encounters and exchanges, their work and living conditions are no longer typical of either their own home or that of those whom they meet, but emerge uniquely out of the sea-changes of shared experience. One illustration appears with the aftermath of England's seventeenth-century civil wars. The suppression of the lower classes' desires for political recognition did not destroy these ideals of millenarian change. The men whose democratic yearnings had been suppressed were now estranged from their former lives and they drifted to the urban ports, like London and Bristol, and then out to sea as the cogs in Britain's emerging imperial navy. While it was not the British elite's intention to seed radicalism across the oceans, this is what occurred as sailors transmitted anti-authoritarian ideals through the chain of Atlantic harbors. Increasingly delocalized from their English origins, these claims became part of a polyglot common sense as the circumatlantic became its own non-national generator of ideas. Circumatlantic social formations and cultural outlooks are brought into each land via the harbors. From the ports, these practices become diffused throughout a domestic territory through regional work-flows and commodity chains. Thoreau's *Walden*, with its lyrical celebration of self-reliance metaphorized by an uncontaminated land-locked pond, has often been highlighted as an exemplar of literary nationalism. Yet Thoreau learns these attitudes as he receives the tradition of radical groups, like the Levelers and Ranters, who were suppressed at the end of the English Civil Wars and whose ideas were then carried abroad by the oceanic flows. Even the Harvard-educated Thoreau responds to the notions more as common sense reasoning sparked off by the view of immigrants than in terms of a history of ideas learned in the burrows of the collegiate library. Additionally, Walden is distinctive only when Thoreau can compare his existence there to that of the Irish immigrants who are brought in to mine the region's natural resources for a distant trade in consumer goods. The Irish provide Thoreau not only with the actual material for his housing, but also with the conversations that spur his contemplations, so that *Walden*'s composition is defined by a global frame of reference.

African slavery furnishes a similar example. In the eighteenth century Africa, like Europe, was composed of a heterogeneous mosaic of socio-political regimes, ranging from strongly demarcated absolutist kingdoms to small republic-like, village-centered micro-states. Slavery threw the continent's differences into even sharper relief, since many of those captured came from outside the social elites and were unlikely to have previously encountered Africans outside of their family, regional, and linguistic groups. Once captured and collected in the coastal holding pens and the slave ships' Middle Passage, the kidnapped Africans engaged in patterns similar to those of all immigrant groups. Some kept close to their regional and linguistic compatriots and exaggerated the cultural assumptions of their locality to preserve their distinction from other Africans; some intermingled with other groups and began sharing different folk beliefs and customs. The various stages of the slave process created a spectrum of identities that cannot simply be traced back to "Africa," since the Atlantic circulation created a new realm and a synthetic black identity that never existed in Africa in the first instance.

The circumatlantic effect of cultural syncretism among these different Africans enabled second-wave elaborations that also glued groups together across ethnic and racial lines. Most antebellum European immigrants came from either the urban lower classes or barely urbanized groups that had been dispossessed from their agrarian life-world as a result of violent enclosures, the ravages of Catholic–Protestant conflicts, or the demographic scarcities caused by an increasing population. Many of these Europeans retained a mixture of folk-beliefs and devotional icons that urbanized elites had abandoned as atavistic. As expatriates traveled through the circumatlantic, their hinterland beliefs were reinforced as different groups recognized the shared nature of their superstitions. African fetishes and religious customs, like voodoo, fascinated Europeans because of their similarity to European peasant beliefs, for example, the tradition of Catholic reliquaries. As Irish and Africans, both colonial subordinates to British imperial Protestantism, not only often lived and worked together in new lands, their cultural practices intermingled in the pre-Civil War period to form new cultural manifestations like minstrelsy, tap-dancing, and other styles of fancy dress. Frederick Douglass' slave narrative consistently indicates how he relied on Irish youth and port laborers for encouragement and examples of an extranational identity, which he desires as a slave striving for emancipation.

It would be wrong to paint a picture of these circumatlantic encounters as invariably ones of joyous harmony, mutually enabling hybridity, and consensual pluralism. It would be equally wrong, though, to overlook how different groups within the oceanic stream responded to its opportunities for forging a shared set of cultural assumptions. Mark Twain's retrospective *Adventures of Huckleberry Finn* illustrates, for instance, that while antebellum Huck and Jim may come from opposite racially defined poles, they also exchange mutually reinforcing folk-beliefs. What originally may have been Celtic and African superstitions fuse to create a heterogeneous mixture that is neither. Jim's fantasy of being ridden by witches combines African ideas of bodily possession with European peasant fears of night-riding covens. As Huck and Jim travel together, their Mississippi is more than simply a line through the American continental mass; it also stands as the Western waterway flowing into the circumatlantic's oceanic pathways. Once these exchanges enter into the aquatic circulation, they continue to spiral around the Atlantic's contours, establishing and augmenting a pattern of exchanges that is increasingly difficult to classify as belonging to any homogeneous regional culture.

Racial relations are readily susceptible to a circumatlantic approach, since the flesh trade and the Northern supply of inexpensive food and clothing to Southern and Caribbean slave markets were crucial to the US economy. Yet beyond matters of race, every convulsion of social and political life within the oceanic matrix created an impression elsewhere. The early 1850s have long been recognized as a period of exceptional literary production in the United States, so much so that one scholarly generation referred to it as the American Renaissance, as if to compare it to Europe's emergence from centuries of stultified social and cultural development. In fact, this spell of heightened literary production is not specific to the United States: the period was a time of dense literary and cultural production throughout Europe. The spur to this outburst of creativity was provided in large part by the events leading up to and beyond the pan-European "springtime of revolutions" in 1848, which brought writers, artists, and students into alliance with working-class rebellion in ways that had not been the case for the prior phase of democratic revolutions in the 1790s. The canonical male writers of the mid-nineteenth century, including Hawthorne, Whitman, and Melville, produced what they considered their masterworks within the environment created by the waves of global political liberation and repression. *Moby-Dick*'s Ahab can be read as a study on Louis Bonaparte's popular authoritarianism as much as a commentary on any local display of militaristic mania. While the War of Independence may have politically separated the United States from Europe, the centuries-long conflict between England and France, and to a lesser degree Spain, was played out on American shores as the overlapping of imperial interests continually determined the shape of the continental United States' expansion and self-image.

One mode of circumatlantic transmission occurs through highly codified and institutionalized forms of exchange, as when writers, journalists, and artists transport each other's ideas, generic conventions, and rhetorical styles. These exchanges are often the most clearly recognizable to later students, but they are not always the most influential among the broad mass of past society, or representative of those social groups distanced from the dissemination of official culture. Since middle-class writers are often reluctant to acknowledge the productive vitality of the lower social strata, popular concerns are often represented in narratives as marginal details, seemingly ornamental flourishes that do not seem necessary to the main exposition. The problem is complicated by the fact that many of the circumatlantic exchanges were ones that actively resisted dominant institutions of class privilege, so that demophobia, the fear and hatred of the mass, contributes further to the silencing of popular history. Only recently have we begun recognizing the Haitian Revolution's deep impact on the West through fears of slave rebellion, distaste about miscegenation, and foreign policy concerns to assert control over the Western hemisphere lest the firebrands of black revolution spread beyond the Caribbean.

If one often has to read against the grain to excavate non-elite histories, their effects can be typically found in the shifts in ideas about the body. Because the primary means of our interaction with global developments is not party politics or high culture, but the foreign commodities that we digest, wear, or otherwise consume, discourses about the body are the ones often most susceptible to registering the impact of far-away events. Through the eighteenth and nineteenth centuries, politically progressive ideas about mass democracy and socialism were often bundled with and conveyed through para-scientific investigations into the body, ranging from phrenology and mesmerism to vegetarianism and temperance. When complaints about these new trends and fascinations appear, they often mediate concerns about more substantive social changes that have been silenced in official discourse. Poe's "The Man That Was Used Up" ostensibly acts as a satire on the way in which formerly luxurious items that were previously available only to a small, wealthy elite have become more easily purchasable objects of fashion. The story also indicates an anxious recognition that even the most intimate acts and personal behavior of Americans are determined by events far away that seem to dissolve the clear boundaries of the nation's jurisdiction. Poe uses the story's continual joking muted pronunciation of the man's name to illustrate how subaltern experiences are literally choked off from public recognition by the knowledge elites of the eastern seaboard. Superficially about modernity's obsession with commodities, Poe's tale also registers how a collective unconscious is formed by metanational events. Excavating these features of the past requires close attention to be paid to events occurring throughout the matrix, leading to heightened awareness of how events in Africa, South America, the Caribbean, and the New World are interlocked.

Literary and cultural studies tend to equate continuity with importance. A text easily gains credibility when it demonstrates its conversation with prior works. For a non-nationalist study, we must respect the brevity and discontinuity of effects as much as cultural continuity. One generation cannot always clearly indicate the source of its ideas if this influence emerges from the constantly mobile circulation of references and experiences within the global system. The challenge for a post-nationalist study will be to forge the analytic tools appropriate to the Atlantic's avenues of experience. Soon we may no longer speak of American Studies but rather of the location of America within the Western oceanic matrix.

Stephen Shapiro

FURTHER READING

Braudel, Fernand (1992a). *The Mediterranean and the Mediterranean World in the Age of Philip II*, trans. Siân Reynolds. Berkeley: University of California Press. (First publ. 1949.)

Braudel, Fernand (1992b). *Civilization and Capitalism, 15th–18th Century*, 3 vols., trans. Siân Reynolds. Berkeley: University of California Press. (First publ. 1982–6.)

Burton, Antoinette M. (2003). *After the Imperial Turn: Thinking with and through the Nation*. Durham, NC: Duke University Press.

Engerman, Stanley L., ed. (1996–2000). *The Cambridge Economic History of the United States*, 3 vols. Cambridge, UK: Cambridge University Press.

Ignatiev, Noel (1995). *How the Irish Became White*. New York: Routledge.

Linebaugh, Peter (1991). *The London Hanged: Crime and Civil Society in the Eighteenth Century.* London: Penguin.

Linebaugh, Peter, and Rediker, Marcus (2000). *The Many-Headed Hydra: Sailors, Slaves, Commoners, and the Hidden History of the Revolutionary Atlantic.* Boston: Beacon.

Lipsitz, George (2001). *American Studies in a Moment of Danger.* Minneapolis: University of Minnesota Press.

Louis, William Roger, ed. (1998–9). *The Oxford History of the British Empire*, 5 vols. Oxford: Oxford University Press.

Pease, Donald E., ed. (2002). *The Future of American Studies.* Durham, NC: Duke University Press.

Roach, Joseph (1996). *Cities of the Dead: Circum-Atlantic Performance.* New York: Columbia University Press.

Rowe, John Carlos, ed. (2000). *Post-Nationalist American Studies.* Berkeley: University of California Press.

Wallerstein, Immanuel (1974). *The Capitalist World-Economy.* Cambridge, UK: Cambridge University Press.

Wallerstein, Immanuel (1974–89). *The Modern World-System*, 3 vols. San Diego: Academic Press.

12

Other Languages, Other Americas

Kirsten Silva Gruesz

Contemporary performance artist Guillermo Gómez-Peña, insisting that we live in an essentially borderless hemisphere, locates one of his monologues in "this troubled country mistakenly called America" – a refrain he twists throughout the piece. Yet for most in the United States it remains a given that America is synonymous with the United States: an assumption not shared by hundreds of millions of Latin Americans, among others, who are more skeptical of the national tendency toward grandiosity. If we attempt to uncouple the link by which the two are made one in common speech – taking "America" to mean a region, not a nation or a high-minded ideal – some unexamined assumptions may disintegrate: among them, that American literature must be written in English; and that the US experience of cultural decolonization is unique in the New World.

In a 1978 essay disingenuously called "What is American Literature?" William Spengemann anticipated both of these challenges. He pointed out that since the discipline of American Literature studied cultural artifacts from the colonial period, their Americanness could not logically derive from the nation-state, although presuppositions about US identity were often projected onto them anachronistically. The implicit definition of the field thus seemed to be "literature written in any place that is now part of the United States or by anyone who has ever lived in one of those places" (Spengemann 1989: 9). Yet both the working curricula and the grand themes of the field were centered on far fewer texts than such a definition would suggest, since scholars also tended to construct the narrative of literary history with reference to only the most valorized literary genres. "By identifying America with the United States," Spengemann added, "we forgo any possibility of comparing the developments of English, French, Spanish and Portuguese literatures in the New World, although some knowledge of these parallel developments would seem indispensable to our expressed aim of measuring the impact that America has had upon literature" (p. 12). By the same token, he points out that it makes no sense to exclude "works written in the United States in other languages, or works written in English outside the present boundaries of the United States, although any number of these may be American in some essential aspect" (p. 15).

By calling attention to the implicit pact of monolingualism within the field, Spengemann was returning to an originary and in some ways more inclusive approach to American literature that prevailed prior to the New Criticism and that movement's repudiation of the emphasis on historicizing. The final volume of *The Cambridge History of English and American Literature* (1907–21) includes lengthy chapters on writings in German, French, Yiddish, and "aboriginal languages"; and despite the *History*'s exclusion of Spanish, scholars in New Mexico were at the same time editing and preserving writings from that area dating back to the seventeenth century. H. L. Mencken's *The American Language* (1921) also has an appendix on the influence of non-English "dialects," this time including Spanish. With few exceptions, however, these postscripts were ignored by the newly institutionalized discipline of American Literature, and at the time Spengemann's essay was first published its propositions seemed merely curious. In the late 1980s, however, the rise of the New Historicism brought new attention to texts that earlier would have been scorned as paraliterary and marginal, thus breaking the stranglehold of the limited canon of which Spengemann had complained. At the same time, critiques mounted by feminists and other commentators of the post-Civil-Rights era cracked open the fiction of a unitary national experience, launching a broad-based effort to make the US canon more inclusive. Yet even then this work remained focused on English-language texts and stayed within the borders of the United States. Of the several provocations in Spengemann's essay, the insistence on incorporating other languages and other Americas has been the last to find its audience – but here, too, his essay has proved prescient.

By the mid-1990s an old historical debate – Do the Americas have a common history or culture? – had been renewed, but with a distinctly anti-imperial bent. Using the vocabulary of ethnic studies and post-colonial theory, seminal work by Vera Kutzinski, José David Saldívar, Lois Parkinson Zamora, and Hortense Spillers, among others – spurred on by such novel spatial topoi as the Black Atlantic and the circum-Caribbean – inspired new transnational research. Meanwhile, scholars associated with the "Recovering the US Hispanic Literary Heritage" project at the University of Houston and the "Languages of What Is Now the United States" project at Harvard had began the arduous task of collecting and analyzing forgotten non-English literary works. In 1998 Janice Radway, then president of the American Studies Association, used the platform of the annual meeting to call into question the very name of the association, arguing for multilingual programs and "the fostering of a relational and comparative perspective" on things American (Radway 1999: 24). Clearly, the time has come to see "America" not as a fixed term of national belonging that presumes a consensual understanding of US experience, but as a historically contingent and culturally fraught marker. To read these ever-changing meanings, it seems imperative to bring extranational works, as well as non-English texts produced within the nation, into conversation with canonical texts and authors. Because fiction is an imaginative form that contains larger social and political desires as well as repressive energies, the introduction of such texts promises to tell us something about how "America" functions as a form of exclusion as well as inclusion. In this brief overview I will treat domestic non-English productions first, following this with an abbreviated sketch of alternate New World literatures that offer provocative points of comparison.

Limiting the plethora of languages spoken in the new nation was not one of its originary traditions of exclusion. As Marc Shell notes, "Inside and outside the often changing borders of the American colonies between 1750 and 1850, if ever there were a polyglot place on the globe – other than Babel's spire – this was it" (Shell 2002: 4). With the persistence of several hundred indigenous, and African, languages; with well-established German, Gaelic, and Welsh speakers; with other European-language speakers emigrating in large numbers; and with the acquisition of huge swaths of territory populated by French and Spanish speakers, the analogy of Babel was used more and more frequently as the century progressed. Observers of the time worried, as they do today, that a multilingual nation was antithetical to democratic consensus. But the degree of hostility toward non-English languages in public life that we associate with contemporary debates on immigration and bilingual education did not really appear until the late nineteenth century, reaching its peak during the xenophobic years of World War I. Prior to that, local examples like the bilingual schools in heavily German areas of Pennsylvania and the Spanish–English consti- tution of the new state of California remind us that tolerance of civic multivocalism was more widespread in the nineteenth century than it is now. These public practices have counterparts in the written record: a sizable body of writings in languages other than English stands as a counter-story to the historical amnesia and presentism of our age.

This growing suspicion of language difference as inherently anti-democratic ex- plains, in part, the paucity of previous scholarship on non-English writings. Shell suggests provocatively that the fetishization of race as the only significant form of difference in US life has subsumed attention to language, noting that "forgetting language difference – and hence, more critically, partly suppressing the category of 'language' itself – is still the urgent component of unofficially anglophone America's understanding of itself" (Shell 2002: 19). Practically speaking, the neglect also stems from the difficulty of accessing the works themselves. Although some nineteenth- century book publishers (notably the house of Appleton) ventured into the foreign- language market, the primary means of distribution for non-English fiction was through serially published *feuilletons*, some locally authored and some copied from elsewhere. Dozens of newspapers in Spanish, French, and German were in evidence during the 1850s; New Orleans alone had three French papers. Many languages that were widely *spoken* during this period left scantier written records, and many publica- tions preferred other literary forms to fiction. Nonetheless, examples of most genres popular in the novel's early period can be found in these non-English sources – although not all have survived the ephemeral form in which they were published, and only a few of those have been excavated and made available to a wide audience.

One of the earliest and most ambitious of these fictions is the anonymously published novel titled, in Spanish, *Jicoténcal* (a recent English translation follows the Nahuatl orthography: *Xicoténcatl*). Published in 1826, the same year as *The Last of the Mohicans*, *Xicoténcatl* – a historical romance of the Spanish conquest of Mexico – invites comparison to Cooper's frontier epics, despite the distant chronological setting. It features Romantic landscapes; an even nobler group of "savages" than Cooper's; and an underlying sense of nostalgia for what is lost in moments of sweeping historical change. Although *Xicoténcatl* has always claimed a place as one of the earliest Spanish American novels, its publication in Philadelphia and its patronage by William Cullen Bryant argue for its inclusion in a North American canon as well, even as its authorship remains mysterious. The most likely candidates, interestingly, are not Mexican but Cuban. The frontrunner is Félix Varela, an abolitionist priest whose opposition to Spanish colonial governance led him to a decades-long exile in the United States; another possibility is José María Heredia, the radical poet and editor associated with Bryant (see Leal 1995 for a discussion of the authorship question). *Xicoténcatl* anticipates the vogue of "Aztequiana" that would follow Prescott's *History of the Conquest of Mexico*: the novel portrays the Mexican natives as honorable, handsome, and enlightened people, in stark contrast to the rapacious Cortés and his henchmen. It focuses on the crucial decision of the Tlaxcalans – a powerful tribe uneasily gathered within the Aztec empire – to support the Spanish invaders and thereby aid the unlikely capture of Mexico City. Borrowing overtly from a historical chronicle, *Xicoténcatl* is just as concerned with questions of political philosophy as it is with constructing a usable past for the New World, with characters debating the merits of imperial (Spanish/Aztec) versus republican (Tlaxcalan) forms of government.

In this version of colonial history, Cortés conquers not because of the advantages of gunpowder and horses, nor because of native superstition, but because he capitalizes on the inner divisions within the Tlaxcalan Senate and its leaders. The novel's hero Xicoténcatl, son of a respected Tlaxcalan senator, tries and fails to form a pan-Mexican alliance against the Spanish. In following the will of the Senate rather than his own military instincts, he shows himself a true democrat, but this same virtue allows the corrupt senator Magiscatzin to betray him. Parallel to this political intrigue runs a sentimental plot involving Xicoténcatl's betrothed, Teutila, and the two Spaniards – one good, one bad – who capture and attempt to seduce her. Philosophical rather than sensational, the novel understands beauty as an index of virtue, and the moral conduct of individuals as a measure of just government. Like other antebellum US fiction, *Xicoténcatl* imagines the doomed lovers within a kind of natural aristocracy that complicates its claims to political equality. Whereas the traitor Magiscatzin "sacrific[es] his country to private resentments" (Anon. 1999: 34), Xicoténcatl refuses to trade Teutila's freedom for military help to the invaders, and in doing so demonstrates his nobility: "The voice of the nation is the only one that the republic's soldier ought to hear," he says righteously, even as guards tear Teutila away from him. "Oh, my country! How you test my love for you!" (pp. 76–7). Love of country and of one's beloved require the same capacities of feeling, joining family and nation in a familiar synecdoche.

Xicoténcatl is steeped in familiar Romantic tropes, from the sublime landscapes that characterize Mexico, "a nation overflowing with the gifts of Nature" (Anon. 1999: 15), to the response of the natural world to the ethno-racial devastation about to be wrought upon the peace-loving Tlaxcalans: a lightning bolt splits an ancient mahogany tree near the novel's beginning, signaling the tragedy to come. Native Mexicans, called "Americans" in contrast to "Europeans," are portrayed as thoughtful deists, worshipping the principle of beauty in Nature rather than pagan idols that might repel a Christian reader. "[U]ncorrupted by the arts of civilivation" (p. 20), the Tlaxcalans know instinctively to "adore the creator of all that exists," and both Teutila and Xicoténcatl parry theological questions from a Spanish priest in a convincing way. In matters of politics, as in morality, the Tlaxcalans are clearly ahead of the Spaniards: their statehouse or "national building" inspires awe in even the lawless Cortés. Meditations on the rise and fall of empires – another Romantic topic – make way for more theorizing on the virtues of self-government. Xicoténcatl warns the confederation of tribes allied under Moctezuma, "When internal divisions destroy the unity of a people, they inevitably become the victims of their enemies . . . I call on all nations! If you love your freedom, gather together all your interests and your forces" so that the enemy will not "enslave you when you are disunited" (p. 79).

Xicoténcatl thus serves as a kind of multicultural mediator: he defends his betrothed, a non-Aztec, and otherwise tries to transcend tribal loyalties. One of Moctezuma's captains, turns this into an exemplary quality: "humanity calls upon you for your services, and an entire world turns to you as its liberator" (Anon. 1999: 84). Although Xicoténcatl fails at this, he is clearly meant to be an avatar of future leaders in the American hemisphere, whose ideal republicanism lends a historical genealogy to struggling nineteenth-century nations. Locating the struggle between democratic and autocratic tendencies within an indigenous past, the novel both celebrates the newly independent condition of the Americas, and warns them against the internal divisions that can doom a republic. If the author was indeed a Cuban independence partisan, his identification with a history of Mexican anti-imperialism is then a gesture at this larger hemispheric community, including the United States in which he apparently took refuge. The themes of patrimonial obligation and national reconciliation through romance – the novel ends with a sentimental scene between Cortés and Marina – link *Xicoténcatl* to contemporaneous North American texts in which Native Americans figure as mediators of old and new, who serve to consecrate the presumably more virtuous republican formations on the continent.

While political exiles were significant in fostering Spanish-language print communities in cities like Philadelphia, New York, and New Orleans, Mexicans in the border zones established local presses even before the acquisition of their territories by the United States. After 1848 Spanish newspapers were sites of engagement with, and often resistance to, the newly dominant culture. With their promised citizenship rights abrogated and their language increasingly shut out of public life, *californios, tejanos*, and *nuevomejicanos* were, as many contemporary Chicano/a scholars argue, effectively a colonized people within the republic. Although no known Spanish-language novels were published in book form in the United States between 1826 and 1892 (María Amparo Ruíz de Burton's postwar romances of the *californios* were written in English), *folletines* did convey fiction to readers of these newspapers. None have yet been made available, but with ambitious recovery efforts like the "US Hispanic Periodical Literature" project underway, that gap will certainly be filled soon.

French-speaking Creoles in Louisiana often expressed a similar sense of linguistic embattlement and cultural defensiveness in response to the increasing dominance of Anglo-American culture there. Despite the racial divide within Creole culture, French-speaking free persons of color in New Orleans enjoyed a higher rate of literacy at midcentury than did their white English-speaking counterparts. The earliest extant fiction produced within this group also counts as the first by an African American writer: Victor Séjour, who left his native New Orleans at nineteen. "Le Mulâtre" (The mulatto), published in Paris in 1837, is set in pre-revolutionary Haiti and recounts the tragic story of Georges, the good-hearted son of a mysterious African woman who dies when he is young, keeping the secret of his paternity by forbidding him from looking at a portrait she has saved of his father. Georges fearlessly saves his master Alfred from an assassination plot, but Alfred becomes smitten with the mulatto's "voluptuous" wife Zélie. When Zélie fights off Alfred's advances and accidentally injures the master, he condemns her to death – and Georges, who accuses the master, shares her sentence. After her lynching Georges joins the maroons and plots his revenge: to kill Alfred, but not until "dear and precious ties bound him to the world" (Séjour 1837: 173): that is, after he too had acquired a wife and child. Georges avenges himself by killing the wife and then his former master; but with his dying breath Alfred lets loose the secret that he is Georges's father, and the unhappy mulatto apparently then kills himself. Like many later fictions, "Le Mulâtre" uses the theme of closeted racial mixing to undermine theories of African inferiority, locating the troubles of a whole society within a single family to intensify its message. Lingering on gruesome details, melodramatic coincidences, and sensational scenes, the tale is also profoundly psychological: its moral burden is to explain how slavery's worst offenses are lodged against the emotions and character.

Although Séjour's story first appeared in France, New Orleans publications were rich in *feuilletons* that are only now being mined. In a gothic tale called "Fantômes" by Louis Placide Canonge, published in *L'Abeille* in 1839, a young Creole man returning from Paris expresses his disaffection and boredom in the "colony" by falling for a local charmer who is already engaged. Supernatural signs point to their tragic fate: to die together at the very moment of her marriage. *Le Courrier de la Louisiane* nurtured a stable of local writers during the mid-1840s, including the very early work of Alfred Mercier, who would become a key figure in the *Athénée louisianais* after the Civil War. One of the most interesting appears to be Alexandre Barde, an émigré journalist whose command of multiple genres sets him apart from other less prolific writers (see

Bruce 2003 for a discussion of the problem of authorship). The tales attributed to Barde, many set among the French and Spanish populations of New Orleans who lived in merry mockery of Anglo rule, range from the burlesque to the gothic to the archly ironic, in a tonal trajectory not unlike that of Poe. Barde also contributed numerous biographical and historical articles to the *Courrier*. He published a serial novel about pirates in the Americas in 1848, most of which has been lost, and later ran a newspaper in western Louisiana. More will undoubtedly be uncovered about Barde's career, as well as that of his fellow editor, Hypolite de Bautée ("D'Artlys"), whose serial novel *Soulier rouge* (1849) tells of a Frenchman who allies with a Choctaw chief and marries into the tribe. Another Creole author, M. Amédée Bouis, contributed to this Indianist literature with *Le Whip-Poor-Will; ou, les pionniers de l'Oregon* (1847).

The most popular Creole historical novelist was Charles Testut, who made use of the crossover historian Charles Gayarré's materials about the Louisiana past. His novels include *Saint-Denis* (1845), a historical romance partially set in New Mexico; *Calisto* (1849), which treats the fate of an aristocratic family that emigrates to New Orleans; and *Le Vieux Salomon* (written in 1858, but not published until 1877), a reformist novel that parallels *Uncle Tom's Cabin* in many respects, including the saintly title character. Testut also experimented with that most popular midcentury genre, the urban mystery novel (see chapter 16 by Shelley Streeby in this volume). His *Les Mystères de la Nouvelle-Orléans* began appearing in 1852, wandering into obscure discussions of occultism rather than capitalizing on its local setting. Given the city's heterogeneous and multilingual population, it is no wonder than many writers – among them Ned Buntline, one of the most successful of all in this genre – located their "mysteries" novels in New Orleans. The oddest and most fascinating of them is Ludwig von Reizenstein, a Bavarian-born architect and engineer who was part of the great wave of Germans to emigrate to the Ohio and Mississippi river valleys in 1848.

Reizenstein's *Die Geheimnisse von New-Orleans*, serially published in the *Louisiana Staats-Zeitung* between 1854 and 1855, actively courted a female readership whom he addressed directly as the novel was being published. It also interpolated current events into the plot of a novel that was obviously still being revised. Reizenstein thus engaged in an unusually dialogic relationship with his readers: spinning scandals and rumors as new chapters appeared, *The Mysteries of New Orleans* smacks of the *roman-à-clef* and (according to Steven Rowan's exhaustive research) incited much speculation about the true identities of his pleasure-loving characters, particularly the German lesbian Orleana and her Creole lover Claudine. The cityscape that emerges from its pages is strongly multicultural and dizzyingly multiracial. In the Second District (today's French Quarter), for example, "the skin color grows browner...and the teeth whiter...[m]oustaches are in finest flower" (Reizenstein 2002: 379) among the dapper Creoles, many of whom are clearly racially mixed. This stew of varying physiognomies, values, and ideas is the perfect hatching point for the novel's loosely constructed conspiracy plot, which follows an extended family of German aristocrats as they are pulled down into indigence by the cleverer criminal characters. Yet the real crime, Reizenstein suggests, goes deeper: "New Orleans would long since have become a Venice if an invisible hand had not punished it in many a year for a crime that meanness and selfishness has held to be a necessary evil": that is, the slave economy underlying the region's prosperity (p. 193). The punishment is a nearly apocalyptic epidemic of yellow fever, which sweeps away even the relatively innocent Germans.

The main villain of *Mysteries of New Orleans*, the Hungarian Lajos Est***, is unrepentingly evil, as is the obligatory lecherous priest who helps him; but some of his cohorts are more originally cast. The teenaged mulatta Merlina Dufresne, who runs a gambling den, shows a cleverness and canny use of her sexuality that contrasts her with the dozens of tragic mulattas who populate Anglo-American fiction. Another Afro-Creole woman runs a bordello specializing in mulattas and mestizas, whose various admixtures are described with a degree of precision that can only be satirical. Sulla, a con artist who takes advantage of striving black families trying to purchase their freedom, is another morally complex African American character who later duels with Lajos over Merlina's favors. The novel does contain some stereotypical portraits of blacks played to comic effect – the young Tiberius, for instance, whose precocious sexuality leads him to seduce a German maid in the house's cistern – but overall, the variety of African American characters is unusual for the period.

Interracial sex can fairly be said to be one of the great preoccupations of the novel: its larger plot has to do with the "bewitching" of Emil, a German architect, who runs off with the mulatta Lucy to conceive a child destined to be the savior of his mother's race. The "hidden hand" orchestrating these events is Hiram the Freemason, who leads the couple to the source of the Red River to gather a plant that spreads yellow fever. Here, Hiram prophesies that when Lucy's child, to be named Toussaint L'Ouverture, starts a black revolution in the year 1871 the mysterious plant will no longer have this power, "and New Orleans will be free from that plague of fever" (Reizenstein 2002: 417). As the novel closes Emil, Lucy, and their young son are headed for Haiti, while the rest of the characters suffer through the epidemic Hiram has set in motion. Although New Orleans pays for the sin of slavery, the novel makes it clear that the city is merely a scapegoat for the wrongs of the nation as a whole. New Orleans has a reputation for decadence, says Reizenstein, yet at least it is not guilty of the repression that characterizes the rest of the country: "*{M}uch is forbidden, but much is also tolerated.* This makes New Orleans the freest city in the United States," compared to "the straightlaced and the hypocritical sinners of eastern and western cities, to whom New Orleans is nothing less than the Sodom and Gomorrah" (p. 130, emphasis in original). The nation as a whole is clearly implicated in the "sin" Hiram sets out to punish: one allegorical scene shows the scurrilous Bald Eagle of America, whose "favorite flesh now is the flesh of black people," cackling with his "bride," the Nebraska Owl – a reference to the compromise of the Kansas–Nebraska Act – while the Louisiana Pelican weeps.

Reizenstein's later repudiation of the novel – he tried to suppress its publication in book form – suggests that it should be seen not as a well-thought exercise in abolitionist sentiment but a reflection of Whiggish anxieties about containing the contagion of social disorder inherent in slave societies, as the reference to Haiti indicates. Other German-language writers shared his attraction to the urban mysteries genre as an entertaining way to confront US racial taboos that were new to them, and to contrast European notions of class with American ones. According to Werner Sollors, the few surviving chapters of an anonymous *Mysteries of Philadelphia* in 1850 display such concerns, as does Emil Klauprecht's *Cincinnati, oder Geheimnisse des Westens*, published simultaneously with Reizenstein's in 1854–5. Klauprecht's massive novel, with its labyrinthine plot and hard-to-follow dialogues, is a less compelling read, but its vivid details of antebellum political debates and of the many national types to be found in the new cities of Ohio are fascinating. In *Cincinnati, or the Mysteries of the West*, New Orleans plays its traditional role as the site of slavery's worst distortions of human nature: there are cruel overseers, exotically seductive Creole women of all racial combinations, and martyred slaves. At the same time, however, free blacks gather in their own hotel to venerate their heroes: Toussaint, Douglass, Cinqué. Stock Indian characters appear, yet a politician is derided for his participation in the theft of land from and legalized massacre of the Cherokees.

In addition to his own immigrant experience, Klauprecht no doubt incorporated details about life in the western part of the nation gleaned from the bestselling works of "Charles Sealsfield" (Karl Postl), which appeared between the late 1820s and the early 1840s. These thinly fictionalized travel writings, later carried on by Friedrich Gerstäcker, were designed to titillate European interest in the adventurous possibilities of life in the New World. Several as yet untranslated novels render the German immigrant experience in less sensational ways than Reizenstein and Klauprecht. Otto Rupius's *Der Pedlar* (1857) and its sequel concern immigrants who try their luck first in New York and then in the Deep South, while Reinhold Solger's *Anton in Amerika* (1862) is a critical novel of manners set in money- and status-conscious New York. During and after the Civil War, Freidrich Strubburg wrote a series of novels about the evils of slavery; in the most popular of them, *Carl Scharnhorst* (1863), a white man befriends and eventually frees an African American boy.

The same year marked the publication of the one surviving tale of New Orleans educator and journalist Joanni Questy, a free person of color who wrote in French. In the remarkable "Monsieur Paul," the narrator befriends the title character on a dark night in New Orleans as they share cigars. When the narrator comes to call at his home, the nervous Monsieur Paul, who is white, observes with some shock that the narrator is a light-skinned Afro-Creole – a detail he hadn't noticed in the dark street. Rather than falling back on protocol and ejecting him, however, Paul brings forward his own wife – a mulatta who is passing for white because "the inflexible and tyrannical law of your country does not recognize the validity of my marriage." Driven half-mad by the burden of keeping such a secret, Paul is forced to duel with an Anglo-American who has challenged his wife's racial honor, and dies. The once-prosperous family ends tragically, while the narrator departs for the freer lands of Haiti and Mexico, taking Paul's domestic slave with him.

As Questy's tale suggests, the rest of the Americas – and in particular the Caribbean slave empire – appears in US fiction sometimes as a vivid counter-example to the social order in the South, and sometimes as its uncanny double. The revolutions in Saint-Domingue resonate not only in *Blake* and *Uncle Tom's Cabin*, but in novels produced in the rest of nineteenth-century Latin America, particularly Cuba and Brazil, with their delayed emancipations. *Sab*, Gertrudis Gómez de Avellaneda's 1841 novel about unrequited love between a mulatto slave and the white heiress who is his cousin, establishes race relations as the central theme in Cuban fiction despite being banned in that colony. Golden-haired and blue-eyed, Sab is out of place among his peers, yet his increasing consciousness of slavery as a moral evil leads him to organize a minor rebellion. His primary power, however, is sentimental: the purity of his devotion to Carlota earns him eternal fame among legions of female followers. The other pole star of the Cuban novel is Cirilo Villaverde's *Cecilia Valdés*, the first part of which appeared serially in 1839, to be completed and revised in 1879 and again in 1882. A multitiered social drama, it integrates the recent history of the Escalera slave revolt and brings in the real figure of the martyred poet Plácido; Villaverde's delayed revisions to the novel reflect his increasingly radical anti-slavery views. Cecilia, like Sab and like Plácido himself, is a tragic mulatta, whose inability to overcome the color lines that defy the heart's logic nonetheless inspires other characters to re-examine the bases of their own racial privilege.

The theme of mixed blood also characterizes Brazil's early novels, in which the questions of African slavery and Indian repression – the joint foundations of its national prosperity – are often intermingled. Joaquim Manuel de Macedo's *A moreninha* ("The little dark girl") of 1844 sentimentalizes the issue of color prejudice though a character of mixed black and Indian blood; later, Antonio Teixeira e Sousa (himself a mestizo) reimagined its plot in his bestselling *Maria ou a menina roubada* ("Maria, or the stolen girl"). But it is the Indianist novels of politician José de Alencar – *O Guarani* (1857) and *Iracema* (1865) – that stand as Brazil's "foundational fictions," to use Doris Sommer's famous phrase. Like *Xicoténcatl*, the serially published *O Guarani* sets its romance in the colonial period. White Portuguese nobles fall in love with Indian kings and passionate mestizas, establishing a historical grounding for a mixed-race nation experimenting with elements of both democratic and monarchical forms of government. In *Iracema* (an anagram of "America") the object of desire is an Indian princess, whose mixed-race son with her Portuguese husband is clearly meant to found a new nation, while the mother herself fades quietly away. Even when race lies veiled in Latin American novels, as it is in the crypto-Jewish body of the heroine of Jorge Isaacs' *Maria* (1867), the theme of divided families persists, solving imaginatively the political disunity that plagued many of the new republics throughout the century. In the Argentine José Mármol's romance *Amalia* (1851), for instance, the heroine's forbidden but inevitable love-match belongs to the opposing political party.

Canada, too, has its tradition of the reconciliation romance with characters that allegorize the major colonial powers: the English, the French, and the often well-organized indigenous populations they encountered. Prior to the unification of the Canadian territories in their current configuration in 1867, Anglophone and Franco-phone writers alike took as their main theme the mediation between the different cultural and religious legacies left by the rival European powers. The Québécois sense of being a defeated, subordinated people, particularly after the failure of French challenges to British authority in 1837–8, is comparable in some respects to that of the Spanish- and French-speakers who were incorporated into the United States, although Montréal sustained an independent print culture for much longer than New Orleans. Themes of racial integration and the historical destiny of the New World appear in Canadian fiction to the same extent as in the United States, and the genre of the historical novel likewise promised to do the ideological work of sorting out these complex alliances. Canadian writers imagined their "others" as Indian, French, or – in the case of John Richardson – Yankee. Richardson, the writer who most effectively capitalized on the events that split British North America in the late eighteenth century, had volunteered to fight with Tecumseh in the War of 1812 and helped raise the British flag over Fort Detroit. Captured by US forces and held as a prisoner of war in Kentucky, he later traveled to the West Indies and to Europe, where he was inspired by Cooper's success to write *WACOUSTA; or, The Prophecy: A Tale of the Canadas* (1832). With its broadly drawn Indian characters, both good and bad, it was widely pirated in the United States and adapted for the stage. Richardson followed up with a sequel, *The Canadian Brothers; or, The Prophecy Fulfilled*, in 1840, the year the Act of Union brought the French and English territories together for the first time, but found his fortunes as an author limited in Canada. Despite his loyalist sympa-thies, he then struck out for New York, where he wrote potboilers, lowbrow historical fictions, and biographies under contract before fading into obscurity in the 1850s. Given Richardson's expansive relationship to North America as a whole and his acute responsiveness to the fictional trends of the day, his work deserves to be treated more extensively and within the transnational framework his novels themselves convey.

Women novelists played at least as important a role in English Canada as they did in the United States, and even before Richardson, Julia Beckwith Hart anticipated his attempt at crossover success. Her first book, *St. Ursula's Convent, or, the Nun of Canada* (1824), a sensational tale set in Québec, was the first Canadian-authored novel to be published there, capitalizing on the dual fascination and repulsion of Anglo Protest-ants toward French Catholics. After relocating to upstate New York, however, Hart turned to the historical novel. *Tonnewonte; or, the Adopted Son of America* (1824–5) went through three editions and compares favorably to the tragic indigenous romances of Child and Sigourney. Another crossover success was Mary Early Fleming, a New Brunswegian who published numerous short stories and short novels in New York periodicals in the 1850s under the pseudonym of "Cousin Mary Carleton," capitaliz-ing on her knowledge of "exotic" French Canada. Women writers seemed particularly drawn toward Québec as a setting for romances of familial and national reconciliation: the outstanding example is Rosanna Mullins Leprohon, a native of Montréal. *Antoinette de Mirecourt; or, Secret Marrying and Secret Sorrowing. A Canadian Tale* (1864) explores social class as a function of language and religion. Although few Canadian novels in English were translated into French, Leprohon's were – a sign of her ability to pass fluidly over that cultural divide.

While many Anglo-Canadian writers had to seek publication venues in England and the United States, Francophone writers benefited from a well-established press culture in Montréal that was particularly vibrant during the 1840s and 1850s. A gothic portrait of Québécois superstitions appeared in 1837 under the title *L'influence d'un livre* by the young Philippe Aubert de Gaspé *fils*. (Curiously, Aubert de Gaspé's father would publish the definitive historical novel of French Canada, *Les anciens Canadiens*, in his old age in 1863.) Writers like Henri-Émile Chevalier earned popularity with racy tales of colonial adventure and interracial romance bearing titles like *La Huronne de Lorette* (1854), *L'Île de sable* (1854), the inevitable *Les Mystères de Montréal* (1855), and *La Fille des Indiens rouges* (1866), the last of which was set among the Inuit. Potboilers aside, however, French Canadian social novels tended toward the nostalgic. Following the model of Patrice Lacombe's *La Terre paternelle* (1846), the Québécois *roman paysan* developed an anti-modernist ideology, showing how a farm family comes near ruin by moving to the city; Pierre Chaveau's *Charles Guérin* (1853) was an even more popular example of the form. Both novels expressed the kinds of anxiety about rural displacement one finds in US local color fiction of the late nineteenth century, but stress the theme of ethno-religious embattlement as well. Rather than urging open rebellion against British political dominance, Québécois fiction takes solace in the nostalgia that was to be epitomized by *Les anciens Canadiens*, and in a kind of sacralization of French-language culture which would arguably become its own form of resistance.

Until recently, Canadian literary histories were divided into Francophone and Anglophone traditions, and little comparative work was undertaken. Neither this "separate spheres" approach nor the monolingual practice of US scholars does justice to the densely interwoven experiences of different language groups in the Americas who saw themselves as part of print communities that transcended national borders. With the uncovering of so many interesting texts in other languages, Americanists might now begin to imagine more ambitious ways of theorizing, for example, the racial politics of sentiment and the relationship between nation and narration. The very obscurity of many of these texts is proof that language difference, like other forms of difference, is also subject to power structures, in the form of institutions of remembering (and forgetting) the past of this country, this continent, this hemisphere; all mistakenly – but indelibly – called America.

REFERENCES AND FURTHER READING

Anon. (1999). *Xicoténcatl: An Anonymous Historical Novel about the Events Leading up to the Conquest of the Aztec Empire*, trans. Guillermo Castillo-Feliú. Austin: University of Texas Press. (First publ. 1826.)

Bruce, Clint (2003). "Les Feuilletons du *Courrier de la Louisiane*: les années Jérôme Bayon (1843–1849)" [The serial novels in the *Louisiana Courier*: The Jerome Bayon years (1843–1849)]. In *Bibliothèque Tintamarre: uvres louisianaises sur internet*. http://www.centenary.edu/french/courrier/index.html. Accessed 30 Aug. 2003.

Klauprecht, Emil (1996). *Cincinnati, or the Mysteries of the West*, trans. Steven Rowan. New York: Peter Lang. (First publ. 1854–5.)

Leal, Luis (1995). "Introducción." In Luis Leal and Rodolfo J. Cortina (eds.), *Jicoténcal*, vii–xlvii. Houston: Arte Público. (First publ. 1826.)

Questy, Joanni (1863). "Monsieur Paul." In *Bibliothèque Tintamarre: uvres louisianaises sur internet*. http://www.centenary.edu/french/textes/paul.html. Accessed 30 Aug. 2003.

Radway, Janice (1999). "What's in a Name?" Presidential Address to the American Studies Association, 20 Nov. 1998. *American Quarterly* 51: 1, 1–32.

Reizenstein, Ludwig von (2002). *The Mysteries of New Orleans*, trans. Steven Rowan. Baltimore: Johns Hopkins University Press. (First publ. 1854–5.)

Rowan, Steven (2002). "Introduction." In Ludwig von Reizenstein, *The Mysteries of New Orleans*, trans. Steven Rowan, xiii–xxxiii. Baltimore: Johns Hopkins University Press.

Séjour, Victor (1837). "Le Mulâtre/The Mulatto." In Marc Shell and Werner Sollors (eds.), *The Multilingual Anthology of American Literature*, 146–81. New York: New York University Press.

Shell, Marc (2002). "Babel in America." In Marc Shell (ed.), *American Babel: Literatures of the United States from Abnaki to Zuni*, 3–33. Cambridge, Mass.: Harvard University Press.

Sollors, Werner (2002). "Ferdinand Kürnberger's *Der Amerika-Müde* (1855): German-language Literature about the United States, and German-American Writing." In Marc Shell (ed.), *American Babel: Literatures of the United States from Abnaki to Zuni*, 117–32. Cambridge, Mass.: Harvard University Press.

Sommer, Doris (1991). *Foundational Fictions: The National Romances of Latin America*. Berkeley: University of California Press.

Spengemann, William (1989). *A Mirror for Americanists: Reflections on the Idea of American Literature*. Hanover, NH: University Press of New England.

PART II
Forms of Fiction

13

Literary Histories

Michael Drexler and Ed White

A familiar argument about early American fiction goes like this. A host of sociological factors conspired to make fiction-writing difficult or unlikely: an underdeveloped economy of subsistence and manufactory, limited leisure for writing and reading, poor production and distribution systems, neglect of bellelettristic culture, and various cultural prohibitions against fiction all resulted in the absence of the necessary infrastructure to support the development of fiction. Additionally, America was not culturally mature enough to produce serious fiction. Persistent parochialism and the late emergence of national culture, a tendency to ape European forms, crude privileging of pragmatic or didactic writing, and uncertainty about the New World content of fiction meant that what was produced was embarrassingly coarse. The earliest examples of fiction – the clumsy works of the 1790s – merely foreshadow the writing of quality that finally emerged in the 1830s.

Mercifully, the scholarship of recent decades has chipped away at these assumptions. The popularity of imported European novels, for instance, or the success of a work like Rowson's *Charlotte Temple*, suggest that claims about the missing American audience are exaggerated. More serious challenges have questioned the basic assumptions behind this dog-eared narrative. Might not the perceived crudeness of early American fiction reflect anachronistic esthetic standards inherited from the nineteenth-century novel?[1] And what if our very concept of "fiction" is too narrow? Various critics have suggested that works traditionally deemed nonfictional – Crèvecœur's *Letters from an American Farmer* or Dr. Alexander Hamilton's *History of the Tuesday Club* – must be read as innovative fictional experiments, inviting us to rethink the early trajectories of American letters.[2] Such arguments invite us to consider a less commonsensical definition of fiction that informed an earlier formal–generic criticism – the view that fiction is "any work of literary art in a radically continuous form, which almost always means a work of art in prose" (Frye 1957: 303). With this more expansive definition, we find fiction doing quite well before the 1790s. Travel narratives, provincial histories, ethnographies, captivity narratives, pamphlets, satires, conversion stories – the list speaks to an astounding proliferation of fiction in the last century of English colonization. That this *colonial* phase of American fiction largely remains invisible speaks to conceptual obstacles impeding a colonial literary history: pre-revolutionary writings are today still read as documentary auxiliaries to the history of settlement. Our concern in this essay, however, is with our subsequent understanding of antebellum fiction, and we begin with a few theses which suggest a productive revision of the old story.

Our starting point is that the dominant prose tradition of late colonial America amounted to a series of locally developed historiographic formulas. Ethnographies, captivity narratives, provincial histories, imperiographies: these were the constituents of early American fiction. Traditions of more imaginative, less obviously realist writing – what we would commonsensically call "fiction" – emerged from experimental adaptations of pre-existing colonial genres of historiography. These adaptations, partially pursued under the growing influence of European fiction in the narrow sense, were primarily attempts to address, even *solve*, historical problems inadequately treated by traditional genres. That is, early fictional innovators sought to develop historiographic conventions in more imaginative formats in order to better capture the confusing processes of New World development. The American "failures" to duplicate British and continental European forms were less second-rate knock-offs than attempts to develop properly New World imaginative genres. If these peripheral innovations did not "succeed" by establishing counter-traditions or influencing the European core, this is less a sign of American esthetic inferiority and more a matter of the hegemony of European conventions. Consequently, the very idea of an early American literary history has a double resonance, for early national "fiction" is commonly "literary history": an attempt to extend or develop history in an imaginative fashion. At the same time, any literary history must explore the synergy between "history" and "literature," fictional currents that were hardly discrete in the eighteenth century. An appreciation of this relationship should allow us to engage with a critical tradition (best exemplified by Lukács) of tracing the formation of imaginative fiction via the historiographic imaginary. While the following pages do not give a complete picture of this literary-historical dynamic, we hope to illuminate some examples of that interplay while sketching the outlines of what a better history of early American fiction might look like.

We might usefully begin with the career of Charles Brockden Brown, a writer exceptional for the volume of his output (more than 5,000 pages), its generic scope, and its self-reflexive interest in literary and historiographic modes. Over nineteen years, from 1792 to 1811, he wrote six novels, numerous serialized columns and short narratives, poems, literary reviews and essays, historical narratives, political commentary, biographies, and translations. Until recently, Brown's reputation rested solely on appraisal of his novels, primarily those written in the creative burst of 1798–1801, though even critical reception of these has been mixed. Traditionally, these novels are viewed as intriguing failures to adapt the Godwinian mode to New World concerns. But after producing his quartet of *Wieland, Arthur Mervyn, Ormond,* and *Edgar Huntly,*

Brown abandoned the novel form in favor of editorial and historiographic tasks. This rejection of the novel has long registered as a retrenchment from generic innovation, evidence of Brown's esthetic immaturity, and a marker of his political conservatism (see Watts 1994; Christopherson 1993). Accordingly, his 1807 assessment of novels, whose readers would "often be deluded by estimates of human life and happiness that are calculated upon false foundations," seems to reveal a moralizing retreat from fiction and an abandonment of those "wild narratives of the imagination" pursued in his younger days (Brown 1807a).

But we might view this career differently. Rather than rejecting the fad for novels, Brown found the utility of the European-dominated form to be exhausted, inadequate to the conceptual problems of contemporary life more effectively treated in other historiographic modes. Rather than making a conservative retreat from the novel, Brown pursued a progressive elaboration of a narrative theory, already evident in his earliest prose, in the link between history and fiction. Originally, the attraction of novels resided not too far from the draw of historical narrative: both, he maintained, offered compensation for the "tameness and insipidity of common life and common events" (Brown 1807a: 410). The proximate appeal of the novel and history-writing warranted a synthesis that Brown appreciated in the "fictitious biographies" of Richardson and Fielding (see Brown 1804); the desired synthesis of the life-events of marginal, unremarkable personages with the grand sweep of historical movements obviously prefigured the work of Walter Scott as well. But whereas the novel tended to feed imaginative fancy with the repetitions of stock tropes – the "terrific" or the "romance" – a deeper, more valued variety lay in historical accounts which, if not factually verifiable, were at least tested by the limits of probability. It is critical to recognize that the difference between historiography and the novel was *not* the difference between fact and fiction. Brown continued to spin fictitious narratives; however, released from the expectations of the conventional novel form, he was free to broaden the reach of fictional experimentation by dressing his narratives in the garb of the discovered letter, the secret history, or the annals of the undiscovered country.[3] If Defoe, Behn, and others had earlier spun fictional narratives out of similar cloth, claiming that their narratives had a basis in fact in order to win public interest in an emergent genre, Brown effectively returned to these pre-novelistic historiographic modes to revitalize what he saw as a predictable and consolidated narrative form at the century's end.

History surpassed the novel in its possibilities, and, having departed from the novel form, Brown devoted himself to refining the presentation of historical narrative while chronicling the differentiation of historiographic modes. This project had the added benefit of offering a vigorous defense of the value of New World writing. His last publishing venture, *The American Register, or General Repository of History, Politics, and Science*, testifies to Brown's attempt to make American writing more visible to the broader community of English readers, while theorizing its world position as well. In a comparative essay entitled "A Sketch of American Literature for 1807," for instance, Brown published lists of US writing under distinct generic "departments," including history, politics, military books, law, poetry and drama, and theology to parallel British publications. American productions in these areas were distinct from their British counterparts. Yet in writing about fiction he provided no "department" for the American novel, while British novels were called "*home*" productions (Brown 1807b, c). And even these made up only a fraction of novels consumed by English-language readers, most having been "naturalized" from French and German authors. The implications were clear: national distinctions were insignificant to the novel form, with Anglo-American productions a small and dominated subset of continental European fiction. In world production, the peripheral US novel could not hold its own as an innovative genre. Further, foreshadowing Franco Moretti's recent theorization of world literature (Moretti 2000, 2003a, b), Brown implied that original development could thrive only in the less dominated historiographic genres. Novels were cosmopolitan, in a negative sense: the US novel was feeble because of the novel's international success. The peripheral society needed the peripheral genres in which "history" could out-imagine the novel.

The career of "Connecticut Wit" David Humphreys offers another case of an apparent paradigmatic opponent of "fiction." This staunch Federalist devoted his literary career to the production of Augustan verse, patriotic biography, and anti-Jacobin satire. Not only did he never venture into what we normally call "fiction," he presented familiar arguments against "the reveries and fictions which have been substituted by hacknied writers in the place of historical facts": repeatedly exposed to "[t]he lie," the fiction reader would eventually "run into the opposite extreme, and give up all confidence in the annals of ancient as well as modern times" (Humphreys 2000: 6–7). Yet this picture is complicated by a survey of his *Essay on the Life of the Honourable Major-General Israel Putnam*, which Humphreys trumpeted as "the first effort in Biography that has been made on this continent" (p. 2). What is fascinating about this work is the sharp stylistic and generic divide between its two halves, examination of which reveals some of the challenges in the literary-historical enterprise.

The work's first half, treating Putnam's background and experiences in the Seven Years War, offers an assemblage of colonial genres: a gothic tale of a wolf hunt in a cavern of "horror" (Humphreys 2000: 14–17); tales of military heroism (pp. 23–30); a captivity tale (pp. 42–8); the story of an attempted seduction of a captive Anglo-American woman by a French officer (pp. 48–53); and a Plutarchan sketch of Putnam, Cincinnatus-like, leaving his plow (p. 67). Clearly Humphreys could not present the subjectivity of his protagonist without recourse to the most popular fictional conventions. Yet the second half, uneasy with colonial genres, takes a drastically different approach, becoming a pastiche of revolutionary documents: a congressional declaration (p. 76); Washington's orders to Putnam (pp. 77–9); a prohibitionary decree (p. 80); various public orders (pp. 81, 95–6, 99); a military address (p. 121); and military correspondence (pp. 105, 106–7, 108, 113, 118–19, 124–6). Interspersed with these are a description of a painting of Bunker Hill (p. 73), excerpts from Barlow's "Vision of Columbus" (p. 73–4), and, in a footnote, a 22-stanza satire by

Francis Hopkinson (pp. 83–7); and the work concludes with Washington's laudatory 1783 letter to Humphreys at the close of the war (pp. 124–6). The stylistic shift allows us to trace some of the tensions shaping American fiction. For the early Putnam is a character of the imperial periphery and thus of literary innovation: his primary conflicts are with beasts, cowards, Indians, and rakes; his principal settings the howling wilderness, the pastoral farm, or the French city of sin (Québec); and he thrives as a walking almanac of a "rural philosopher" (p. 18). But the Putnam of the second half represents the new center of power as he becomes a military and social leader. Consequently he can no longer be the character-in-formation displaying rebellion and independence. In literary terms, the narrative suggests that colonial genres reach a definitive terminus, the Revolution, after which authors aspiring to world status must deploy less parochial forms like the command, the decree, the manifesto, the encomium, or the tableau – all "centripetal" forms, in Bakhtin's terms. It is revealing that Humphreys tucks Hopkinson's satire into a footnote – a visible symptom of generic repression.

In a sense, then, Humphreys' biography illustrates some of the implications of Brown's analysis, despite his apparent distance from that author. Like Brown, Humphreys sought the innovative blend of imaginative colonial genres in a fictional mode distinct from the European novel. The "essay" of his title was no austere marker of nonfiction but rather an insistence on the imaginative project of fiction. And if Humphreys was clearly capable of crafting an adventure story along the lines of the historical novels of the 1820s, he insisted instead on pursuing a different direction, away from the hegemonic European forms. Such a turn was less failure than refusal, an attempt to make central the transition to the hierarchic republican forms thriving on the world periphery. He sought a cumulative form of fiction that might indulgently take readers from a remembrance of things colonial to the mature subjectivity of republican meritocracy, in each case remaining true to New World genres. The *Essay* thus offered "literary history" in both the aforementioned senses: a combination of imaginative and historiographic modes, presented in a historical *précis* of American genres.

The literary-historical hybrids of American fiction were grounded in a sometimes implicit, often explicit self-theorization of America's marginal position in "world" fictional production, for which a commitment to historiographic adaptation was an essential counter-response. But how did this global sphere affect the fictional adaptations of historiography? We can again approach this question with reference to Brown, whose first major novel, *Wieland*, offers an interesting engagement with *local* history. Its immediate inspiration was Robert Proud's *History of Pennsylvania*, one of a slew of post-revolutionary provincial histories. Focusing on the colonial era, Proud insisted that the 1750s marked "the golden days of *Pennsylvania*" before the lapse of the Paxton Riots of 1763–4 (Proud 1797: 7). At that moment, "certain most furious zealots" aroused a band of "*armed demi-savages*" to commit "the most horrible *massacre*" of local Indians (p. 326). The resulting "spirit of faction…infected the minds of many," proving a "sorrowful presage of the approaching change" of the

Revolution (pp. 329–30). Proud's Tory account of colonial "madness," "enthusiasm," and massacre would serve as the kernel for *Wieland*, a novel carefully set in the time and countryside of the Paxton Riots. Brown hints at his approach in a 1799 assessment of Proud, praised as "the humble, honest, and industrious compiler" for carefully preparing the building materials "in the order in which they will be successively required by the builder" (Brown 1992: 26). Here the proper building blocks are the constituent regions and populations of Pennsylvania, the decisive episode the Paxtoneers' rural insurrection. For the uprising was no arcane detail of Pennsylvania's past, but a case study of a worldwide phenomenon – the rural uprising – evident not only in post-revolutionary America (in the Shays, Whiskey, and Wyoming conflicts) but also in Haiti, Ireland, and France. Consequently, the tendency to read early American fiction as a series of national allegories risks eliding the historiographic method linking local inspiration to global analysis. Like Proud, Brown used the provincial historians' building blocks, reworked in imaginative form, to explore the dynamics of seemingly incomprehensible rural insurgencies.

A similar route was taken in Tabitha Tenney's *Female Quixotism*, a novel whose Pennsylvania countryside setting and political–sentimental discourse displays a profound concern with the recent Fries Rebellion, the details of which were circulated in the documentary collection *The Two Trials of John Fries*. Dorcasina Sheldon's final renunciation of her sentimental fervor strongly echoes Fries's plea for mercy. "I have passed my life in a dream, or rather a delirium," she writes, much as Fries confessed to President Adams that he "is one of those deluded and unfortunate men … [who] solicits the interference of the President to save him from an ignominious death, and to rescue a large, and hitherto happy family, from future misery and ruin" (Tenney 1992: 320–3; Anon. 1800: 130, 135). Like Brown, Tenney started not with a national allegory but with a local Pennsylvanian insurrection before moving on to what she viewed as the transnational cultural dynamics of Jacobin sentimental violence. The contrast with the novel's British counterpart, Charlotte Lennox's *The Female Quixote*, is telling, for rather than address the quixotic individual she examined the "ism" expressed most recently in France and Haiti. While this imaginative circuit from local history to an eighteenth-century world-systems theory highlights the tremendous significance of insurrectionary movements for the period's literature, its literary-historical implications are more far-reaching. For to deplore the limited character development of these works is to miss the point. *Wieland* and *Female Quixotism*, like many other fictions of the time, were concerned less with individual character depth than with the dynamics of insurgency in particular geopolitical *settings*. Consequently each novel attempted a historical analysis or problem-solving that contemporary US readers would have connected with political upheavals of the time. In short, these novels were conceived as historiographic projects elaborating affiliated forms of historical prose (the provincial history, the trial record) rather than following the established conventions of British prose.

A slightly different synergy is evident in the work of Hugh Henry Brackenridge, whose famously expanding *Modern Chivalry* is frequently criticized for weak character development and plot cohesion. We might approach *Modern Chivalry* through Brackenridge's fictional project of the 1790s, *Incidents of the Insurrection*, a work ostensibly justifying his involvement in the Whiskey Rebellion. What is striking about *Incidents* is its numerous parallels to the later historical novel tradition: a "mediocre" protagonist who is the "hub" around whom events flow; the search for a "middle way" or "neutral ground" within a conflict; depiction of this middle way as a crucial "cultural development"; characterization following "historical–social types"; a "retrogressive" plot driven by the constant overcoming of impediments; major historical figures appearing tangentially, but humanized rather than heroized; emphasis upon the interaction "between 'above' and 'below'"; compression and intensification of events; and the geopolitically marginal context (Lukács 1983). Here Brackenridge mapped the conflict between democratic backcountry yeomen and republican littoral elites, presenting himself as the seeker of the middle way; he chronicles the ebbs and flows of the uprising, complete with humanizing cameos by Hamilton and Washington in a spectacular meeting of "above" and "below." In short, Brackenridge wrote something very similar to a Walter Scott novel, but *twenty years earlier*; and we should certainly read *Incidents* as one of the innovative fictions of the period.

Twenty years later, Brackenridge insisted, in *Modern Chivalry*, that *Incidents* was less an account of an isolated event than "a picture of a people broke loose from the restraints of government, and going *further than they had intended to go*"; and he wished his book back in print to speak to the secession movements of the 1810s (Brackenridge 1962: 765–6, emphasis in original). The comments suggest continuities between *Incidents* and *Modern Chivalry* that are at first hard to track: the latter has no continuous plot tracing a definitive conflict. Nonetheless, in its smaller episodes it characteristically traces conflicts between political and cultural extremes, high and low cultures, the search for a middle ground, repeated impediments, and actual historical personages mingling with stock character types. So what was the historiographic model for the work? In his *Law Miscellanies* (1814) Brackenridge declared his ambition to draft a "Pennsylvania Blackstone," a detailed legal commentary on juridical issues, and we might usefully read *Modern Chivalry* as a "comic Blackstone," mapping a vernacular common law of ideological impulses and reactions that lay the cultural foundations for formal legal-political decisions. In this light, the oddity of *Modern Chivalry* – its constant serial expansion from 1792 to 1815, and the resulting stylistic "inconsistencies" – is far from a literary flaw: it is instead a historiographic achievement mapping the ideologemes of everyday adjudication. With the legal history as model, *Modern Chivalry* snaps the confines of the bourgeois novel to offer an imaginative anatomy of cultural interpretation in the early republic.

One further illustration from Brown's career suggests further experimental routes open to early American writers. Having abandoned the framework of the European novel, Brown devoted much of the next decade to grand-scale experimentation with macro-historical traditions in a series of historical sketches. One segment, published in Dunlap's biography of Brown as "Sketches of the History of the Carrils and Ormes," covers centuries tangentially unified by the history of several elite families.[4]

Brown's focus, though, is the major structural determinants of culture, from "the management of agriculture to the logic and effects of political, military, artistic, and ecclesiastical culture" (Barnard forthcoming). It is as if Brown sought to write a grand global fiction in which "events" span decades and "society" is the major character, whose qualities include architecture and music. The sketches are striking illustrations of the historiographic–literary synergy, betraying the influence of Machiavelli's historical method. Brown's own "machivelliads" drew on republican institutional analyses to produce counterfactual historical fictions comparable to *The Florentine Histories*, though explicitly imaginative. The neglect of these works has left an unfortunate gap in our literary history, not least for our appreciation of a transnational macro-historical track in early American fiction.

The United States' theorization of its position in world literature, the fictional experimentation with colonial genres, the innovations with local or macro-histories – all suggest an expanded account of American literary development with which we might not only move beyond conventional censures of the so-called first novels of the 1790s but also complicate our picture of canonical successes. Take the career of Washington Irving, for example, extending from the Jonathan Oldstyle letters of 1802 to the biographies of Mohammed and Washington in the 1850s. His career, apparently focused on the two tracks of "sketches" (*Salmagundi, The Sketch-book of Geoffrey Crayon, Bracebridge Hall, The Alhambra*) and "histories" (*Knickerbocker's History of New York, The Life and Voyages of Columbus, The Conquest of Granada, Adventures of Captain Bonneville*), further illustrates the early republican failure to produce a true novel, famously attributed to Irving's inability to escape European influences. Yet we would suggest that the parodic *History of New York*, the satirically narrated *Conquest of Granada*, and even the various sketch-books taken as fictional unities, signal a refusal to accept the novel's recognized conventions, and continued attempts to develop innovative fictional–historical hybrids, whether in the sketches' episodic engagement with local history or the experimental reworkings of discovery and colonization. Clearly our canonical literary history can gain much from a thoughtful reconsideration of earlier innovations and resistances.

We want to conclude with some brief speculations about Atlantic fiction, explored in recent years primarily to stress the continuities between British and US writing. Yet while colonial and post-revolutionary American writers clearly perceived the hegemony of European letters, the project of historiographic experimentation prompted spatial and temporal connections to the broader Atlantic basin, which should be examined with greater specificity. For instance, the North African Barbary coast – "Algeria" in American parlance – became a literary focal point following the capture, enslavement, and ransom of American sailors in the region. Within the sphere of global mercantile enterprise and the circumatlantic slave trade, Algerine captivity literature reinvigorated the old colonial formula of the Indian captivity narrative while offering a bridge to the new republican critiques of African chattel slavery. The result was a partial equation of the marginal United States with the North African Atlantic rim, and a literature exploring the servitude of the periphery.

One of the first works to respond to this global–cultural mapping was Franklin's innovative "Sidi Mehemet Ibrahim" of 1790, a fictionalized political pamphlet imagining republican anti-slavery arguments within the breakaway "Erika" sect. Such stylistic experiments would become popular and take a prominent position in US writing, in works like Mathew Carey's *A Short Account of Algiers* (1794) and John Stevens' *An Historical and Geographical Account of Algiers* (1797). More significant, perhaps, were the innovations of Royall Tyler and Susannah Rowson, prominent figures in the emergence of a US literary culture. Each had initially written popular works – "The Contrast" and *Charlotte Temple* respectively – inspired by the revolutionary contrast between the new republic and its former Atlantic metropole. And each quite naturally turned to the Algerian sphere, Rowson writing "Slaves in Algiers" (1794) and Tyler *The Algerine Captive* (1797). Like Franklin's piece, these works crafted ironic parallel histories to explore problematic republican issues resurfacing around the Atlantic rim. Rowson's work proved particularly innovative, drawing on the harem as a metaphor for marital and sexual inequality in Anglo-American society to envision a geopolitical historiography of domesticity. This "Algerian" movement thus combined the most innovative features of US fictional experimentation: a melding of historiographic, colonial, and European styles and forms, and a vernacular theorization of global (or at least "Atlantic") culture from a peripheral perspective.

The challenge for contemporary literary history, then, is to resist the assessment of American fiction in the cramped, anachronistic framework of national fiction. Rather than seeking the most European of American novels as the pinnacle of fictional achievement, we might consider an alternative literary history in which a work like Leonora Sansay's *Secret History; or, the Horrors of St. Domingo* takes center stage. In his 1808 survey of American publications, Charles Brockden Brown catalogued this work in the department of "history" – a sign of his appreciation as much as it is a marker for today's critical bafflement. For Sansay's work defies conventional generic expectations in fascinating ways. Written as a series of letters from a lady of Philadelphia to the infamous conspirator Aaron Burr, Sansay's text offered a hybrid of personal writing, sentimental narrative, historical explanation, and ethnographic survey; the epistolary form allowed for the vertical integration of a variety of historiographic modes to relate a complex account of revolutionary violence, European tyranny, and nascent anti-colonial movements across the Caribbean from Haiti and Cuba to Jamaica and Philadelphia. The result was a stunning sentimental tour of the cataclysmic final stages of the Haitian Revolution, in one of the most innovative and trans-American works of early republican America. Brown's classification suggests that, without dismissing the marital plot as excuse or device, he found in the *Secret History* a valuable contribution to a distinctive New World tradition of historical fiction. We could do worse than to follow Brown's project of a new conceptualization of early American fiction. Attuned to the Atlantic battle over literary forms, and resistant to *ex post facto* generic conventions, we might find early American fiction an innovative guide to cultural mapping rather than a collection of crude New World knock-offs.

NOTES

1 An excellent example of such an argument is the discussion of *Arthur Mervyn* in Warner 1990: 151–76.
2 On Crèvecœur's *Letters* as a *"bildungsroman* of sorts,"* see Rice 1993; on Hamilton's *History* as a "comic novel" influenced by the anatomy, see Micklus 1990.

3 See, for example, his pamphlet *An Address to the Government of the United States . . .* (Brown 1803), which uses the ruse of a discovered letter to present a historical analysis of the state of the territories beyond the Mississippi.
4 For an introduction, see the excellent overview offered by Barnard 2004.

REFERENCES

Anon. (1800). *The Two Trials of John Fries, on an Indictment for Treason; Together with a Brief Report of the Trials of Several Other Persons, for Treason and Insurrection . . .* Philadelphia: William W. Woodward.

Barnard, Philip (2004). "Culture and Authority in *The Historical Sketches.*" In Philip Barnard, Mark L. Kamrath, and Stephen Shapiro (eds.), *Revising Charles Brockden Brown: Culture, Politics, and Sexuality in the Early Republic,* 310–31. Knoxville: University of Tennessee Press.

Brackenridge, Hugh Henry (1962). *Modern Chivalry,* ed. Claude M. Newlin. New York: Hafner. (First publ. 1792–1815.)

Brown, Charles Brockden (1803). *An Address to the Government of the United States, on the Cession of Louisiana to the French: And on the Late Breach of Treaty by the Spaniards; Including the Translation of a Memorial, on the War of St. Domingo, and Cession of the Mississippi to France, Drawn up by a French Counsellor of State.* Philadelphia: John Conrad & Co.

Brown, Charles Brockden (1804). "For the Literary Magazine. Fielding and Richardson." *Literary Magazine* 2: 15 (Dec.), 657–9.

Brown, Charles Brockden (1807a). "For the Literary Magazine. On the Cause of the Popularity of Novels." *Literary Magazine* 7: 45 (June), 410–12.

Brown, Charles Brockden (1807b). "General Catalogue and View of British Publications for the Year 1806." *American Register; or the General Repository of History, Politics and Science,* vol. 1, 173–86.

Brown, Charles Brockden (1807c). "A Sketch of American Literature for 1807." *American Register; or the General Repository of History, Politics and Science,* vol. 1, 149–62.

Brown, Charles Brockden (1992). *Literary Essays and Reviews,* ed. Alfred Weber and Wolfgang Schäfer. New York: Peter Lang.

Christophersen, Bill (1993). *The Apparition in the Glass: Charles Brockden Brown's American Gothic.* Athens, Ga.: University of Georgia Press.

Frye, Northrop (1957). *Anatomy of Criticism: Four Essays.* Princeton: Princeton University Press.

Humphreys, David (2000). *An Essay on the Life of the Honourable Major-General Israel Putnam: Addressed to the State Society of the Cincinnati in Connecticut and Published by their Order,* ed. William C. Dowling. Indianapolis: Liberty Fund.

Lukács, Georg (1983). *The Historical Novel,* trans. Hannah Mitchell and Stanley Mitchell. Lincoln: University of Nebraska Press. (First publ. 1937.)

Micklus, Robert (1990). "Introduction." In Robert Micklus (ed.), *The History of the Ancient and Honorable Tuesday Club,* vol. 1, xv–xxxiv. Chapel Hill: University of North Carolina Press.

Moretti, Franco (2000). "Conjectures on World Literature." *New Left Review,* 2nd ser., 1, 54–68.

Moretti, Franco (2003a). "More Conjectures." *New Left Review,* 2nd ser., 20, 73–81.

Moretti, Franco (2003b). "Graphs, Maps, Trees." *New Left Review,* 2nd ser., 24, 67–93.

Proud, Robert (1797). *The History of Pennsylvania, in North America, from the Original Institution and*

Settlement of That Province, under the First Proprietor and Governor William Penn, in 1681, Till after the Year 1742..., 2 vols., vol. 1. Philadelphia: Zachariah Poulson, Jr.

Rice, Grantland S. (1993). "Crèvecœur and the Politics of Authorship in Republican America." *Early American Literature* 28: 2, 91–119.

Sansay, Leonora (1808). *Secret History; or, the Horrors of St. Domingo, in a Series of Letters, Written by a Lady at Cape Francois, to Colonel Aaron Burr*. Philadelphia: Bradford & Inskeep.

Tenney, Tabitha Gilman (1992). *Female Quixotism: Exhibited in the Romantic Opinions and Extravagant Adventures of Dorcasina Sheldon*, ed. Jean Nienkamp and Andrea Collins. New York: Oxford University Press. (First publ. 1801.)

Warner, Michael (1990). *The Letters of the Republic: Publication and the Public Sphere in Eighteenth-Century America*. Cambridge, Mass.: Harvard University Press.

Watts, Steven (1994). *The Romance of Real Life: Charles Brockden Brown and the Origins of American Culture*. Baltimore: Johns Hopkins University Press.

14

Breeding and Reading: Chesterfieldian Civility in the Early Republic

Christopher Lukasik

Civility appears as an integral, yet complicated feature of the political and social transformations of the pre- and post-revolutionary periods in America. On the one hand, the discourse of politeness – with its structure of genteel deference, its historical association with the corrupt courts of Europe, and its emphasis on a politics of deceit and individual manipulation – has been identified as antithetical to the disinterestedness and egalitarianism of civic republicanism (Wood 1991; Warner 1990). On the other, civility's culture of performance – its textually and visually reproducible codes of conduct, and its ties to commercial self-interest – has been read as instrumental to the role-playing bourgeois self of post-revolutionary economic liberalism. Civility's anti-republican values of sociability, formality, and exclusivity survived the Revolution's more radical impulses by retreating into private society (Shields 1997), where their eventual diffusion as "vernacular gentility" (Bushman 1992) aided the formation of middle-class identity in antebellum America (Halttunen 1982).

Perhaps no text was more responsible for the downward distribution of civility in post-revolutionary America than Lord Chesterfield's *Letters* to his son (1774; Stanhope 1932). When the various authorized and unauthorized editions, adaptations, and abridgments are counted, the *Letters* went through no fewer than thirty editions in America between 1775 and 1800 (Gulick 1979), prompting Richard Bushman to appoint Chesterfield as "the foremost teacher of fine manners in the eighteenth century" (1992: 30) and Karen Halttunen to pronounce the *Letters* "the most important influence on nineteenth-century American etiquette" (1982: 94). In what follows, the discourse surrounding Chesterfield's *Letters* in post-revolutionary America appears as a key element in the survival of genteel social distinction. The initial cultural response to Chesterfield – particularly the specific reference to Chesterfield in the literary depiction of the seducer – may have helped civility reimagine and retain its pre-revolutionary function in structuring social relations in two ways. First, the visibility of social distinction is relocated away from the genteel performances of the body and on to the permanent and unalterable features of the face; and second, civility's anti-republicanism becomes associated with immorality, dissimulation, and self-interest (especially rapid social and political mobility) rather than exclusivity.

Although the democratization of genteel culture propelled by Chesterfield's *Letters* undoubtedly threatened the exclusivity of polite society, it was Chesterfield's immorality – especially his equation of social power with the capacity to dissimulate one's permanent character – that critics targeted for censure. "Politeness... like lord Chesterfield's," the Reverend John Bennett explained to the 1792 readers of *American Museum*, was entirely "made up of dissimulation" (1792a: 139).[1] Bennett wished that "the memory of his immoral graces, and his refined dissimulation" would "sleep for ever with him in his grave" (1792b: 5). Likewise, John Burton warned American readers in 1794 that Chesterfield's two "grand maxims are – to conceal his own opinions, but artfully to discover those of the persons with whom he should have any concerns – and to disguise his own temper, but, by exciting the passions of others ...profit by their imprudence" (Burton 1794: 259). According to Burton, Chesterfield's *Letters* did little more than endorse "the practice of dissimulation for the purpose of promoting his worldly interest" (p. 258). His immoral "creed" of "hypocrisy, fornication, and adultery," the 1786 *New Haven Gazette and Connecticut Magazine* protested, enlisted "the graces of civility" in the pursuit of self-interest (Anon. 1786: 327). If gentility had been characterized formerly by pleasing others, now it was in danger of being epitomized by pleasing oneself. Whether those personal pleasures were defined in terms of political, commercial, or sexual interests, Chesterfield's model of genteel conduct opposed the republican ideal of civic virtue based upon disinterest (Lewis 1987: 690).

As members of the post-revolutionary elite such as Mercy Otis Warren lambasted Chesterfield's promotion of genteel dissimulation in the American press, others, such as an anonymous author from Easton, Maryland, urged the public to consider the effects Chesterfield might have on those who lacked the moral character necessary to discern "that under a theory of politeness would be introduced a system at professed variance with our morality" (Anon. 1791: 89). The author nervously predicted to his readership that "The arts of printers will disseminate the work in places where its test, public opinion, cannot accompany it – it may be read in the country; and if there are colonies at a distance, where the vibrations and operations of public opinion can be but feebly felt, such a book will there find admission, and, if as artful as these letters, may be relished" (p. 90). As both people and print exceeded the reach of existing institutional sources of moral authority – such as family, school, and church – the spread of Chesterfieldianism exacerbated concerns about uninstructed reading practice.

The widespread adoption of Chesterfield, our anonymous author from Easton concluded, should also remind people "to guard against deception," for "the same people who could be polite" might also be, at the same time, indecorous and dishonest (Anon. 1791: 91). Indeed, those who hid behind the mask of genteel dissimulation,

John Burton observed, often "assume a deportment, contrary to their station; and step out of their own sphere in order to act a part for which they are not qualified, by genius, education, or fortune" (1794: 256). "They, who behave in a manner unbecoming their situation, and assume a part in the great drama of life, not adapted to their abilities or station," Burton reasoned, "must unavoidably incur the censure of affectation" (p. 266). With the demise of legally enforced sumptuary distinction, the rise in material wealth among the middling classes, increased immigration from Europe, and the rapid growth of a print culture that made the codes for gentility more broadly accessible, the distinction between elite and non-elite was deteriorating in 1790s America. As one historian recently put it, "By the end of the eighteenth century, fears about dissimulation suffused American culture" (Bullock 1998: 254). It seemed as if any man, even the most vulgar and immoral, could pass himself off as a gentleman so long as he had a little wit and learning, a fashionable appearance, and a well-rehearsed genteel persona (Shields 1997: 276). If supporters reasoned that the publication of Chesterfield's *Letters* promised a republic of refined gentlemen, critics responded by claiming that Chesterfieldianism was threatening to deliver a nation of duplicitous rakes, seducers, and rogues.

The spread of Chesterfieldianism also further underscored the necessity and value of discerning the character of men and women in public (especially if they were to be considered as potential sexual or commercial partners), and reading books was considered vital to one's success in this endeavor. Reading men and reading books were understood as equivalent practices at the end of the eighteenth century. "To know mankind well," as Chesterfield himself remarked, "requires . . . as much attention and application as to know books, and, it may be, more sagacity and discernment" (Stanhope 1932: vol. 3, 779). Such discernment was especially crucial for young women, whose education emphasized "the associative link between deciphering human and literary characters" (Barnes 1997: 59). Erasmus Darwin, for example, urged governesses to select novels carefully so that their pupils could see "human nature in all the classes of life . . . as it really exists" (1798: 49). Although reading novels could never replace life experience, reading the wrong ones could confound it.

As Darwin's remarks suggest, the only reading considered more dangerous than Chesterfield's *Letters* in early America was novel-reading. If the *Letters* were criticized for producing a nation of immoral, dissembling, self-interested, and upwardly mobile young men, then novels, particularly European romances, were condemned for preparing their readers to be seduced and impoverished by such men.[2] *The Juvenile Mirror and Teacher's Manual* (1812) of New York, for example, claimed that novels "are unhappily calculated to seduce the unsettled minds of young persons" and to "encourage false views of life" (p. 69). "The most profligate villain that was bent on the infernal purpose of seducing a woman," Concord's *New Star* lamented, "could not wish a symptom more favorable to his purpose, than an imagination inflamed with the rhapsodies of novels" (Anon. 1797: 3). In 1801 Nathan Fiske placed novels in the same subversive class of books as Chesterfield's *Letters*, complaining that

Chesterfield, with all his nobility, with all his brilliant powers, and all his external graces, betrays an ignoble mind, and an impure heart. There are herds of novelists whose representations of life and manners tend to mislead the unwary youth of both sexes. The writings of these, and many other authors, are too well calculated to add new encouragements [*sic*] to licentiousness, and new difficulties to virtue. (Fiske 1801: 153)

Most novels, according to their opponents, took advantage of the undiscerning or inattentive reader by offering a "misrepresentation of human character and human life" (Anon. 1804: 332), or, worse yet, by depicting "characters which never existed and never can exist" (Anon. 1792: 225). As a result, these novels were understood as encouraging their readers "to cherish expectations that can never be realized, and to form notions of each other, which painful experience will every day refute" ([Cento] 1805: 8). "By the magic wand of the genius of romance," one author remarked, "the daughter of a cottager is exalted into a countess, and the labourer at the anvil and the mine soon graces the court and the drawing room" ([Cento] 1805: 8). As the above example demonstrates, romance novels were castigated in particular because they were thought to offend, just as Chesterfield did, in disturbing "the distinctions of rank" ([Cento] 1805: 8).

Besides misrepresenting the actual community by disregarding the limitations of rank in their fictionalized one, romance novels were also denounced for debilitating the minds of their readers. Reading romance novels, the theory went, enfeebled the mind, making it more likely to accept the imaginative projection of a person's character rather than the more "rational" assessment offered by one's community or family. Such romantic fiction, wrote one critic in 1792, "naturally prepares the mind for the admittance of vicious ideas," especially when "the warm representation painted in the novel" is "read in the privacy of retirement" (Anon. 1792: 225).[3] Thus, the negative effects of reading romance novels were twofold: they distributed false images of people within a fictional community; and, in doing so, they weakened the reader's mind, rendering it more likely to receive such false views as true in his or her subsequent experiences in the actual one. The effects were imagined to be so severe that "A young person habitually and indiscriminately devoted to novels," as the Reverend Samuel Miller remarked, "is in a fair way to dissipate his mind, to degrade his taste, and to bring on himself intellectual and moral ruin" (1803: 179).

The idea that reading romance novels could adversely affect the imaginations of their readers, making them vulnerable to the same type of deception that dissembling seducers practiced, however, was not restricted to the minds of ministers; it also filled the pages of early American novelists. Hannah Foster's didactic novel *The Boarding School* (1798), for instance, regrets how the "romantic pictures" of novels "fill the imagination with ideas,... pervert the judgment, mislead the affections, and blind the understanding" (Foster 1798: 18). Such symptoms plague the mind of Dorcas Sheldon in Tabitha Tenney's anti-romance-novel novel *Female Quixotism* (1801). Part satire, part didactic tract, *Female Quixotism* demonstrates how Dorcas' unregulated novel-reading – diagnosed as a chronic case of "novel-mania" (Tenney 1992: 57) – and her "thousand pounds a year" (p. 14) estate make her a prime target for a seemingly endless supply of dissimulating seducers.

The near-omnipresence of dissimulation within this period's literature makes it hardly coincidental that the same type of Chesterfieldian dissembler criticized by ministers and moralists also preoccupied the nation's dramatists and novelists at the end of the eighteenth century.[4] Post-revolutionary authors – from Susanna Rowson to Charles Brockden Brown – were obsessed with dissimulation not only because it threatened the stability of domestic patriarchy by facilitating actual seductions, but also because of an uneasiness with how books were affecting the way people represented themselves and read others in public. William Dunlap's Oxford-educated murderer in *American Shandyism* (1789) and the exceptionally well-read highway robber in Tenney's *Female Quixotism* are but two examples of how the seducing male dissimulator deployed genteel manners and book-smarts to conceal his low social standing and criminal behavior.[5] Similarly, Royall Tyler's *The Contrast* (1787) reveals the problem when Chesterfieldianism is distributed to and by a dissembling white male who finds himself excluded from his former modes of social distinction – money and family. In addition, Foster's *The Coquette* (1797) specifically identifies its financially challenged seducer, Peter Sanford, as a "Chesterfieldian" (Foster 1996: 194), and William Hill Brown's *The Power of Sympathy* (1789) admonishes its readers to beware of men like Sanford who compose themselves "on the Chesterfieldian system" (Brown 1996: 53).

The specific invocation of Chesterfield by these and other post-revolutionary authors was an effort to distinguish and distance the social effects of reading their works (and of reading literature in general) from the negative social effects associated with reading books such as Chesterfield's *Letters* and romance novels. While texts like the *Letters*, countless conduct manuals, and courtesy books strove to refine the mostly male uncouth, they were also blamed for producing the performances of upwardly mobile dissimulators. In response, post-revolutionary novelists such as Hugh Henry Brackenridge, Foster, and Tenney turned to the principles of less voluntary and more corporeal discourses of moral character – such as physiognomy (which read a man's permanent moral character from his unalterable facial features) – in order to counteract the dissimulation associated with books such as Chesterfield's *Letters* and to curb the rapid social and political mobility of the men who read such books. Unlike European romances, which were said to facilitate dissimulation by adversely affecting the minds of their readers, early American seduction novels like *The Coquette* and *Female Quixotism* promised pictures that would edify, not seduce, the imaginations of their readers, and the corporeal legibility of character was a significant feature of that didacticism.

In *The Coquette*, Foster specifically identifies the seducer's dissimulation with Chesterfieldian performances on the one hand and the use of physiognomy as a potential counter-practice to them on the other. The episode takes place near the end of the novel, in letter 51, when the formerly coquettish, but now reclusive, Eliza Wharton sits alone in her bedroom fawning over a portrait of her beloved Peter

Sanford. The miniature reflects Eliza's misplaced intimacy, and Sanford's pictorial presence in her private "chamber" (Foster 1996: 194) anticipates the ill-fated union that he and Eliza will share in person later. But for her more discerning friend Julia Granby, the painting possesses a quite different meaning. When Julia enters the room, Eliza asks her, "You pretend to be a physiognomist, . . . what can you trace in that countenance?" (p. 194). In response, Julia scrutinizes the portrait's face and instantly identifies what Eliza has been unable to see throughout the novel: that her beloved is "an artful, designing man" and that "he looks . . . like a Chesterfieldian" (p. 194).

Of course, at this moment in the narrative, Julia's identification of Sanford as an "artful, designing man" is hardly a revelation. Virtually everyone in the novel, its readers included, is aware that Sanford is a man of "known libertinism" (Foster 1996: 168). They warn Eliza *ad nauseam* that Sanford is a "profligate man" (p. 116), "a professed libertine" practiced in "the arts of seduction" (p. 119), a "second Lovelace" (p. 134), "an artful debauchee" (p. 147), an "assassin of honor" (p. 154), and "a deceiver" (p. 171). Even Sanford himself joins the chorus when he admits to his confidant Deighton that Eliza's "sagacious friends have undoubtedly given her a detail of my vices" so that "she can blame none but herself, since she knows my character" (p. 149). While Eliza's choice of intimacy with Sanford is notoriously difficult to understand, it does appear that one reason she chooses not to listen to her friends and family is that she believes Sanford is capable of being reformed, whereas her community does not. What Foster seems to emphasize in the community's failure to prevent Eliza's seduction is not its inability to communicate that Sanford is a rake, but rather its failure to communicate that he will *always* be a rake. Eliza can disregard Sanford's past "scenes of dissipation" because she believes that his moral character will be different in the future. Eliza embraces the adage that "*A reformed rake makes the best husband*" (p. 146), whereas her foil, Julia, has "no charity for these reformed rakes" (p. 202). After Sanford marries another woman for money, Julia begs Eliza to recognize that "marriage has not changed his disposition" (p. 209), it has merely given him the means to indulge it. The eventual success of Sanford's seduction of Eliza therefore represents a more general failure in the communal norms of gentility to establish the permanency and visibility of immoral character in a person who, externally at least, appears like "a finished gentleman" (p. 119) of virtue.

What makes Julia's physiognomic reading of Sanford's portrait so significant, then, is not her assessment of his character – which everybody already knows – but rather her attempt to identify Sanford's seemingly innate immorality with his face. If Julia's physiognomic assessment of Sanford differs from that expressed by the novel's chorus of ineffectual monitors, it is because she appears to derive her knowledge of Sanford's character not so much from his past conduct or his present performances – which he, of course, can adapt to his own interests – as from his unalterable facial features. In fact, Julia is "astonished" that Eliza's "penetrating eye, has not long since read his vices in his very countenance" (Foster 1996: 202). When Eliza first solicits Julia's expert opinion regarding the miniature, she does so presumably in the hope that her friend's physiognomic reading of the portrait's face will discover aspects of Sanford's moral character different from those being circulated by the community and more in line with her own romantic image of him (p. 190). Instead, Julia's words confirm the community's image of Sanford – but beyond that, they also naturalize that image. Sanford's immorality now becomes more than a series of unwise decisions; it is essential to him.

While Julia is no more successful than the community in preventing Eliza's seduction, her late entrance into the novel and the fact that her physiognomic reading occurs after Sanford has already symbolically penetrated Eliza's chamber assures us that her remarks are meant more for us than for Eliza. If Sanford's mastery of Chesterfieldian politeness helps him to satisfy his sexual urge for seduction and his economic need for marriage, Julia's physiognomic discernment informs the novel's readers of the value of seeing through such performative masks. As Foster reiterates throughout *The Coquette*, Sanford's mastery of the genteel codes of politeness enables him to "assume any shape" (Foster 1996: 121) before Eliza, and his seduction depends largely upon his ability to charm her eye (p. 122) and cast "a deceptious mist over her imagination" (p. 111). Eventually, Eliza's "disturbed imagination" (p. 191) deteriorates to the point that she is unable to describe the incidents of her life to her friends without evoking scenes from "a novel" or "romance" (p. 190). In contrast, "the powerful gaze of Julia Granby" (Waldstreicher 1992: 215) and her "inquisitorial eye" (p. 211) are epitomized by rational reflection. The difference between reading novels and becoming the unfortunate victims of them, readers learn, is the difference between Julia's "reflecting and steady mind" (Foster 1996: 241) and Eliza's "en-feebled...mind" (p. 222); the difference between Julia's model of reading moral character from Sanford's face and Eliza's model of reading it from his performances.

Julia's physiognomic reading of Sanford's portrait is odd, however, in that it lacks any detailed physical description. Such an omission raises the possibility that Julia might have identified the portrait's character as a "Chesterfieldian" from her previous knowledge of his character rather than from his face. The manner in which the scene unfolds encourages this interpretation, since Julia deduces that the portrait depicts Sanford – she says "I guessed whose it was" (Foster 1996: 194) – before she divulges what character she sees in his countenance. Although Foster does not disclose how Julia is able to guess that the image belonged to Sanford, it is probable that some account of his reputation would have been included in Julia's previous correspondence with others in the novel (such as the letter Lucy writes inviting her to visit Eliza: see letters 48 and 49). Whether or not Julia practices physiognomy – in the sense of producing an accurate reading of moral character from the details of Sanford's portrait – seems secondary here to the fact that she uses the logic of physiognomy to substantiate her desire to make his vice visible and ineradicable by associating the immorality of his known character to his face. In this sense, Julia's remarks affirm what Allan Sekula has said elsewhere about physiognomy's later relationship to portrait photography: that its popular hermeneutics of the body "was instrumental in constructing the very archive [it] claimed to interpret" (Sekula 1986: 12). For physiognomy was as much a practice of creating faces as it was a method for interpreting them. In the portrait scene, Foster appears less interested in the validity of specific physiognomic readings than she is in physiognomy's discursive potential as a counter-practice to Chesterfieldian dissimulation. Hardly a criticism of the patriarchy, as many critics have claimed, *The Coquette* instead recommends physiognomy's desire for a permanent, involuntary, and visible relationship between moral character and the face as a means to insulate the marital structures of patriarchal society from Chesterfieldians whose wealth was as false as their manners.[6] *The Coquette* establishes the didactic seduction novel's value for its largely feminine readership and defends the genre from those critics who sought to equate it with the romance by promoting a more rational and less imaginative reading practice.

Julia's exemplary reading practice (of portraits, letters, and men) also suggests that the kind of protean image manipulation that Sanford practices so well as he seduces – that capacity to "cast a deceptive mist" over the imagination – is no longer exclusive to the world of masculine gentility. Julia becomes an exemplary female character for Foster since she has mastered both reading practices: of books and of men. Julia's epistolary reading enables her to identify Sanford as the portrait's original, while her physiognomic discernment allows her to assign a permanent moral character to his face. Even as such physiognomic discernment promises to protect the patriarchal social order in *The Coquette* from the threat of upwardly mobile, dissembling white males, it also elevates the social power of women within that system by attempting to make positive claims for their reading and their minds.[7] What is potentially, and somewhat pragmatically, attractive to established gentry about an exemplary female character like Julia is that her social power need not be defined in opposition to her subordinate status as a woman within the system of domestic patriarchy, but may rather be a product of her ability to determine the character of men operating within it.[8]

As the previous remarks suggest, the negative response to Chesterfield's *Letters* in the post-revolutionary press and the specificity of Chesterfieldianism in the post-revolutionary literary depiction of the seducer reflect a concern with the distributive effects of print itself and its threat to the residual social order of colonial gentility. Yet, by attacking Chesterfieldianism for its immorality, dissimulation, and self-interest, particularly its encouragement of social mobility, these texts shifted the focus on the anti-republican elements of civility away from its exclusivity. In short, they made Chesterfieldianism's democratization of genteel culture appear anti-democratic. Civility's formerly anti-republican value of exclusivity was maintained, despite the diffusion of its manners, by relocating the visibility of social distinction from the genteel, yet voluntary performances of the body to the more involuntary features of the face. Although physiognomy would eventually be succeeded by phrenology as the antebellum period's scientific discourse of permanent moral character, the persistence of the logic of physiognomic distinction within the works of Cooper, Melville, Hawthorne, and Stowe indicates its centrality to the development of the novel in America and it demonstrates the degree to which that logic and its emphasis on reading the face for a person's permanent and essential character might have anticipated the emergence of racial and ethnographic difference as instruments for social organization in nineteenth-century America.

NOTES

1 The *American Museum* reprinted "Letter XII: On Politeness" from Bennett's didactic *Letters to a Young Lady*. No fewer than six American editions of the *Letters* were published by 1811, each calling upon readers "to burn" Chesterfield's books (Bennett 1791: vol. 2, 50).

2 For an alternative account of the early American novel and dissimulation, see Rice 1997: 147–72.

3 For more on how novel-reading left "the mind so softened," see D.S. 1791: 141.

4 Jan Lewis also notes how the pages of republican literature are filled with deceivers and coquettes, but she explains their ubiquitous presence in literature as describing a social problem that print culture reflects rather than causes; see also Bell 1974.

5 One might also include the impostor Craig and the master actor, Ormond, in Charles Brockden's Brown's *Ormond* (1799), the bivocalist Carwin in Brown's *Wieland* (1798), the designing Sinisterus Courtland of Judith Sargent Murray's *The Story of Margaretta* (1798), and a whole range of forgers and counterfeiters too long to identify individually

6 See Davidson 1986; Smith-Rosenberg 1988; Harris 1995. See also Stern (1997), who proposes an alternative reading of *The Coquette* that refuses the traditional conduct-book reading of the novel (where Eliza serves as the negative exemplar), but retains the force of the socially conservative inflection of the book all the same.

7 Sarah Emily Newton also reads Foster and Rowson within the tradition of "usable fiction" whose works placed the responsibility for seduction on the failure of independent women to judge men for themselves (1990: 138–67).

8 Julia's active, if still limited, agency is consistent with what Gillian Brown has identified as the structure of liberal consent found within seduction stories like *The Coquette*. According to Brown, this structure reconfigures consent to signify women's membership in the social contract. "Women's participation in the social compact," Brown argues, "does not necessarily serve the rights of women, particularly if female members of society espouse only long-standing androcentric views of class, courtship, marriage, and family" (2001: 143).

REFERENCES

Anon. (1786). "New Office of Initiation for All Youths of the Superior Class. Lord Chesterfield's Creed." *New Haven Gazette and Connecticut Magazine* 1: 42 (30 Nov.), 327–8.

Anon. (1791). "Remarks on Chesterfield's Letters." *American Museum* (Feb.), 89–91.

Anon. (1792). "Character and Effects of Modern Novels." *Universal Asylum and Columbian Magazine* 9, 225.

Anon. (1797). "Novels." *New Star* 1: 1 (11 April), 3.

Anon. (1804). "The Reading of Novels." *Weekly Visitor or Ladies' Miscellany* 2: 94 (21 July), 332.

Barnes, Elizabeth (1997). *States of Sympathy: Seduction and Democracy in the American Novel*. New York: Columbia University Press.

Bell, Michael Davitt (1974). "'The Double-Tongued Deceiver': Sincerity and Duplicity in the Novels of Charles Brockden Brown." *Early American Literature* 9: 2, 143–63.

Bennett, John (1791). *Letters to a Young Lady . . . ,* 2 vols. Hartford, Conn.: Hudson and Goodwin.

Bennett, John (1792a). "Letter XII: On Politeness." *American Museum* (April), 139–40.

Bennett, John (1792b). *Strictures on Female Education: Chiefly as it Relates to the Culture of the Heart*. Norwich: Ebenezer Bushnell.

Brown, Gillian (2001). *The Consent of the Governed: The Lockean Legacy in Early American Culture*. Cambridge, Mass.: Harvard University Press.

Brown, William Hill (1996). *The Power of Sympathy*. New York: Penguin. (First publ. 1789.)

Bullock, Stephen (1998). "A Mumper Among the Gentle: Tom Bell, Colonial Confidence Man." *William and Mary Quarterly* 55: 2, 231–58.

Burton, John (1794). *Lectures on Female Education and Manners*. New York: [Samuel Campbell].

Bushman, Richard (1992). *The Refinement of America*. New York: Vintage.

[Cento] (1805). *Literary Magazine and American Register* 4: 22 (July), 7–8.

D.S. (1791). "Extract of a Letter from a Lady in Jamaica, to her Friend in Pennsylvania; On Novel Reading." *Universal Asylum and Columbian Magazine* 6 (March), 141–2.

Darwin, Erasmus (1798). *A Plan for the Conduct of Female Education*. Philadelphia: J. Ormond.

Davidson, Cathy N. (1986). *Revolution and the Word: The Rise of the Novel in America*. New York: Oxford University Press.

Fiske, Nathan (1801). *The Moral Monitor*. Worcester, Mass.: I. Thomas.

Fliegelman, Jay (1993). *Declaring Independence*. Stanford: Stanford University Press.

Foster, Hannah Webster (1798). *The Boarding School*. Boston: I. Thomas and E. T. Andrews.

Foster, Hannah Webster (1996). *The Coquette*. New York: Penguin. (First publ. 1797.)

Gulick, Sidney (1979). *A Chesterfield Bibliography to 1800*, 2nd edn. Charlottesville: University Press of Virginia.

Halttunen, Karen (1982). *Confidence Men and Painted Women: A Study of Middle-Class Culture in America, 1830–1870*. New Haven: Yale University Press.

Harris, Sharon M. (1995). "Hannah Webster Foster's *The Coquette*: Critiquing Franklin's America." In Sharon M. Harris (ed.), *Redefining the Political Novel: American Women Writers, 1797–1901*. Knoxville: University of Tennessee Press.

The Juvenile Mirror and Teacher's Manual (1812). New York: Smith & Forman.

Lewis, Jan (1987). "The Republican Wife: Virtue and Seduction in the Early Republic." *William and Mary Quarterly* 44: 4, 689–721.

Miller, Samuel (1803). *A Brief Retrospect of the Eighteenth Century*, 2 vols. New York: T. & J. Swords.

Newton, Sarah Emily (1990). "Wise and Foolish Virgins: 'Usable Fiction' and the Early American Conduct Tradition." *Early American Literature* 25, 139–67.

Rice, Grantland (1997). *The Transformation of Authorship in America*. Chicago: University of Chicago Press.

Sekula, Allan (1986). "The Body and the Archive." *October*, 3–63.

Shields, David S. (1997). *Civil Tongues and Polite Letters in North America*. Chapel Hill: University of North Carolina Press.

Smith-Rosenberg, Carolyn (1988). "Domesticating Virtue: Coquettes and Revolutionaries in Young America." In Elaine Scarry (ed.), *Literature and the Body: Essays on Populations and Persons*, 160–84. Baltimore: Johns Hopkins University Press.

Stanhope, Philip Dormer, Fourth Earl of Chesterfield (1932). *Letters*, ed. Bonamy Dobrée, 6 vols. New York: Viking. (First publ. 1774.)

Stern, Julia A. (1997). *The Plight of Feeling: Sympathy and Dissent in the Early American Novel*. Chicago: University of Chicago Press.

Tenney, Tabitha Gilman (1992). *Female Quixotism: Exhibited in the Romantic Opinions and Extravagant Adventures of Dorcasina Sheldon*, ed. Jean Nienkamp and Andrea Collins. New York: Oxford University Press. (First publ. 1801.)

Waldstreicher, David (1992). "'Fallen under my Observation': Vision and Virtue in *The Coquette*." *Early American Literature* 27: 3, 204–18.

Warner, Michael (1990). *The Letters of the Republic: Publication and the Public Sphere in Eighteenth-Century America*. Cambridge, Mass.: Harvard University Press.

Wood, Gordon S. (1991). *The Radicalism of the American Revolution*. New York: Vintage.

15

The American Gothic

Marianne Noble

In his 1856 novella "Benito Cereno," Herman Melville imaginatively fleshed out a true story about a slave revolt that occurred on board the slave ship *The Tryal* in 1799. He had read the story in a memoir written by Amasa Delano, a ship's captain who described coming across the vessel in distress off the coast of Chile. Unbeknown to Delano, the ship had been taken over by the slaves on board, and when he boarded her to provide assistance, the slaves feigned submission to the ship's captain, Benito Cereno. The ringleader of the plot, Babo, played the role of his captain's trusty valet, sticking closely to him as though to protect his beloved, ailing master. Numerous glitches in the performance of blacks and whites alike generated confusion and mounting anxiety for Delano. Finally, though, he realized what was actually going on, pitched battle against the slaves, overpowered them, and brought them to Lima for prosecution and execution or re-enslavement.

A centerpiece scene of Melville's novella presents a tableau in which Babo performs what he presents as a daily ritual, the shaving of Benito Cereno. The scene has extraordinary symbolic power. The reality it presents is an enraged and vindictive slave with a razor-sharp blade at the throat of his former master, who nearly faints in terror when the slave actually draws his blood. However, an American looking on with blissful unawareness sees nothing but the beauties of relationships founded on natural bonds of submission and domination. Though he has an uneasy feeling that he cannot identify, Delano takes comfort from seeing the slave so tenderly shaving the master he loves, seeming to enjoy his natural role of serving his superiors. Though Delano is looking right at a scene of tremendous latent violence, he sees only "a certain easy cheerfulness, harmonious in every glance and gesture," which he believes characterizes negroes in general, as well "docility arising from the unaspiring contentment of a limited mind, and that susceptibility of blind attachment sometimes inhering in indisputable inferiors" (Melville 2002: 70–1). What most interests Melville is the presence of intellectual blinkers that prevent Delano from seeing what is directly in front of him.

This scene can be seen as representing one of the deepest fears haunting the American mind in 1856, a year poised evenly between the passage of the fugitive slave law and the Civil War. The shaving tableau captures the nuances of the tension that characterized this time, captures an uncanny fear in whites of a disjunction between appearances and a suspected reality – the fear that the seemingly happy order could crumble at any moment, revealing resentment and rage boiling over into a wave of violence. The famous abolitionist Thomas Wentworth Higginson observed as much in an essay he wrote at about the same time that Melville wrote "Benito Cereno." Meditating upon the 1831 slave rebellion of Nat Turner, Higginson writes, "those dusky slaves, so obsequious to their master the day before, so prompt to sing and dance before his Northern visitors, were all swift to transform themselves into fiends of retribution now" (1994: 1893). Like Melville, Higginson is intrigued by an uncanny sensation caused by the gap between an ongoing normality and a feeling that the tables could turn at any moment. Interested to pinpoint the precise nature of this uncanny feeling, he turns to a lengthy quotation from an anti-slavery politician, "the eloquent James McDowell," who in January 1832 debated the meaning of the Nat Turner slave rebellion with Southerners. McDowell claimed that Nat Turner had "banished every sense of security from every man's dwelling" because of "the suspicion eternally attached to the slave himself, – the suspicion that Nat Turner might be in every family; that the same bloody deed might be acted over at any time and in any place." He identified a particularly uncanny aspect to this fear, insisting that the slaveholding population "prefer[red] any thing rather than the horrors of meeting death from a domestic assassin" (quoted in Higginson 1994: 1899). This deep, constant anxiety that every Southern family might have a domestic assassin in its midst characterizes the uncanny of 1856. People of both North and South feared that the day of retribution at the hands of slaves was not far away. And it is that which makes the shaving scene so successful an allegory of its day.

The shaving tableau, and its allegorical meaning, not only captures its day; it also crystallizes the goals and methods of American gothic literature. Ever since this fractured nation was born – dedicated to the principle that all men are created equal but denying citizenship and even humanity to all but white middle-class males – US literature has striven to represent that schism. And no genre has been more enabling for this effort than the gothic. US gothic literature tells tales of black animals buried alive inside house walls; women locked in their homes by predatory fathers and uncles; vengeful Indians stalking white children in underground caves; corpses rotting in the cellars of gorgeous mansions; alcoholic husbands who murder their long-suffering wives; old genteel families crumbling beneath the weight of ancestral guilt and incestuous longing; white women trapped and cornered by savage black beasts. Of course, there are the other stories as well – stories of good boys whose virtue is rewarded with wealth; slave-owners who free their slaves once they under-stand the piteousness of their plight; girls whose deepest desires are met by marriage to powerful men who protect and love them. But the gothic is driven by the impetus to reveal the counter-narrative to these optimistic stories. In a nation whose dominant narrative says, "This nation provides equal opportunity and justice for all and is bound together by fraternal love," gothic literature reveals a different picture of US history. It reveals the history of blacks enslaved, worked to death, and denied sexual privacy. It unveils the history of Indians annihilated with bullets and smallpox, or shoved off their own land to one frontier and then another still further away. It tells the story of domestic workers gagged and beaten by their employers. It exposes the indignity and rage of brilliant women forced to find the meaning of their lives stirring puddings and hemstitching diapers. To be sure, such exposures do not *require* the gothic: sentimentalism, realism, naturalism, modernism, and post-modernism can all tell these tales as well. What the gothic achieves remarkably well is the act of unveiling. It exposes the existence of repudiated counter-narratives beneath genial fictions. It insists that this montage of simultaneous and opposed narratives characterizes America itself. That is what makes the gothic so American. And that is what makes the shaving scene in "Benito Cereno" – with its overlapping narratives of geniality and murderous rage – so emblematic of American gothic in general.

This essay offers a theory of the political work of early American gothic literature. I concentrate on "Benito Cereno" as a way of focusing my presentation of this theory. But my intention is that the insights afforded by close consideration of "Benito Cereno" will serve as a model that exemplifies more broadly the work of American gothic literature across this period. As I have just shown, the novella crystallizes an uncanny fear of slave rebellion in 1856. Throughout American literature the gothic similarly crystallizes fears particular to its cultural moment. The gothic enables us to understand what a society fears.

The American gothic is above all a psychological genre: it explores the nature of personal identity within the social structures unique to the United States. Whereas previous generations of critics have argued that American gothic distinguishes itself from European gothic through an interest in human psychology *as opposed to* politics or history, scholars today insist that its psychological orientation is itself about national history, as that history is experienced and enacted by individual people. While Melville's primary interest in "Benito Cereno" is the extraordinary psyche of Amasa Delano, that psyche is of interest for its deep meaning in the context of American nationalism and American history. Like so much American gothic, the story Melville crafted probes deeply into the psyche of one man's self-delusion, and in doing so, it allegorically explores the self-delusiveness of "Americans," portraying them as cheerful men disposed to philanthropic benevolence who cannot understand or even see the resentment of those around them.

Many American gothic narratives that explore national history through personal identity focus upon a psychic operation that psychological theorists have called "abjection." Indeed, the representation of abjection is frequently the link between the individual portraits and their larger cultural meaning. Julia Kristeva coins the term "abjection" in *Powers of Horror* (1982). For her, it refers to a primary psychic operation performed by all infants. Before they can define who they *are*, they must negate all of the possible attachments and identifications that symbolize who they are *not*. The primary negation is of the mother. Before a child can develop his understanding of his own unique existence, he must shove away the mother. Not me, the child insists. But the self thus constructed is dangerously indebted to the very things it is not for its definition – they are a crucial, albeit negated part of the self, haunting with a sense of lost wholeness, lost erotic attachment. We therefore have a love–hate relationship with our own abjects. We fear the abject, Kristeva writes, because it "disturbs identity, system, order. What does not respect borders, positions, rules. The in between, the ambiguous, the composite" (1982: 4). But on the other hand, we love it for the euphoric transcendence and wholeness it promises. Judith Butler has borrowed this term "abjection" to signify a similar process that works at the level of an entire culture. The dominant narratives defining a society and its values are constructed through repudiation or negation of possible alternatives posed by "others" within that society. The key to understanding abjection is to recognize that the abject – the negated "other" – is a central component of identity, albeit central through denial rather than acclamation.

American gothic literature explores the many ways in which abjection is central to Americans' senses of themselves as individuals and as Americans. We find a clear example of this process in "Benito Cereno." Amasa Delano conceives of himself as a generous, affable, egalitarian sort of fellow. As Melville writes,

> Captain Delano's nature was not only benign, but familiarly and humorously so. At home, he had often taken rare satisfaction in sitting in his door, watching some free man of color at his work or play. If on a voyage he chanced to have a black sailor, invariably he was on chatty, and half-gamesome terms with him. In fact, like most men of a good, blithe heart, Captain Delano took to Negroes, not philanthropically, but genially, just as other men to Newfoundland dogs. (2002: 71)

Delano's fondness for negroes is part of his generally gamesome, familiar, benign sense of himself. However, that self-conception is actually constructed through negation of the humanity of those same negroes, as the comparison of them to Newfoundland dogs makes clear.

The following passage makes even clearer the relationship between Delano's identity and the abjection of negro subjectivity. In it, Delano is experiencing an uncanny sensation provoked by an inability to conform the scene before him to his sense of how the world is ordered:

> All this is very queer now, thought Captain Delano, with a qualmish sort of emotion; but as one feeling incipient seasickness, he strove, by ignoring the symptoms, to get rid of the malady. Once more he looked off for his boat. To his delight, it was now again in view, leaving the rocky spur astern.
>
> The sensation here experienced, after at first relieving his uneasiness, with unforeseen efficiency, soon began to remove it. The less distant sight of that well-known boat – showing it, not as before, half blended with the haze, but with outline defined, so that its individuality, like a man's, was manifest; that boat, Rover by name, which, though

now in strange seas, had often pressed the beach of Captain Delano's home, and, brought to its threshold for repairs, had familiarly lain there, as a Newfoundland dog; the sight of that household boat evoked a thousand trustful associations, which, contrasted with previous suspicions, filled him not only with lightsome confidence, but somehow with half humorous self-reproaches at his former lack of it.

"What, I, Amasa Delano – Jack of the Beach, as they called me when a lad – I, Amasa; the same that, duck-satchel in hand, used to paddle along the waterside to the school-house made from the old hulk; – I, little Jack of the Beach, that used to go berrying with cousin Nat and the rest; I to be murdered here at the ends of the earth, on board a haunted pirate-ship by a horrible Spaniard? – Too nonsensical to think of! Who would murder Amasa Delano? His conscience is clean. There is some one above.... What a donkey I was.... Ha! glancing toward the boat; there's Rover; a good dog. (Melville 2002: 64–5)

Delano feels queasy at his inability to make sense of what is going on around him, but, rather than concede that he needs a new interpretative framework, he attempts to alleviate his queasiness through a more firm abjection of the alternative truths staring him in the face. He does this by "ignoring the symptoms" in the hopes that the malady will go away. Melville further portrays the process of abjection by imagining that Delano calms himself through contemplating his boat, which, with its "outline defined," manifests "its individuality." All is a cognitive "haze" for him until he sees a familiar "individuality," which triggers for him feelings of comfort and assurance, suggesting by extension that the familiar outlines of all things have always been correct. He casts off his uncanny fear by telling himself that boundaries are not unstable, that identities are secure. However, the key act he performs to restore calm is an abjection implicit in his comparison of the boat, Rover, to a Newfoundland dog, which as we have seen, is a metaphor he uses for negroes. Delano finds comfort not only in his well-known, dog-like boat, but metonymically, in his assurance of the dog-like nature of negroes. Through this metonymy, Delano reassures himself that the negroes on board the mysterious boat pose no threat – they do not have the minds nor natures for it. They are "good dog[s]." This is not a conscious association, but it comforts him all the more powerfully for its unconsciousness.

This abjection of the humanity of negroes relaxes Delano because it enables him to secure his own identity. After reassuring himself that the world is as he has always believed it, he turns to a fascinating mental rehearsal of the key features of his identity. He is not going to be murdered. He is not the type to be implicated in a diabolical plot. He is normal, an innocent, boyish man: little Jack of the Beach, a boy who paddled outside the schoolhouse, and used to go berrying with his cousin. These images define how Delano thinks of himself. What Melville exposes – more brilli-antly than any writer I know of – is how tenuously this sense of himself rests upon the unstable foundation of abjecting negro humanity. Melville exposes how personal identity is hinged to the social order, so that when epistemology flounders under pressures from abjected social groups, so does personal identity.

"Benito Cereno" suggests an analogy between the consolidation of Delano's indi-viduality through abjection of black subjectivity and the construction of American national identity. Just as Delano rationalizes his own dominance of blacks by negating the capabilities of blacks, so too white American men are masters in the United States through abjection. That abjection happens at the level of narrative: certain stories are told (such as that blacks are naturally inferior and know it) and others are not (such as that blacks are just as capable as whites of logic, resentment, and the careful plotting of murderous revenge). The natural inferiority of blacks is a key component of the dominant stories Americans have told about their national identity, stories that Jared Gardner calls "master narratives." By presuming that blacks are inferior and by repressing signs to the contrary, white Americans can believe other parts of the master narrative – that blacks find servitude to whites to be natural and pleasant; that those in power are neither cruel nor unfair; that they are, on the contrary, the nicest people in the world, on good terms with everybody; that they are likable innocents whose consciences are clean and who, like children, feel malice toward none and charity toward all. Toni Morrison similarly proposes in *Playing in the Dark: Whiteness and the Literary Imagination* that a spectral Africanist presence is the defining feature of American literature, a tradition haunted by representations of chained or subjugated black figures. She demonstrates how the image of a chained black serves throughout mainstream US literature as the negative enabling a white subject to know himself as free and authoritative.

A great deal of American gothic literature explores or reveals the abjection of black subjectivity. Crèvecœur's *Letters from an American Farmer* (1782) is a good example. This collection of letters, purporting to be written by a farmer named James to a European friend, is renowned for asking, and answering, the question, "What is an American?" In his answer, Crèvecœur suggests that an American is a landowning person of mixed national (though all European) origin who is on good terms with everyone. His doors are left open, and even Indians feel free to come in and say hello. However, in a letter near the end of the series, James is visiting a Southern plantation and, out on a walk, he comes across a slave who is being tortured to death by being confined to a small cage hung from a tree.

> I shudder when I recollect that the birds had already picked out his eyes; his cheek bones were bare; his arms had been attacked in several places, and his body seemed covered with a multitude of wounds. From the edges of the hollow sockets and from the lacerations with which he was disfigured, the blood slowly dropped and tinged the ground beneath. (Crèvecœur 1994: 834)

The narrator finds this gothic spectacle horrifying – he does not approve of slavery or torture – but he cannot put the slave out of his misery by shooting him because he does not have a bullet. And so, sadly, he leaves him, puts him out of his mind, and joins the slave's owner for dinner, a meal that, as Teresa Goddu points out in her influential discussion of this scene, was made possible by slave labor. Crèvecœur did not intend this episode to be a key part of his definition of an American, but the eruption of the gothic into Crèvecœur's generally sunny portrait of American identity is another example of abjection at work in defining the American. Americans think of themselves as freedom-loving, affable, plain, honest, sympathetic folk; when confronted with evidence to the contrary, they avert their eyes rather than revise their master narratives and take steps to ameliorate things. As Teresa Goddu, Justin Edwards, Priscilla Wald, Lesley Ginsberg, Joan Dayan, Robert K. Martin, and many others have demonstrated, abjection of black subjectivity is prominently featured in the works of such authors as William and Ellen Craft, Frederick Douglass, Edgar Allan Poe, and Nathaniel Hawthorne. Decades ago, Leslie Fiedler argued that the gothic is *the* American genre par excellence, and that its most important theme is the guilty secret of slavery, a secret in full view. As in the shaving tableau in "Benito Cereno," Americans have always refused to look at what is in front of them. The gothic restores the repressed to consciousness.

Abjection of Native American subjectivity has also historically defined American identity, and it therefore also figures prominently in American gothic literature. Renee Bergland has demonstrated that US literature is haunted by Indian ghosts, spectral presences that signify the nation's primal guilt over the sin at the heart of its origin: the theft of the entire body of land from its prior inhabitants. As Bergland writes, "Americans are obsessed with Native Americans...everyone who tries to imagine himself or herself as an American subject, must internalize both the colonization of Native Americans and the American stance against colonialism. He or she must simultaneously acknowledge the American horror and celebrate the American triumph" (2000: 16). This irreconcilable dualism, and its allied anxiety, pervade early American literature. Consider, for example, Hawthorne's haunted house story, *House of the Seven Gables* (1851). At one point Hawthorne imagines a palace, full of gorgeous rooms, including one with a dome through which one can gaze, unimpeded, at heaven itself. In the basement, though, lies a half-decayed corpse. Hawthorne explicitly compares this house to a man with a heinous deed in his background. The narrator wonders whether any number of generous acts committed by a man like this can compensate for his criminality, and whether a beautiful house with a corpse in its basement will ever stop smelling bad; the answer to both these questions is "no." Hawthorne's exploration of individual identity in this novel is – as in so much American gothic – equally an exploration of national identity. The thrust of the novel suggests an analogy, of which Hawthorne may not have been fully conscious, between the image of the house and the United States: the nation is a beautiful, sunny, charitable, benevolent society with direct access to God, but it is nonetheless erected upon a foundation of theft and racial annihilation. There is a corpse in the nation's basement, and it is the corpse of defrauded and annihilated Native Americans. Obliquely, then, the nation stands condemned in this gothic tale of a house haunted by those from whom the land was stolen. Surely it was in a dramatically different mood that Hawthorne wrote years later, in the preface to *The Marble Faun*: "No author without a trial, can conceive of the difficulty of writing a romance about a country where there is no shadow, no mystery, no picturesque and gloomy wrong, or anything but commonplace prosperity, in broad and simple daylight, as is happily the case with my dear native land." Here he sounds more like Captain Delano than the younger author who had brooded over the burdens of the nation's dark Puritan legacy and his own descent from the hanging judges at the Salem witch trials.

In America as in Europe, the gothic is also a literary response to the Enlightenment, an era that dramatically revised people's understandings of social order, political authority, and the role of individuality. Whereas power had formerly been concentrated in a king or feudal landlord, the Enlightenment saw the rise of a form of social order in which power was disseminated among the people themselves. People now believed they were capable of self-regulation, that government was properly immanent, rather than transcendent. The epoch witnessed the rise of middle-class values, in opposition to the more aristocratic caste system of earlier times. It further marked a new belief in the value of each and every individual, an importance fully realized in the development of political democracies. This belief is enshrined in the American Declaration of Independence, which posits the self-evident nature of the claim that all men – peasants as much as the King – are created equal and have a natural right to pursue their own happiness.

Michel Foucault, however, has theorized the dark side of this political dream. As he has famously argued, modern Western people are not as free as their cherished documents and ideologies lead them to think they are. Power has not been relaxed; instead, it has merely changed modes. People in modern Western societies are controlled not by repression but by internal self-subjugation. We acquiesce in power not because we are forced to but rather because our subjectivities are created in such a way that we welcome it. Power leaves us free to pursue our desires only because our desires themselves have been predetermined. Our homes and families are not refuges from this internalization of oppression; to the contrary, they indoctrinate us to be the agents of our own oppression.

Gothic literature arose at the same time as this new mode of power was coming into being, and it gives voice to the nightmarish aspects of the Enlightenment dream. It does so by fetishizing the symbols of the outmoded forms of power that the new liberal society had repudiated. Gothic fictions are typically set in the feudal era; their spirit originated in the gothic architecture of a society regulated by physical force and centralized in the person of a king or lord – castles with dungeons, heavily fortified walls, chains, and instruments of torture. Also prominently featured in gothic literature are other repudiated aspects of the pre-modern social order: monasteries, convents, and a preoccupation with the evils of Catholicism; degraded members of the aristocracy and clergy; madhouses devoted to confinement, not cure. The gothic focuses upon these relics of the earlier era as a way of restoring to consciousness the disorder imperiling the rational presumptions of the Enlightenment.

A good example of how gothic literature fetishizes symbols of pre-modern social regulation appears in another representative passage from "Benito Cereno." In it, Delano meets one of the other slaves, a "gigantic black" named Atufal. "An iron collar was about his neck, from which depended a chain, thrice wound round his body; the terminating links padlocked together at a broad band of iron, his girdle." These chains epitomize the gothic: they are heavy and confining, and the iron girdle (at the slave's groin?) vaguely suggests torture. They represent the cruelty and repression of a former era that modern people have repudiated in accordance with their belief in the inalienable right to individual liberty. Captain Delano is not comfortable with these locks and chains favored by the aristocratic Spaniard. On his own boat, he finds that discipline, enforced by subordinate deck-officers, achieves a "quiet orderliness." Indeed, he contrasts the disordered relations among Cereno's crew to his own "comfortable family of a crew." Because his system prevents most eruptions of disorder, Delano does not need locks and chains. He can rule with a friendly American style that makes the burdens of subjugation feel light both to him and to the members of his community. Discipline enables Americans to cast off the mien of ruler and see themselves as nothing more than boyish innocents, having little in common with debilitated, torture-loving Spanish autocrats. The fact is, Delano is not comfortable with slavery. Like Crèvecœur, he believes in freedom. Thus, when Babo expresses loyalty, Delano cries out, "Don Benito, I envy you such a friend; slave I cannot call him." Delano would much rather believe that Babo serves Benito Cereno out of his own free will, which is why he cannot call Babo a slave. He cannot tolerate the remarkable unfreedom beneath his cherished vision of a freedom-loving society. The gothic image of Atufal draped in chains and padlocks uncomfortably clashes with his optimistic view of a free social order. The archaic symbols of power so beloved of gothic writers restore to attention the forms of repression that are buried but not dead.

A great deal of American gothic – particularly early American gothic – responds to the anxieties raised by the new forms of social control. This is not surprising, of course. With the Revolution only a few years behind them, and ratification of the Constitution having occurred only in June 1788, early American writers registered the fear that self-regulation would fail to order the new society, or else the fear that repression was only being redefined, not abolished. Charles Brockden Brown, one of America's earliest gothic writers, explores this anxiety in *Wieland*, subtitled "An American Tale" (1798). The novel portrays a ventriloquist by the name of Carwin who maliciously and secretly projects his voice to Theodore Wieland, pretending to be the voice of God telling him to kill his family. He also projects it to Henry Pleyel, pretending to be the voice of Clara, Pleyel's beloved, *in flagrante delicto* with Carwin himself. These vile pranks destroy the Wieland family and torture the survivors. In this novel, Brown is particularly concerned with the political and philosophical implications of Carwin's ventriloquism. If people's senses are so unreliable that they can be brought to believe that their beloved is cheating on them or that God has told them to slaughter their families, then how can a democracy possibly work? Given that the human mind is so fallible, how can government by the people work? Foucault posits that self-government requires the molding of people's wills in such a way that their desires coincide with the larger good. But the trope of ventriloquism in *Wieland* registers the anxiety that people might not have the *right* beliefs instilled in them. As Pleyel says to Clara, Carwin had sought "to make your will the instrument by which he might bereave you of liberty and honor." That, according to Foucault, is precisely the nature of liberal government: individuals' own wills deprive them of their liberty. But in *Wieland* Brown indicates an anxiety particular to his day: that the will of the people could be manipulated in *other* ways that would be detrimental to the union. In his introduction to *Wieland*, Jay Fliegelman (1991) suggests that Brown was prompted to write the novel by a crisis over inflammatory journalism: a proliferation of partisan newspapers made many leaders anxious that the voting mass of readers would have the points of view of various factions ventriloquized into them, as it were. Democracy was precarious indeed. In this novel, the gothic explores the fears of its collapse.

While the gothic has been a staple of American literature since the Revolution, the works of the country's most famous gothic author, Edgar Allan Poe, have traditionally been seen as oddly detached from the mainstream of American literature. His works are more obviously part of the European tradition, making extensive use of the European conventions of castles, debauched aristocrats, and remote settings, such as the Spanish Inquisition. They seem more interested in psychology and esthetics than in the nationalist and historical concerns that preoccupied such authors as Brown, Crèvecœur, Hawthorne, and Melville. And Poe has influenced and impressed European writers, such as Baudelaire, more than he has Americans. But more recent scholarship, such as Rosenheim and Rachman's collection (1995), emphasizes Poe's embeddedness within American culture, his responsiveness to it rather than his alienation from it. Joan Dayan, for example, has argued that Poe's obsession with characters that die but then come back to life constitutes a meditation upon how the courts defined "a person" when confronted with issues like slavery, which clearly complicated that definition. Poe's living-dead characters, she argues, can be read as "legal personalities" that probe the distinction between actual and legal existence. She points to court cases that distinguished between the physical persons of slaves and "legal personhood," which she defines as "the social and civic components of personal identity." Such personhood was denied to slaves: "So far as civil acts are concerned, the slave, not being a person, has no legal mind, no will which the law can recognize," an 1861 court decision asserted (1999: 410). Dayan argues that legal pronouncements like this one subject slaves to civil death. But since the slaves under discussion are in fact alive, the result is a form of living death, a state of being that Poe explores in stories of the living dead, such as "The Fall of the House of Usher," "Ligeia," and "The Tell-Tale Heart."

There is not space here to explore the myriad instances and forms of early American gothic. Key figures include Edgar Allan Poe, of course, but also Charles Brockden Brown, Hector St. John de Crèvecœur, Henry Dana Sr., Washington Allston, John Neal, James Fenimore Cooper, Nathaniel Hawthorne, Herman Melville, Harriet Beecher Stowe, George Lippard, Harriet Spofford, Alice Cary, Harriet Jacobs, Harriet Wilson, Emily Dickinson, and Louisa May Alcott. Nor is there room to explore the other pleasures and themes of early American gothic, the largest gap being women's gothic literature. Politics is not the only lens through which early American gothic can fruitfully be explored, though it is a particularly valuable one. In large part, that is because the action of repression is so frequently instigated by ideologies disseminated by people with a vested interest. American gothic explores those interests and their darker implications for the people influenced by them. Above all, it insists that the clash between cheerful ideology and a darker social reality is the central fact of American political life. It is for that reason that the gothic has always been a central fact of American literary history.

REFERENCES AND FURTHER READING

Bergland, Renee L. (2000). *The National Uncanny: Indian Ghosts and American Subjects.* Hanover, NH: University Press of New England.

Crèvecœur, J. Hector St. John de (1994). *Letters from an American Farmer* (first publ. 1782). Excerpted in *The Heath Anthology of American Literature*, 2nd edn., vol. 1. Lexington, Mass.: Heath.

Dayan, Joan (1999). "Poe, Persons, and Property." *American Literary History* 11: 3 (Fall), 405–25.

Edmundson, Mark (1997). *Nightmare on Main Street: Angels, Sadomasochism, and the Culture of Gothic.* Cambridge, Mass.: Harvard University Press.

Edwards, Justin D. (2003). *Gothic Passages: Racial Ambiguity and the American Gothic.* Iowa City: University of Iowa Press.

Fliegelman, Jay (1991). "Introduction." In *Wieland and Memoirs of Carwin the Biloquist*, vii–xliv. New York: Viking Penguin.

Gardner, Jared (1998). *Master Plots: Race and the Founding of an American Literature, 1787–1845.* Baltimore: Johns Hopkins University Press.

Ginsberg, Lesley (1998). "Slavery and the Gothic Horror of Poe's 'The Black Cat.'" In Robert K. Martin and Eric Savoy (eds.), *American Gothic: New Interventions in a National Narrative*, 99–128. Iowa City: University of Iowa Press.

Goddu, Teresa A. (1997). *Gothic America: Narrative, History, and Nation.* New York: Columbia University Press.

Gross, Louis S. (1989). *Redefining the American Gothic: From* Wieland *to* Day of the Dead. Ann Arbor: UMI Research Press.

Hayes, Kevin J., ed. (2002). *The Cambridge Companion to Edgar Allan Poe.* Cambridge, UK: Cambridge University Press.

Hendershot, Cyndy (1998). *The Animal Within: Masculinity and the Gothic.* Ann Arbor: University of Michigan Press.

Higginson, Thomas Wentworth (1994). "Nat Turner's Insurrection." Excerpted in *The Heath Anthology of American Literature*, 2nd edn., vol. 1. Lexington, Mass.: Heath. (First publ. 1861.)

Kristeva, Julia (1982). *Powers of Horror: An Essay on Abjection*, trans. Leon S. Roudiez. New York: Columbia University Press.

Martin, Robert K., and Savoy, Eric, eds. (1998). *American Gothic: New Interventions in a National Narrative.* Iowa City: University of Iowa Press.

Melville, Herman (2002). "Benito Cereno" (first publ. 1856). In *Melville's Short Novels*, ed. Dan McCall. New York: Norton.

Morrison, Toni (1993). *Playing in the Dark: Whiteness and the Literary Imagination.* New York: Vintage.

Reynolds, David S. (1988). *Beneath the American Renaissance: The Subversive Imagination in the Age of Emerson and Melville.* New York: Knopf.

Rosenheim, Shawn, and Rachman, Stephen, eds. (1995). *The American Face of Edgar Allan Poe.* Baltimore: Johns Hopkins University Press.

Samuels, Shirley (1996). *Romances of the Republic: Women, the Family, and Violence in the Literature of the Early American Nation.* New York: Oxford University Press.

Wald, Priscilla (1995). *Constituting Americans: Cultural Anxiety and Narrative Form.* Durham, NC: Duke University Press.

Wardrop, Daneen (1996). *Emily Dickinson's Gothic: Goblin with a Gauge.* Iowa City: University of Iowa Press.

16
Sensational Fiction

Shelley Streeby

Nineteenth-century sensational fiction is an international genre, and there is a substantial critical literature on British and French sensational forms, including penny dreadfuls, the *roman-feuilleton*, and novels by writers such as George Sand, Eugène Sue, Wilkie Collins, and Mary Braddon. In the United States, however, sensational fiction has only recently emerged as a category in nineteenth-century literary studies, and only a small number of examples of what is perhaps the most popular genre of US fiction of its time are currently in print. In the late 1980s Michael Denning, in *Mechanic Accents* (1987), and David Reynolds, in *Beneath the American Renaissance* (1988), made important contributions to the project of retrieving and analyzing a forgotten archive of bestselling sensational fiction, including vast numbers of newspapers, story papers, pamphlet novelettes, and dime novels. This archive and the critical discussion that emerged in the 1990s, along with work in allied fields such as theater and film studies, labor history, ethnic and cultural studies, and sexuality and gender studies, made "sensation" a key word for scholars of nineteenth-century US literature.

Sensational fiction can be defined in part by its position within the nineteenth-century US literary field. To understand that position, we must consider its typical forms of publication, its cheap price relative to other forms of literature, its possible audiences, and its lowly place within emerging literary hierarchies, somewhere beneath the literature of the "American Renaissance" and the bestselling sentimental novels of the time. There is a risk in overstating differences between competing literary formations, however, for these three literary tiers cannot always be neatly distinguished from each other: canonical authors such as Melville, Hawthorne, and Poe wrote fiction that could be called sensational, as did many of the women writers of the era, such as E. D. E. N. Southworth, Metta Victor, and Louisa May Alcott, although the latter are more often considered in relation to literary sentimentalism. Furthermore, both sentimental and sensational fiction participated in a larger ensemble of discourses on sentiment and sensation and on individual and political bodies that can in part be traced to the "cultures of sensibility" of eighteenth-century Europe. It is therefore not surprising that sentimentalism and sensationalism share much and in part overlap.

Sensational fiction can also be defined as a form of popular melodrama with close ties to other "low" nineteenth-century genres of physical entertainment such as theatrical melodrama, blackface minstrelsy, and Barnum's freak show. Like melodrama more generally, as defined by Linda Williams, sensational fiction emphasizes temporal coincidences, stages moments of truth that expose villains and recognize virtue, and tries to move its audiences to experience intense feelings, such as thrill, shock, and horror. Indeed, literary critics have often worried over the manipulative, visceral, and voyeuristic aspects of sensational fiction's appeal to readers, and they have sometimes concluded that such a structure of feeling displaces or fatally compromises any political critique. The cross-dressing and other scenes of bodily masquerade and transformation that were ubiquitous in theatrical melodrama and the minstrel show are also central to sensational fiction, making this literature a rich repository of changing ideas about sexuality, gender, class, and race. Finally, all of these forms of sensational entertainment emerged in the context of nineteenth-century urban and imperial US modernity. Drawing especially on Walter Benjamin's ideas, recent work on the nineteenth-century city in a variety of disciplines has built on the thesis that the urban environment of capitalist modernity altered the human "sensorium" and inaugurated new modes of perception that affected the cultural forms that emerged in its wake. We could therefore understand sensational fiction as a typical product of the urban popular cultures that were shaped by this new sensorium, with all of its shocks, thrills, and sensational intensities. While the genre's urban origins make questions about the existence and significance of such a sensorium especially interesting, however, the popularity of both urban and imperial sub-genres of sensational literature also suggests how central the city/empire nexus was in the nineteenth-century United States. That is, many authors of sensational fiction wrote both "mysteries of the city" novels and stories about imperial adventures in the US West and the Americas, and this double emphasis reveals some of the many connections between city and empire during this era of US capitalist modernity.

Sensational fiction became popular in the United States during the 1830s and 1840s, in the wake of a print revolution that made cheap reading material available to many more readers in the rapidly expanding nation. Steam-driven presses and innovations in paper-making technology made it possible to produce larger editions at cheaper prices than ever before, and papers and books circulated more widely during these years as railroads began to connect different parts of the nation. Much of this literature was initially published in northeastern cities such as New York, Philadelphia, and Boston, but other publishing centers emerged in the decades that followed. Following the US–Mexican War of 1846–8 sensation fiction traveled west, inspiring writers such as California's John Rollin Ridge to give the genre a try. After the Civil War, sensational fiction continued to flourish, notably in the form of dime novels produced under industrial conditions by firms such as Beadle and Adams.

Sensational fiction circulated in a variety of forms. In many cases, a narrative would be serialized in a story paper, sometimes more than once, and then reprinted as a cheap pamphlet novel or a dime novel. Story papers were cheap eight-page weeklies that began to flourish at the end of the 1830s. In the 1840s, papers such as the *Flag of our Union*, the *Flag of the Free*, and the *Star Spangled Banner* juxtaposed sensational narrative episodes with editorials, letters to the editor, advice, and often coverage of the US–Mexican War based on the news in penny dailies. During this period authors such as George Lippard and Ned Buntline were able to launch their own story papers. Later, in the 1850s and 1860s, new family story papers emerged, some with circulations in the hundreds of thousands, such as the *New York Ledger*, the *New York Weekly*, *Saturday Night*, and the *Fireside Companion*. In 1860 Beadle and Adams marketed the first dime novel, and in 1870 they began to issue a story paper, the *Saturday Journal*. So throughout much of the century, sensational fiction was part of a larger textual commodity, the story paper, which in some cases had close ties to the social movements of the period but was increasingly an important part of an emergent mass culture, one that targeted a broad audience that cut across classes.

The serialized form of much of this fiction contributed to its sensational appeal. Because publishers tried to present suspenseful stories that would help to build circulations, individual episodes often end with a melodramatic event or action scene designed to make readers anxious to buy the next installment in order to find out what happened next. This helps to explain why sensational fiction is so episodic and why its narrative pace is so frenetic. The serialized structure also meant that while a particular story was running in one of these papers the author could shape it in response to news of politics, crime, scandals, and war, and even to letters from readers. New prize competitions also helped to establish the defining characteristics of the genre as publishers called for certain types of stories, authors came up with their ideas, and readers reacted. In the late 1840s, the *Flag of our Union* was one of the first story papers to feature such a competition for "exciting," "highly readable and entertaining" sensational fiction, and to include a lurid illustration next to segments from prize-winning tales.

Hundreds of writers, most of them now forgotten, produced sensational fiction during the nineteenth century, and, as Denning suggests, over time the "trend was toward industrial production based on division of labor and corporate trademarks, the pseudonyms of the market" (1987: 23). Despite this trend, however, many authors of sensational fiction became literary celebrities, especially in the early decades. During the 1840s and 1850s, Lippard and Buntline were two of the most popular and prolific writers of sensational fiction. Lippard produced numerous bestsellers, including several "mysteries of the city" novels, such as *The Quaker City; or, The Monks of Monk Hall* (1845), *The Killers* (1850), *The Empire City; or, New York by Night and Day: Its Aristocracy and its Dollars* (1850), and *New York: Its Upper Ten and Lower Million* (1853). He also wrote two US–Mexican War romances, *Legends of Mexico* (1847) and *'Bel of Prairie Eden* (1848). Buntline was even more prolific: his sensational novels ran into the dozens, including *The Mysteries and Miseries of New York* (1848),

Figure 16.1 "The Widow's Hope." Painted by T. M. Joy and engraved by J. F. E. Prudhomme. Frontispiece from S. G. Goodrich (ed.), *The Token and Atlantic Souvenir, A Christmas and New Year's Present* (Boston: Otis, Broaders, & Co., 1839). Collection of Shirley Samuels.

Three Years After (1849), *The B'hoys of New York* (1850), *The G'hals of New York* (1850), and *The Convict* (1851). He also produced two US–Mexican War novels, *The Volunteer* (1847) and *Magdalena the Beautiful Mexican Maid* (1846), several sensational stories set in the Caribbean, such as *Matanzas; or, A Brother's Revenge* (1848), *The Mysteries and Miseries of New Orleans* (1851), and *The Black Avenger of the Spanish Main; or, The Fiend of Blood* (1847), and several more about the US West, notably *Buffalo Bill, the King of Border Men* (1869).

Both Lippard and Buntline were active participants in the urban public spheres of their time, and the career trajectories of both reveal linkages among the new urban cultures, journalism, theater, and sensational fiction. Lippard started out as a writer for the penny papers in Philadelphia, but soon thereafter began to publish stories and novels. Then, in 1845, his "mysteries of the city" novel *The Quaker City* became a great success; so much so that city officials banned a theatrical adaptation of it that was set to open in Philadelphia because they feared that the performances might provoke riots. The popularity of *The Quaker City* allowed Lippard to become a working-class advocate who dedicated his story paper and novels to the causes of labor and land reform. Toward the end of his short life (he died of tuberculosis in his early thirties) he developed a secret society, the Brotherhood of the Union, to promote those causes. Buntline, for his part, worked as a writer for the story papers in Boston and then in New York, where he participated in the city's nativist and temperance movements, which he championed in his story paper and his fiction. He also figured prominently in the Astor Place theater riots, for which he was briefly imprisoned. Buntline's New York novels, moreover, inspired the "Bowery b'hoy and g'hal" theatrical melodramas that were all the rage in that city at midcentury, and later in his life he wrote and performed in plays about Buffalo Bill based on his own novels.

As the titles of Lippard's and Buntline's novels suggest, sensationalism was a capacious genre that borrowed from and incorporated many other sub-genres, including crime and war literature, stories of urban underworlds, seduction narratives, historical romances, legends of the American Revolution, southwestern frontier humor, picaresque novels, the gothic, horror, and what we might call early science fiction, among others. Two of the most popular and important sub-genres, however, were the urban gothic or "mysteries of the city" novel and the imperial adventure story.

Since the late 1980s, perhaps in response to Denning's argument that earlier critics had overemphasized dime novels about the frontier and pioneer life and had thus overlooked urban literature, much of the scholarly work on sensational fiction has focused on mysteries of the city novels. During the 1840s these novels attained an impressive popularity in Paris, London, New York, Philadelphia, and many other places. Eugène Sue's 1842 *Mystères de Paris* served as a prototype for many of the variations that followed. Sue's novel, which was serialized in the *Journal des débats* and eventually became thousands of pages long, "opened to popular novelistic treatment," according to Peter Brooks, "a certain urban topography and demography, of crime and social deviance, finding and exploiting a new form of the narratable" (1984: 147). While Sue included multiple plotlines, foregrounded melodramatic contrasts between high life and low life, and introduced scores of characters with deviant sexualities in his efforts to map this new urban terrain, the prostitute Fleur-de-Marie was an especially important character, for Sue used her body as a figure for the corruption of the capitalist city. Like many mysteries of the city novels, in other words, *Les Mystères de Paris* both exploits new urban topographies and attempts to document social and economic disparities and urban misery. As Brooks suggests, while the novel is in part a slumming narrative that offers a bourgeois perspective on the underworld of the lower classes, Sue was transformed by the experience of writing it and eventually became a socialist deputy who represented working-class districts of Paris.

Although the US versions of the mysteries of the city novel do not comprise a unified body of work, many of them similarly combine lurid voyeurism and social activism as they map urban terrain, and most use women's bodies as figures for urban corruption and exploitation. Lippard's *The Quaker City* was the bestselling US adaptation of the sub-genre; Buntline's New York novels constitute later versions, and at least fifty others, with different local variations and written by authors such as George Thompson, Henri Foster, and A. J. H. Duganne, appeared in the story papers of the era. Lippard's trajectory could be compared to Sue's, since the success of *The Quaker City* encouraged him to become an advocate of the working classes, and Buntline's New York novels also promoted the nativist and temperance movements that he championed through other channels; but in novels such as George Thompson's *Venus in Boston* (1849), *The House Breaker* (1848), and *The Gay Girls of New York* (1853), urban activism and reform are for the most part displaced by a voyeuristic vision of the city that exploits episodes of sex and violence while detaching them from a larger world of urban social movements and associations.

The Quaker City, like many other sensational novels, was loosely based on a penny-paper account of urban crime; in this case, the 1843 murder of Mahlon Heberton by Singleton Mercer, whose sister had been seduced and abandoned by Heberton. While this event is the basis for only one of the many complicated plots in the novel, it is especially significant because, for Lippard, seduction and rape are master metaphors used to comprehend the many forms of inequality that thrive in the industrializing metropolis. In part, this emphasis on endangered women's bodies corresponds to the political agitation within urban reform and working-class movements of the 1840s surrounding the campaign to make seduction a criminal offense. For Lippard and for many other reformers, this project was important because they believed that poor and working-class women were especially vulnerable to sexual violence at the hands of wealthy men. As Lippard stated in his introduction to *The Quaker City*, his guiding idea was that "the seduction of a poor and innocent girl, is a deed altogether as criminal as deliberate murder." But over the course of the novel seduction takes on added meanings as endangered women's bodies are deployed as symbols of the injustices suffered by the poor and working-class people of the city. In this way, the labyrinthine party-house Monk Hall, where rich Philadelphians meet to drink, gamble, and have sex, becomes a figure for the city's secret life.

As this summary of the narrative structure of *The Quaker City* suggests, gender and sexuality are important issues in mysteries of the city literature partly because women's bodies are symbolically central to it. When sensational writers make the bodies of endangered women and prostitutes into symbols of urban problems, they participate in a larger set of discourses on sensation, notably including Lockean sensational psychology, in which women are strongly identified with the nerves, the body, and the passions, and are therefore constructed as perpetually vulnerable and endangered. This gendered psychology, as well as the sensationalists' focus on deviant sexuality as a sign of urban corruption, could lend support to efforts to police and regulate the behavior of women, especially the poor and women of color, as well as that of male seducers. As this last point implies, ideas about manhood are also at stake in mysteries of the city literature, which tends to pit male social types who are representatives of larger social formations, classes, races, and nations, against each other in order to compare different models of manhood and to stigmatize certain types of men, especially wealthy men. This narrative convention has implications for sexuality as well as gender, since within such romantic triangles the relationships between men are often as intense and significant, if not more so, than those between the men and the woman. While sensational mysteries of the city literature often explores the intensities of homosocial and homoerotic triangles, however, it also echoes an anti-urban strain in many antebellum reform movements that recasts the forms of mixing and public association made possible by the city as threats to the home and to public safety, and therefore as threats to an emergent domestic order.

It could be argued that mysteries of the city novels and other sub-genres of sensational fiction explore and exploit the problem of embodiment in the face of US liberal capitalism's emphasis on disembodied abstraction. That is, if the ideal of a rational–critical public sphere and a liberal citizen–subject depends upon the transcendence of that subject's body as well as the particularities of material and economic life, then sensational fiction dwells on the bodies and material particularities that are disallowed by such liberal ideals. It is therefore not surprising that, along with gender and sexuality, class and race emerge as two central tensions in mysteries of the city literature. One of the organizing premises of this sub-genre is that economic differences divide the city into an upper ten and a lower million, and sensational urban fiction maps these disparities by foregrounding particular types of bodies – the corrupt libertine, the endangered virgin, the prostitute, and the heroic mechanic, to name a few. While villains are known as such because they outrage and inflict various kinds of violence on bodies, victims and heroes are partly identified through displays of virtuous suffering, which ostensibly aim to mobilize the sympathies of its audience in behalf of the lower million but almost always focus in particular on poor and working-class white bodies. Sensational fiction also acts as a racializing discourse when it attributes innate differences to different types of bodies, as it sometimes does: for instance, in mysteries of the city literature that catalogues urban ethnic and racial types, or in urban crime plots that focus on racialized criminals. This tendency is especially pronounced in the work of writers with nativist and pro-slavery sympathies such as Ned Buntline. In novel after novel, Buntline defines the native-born white working-class body by opposition to a host of threatening racialized and foreign bodies. And George Thompson, who is relatively uninterested in white working-class activism, still uses racialized bodies as a source of horror, as in his representation of the black criminal Flash Bill as a hyper-embodied rapist and murderer in *The House Breaker*.

The racial politics of the genre are also on display in the imperial adventure fiction that flourished during the same years in which mysteries of the city novels attained wide popularity. Many of these sensational narratives focus on US–Indian conflicts, from colonial wars to more recent conflicts such as those with the Seminole Indians in Florida. Stories of explorers and adventurers in the US West, such as Charles Averill's novels about Kit Carson, were also extremely popular, as were thrilling tales of outlaws and bandits such as the Gold Rush legend of Joaquin Murrieta, which John Rollin Ridge turned into a cheap novel. After Beadle & Co. began to issue dime novels in 1860, women writers such as Ann Stephens and Metta Victor authored almost one-third of the novels published during the firm's early years, and many of these took the form of Western adventure. In other cheap novels the circumatlantic world is the backdrop for sensational sub-genres such as Caribbean pirate tales and maritime romances, and still other novels address such topics as Cuban filibustering, the conquest of Mexico, and revolution in Peru. But especially during the late 1840s,

US–Mexican War fiction was one of the most popular of the sensational imperial adventure sub-genres, with dozens of war novels, including two each by Buntline and Lippard, being published in the story papers during this period.

Most of these war novels are international romances in which the hero is a US military officer and the heroine is a Mexican woman of European, not Indian, descent. In these romances, as in mysteries of the city literature, women's bodies are symbolically central, but here it is the woman's body as symbol of the nation and race that is of interest. Also similarly, the romances often feature rivalries between different types of "manly" and "unmanly" men, and many of the latter are seducers or rapists. The Mexican War romances often contain a queer plot twist, however, for in several cases the Mexican woman masquerades as a man and fights for the Mexican army until her newly awakened love for the US soldier compels her to reveal her gender. Although some of these novels end with a marriage between hero and heroine, in other novels marriage is delayed or blocked by war-related events. If conclusions that end in marriage imply that at the end of the war the US should annex all or part of Mexico, the more ambiguous and even tragic endings suggest doubts and uncertainties about whether Mexican territory, and especially whether large numbers of Catholic and non-white Mexican people, can or should be incorporated into the so-called Anglo Saxon nation.

In addition to international romance, some of this fiction includes action scenes modeled on accounts of the war that were published in the papers. The titles and subtitles of sensational war novels often refer to places where famous battles took place, such as Buena Vista and Monterrey, and international romances are frequently set at or near battle sites. While attempts to represent the horrors of war in anything like a realistic fashion are relatively rare in this literature, Lippard's two war novels contain lurid and detailed sensational representations of battles such as the assault on Monterrey, where US soldiers moved to take control of the city by invading Mexican homes, knocking down walls, and then moving on to the next house. Although both novels idealize white US heroes and demonize racialized Mexicans, Lippard does sometimes focus on Mexican losses and on the suffering of Mexican people, as when he represents two sisters whose father and brother are killed at Monterrey. While one of the dominant projects of sensational imperial adventure fiction is to celebrate white US American manhood, several novels, like these two, also include moments when characters question the war by calling it an invasion of Mexico or suggesting that it was fought to extend slavery's territory. While the dominant note in this fiction is support for the war and especially for the US troops, the moments of doubt and contradiction that it sometimes voices echo the many contemporaneous criticisms of the war, which could be compared to the Vietnam War in terms of the opposition that it provoked among US Americans.

During the 1840s most sensational authors were male, but in the 1850s and 1860s more women began to publish bestselling sensational fiction. E. D. E. N. Southworth, who was perhaps the century's most popular writer, published more than sixty novels in the story papers, especially in Robert Bonner's *New York Ledger*. From 1854 until she wrote her final novel more than thirty years later, T. B. Peterson, who published some of Lippard's novels and was the nineteenth century's major publisher of cheap sensational books, issued almost all of the US editions of her work, including her most famous novel, *The Hidden Hand* (1859), a sensational story of female adventure. While most of this novel's action is set in Virginia, it also includes important mysteries of the city and US–Mexican war sub-plots. In the beginning, the heroine Capitola is discovered in New York City dressing as a boy and selling newspapers in order to survive (Southworth lifted this idea from a newspaper that contained a story about a cross-dressing newsboy), and the conclusion crucially involves the battlefields of Mexico, since Herbert Grayson, Capitola's love interest, participates in the war. Although Grayson becomes an officer, his friend Traverse Rocke is soon sorry he enlisted, partly because of the onerous and despotic military discipline, but also because he feels that it is wrong to "[invade] another's country."

Southworth can be classified as a writer of sensational fiction because of her publishers, because of the exciting, melodramatic, and multiple adventures that she incorporated into the complicated plots of her novels, and because of her style and subject matter. For most critics, however, then as now, it was by no means a compliment to call a writer's work sensational, and Southworth and other women authors received additional criticism for adopting a sensational style to address topics that were beyond the pale of middle-class white womanhood. Louisa May Alcott seemingly anticipated and sought to defuse in advance such criticism, for she used an ambiguous pseudonym, A. M. Barnard, when she published several sensational stories in *Frank Leslie's Illustrated Newspaper* and the *Flag of our Union* during the 1860s. Perhaps the most famous of these is the novella "Behind a Mask; or, A Woman's Power" (1866), the story of a governess and former actress who performs and manipulates gender stereotypes and thereby fools her employers and marries above her station. Although critics have generally agreed that sensational fiction allowed Alcott to express emotions that she had to subdue and control in her sentimental domestic fiction, they have debated the question of whether these stories critically interrogate or reinforce nineteenth-century gender roles. Similar questions might be asked about "Pauline's Passion and Punishment" (1863), another narrative that was published in Leslie's weekly. In this story the main character, Pauline, who works as a companion to the daughter of a Cuban plantation owner, also plays a part, but this time she does so in order to take her revenge on a lover who had formerly abandoned her in order to marry a wealthy woman. If critics have disagreed about the deconstructive potential of these stories, Alcott herself seems to have worried that they might adversely affect her literary reputation, for she soon stopped writing them; and in *Little Women* (1868) Professor Bhaer famously calls Jo's story-paper fiction "bad trash."

While gender is clearly a central concern in Alcott's sensational stories, issues of nation, empire, and race are also significant. In "Pauline's Passion and Punishment," for instance, Alcott describes Pauline as a north European type of woman – her "carriage" reveals "the freedom of an intellect ripened under colder skies" – while

Manuel, the Cuban man with whom she eventually falls in love, is defined by his "southern blood." And although Alcott tried to distinguish her sensation fiction from anti-slavery tales such as "M.L." (1860) and "An Hour" (1864), which were published in the anti-slavery newspaper *The Commonwealth*, there is considerable overlap between the two forms of literature, for both are melodramatic in structure and both address controversial topics such as interracial desire and marriage: "M.L." is about a marriage between a white woman and a mixed-race man from Cuba, while "An Hour" condemns slavery by focusing on an island slave revolt and the blocked romance between a slave woman and her dying master's son.

This convergence between Alcott's sensation fiction and her anti-slavery melo-dramas raises questions about the intersections between sensational fiction and anti-slavery literature more generally. Although Harriet Beecher Stowe's abolitionist novel *Uncle Tom's Cabin* (1852), for example, is usually classified as sentimental literature, Stowe drew on both sentimental and sensational devices and conventions in writing it. While Little Eva's deathbed scene exemplifies the sentimental emphasis on the redemptive qualities of the dying white child, other episodes, such as Eliza's thrilling escape over the ice, or the scenes where Cassy manipulates Legree's fears by making him think his house is haunted, suggest a more sensational structure of feeling. Other anti-slavery novels that include sensational elements include William Wells Brown's *Clotel; Or, The President's Daughter* (1853), which is about the horrors of slavery as they are experienced by a slave woman who is one of Jefferson's descendants (a plot that Lippard also incorporated into his mysteries of the city novel *New York*), and Martin Delany's *Blake; or, The Huts of America* (1859), which was originally serialized in the *Anglo-African Magazine* and which focuses on its hero's efforts to foment slave insurrections in the US South and Cuba.

Sensational elements can also be identified in the literature produced by canonical authors such as Poe, Hawthorne, and Melville. Poe's sensationalism derives in part from his interest in urban modernity, as it is manifested in his crime fiction and in stories such as "The Man of the Crowd" (1840), but the emphasis in many of his other tales on the horrors of the body's corporeality and materiality also recalls the sensa-tional bodies of the era's cheap literature. The sensational foundations of Hawthorne's *House of the Seven Gables* (1851), on the other hand, can be discerned in the novel's focus on class divisions, a mysterious lost inheritance, and the crimes of the past. And Melville's *Pierre; or, The Ambiguities* (1852) starts out as a sentimental novel about an elite rural family and then turns into a sensational mysteries of the city story when Pierre and his two companions – his childhood sweetheart Lucy and his newly discovered half-sister Isabel, to whom he is strongly attracted and who has been working as a lowly seamstress – move to a desperately poor neighborhood in New York City. This move allows Melville not only to gesture toward the emerging class disparities that were a central concern in urban sensational fiction, but also to explore alternative formations of gender, family, and sexuality through the novel's romantic triangles and its sensational treatment of Pierre's unconventional domestic arrange-ments. Although many more connections between sensational fiction and canonical literature, as well as between sensationalism and other literary and cultural discourses, may be traced in the years to come, the most important task for future generations of scholars is to recover and discuss more of the huge body of sensational fiction that remains unread, for what has been retrieved up until now is still only a small part of a much larger whole.

REFERENCES AND FURTHER READING

Alcott, Louisa May (1995). *Louisa May Alcott Unmasked: Collected Thrillers*, ed. Madeleine Stern. Boston: Northeastern University Press.

Alcott, Louisa May (1997). *Louisa May Alcott on Race, Sex, and Slavery*, ed. Sarah Elbert. Boston: Northeastern University Press.

Anthony, David (1997). "The Helen Jewett Panic: Tabloids, Men, and the Sensational Public Sphere in Antebellum New York." *American Literature* 69: 3, 487–514.

Barker-Benfield, G. J. (1992). *The Culture of Sensibility: Sex and Society in Eighteenth-Century Britain*. Chicago and London: University of Chicago Press.

Brodhead, Richard (1993). "Starting Out in the 1860s: Alcott, Authorship, and the Postbellum Literary Field." In *Cultures of Letters: Scenes of Reading and Writing in Nineteenth-Century America*, 69–106. Chicago: University of Chicago Press.

Brooks, Peter (1984). "The Mark of the Beast: Prostitution, Serialization, and Narrative." In *Reading for the Plot: Design and Intention in Narrative*, 143–70. New York: Knopf.

Brown, Bill, ed. (1997). *Reading the West: An Anthology of Dime Westerns*. Boston and New York: Bedford.

Coultrap-McQuin, Susan (1990). *Doing Literary Business: American Women Writers in the Nineteenth Century*. Chapel Hill and London: University of North Carolina Press.

Denning, Michael (1987). *Mechanic Accents: Dime Novels and Working Class Culture in America*. New York and London: Verso.

Elmer, Jonathan (1995). "Poe, Sensationalism, and the Sentimental Tradition." In *Reading at the Social Limit: Affect, Mass Culture, and Edgar Allan Poe* , 93–125. Stanford: Stanford University Press.

Lippard, George (1995). *The Quaker City; or, The Monks of Monk Hall. A Romance of Philadelphia Life, Mystery and Crime*, ed. David Reynolds. Amherst: University of Massachusetts Press. (First publ. 1845.)

Looby, Christopher (1993). "George Thompson and the Romance of the Real: Transgression and Taboo in American Sensation Fiction." *American Literature* 65: 4, 651–72.

Lott, Eric (1993). *Love and Theft: Blackface Minstrelsy and the American Working Class*. New York: Oxford University Press.

Nelson, Dana D. (1998). "Gynecological Manhood: The Worries of Whiteness and Disorders of Women." In *National Manhood: Capitalist Citizenship and the Imagined Fraternity of White Men*, 135–75. Durham, NC, and London: Duke University Press.

Post-Lauria, Sheila (1996). "(Un)Popularity: Moby Dick and Pierre." In *Correspondent Colorings: Melville in the Marketplace*, 123–47. Amherst: University of Massachusetts Press.

Reynolds, David S. (1988). *Beneath the American Renaissance: The Subversive Imagination in the Age of Emerson and Melville*. Cambridge, Mass., and London: Harvard University Press.

Saxton, Alexander (1990). *The Rise and Fall of the White Republic: Class Politics and Mass Culture in Nineteenth-Century America*. New York and London: Verso.

Slotkin, Richard (1985). *The Fatal Environment: The Myth of the Frontier in the Age of Industrialization, 1800–1890*. Middletown, Conn.: Wesleyan University Press.

Southworth, E. D. E. N. (1988). *The Hidden Hand, or Capitola the Madcap*, ed. Joanne Dobson. New Brunswick, NJ: Rutgers University Press. (First publ. 1859.)

Streeby, Shelley (2002). *American Sensations: Class, Empire, and the Production of Popular Culture*. Berkeley: University of California Press.

Thompson, George (2002). *"Venus in Boston" and Other Tales of Nineteenth-Century City Life*, ed. David Reynolds and Kimberley Gladman. Amherst: University of Massachusetts Press.

Williams, Linda (2001). *Playing the Race Card: Melodramas of Black and White from Uncle Tom to O. J. Simpson*. Princeton and Oxford: Princeton University Press.

17

Melodrama and American Fiction

Lori Merish

Compared to the sentimental and the sensational – affect-generating literary languages with which it shares many similar, overlapping characteristics – melodrama has received little focused critical attention in late eighteenth- and early nineteenth-century American literary studies. To be sure, American theater historians, from David Grimsted's groundbreaking *Melodrama Unveiled* to Bruce McConachie's *Melodramatic Formations*, have examined the widespread influence of stage melodrama in nineteenth-century America (especially between 1820 and 1870) as a language of political protest and a form of popular working-class culture.[1] But while scholarship in British literary studies has for several decades examined the relationship between melodramatic theater and literature, often focusing on melodrama's inscriptions of social class (e.g. the work of Martha Vicinus and Elaine Hadley), there has been little work on what John Belton has termed the "melodramatic mode" as it informs and is mobilized in American literature.[2] This essay will address this critical absence, drawing on recent work by Eric Lott and Linda Williams that finds in melodrama what Williams calls a "racially based" form of representation.[3]

Characterizing the American melodramatic mode as an explicitly gendered language for representing social differences, this essay examines the relevance of melodrama for understanding early American fiction, including the plot and thematic devices of this fiction as well as some of its characteristic formal and rhetorical features. Three literary texts anchor my discussion: Hawthorne's *The Blithedale Romance*, a text which foregrounds the melodramatic imagination as male fantasy; Stowe's *Uncle Tom's Cabin*, a text that both explicitly racializes melodrama and challenges its masculine bias by incorporating an innovative idiom of maternal melodrama; and Southworth's *The Hidden Hand*, a text that self-consciously parodies melodramatic gender scripts, and in which melodrama's historically resonant class critique is refracted through race and an explicitly racialized cast of characters. In antebellum America, the interdependence of theatrical and fictional melodrama was both pronounced and complex: the melodramatic vocabulary of the stage widely influenced American fiction, while several of the era's most popular texts (including *Uncle Tom's Cabin* and *The Hidden Hand*) were adapted as theatrical melodramas that proved wildly popular.

Melodrama's formal characteristics have been enumerated by several critics: a starkly defined, manichean conflict between good and evil, salvation and damnation; the personification of these polarized moral absolutes in stock characters, especially the virtuous young woman, the noble hero who rescues the heroine, and the satanic villain (whose villainy is often disguised by his elite standing and is generally expressed as a sexual threat); the elaboration of conventional narratives of familial dispersal and reunion; an emphasis on the revelation of hidden actions and moral dimensions (what Peter Brooks terms melodrama's "moral occult"); a rhetorical style characterized by expressions of highly charged emotion though hyperbolic utterances and grandiose gestures; and a tendency to convey vivid emotional effects in pictorial tableaux.[4]

Most definitions note a concentration on plot at the expense of complex character-ization, which gives melodramatic texts an episodic quality and can create a diffuse narrative structure.[5] Typified by a sensational, rapid succession of implausible actions, melodramatic plot contrivances include miraculous coincidences and striking rever-sals: as one antebellum critic noted, melodrama not only depicted characters "better than saints, or worse than devils," but situated its simplified characters in circum-stances that "outrage all probability."[6] These plot devices especially facilitate plots of recognition and reconciliation:[7] melodramas feature masked relationships and dis-guised identities, characters with mysterious parentage and origins, babies switched in their cradles or abducted, princes disguised as peasants and blackguards as nobles; the trope of recognition is especially enacted in the plot of familial separation and return.[8] The melodramatic mode is not reducible to any single thematic formula, as Elaine Hadley observes,[9] yet the theme of female sexual endangerment – in its usual incarnation, a narrative of a virginal maiden seduced by an aristocratic rake – was a staple of melodramatic literature, especially domestic melodrama, the most popular sub-genre on the stage (and in literary texts) by the 1830s. Although certain variants of American theatrical melodrama (such as the celebrated Edwin Forrest vehicles) centered on masculine virtue and heroism,[10] most melodramas foregrounded feminine virtue and relied upon a conventional vocabulary of sexual difference. As Mary Poovey observes, "For its characters and its [usual] plot, melodrama assumes both the naturalness of female dependence and the sexual double standard; if male sexuality were not aggressive and predatory, . . . and if females were not innocent, vulnerable, and valuable precisely in this vulnerable innocence, villainy would assume a different guise and plots would not tell of innocence persecuted and then saved."[11]

In his study of the rise of American stage melodrama as a national cultural form, Grimsted identifies a formulaic "melodramatic structure" reproduced in most mid-nineteenth-century plays; the structure was so consistently followed that "one com-petent dramatist's plays were scarcely distinguishable from another's . . . in character, structure, and sentiment." Most melodramas present an unprotected virtuous female (the heroine is almost always motherless, her father usually absent or incompetent) pursued with diabolic subterfuge and occasional violence by the villain. Often a votary of "fashion" and almost always tainted with foreign blood, the villain is wholly committed to what one dramatist called "shattering virtue's temple" and satisfying his lust. While the heroine is regularly described in imagery of divinity (e.g., "heavenly maid," "chaste-eyed angel"), the villain is cast in the language of satanic deception, a characterological opposition elaborated through a gendering of plot. In contrast to the villain, who actively plans and enacts his foul designs, the heroine is characterized by extreme vulnerability and passivity; in a gesture of self-nomination characteristic of melodrama, one heroine sighs, "I can only wait patiently for the storm to burst on my head and trust to heaven for deliverance."[12]

Mediating between these two positions is a third: the villain is defeated, and the young woman rescued from sexual misfortune, by the saving ministrations of the virtuous, manly hero. Like the heroine, he is an idealized character: courageous, faithful, virtuous, chaste, and often rural-born. Notably, Grimsted observes,

> the hero proved his goodness, as the villain his evil, primarily by his attitude toward "defenseless woman, . . . that sex that nature formed us to defend." No hero tolerated so much as joking mention of a desire to do any woman wrong; such a thought was sure to drive him, depending on his temperament, either to anger or a sermon.[13]

Melodramas flourished on the American stage: French, English and German melodramas appeared in America starting in the late eighteenth century, and the native melodrama discussed by Grimsted was fostered by theater directors, playwrights, and actors.[14] Its influence can be seen throughout American fiction from this period: even in texts in which the melodramatic is not the dominant mode of literary expression, melodramatic characterization, motifs, and plot devices appear with great frequency.

Much American fiction from this period bears traces of the melodramatic: the delineation of characters as manichean opposites or moral absolutes; a heightened rhetoric characterized by hyperbole, grandiose antithesis, declamatory statements, and the expression of intense feeling; and an emphasis on emotionally charged gestures and tableaux (especially domestic tableaux) as privileged, revelatory fictional signs; while fictional plots often involve dilemmas of recognition, invoking the temporary veiling and ultimate recognition of moral character. Several novelistic sub-genres, from the revolutionary-era seduction novel of Rowson and Foster, with its plot of virtue on trial, to the quintessentially "American" genre of romance, with its investment in symbolic characterization and what Richard Chase identifies as a fundamental manicheism, share features with – when they are not directly indebted to – melodramatic representation.[15]

Tellingly, Nina Baym has described the romances of Cooper, Melville, and others as "melodramas of beset manhood"; they seem close kin to the heroic stage melodramas McConachie examines. Hawthorne's great romances, especially *The House of the Seven Gables* and *The Blithedale Romance*, reference, while often complicating, melodrama's stock characterizations and plots of persecution and sexual endangerment. Similarly, much of what we understand as the sentimental mode derives from the melodramatic inscription of virtuous feeling; what Brooks identifies as the new "aesthetics of embodiment" associated with melodrama, where the body is "emblematized" or "seized by meaning," illuminates sentimental modes of embodiment and the acute moral legibility of the sentimental body.[16] Thus, even that exemplary sentimental novel, Susan Warner's *The Wide, Wide World*, contains melodrama's telling incident: Ellen's encounter with the sadistic clerk Mr. Saunders, and her breathtakingly timely rescue by her virtuous "brother" and eventual suitor John Humphreys, is stereotypically melodramatic.[17]

Fanny Fern's *Ruth Hall* marks its departure from sentimental convention in melodramatic terms: Ruth barely escapes the melodramatic suffering and characteristic demise of the sentimental seamstress to wrest control of her own plot – notably, as a writer, who uses her razor wit to critique heterosexual relations and imbue women's stories not with pathos but with humor. And while Stowe echoed clerical opponents of the stage in her view of theatrical entertainments (refusing to pen a stage adaptation of *Uncle Tom's Cabin* herself, she attended one performance of the play hidden under a shawl), the famous set-pieces of her novel – Eliza crossing the ice, Little Eva's death, Uncle Tom's death – are profoundly influenced by the melodramatic imagination.[18] While, as Mary Kelley has influentially argued, domestic authors claimed the novel as their oratorical platform, they also embraced it as their theatrical stage – adapting the publicity of domestic melodrama to the private realm of the fictional page.[19] What Richard Brodhead describes as the constitutive theatricality of domestic fiction is illuminated by the melodramatic context from which that literature emerged.[20]

Influential in theatrical and literary popular cultures, melodrama supplied a highly charged language whose moving effects were mobilized in political discourses as well.[21] Discussing the uses of melodrama in British political discourse, specifically in debates surrounding the poor laws, Elaine Hadley argues that melodrama activates ethical norms associated with a patriarchal social order and what E. P. Thompson has described as a "moral economy": invoking a traditional, rural social order based on the economic and social interdependence of the different "orders" (e.g. laborers and landlords) and mutual responsibilities and duties, melodrama documents the erosion of this paternalist social vision. Focusing typically on the moral lapses of elites, the melodramatic mode offers a conservative critique of market individualism and class society at the moment of their historical emergence.[22] The melodramatic vision of class paternalism (and conservative critique of market culture) was itself highly contested in Jacksonian America, with its oft-proclaimed egalitarian, democratic relations among (white) men; it is most clearly associated with pro-slavery writers such as George Fitzhugh, who – tellingly – includes the English poet Thomas Hood's "The Song of the Shirt," with its melodramatic portrait of the downtrodden needle-worker, in his defense of slavery, *Cannibals, All!*[23] Reformers of various stripes seized upon the affective power of the melodramatic mode to relate social evils.

Appropriating melodrama's stark dramaturgy of good and evil, salvation and damnation, moral reformers in particular employed melodramatic representation to illuminate and interpret the occulted moral dimensions of social life.

In Jacksonian political and social discourses, the melodramatic mode was thus deployed to suit a range of social and political contexts. In particular, melodrama's gendered vocabulary of sexual exploitation was employed by a range of writers: middle-class reformers and radical working men who envisioned villainous "lords of the loom" and predatory overseers victimizing helpless factory girls and impoverished seamstresses; temperance advocates who depicted women and children terrorized and abused by their would-be protectors transformed into drunken villains, themselves enslaved by the "demon rum"; urban moral reformers such as members of the Magdalen Societies who protested the crime of seduction in melodramatic terms; and abolitionists who denounced the "peculiar institution" by focusing, melodramatically, on the sexual persecution and physical abuse of slave women and girls (the "tragic mulatta," who dies as a consequence of her sexual dishonor, has an expressly melodramatic pedigree). Foregrounding the sufferings of the "helpless and unbefriended" while distancing that suffering from newly enfranchised, politically empowered white males,[24] these writers expressly align melodramatic victimization with women, feminized members of the working class (particularly seamstresses), and feminized slaves.[25]

Melodrama's gendered logic is acutely evident in Hawthorne's *The Blithedale Romance*. The text not only evinces melodrama's preoccupation with a "moral occult," a penchant for interpreting everyday events to glean hidden moral meanings; *Blithedale* also employs explicitly melodramatic characterization and plotting. And while several critics have commented on Coverdale's penchant for spectatorship and the language of theatricality that infuses his imagination, none have noted the specifically melodramatic quality of the *Blithedale* narrator's spectatorial and theatrical fantasies. Coverdale repeatedly encodes his visual experience in melodramatic terms; in particular, his voyeuristic fascination with what he terms his "private theater" (p. 48) of characters (Zenobia, Priscilla, and Hollingsworth), as well as his obsession with unearthing dark secrets, masked relationships, and hidden crimes, reveal the influence of the melodramatic imagination.[26]

Blithedale borrows several elements from stage melodrama: in particular, the subplot involving the villain Westervelt (complete with black coat and sham gold teeth), the pale, motherless, and unprotected maiden Priscilla (whose victimization, notably, is expressly sexualized), and the ineffectual, indeed ruined, father Old Moodie/ Fauntleroy (who owes his weakness, melodramatically, to secret crimes perpetrated in the past) reads straight out of the melodramatic repertory. More generally, the frequent appearance in Hawthorne's fiction of spectacles and set-pieces (exemplified by the scaffold scenes in *The Scarlet Letter* and the "Eliot's pulpit" and theater scenes in *Blithedale*), scenes dramatically marked by heightened rhetoric and emotion in which moral truths are revealed, and especially his fascination with the emerging (and highly gendered and eroticized) performance culture of mesmerism, suggest the impact of melodramatic theatricality on his fiction.

Constructing Priscilla as wronged maid and innocent victim, Hawthorne's narrative in some sense aims to complete the melodramatic formula and determine who the melodramatic "hero" – and Priscilla's rescuer – will be. (Hollingsworth, of course, appears to fulfill this role in the text; but Coverdale consistently attributes to his rival the role of seducer/villain. Reprising what Joseph Roach terms the "mortgage melodrama," Coverdale envisions Hollingsworth in cold, calculating pursuit of Zenobia and then Priscilla's fortune, which he wishes to appropriate to his own egotistical purpose – erecting a reformatory for prisoners in the location of the reformers' commune – a purpose that is, notably, hidden from the rest of the Blithedale community.[27]) But by narrating *Blithedale* in first person and making the urge to melodramatize Priscilla's story Coverdale's own, the text both equates the melodramatic imagination with male fantasy and ironizes that fantasy through Coverdale's pained interiority. For Coverdale's oft-noted skepticism and ambivalence extend to the revelatory power and certainty of melodrama's "moral occult." While the Blithedale utopia, like the Veiled Lady herself, would appear to manifest the sacred in an otherwise profane world, Coverdale oscillates between investing in those spiritual truths and repudiating them as mere "humbug" (p. 5). The melodramatic mode is both reworked and problematized in Hawthorne's fictional text.

While Priscilla is largely trapped within the melodramatic plot – at least until the final, subversive chapter, where the power relations of the text's melodramatic "white slave" narrative appear spectacularly reversed – the character of Zenobia is also melodramatically inflected. Repeatedly figured as an actress, the larger-than-life Zenobia at times appears to break free of melodrama's gendered limits to attain the stature of tragic heroine; however, she is repeatedly reduced by Coverdale to a few stock melodramatic roles. In particular, while Zenobia regularly and eloquently challenges the debilitating domestic limits of women's position in antebellum society – and Coverdale himself acknowledges that the "sphere of ordinary womanhood was narrower than her development required" (p. 190) – he melodramatically interprets the tragedy of Zenobia's life in the highly personal terms she herself so roundly repudiates. In Coverdale's imagination, Zenobia oscillates between two highly melodramatic positions: that of a young woman wronged (marked by a secret sexual past with Westervelt, seduced and abandoned by Hollingsworth), and that of a conniving procuress (delivering Priscilla to Westervelt to preserve both her lover and her fortune, she is subsequently punished for this "unfeminine" and immoral act).

Zenobia's death – an act of renunciation and revenge that Coverdale reads as highly theatrical – extends the text's melodramatic logic: Zenobia herself is punished for her transgressive agency, while her death becomes an inescapable token of moral culpability for the treacherous Hollingsworth. (In another sense, Zenobia's sacrificial death inhabits what Franco Moretti describes as the melodramatic time frame of "too late"; and it relegates her to the silence Brooks terms melodrama's "text of muteness.") But if Zenobia's body is, for Coverdale, melodramatically "seized by meaning" both in life and in death, Zenobia resists, and indeed critiques, Coverdale's efforts at moral interpretation, which she equates to a kind of masculine sexual violence. From the outset, Zenobia frustrates Coverdale's efforts to "penetrate" the "mystery of [her] life" (p. 47) – a melodramatic impulse that she turns back on to Coverdale himself. Zenobia thus provides a commentary on the melodramatic mode that calls into question both its moral authority and its gendered conventions.

Jane Tompkins has argued in melodrama's own terms that traditional narratives of antebellum literary history assign "Hawthorne and Melville the role of heroes, [and] the sentimental novelists the role of villains," yet both were indebted to the melodramatic imagination.[28] Two texts from the period, Harriet Beecher Stowe's *Uncle Tom's Cabin* and E. D. E. N. Southworth's *The Hidden Hand*, exemplify various ways in which women writers used and revised the melodramatic mode and its characteristic gender investments. Notably, both of these immensely popular texts were adapted as stage melodramas, a fact that suggests their special compatibility with – and, indeed, influence by – the melodramatic imagination.

Melodrama left a deep impress on *Uncle Tom's Cabin*. Stowe's penchant for character types that personify good and evil and, in general, her preoccupation with illuminating the occulted moral dimensions of social life – embodied here in the abhorrent traffic in persons (an institution that, in one character's words, "comes from the devil") – define the text's melodramatic sensibilities.[29] In a sense, what Robyn Warhol terms Stowe's "engaging narrator" performs for the reader melodrama's interpretive work, explicitly drawing out the text's moral meanings.[30] Importantly, Stowe extends the gendered tropes of melodrama into the realm of race relations: recuperating blackness through an ideology of "romantic racialism," Stowe reverses melodrama's traditional racial meanings. In Stowe's racial melodrama, villainous (white) men, from the unfeeling Haley to arch-villain Simon Legree, pursue their nefarious designs by victimizing an expanded array of the "helpless and unbefriended," especially feminized black men such as the Christlike martyr Uncle Tom (a figure "gentle as a child" [p. 204] whose melodramatic demise before George Harris arrives to free him painfully exemplifies the "too late" of melodramatic temporality), vulnerable black women such as Prue, and little children such as Eva St. Clare (depicted as a kind of moral barometer – the sufferings of slavery "sink into her heart" and kill her) and the novel's many brutalized slave children.

The peculiar institution's mortal costs are borne by these characters, who are marked as slavery's sacrificial victims – and the text points toward a redemption that is eschatological as well as social and historical. Furthermore, in *Uncle Tom's Cabin*, melodrama's characteristic narrative of familial dispersal and return is expressly racialized: slavery's greatest tragedy is the separation of families, particularly mothers and children; and the concluding tableau reunites the African American family (returning Cassy to Eliza, Emily de Thoux to her brother George Harris), "drawn together by the singular coincidence of their fortunes" (p. 371) – a melodramatic conclusion only possible, in Stowe's text, in the extranational space of Canada.

Spectacularly inverting melodrama's racial meanings, *Uncle Tom's Cabin* also transforms its gender content. By incorporating into her text the idiom of "sentimental power," Stowe gives women greater latitude of agency and characterization. Most importantly, she introduces the language of maternal melodrama, with its thematic of maternal separation and return, into her analysis of racial politics.[31] Importantly, the affective ingredients of maternal melodrama – grief over the loss of one's children, and heroic resolve to retain them – constitute the site of the novel's interracial sympathy and (feminine) activist potential.[32]

The novel uses these materials most prominently in Eliza's love for her son. Her refusal to allow their separation motivates her heroic escape from slavery; as Linda Williams points out, it affords an "empowerment" that differentiates her from earlier melodramatic heroines.[33] The revisionist potential of maternal melodrama is especially evident in the text's treatment of Simon Legree. Stowe's Legree, like Hawthorne's Westervelt, is a classic melodramatic villain – and, as with Westervelt, his threat (directed toward Emmeline and Cassy) is explicitly sexual. While he aims to enact his melodramatic designs, he finds himself instead confined within Cassy's own gothic (maternal) melodrama. With sensational effects (complete with creaking ceilings), she simulates the haunting presence of Legree's dead mother. In this version of maternal melodrama, mothers return from the grave to reclaim their children. By stage-managing her own (melo)dramatic plot, Cassy manages to escape Legree and, in the end, become reunited with her own long-lost children.

Like much serial fiction from the period, Southworth's *The Hidden Hand* strongly bore the imprint of the melodramatic imagination.[34] Serialized in Robert Bonner's *New York Ledger* in 1859, *The Hidden Hand* incorporates a dizzying array of melodramatic plot contrivances and an expansive cast of melodramatic heroines (e.g. Clara Day and the virtuous seamstress, Marah Rocke), heroes (e.g. Traverse Rocke and Herbert Greyson), and villains (most notably, Black Donald and Gabriel Le Noir). The text's investment in melodramatic convention is evidenced in its many references to theater, its incorporation of several courtroom scenes (as Brooks notes, a staple of melodrama) and similar scenes of moral unmasking, and its inclusion of an array of sensational incidents (murder, kidnapping, illicit seizure of property, forced captivity – including entrapment in an insane asylum – and attempted rape); in addition, its heroine Capitola Le Noir (familiarly known as Cap Black) is repeatedly figured as an actress. But the text is especially notable for the way it ironizes the melodramatic mode, particularly its gendered vocabulary of virtue and vice, passivity and activity, a vocabulary – as the characters' very names indicate – thoroughly racialized in *The Hidden Hand*.[35] Indeed, though in a tone quite distinct from the evangelical sensibility of Stowe's novel, *The Hidden Hand* aligns melodrama's "moral occult" with the hidden crimes against person and property perpetrated under slavery.

To an extraordinary degree, *The Hidden Hand* self-reflexively comments on melodramatic forms. In doing so, it reveals how thoroughly familiar melodramatic codes were to its antebellum readers, while – by calling attention to its own artifice and fictionality – encouraging those readers to adopt a distanced, critical stance. Throughout the novel, characters reiterate melodramatic clichés such as "your money or your life" during dramatic situations, and measure their own emotional reactions against those featured on the stage. For example, when one character's estranged nephew is unexpectedly restored to him, he declares, "I am not sentimental, nor romantic, nor melodramatic, nor anything of that sort. I don't know how to strike an attitude and exclaim – 'Come to my bosom, sole remaining offspring of a dear, departed sister,' or any of the like stage-playing."[36] Ironizing, even mocking melodramatic conventions, the text unsettles them; at the same time, it adapts melodrama's traditional class critique to the arena of contemporary gender and racial politics.

The primary instrument of the text's melodramatic revisionism is Southworth's heroine herself.[37] Quite unlike any passive, virginal melodramatic heroine, the cross-dressing Capitola seizes the power to generate plot typically afforded to the villain in melodrama. Staging scenes of her own devising (e.g. a mock wedding scene, in which she poses as Clara Day to foil Le Noir's nefarious designs, and a duel with villain Craven Le Noir, in which she forces confession of his abuse of her name), Capitola is the text's primary agent of moral unmasking; and what she unmasks is the injustice of male power. Especially notable is Cap's reworking of melodrama's stock theme of seduction and female sexual endangerment.[38] While the plot of attempted seduction appears repeatedly in Southworth's text (e.g. in the story of Marah Rocke and Clara Day), and Cap herself testifies that she was sexually threatened on the New York streets, Cap refuses to be entrapped by codes of female sexual victimization: she refuses confinement in her guardian's home as a way to ensure her safety; and she asserts her right to defend herself from male attack – be it physical assault or verbal attack on her "honor." In an important sense, Cap refuses to be defined by melo-drama's gender codes; and she claims for herself the power to "rescue" other women from male abuse, assuming in a key sequence of the text (to cite one example) the role of rescuing, chivalric hero to Clara's innocent victim.

Raised on the New York streets, regularly lapsing into the working-class vernacular of street-boy slang, Capitola presents a subaltern (and racialized) class position from which melodrama's gender scripts can be rewritten. This is especially evident in an encounter between Cap and the local minister, arranged by her guardian Major Warfield, who enlists the minister's moral authority in his efforts to "manage the capricious little witch" (p. 180). Recognizing at once that she "shall be lectured by the good parson," Cap resolves to foil his efforts of moral interpretation and inscrip-tion. Exhibiting "the decorum of a nun," Capitola performs the part of a seduced woman and regretfully leads the minister through a "confession" of past sexual indiscretions – thus gratifying her "respectable" male interlocutor's evident desire for sexual narrative (and prurient interest in female sexual transgression), and dis-rupting the melodramatic formula that would cast her as innocent maid in need of patriarchal protection.

Skillfully employing *double entendre* to manipulate the terms of the seduction narrative, Cap allows the minister to find the meanings he both seeks and fears: confiding, "I have been very indiscreet, and I am very miserable!" (p. 183), Cap builds narrative suspense through heightened rhetoric: "I'm going to inform you, sir! And oh, I hope you will take pity on me and tell me what to do; for though I dread to speak, I can't keep it on my conscience any longer, it is such a heavy weight on my breast!" (p. 184). Positioning the minister as privileged confessor while reminding him that she "had no mother," Cap relates how she first met one Alfred Blenheim "walking in the woods" and she has since met him countless times, confessing that he is now "hid in the closet in my room" (184–5): "I hope you will forgive me, sir! But – but he was so handsome I couldn't help liking him!" (p. 184). When the pastor exclaims with "deepest horror" in terms wholly conventional and moralistic – "did you not know . . . the danger you ran by giving this young man private interviews . . . ? Wretched girl! Better you'd never been born than ever so to have received a man!" (p. 185) – Cap turns the tables on him. In doing so, she aligns the sexual corruption of the alleged seducer with the minister's illicit assumptions. Revealing that Alfred Blenheim is a "poodle that strayed away from some of the neighbor's houses," Capitola takes exception with what she envisions as the minister's depraved taste for sexual scandal. "Man! I'd like to know what you mean by that, Mr. Goodwin! . . . I – I give private interviews to a man! Take care what you say, Mr. Goodwin! I won't be insulted! No, not even by you!" (pp. 184–5). The distressed minister has no advice for Warfield other than to "thrash that girl *as if she were a bad boy* – for she richly deserves it!" (p. 185, emphasis added).

Addressing the frequency of stories of "seduction and betrayal" among existing testimonials by antebellum prostitutes (most of whom were interviewed by moral reformers), historians have suggested that these women often framed their sexual experience melodramatically because they knew that was what their interviewers expected – it conformed to middle-class gender stereotypes (of passive and asexual women) and would readily garner sympathy from their listeners.[39] Capitola brilliantly ironizes this conventional scene of melodramatic narrative transmission, destabilizing the gender stereotypes – of middle-class/male "protection" and female sexual ignorance, passivity, and "modesty"– activated within it.

Notes

1 David Grimsted, *Melodrama Unveiled: American Theater and Culture 1800–1850* (Berkeley: University of California Press, 1987); Bruce A. McConachie, *Melodramatic Formations: American Theater and Society, 1820–1870* (Iowa City: University of Iowa Press, 1992). In America as in England, melodramatic theater's audience came from all social strata, though its greatest popularity and support lay among the urban working classes; see Michael R. Booth, *English Melodrama* (London: Herbert Jenkins, 1965), 13. On melodrama as popular, working-class form, see McConachie, *Melodramatic Formations*, and David Grimsted, "Melodrama as Echo of the Historically Voiceless," in Tamara K. Hareven (ed.), *Anonymous Americans* (New York: Prentice-Hall, 1971), 80–98.

2 Martha Vicinus, "'Helpless and Unbefriended': Nineteenth-Century Domestic Melodrama," *New Literary History* 13 (Fall 1971), 127–43; Elaine Hadley, *Melodramatic Tactics: Theatricalized Dissent in the English Marketplace, 1800–1885* (Stanford: Stanford University Press, 1995); John Belton, *American Cinema/American Culture* (New York: McGraw-Hill, 1994).

3 Linda Williams, *Playing the Race Card: Melodramas of Black and White from Uncle Tom to*

O. J. Simpson (Princeton: Princeton University Press, 2001); Eric Lott, *Love and Theft: Blackface Minstrelsy and the American Working Class* (New York: Oxford University Press, 1993). Melodrama's conventional, symbolic association of whiteness with virtue, and blackness with villainy, made it readily available to racial encoding and revisionism.

4 Peter Brooks, *The Melodramatic Imagination: Balzac, Henry James, and the Mode of Excess* (New Haven: Yale University Press, 1995), viii.

5 Indeed, as Martha Vicinus notes, "character development is irrelevant to melodrama"; instead, in assessing melodrama, we need to "retrain our expectations and sensibilities to focus upon action and plot" ("'Helpless and Unbefriended,'" 134).

6 As quoted in Grimsted, *Melodrama Unveiled*, 195.

7 Peter Brooks notes that melodrama employs "the dramaturgy of virtue misprized and eventually recognized. It is about virtue made visible and acknowledged, the drama of a recognition" (*Melodramatic Imagination*, 27).

8 Grimsted, *Melodrama Unveiled*, 196. John Cawelti perceptively notes that melodrama is characterized by what he terms an "aesthetic of simplification and intensification": an episodic simplicity centering on moments of crisis (the threat of death, violence, sudden impoverishment, various forms of moral temptation), and the intensified emotional effect of these incidents conveyed through a simplified esthetic of character types, tableaux, and set-pieces. See his discussion of "social melodramas" in *Adventure, Mystery and Romance: Formula Stories as Art and Popular Culture* (Chicago: University of Chicago Press, 1973), 265.

9 Hadley, *Melodramatic Tactics*, 230 n. 10.

10 McConachie, *Melodramatic Formations*.

11 Mary Poovey, *Uneven Developments: The Ideological Work of Gender in Mid-Victorian England* (Chicago: University of Chicago Press, 1988), 83.

12 Grimsted, *Melodrama Unveiled*, 171, 175, 176, 177, 174.

13 Ibid., 181

14 Ibid., 1–21.

15 One of the traits Chase attributes to the romance tradition is "a tendency toward melodrama and idyl": *The American Novel and its Tradition* (Garden City, NY: Doubleday, 1957), ix.

16 Brooks, "Melodrama, Body, Revolution," in Jacky Bratton, Jim Cook, and Christine Gledhill (eds.), *Melodrama: Stage, Picture, Screen* (London: British Film Institute, 1994), 18. Several scholars have noted the historical connection between the two modes; for example, Pixérécourt, usually identified as the founder of French melodrama, was directly influenced by Richardson's fiction.

17 *The Wide, Wide World*, ed. Jane Tompkins (New York: Feminist Press, 1987), 396ff. Although Ellen is not the typical melodramatic heroine – she undergoes real character development; hers is a *bildungsroman* or, more precisely, a conversion narrative, not a melodrama – Warner's novel is capacious enough to include this revelatory incident, by way of defining her relationship with John. Indeed, that relationship is an extension of the melodramatic logic of this scene: sentimental novels rarely escape the constitutive paternalism of the melodramatic imagination.

18 Grimsted, *Melodrama Unveiled*, 24; Cawelti, *Adventure, Mystery and Romance*.

19 *Private Woman, Public Stage: Literary Domesticity in Nineteenth-Century America* (New York: Oxford University Press, 1983). As Kelley observes, "respectable" middle-class women were not expected to mount the oratorical platform; nor were they expected to attend theatrical performances – a fact that clearly informed women writers' mediated, textual use of melodramatic materials.

20 "Veiled Ladies: Toward a History of Antebellum Entertainment," in *Cultures of Letters: Scenes of Reading and Writing in Nineteenth-Century America* (Chicago: University of Chicago Press, 1993), 48–68.

21 As Hadley demonstrates in the British context, "melodrama's familial narratives of dispersal and reunion, its emphatically visual renderings of bodily torture and criminal conduct, its atmospheric menace and

providential plotting, its expressions of highly charged emotion, and its tendency to personify absolutes like good and evil were represented in a wide variety of social settings": *Melodramatic Tactics*, 3.

22 *Melodramatic Tactics*. Looking explicitly at domestic melodrama, Martha Vicinus argues that these plays offered an influential vocabulary for representing changes wrought by the industrial revolution. Vicinus contends that domestic melodrama comprised an esthetic response to the traumas of the industrial revolution; its heroines, "helpless and unbefriended," reflected the feelings of loss of working-class people faced with the destruction of traditional values. Noting that melodramatic theater and literature had particular appeal for "the working class and women, two groups facing great dangers without economic power or social recognition," Vicinus argues that "domestic melodrama by its very nature is conservative, however subversive its underlying message. It argues for the preservation of the family and its traditional values – a binding in of the errant son or unforgiving father or wayward daughter": " 'Helpless and Unbefriended,' " 141.

23 George Fitzhugh, *Cannibals All! or, Slaves Without Masters*, ed. C. Vann Woodward (Cambridge, Mass.: Harvard University Press, 1988).

24 On the feminization of dependency during this period, see Nancy Fraser and Linda Gordon, "A Genealogy of 'Dependency': Tracing a Keyword of the U.S. Welfare State," in Nancy Fraser, *Justice Interruptus: Critical Reflections on the "Postsocialist" Condition* (New York: Routledge, 1997), 121–49.

25 On the melodramatic portrait of the sentimental seamstress, see Lori Merish, "Representing the 'Deserving Poor': The 'Sentimental Seamstress' and the Feminization of Poverty in Antebellum America," in Debra Bernardi and Jill Bergman (eds.), *Our Sisters' Keepers: Theories of Poverty Relief in the Work of 19th-Century American Women Writers* (forthcoming from University of Alabama Press). On the feminization of slave suffering in abolitionist literature, see Elizabeth Ammons and Jenny Franchot, "The Punish-

ment of Esther: Frederick Douglass and the Construction of the Feminine," in Eric Sundquist (ed.), *New Literary and Historical Essays on Frederick Douglass* (New York: Cambridge University Press, 1990), 141–65.

26 Nathaniel Hawthorne, *The Blithedale Romance* (New York: Penguin, 1983), 48. All further references to the text are to this edition. As Coverdale frankly states, Hollingsworth, Zenobia, and Priscilla "were separated from the rest of the Community, to my imagination, and stood forth as the indices of a problem which it was my business to solve"; attempting to "penetrate" their "secrets," Coverdale secretly observes them, hoping they'll "give themselves away" (pp. 69, 48).

27 Joseph Roach, *Cities of the Dead: Circum-Atlantic Performance* (New York: Columbia University Press, 1996).

28 Jane P. Tompkins, "The (Other) American Renaissance," in Walter Benn Michaels and Donald Pease (eds.), *The American Renaissance Reconsidered* (Baltimore: Johns Hopkins University Press, 1985), 35.

29 Harriet Beecher Stowe, *Uncle Tom's Cabin* (New York: Norton, 1994), 193. All further references to the text are to this edition.

30 Robyn R. Warhol, "Toward a Theory of the Engaging Narrator: Earnest Intervention in Gaskell, Stowe, and Eliot," *PMLA* 101: 5 (1986), 811–18.

31 This language in Stowe's text surely owes some of its resonance to the slave code, in which the child follows the condition of its mother.

32 On maternal melodrama, see e.g. the essays in Christine Gledhill (ed.), *Home is Where the Heart Is: Studies in Melodrama and the Woman's Film* (London: British Film Institute, 1987), and Ann Cvetkovich, *Mixed Feelings* (New Brunswick: Rutgers University Press, 1991).

33 *Playing the Race Card*, 61.

34 As Mary Noel notes, serial fiction was a literature of "remarkable coincidence," and "time-worn" melodramatic plot devices – "the forged letter, the birthmark, the drug that would give the semblance of death, the accidental meeting, the two unrelated characters who looked exactly alike," and especially "the Grand Reunion theme," in

which far-flung relatives are miraculously restored to one another – comprised its narrative vocabulary. According to Noel, "the greatest triumph of the Grand Reunion theme was 'The Hidden Hand' of Mrs. Southworth": see *Villains Galore: The Heyday of the Popular Story Weekly* (New York: Macmillan, 1954), 146.

35 On racial encoding in Southworth's novel, see Katherine Nicholson Ings, "Blackness and the Literary Imagination: Uncovering the Hidden Hand," in Elaine K. Ginsberg (ed.), *Passing and the Fictions of Identity* (Durham, NC: Duke University Press, 1996), 173–99.

36 E. D. E. N. Southworth, *The Hidden Hand*, ed. Joanne Dobson (New Brunswick: Rutgers University Press, 1988), 55. All further references to the text are to this edition.

37 In his study of American stage melodrama, David Grimsted has identified the melodramatic "type" of the "lively girl," a character of humble social position who regularly appeared in low-comedy sub-plots and who would characteristically mock stage conventions; in Capitola, Southworth elevates the figure of the "lively girl" to the central narrative role usually assigned to the virtuous (and passive) melodramatic heroine. In doing so, she establishes Cap as a figure through which to comment on as well as revise generic conventions. See David Grimsted, *Melodrama Unveiled*, 185.

38 The plot structure Grimsted identifies as conventional in American stage melodrama is reproduced, as well as significantly revised, in *The Hidden Hand*: there are two distinct erotic triangles of the sort Grimsted describes, as well as a seemingly proliferating cast of male villains; but in both of these erotic plots the emphasis on female passivity and vulnerability, as well as the insistence on heroic male "protection" of women's chastity, are dispensed with. Southworth's revisionist text, like the melodramas Grimsted discusses, foregrounds female sexuality as its primarily narrative problematic. But in *The Hidden Hand*, the forms of male authority and the binaristic model of gender – of male agency and knowledge, and female passivity, modesty, and "innocence" – characteristic of the melodramatic mode are fundamentally called into question, subjected to a destabilizing and self-reflexive irony.

39 Barbara Meil Hobson, *Uneasy Virtue: The Politics of Prostitution and the American Reform Tradition* (New York: Basic Books, 1987).

18

Delicate Boundaries: Passing and Other "Crossings" in Fictionalized Slave Narratives

Cherene Sherrard-Johnson

This peculiar phase of Slavery has generally been kept veiled: but the public ought to be made acquainted with its monstrous features, and I willingly take the responsibility of presenting them with the veil withdrawn. I do this for the sake of my sisters in bondage, who are suffering wrongs so foul, that our ears are too delicate to listen to them.

Lydia Maria Child's clever preface to Harriet Jacobs' *Incidents in the Life of a Slave Girl* (1861) asserts her empathy for her "sisters" in bondage, while at the same time promising to rend in two the veil of decorum shielding women's delicate ears from slavery's atrocities. On the one hand, Child draws the veil aside; on the other she reinforces the boundary between propriety and disclosure, foreshadowing Jacobs' own cautious dance. Both writers' reluctance to reveal too much must be balanced by their duty to relay the harshness of the enslaved woman's condition. Though replete with fictive elements, including the invention of her narrative persona Linda Brent, Jacobs' narrative depends for its authenticity on her ability to prove its first line: "Reader, be assured this is no fiction" (2000: 1). Fictionalized slave narratives, while derived from a genre that deftly interweaves witnessing, experience, autobiography, and artifice, can transcend Jacobs' limitations by partaking of fiction's full arsenal, including intertextual and historical referents, while maintaining a narrative authority that reinforces the efficacy of their writing.

Hannah Crafts' newly published *The Bondwoman's Narrative* (1853–61) and William Wells Brown's *Clotel; or, The President's Daughter* (1853), formerly thought to be the first novel by an African American writer, portray two kinds of crossings in novels that take the form of fictionalized slave narratives. The first is their rendering of the escape, crossing the boundary line from slavery into freedom, a line which after the passage of the fugitive slave law in 1850 must be continually redrawn. The second is the crossing of the color line – passing from one race to another. The fictionalized slave narrative allows them to critique the peculiar institution while maintaining their safe distance from recapture. These literary fugitives negotiated and transgressed the boundaries of national citizenship and humanity through their own literal crossings of the Atlantic and the Mason–Dixon line, respectively, and their literary crossings of the boundary between fact and fiction. Because both novels draw heavily on the hybridized slave narrative genre, this essay pays special attention to the moments when the narrative itself crosses the boundary between its representation of truth and fiction.

When contained within fictional narratives of escape, stories of racial passing and miscegenation take on a sensational role that titillates readers while simultaneously illustrating the malleability of racial identity and the presumption that slavery is limited by epidermal boundaries. Both *The Bondwoman's Narrative* and *Clotel* showcase characters whose white skin jars with their enslaved condition. Within the logic of these novels, and according to the customs and laws of the United States, that whiteness guarantees neither freedom or citizenship. In *Clotel*, the heroine appears on the auction block "with a complexion as white as most of those who were waiting with a wish to become her purchaser" (Brown 1853: 47). In *The Bondwoman's Narrative*, the narrator describes herself as "almost white," with barely a trace of "the obnoxious descent" that enforces her servitude. Dwight McBride, in identifying the body of the slave as "both singular and collective," explains that while white bodies can "signify individuality," black bodies, as a result of their "limited access to the category of the individual," almost always function as representative bodies (2001: 10–11). By rendering the white slave as spectacle, Brown and Craft bridge the opposition identified by McBride. The enslaved status of their characters constructs them as representatives, yet their individual whiteness threatens slavery's social and legal practices precisely because it prevents them from completely embodying the collective. Brown's mulatta heroine is the vehicle for his exploration of slavery's sexual exploitation of women, and the nation's complicity, epitomized by Clotel's father, Thomas Jefferson, in her own suicide and her daughter's exile. The mulatta narrator in *The Bondwoman's Narrative* plays a central role by using her mediating status to function as a confidant (of both her mistresses and her fellow slaves) who critiques the complex circumstances that precipitate the mulatta's too often tragic fate.

By inhabiting the borders of fact and fiction, interweaving intertextual and historical references and thematic tropes, fictionalized slave narratives allow their authors to privilege, rather than to destroy, the restrictions of the veil of propriety and deception identified in Child's preface. Their writing tests the delicate boundaries of the veil, allowing readers to understand the slave narrative as a genre that foregrounds autobiographic testimony and protest, but also, and most importantly, as a blueprint for early black fiction. Ann duCille describes *Clotel* in this way: "It is fiction, but to be of value to its tradition, it must be readable as fact, because African-American literature is forever fixed in a documentary relation to the real world" (2000: 258). Though fictional slave narratives do serve a documentary function and feature several authenticating witnesses, it is ultimately their narrators who control the shape and substances of their story. This chapter considers scenes of boundary crossing (legal, national, social) and passing (racial, gender, class) within the broader context of how these novels "pass" self-consciously as slave narratives, while fully engaging fictive and novelistic strategies. After illustrating how *Clotel*'s vacillation between fact and fiction reveals Brown's role as witness, editor, and artist, this essay uses his narrative framework to conduct a more thorough exploration of the newly discovered *The Bondwoman's Narrative*.

"This, reader, is an unvarnished narrative"

So William Wells Brown reminds his audience throughout his audaciously titled 1853 novel *Clotel; or, The President's Daughter*. Similarly to the novel, the title walks a precarious line between oral history, written history, and artistic license. *Clotel* relays the story of the perilous antebellum adventures of the two daughters of the slave Currer and Thomas Jefferson. By aggressively naming Jefferson, and not just an anonymous "president," as the progenitor of his heroines, Brown indicates that the common practice of sexual exploitation of black female slaves by their white master is practiced by the highest social echelons, while also reinforcing the common belief that Jefferson quite possibly fathered children with Sally Hemings, a slave who was also his wife's half-sister, as the oral history of her descendants, and now DNA evidence, appears to bear out.

The structure of *Clotel* revolves around several sub-plots that include the experience of other minor slave characters, religious conversion and its link to anti-slavery activism, as well as the central tragic story of the title character. Yet despite its clear indebtedness to sentimentality, Brown's *Clotel* is threatening precisely because it extends beyond the boundaries of truth into fiction. Instead of beginning with a brief portrait of Clotel's childhood, as Brown does in his own narrative and as is common in most slave narratives, he commences with a sensationalized portrayal of an auction. The diction in this scene relays the eroticism with which he infuses his portrayal of nearly white enslaved women throughout the novel. In our first vision of the title heroine, she creates "deep sensation amongst the crowd": "There she stood, with a skin as fair as most white women, her features as beautifully regular as any of her sex of pure Anglo-Saxon blood, her long black hair done up in the neatest manner, her form tall and graceful, and her whole appearance indicating one superior to her condition" (Brown 1853: 9).

Brown includes this early scene on the auction block, encoded with anti-slavery rhetoric and narrative strategies, to evoke sympathy from free white women for the plight of enslaved black women. The by-product of Brown's endeavor is that it established a standard of beauty that the majority of mulatta characters evince. Several characteristics attract attention: the reference to blood, skin color comparable to the whitest of white women, the woman's graceful and neat deportment, and the incongruity of her physical form and her enslaved status. In the subsequent auction, her various aspects are itemized and attributed monetary value until finally her "chastity and virtue," along with the irresistible information that she has "never been from under her mother's care," results in a sale price of "fifteen-hundred dollars" (Brown 1853: 48). In *Clotel*, both the tragic central characters and other heroic figures are, as Brown was, mulatto with heavily emphasized Anglo features. Conferring external whiteness as a strategy for gaining sympathy also tends to reify hierarchies of the slave system, particularly when Brown juxtaposes Anglo-identified mulattos with figures like Pompey, who is "no countfit," but the "genewine artekil," with his large features, woolly hair, and white teeth (p. 51). Brown's description of the wrongfully enslaved German-born Salome as "perfectly white" invites comparison with Clotel and her sister Althesa. Though legally black, they are indistinguishable in features and by association rationally should not be held in bondage on account of their skin color. The obvious danger here is that Brown's examples imply that slavery is somehow more befitting to darker slaves.

Though Brown's *Clotel* draws heavily on Lydia Maria Child's *The Quadroons*, especially in chapters 4, "The Quadroon's Home," and 15, "Today a Mistress, Tomorrow a Slave," he makes some significant alterations. Child's story bears out the classic plotline of the tragic mulatta through the characters Rosalie and her daughter Xarifa. Though a merchant's daughter, Rosalie cannot marry her white lover Edmund because of her black blood. Instead, like Clotel, who enters a union "sanctioned by heaven, although unrecognised on earth," Rosalie becomes Edmund's lover and bears him a daughter (Brown 1853: 63). Unfortunately, as with Clotel, Rosalie loses Edmund to a woman of his own race. Rebuked by his infidelity, she dies of a broken heart. Her daughter also hopes to marry her white lover, but when it is discovered that her grandmother was a slave, she is remanded into slavery. Her lover dies trying to save her, and Xarifa becomes "a raving maniac." Though Clotel's first union ends with both herself and her daughter Mary being sold, instead of dying of love, Clotel achieves her freedom with the objective of locating her daughter. Only when "all hope of seeing her [daughter] now had fled" (Brown 1853: 181) and she is faced with recapture, does she plunge herself, Ophelia-like, into the waves of the river, causing the narrator to remark austerely: "Thus died Clotel, the daughter of Thomas Jefferson, a president of the United States: a man distinguished as the author of the Declaration of American Independence, and one of the first statesman of that country" (Brown 1853: 182). In this way, despite the sentimental diction used to describe Clotel's suicide, the narrator implicates the nation in Clotel's tragic death. In addition, her suicide allows her – albeit limited – agency: her decision to die rather than return to slavery raises her stock as a tragic heroine whose death is precipitated by the brutal effects of slavery rather than female hysteria or the "warring blood" affliction presumably inherent to mulattos. Furthermore, Clotel's daughter Mary ultimately finds freedom and marriage abroad with her black lover George.

Along with myriad intertextual references, Brown uses historical data and details from oral and written slave narratives to craft his many-voiced novel. He includes details from William and Ellen Craft's widely publicized and daring escape, which he himself would pen as amanuensis in *Running a Thousand Miles for Freedom* (1860), in his dramatization of Clotel's flight:

> Under the assumed name of "Mr. Johnson," Clotel went to the clerk's office and took a private state room for herself, and paid her own and servant's fare. Besides being attired in a neat suit of black, she had a white silk handkerchief tied round her chin, as if she was an invalid. A pair of green glasses covered her eyes; and fearing that she would be talked to too much and thus render her liable to be detected, she assumed to be very ill. (Brown 1853: 139–40)

Following Ellen's escape with her husband William, a portrait of her disguised as a white invalid was widely circulated. That Brown borrows the specifics of Ellen's male costume suggests a conscious fluidity between fact and fiction. Yet when the historical or literary referent does not conform to Brown's fictional agenda, he has no qualms about altering it. For instance, he reproduces the text from a statement he penned four years prior for *The Non-Slaveholder* (1849) that relays an observer's peculiar reading of an encounter with Ellen and William. By recycling the true story of the Crafts' escape as Clotel's fictional escape, Brown relies on public recognition to bolster the claim he makes at the end of the section: "This, reader, is no fiction; it actually occurred in the railway above described" (1853: 144). This knowing inclusion also has the effect of sensationally moving the plot forward while simultaneously stretching the boundaries of race and gender categories. Despite the conscientious observer's acknowledgement of something "mysterious and unusual" about the cross-dressing Clotel, and his detection of her "low, womanly voice," he mistakes her complexion for a "darkness" that "betokened" Spanish extraction (p. 142). Though Brown includes nearly the entire text of the described encounter, he curiously excises the final two sentences of the observer's statement from his novel. While it is clear why he would not include a sentence that reveals the two travelers as the Crafts, his omission of the comment that Clotel/Ellen was either a "woman or a genius" diminishes the ingenuity of the disguise. Instead of crediting the female subject's artifice and initiative in his fictional refashioning, the emphasis is on the skin color and voice – physical aspects that have not been altered (p. 9). Despite this unfortunate effect, the omission still underscores the malleability of race and gender categories by allowing the cross-dressing performance to go undetected.

An Inscrutable Witness: Hannah Crafts' Literary Alchemy

Unlike *Clotel*, whose author is easily verifiable, questions persist regarding the authenticity and the identity of the author of the newly published *Bondwoman's Narrative*. Should the narrative prove to be a penned by a white author, despite the claims of several prominent scholars, such as William Andrews, who asserts that "[the narrator] is a product of an African American woman's experience and imagination,"

Figure 18.1 Runaway slave. From Olin Library, Cornell University.

or a free person of color, it nevertheless still fits the category of fictionalized slave narrative (in Gates 2002). Despite the questions of authorship, this work merits interrogation precisely because it defies our understanding of black literary history by allowing us insight into the process of writing, acquisition of intertextual references, and eclectic borrowing in antebellum American literature.

One of the first indications that *The Bondwoman's Narrative* is unique among fictionalized and actual slave narratives is the narrator's frank, nonsensational representation of the condition of slavery: "The life of a slave at best is not a pleasant one, but I had formed a resolution to always look on the bright side of things, to be industrious, cheerful, and true-hearted, to do some good though in an humble way, and to win some love if I could" (Crafts 2002: 11). Contrast this passage with Linda Brent's convictions that "Death is better than slavery" (Jacobs 2000: 62), and that slavery is "far more terrible for women" (p. 77). The narrator (hereafter referred to as Hannah to distinguish her from the author, who will be referred to as Crafts) makes a more "realist" resolution to construct a life for herself within the patriarchal system. Her intention to endure is at odds with most fugitive and abolitionist authors' insistence on the intolerable nature of slavery. Interestingly enough, Hannah's determination to "look on the bright side" resonates with the comment by the author and former slave Elizabeth Keckley in her postbellum slave narrative *Behind the Scenes. Or, Thirty Years a Slave and Four Years in the White House* (1988) that "Slavery had its dark side as well as its bright side," an ambivalent characterization presumably possible because Keckley's narrative was published after emancipation, but one that also distinguishes her among female slave authors.

Like Brown's *Clotel, The Bondwoman's Narrative* relays several slaves' experiences; however, the author presents these tales through scenes of storytelling where the subjects confide in the narrator. Hannah is quite comfortable in the role of distant observer/spectator that is usually occupied by male narrators; she seizes the gaze, using it to both contain her narrative and critique slavery's patriarchal tendencies. In this early scene, she establishes her acute methods of observation: "I have said that I always had a quiet way of observing things, and this habit grew upon me, sharpened perhaps by the absence of all elemental knowledge. Instead of books I studied faces and characters, and arrived at conclusions by a sort of sagacity that closely approximated the unerring certainty of animal instinct" (Crafts 2002: 27).

Later, we discover that while Hannah is literate, literacy does not have a primary place in her life as it does in Jacobs' and Douglass' process of self-realization and emancipation. Contrary to Douglass' pronouncement that reading "enabled [him] to utter [his] thoughts" (1995: 24), Hannah emphasizes that a study of "faces and characters" is a more reliable survival skill. This distinction becomes ever more curious given that Crafts is careful never to portray Hannah reading any book but the Bible, even though Crafts' intertextual references indicate that she is extremely well read in secular literature.

Hannah acknowledges, without humility or discomfort, that she is addressing her audience from the specific, privileged position of a house slave and not as a representative for her "sisters in bondage":

> That toil unremitted unpaid toil must be my lot and portion, without even the hope or expectation of any thing better. This seemed the harder to be borne, because my complexion was almost white, and the obnoxious descent could not be readily traced,

though it gave a rotundity to my person, a wave and curl to my hair, and perhaps led me to fancy pictorial illustrations and flaming colors. (Crafts 2002: 6)

This passage is indicative of Hannah's tendency to assert her individuality in order to distinguish her from other enslaved Africans. For instance, though several of the stories she relays feature the adventures of women easily identifiable as tragic mulattas, she remains exempt from this particular appellation despite her physiological resemblance. A revealing description of her mistress establishes Hannah as a keen reader of miscegenation:

I was studying [my mistress], and making out a mental inventory of her foibles, and weaknesses, and caprices, and whether or not she was like to prove an indulgent mistress. I did not see, but I felt that there was mystery, something indefinable about her. She was a small brown woman, with a profusion of wavy curly hair, large bright eyes, and delicate features with the exception of her lips which were too large, full and red. (Crafts 2002: 27)

This portrayal of Hannah's mistress, who we later discover is passing for white, is consistent with Brown's representation of the mulatta in *Clotel* and prefigures later fictive portrayals of the ambiguously raced passing subject. Hannah styles herself as a reliable judge of her mistress's character as well her suspicious features: "wavy curly hair" similar to her own, and lips "too large, full and red." Her ability to discern and anticipate the actions of others is part and parcel of her survival arsenal.

Hannah's adventures with her passing mistress bear more in common with Clotel and Althesa's respective experiences in chapters 15, aptly titled "Today a Mistress, Tomorrow a Slave," and 23, "Truth Stranger than Fiction," of Brown's novel than with Jacobs' famous preference for the penitentiary over living with a "an unprincipled master and a jealous mistress" (2000: 31). The place of the archetypal jealous mistress in *Clotel*, who "regards every quadroon servant as a rival," is taken by Hannah's more vulnerable mistress, who is sought after by a sinister, Dickensian slave speculator aptly named Mr. Trappe (Brown 1853: 119). Like Clotel and Althesa, Hannah's mistress is exposed as the daughter of a slave: "whoever might be her paternal relative, her mother was a slave then toiling in the cotton [fields] of Georgia" (Crafts 2002: 44) – and therefore, like Jefferson's "daughters," she must "follow the condition of her mother" (Brown 1853: 170). Ultimately, Hannah's mistress expires before she faces the fate of Jefferson's descendants, who are portrayed with Brown's titillating diction as "trembling, blushing and weeping; compelled to listen to the grossest language, and shrinking from the rude hands that examined the graceful proportions of their beautiful frames" (1853: 171). In a fascinating turn of events, Hannah and her mistress take flight (despite Hannah's misgivings), departing "hand in hand" through "the wide expanse of [field] and forest and meadow, crossed by intersecting roads, and hurr[ying] away" (Crafts 2002: 51). So miserable are their circumstances while in hiding that they "lost all resemblance to human beings," and upon discovery future "flight" becomes "out of the question" (p. 68). Contrary to slave narrators like Frederick Douglass, who cagily refuses to reveal his path to freedom for fear of compromising the route for those who might follow, Hannah relays the perils and tribulations of their journey in great detail, almost as a deterrent to those who might seek freedom in a similar fashion.

Among the ways in which Crafts empowers and distinguishes Hannah is showing her stealthily gazing at portraits in her master's gallery at Lindendale plantation. When caught, she admits that she was "looking at the pictures" to an interrogator who remarks: "as if such an ignorant thing as you would know any thing about them" (Crafts 2002: 17). Yet for Hannah, gazing upon these portraits allows her to inhabit the spectator's role as she "enter[s] a new world of thoughts, and feelings and sentiments" (p. 17). Like Jacobs, who finds empowerment in her "loophole of retreat," Hannah affirms that she "was not a slave with these pictured memorials of the past" (p. 17). Neither could the portraits "enforce drudgery, or condemn me on account of my color to a life of servitude. As their *companion* I could think and speculate. In their presence my mind seemed to run riotous and exult in its freedom as a rational being, and one destined for something higher and better than this world can afford" (p. 17). It is not in the reading of books, but in her confrontation of the inanimate, and therefore impotent, faces that Hannah finds self-awareness and empowerment.

Despite her continual claims that she is sustained by her faith, it is Hannah's ability to insert herself as a reliable judge of character that allows her to persist under slavery's heel. Not only does this authority empower her to outwit, and outlive, her masters and mistresses, it protects her from the fate normally attributed to attractive mulatta women like herself. In fact, it is only when she might be compelled into a forced marriage, an institution which she believes "in a state of servitude . . . must at best be of doubtful advantage" (Crafts 2002: 131) that she is motivated to plan her final escape:

> Had Mrs. Wheeler condemned me to the severest corporeal punishment, or exposed me to be sold in the public slave market in Wilmington I should probably have resigned myself with apparent composure to her cruel behest. But when she sought to force me into a compulsory union with a man whom I could only hate and despise it seemed that rebellion would be a virtue, that duty to myself and my God actually required it, and that whatever accidents or misfortunes might attend my flight nothing could be worse than what threatened my stay. (p. 207)

It is not so much the state of slavery, but that of enforced matrimony, in particular sexual subordination to one she feels is beneath her in the slavocracy, a field slave who resided with "the vile, foul, filthy inhabitants of the huts," that Hannah finds a "horror unspeakable" (p. 205). Indeed, it appears that the author intends us to understand that the condition of slavery, however demeaning, is simply a fact of women's lives. Mr. Trappe tells her and her mistress as much:

> We are all slaves to something or somebody. A man perfectly free would be an anomaly, and a free woman yet more so. Freedom and slavery are only names attached surrepti-

tiously and often improperly to certain conditions. They are mere shadows the very reverse of realities, and being so, if rightly considered, they have only a trifling effect on individual happiness. (p. 97)

Though Hannah observes that Mr. Trappe relays this information as if her mistress were "a mere machine he was discussing and analysing," there are times when she too seems resigned to her enslaved condition. This same cynicism appears to shield her from the fate of the tragic mulattas in the novel, including that of her passing mistress, who dies before she can be sold while Hannah stoically endures her transference.

While often cloaking her own experiences in enigma, it is a common practice of Hannah's to willingly relay the gory details of others' experiences without fear of reprisal. As such, we find scenes in *The Bondwoman's Narrative* that would most likely have been excised from publication had an eagle-eyed abolitionist like Child been looking over her shoulder. For instance, she uses erotic language similar to Brown's to portray the plight of not one, but an entire coven of tragic mulattas. She views these "helpless victims of [their master's] sensuality" as childlike dependants and contrasts the sensationalism of their condition with her own pragmatism. Through a conversation with the slave girl Lizzy, with whom she served at Lindendale, Hannah relays a brutal act committed by one the "youngest and most beautiful" of Master Cosgrove's mulatta harem when she is faced with being sold away from her master:

she snatched a sharp knife which a servant had carelessly left after cutting butcher's meat, and stabbing the infant threw it with one toss into the arms of its father. Before he had time to recover from his astonishment she had run the knife through her own body, and fell at his feet bathing them in her blood. (Crafts 2002: 177)

While portraits of slave mothers' suicides do appear in fictive and factual slave literature, not until Toni Morrison's *Beloved* would an author portray infanticide in such raw detail. Yet strangely, in contrast to Morrison's fictional portrayal of Margaret Garner's desperation, Crafts sees these "dove-like" women as patently unfit for freedom. When another of Cosgrove's mistresses is freed, an overseer observes that the slave would likely furnish "food for the vultures" (p. 184).

Contrary to *Clotel*'s auction scene, in which shivering beauties are appraised before the scalding eyes of spectators, Crafts allows Hannah to retreat while Mr. Trappe barters with Saddler for a good price. Unlike Clotel's excessive beauty, Hannah's appearance is realistically downplayed; her would-be purchaser views her as "excessively homely," while Mr. Trappe merely protests that "you won't find a nicer bit of woman's flesh to be bought for that money" (Crafts 2002: 103). Mr. Trappe also downplays Hannah's proclivity for escape, explaining that she was unduly influenced by her disobedient mistress. After recounting an incident in which a prior purchase "jumped into the river when she found that her child was irretrievably gone," Saddler concludes that he will purchase Hannah, not because of the valuable virtue which garners such a high bid for Clotel, but because she "has no child" (p. 105). Crafts highlights the crass realism of the business of slavery without the pathos evident in Brown's representation of Clotel's suicide, in which she "clasped her hands convulsively, and raised them, as she at the same time raised her eyes towards heaven, and begged for that mercy and compassion there, which had been denied her own earth; and then, with a single bound, she vaulted over the railings of the bridge and sunk for ever beneath the waves of the river!" (p. 182).

Only at the conclusion of her sale does Hannah evince an emotional response. Her tears are quickly staunched by the unsolicited advice from her new owner that "some of [his] girls have done first rate" and that possibly Hannah might win her freedom through marriage, as others of his female slaves sold into New Orleans' infamous market have done (Crafts 2002: 110). Despite her prior leap for freedom, her new masters read Hannah as one "who can be trusted." She proves this to be true soon after her sale, when she readily admits her enslaved status to her rescuers after her master is killed in a carriage accident. Though her confession and explanation seem implausible (she tells the reader that her "better nature prevailed"), her actions underscore her belief that freedom in and of itself is not a sufficient end (p. 116). Time and time again the reader must infer that Hannah would rather live comfortably in servitude than be free to dwell in squalor.

Despite Hannah's occasional acquiescence, she also plays a trickster's role, demonstrating yet another way in which *The Bondwoman's Narrative* deviates significantly from the slave narrative plot trajectory. Frances Smith Foster notes that such "survival techniques, with which the oral literature is especially replete such as tricking the master out of additional food, hustling clothing and gifts by exploiting the prejudices of whites, and using their mother wit to avoid any number of unpleasant situations are rarely revealed" (1979: 99).

However, to survive within the slave system, Hannah does deploy a trickster's methods. Her actions depict a consistent willingness to assert her pride and individuality within the confines of her enslaved status. For instance, Hannah portrays her relationship with her final mistress Mrs. Wheeler in this way: "Between the mistress and her slave a freedom exists probably not to be found elsewhere. A northern woman would have recoiled at the idea of communicating a private history to one of my race, and in my condition, whereas such a thought never occurred to Mrs. Wheeler" (Crafts 2002: 150).

Taking advantage of her mistress's underestimation of her, Hannah applies coveted face powder to her mistress's face before the latter petitions for a lucrative political office on behalf of her husband. Unfortunately, the "very fine, soft, and white" powder renders Mrs. Wheeler's face "as black as Tophet" (Crafts 2002: 166). This incident obliterates all her husband's political aspirations, forcing the Wheelers to leave Washington DC in disgrace. When questioned about the powder, Hannah replies that she "saw in the newspapers some accounts of a chemist who having been jilted by a lady very liberal in the application of powder to her face had invented as a method of revenge a certain kind of smelling bottles, of which the fumes would suddenly

blacken the whitest skin provided the said cosmetic had been previously applied"
(p. 167).

When Hannah is confronted as to why she did not reveal this knowledge she
stammers: "I – I – didn't think of it" but her mistress does not believe her and neither
do we. While Hannah may enjoy her mistress's embarrassment, her denial indicates
that she does fear punishment; furthermore, because she prizes safety and comfort over
the potential, yet intangible, rewards of freedom, she designs the ruse merely to assert
her superiority over Mrs. Wheeler, rather than to facilitate her own escape.

The study of fictionalized slave narratives expands the boundaries within which we
presume actual slave narratives belong. That the authors of *Clotel* and *The Bondwoman's
Narrative* saw a fusion of fact and fiction as the ideal method for conveying their
political sentiments, and drawing their individual characters, is what renders this
unique genre of nineteenth-century writing appealing to scholars as well as modern
authors such as Toni Morrison and Octavia Butler, who have written what scholars
now interpret as *neo*-slave narratives. Ultimately, while Brown's novel became a
blueprint for the African American novel, Crafts' narrative demonstrates that the
slave narrative "blueprint" is by no means a static form but a dynamic one, ever
evolving in the minds of the witnesses to slavery's horrors and those who penned their
stories.

REFERENCES AND FURTHER READING

Brown, William Wells (1853). *Clotel; or, The President's Daughter*. New York: Modern Library.

Child, Lydia Maria (1849). *Fact and Fiction: A Collection of Stories*. Boston: J. H. Francis.

Crafts, Hannah (2002). *The Bondwoman's Narrative*, ed. Henry Louis Gates, Jr. New York: Warner. (First publ. 1853–61.)

Douglass, Frederick (1995). *Narrative of the Life of Frederick Douglass, an American Slave*. New York: Dover.

duCille, Ann (2000). "Where in the World is William Wells Brown? Thomas Jefferson, Sally Hemings, and the DNA of African-American Literary History." *American Literary History* 12: 3 (Fall), 443–62.

Fabi, M. Giulia (1993). "The 'Unguarded Expressions of the Feelings of the Negroes': Gender, Slave Resistance, and William Wells Brown's Revisions of *Clotel*." *African American Review* 27: 4 (Winter), 639–54.

Foster, Frances Smith (1979). *Witnessing Slavery: The Development of Antebellum Slave Narratives*. Westport, Conn.: Greenwood.

Gates, Henry Louis, Jr. (2002). *The Bondwoman's Narrative: An Educational Companion*. Ann Arbor, Mich.: XanEdu.

Jacobs, Harriet A. (2000). *Incidents in the Life of a Slave Girl, Written by Herself*. Boston: Harvard University Press. (First publ. 1861.)

Keckley, Elizabeth (1988). *Behind the Scenes. Or, Thirty Years a Slave and Four Years in the White House*, intr. James Olney. New York: Oxford University Press, 1988. (First publ. 1868.)

McBride, Dwight (2001). *Impossible Witnesses: Truth, Abolitionism and Slave Testimony*. New York: New York University Press.

19

Doctors, Bodies, and Fiction

Stephanie P. Browner

Some time around the end of the eighteenth century, as scholars have shown, Western thinking about the body changed: the self was decorporealized, and the body became a material object to be mastered through empirical observation. In the United States this meant that the body replaced the soul as a locus of debate, disease loomed larger than damnation as a worrisome threat, and the doctor supplanted the minister as the most esteemed authority in the nation. It also meant that the body was often valorized, and many came to believe that by knowing the body empirically, men and nations might better manage the diseases, discord, differences, and carnivalesque excesses that democracy seemed to license.

Medicine's claims to somatic expertise and managerial talents did not, however, go uncontested. Although wealth, family connections, and access to power allowed elite medical leaders to create policies and institutions (schools, societies, and hospitals) that made professional medicine's authority legitimate, visible, and exclusive, the popular press often pilloried those who used these channels as aristocrats, cashing in on their social position. In 1833, for example, a New York newspaper called for the end to "mystification and concealment – wigs, gold canes, and the gibberish of prescriptions." State legislatures concurred: in 1800 almost all states had medical licensing regulations, and in 1860 almost none had such laws. There were also worries about the violence inherent in medicine's drive to epistemological mastery, about science's equation of rational disinterest with white, educated masculinity, and about the damage to individual bodies and to somatic meaning that might be done as science installed its peculiar understanding of the body.

All of these concerns show up in fictional portraits of doctors. Literature in these years had its own professional and class aspirations, and in fictional representations of doctors we can see both the extraordinary faith the nation put in professional medicine's capacity to unravel and manage the mysteries of the human body, and the nation's deep anxieties about scientific materialism and how science might gain and use somatic knowledge. What follows, then, is a survey of a handful of texts that bring to the fore both fiction's involvement in the construction of professional authority and fiction's resistance to the medicalized body and to the loss of democratic possibility that comes with professionalism.

In an essay published in the January 15, 1788 issue of the *New York Packet*, "Publius" (James Madison in this case) suggests that the nation should put its trust in experts in much the same way as a patient trusts his doctor. Anxious about factions and unrestrained popular rule, Madison likens the nation to a patient with a "disorder daily growing worse." The cure, he explains, depends upon the patient "coolly revolving his situation, and the characters of different physicians," and then selecting and calling in "such of them as he judges most capable of administering relief, and best entitled to his confidence." For Madison, national instability is akin to disease, and, as the ill man calls in a medical expert, so the country must call in political experts. Citizens have the right to choose their government and patients have the right to choose their doctors; but once a choice is made, citizens and patients alike should, unless there is good reason to the contrary, follow the advice of the experts – the professionals in whom they have put their trust. Smart patients and smart citizens, Madison suggests, allow professional experts to manage their bodies and the nation.

Twelve years later, Charles Brockden Brown takes up this oft-made argument for expertise as the antidote to disorder. In *Arthur Mervyn, or Memoirs of the Year 1793*, Brown chronicles the troubles plaguing the young nation. Financial speculation, defaults, and insolvencies reveal the instability of a market economy; an influx of Santo Domingoans offers a disturbing reminder of slave rebellions abroad and the injustices of slavery at home; and secrecy, lies, dissimulation, and plagiarism suggest that language itself is unreliable – a deeply unnerving possibility in a nation founded by a declaration (Goddu 1997). As both ultimate emblem and irrefutable evidence of the nation's ill-health, there erupts an outbreak of yellow fever in the nation's capital. In response both to the very real horrors of the 1793 summer of fever and death in Philadelphia and to the less tangible but equally unsettling economic, social, and psychic threats to civic health posed by urbanization and unbridled commerce, Brown offers the figure of the good doctor.

Doctor Stevens brings to his work both the sympathy valued in eighteenth-century moral philosophy and the detachment of science (Waterman 2003). He takes in the fever-stricken Mervyn and ministers to the city's sick and dying. He also stands apart from the rumors, fear-mongering, and financial machinations all around him, protecting himself and his family through rational self-management of body and mind: "cleanliness, reasonable exercise, and wholesome diet." Brown valued the scientific approach – he was good friends with the founders of the nation's first medical journal, *The Medical Repository* – and, as he notes in the introduction to *Arthur Mervyn*, by writing about that "calamitous" summer of 1793, he hoped to "methodize his own reflections" and to call forth " benevolence," "disinterestedness," and "intrepidity." The moral observer, Brown hoped, might inspire in others "the spirit of salutary emulation," and within the novel the doctor's steady composure is an effective antidote that restores Mervyn to "life and health." In fact, as the frame narrator of the first two thirds of the novel, the doctor seems to promise the possibility that national disorder might be written as a medical case history of health restored.

Notably, the second half of the novel, published two years after the first half appeared, is less certain about the efficacy of medical expertise. Now, Mervyn's attempts to do good are repeatedly foiled; the authenticity of his story is undermined as the doctor hears contradictory accounts from others; and the bewildering plot of conflicting information, misreadings, deception, forgeries, lost and found letters, and willful obfuscations is never fully untangled. The promise offered by the doctor's stable narrative presence crumbles when we begin to suspect that the entire tale is told by Mervyn. As it turns out, national disorder cannot be encapsulated as a case history of disease diagnosed, managed, and cured.

In his tales of medical ambition, Nathaniel Hawthorne also explores the limits of medical expertise; and he challenges new developments in medicine's understanding of the body. Between 1815 and 1860 more than 1,000 US physicians traveled to Paris, where they were schooled in the latest clinical methods, pathology theories, and physical examination techniques. They learned to value visible, anatomical signs over the patient's story, and some joined in the efforts of French physicians to derive an arithmetical structure for medical language by plotting patients' description of pain, nausea, and aches against what the doctor could know through direct examination (visible, measurable signs such as flush, temperature, pulse, breathing rate, and lesions). Increasingly, physical examinations of the body (living or dead) were understood simply as encounters between science and its object of inquiry, and the notion of the body as property came to permeate medical discourse. In the United States, medical schools began to advertise their somatic wealth. Some proclaimed the plenitude of cadavers at their schools; Southern schools touted their easy access to the bodies of deceased slaves; and part of the appeal of studying in Paris lay in the French capital's capacity to offer greater access to bodies – alive and dead – in clinics and in pathology laboratories than was possible in the United States.

In "The Birth-mark" Hawthorne taps popular worries about medicine's desire to know the body and medicine's inclination to think of the body as an assemblage of parts. The small red handprint on Georgianna's cheek can be read, as critics have suggested, as a metonym for creativity, female sexuality, imperfection, or mortality, but it functions also, and perhaps most simply, synecdochically for Georgianna's body. In fact, not only does the part represent the whole, but the part cannot be separated from the whole. And herein lies Aymer's failure: in thinking of Georgianna's birthmark as something he can remove without regard for its relationship to the patient's whole being, Aylmer fails to understand that the mark on her cheek is of the body. It cannot be plotted or translated, and it cannot be erased without annihilating the body that bears it.

The tale does not deny somatic meaning. Indeed, the mark reveals a commitment to somatic signification, and to Hawthorne's participation in a fantasy of the body as a legible text. Medicine, too, participated in that fantasy. The lesion, discovered in living bodies in the wards at La Pitié and in the cadavers of the pathology laboratory, was, for medicine, the body writing itself, revealing its secrets in visible signs. Expertise in this somatic language was central to medicine's claim to authority. Hawthorne, however, in a challenge to that authority, revises medicine's stable, knowable lesion, making it a coy somatic text that yields no definitive meaning and yet is endlessly meaningful. Hawthorne's tale, like medicine, fantasizes that with its visible signs the body is asking to be read. But Hawthorne rejects medicine's fantasy of empirical somatic knowledge, and offers instead romance and linguistic play as a mode of knowing the body, and one less likely to do violence to the body and its meanings.

In "Rappaccini's Daughter," Hawthorne again challenges medicine's expertise, but also finds medicine's willingness to probe the body's darkest recesses thrilling. The later tale is darker: a birth-mark on the skin is now a poison within; a body that writes desire on its surface is now a body that kills with its breath. While "The Birth-mark" recounts a medical experiment as it is planned, the later tale begins with the experiment *in media res*. In the earlier tale, the physician hopes to purify a besmirched body; in "Rappaccini's Daughter" he has bred a new body, a "commixture," an "adultery," a "monstrous offspring of man's depraved fancy" (Hawthorne 1974b: 110, 124). The later tale considers not medicine's failed territorial raid upon female sexuality, but rather medicine's successful colonization of the body's interior, that "dim region beyond the daylight of our perfect consciousness" (p. 114).

The tale is set at the moment of modern medicine's birth (sixteenth-century Padua); Rappaccini is probably modeled on Padua's most famous anatomist, Andreas Vesalius, who arrived in Padua in 1537 and published his masterpiece, *De humani corporis fabrica*, in 1543; and Baglioni represents Galenic medicine and the staid academic world Vesalius challenged.[1] In most histories, Vesalius is a champion of empirical, scientific methods, but in Hawthorne's account of Paduan science medicine's violation of the body is not redeemed by the knowledge it constructs. The tale invokes Renaissance notions of the body's interior as a continent ripe for exploration and colonization, and as Renaissance anatomists put their names upon body parts, so Rappaccini colonizes his daughter's body. The result, however, is not somatic mastery. Vesalius may have wielded the scalpel himself when he taught anatomy and eagerly plunged his hands into messy dead bodies, but his masterpiece, a text engraved and printed by some of the best craftsmen of the day, ordered and beautified somatic materiality. By contrast, Rappaccini's masterpiece, his daughter's body, is a "wonder of hideous monstrosity" that underscores not the glories of medical mastery over the somatic, but rather the estranged body created by medical knowledge. Beatrice is beautiful, yet artificially brilliant, and her breath bespeaks a somatic interior that Rappaccini's science has made a place of poison and death.

Undoubtedly, Hawthorne wants us to condemn what the father has done to his daughter; and yet Rappaccini also offers a view of the body Hawthorne values. By remaking his daughter's body, Rappaccini revises the idealized image of the pure, transcendent female body, suggesting instead that all bodies, even female bodies, are organic matter that will ripen, putrefy, and die. In fact, Rappaccini's passion for direct, sensory knowledge of the "hue and perfume" of "malignant influences" makes him akin not only to Vesalius but also to nineteenth-century pathologists. He shares with them a fascination with the sights and smells of disease, and his intimacy with dangerous plants parallels the "morbid education of the senses" that was essential to clinical medicine (Porter 1997: 312). Similarly, Giovanni's training in the sensory world of Rappaccini's garden laboratory is akin to nineteenth-century medical education at the Hotel-Dieu, La Pitié, and other Parisian hospitals where instruction included "drilling students to interpret the sights, sounds, and smells of disease" (Porter 1997: 312). For Hawthorne, this work is creative as well as awful. Thus, although Rappaccini's fanatical devotion to discovering the secrets of poisons surely played upon popular fears of a medical profession which seemed to some nineteenth-century observers to be obsessed with disease and death, and Hawthorne would have us recoil from Rappaccini's work, he also seems to delight in the "pale man of science" who devotes, "as might an artist," an entire life to "achieving a picture" of the mortal human body (1974b:126). The pathologist's portrait of the diseased body is, for Hawthorne, both "terrible" and "beautiful" (p. 127), and in the discourse of disease Hawthorne finds a "symbolic language" that richly renders the "thrill of undefineable horror" that attends intimate somatic knowledge (pp. 98, 121). Rappaccini's interest in poisons is, in the end, more interesting and preferable to Aylmer's desire for purity.

As foils to Rappaccini, Hawthorne offers two other medical men in the tale, Baglioni and Giovanni, both of whom fail because they cannot think beyond reductionist medical or moral paradigms. Giovanni is convinced that Beatrice's body says something about her character. He insists upon a moral interpretation of her somatic signs, and he is beholden to the literary convention in which character is writ upon the body. He is a callow young man who fails in love because he cannot accept that a pure spirit might inhabit a sick body. Baglioni understands the body as mere matter, and his antidote kills rather than cures Beatrice precisely because he has reduced her condition to a physical problem, like Georgianna's birthmark, that can be cured with the right chemical brew. Rappaccini, by contrast, knows better. His own "inward disease" marks him as a man willing to confront the reality that we inhabit mortal bodies with dark, diseased interiors. Thus, although Renaissance anatomy and nineteenth-century pathology might be charged with stealing the body's interior from religion and with colonizing and poisoning the body's interior landscape, Hawthorne also finds in pathology an alluring and profoundly untranscendent body that is a suitable house for an interiority more complicated than any encompassed by clichéd notions of a "pure soul within."

Like Hawthorne, Herman Melville interrogates science's claim to disembodied objectivity. Based on Melville's fourteen months' service on a US Navy frigate, *White-Jacket* offers a scathing, vitriolic satire of the head surgeon of the fleet. In many ways Cadwallader Cuticle, MD, is a caricature of the mad doctor: he is accomplished; he has bizarre, grotesque interests; he is oblivious to the morbidity of his work; and his withered body testifies to his intellectual passions. But Cuticle is also more than a stock character. Melville devotes four chapters (more than to any other character) exclusively to the fleet surgeon; "The Operation" is the longest chapter in the book; and we know that Melville went out of his way to make the information in these chapters accurate. The portrait of the surgeon is also noteworthy because it is the only one in *White-Jacket* to depart radically from its historical counterpart. The real surgeon on the *United States* in 1843 was widely admired as a skillful physician and a good administrator; but instead of honoring this man, Melville develops at length, with what one critic has called a "maniacal exactitude of language," a satirical portrait of a cruel man (Dimock 1989: 317).

In part, the satire skewers professional careerism, but the vitriol is aimed also at challenging widely held assumptions about the relationship between mind and body, intellect and brawn, rationality and physicality. Throughout much of the nineteenth century these polarized notions were used in both crude and subtle ways to map distinctions between male and female, white and non-white, upper and lower classes. As Robyn Wiegman notes, an "asymmetry of corporeality" dominates habits of representation in the nineteenth century: the category of citizen is essentially bodiless, while other categories – women, non-whites, and workers – bear a burden of a heightened corporeality (Wiegman 1995: 6). On the surface, Melville seems to indulge this kind of thinking. In *White-Jacket* the common sailor is "of the body" in a way officers are not. Sailors suffer constant physical discomforts, labor at work that does not renew and is not adequately compensated, endure frequent floggings, and live under the looming threat of the death penalty. In short, the sailor's body is the primary site of his oppression. This may, at times, reduce the sailor to being a mere body, but it also makes the sailor's body a ready site for fraternity, rebellion, and nobility. Friendships on the *Neversink* nurture what one critic calls a "democratic eros," and in a moving account of what he calls the "Rebellion of the Beards," Melville rewrites the 1842 Somers mutiny as a tale of the common seaman's physical nobility (Martin 1986).

In the context, then, of oppressed but noble sailor bodies, the fleet surgeon's pathetic body takes on particular significance. Melville seems to accept the popular notion that mind and body are in opposition. Sailors are lusty and Cuticle is physically decrepit, we are given to understand, because his intellectual pursuits have taken a toll on his body. But Cuticle's body is not simply one that has been worn away and thus rendered less present, visible, or significant. Indeed, the rhetoric Melville lavishes on describing Cuticle's attenuated body suggests that for him, as for Hawthorne, the intellectual interests of a medical man not only vitiate his body but also inscribe it with medicine's peculiar obsessions. Aylmer's trembling, impotent body, for example, bespeaks medicine's displaced, prurient fascination with female sexuality, and Rappaccini's sickly, odiferous body is both a direct result of his botanical experiments and a powerful symbol of the dark interiority pathology presupposes. Cuticle's body also testifies to medicine's morbid interest. His missing body parts gesture humorously to the role of dissection in nineteenth-century medicine, to medicine's interest in disease and decay as well as health, and to Cuticle's own eagerness to collect parts and to amputate. The surgeon's nearly dead body reminds us that it is "largely through interrogation of the dead that doctors aspire to know the diseases of the living" (Arnold 1993: 6).

In addition, Cuticle's attenuated body gestures to medicine's habit of locating itself in what Denise Albanese has called "an artificial space of evacuated materiality" (quoted in Nelson 1998: 123). Although all human individuals, including doctors and scientists, dwell in idiosyncratic corporeal bodies, scientific knowledge claims to transcend the distractions and unreliability of embodiment. Moreover, in the nineteenth century the observer was, almost by definition, a white, upper-class professional man, and thus his body remained outside the frame of reference as science reproduced its authority in "captioned and ever-multiplying displays" of the bodies of others (Nelson 1998: 103).

Cuticle's body suggests a very different image of science. His body is, like those he works on, profoundly material. In fact, Melville is so taken with the humor of Cuticle's patchwork body as a mirror image of the bodies created by medical discourse (the body understood as parts and not as a whole) that he has the surgeon remove his jacket, his kerchief, his false eye, his false teeth, and his wig before beginning an amputation. With this darkly humorous dismantling, the professional becomes literally and ironically "disembodied" and thus becomes a grotesque, carnivalesque body – a parodic image of the idealized classical body. At the moment of surgery, Cuticle is not an emblem of disembodied rationality but a brutal, fragmentary, corporeal man, and Melville devotes some of his most maniacal exactitude of language to suggesting that the surgeon is as much "of the body" as his patient while being, at the same time, much less of a man. Indeed, the fleet surgeon – a figure of naval, professional, and scientific authority – presides over hangings and floggings, operates a sick bay in the bowels of the ship while officers promenade on the deck above, and cuts off a sailor's leg simply to flaunt his surgical skills. Melville's bitterness is palpable: this fragment of a man is authorized to preside over the destruction of bodies and the fragile democratic fraternity that common sailors forge among themselves.

By the time *White-jacket* was published, the medical profession was at its nadir. Between 1830 and about 1870, with the rise of anti-elitist sentiments, the liberal professions (law, medicine, and ministry) lost prestige and power, even though all three continued to garner some respect and to build institutional power.[2] During these years professional medicine's alliance with wealth and political power became increasingly suspect, and anti-elitist rhetoric detected power plays everywhere – in scientific language, in the display of diplomas and certificates of society membership, and in the class affiliation of elite doctors. The most popular domestic medicine manual of the day, for example, announced on the title-page that it was written "In Plain Language, Free from Doctor's Terms" (Gunn 1860). Similarly, a regular full-page advertisement in *Harper's Weekly* for Graefenberg tonics derided elite physicians for their dependence upon the trappings of professionalism.

In response, regulars scaled back some of their professionalizing efforts; many retreated from their commitment to licensing regulation, and schools lowered entrance and graduation standards. And yet, many regulars, including the founders of the American Medical Association, continued to believe that they had a peculiar claim to veneration and confidence based on the fact that they were men of good character, indicated in part by their cultural refinement.[3] As Pierre Bourdieu suggests, an "aristocracy of culture" often permeates a society's class distinctions, affirming the "moral excellence" of those with a "capacity for sublimation" (1984: 7). US physicians often demonstrated their membership in the aristocracy of culture by returning from study abroad (trips that carried considerable cachet) with a taste for European highbrow culture. John Morgan, often called the father of American medicine, returned from his European travels with the beginnings of an art collection (paintings, engravings, and original manuscripts); Benjamin Rush met Europe's cultural luminaries during his trip; and physicians who studied in Paris often flaunted what one doctor called "Parisian polish," using French phrases and resisting a re-acculturation to the "provincial manners" of the United States (Warner 1998: 40).

Highbrow literary magazines often endorsed this image of the refined, educated, kind, ethical physician. An 1843 editorial in *The Southern Literary Messenger*, for example, insisted that, contrary to popular opinion, doctors are religious men and never hard-hearted (Anon. 1843). In 1852 *The New Englander* published an address in which Yale medical professor Worthington Hooker explained that the professional doctor is distinguished not so much by successful treatment (perhaps an attempt to respond to the fact that regulars did not have a higher rate of cures than irregulars) but by his character (Hooker 1852). And the next year *Putnam's* ran two articles championing doctors for their kindness, common sense, and steadiness (Anon. 1853a, 1853b). Fictional portraits often concurred, representing the doctor as a liberal, upper-class gentleman who brings stability to the world he inhabits. He can encounter the bizarre, the exotic, the Other, and yet remain untainted; and he can bring order to worlds riven by property disputes, contested wills, and the breakdown of class boundaries. In many stories, the virtues of the professional doctor are also the virtues elite fiction claimed for itself as it established an authority premised upon a distinction between itself and the "low" character and illegitimacy of popular and populist genres such as dime novels and sensational fiction.

And yet, some stories challenged the politics of refinement.[4] In Rebecca Harding Davis's 1861 *Atlantic* story, "Life in the Iron Mills," the doctor fails to understand the somatic realities of class oppression. Davis puts bodies shaped by class at the center of her story. The mill workers are "brawny" and half-naked, or hunchbacked and ravaged. The mill-owner's son refers casually to the workers as "his hands," which they are since it is their labor that creates his wealth. And Mitchell, a Northern well-to-do cynical philosopher, has the body and aesthetics of his class: the well-built body of an "amateur gymnast," an "anatomical eye" from time spent in gymnasiums, and a refined "white hand" adorned with "the bloody-glow of a red ring" (Davis 1861: 51). Hugh Wolfe, a hungry, desperate ironworker with a talent for sculpture, understands well the class politics of somatic esthetics: he is painfully aware of the contrast between his own flesh, "muddy with grease and ashes," and "the pure face, the delicate, sinewy limbs" of Mitchell (p. 58).

The doctor's part in the story is small but significant. Although he should be smart and sensitive about bodies and what they mean, including the statue of a nude woman that Hugh has made out of korl (iron refuse), Dr. May is the most obtuse of all the characters. Initially, he understands the power of the statue to lie in artistic mastery; then he is eager to point out anatomical inaccuracies; ultimately he is vexed and puzzled. He is moved by the statue, and by his encounter with a degraded worker with artistic talent; he sighs, "a good honest sigh, from the depths of his stomach" (Davis 1861: 55); and he explains to Hugh that a "man may make himself anything he chooses." Thus the doctor puts himself at ease with a "glowing" sense of "his own magnanimity" (p. 56).

Although Davis is clearly suggesting that most philanthropy is empty talk, she allows that the doctor is, in fact, magnanimous, and that the possibility of self-making is exactly what Hugh hungers for: "The puddler had drunk in every word, looking through the Doctor's flurry, and generous heat, and self-approval, into his will." But will is precisely what the doctor lacks, and this intimate moment between grimy worker and kind-hearted town physician collapses when the doctor rejects the puddler's plea for fraternity. When Hugh asks, "Will you help me?" the doctor turns to his companions and laments, pathetically, "I have not the means" (Davis 1861: 56). The doctor cannot think or feel his way out of his class privilege, and he refuses to spend any money on salving his conscience.

In an 1853 *Putnam's* short story Charles Frederick Briggs, co-founder and editor of *Putnam's*, also indicts the well-to-do physician for a failure to risk his class privilege to help another.[5] In "Elegant Tom Dillar" a doctor "outs" his daughter's fiancé for his secret career as a minstrel dancer. Tom Dillar is a rich man of European ancestry who is duped into making a bad investment and yet returns to high society a few months later rich and elegant once again. No one knows how he makes his living until the doctor discovers and tells everyone that Tom is passing as an Irishman who blacks up and takes top billing as a star minstrel dancer.

Inverting the literary habit of reducing the poor to metonymic body parts, Briggs makes Tom an impressive somatic genius who finds personal and professional fulfillment on the minstrel stage. In many ways, Tom's identity is remarkably fluid: an elegant fellow who is wronged by all, then an unshaven, destitute homeless man no one recognizes, he remakes himself three or four times. He might be a trickster figure, but he practices no tricks: he simply proposes to make his living as a professional artist, a song-and-dance man in a minstrel show, and the story celebrates Tom's talents by elevating minstrelsy to a reputable profession. That Tom sees how to use his talent for music and dance to make money testifies to his resourcefulness, and suggests that he is as American as the dollar that his last name invokes.

The doctor, by contrast, gains his authority not through somatic talents but through his professional identity as a man of good character and of cultural refinement. Indeed, the doctor has the power to expose Tom not because of his medical expertise but because of his class privilege. Dr. Laurens goes to the opera, as man of refinement should, but he prefers minstrelsy and often enters through a backdoor to catch a show. Thus, when he is called to attend Tom after he has fallen, the doctor risks exposing his own low-class taste for minstrelsy. But he also knows that he is, in the end, protected by his professional identity: when the opera is not on, he can slum it and indulge in this quintessential American art form.[6] Tom, however, cannot with impunity be associated with minstrelsy; his social status is more vulnerable. Thus, when the doctor tells Tom's secret at the Manhattan Club, he knows that this will result in Tom's expulsion from the ranks of the city's socialites.

The class and somatic politics of high and low culture are at the center of the story. At the opera, Dr. Laurens maintains professional composure: he listens to the "prima donna as though she were a patient." But minstrelsy, and in particular the "incomparable Higgins," makes him lose his self-possession. He "never fail[s] to drop in" when Higgins/Tom performs, which was "nearly every night," and it is clear that minstrelsy can make a refined, elite physician responsive to the art and body of the Other.[7] In fact, it is the doctor's great pleasure in Tom's talent that makes his betrayal so ugly. Although Dr. Laurens is entertained by the talent on the minstrel stage (and perhaps titillated by minstrelsy's somatic crimes against established social codes), he refuses to act on the democratic potential of fascination with the Other. As he knows, a man performs his class identity through his esthetic choices, and he must not let his low taste contaminate his family: Tom may ravish him, but not his daughter.[8] Thus, when called in his professional capacity to attend the body of the fallen minstrel, the doctor does not give Tom the same kind of attention he gives the opera diva. Rather, he asserts his authority, rejects Tom's talents for play, deception, and fluidity, and casts him out. The moral energy of the tale reaches its climax in a condemnation of the doctor for betraying a body he so admires and for capitulating to anti-democratic ideologies that would fix race, class, and national identities upon the body.

By the end of the nineteenth century, medicine would be the most prestigious and lucrative profession in the nation. Indeed, the rise of a culture of professionalism and the establishment of a habit of somatic empiricism are perhaps two of the most enduring legacies of the century. Fictional portraits of doctors speak to the shifting terms and dynamics of these emerging enterprises, and they testify to the role of fiction in negotiating what the body means, and how, and whom society will authorize to enter the sickroom, attend the ailing body, and witness at the deathbed.

Notes

1 The work at Padua began with Alessandro Benedetti's "The Account of the Human Body: Or Anatomy" (1502). Soon after this several other anatomical texts appeared, and in 1531 a dissection manual by Galen was rediscovered and published. A major recovery from classical medicine, "On Anatomical Procedures" revealed that Galen had extrapolated from animal dissections for his knowledge of human anatomy. Now, anatomists could honor Galen and follow his injunction to dissect and thus to see for themselves – the very definition of "autopsy." But they could also make their own reputations by correcting Galen and contributing to a more accurate map of the human body. With these opportunities suddenly

available, anatomy became, like geography, a field in which new worlds beckoned and parts had to be named. Like a lucky discoverer who memorializes himself by putting his name on a strait, a lake, or continent, the anatomist might discover and put his name upon an organ, a vessel, a tube. Fallopio and others achieved such fame. Vesalius came to Padua in 1537 as a young physician expert in dissection. Since dissection had never been mandatory for medical students, his appointment was a bold move calculated to confirm the university's dominant role in the new field of anatomy (Porter 1997).

2   Historians have given much thought as to why the professions lost prestige and authority in these years. Some point to the extension of political democracy, including expansion of the franchise and an increase in the election of commoners to political office. Others note that a rapidly growing market made suspicion rather than confidence a model for all social interactions. Faith in the progressive working of a *laissez-faire* market was widespread during the reign of Andrew Jackson and his chosen successor Martin van Buren, even though in these same years class inequalities hardened. Thus, although these were years marked by both depression and rapid capitalist expansion, there was a popular conviction that no man or class should have special privileges. Populists failed to note that what seemed like a level playing field (i.e. no market regulation) did not necessarily mean that all entered into the market as equals (Larson 1977).

3   The AMA was founded, in part, in the hope of bolstering the profession's reputation, and although many, including the first president, were able to enter the profession because entrance barriers had been lowered, he and others sought to articulate the grounds on which the profession might elevate itself and once again earn the confidence of the nation (Haber 1991).

4   As Nancy Glazener notes, critiques of class politics in nineteenth-century literary magazines served many purposes, including the suggestion that literature is objective and disinterested – virtues that then validated it as a critical, independent discourse free of suspect class allegiances (Glazener 1997).

5   Briggs 1853: 525–30. For a reprint and fuller version of the commentary I offer here, see Browner 2001.

6   Notably, while *Putnam's* offered ample coverage of opera in a regular "Music" column, it did not comment on minstrelsy or other popular theatre, with the sole exception of J. J. Trux's 1855 article, "Negro Minstrelsy: Ancient and Modern."

7   In noting the democratic energy of minstrelsy, I do not mean to overstate the case. As Eric Lott notes, minstrelsy "divested black people of control over elements of their culture," and "Elegant Tom Dillar" may suggest that only when a European aristocrat "does" black culture does it becomes art refined enough for a professional man to find interesting. But Briggs's story also, in detailing the doctor's eagerness to see Higgins every night, testifies to a "profound white investment in black culture" (Lott 1993: 18).

8   See Lott 1993: 149, for a discussion of vulgarity and the libidinal body politics of minstrelsy. Lott also notes the homosocial bonds across race lines that minstrelsy explores and the gesture to gender-bending in some performances. Dr. Laurens' willingness to allow himself but not his daughter the somatic pleasures of minstrelsy speaks to the homoerotic undertones in minstrelsy.

References

Anon. (1843). "Short Essays on the Medical Profession" *Southern Literary Messenger* 9, 297.

Anon. (1853a). "Doctors." *Putnam's* 2, 66–71.

Anon. (1853b). "The Medical Profession." *Putnam's* 2, 315–18.

Arnold, David (1993). *Colonizing the Body: State Medicine and Epidemic Disease in Nineteenth-Century India.* Berkeley: University of California Press.

Blake, John B. (1980). "Anatomy." In Ronald L. Numbers (ed.), *The Education of American*

Physicians, 29–47. Berkeley: University of California Press.

Bourdieu, Pierre (1984). *Distinction: A Social Critique of the Judgment of Taste*, trans. Richard Nice. Cambridge, Mass.: Harvard University Press.

Briggs, C. F. (1853). "Elegant Tom Dillar." *Putnam's* 1, 525–30.

Brown, Charles Brockden (1998). *Arthur Mervyn, or Memoirs of the Year 1793*. New York: Library of America. (First publ. 1800.)

Browner, Stephanie (2001). "Documenting Cultural Politics: A *Putnam's* Short Story." *PMLA* 116: 2, 397–405.

Davis, Rebecca Harding (1861). "Life in the Iron Mills." *Atlantic Monthly* 7, 430–51. Repr. as *Life in the Iron Mills* (Bedford Cultural Edition), ed. Cecelia Tichi. Boston: Bedford, 1998.

Dimock, Wai Chee (1989). *Empire for Liberty: Melville and the Poetics of Individualism*. Princeton: Princeton University Press.

Foucault, Michel (1975). *The Birth of the Clinic: An Archeology of Medical Perception*, trans. A. M. Sheridan Smith. New York: Vintage.

Glazener, Nancy (1997). *Reading for Realism: The History of a US Literary Institution, 1850–1910*. Durham, NC: Duke University Press.

Goddu, Theresa A. (1997). *Gothic America: Narrative, History, and Nation*. New York: Columbia University Press.

Gunn, John C. (1860). *Domestic Medicine*. New York: Saxton, Barker & Co.

Haber, Samuel (1991). *The Quest for Authority and Honor in the American Professions, 1750–1900*. Chicago: University of Chicago Press.

Hawthorne, Nathaniel (1974a). "The Birth-mark" (first publ. 1843). In *The Centenary Edition of the Works of Nathaniel Hawthorne*, ed. Fredson Bowers, L. Neal Smith, John Manning, and J. Donald Crowley, vol. 10: *Mosses from an Old Manse*. Columbus: Ohio State University Press.

Hawthorne, Nathaniel (1974b). "Rappaccini's Daughter" (first publ. 1844). In *The Centenary Edition of the Works of Nathaniel Hawthorne*, ed.

Fredson Bowers, L. Neal Smith, John Manning, and J. Donald Crowley, vol. 10: *Mosses from an Old Manse*. Columbus: Ohio State University Press.

Hooker, Worthington (1852). "The Present Mental Attitude and Tendencies of the Medical Profession." *New Englander* 10. Repr. as *Inaugural Address*, New Haven: T. J. Stafford.

Larson, Magali Sarfatti (1977). *The Rise of Professionalism: A Sociological Analysis*. Berkeley: University of California Press.

Lott, Eric (1993). *In Love and Theft: Blackface Minstrelsy and the American Working Class*. New York: Oxford University Press.

Madison, James (1982). "Federalist #38" (first publ. 1788). In *The Federalist Papers*, ed. Garry Wills. New York: Bantam.

Martin, Robert K. (1986). *Hero, Captain, and Stranger: Male Friendship, Social Critique, and Literary Form in the Sea Novels of Herman Melville*. Chapel Hill: University of North Carolina Press.

Melville, Herman (1970). *White-Jacket, or The World in a Man-of-War* (first publ. 1850). In *The Writings of Herman Melville*, Northwestern-Newberry Edition, ed. Harrison Hayford, Hershel Parker, and G. Thomas Tanselle. Evanston, Ill.: Northwestern University Press.

Nelson, Dana (1998). *National Manhood: Capitalist Citizenship and the Imagined Fraternity of White Men*. Durham, NC: Duke University Press.

Porter, Roy (1997). *The Greatest Benefit to Mankind: A Medical History of Humanity*. New York: Norton.

Warner, John Harley (1998). *Against the Spirit of System: The French Impulse in Nineteenth-Century American Medicine*. Princeton: Princeton University Press.

Waterman, Bryan (2003). "*Arthur Mervyn's* Medical Repository and the Early Republic's Knowledge Industries." *American Literary History* 15: 2, 213–47.

Wiegman, Robyn (1995). *American Anatomies: Theorizing Race and Gender*. Durham, NC: Duke University Press.

20

Law and the American Novel

Laura H. Korobkin

As Charles Hansford Adams has noted, the "great dilemma of America's formative years" between the Revolution and the Civil War was the conflict "in the national conscious-ness between the claims of self and community," a dilemma that, he argues, was "most frequently resolved into a national conversation about law" (1990: 2–3). Indeed, from their earliest days Americans have understood themselves through such law-inflected ideas as individualism, equality, and citizenship. From the start too, to read an American novel has been to participate in this continuing cultural conversation. Whether cast as jurors in Charles Brockden Brown's challenge to Enlightenment theories of knowledge and governance in *Wieland*, challenged to respond to Harriet Beecher Stowe's impas-sioned yet carefully analytical dramatizations of sufferings inflicted by the fugitive slave law and pro-slavery judicial decisions in *Uncle Tom's Cabin* and *Dred*, or disturbed by the abusive use of the law's power against helpless women and poor soldiers in the sub-plots of E. D. E. N. Southworth's popular *The Hidden Hand*, readers of antebellum American fiction were engaged by legal issues almost whenever they picked up a new novel. If novels have helped to shape Americans' opinions about a range of legal issues, the law has also shaped the development of the novel, especially its structural emphasis on the problematics of agency, the juror-like role of readers, and American fiction's almost obsessive focus on the individual's relation to authority.

We use the word "law" frequently and casually, but what do we really mean? In this essay it is used to mean three distinct concepts: legal process, legal texts, and legal doctrines. Legal process is lawsuits and trials; its focus is on evidence and proof, testimony and argument, confrontation and conflict, verdict, appeal, and sentence. It is the trial as theater, the courtroom as key arena where dramas of power – and powerlessness – are enacted; the trial as oppositional storytelling contest, with jurors as readers and judges. Legal texts are the written artifacts of law. They include judicial opinions and statutes; documents from the Constitution to the fugitive slave law, from the transcript of a deposition to the wording of a restraining order. While such texts are, of course, often part of legal process, and articulate legal doctrines, they appear separately here to emphasize both their materiality and their distinct linguistic character: they speak through the specialized, empowered language that separates them from other forms of discourse and through vivid narratives and arguments that connect them to such other discursive forms as the sermon, the editorial, the political speech, and the novel. Legal doctrines, the most abstract aspect of law to be treated here, are the shifting set of legal ideas that hold the American social and political contract together and become flashpoints for political and cultural controversy. Legal doctrines include the concept of natural law that informs the Declaration of Independence and the early republic's notions of an ideal society; the concept of equality that makes every American, at least theoretically, an equal participant in the rights and obligations of citizenship; and the various analytical doctrines by which slavery was legally rationalized, legitimated, and attacked.

While these aspects of law are separated for the purposes of this essay, they are so interdependent that they may best be thought of as names for varying angles of vision into the object of examination. Many significant works of literature, like Melville's "Benito Cereno," engage all three. The remainder of this essay uses these three facets of law to examine representative major and minor examples of American fiction from the 1790s to the Civil War, including Charles Brockden Brown's *Wieland* (1798), James Fenimore Cooper's *The Pioneers* (1823), John Neal's *Rachel Dyer* (1828), Harriet Beecher Stowe's *Uncle Tom's Cabin* (1852) and *Dred* (1856), Herman Melville's "Benito Cereno" (1855), and E. D. E. N. Southworth's *The Hidden Hand* (1859).

Legal Process: The Juridical Novel

Six pages into Charles Brockden Brown's *Wieland* (1798), Clara Wieland pauses in her letter-writing to warn that "if my testimony were without corroborations, you would reject it as incredible. The experience of no human being can furnish a parallel." The story she is beginning to tell, whose gothic elements will include mysterious, disembodied voices, violent multiple murders, ventriloquism, madness, accusations of sexual licentiousness, and Clara's own nearly fatal breakdown, does indeed venture far beyond any ordinary reader's experience. In challenging readers to make sense of this disordered world, Brown's narrator addresses us – and the novel's characters frequently address each other – as jurors deciding a case, decision-makers who must sort through conflicting, often misleading evidence to reach an appropriate verdict. Like Nabokov's Humbert Humbert, Clara is both witness and lawyer, both a biased testifier to events she experienced and an "interested" attorney interpreting and arguing the meaning of those events. The novel's plot becomes a series of trials (including one real one), saturated by a vocabulary of evidence, inference, testimony, and judgment, implicating readers in its forensic process and requiring them to reach verdicts not only about questions of criminal responsibility, but also about the credibility and sanity of Clara herself and, ultimately, the reliability of any judgments in such a bewildering world.

As Jay Fliegelman and Roland Hagenbuchle have effectively argued, Brown's novel challenges Enlightenment theories of knowledge and rationality, like Locke's, by presenting a world in which ordinary rules and assumptions do not apply (Fliegelman 1991; Hagenbuchle 1988). Information obtained directly by the senses (voices, lights) is not what it appears to be, and the human mind, instead of being a splendidly rational instrument that can know, order, and control the world, is unstable, vulnerable, tending toward inward collapse. Significantly, Brown complicates gothic fiction's attack, in the wake of the French Revolution, on the possibility of the rationally governed self or nation by casting the reading experience as a forensic process, one in which the problem of irrationality becomes the impossibility of connecting evidence to inference as narrative events become testimonial sequences. A trained but nonpracticing lawyer, Brown uses the structure of the trial to place special demands on his reader–jurors. Despite the extreme difficulty of assessing testimonial credibility, and the incorrect inferences we inevitably draw from evidence constructed to mislead, we as readers cannot abandon our juridical roles; we are implicated by the novel's structure in the critical project of reaching judgment. If we persist, we can do so, though our verdict must be returned in the face of lingering, eroding doubts.

Brown's novel establishes the tradition in American fiction of using the analogy to trial process to foreground contemporary legal issues, to emphasize the distance between the unrepresentable reality of "what happens" and the shaped, linguistic narrative testimonies through which events reach us, and to entangle readers in the uncertain but necessary quest for judgment. In *Rachel Dyer* (1828) John Neal echoes *Wieland*'s sense of the law as an insufficient bulwark against the forces of irrationality and prejudice. In lengthy speech-filled courtroom scenes designed to elicit outrage on the part of the reader–juror, Neal's fevered novel about the Salem witchcraft trials dramatizes the lack of such procedural safeguards for defendants as the presumption of innocence, court-appointed counsel, compulsory process, and sworn testimony. The vulnerability of inadequately protective process to the biases and frenzy of 1692 becomes the springboard for Neal's implicit attacks on contemporary American criminal procedures. Though improved since colonial days, criminal process was still, in Neal's view, weak and ineffective. In the 1840s, Brown's gothicism and forensic positioning are employed by Edgar Allan Poe in tales like "The Tell-Tale Heart" (1843) and "A Cask of Amontillado" (1846), whose warped confessional narrators situate readers as jurors assessing credibility on the basis of a one-sided, unreliable evidentiary presentation. Though his tales avoid the courtroom, along with most other machinery of explicit legal process, they mimic the form of criminal defendants' testimony, providing the evidentiary basis for reader–jurors to analyze criminal psychology and to make inferences that enable the construction of alternate, more accurate narratives of events and motives.

Legal process is also the dramatic display of governmental power over the individual, as in the familiar opening scene from Hawthorne's *The Scarlet Letter*, where Hester Prynne, displayed to an unsympathetic crowd, listens as the magistrates make her lifetime letter-wearing sentence a terrifying disciplinary example. Though the law is formally neutral and ideally just, it has all too often been infected by discrimination based on race, gender, or class, its enforcement machinery wielded in a complex partnership between governmental entities and the powerful groups that sustain them. From *Rachel Dyer* to *Billy Budd* to *Native Son*, novels have turned to the theater of power in the courtroom to dramatize concerns about public authority, their representations shaped by the cultural context of the moment of fictional production.

While American fiction is often thought of as supporting the viewpoints of those who live as outsiders to power, such is not always the case. In *The Pioneers* (1823) James Fenimore Cooper offers a qualified paean to the potential benefits for American civilization if the educated, landed classes continue to control government, property development, and the unruly propensities of the poor. In his first literary appearance, the aged Natty Bumppo may be an omnicompetent woodsman animated by an inner, natural sense of law and ethics, a model of self-reliance and environmental awareness, but he is also the illiterate former servant of an aristocratic Englishman, a man who would never consider himself the social equal of the Temples, the novel's present and future American dynasty. When Cooper puts Natty on trial for shooting deer out of season (a violation not of "natural" but of "civilized," community-based law), and for resisting arrest with a firearm, Leatherstocking's articulation of his homespun, nature-based individualism ("I trouble no man; why can't the law leave me to myself?") wins generations of sympathetic readers; but it is, finally, Judge Temple's vision the novel reinforces. "Would any society be tolerable," he asks, "where the ministers of justice are to be opposed by men armed with rifles? Is it for this that I have tamed the wilderness?"

Temple speaks to the community's needs to ensure a flourishing, peaceful future. Recognizing that laws designed to curb the unruly mob must occasionally bang up against an atypically self-regulated individual like Natty, Temple willingly exacts the price of Natty's temporary imprisonment to gain the benefit of an effective rule of law. Individualism, resistance to authority, and the theoretical universality of inner natural law are attractive ideas with significant currency in Cooper's America, and the self-reliant Natty is surely Cooper's best-known literary legacy; but the novel ultimately supports Cooper's belief that prosperity requires law (and judgeships) to be in the hands of those whom education and rank have best fitted to handle power. If the union of Temple's daughter and Oliver Effingham secures the novel's generally optimistic ending, it is notably achieved only when imputations of Effingham's Indian blood and low-class birth are effaced and he is revealed to be the son of Temple's lost friend and the rightful heir to his lands. For Cooper, a cranky conservative and tireless litigator, the legal events of arrest, trial, and imprisonment provide ideal plot devices through which to dramatize and evaluate competing claims for power and authority in America's rapidly expanding commercial arena.

In the hands of other authors, legal process dramatizes the victimization of the powerless. In *The Hidden Hand* (1859), bestselling author E. D. E. N. Southworth undershadows her rollicking anti-sentimental plot by bringing minor characters into first the Orphans Court and then a military court martial. In both cases, the villainous

Colonel Le Noir treats the government's powerful hands as mere extensions of his own, bribing a probate judge to disregard the dying wishes of a gentle heiress's father, and later trumping up a capital case against her equally gentle and passive lover, a soldier in the Mexican War. While both cases eventually end happily, with the lovers blissfully united in the final chapter, Southworth's hard-headed initial courtroom scenes here, as in her 1876 blockbuster *Ishmael*, graphically depict both the reality of legal corruption and the legal disabilities of women and the poor. By presenting parallel cases, Southworth equates the antebellum American woman's legal vulnerability with the powerlessness of the impoverished military underclass; for both, the law is just corrupt enough, just weak enough, to permit the strong to wield its enforcement powers for their own purposes. In ways that parallel Melville's construction of crime in *Billy Budd*, Southworth's legal cases foreground questions of agency: the heiress's sweet submissiveness to the law of guardianship is passive kin to her lover's helplessly unintentional commission of the capital crime of sleeping on duty after being ordered awake for days on end. Not just unassertive but even unintentional non-acts can trigger adverse legal consequences that can be reversed only through the intervention of energetic agents, empowered characters like Southworth's heroine, Capitola the madcap (who helps to vindicate the heiress), or Capitola's lover, Herbert Greyson (a colonel in the Mexican War who intervenes to influence the court martial's verdict). In Southworth's fiction, the law is not so much the instrument of governmental and political oppression as it is the tool of choice for the strong to legitimate and consolidate their control of the weak. Justice therefore depends on the coincidence of power and goodness; happy endings can be achieved only when the strong happen also to be ethical.

In "Benito Cereno" (1855), Herman Melville uses legal process as Brockden Brown did, to structure in unspoken ways the reader's relationship to the main character's perceptions. Once again, readers are situated implicitly as jurors who must struggle to assess difficult, misleading evidence that the novel's primary reflector evaluates unsuccessfully. In this dark, often terrifying novella Melville questions the objectivity – indeed, the viability – of contemporary legal process, suggesting that in America in the 1850s racial assumptions and stereotypes (along with assumptions about the "naturalness" of class and gender hierarchies) are so deeply embedded in the consciousnesses of even the most well-meaning, "benevolent" Northerners that it is simply impossible for either the sufferings or the capacities of blacks to be appreciated.

Basing his tale on the actual memoirs of Amasa Delano, Melville creates a fictional Delano, a Massachusetts ship's captain who, like his historical counterpart, encounters a ship in disarray off the coast of South America but fails to recognize that the blacks have violently rebelled and now control the ship. Boarding the boat to assist the stricken captain, crew, and supposed cargo of slaves, Delano hears tales of storms and woe, sees blacks go unpunished for violence to whites, but also sees performances of black deference to whites, including the seemingly faithful servant Babo (really the rebellion's mastermind) tending the nervous, invalid Captain Cereno. Repeatedly,

Delano becomes suspicious, suspecting foul play, but just as repeatedly, as James Kavanagh has brilliantly shown, he calms himself with "tranquilizing" thoughts of his own comfortable superiority, dismissing his momentary glimpses of black authority by reflecting that the blacks "were too stupid," at their best mere Newfoundland dogs, an attitude that permits Delano's mind to "feel and live its own ruthlessness as 'innocence' and 'moral simplicity'" (Kavanagh 1988: 357).

Recent critics have turned the tide away from examining what Delano sees (the spectacle of allegorical "evil" that fascinated earlier critics) toward historically grounded arguments that target the way Delano's complacent ideology of racial and class superiority *prevents* him from seeing. Significantly, Melville constructs this critique as a form of trial at which the problem is not so much the discriminatory presentation of evidence as the unconscious, disabling biases of the jury. As a juridical fact-finder, Delano cannot make the reasonable evidentiary inference of black authority because his experience of the world, his "common sense" understandings and assumptions, are hopelessly warped by cultural conditioning. As reader–jurors, we duplicate Delano's attempts; our recognition of Delano's inadequacies should trigger an examination of our own. Like Brown, Melville implies the analogy to jury deliberation to demonstrate the difficulty, in or out of the courtroom, of judging the world around us accurately, here especially in matters of race. Where Brown engages eighteenth-century theories of evidence and understanding, Melville refers obliquely to contemporary slave rebellions and the fundamental legal challenge of recognizing the slave as a person rather than a piece of property. Yet finally, his point is not so much an attack on specific legal doctrines or cases, as Brook Thomas and Michael Paul Rogin have argued in linking "Benito Cereno" to the fugitive slave decisions of Melville's father-in-law, Massachusetts Chief Justice Lemuel Shaw, but a general challenge to the possibility of overcoming unacknowledged racist ideology (Thomas 1987; Rogin 1983).

Legal Texts: Interactions of Legal and Literary Discourse

Delano's sailors violently retake the renegade slave ship in "Benito Cereno" and sail it to Lima, where an official investigation is conducted. Melville's third-person narrative then shifts at length to a fictional transcript of depositions, complete with official oaths and linguistic solemnities. Melville's deployment of this narratively discontinuous text, though based on the historical record and participating in the tradition of authenticating fiction with "official" documents, also brilliantly consummates the tale's legal framework by shifting away from dynamic, deliberative trial process to the post-trial textual reification of racial bias in empowered permanent records. In moving from metaphorical to "actual" legal case, Melville highlights the dangers of textuality. If the earlier narrative's account of evidence from Delano's viewpoint requires reader–jurors to construct the slaves' exculpatory narrative inferentially from small textual hints, the official legal record's one-sided account invites parallel

investigation (and contains evidence of white brutality to captured, manacled blacks)
but reminds us that the verdict – and punishment – are already accomplished; what
survives will be only the self-justifying records of those in power.

Though the court believes certain facts "because the negroes have said it," it never
equates credibility with the legal rights of selfhood by considering that the captured
Africans' resort to violence to obtain freedom might be lawful (although the American Supreme Court accepted such a rationale in the 1839 *Amistad* case). As Carolyn
Karcher has shown, Melville's "transcript" notes that some of Cereno's testimony,
initially "held dubious for both learned and natural reasons," was believed only when
corroborated by other witnesses; otherwise, the tribunal "would have deemed it but
duty to reject" it as the product of an unstable mind (1992: 215). Like the testimony
Clara Wieland knows will not be believed without corroboration, Cereno's testimony
appears counter-intuitive; Babo's brilliantly inventive plots and performances contradict the presumption of black mental inadequacy required by contemporary racial
theories. Melville's keen recognition of the power of culturally constructed assumptions is demonstrated when the court momentarily bows to the cumulative impact of
consistent white testimony, but never questions its underlying belief in the purported
teachings of the "learned" and the "natural," culture and biology.

In *Law and Letters in American Fiction*, Robert Ferguson (1984) has influentially
demonstrated how mutually constitutive the professions and subject matters of law
and literature were before the Civil War. Yet by limiting himself to writers with legal
training, Ferguson necessarily excludes women, and thus works like Harriet Beecher
Stowe's *Dred* (1856), a novel more soaked in legal issues, arguments, and texts than
any other before or since. When Stowe's *Uncle Tom's Cabin* (1852) outsold any previous
novel, inciting waves of sympathy for slaves' sufferings, outrage at the fugitive slave
law, and calls for the abolition of slavery, a chorus of pro-slavery voices attacked her as
a fantasizer, calling her depictions of slavery unrealistically harsh, the product of a
passionate but uninformed imagination. In response, Stowe published *The Key to Uncle
Tom's Cabin* (1853), a nonfiction compendium of sources for the novel's major
characters and events, supplemented by correspondence and narratives recounting
abuses of slaves, slave-state laws, legal decisions granting slave-owners virtually
unlimited power over their slaves, advertisements for runaways emphasizing permanent scars, and documentation of American churches' widespread approval of slavery.

When Stowe came to write *Dred*, she solved the problem triggered by *Uncle Tom's
Cabin* in a risky, original way: she folded into her text at key moments the entire texts
of shocking pro-slavery legal documents, including an influential appeals court
decision, a state statute, and a court order authorizing slave-catchers to "kill and
destroy" escaped slaves "by such means as he or they may think fit" without fear of
prosecution. Her plot, circling back continually to an examination of slavery's legal
aspects, refers frequently to real events, like the murder of Elijah Lovejoy, mimics real
cases decided under slave law, like that of Margaret Garner (whose murder of her
children would later inspire Toni Morrison), and analyzes the racial implications of
law-related documents like the Constitution. As if that were not enough, she adds

legal footnotes and three law-related appendices. *Dred* might be a novel, but it is so constrained by documented historical and legal facts that no reader could challenge its veracity.

To appreciate the extraordinary hybrid text Stowe produced, we need to remember how American culture characterized and differentiated law and literature in her day. Law was understood to be factual, objective, rational, political, empowered, and overwhelmingly male; it spoke its own language, in contexts that limited most legal texts to a restricted, legally educated audience. Novels, especially the sentimental "women's literature" with which Stowe was associated, were to be fictional, subjective, emotional, domestic, gentle, and female. If she engages with a contemporary issue like slavery, the female novelist is assumed to work through passion rather than intellect, to reduce legal complexities to a melodramatic world of heroes and villains, violence and victims, and to elicit intense responses by stirring up readers' emotions. Even recent admiring critics of *Uncle Tom's Cabin* like Jane Tompkins perpetuate the image of Stowe as the ultimate sentimentalist, though others, notably Gregg Crane, have demonstrated the novel's nuanced analyses of higher law – the doctrine that just laws must conform to a moral and religious imperative that stands above the law of the land (Tompkins 1985; Crane 2002).

In *Dred*, however, Stowe simply breaks the rules for what a "woman's" novel – or indeed *any* novel – should be. Unlike novels based on celebrated cases that attempt imaginatively to understand a murderer's psychology, or dramatize how racism precludes freedom and justice – *McTeague, An American Tragedy, Native Son* – Stowe refuses to maintain a distinction between fact and fiction, to limit her novel's claim on readers by leaving them the option of dismissing her story as "mere" fiction. As a result, she gives up at key points the novelist's traditionally uncircumscribed creative latitude to shape events and outcomes as her moral imagination requires. Yet she also chooses not to make her book the maximally accurate novelization of a real case, as Norman Mailer would do over a century later in *The Executioner's Song*. Instead, she redefines fictional discourse as continuous with – indeed, at times indistinguishable from – the texts and rhetoric of law, and thus capable of moving seamlessly from one to the other. In *Dred*, Stowe weds her own story of an idealistic lawyer, a family of four siblings (two of whom are excluded by the law's fictions from sharing the freedom and status of their all-white sister and brother), and a mysterious, apocalyptic slave rebel, not just to a series of sensational legal cases but to legal discourse itself. For her large public readership, the novel furnishes an accessible pathway to the rhetoric and substance of law, to texts that would usually be read only by white male lawyers and the few others interested in particular cases.

At the heart of *Dred* is a fictional case in which the owner of a slave sues a man who has leased the slave's services, for having shot and injured the slave when she fled to escape punishment. The slave, Milly, is Stowe's creation, as are the circumstances of the injury, the lawyer's compassionate, successful argument on Milly's behalf in the trial court, and the complex relationship between that lawyer and his father, the appeals court judge who orally delivers the appellate decision that reverses the jury's verdict. But the decision itself is simply – and virtually completely – the text of *State v. Mann*, a significant 1829 South Carolina case Stowe had discussed in the *Key*, holding that "the power of the master must be absolute, to render the submission of the slave perfect," an unsentimental declaration that masters must have the legal right to use violence against slaves because only brute force and power without recourse can produce unrebellious obedience. To a reader, the novel's flow is uninterrupted; the actual Judge Ruffin's decision becomes the fictional Judge Clayton's, just as elsewhere in the novel Stowe's characters speak through, or react to, real legal events and arguments. Judge Clayton's son resigns from the bar, refusing to practice law where such abuses are condoned, devoting himself instead to legal reforms to benefit slaves and, eventually, bring about abolition. As everywhere in this novel, both the younger Clayton's frustrations and his hope for redemption are legal; the world of *Dred* is governed not by religion, emotion, or woman's strength, but by law. *Uncle Tom's Cabin* famously ends with Stowe's injunction to readers to "feel right" about slavery, making condemnation of slavery and recognition of slaves as human beings the first order of business; *Dred* takes a turn toward practical law, directing us to repeal and enact specific statutes and rights.

An 1829 South Carolina decision is not a text many Americans would ordinarily encounter, though some anti-slavery publications did print important cases. By putting it in the hands of thousands of novel readers, Stowe expands the forms of discourse with which Americans engaged as they thought through the Kansas–Nebraska Act or the prospects for abolition. With the novel as medium, readers added the law's own normally arcane texts to the newspapers, periodicals, speeches, and stories that clamored for their analytical attention. It is significant that, if *Dred* definitively claims the novel as a powerful, legitimate participant in the nation's public discussions of slavery law and policy, it also forces readers to confront the actual pro-slavery legal texts which maintained the institution, texts stripped of the rhetoric of affection and protectiveness used by slave-owners in public debates.

Legal Doctrines: Fiction and Substantive Law

As the discussion above suggests, American novelists have been drawn to the law's adversariality and theatricality, to its processes of narrative presentation, evidentiary evaluation, and juridical verdict as well as to the empowered pronouncements of legal texts. Inevitably, the novel's recourse to law brings with it dramatizations of complex legal doctrines. A few of the novel's engagements with areas of substantive law are especially relevant. One is the early republic's investment in the theory of natural law and therefore in the potential for a nation of equal, self-regulating citizens. This idea became the fulcrum first for Charles Brockden Brown's destabilizing challenges to the possibilities of natural order and authority in the new nation and then, several decades later, for James Fenimore Cooper's troubled conclusion that Natty Bumppo's anti-authoritarian individualism is the unrepresentative product of a vanishing wilderness culture that must yield to a centralized, empowered rule of law if the criminal propensities and "wasty ways" of the mass of men are to be successfully governed.

The ultimately divine origin of natural law links it to a second major legal theme, the doctrine of higher law. Preached by abolitionists in essays and sermons, higher law is brilliantly dramatized in Stowe's novels as the proper basis not just for religious but for secular laws that would work to transform the harsh inequities of slavery into a just, Christian society. A separate essay might take up other legal ideas that are significant to literature during this period, including the law of property and inheritance (in works like *The Pioneers*, Hawthorne's *The House of the Seven Gables*, and Melville's *Pierre*), the legal status of women and minorities (*Ishmael* and Jacobs' *Incidents in the Life of a Slave Girl*, as well as *Uncle Tom's Cabin* and *Dred*), or the vulnerability of democracy to official oppression and demagoguery (Hawthorne's *The Scarlet Letter*, Melville's *Mardi* and *Moby-Dick*). Fortunately, much excellent recent work has been done that uses careful historical analyses of substantive legal trends, ideas, cases, and conflicts to frame literary readings.

Several of the best law-and-literature critics begin with fine discussions of the importance of law to early American literature and culture; they include Robert Ferguson, whose study of legally trained authors emphasizes the degree to which eloquence, classical learning, esthetic interests, and literary output were considered not just consistent with, but appropriately part of the lawyer's vocation (1984: 3–84); Jay Fliegelman, whose *Prodigals and Pilgrims* (1982) examines at length the revolutionary era's vexed search for a concept of legitimate and lasting political authority on which to base a new American identity; and Charles Hansford Adams, who situates Cooper's obsession with law as the basis of individual identity by carefully tracing how much "the law was intimately connected with the very idea of the nation," as newly created Americans struggled to decide whether law impeded, or enabled, the growth of the individual (1990: 3, 1–24).

On the antebellum context, Sacvan Bercovitch's *The Rites of Assent* (1993) examines Emerson, Hawthorne, and Melville, among others, through an incisive study of the development of liberalism in an era of agitation about slavery, dissolution of the union, and the meaning of individuality. Brook Thomas' *Cross-Examinations of Law and Literature* (1987) offers productive readings of Cooper, Hawthorne, Stowe, and Melville by matching their texts with contemporary legal conflicts and cases they both responded to and influenced, while Gregg Crane offers the best legally informed analysis of the development of higher law jurisprudence and its links to the antebellum literary context (2002: 12–55). On the period as a whole, Wai Chee Dimock's *Residues of Justice* (1996) traces interactions of literature and law with philosophical theories of justice and the concept of commensurability; the three essays in Smith, McWilliams, and Bloomfield's *Law and American Literature* (1983) offer a fine overview that expands from early American legal history to include analyses of literary lawyers as well as modern literary representations of criminal defendants as victim–perpetrators; and Perry Miller's overarching analysis of "The Legal Mentality" in his seminal *The Life of the Mind in America* continues to ground virtually all later work (1965: 99–265).

REFERENCES AND FURTHER READING

Adams, Charles Hansford (1990). *The Guardian of the Law: Authority and Identity in James Fenimore Cooper*. University Park: Pennsylvania State University Press.

Bercovitch, Sacvan (1993). *The Rites of Assent: Transformations in the Symbolic Construction of America*. New York: Routledge.

Crane, Gregg D. (2002). *Race, Citizenship, and Law in American Literature*. Cambridge, UK: Cambridge University Press.

Dimock, Wai Chee (1996). *Residues of Justice: Literature, Law, Philosophy*. Berkeley: University of California Press.

Dobson, Joanne (1986). "The Hidden Hand: Subversion of Cultural Ideology in Three Mid-Nineteenth-Century American Women's Novels." *American Quarterly* 38, 223–42.

Ferguson, Robert A. (1984). *Law and Letters in American Culture*. Cambridge, Mass.: Harvard University Press.

Fliegelman, Jay (1982). *Prodigals and Pilgrims: The American Revolution against Patriarchal Authority, 1750–1800*. Cambridge, UK: Cambridge University Press.

Fliegelman, Jay (1991). "Introduction." In *Wieland and Memoirs of Carwin the Biloquist*, vii–xliv. New York: Viking Penguin.

Hagenbuchle, Roland (1988). "American Literature and the Nineteenth-Century Crisis in Epistemology: The Example of Charles Brockden Brown." *Early American Literature* 23, 121–51.

Hedrick, Joan D. (1994). *Harriet Beecher Stowe: A Life*. New York: Oxford University Press.

Karcher, Carolyn (1992). "The Riddle of the Sphinx: Melville's 'Benito Cereno' and the *Amistad* Case." In Robert E. Burkholder (ed.), *Critical Essays on Herman Melville's "Benito Cereno"*, 196–229. New York: G. K. Hall.

Kavanagh, James H. (1988). "The Hive of Subtlety: 'Benito Cereno' and the Liberal Hero." In Sacvan Bercovitch and Myra Jehlen (eds.), *Ideology and Classic American Literature*, 352–83. Cambridge, UK: Cambridge University Press.

Miller, Perry (1965). *The Life of the Mind in America from the Revolution to the Civil War*. New York: Harcourt, Brace & World.

Rogin, Michael Paul (1983). *Subversive Genealogy: The Politics and Art of Herman Melville*. New York: Knopf.

Smith, Carl S.; McWilliams, John P.; and Bloomfield, Maxwell (1983). *Law and American Literature: A Collection of Essays*. New York: Knopf.

Sundquist, Eric (1999). "'Benito Cereno' and New World Slavery." In Sacvan Bercovitch (ed.), *Reconstructing American Literary History*, 93–122. Cambridge, Mass.: Harvard University Press.

Thomas, Brook (1987). *Cross-Examinations of Law and Literature: Cooper, Hawthorne, Stowe and Melville*. Cambridge, UK: Cambridge University Press.

Tompkins, Jane (1985). *Sensational Designs: The Cultural Work of American Fiction 1790–1860*. New York: Oxford University Press.

21
Labor and Fiction

Cindy Weinstein

Henry David Thoreau's *Walden* (1854) is about labor from a variety of perspectives, whether in its most tangible embodiments (the concrete materials that are required to build his shelter) or in its most poetic manifestations (the esthetic impressions that go into the composition of his book). Thoreau's account of his attempt to "get my living honestly" (1986: 71) is clearly not fiction, but his Transcendentalist revision of labor reflects overtly upon the relation between labor and the creative process, which, of course, includes the art of making fiction. *Walden* is a relentless screed against industrialization, against specialization, against idleness, against drudgery, against slavery. It is one man's attempt to critique all that he sees wrong with antebellum systems of production and consumption, both within and without the domestic realm, and to create a different model of labor that is fulfilling, self-sustaining, bare, meditative, physical, and esthetic.

Walden enacts Thoreau's idyl of labor, as the literal and conceptual aspects of his life and art reproduce the rhythms and transformations of the natural world. The chapter entitled "The Bean-Field," for example, is a meditation on the "curious labor" (Thoreau 1986: 200) of hoeing beans, which includes not only a tabulation of expenditure and income for that very purpose, but a statement of poetic intention as he characterizes his "daily work" as "making the yellow soil express its summer thought in bean leaves and blossoms" (p. 202). Labor, if rightly practiced, is both a necessary fact (to survive, one must work: "he that does not eat need not work" [p. 270]) and a foundation for creative expression. Thoreau, in other words, strives to make inextricable his work as farmer, builder, hunter, poet, and writer, and "the work" that we read; that is, *Walden* itself.

Indeed, whether its declared subject matter is bean-fields, leaves of grass, or white whales, much American literature in the mid-nineteenth century is haunted by an idealized conception of labor, what Thoreau calls "a very *agricola laboriosus*" (1986: 202), whose roots may be traced to Thomas Jefferson's agrarian paeans in *Notes on the State of Virginia* or J. Hector St. John de Crèvecœur's *Letters from an American Farmer*, where the body and mind allegedly flourish through contact with the land and its endless fecundity. One of the keenest observers of American society, Alexis de Tocqueville, however, hypothesized a different and less rosy linkage. In *Democracy in America* (1835), he notes that in contrast to aristocratic societies where "the notion of profit is kept distinct from that of labor," the "equality of conditions" in America "not only ennobles the notion of labor, but raises the notion of labor as a source of profit" (1945: 161). For many authors of the antebellum period, including Thoreau, Herman Melville, Nathaniel Hawthorne, and Harriet Beecher Stowe, not to mention writers of slave narratives such as Frederick Douglass, Harriet Jacobs, and Solomon Northup, De Tocqueville's analysis of the rupture of the connection between work and salvation and its replacement by one between work and economic accumulation for its own sake correctly registers a central failure of American society. Their texts attempt to restore work to its inherently salvific origins by critiquing how labor "has been so minutely subdivided and peddled out," as Ralph Waldo Emerson writes in "The American Scholar" (1837), that "man is metamorphosed into a thing" (1982: 84).

Over and again, literature reveals how the ennobling potential of labor gets lost as it becomes the mechanism for turning people into things, whether the blank maids in Melville's allegory of industrial sterilization, "The Paradise of Bachelors and Tartarus of Maids" (1855), the slaves on Legree's plantation, or the fate of William Craft's siblings as told in "Running a Thousand Miles for Freedom" (1860), whose "master wanted money, so he sold my brother and then mortgaged my sister" (Craft 1969: 276). That slaves *were* things, according to slave law, makes the representations of labor in slave narratives especially interesting. Is it possible for a slave narrative to configure work as anything other than a sign of the slave's complete bondage and alienation? The slave's brutal state of being (or nonbeing), combined with the fact that the parents' reproductive labors – their children – were also defined as things to be sold in the market, adds yet another dimension to the problematic valuation of work in slave narratives. Whereas slave narratives make absolutely clear the pernicious nexus between slave labor, reproduction, and profit, sentimental fictions of the antebellum period, by and large, present yet a different view of their protagonists' labors. Although many sentimental heroines and heroes display a strong work ethic (Gerty of Maria Cummins' *The Lamplighter* [1854], Augusta of Maria McIntosh's *Two Pictures; or, What we Think of Ourselves, and What the World Thinks of Us* [1863], and Eoline of Caroline Lee Hentz's *Eoline, or Magnolia Vale* [1852] are teachers; Ishmael Worth of E. D. E. N. Southworth's *Self-Raised, or From the Depths* [1863] and Marcus Warland of Hentz's *Marcus Warland* [1852] are both lawyers), the significance and arduousness of their vocations pale in comparison to the labor of piecing together a new family out of the shards of their original one.

The conditions of its own production (as well as the obstacles to it) are very much the subject of Thoreau's text, and although *Walden* may stand out by virtue of the eloquence with which it self-consciously reflects upon those conditions, the fact is that many texts and many genres are similarly preoccupied. In what follows, I want to delineate how key canonical fictions of the period, slave narratives, and sentimental novels not only represent their characters and their labor, but examine and extend how readers might identify and evaluate alternative kinds of labor, including the rigors of writing, the difficulties of attaining freedom when confined to a life of bondage, or the task of making a family in the absence of consanguineous relations.

Some of the most scathing literary indictments of labor in antebellum society can be found in the fiction of Melville and Hawthorne. Surely, Bartleby's famous words, "I would prefer not to," apply to any number of characters whose labors are mentally stupefying and/or physically harmful: the sailors aboard *White-Jacket*'s (1849) *Never-sink*, the crew of the *Pequod*, Hawthorne in the Custom House sketch of *The Scarlet Letter* (1850), and Miles Coverdale of *The Blithedale Romance* (1852), whose "commitment to lessen the laboring man's great burthen of toil" (Hawthorne 1983: 19) is as problematic as his interest in the "theories of equal brotherhood and sisterhood" (p. 24) upon which Blithedale is organized. These texts, like Thoreau's, are especially powerful because their critique of labor, convincing as it may be, acts as the spur for an even more devastating self-critique, which then becomes an opportunity to reflect upon the ways in which the labor of writing depends upon the very conditions that are being diagnosed as the problem. The maids in Tartarus, after all, produce the paper that not only allows the barristers in paradise to conduct their legal affairs, but also provides Melville himself with an essential ingredient for his labors. At the same time, these writers' art often strives to offer an alternative model of production – more precisely, esthetic production – that would undo the damaging effects of alienated labor. The symphony of voices, genres, and texts in *Moby-Dick* (1851), or the beautifying labors Hester lavishes upon her scarlet letter, allowing its significations as well as those of the novel to metamorphose endlessly, would be two of the most famous examples.

I will focus my attention here briefly on Hawthorne's *The Blithedale Romance*, which is of particular interest on the question of labor because, like Thoreau's venture at Walden, the experiment at Blithedale (the utopian community of Brook Farm, historically speaking, to which Hawthorne belonged for a short while in 1841) represents an attempt, based on the writings of the socialist Charles Fourier, to conjoin the labors of the body with those of the mind. Thus the narrator, Coverdale, writes: "Each stroke of the hoe was to uncover some aromatic root of wisdom, heretofore hidden from the sun" (Hawthorne 1983: 65). But unlike Thoreau's relentless "labor which yielded an instant and immeasurable crop" (1986: 204) in the form of both beans and figurative language, Hawthorne's characters (as well as Hawthorne himself who, in a letter written at Brook Farm to his fiancée, Sophia Peabody, noted that "this present life gives me an antipathy to pen and ink" [1983: viii]) fare considerably better with "delectable visions of the spiritualization of labor" (p. 65) than with the real thing. With characteristic irony, Coverdale finds little to support the Transcendentalist's belief in the creative forces to be unleashed by laboring upon the land, and on the contrary propounds the idea that a separation between "the yeoman and the scholar" is a necessary one: "the clods of earth, which we so constantly belabored and turned over and over, were never etherealized into thought. Our thoughts on the contrary were fast becoming cloddish.... Intellectual activity is incompatible with any large amount of bodily exercise" (p. 66). Far from providing the material basis for mental ennoblement, then, physical labor is a conduit for nothing except more physical labor. As with all of Coverdale's statements, laced with irony, elitism, and retrospective condescension as they are, it is important to remember that without Coverdale's experiences at Blithedale (and Hawthorne's at Brook Farm?), the narrative of Blithedale would not have been written. Manual labor of the kind engaged in by "the swinish multitude" (p. 20) is therefore necessary to manual labor of a different kind, which is to say literary production, if only as a category of labor which enables Coverdale, the poet in the group, to produce an alternative or, more precisely, what seems like an alternative to that multitude's mind-numbing labors. Unlike Thoreau or Melville, though, whose texts hold out the possibility that, even in the face of everything that is wrong with labor in their society, labor can be a source of spiritual and creative expression, *The Blithedale Romance* harbors no such conviction. What Coverdale endorses in his personal abnegation of labor (others, of course, must work in order that he can so abnegate) is an embrace of leisure, a spectatorial and consumerist state of being – clearly, not the redefinition of leisure that Thoreau seeks to accomplish in *Walden* – that he hopes will elude the fate of reification predicted by Emerson but instead turns everyone, including himself, into the very "thing" that he is trying to escape.

Coverdale can escape from physical labor because he makes enough money through his writing; in addition to which, he is not a slave. This obvious point becomes relevant once we shift the focus from the canonical fictions of Hawthorne, Melville, and Thoreau to slave narratives, where the prospect of leisure is severely circumscribed, to put it mildly, the notion of labor as inherently spiritualizing is similarly problematic, and the goal of escape involves not the pleasures of spectatorial consumption, but the avoidance of physical punishment, the redefinition of oneself from thing to person, and the reclamation of one's labor as one's own. Of course, slave narratives discuss and deplore the conditions of labor on the plantation and in the household; but I am particularly interested in examining how the labor of writing the slave narrative becomes the medium through which the slave attempts to overcome the alienation of her labor and, in the process, endeavors to own herself. One might choose any number of slave narratives that meditate on the relation between slave labor and the labor of producing a slave narrative – Frederick Douglass' *Narrative of the Life of a Slave* (1845) or Harriet Jacobs' *Incidents in the Life of a Slave Girl* (1861) immediately come to mind; but Solomon Northup's *Twelve Years a Slave* (1853) is an especially interesting example, not least because Northup had the experience of being a free laborer in upstate New York before he was kidnapped and sold into slavery near the Red River in Louisiana (the complete title of his narrative is *Twelve Years a Slave. Narrative of Solomon Northup, a Citizen of New-York, Kidnapped in Washington City in 1841, and Rescued in 1853, from a Cotton Plantation near the Red River in Louisiana*). Northup's narrative is also fascinating because his method of storytelling continuously, indeed compulsively, calls attention to his awareness that though the incidents in the story happened to him, he will never know all of the details of his capture and liberation. His labors on the plantation, and those of his fellow slaves, are a central preoccupation of the narrative, but equally central is a metanarrative, which is the labor of producing and possessing his story. Like Thoreau's, Northup's narrative is not fiction, but just as the representations of labor in *Walden* help us towards a more satisfying explanation of labor in key antebellum fictions, so too Northup's slave narrative establishes a set of concerns regarding labor through which many sentimental fictions of the period will articulate their own ideas about it.

Northup, a free black man living in New York with his wife and three children, opens his narrative with an account of his various employments, all of which reveal a strong work ethic. He does repair work on the Champlain Canal; he transports timber from Lake Champlain to Troy; he is familiar with agricultural labors; he drives a hack; and he excels in playing the violin, which leads to several engagements and monetary remuneration. He is eventually kidnapped by two men who persuade him to join them en route to New York, and eventually Washington DC, in order that he can earn money by playing his violin in their circus company. He agrees and, days later, finds himself drugged and chained in a slave pen around the corner from the Capitol, and then turned into a slave for the next twelve years of his life. One of the first lessons that Northup's captors teach him while in the slave pen is that to reveal his identity as a free man is to risk death. Each time he speaks the truth about himself, he is viciously punished, until he finally understands that the truth will not set him free, but rather that some combination of exposure and concealment will be necessary for his escape.

Those twelve years of, quite literally, self-denial are Northup's subject, and his account shares many of the generic conventions of slave narratives, including representations of barbaric physical violence done to himself and others, the necessity of concealment in order to effect one's liberation (resonant with Jacobs' years in her grandmother's garret), and the unthinkable family separations that form the bedrock of the slave system and the psychic torture it inflicts. Having become "perfectly familiar with the art and mysteries of rafting" (1968: 8) during his work on the canal, Northup proves to be a particularly valuable slave, although that in no way guarantees immunity from physical abuse. At one point in his narrative, after his original name has been taken away and his slave name, for the moment at least, is "Ford's Platt," Northup writes that he was "pronounced the 'smartest nigger in the Pine Woods' – in fact I was the Fulton of Indian Creek" (p. 71); and later, when describing his musical abilities, he confesses, "at the expense of appearing egotistical . . . that I was considered the Ole Bull of Bayou Boeuf" (p. 165). Throughout this account we learn of his expertise, ingenuity, and creativity; and even though he "must toil day after day" (p. 92), without reward, recompense, adequate blankets, or food, his narrative registers evidence of another dimension to his labor. He writes: "my thoughts, for twelve years, turned to the contemplation of my escape" (p. 212). Once a slave, he must add "escape" to his list of labors which includes picking cotton, clearing cane, gathering corn, and somehow always finding that "the labor of the day is not yet ended" (p. 127). Thus, at the same time as his narrative depicts and descries the horrific conditions endured by slave laborers in the South (about his master Epps, Northup writes, "Ten years I toiled for that man without reward. Ten years of my incessant labor has contributed to increase the bulk of his possessions.... I am indebted to him for nothing, save undeserved abuse and stripes" [p. 138]), Northup's labor does not end there. He is always on the lookout for potential sympathizers who might assist him in his plans for escape, strategically plying them with hints and suggestions as to his true status as a free black man kidnapped into slavery, and he desperately tries to contact friends and family in the North, even going so far as to make his own pen and ink.

The image of Northup "manufactur[ing] a pen," making ink, and meeting "with the good fortune of obtaining a sheet of paper" (1968: 175) only after being a slave for nine years is significant because it demonstrates how the very act of writing, and the implements necessary for it, must remain outside of the slave's grasp in order for the peculiar institution to continue. Written expression is off-limits, as are books (Douglass, Fanny Kemble, and Stowe all note that teaching a slave to read is illegal in the South), as is the post office. The slave narrative is thus aptly named because it is a text (and a genre) dedicated to making a narrative out of an experience that stifles expression. Like many slave narrators, conscious of transgressing the potentially racist limits of their white audience, Northup is careful not to appear too confident. He speaks of scenes as "imperfectly described" (p. 162), or prefaces incidents with the phrase, "if I remember rightly" (p. 71). There is, however, a more profound sense of hesitation, of belatedness, and of incomplete knowledge in Northup's narrative, and his text works hard to close the epistemological gap between his own experience as a slave and his representation of it. Such closure, however, is not to be his, because everything from the names of his kidnappers to the fate of his rescuer, Bass, remains unknown: "their names, as they afterwards gave them to me, were Merrill Brown and Abram Hamilton, though whether these were their true appellations, I have strong reasons to doubt" (pp. 12–13); "Whither he [Bass] is now gone, I regret to be obliged to say, is unknown to me" (p. 205). The elusiveness of complete knowledge is matched in the narrative by an ambiguity about time. About his nemesis Burch, the man who purchases him from his original kidnappers, Northup has this to say: "His name was James H. Burch, as I learned afterwards – a well-known slavedealer in Washington, and then, or lately, connected in business, as a partner, with Theophilus Freeman, of New Orleans.... Both of these men still live in Washington, or did, at the time of my return through that city from slavery in January last" (p. 21). Northup's self-conscious uncertainty about the status of the persons in his narrative ("then, or lately," "still live ... or did") is undoubtedly connected to the fact that he "learns afterwards" the name of his torturer, as well as a host of other details about his story. Northup's "constant labor" (p. 163) on the plantation constitutes one element of his "endless labor" as a slave; one must also add as another his determination to get his identity back, to become Northup once more rather than Platt, or Steward, or Tibeats (just some of the names he accumulates in the course of his enslavement). This, too, involves a list of Herculean tasks, demanding his own intelligence and strength, as well as the efforts of people such as Governor Hunt of New York and Supreme Court Justice Nelson. Then there is the work of putting together the pieces of a story that is at once his and yet forever out of his reach.

Northup's narrative, like so many antebellum texts, begins with a separation from his family. *Uncle Tom's Cabin* (1852) and *Incidents in the Life of A Slave Girl* are, perhaps, the most famous diagnoses of how slavery is founded on reproductive dispossession, but the sundering of domestic ties is instrumental to any number of novels, including Maria Cummins' *The Lamplighter*, Susan Warner's *The Wide, Wide World* (1850), Mary Jane Holmes' *'Lena Rivers* (1856), Caroline Lee Hentz's *Ernest Linwood* (1856) — the list goes on. It is worth observing that the assault on family is the *donnée* of both slave narratives and sentimental novels. To do so is to acknowledge at once their overlapping concerns (self-possession, escape from punishment, the predicament of the orphaned child) and the markedly different strategies available to them as they attempt to achieve their generic goals. For example, unlike sentimental protagonists whose task is the acquisition of a family based on love rather than consanguinity (and often the two are mutually exclusive), the slave's primary motivation is often the restoration of consanguineous bonds. Also, whereas sentimental protagonists, most of whom are female, are entitled to the benefits of contractual arrangements, such as adoption and marriage, the protagonists of slave narratives often bemoan the fact that slaves are not permitted to enter into such contracts, the marriage contract being a particularly significant deprivation. If one of the goals of slave narratives is reunion with one's family, what might we make of the fact that sentimental fictions, though they often end with the restoration of the middle-class family, do such a persuasive job of demonstrating the biological family's emotional insufficiencies? How do these novels represent the labor of their protagonists, and what might their "cultural work," to invoke Jane Tompkins' fitting phrase, be?

At one point in Maria McIntosh's *Two Pictures; or, What we Think of Ourselves, and What the World Thinks of Us* (1863), the main character reminds herself of the words spoken to her by her guardian: "I have heard Mr. Mortimer say that work was the best cure for unhappiness — let me try it" (p. 222). To be sure, work plays a part in the lives of many sentimental heroines of the period, although their typical labors as teacher, governess, or domestic drudge are usually just that — a temporary part played by the main character until she finds her true role as wife and mother. There are, of course, exceptions to this generic rule, and Fanny Fern's *Ruth Hall* would certainly be the most notable by virtue of the fact that Ruth's role as mother is initially dependent upon her job as writer: a job she never gives up, even when her children are once more safely by her side. That said, however, the more conventional trajectory of the heroine involves parental separation, a series of domestic ties that are either emotionally satisfying or deeply problematic, a stint as a worker of some sort, and eventually a home and children of her own.

This last piece of the narrative — the reproduction of the bourgeois family — has been taken to represent the "cultural work" of sentimental fictions, and yet the families in these texts are usually in such disastrous states that it is difficult to take seriously the notion that the heroine's household will somehow elude the pitfalls of her own original and damaged family. Indeed, if one looks at the entire plots of the novels themselves and not just their conclusions, it becomes evident that they are up to something potentially quite different and radical: the reconfiguration of the family itself. First, they are replete with terms such as "a sort of adopted daughter" or "my foster child-lady," that designate an ambiguity about family relations. Second, characters act as if family relations were decisions to be made rather than biological destiny: "I will not have you call me 'uncle' – I am your father," or "Come with me and be my sister." And third, their plots consistently register a sometimes playful, yet often dangerous ambiguity about names: "she had, in reality, no surname of her own," or "Yes, here is a name, – *the name*, – Ida May!" Sentimental heroines – take, for example Gerty and Ellen Montgomery – are continuously being adopted and re-adopted, losing one last name and getting another (again, reminiscent of the slave narrative), as if membership in one family did not prohibit membership in another. The point is that, like the legal treatises of the period that helped to develop the field of "domestic relations law," or the burgeoning advice literature of the period that assisted mothers and fathers, sisters and brothers in establishing their proper relations both within the family and beyond, or the writings of radical reformers such as Frances Wright and John Noyes, sentimental fictions are preoccupied with the question of what makes a family. Their novels are attempts to extend and redefine *the* central institution of antebellum culture. They do so by making the case that the biological family (the mother usually dies in the first few pages or, if she's lucky, the first few chapters), and the father in particular, is no longer providing the children of sentimental fictions the structural coherence that will give them not only definitive last names but emotional stability. Their texts labor to discover a new kind of coherence for their fictional children (a literary attempt to arrive at what, in the legal realm, was called "the best interests of the child") that is based more on affection than affinity, more on sympathy than salary.

To prove this point, I want to conclude with a brief discussion of *The Wide, Wide World*, Susan Warner's 1850 blockbuster in which Ellen Montgomery is separated from her mother and father, and thereafter can find comfort in the arms of virtually anyone to whom she is not consanguineously related, the evil Mr. Saunders being the exception that proves the rule. One must first acknowledge that Ellen's labors are primarily psychological rather than physical; and, as Tompkins has convincingly demonstrated, they are characterized by tremendous and painful acts of self-sacrifice in the interests of appeasing the often impossibly demanding adults in her life. There is also a victory, however, in that she gets to dispense or withhold her love, as she wishes. The best example of this can be seen when the narrator considers Ellen's response to her father's death. Her father, we recall, is a cruel man, who separates Ellen from her mother in a particularly harsh and unfeeling way. In a novel that gauges Ellen's spiritual development through the depth of her sympathy, it is worth noting that Ellen is neither condemned nor castigated for the remarkable lack of feeling she expresses when Mr. Montgomery dies: "the knowledge of his death had less pain for her than the removal of this fear [that he would take her from "everything good and pleasant"] brought relief" (Warner 1987: 381). Indeed, hers is a world where the love of chosen relations always trumps biological ones (Alice tells Ellen, "you shall be my little sister and I will be your elder sister" [p. 224], and John reminds her, "you know you gave me leave to be your brother" [p. 296]), and Ellen is constantly forced to defend her choices. This redefinition of family, according to the logic of choice and affection, is the "cultural work" of Warner's novel: the point of Ellen's labor, and, more generally, of sentimental novels. Emerson's terms provide a surprisingly useful gloss, if one understands that Ellen's move away from consanguineous relations and toward chosen ones eventuates in her metamorphosis from thing to person.

To be sure, the goal of Ellen's labors in *The Wide, Wide World* differs dramatically from that of labor as treated by Thoreau, Hawthorne, and Northup; but, like their texts, Warner's carries with it the conviction that the interventions of antebellum fiction on the topic of labor – however the author chooses to approach it – are ideologically as well as esthetically significant. Labor is an essential category of experience for authors of the period, whether to be critiqued, extolled, renewed, or redefined. "Where is this division of labor to end?" asks Thoreau (1986: 89). For Thoreau, it temporarily ends with *Walden*; for Hawthorne, it constitutes the very identity of individuals; for Northup, who has experienced self-division through slave labor, it ends (almost) with freedom; and for sentimental fictions, like Warner's, it ends with a family of one's own making.

References and Further Reading

Baym, Nina (1978). *Woman's Fiction: A Guide to Novels by and about Women in America, 1820–1870*. Ithaca, NY: Cornell University Press.

Bromell, Nicholas (1993). *By the Sweat of the Brow: Literature and Labor in Antebellum America*. Chicago: University of Chicago Press.

Brown, Gillian (1990). *Domestic Individualism: Imagining Self in Nineteenth-Century America*. Berkeley: University of California Press.

Craft, William (1969). "Running a Thousand Miles for Freedom; or, the Escape of William and Ellen Craft from Slavery." In *Great Slave Narratives*, selected by Arna Bontemps. Boston: Beacon.

Cummins, Maria Susanna (1988). *The Lamplighter*, ed. Nina Baym. New Brunswick: Rutgers University Press. (First publ. 1854.)

Emerson, Ralph Waldo (1982). "Nature." In *Selected Essays*. New York: Penguin.

Grossberg, Michael (1985). *Governing the Hearth: Law and the Family in Nineteenth-Century Amer-ica*. Chapel Hill: University of North Carolina Press.

Hawthorne, Nathaniel (1983). *The Blithedale Romance*. New York: Penguin. (First publ. 1852.)

Hentz, Caroline Lee (1856). *Ernest Linwood: A Novel*. Boston: John P. Jewett. (First publ. 1856.)

Holmes, Mary Jane (1970). *'Lena Rivers*. New York: Dillingham. (First publ. 1856.)

Langdon, Mary (1854). *Ida May; A Story of Things Actual and Possible*. Boston: Phillips, Sampson & Co.

McIntosh, Maria (1863). *Two Pictures; or, What we Think of Ourselves, and What the World Thinks of Us*. New York: Appleton.

Northup, Solomon (1968). *Twelve Years a Slave*, ed. Sue Eakin and Joseph Logsdon. Baton Rouge: Louisiana State University Press.

Stephens, Marion H. (1972). *Hagar the Martyr; or, Passion and Reality*. New York: Fetridge.

Thoreau, Henry David (1986). *Walden*. New York: Penguin. (First publ. 1854.)

Tocqueville, Alexis de (1945). *Democracy in America*, vol. 2. New York: Vintage. (First publ. 1935.)

Tompkins, Jane (1985). *Sensational Designs: The Cultural Work of American Fiction, 1790–1860*. New York: Oxford University Press.

Warner, Susan (1987). *The Wide, Wide World*. New York: Feminist Press. (First publ. 1850.)

Weinstein, Cindy (1995). *The Literature of Labor and the Labors of Literature: Allegory in Nineteenth-Century American Fiction*. Cambridge, UK: Cambridge University Press.

Weinstein, Cindy (2004). *Family, Kinship and Sympathy in Nineteenth-Century American Literature*. Cambridge, UK: Cambridge University Press.

22

Words for Children

Carol J. Singley

The period following the American Revolutionary War witnessed a significant increase in the production of books for childhood consumption, as well as an increase in the variety of reading material available. Although texts for children had existed in one form or another for centuries, the content of reading material for children and adults was often indistinguishable (Hunt 2001: 29). The proliferation of children's literature as both concept and commodity coincided in the United States with an increase in population that created a greater demand for reading material; improved technology that facilitated the printing, marketing, and distribution of books; the rise of a middle class able and willing to purchase books; and a public school movement. Until the late eighteenth century American publishers took their cues from England, reprinting favorites for children. At that point, however, first in Boston and New York and then in Philadelphia, a flourishing publishing industry grew up, and literature for children formed a large part of it. These material developments were accompanied by the emergence of a new conception of childhood as a distinct phase of life rather than a miniaturized adulthood, and a more sympathetic understanding of the child and its needs. The child as both reader and subject of literature also became emblematic of the new republic, simultaneously inscribing its hopes and fears as the nation entered its first century of independence.

In the period from 1780 to 1865, as in previous ones, literature for children was deeply anchored to prevailing beliefs about the child; in particular, to attitudes toward child-rearing and the child's relationship to God and family. The colonies had always emphasized childhood education and, following the English model, inculcated the importance of obedience to parents and self-control. Prior to independence, reading matter for children included the Bible (which was translated into Indian languages for missionary purposes) and other forms of didactic writing such as sermons, catechisms, doctrinal treatises, histories, natural histories, and biographies. John Bunyan's religious allegory, *The Pilgrim's Progress* (1678, 1684), was read on both sides of the Atlantic and by all ages. *A Little Pretty Pocket-Book*, published in London by John Newbery in 1744, was one of the first commercial books for children to offer amusement; but Americans, among whom the cultural and religious ideologies associated with Calvinism prevailed, favored literature moral in form and content. Calvinist views, which held sway for nearly two centuries, adhered to a view of the child, as of the adult, as innately corrupt and in need of early religious training and strict discipline to achieve repentance and salvation. Although the strength of Calvinism was waning generally by the end of the eighteenth century, the spirit of Jonathan Edwards, who in the 1740s characterized children as "young vipers and infinitely more hateful than vipers," retained currency.

Although production of children's fiction increased in the last two decades of the eighteenth century, English literature continued to exert great influence on American juvenile fiction. In particular, Maria Edgeworth, arguably more popular in the United States than in England, where some considered her too liberal, helped make the transition from strictly Puritan to more generalized moral writing. In *The Parent's Assistant* (1796) and *Moral Tales* (1801), Edgeworth met readers' expectations for children's fiction which was both amply entertaining and suitably instructional, and which continued to emphasize the importance of self-reflection and self-improvement. Lydia Maria Child, author of the advice manual *The Mother's Book* (1831), listed Edgeworth's books among those recommended for children aged from five to sixteen. Edgeworth also struck a chord with American readers with her emphasis on science and learning from experience, her pleasant country settings, and her use of realistic, up-to-date material rather than fairy-tales – which many deemed untruthful, frivolously imaginative, and unnecessarily violent. A distinctly American genre appeared with the publication of *The Tales of Peter Parley, About America* (1827), by Connecticut-born Samuel G. Goodrich. This volume and its sequels met the nation's dual demand for knowledge and entertainment by offering mostly accurate geographical and historical facts in the form of a travelogue by the beloved "old man" Peter Parley.

As the newly formed nation took stock of itself and Puritan standards faded, a vision of freedom and limitless potential entered into literature and views of childhood alike. American literature unabashedly figured itself in the form of the child, emphasizing its nascent goodness and hopeful future. The child thus served an important rhetorical function in the construction of American nationhood. Gradually sensible of their uniqueness, Americans also began defining themselves differently from England. As print technology developed and children increasingly constituted a distinct audience for publishers, many writers noted for adult subjects also turned their hand to juvenile fiction. Benjamin Franklin, for example, published *The Story of the Whistle* in France in 1779 while American ambassador there, retitling the tale *The Whistle: A True Story Written to His Nephew* in a 1793 edition. Renowned American writers of adult fiction not only wrote for children but also often featured children as main characters in their texts. By the mid-nineteenth century "majors wrote for minors" (Griswold 1992: viii), and the line separating juvenile and adult fiction was blurred to the point of being indistinguishable.

The dawn of the nineteenth century saw the first indigenous outburst of creative literature for children. Such literature continued to emphasize the need for obedience, but as juvenile literary forms became more imaginative and entertaining, they also recorded a thirst for experience, the rewards to be gained by ingenuity and initiative, and a sense of adventure. American writer William Cardell, critical of fairy-tales and nursery rhymes, achieved success with his 1824 *The Story of Jack Halyard*, a tale combining adventure with individual and family moral virtue, about a boy who goes to sea after his father dies and who prospers enough to repurchase the family farm. Cardell's *The Happy Family; or Scenes of American Life* (1827), set on the frontier, pointedly asserts the superiority of "American" life. Fiction of the period was highly gendered, with girls trained to replicate the patterns of their mothers by demonstrating domestic virtues and boys encouraged to develop the independence necessary to setting their own course. It was also class-based, the vast majority being written for middle-class and socially aspiring white readers. Native Americans and African American children had conspicuously little to read, although they were frequently constructed as stereotypes in texts that featured them and to which they had little access.

The American novel developed in a literary atmosphere dedicated to history. The proper subject of American literature, early critics believed, was the past; the indigenous narrative form must therefore be the historical novel. Taking this cue and drawing as well on English Romantic traditions, writers such as James Fenimore Cooper, Lydia Maria Child, and Catharine Maria Sedgwick helped to develop the genre of historical romance, which often portrayed the clash of cultures between Anglo settlers and Indians. Cooper's Leatherstocking Tales (1823–41), comprising five novels, became standard fare. Child's novel *Hobomok* (1824) is the first account of intermarriage between whites and Indians in American fiction. However bold the plot, Child subordinates the miscegenation to Anglo hegemony by anglicizing the child of the union of Mary Conant and Hobomok and requiring his assimilation into white society. In her Puritan romance *Hope Leslie* (1827), set in seventeenth-century Massachusetts, Sedgwick both follows and departs from the conventions of the early frontier romance. She rewrites accepted history of the Pequod War, chronicling injustices toward Indians enacted by the Puritan fathers; and she sets a new standard for female heroism by creating a portrait of the young Hope Leslie, who with her resourcefulness, courage, and honesty rivals and at times surpasses her male counterpart, Everell Fletcher. Sedgwick also portrays a variety of girlhood types to complement Hope's character, including the chaste and dutiful Esther, constrained by Puritan codes; Hope's sister Faith, whose marriage to an Indian results in a loving but sterile muteness; and the daunting Indian girl Magawisca, superior to all the characters in bravery, self-sacrifice, and idealism. Sympathetic toward the Indian but also limited in her vision for mixed-race relations, Sedgwick denies Magawisca marriage to Everell and sends her off alone into the forest, suggesting the inevitable decline of native tribes. "My people have been spoiled," Magawisca says at the end of the novel; "the Indian and the white man can no more mingle, and become one than day and night."

Despite new commercial avenues for creative work and a growing taste for entertainment, didactic literature abounded. A spirit of reform seized the nation in the first
half of the century, pressing producers of children's literature to hold to rigidly
defined educational goals and to see literature as a vehicle for the promotion of
religious beliefs, manners, behavior, and morals. Writers instructed children on
matters of faith as well as practical matters of life, encouraging them to be humane
and inveighing against the cruelty of slavery and mistreatment of animals. Prominent
in this respect was the Sunday School movement, which took hold in both England
and the United States in these years. Aimed in particular at the elementary education
of poor children, it distributed religious tracts as well as magazines, journals,
chapbooks, broadsides, and cheap editions. The Sunday School movement flourished
especially in the gap created by rural families' suspicion of the public school system.
With the American revolutionary cause still firmly in mind, they bristled at the
idea of submitting to secular authority (Bingham and Scholt 1980: 156). The
hundreds of volumes of literature published by the American Sunday School Movement, formed in 1824, were multidenominational in scope and helped to keep the
doctrines of religion alive while giving it a gentler face than the preceding Calvinist
sermons and texts.

With the war for political independence won, national attention now focused on
revolution of a domestic kind. A generation of educators and religious leaders,
perceiving a crisis in the family, identified home as the new front and implored
parents to take an active role in the rearing of children. Fathers were reminded not to
neglect their duties as rightful familial patriarchs. Mothers were exhorted to renew
their efforts to teach their children not only hygiene, manners, and religion, but also a
new patriotism that emphasized the positive results of hard work and charity toward
those less fortunate. This new regime, while not abandoning the emphasis on firmness
and obedience to parents so prevalent in Puritan times, called for a more tender
treatment of children. Mothers, singled out because of their presumed innate spirituality and kindness, were adjured to exert piety in the form of prayers and active
persuasion to guide their children. A new romantic cult of childhood developed,
influenced in part by John Locke's emphasis, in *Some Thoughts Concerning Education*
(1693), on education as a means to an end, and by the writings of Jean Jacques
Rousseau (1712–78), who advocated that children should be not only nurtured but
respected. Increasingly, children's natural need of play was indulged; their growth
conceived of as developmental; and their pastimes, clothing, and toys given distinctly
different aspects from the dress and activities of adults. Although middle-class parents
were cautioned throughout the 1830s not to spoil children or indulge them in
frivolous fashions, they were also instructed to discipline their children and instill
Christian values through gentle persuasion rather than fear or force. This new interest
in child welfare produced a voluminous advice literature, which, while not expressly
intended for childhood consumption, was written with them in mind and reflected
concerns in the nation as a whole.

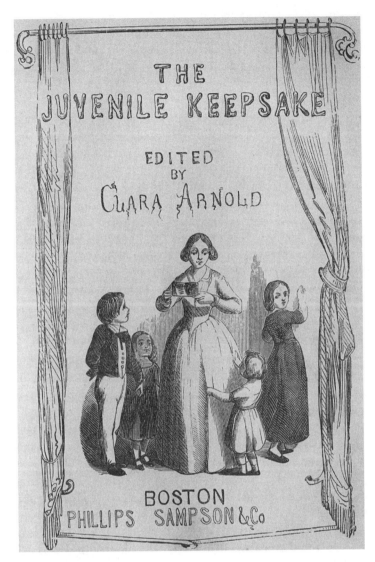

Figure 22.1 Title-page for Clara Arnold (ed.), *The Juvenile Keepsake; A Gift Book for Young People.* (Boston: Phillips, Sampson, & Co., 1853). Collection of Shirley Samuels.

Many authors incorporated the theories of child nurture in their fiction: for example, Lydia Maria Child, Timothy Shay Arthur, and Jacob Abbott penned both advice books and juvenile fiction. Child's domestic manual *The Frugal Housewife* (1829) went through thirty-three American editions. She addressed girls directly in *The Girl's Own Book* (1833), offering practical suggestions for excelling at domestic duties. Her juvenile fiction *Evenings in New England* (1824) implies rather than imposes Calvinist belief, and celebrates family affection and quiet moral improvement. At the forefront of many discussions of child discipline was the issue of corporal punishment, with traditionalists reluctant to relinquish its use as a tool of parental authority and advocates of the new nurture underlining the damage of corporal punishment to the child's will. Catharine Sedgwick, in *Home* (1835), addresses the issue in her depiction of pious parents whose son Wallace, in a fit of rage over his sister's kitten having torn his new kite, throws the kitten into a pot of boiling water. The horrified father, to his credit, invokes precept and example to help his son repent of his temper and vow to be more compassionate and responsible. Avoiding brute force, relying on reason, and buttressing his point with patriarchal authority, the father models in his disciplinary strategy the dominant national outlook.

Influential advice literature of the period also includes *The Young Christian* (1851) by Jacob Abbott, author of the bestselling Rollo books, which based Christian duty on faith, and the writings of Lyman Beecher, which, trusting in the child's innate moral instinct, questioned rigid notions of infant depravity and laid the groundwork for benign attitudes toward childhood. At the liberal extreme were unorthodox proponents of childhood education such as William Ellery Channing and Bronson Alcott, author of *Observations on the Principles and Methods of Infant Instruction* (1830), whose outlooks were Transcendentalist rather than Calvinist. These views were countered in turn by adherents to older, more austere perspectives, such as Heman Humphrey in *Domestic Education* (1840). The overall direction of child-rearing moved from disciplinary force to "disciplinary intimacy" (Brodhead 1988), increasingly centering child-rearing on affection rather than authority. Lydia Sigourney's popular *Letters to Mothers* (1838) emphasized the importance of maternal nurture, in particular, and, portraying the child as a potential angel, described methods by which "the harp might be tuned [so] as not to injure its tender and intricate harmony." Sigourney, rejecting views of the child as erring and recalcitrant, argued for methods of gentle correction that would support rather than thwart the child's natural ebullient state. An important text mediating older, orthodox views and newer, liberal ones is Horace Bushnell's *Views of Christian Nurture* (1847), which held to the doctrine of innate depravity but emphasized the benefits of proper nurture to weed out sin. As Bushnell's book makes clear, writers of the period convinced themselves that they were successfully reconciling traditional Christianity with new freedoms, but both the earlier fundamentalist belief and the newer liberal one envisioned the child in idealistic terms, as a "potential servant of some universal moral imperative . . . ordained by God" (Wishy 1968: 24).

A number of social changes formed the backdrop to mid-nineteenth-century American children's fiction, leading to construction of the child not only as national sign of independence, patriotism, and promise but also as embodiment of increasing national misgiving. Economic and geographic expansion placed issues of racial and ethnic difference in high relief. As city populations swelled with European immigrants, new rifts were created between the affluent and the poor; traditional religious holds loosened in part from conflict with Darwinian theories; and issues over slavery mounted to a critical point. Industrialization and commerce meant more wealth, but only for a segment of the American population. Children of white professionals and businessmen, released from the need to labor, had increasing free time to read and to learn social skills deemed suitable for aspiring ladies and gentlemen. To help them with the new challenges of raising such children, white middle-class parents turned to advice manuals about child-rearing issues, ranging from religious education and domestic arts for girls to horsemanship and bravery for boys. But in the cities the plight of children, especially immigrant children abandoned or neglected by impoverished parents working long hours in factories and debilitated by alcohol and ill-health, was conspicuously different. Responding to these conditions, in 1854 the Children's Aid Society began work on behalf of poor, abandoned, and orphaned children, arranging urban shelters for some and beginning the practice of transporting others via "orphan trains" to farm families in the Midwest and West. Such relocations reflected society's belief that the problems of childhood, environmental in nature, could be ameliorated with wholesome family life.

The temperance movement also took hold, leading to the production of formulaic stories and novels, among them Timothy Shay Arthur's *Ten Nights in a Bar-Room* (1854). The American Temperance Union also appealed to children through the well-funded *The Youth's Temperance Advocate*, distributed through the Sunday Schools until the early 1860s. Temperance literature frequently enlisted scenes of neglect and abuse of children to demonstrate the deleterious effects of alcohol on family life and, at the same time, to suggest the power of the child to convert parents to sobriety and reform society. Such literature constructs the child not only as the object but also as the instrument of reform, but often at a cost that puts the child – especially the female – at risk of sexual abuse, often by the father. In the child's loving ability to convert the drunken father, sometimes explicitly enacted in the bed of a child, these stories "make drunks temperate by transforming what we cannot help but recognize as scenes of pederasty and incest into loving mechanisms of redemption," making the literature "both culturally subversive and culturally conservative" (Sánchez-Eppler 1997: 61). Children were also increasingly enlisted in the growing debate between the North and South over slavery. Anglo-American children – even more so than women, because of their purity and innocence – became powerful advocates for abolition. Two periodicals devoted material to slavery issues: *The Slave's Friend* (1837–9), and *The Youth's Emancipator* (1842–?3). A common trope in these magazines, which enlisted children as advocates of abolition and domesticity, was the pet animal (Ginsberg 2003). The nonwhite child, represented as the conspicuously racialized other, became the means by which the nation posed and pondered the vexed questions of slavery.

By the 1840s American publishers were selling inexpensive paper-bound romances and adventure stories for young readers, many of them pirated from the abundant numbers of English titles available. Best known among American series books published for children were the tales of Jacob Abbott's Rollo, first introduced in 1830s and numbering twenty-eight volumes in all. As indicated by the titles of the first two volumes, *The Little Scholar Learning to Talk* (1835) and *Rollo Learning to Read* (1835), Abbott's emphasis, garnered from Edgeworth, was on practical learning, perseverance, and social adroitness, with matters of religion receding into the background. Abbott takes his hero, full of antics, through experiences from age five onward that test his obedience, forbearance, tolerance, and resourcefulness. Prominent in the Rollo books, as well as in the Franconia series that Abbott first published in 1850, is the need to cooperate with others and submit to legitimate authority, often in the form of a guiding parent or other adult, as well as a characteristically "American" emphasis on making and managing money (Avery 1994: 89). Adopting a gentle tone toward his hero and intent on presenting "quiet and peaceful pictures of happy domestic life," as he described the Franconia series, Abbott was committed in the more than 200 books he wrote for children to positive endings for his protagonists. In this respect his work differs from that of other contemporary fiction writers for children who took more austere stances. The "Oliver Optic" books, written pseudo-nymously by William Taylor Adams, were also immensely popular throughout the 1850s. Adapting for children features of frontier romance found in adult fiction such as Cooper's *Leatherstocking Tales* – lone heroes, damsels in need of rescue, stoic Indians – Optic's books fed an increasing middle-class male appetite for adventure. Adams, an astute entrepreneur, also founded and edited a number of magazines for children, including *Oliver Optic's Magazine, Our Boys and Girls*, and *Our Little Ones*; and he launched the career of Horatio Alger, Jr., whose *Ragged Dick* (1868) became the prototypical "rags to riches" story of the late nineteenth century.

Although inexpensive and sensationalized adventure stories had been available for popular consumption since the 1830s, the Beadle Publishing Company initiated the era of the "dime novel" on a large scale in 1860 with Ann Sophia Stephens' *Malaeska; The Indian Wife of the White Hunter*. Unusual because its subject matter was Indian life, *Malaeska* was full of action and heralded the lucrative market to come in popular fiction for children. Stephens invests Malaeska with natural beauty "beyond expression" and combines lush descriptions of the land with the drama of life-and-death combat. In an opening scene a hunter sits transfixed by the beauty of sunbeams playing on a waterfall when

> the click of a gunlock struck sharply on his ear. He sprang to his feet. A bullet whistled by his head, cutting through the dark locks which curled in heavy masses above his temples, and . . . he saw a half-naked savage crouching upon the ledge of rocks. . . . The spray fell upon his bronzed shoulders and sprinkled the stock of this musket as he lifted it to discharge the other barrel. With the quickness of thought, Jones drew his musket to his eye and fired.

The Beadle Company's second novel, Edward Sylvester Ellis' *Seth Jones; or, the Captives of the Frontier* (1860), became the company's all-time bestseller. Many dime novels capitalized on a national enthusiasm for the frontier, investing children with a sense of individualism and expansive potential, although often at the expense of native peoples.

Periodical literature also proliferated after 1800, first in the form of newspapers and then in monthlies, weeklies, annuals, journals, and magazines. The first periodicals for children were short-lived: *Children's Magazine*, published out of Hartford, Connect-icut, in 1789, lasted only three months; *Youth's News Paper*, begun in New York in 1799, produced only six issues. But by the 1820s American printing, marketing, and distribution had developed sufficiently to support steady publications of children's periodicals. Christmas annuals, given as gift books, became popular in the 1820s. *The Juvenile Miscellany*, founded and edited by Lydia Maria Child in Boston, appeared for a decade beginning in 1826 and published work by some of the period's most noted American writers, including Lydia Sigourney and Sarah Josepha Hale. Hale, famous for "Mary Had a Little Lamb" (1830), succeeded Child as editor of the *Miscellany*. *The Youth's Companion*, begun in 1827, enjoyed great longevity, appearing until 1929. Over the course of the century periodical magazines, promoting as well as reflecting changing societal attitudes toward children and their needs, became more entertain-ing and commercial while still retaining their moral tone. *Parley's Magazine*, begun in 1833 and merged with *Robert Merry's Museum* in 1844, continued until 1872; both were founded by the morally minded but market-savvy writer, publisher, and entre-preneur Samuel G. Goodrich. A number of children's magazines appeared at the end of the Civil War and immediately following it, notably *Our Young Folks* (1865), *The Little Corporal* (1866), *Children's Hour* (1866), *Riverside Magazine for Young People* (1867), *Frank Leslie's Boy's and Girl's Weekly* (1867), *Oliver Optic's Magazine* (1867), *St. Nicholas Magazine* (1873), ably edited by Mary Mapes Dodge, and *Harper's Young People* (1879).

Many bestselling novels of the pre-Civil War period feature children, often orphans, who face the trials of emotional and physical abandonment and through their own efforts and the application of Christian teachings are rewarded with loving homes. The adoption plot permitted a host of adventures because it freed the protagonist from the encumbrances of home and family. At the same time, the process of adoption, often represented as Christian salvation, infused tales with traditional moral messages; and the lost-and-found plot modeled the script for a youthful nation increasingly at home with itself and expecting fulfillment of its infinite promise. In *The Wide, Wide World* (1850), by Susan Warner (the pen-name of Elizabeth Wether-ell), young Ellen Montgomery, after tearfully facing the death of her mother, must draw on inner resources to make her way in the world. She survives the stern Calvinist discipline of her aunt; is comforted by the gentle Christianity of Alice Humphreys; enjoys genteel comforts with the Lindsays; and ends as submissive lady and wife to John Humphreys. Ellen's story recapitulates changes in the construction of American childhood from the seventeenth to the nineteenth century: from an austere Calvinism, in which the child, perceived as innately flawed, is subject to endless correction; to a more benign form of Christianity that emphasizes tender care and self-abnegation; and finally to a commercialized class consciousness that positions the child as both commodity and consumer. Maria Susanna Cummins' bestselling *The Lamplighter* (1854) also describes an orphaned girl, Gerty, who is first rescued by an old lamp-lighter, then adopted by a wealthy blind woman, and eventually reunited with her biological father and childhood sweetheart. A sentimental romance, this novel combines American and European elements: the plot is reminiscent of Old World fairy-tales in which protagonists, severed from their roots, are restored to their rightfully high positions; but it also reflects American initiative, ingenuity, and indomitable spirit. Nathaniel Hawthorne broke new ground with his depiction of Pearl Prynne in the Puritan romance *The Scarlet Letter* (1850). Pearl, whom authorities threaten to remove from her birth mother, exceeds the boundaries society sets for her as emblem of her mother's adultery and shame, and – impish, curious, and insistent– embodies an uninhibited natural, romantic energy that Hawthorne ultimately contains by removing her to England.

Sentimental fiction of the period revels in the gentle child, a staple of the genre, and especially in child death, invested with the power not only to convert individuals but also to effect monumental social change. The cult of childhood death dramatizes the notion of childhood purity too fragile to withstand the onslaughts of an increasingly materialistic, competitive culture, but this preoccupation also reflects the high incidence of juvenile death in nineteenth-century American society. For example, in 1853 in New York alone 49 percent of deaths in all classes were of children under five (Bingham and Scholt 1980: 159). The image of the sacrificial, suffering child seized the literary imagination. Hawthorne protested Puritans' persecution of Quakers in his historical story "The Gentle Boy" (1832), about the death of a boy so pure it is "as if his gentle spirit came down from heaven to teach his parent a true religion." Louisa May Alcott, in *Little Women* (1868), depicts mild-mannered Beth March, whose uncomplaining acquiescence in illness and death both chastises and inspires her three sisters, Jo, Amy, and Meg, as they engage in classic nineteenth-century girlhood struggles to discipline their emotions, develop domestic skills, and open their hearts to serve others with a spirit of selfless Christian charity. The most famous of all nineteenth-century child deaths is that of Little Eva in Harriet Beecher Stowe's *Uncle Tom's Cabin; or, Life among the Lowly* (1852). Promoting her ethos of encouraging the reader to "feel right," Stowe's novel accomplishes simultaneously the aims of domestic fiction – promotion of feminine virtue and spirituality – and the goals of abolition by investing Eva with the power to identify the enslaved Tom as her spiritual counterpart; to effect the conversion of her slave-holding father; and to inspire the reluctant Ophelia's embrace of the orphaned black child Topsy. This novel, while directed at an adult audience, was read by children and adults alike and became an international bestseller. Remarkable at its time for its bold abolitionist stance, the text is notable from today's perspective for a white, middle-class, Protestant woman's vision which predicates eradication of slavery on the association of African American manhood with the child, and which subordinates willful black childhood to the authority of Northern feminine gentility. Yet Stowe's children became effective advocates for abolition precisely because they reinforce the idea that essential racial differences distinguish white from black people (Levander 2004).

Although the Civil War slowed the production of publishing in the United States, especially in the South, the conflict sparked an outpouring of literature, including children's stories, sharply demarcated along lines of gender. Early on, male children frequently appeared as victims rather than actors. The tale of the accidental killing of the pious, patriotic Clarence McKenzie, sentimentalized in the religious publication *The Little Drummer Boy* (1861), circulated widely in the North. Increasingly, however, publishers responded to children's desires to become more active participants in the war by producing adventure stories as well as factual pieces designed to help children imagine what war was like. Charles Carleton Coffin's *My Days and Nights on the Battlefield*, Oliver Optic's *The Sailor Boy* and *The Soldier Boy*, and John Townsend Trowbridge's *The Drummer Boy* (all 1863) fed appetites for action. Horatio Alger (*Frank's Campaign* [1864]) and Harry Castlemon (*Frank on a Gunboat* [1864]) launched their careers with wartime adventure stories. If imagining a child war hero had the intended effect of stirring patriotic fervor, it also produced the unintended result of loosening bonds between child and family, fostering individual exploits rather than responsibilities to family and community, a fact that President Theodore Roosevelt, who read such material as a child, lamented when he gained the presidency at the turn of the century (Fahs 2001: 285). Girls participated in Civil War fiction but were urged to support the effort from behind the scenes by knitting or sewing; if given active roles, such as in Louisa May Alcott's "Nelly's Hospital" (1865), they served as moral inspiration or education for those around them. A singular exception was Jane Goodwin Austin's *Dora Darling, the Daughter of the Regiment* (1864), a female adventure story set in Virginia which, though popularly acclaimed, "was hedged with . . . uncertainty and contradictions" as it attempted "to meld an ethos of adventure with the antebellum ideology of domesticity" (Fahs 2001: 278–9). African American children, seldom the target audience of mainstream publishers, often appeared as caricatures with exaggerated dialects in fiction intended for white children. Although some children's magazines explored the issues of slavery and abolition, they rarely represented new roles for African Americans (Marten 1998: xiv), replicating the ingrained racial and racist attitudes of adults. Only one book, John Townsend Trowbridge's *Cudjo's Cave* (1863) – partially aimed at children and reflecting Northern sympathies – attempted to imagine an African American as a military hero.

The post-Civil War period heralded the "Golden Age" of children's literature, a period lasting until 1914 during which an abundance of first-class American fiction for and about children was published. Reflecting the influence of Charles Darwin's *Origin of Species* (1859), such literature attempts to reconcile competing views of child development at a time when accumulating scientific evidence confronted issues of religious faith. The book most influential in shaping the transition in views on child nurture from 1860 to 1880 was Jacob Abbott's *Gentle Measures in the Management and Training of the Young* (1871). Convinced that children could develop upright moral characters and still retain freedom and a zest for life, Abbott embraced only the more positive features of Darwin. Other writers signaled the emergence of twentieth-century psychology and literary modernism by producing introspective accounts of the child, recapitulating Darwin's developmental theories in their depictions of childhood growth. Significant in this regard is Alcott's *Little Men* (1871), which, by employing scientific theory, "tracks the process by which antisocial children are transformed into bourgeois citizens" (Levander 2000: 29); and *Jo's Boys* (1886), which, ostensibly praising nurture, emphasizes material wealth and lineage as requisite to the achievement of genteel citizenry (Singley 2001). Writers also began to invest children with psychological complexity, precocious sexuality, and the capacity to provoke as well as endure violence, famously in Henry James's *The Turn of the Screw* (1898). In this respect the scenes of cruelty to animals in such sentimental novels as *Home* and *The Lamplighter* can be seen not only as displacements of sexual and domestic abuse but also as precursors of overt acts of twentieth-century societal violence. Finally, juvenile fiction, increasingly commercialized as the nation's economy expanded and following the lead of Abbott and Alger, featured the child as both creator and consumer of wealth and seized upon the materiality of childhood to express both faith in social progress and nostalgia for less complicated times.

References and Further Reading

Avery, Gillian (1994). *Behold the Child: American Children and their Books, 1621–1922.* Baltimore: Johns Hopkins University Press.

Berebitsky, Julie (2000). *Like Our Very Own: Adoption and the Changing Culture of Motherhood, 1851–1950.* Lawrence, Kan.: University Press of Kansas.

Bingham, Jane, and Scholt, Grayce (1980). *Fifteen Centuries of Children's Literature: An Annotated Chronology of British and American Works in Historical Context.* Westport, Conn.: Greenwood.

Brodhead, Richard (1988). "Sparing the Rod: Discipline and Fiction in Antebellum America." *Representations* 21, 67–96.

Brown, Gillian (2001). *The Consent of the Governed: The Lockean Legacy in Early American Culture.* Cambridge, Mass.: Harvard University Press.

Crain, Patricia (2000). *The Story of A: The Alphabetization of America from* The New England Primer *to* The Scarlet Letter. Stanford: Stanford University Press.

Fahs, Alice (2001). *The Imagined Civil War: Popular Literature of the North and South, 1861–1865.* Chapel Hill: University of North Carolina Press.

Ginsberg, Lesley (2001). "The ABCs of *The Scarlet Letter.*" *Studies in American Fiction* 29: 1, 13–21.

Ginsberg, Lesley (2003). "Babies, Beasts and 'Domestic Bondage': Slavery and the Question of Citizenship in Antebellum American Children's Literature." In Caroline F. Levander and Carol J. Singley (eds.), *The American Child: A Cultural Studies Reader.* New Brunswick, NJ: Rutgers University Press.

Goshgarian, G. M. (1992). *To Kiss the Chastening Rod: Domestic Fiction and Sexual Ideology in the American Renaissance.* Ithaca, NY: Cornell University Press.

Griswold, Jerry (1992). *Audacious Kids: Coming of Age in America's Classic Children's Books.* New York: Oxford University Press.

Hunt, Peter (1994). *An Introduction to Children's Literature.* New York: Oxford University Press.

Hunt, Peter (2001). *Children's Literature.* Malden, Mass.: Blackwell.

Hunt, Peter, ed. (1995). *Children's Literature: An Illustrated History.* New York: Oxford University Press.

Levander, Caroline F. (2000). "The Science of Sentiment: The Evolution of the Bourgeois Child in Nineteenth-Century American Narrative." *Modern Language Studies* 30: 1, 27–44.

Levander, Caroline F. (2004). "'Letting her White Progeny Offset her Dark': The Child and the Racial Politics of Nation-making in the Slavery Era." *American Literature* 76: 2, 221–46.

Levander, Caroline F., and Singley, Carol J., eds. (2003). *The American Child: A Cultural Studies Reader.* New Brunswick, NJ: Rutgers University Press.

Marten, James (1998). *The Children's Civil War.* Chapel Hill: University of North Carolina Press.

Marten, James, ed. (1999). *Lessons of War: The Civil War in Children's Magazines.* Wilmington, Del.: Scholarly Resources.

Meigs, Cornelia; Eaton, Anne Thaxter; Nesbitt, Elizabeth; and Viguers, Ruth Hill, eds. (1969). *A Critical History of Children's Literature,* rev. edn. London: Macmillan.

Sánchez-Eppler, Karen (1997). "Temperance in the Bed of a Child: Incest and Social Order in Nineteenth-Century America." In David S. Reynolds and Debra J. Rosenthal (eds.), *The Serpent in the Cup,* 60–92. Amherst: University of Massachusetts Press.

Singley, Carol J. (2001). "The Limits of Nurture in Louisa May Alcott's Adoption Fiction." Paper presented to American Women Writers International Conference, San Antonio, Texas.

Wall, Barbara (1991). *The Narrator's Voice: The Dilemma of Children's Fiction.* London: Macmillan.

Wishy, Bernard (1968). *The Child and the Republic.* Philadelphia: University of Pennsylvania Press.

23
Dime Novels

Colin T. Ramsey and Kathryn Zabelle Derounian-Stodola

At the end of John Ford's 1962 Western *The Man Who Shot Liberty Valance*, a persistent reporter, having just heard the truth about who actually shot the notorious murderer, wads up his notes and tosses them in the trash. His explanation is simple: "This is the West," he remarks matter-of-factly; "when the legend becomes fact, print the legend." The film thus sums up the long and entangled history of the American West and the printed word; and, until the advent of film at the beginning of the twentieth century, no print medium played a bigger role in the creation of the West as a place of legend than the dime novel. Indeed, the dime novel's preference for "legend" over fact was visible even to some who themselves became a focus of the dime novels' legend-making. For instance, in his *Autobiography*, Kit Carson relates the story of his 1849 pursuit of a band of Jicarilla Apaches who had killed a man named James White and captured his wife along the Santa Fe Trail. News of the attack quickly reached a nearby cavalry garrison, and Carson was hired to help track down the raiding party. They caught up with the Apaches, but the soldiers ignored Carson's advice to charge the camp. The Apaches then promptly killed Mrs. White and escaped. Carson describes the scene this way:

> The body of Mrs. White was found, perfectly warm . . . shot through with an arrow. . . . In the camp was found a book, the first of the kind that I had ever seen, in which I was made a great hero, slaying Indians by the hundreds, and I have often thought that Mrs. White would read the same and, knowing that I lived near, she would pray for my appearance that she might be saved. (Quoted in McMurtry 2001: 20)

The sight of the book prompts Carson, apparently surprised at his own fictional celebrity, to muse about the difference between the factual West of his own experience and the legendary West already being created around him in print. As Larry McMurtry writes, at this moment "real life and the dime novel smacked into each other" (2001: 20).

Precursors of the Dime Novel

It is interesting that Carson says the book was "the first of the kind that I had ever seen," thus placing it in an identifiable category easily recognized by his readers: a cheap "Western" in which certain features of plot and character are standardized, predictable, and highly violent. That is, he is describing a typical dime novel. But there is one problem in the scene: Carson's dates don't add up. His search for Mrs. White took place in 1849, but the first true dime novel, *Malaeska; The Indian Wife of the White Hunter*, did not appear until 1860, more than a decade after Mrs. White's death. She couldn't have had a dime novel in her possession.

This inconsistency reveals that the dime novel form is more complex than we might first assume. Though cheap paper-backed fiction had begun to appear as early as the 1830s, the dime novels' nearest precursors were the story papers of the 1840s and early 1850s. These were eight-page weekly newspapers, containing several serialized stories in each number, as well as small amounts of humor, correspondence, and similar miscellaneous items (Denning 1998: 10). Aside from their cheapness, the story papers shared with the later dime novels their sensational and sometimes violent content. Carson was himself featured as a central character in some of the story papers of the late 1840s, and, despite the fact that he calls what he found a "book," it is certainly possible that it was a story paper he discovered next to Mrs. White's body. Furthermore, the story papers' newspaper format made them, like the later dime novels, cheap enough to be affordable even to a pioneer family.

Figure 23.1 Title-page of Ann Stephens' *Malaeska; The Indian Wife of the White Hunter*, as reissued by Beadle in 1860.

In any case, the story papers achieved an extremely wide circulation by the 1850s, numbering into the hundreds of thousands, and, though they certainly contained Western stories with violent plots, they also featured other serials to broaden their appeal to an entire family. Each issue would typically include several different narratives from various genres, including sea stories, historical romances, domestic romances, and of course, Westerns (Denning 1998; Johannsen 1950). Indeed, the story papers' use of multiple generic styles to appeal to a broad audience was adopted by the first true dime novels of the 1860s.

Another precursor of the dime novels was the pamphlet novel of the 1830s and 1840s. These texts, like the story papers, also sold quite well, until increased postal rates put them out of business in 1849 (Denning 1998). Pamphlet novels were also larger than the later dimes, at about six by eight inches, and they were shorter, at roughly fifty pages. Though some cost as little as twelve and a half cents, the more typical cost of pamphlet novels was twenty-five cents or more. The difference in cost may seem inconsequential now, but the more expensive pamphlet novels were still beyond the means of many workers when the average laboring wage was only about a dollar per day (LeBlanc 1996: 14).

This brief review of the dime novels' precursors demonstrates that dime novels cannot be understood without considering, in addition to their typical contents, both their distinctive physical form and the contexts of their production and marketing. As Bill Brown puts it, "the dime Western is…a subgenre that is inseparable from its systematic modes of production and distribution" and is "most recognizable by the standardized packaging" (1997: 6). We must therefore see the dime novels of the 1860s both as falling within an already established market tradition of cheap popular fiction and also as a new form of reading matter. Their novelty was defined by their distinctive marketing practices and by their peculiar mode of rapid, almost industrial production, a system that resulted in generally standardized content.

Packaging and Marketing

In 1860 Beadle & Adams, a former publisher of cheap song and etiquette books, put out *Malaeska; The Indian Wife of the White Hunter* as the first title in their new series "Beadle's Dime Novels." Thus the term "dime novel" was, in the beginning, essentially a brand name (Cox 2000: xiii). Beadle & Adams highlighted the price as a definitive component of their new series: both as a selling point in itself, and also as a marker to distinguish Beadle's product in the wider marketplace. These first dime novels measured four inches by six and ran to about 100 pages each. They were paper-bound, and the backs were an unusual salmon color; and of course, each one cost a dime. The "Beadle's Dime Novels" series was an instant success, and the firm brought out a new title about once every two weeks for the next fourteen years, until it replaced the series with "Beadle's New Dime Novels." Though many of these early dimes had only black-letter text on their covers, fully illustrated covers rapidly became the standard, and they became increasingly lurid as time went on.

Beadle enjoyed such success with its first dime novel series that a number of other publishing houses immediately began putting out their own. For instance, in 1863 Irwin Beadle left his brother Erastus' publishing firm to found a new venture with George Munro, formerly the foreman of Beadle's printing plant. They began putting out "Irwin P. Beadle's Ten Cent Novels" that same year (Cox 2000), though the series became "Munro's Ten Cent Novels" in 1864 during trademark litigation with the original Beadle firm. "Munro's Ten Cent Novels" went on to become the most serious competition for "Beadle's Dime Novels," but the success of the new dime format was such that additional publishers continued to bring out dime novel series of their own, under such titles as "DeWitt's Ten Cent Romances," the Talbot firm's "Ten Cent Novelettes," and so forth.

This rapid proliferation of dime novels in the marketplace led Beadle to offer cheap texts in a new format by the early 1870s in order to stay ahead of the competition. "Beadle's Dime Library" series inaugurated the "library" format: these novels were quartos, about eight by twelve inches, each comprising a single sheet folded four times and then bound and cut to produce a sixteen-page pamphlet of multi-column print. Later, the library format also included octavo pamphlets of thirty-two pages (LeBlanc 1996: 15). Again, other firms soon followed suit, bringing out their own library series. With the revised format, new issues came out even more frequently, often weekly, and prices continued to drop. In the late 1870s Beadle created its "Half Dime Library" and "Nickel Library." Other firms did likewise, bringing out their own nickel series. These nickel novels, however, unlike their earlier dime counterparts, were aimed primarily at adolescent boys, and they were shorter than the dimes, usually about fifty pages.

Ultimately, the expansion of the market in popular fiction turned the dime novel into a generic term that referred to all cheap fiction with paper covers (Cox 2000: xiv). Moreover, whatever the particular cost, the series format was, from the beginning, a marketing technique designed to create a continuing interest in readers/buyers. As Bill Brown notes, "Lists of other novels in the series were printed in each book, and novels in a series made occasional reference to others." That is, the dime novel publishing houses used the series format to "orchestrate consistency and change, the *effect* of stability and the *effect* of novelty" (1997: 22, emphasis in original). Given the ever-expanding number of titles, new material obviously needed to be rapidly produced. The problem, from a marketing standpoint, was managing to meet such a high production demand without losing the important quality of recognizability for readers.

Content, Production, Authorship

Another of the Beadle firm's marketing innovations provided the solution. In 1877 the "Half Dime Library" introduced the concept of the recurring character with Deadwood

Dick (LeBlanc 1996: 16). An almost instant hit, Deadwood was an outlaw and the leader of a band of rogues. He was thus typically depicted as an appealing anti-hero, though in the later of Beadle's thirty-four issues devoted to him, he functioned as a detective as much as an outlaw. He was also instantly recognizable to readers, who understood that a Deadwood Dick dime would feature a dependable complex of additional recurring characters (such as the sometimes opponent, sometimes love interest Calamity Jane) and a standard set of Western settings and narrative situations. Deadwood proved particularly popular, and other firms quickly picked up and extended the recurring character concept. Indeed, in a move that mimicked the story papers of the 1840s, many dime novelists began to employ recurring fictionalized versions of actual Western personalities, such as "Wild Bill" Hickock and Buffalo Bill Cody, and this intermixture of fact and fiction was reinforced through various other complementary series, such as the "Dime Biographies" of actual Western figures (Brown 1997).

As the use of recurrent characters grew, so did the standardization of narrative situation. Though the first dime novels generally engaged a wide variety of settings and scenes, and tended to emphasize relatively complex characterization and the resolution of long-term conflict, dime novel plots increasingly became vehicles for multiple scenes of violent confrontation (Brown 1997). Understandably, the author's role in creating such similar narratives was not seen as a marketable commodity. Thus, for the most part, dime novels were an anonymously or pseudonymously authored discourse in which trademark characters were marketed more prominently than authors (Denning 1998: 20). Around such characters, unnamed "hack" authors could write any number of new stories. However, a small handful of writers achieved relative notoriety for their dime novels. For instance, the writer who invented Deadwood Dick, Edward Wheeler, became quite well known, and his name became valuable in its own right – indeed, so important was it that when he died Beadle suppressed the information and continued to publish titles under his name for some years. Such suppression, and the substitution of narratives by other authors under Wheeler's name, was possible because, by the early 1870s, dime novel production was taking place on a very nearly industrial scale. The large publishing houses had begun to produce their dime novels in what were, in essence, fiction factories. Bill Brown describes the Beadle firm's vertically arranged William Street office this way: "writers composed stories upstairs; below them, editors blue-penciled offensive language and excess words, artists produced illustrations, and typesetters set type; below them ran the presses" (1997: 27). Naturally, such an industrial system of production tended to further denigrate individual authors' creative impulses in favor of adherence to pre-established formulae, even if the occasional author managed innovation nonetheless.

Ultimately, then, we should see the dime novels as a significantly mass-produced form of reading matter that depended upon a set of nearly interchangeable character types and easily reproducible marketing, and employed quasi-industrial production methods that de-emphasized individual authorship. However, despite these facts, we should not dismiss the form as being uninteresting or assume its readers were unsophisticated.

Two Early Beadle Dime Novels

In her feminist critique of Western novels and films, *West of Everything*, Jane Tompkins describes a surprising thematic connection between twentieth-century Western novels and nineteenth-century domestic "sentimental" novels: "The sentimental heroine, always unjustly treated, was forbidden to show her anger; the Western hero, always subject to duress, is forbidden to register his pain. . . . One has to ask why" (1992: 125–7). Why indeed? The similarity Tompkins describes is significant precisely because Westerns and domestic novels appear, intuitively, dissimilar. However, early dime novels, particularly those of the 1860s, followed their story paper predecessors' inclusion of various genres in order to reach as broad an audience as possible.

A case in point is *Malaeska; The Indian Wife of the White Hunter*, by Ann Sophia Stephens, a nineteenth-century magazine editor who was one of the most prolific and popular authors of her day. Like the story papers, *Malaeska* included several stylistic genres, though unlike them, it included this varied content within a single narrative. Stephens' novel marks a point at which the conventions of the domestic fiction often published in the women's magazines were welded onto the narrative conventions that would become the mainstay of dime novel Westerns. *Malaeska*, then, is a kind of "missing link" between genteel nineteenth-century sentimental fiction on the one hand, and later "blood-and-thunder" (Durham 1954–5: 34), dime novel Westerns on the other. *Malaeska* suggests that early dime-novel readers did not always restrict their reading to the kinds of novels which twentieth-century critics have designated, as Nina Baym puts it, "by and about women" (1978: 24) or, correspondingly, by and about men. Stephens, after all, had adapted the dime edition of *Malaeska* from her serialized version published in 1839 in the *Ladies' Companion*.

In fact, the earliest version of *Malaeska* did not even appear as a serial in the *Ladies' Companion*: it was actually published as "The Jockey Cap" in a single issue of the *Portland Magazine* in April 1836. Stephens had founded the *Portland Magazine* in 1834, and she was the magazine's sole editor and its most regular contributor until her family moved to New York in 1837. "The Jockey Cap" version of *Malaeska* is unmistakably a Western, although, as in other early examples of the genre, the frontier – the space between European occupation and Indian country, between "civilization" and "savagery" – is not on the high Western plains, but in New England. The story takes place during the early eighteenth century and concerns the interaction between Indians and European settlers living on the border between Maine and New Hampshire near a large hill called the Jockey Cap. Throughout the story, Stephens juxtaposes an emotionally indirect language of manners with blood-soaked description of battles for survival. The result is a sort of tension between the two levels of discourse which is common to Westerns, especially the dime novel variety. In any case, in "The Jockey Cap," Stephens is quite clearly writing in a genre distinct from the domestic novel.

The main plot of "The Jockey Cap" involves hostilities between Indians and settlers and begins when an Indian fires upon hunter Arthur Jones. Jones kills his attacker and scalps the body. This killing, it appears, will start a war between the settlement and the nearby Indian village. However, another man, Bill Church, decides to travel to the village and prevent the war. Once Church arrives, the reader discovers that he has an Indian wife and child there. Despite his entreaties, the Indians decide to fight, and a terrible battle between the settlement and the Indian village ensues. In the midst of it, the figure of the White Hunter, Bill Church, figures prominently until he encounters his father-in-law, the Indian chief, and they kill each other. In Stephens' schema, then, Indian and white are completely incompatible. If Stephens has created a sexual relationship between Indians and whites, the union is demonstrably untenable; it can not prevent a "savage" war, and it even causes, at least indirectly, the "savage" death of both Malaeska's Indian father and her white husband.

The narrative ends after the battle, when Malaeska finds the bodies of her father and husband and buries them together in a single grave. Its conclusion describes Malaeska more or less haunting the area, making baskets for the settlers, but living apart from both them and her tribe. She is thus utterly disinherited; she has no social status, indeed, no social identity, as either Indian or white. Malaeska becomes a tragic figure, surviving the war itself only to be locked in a no-man's-land between separate and irreconcilable social structures.

Interestingly, it was the disinheritance plot of "The Jockey Cap" that Stephens exploited in her later versions of the tale. By 1839 she had begun writing and editing a women's magazine called the *Ladies' Companion*, and she extended the Malaeska story in its pages. The *Ladies' Companion* version takes the narrative far beyond the point when Malaeska finds her dying husband at the end of the battle, and Stephens here shifts the setting to one more typical of domestic novels, in a kind of "Malaeska takes Manhattan." In the *Ladies' Companion* version (which would ultimately become the dime novel version), the hunter, whose name is now Danforth, actually survives long enough to tell Malaeska to find his parents in Manhattan: "find your way to them, and tell them how their son died, and beseech them to cherish you and the boy for his sake" (p. 31).

In many ways, the subsequent development of the story corresponds to the "over-plot" of nineteenth-century "women's fiction" described by Nina Baym: "[Women's] novels...all tell about a young woman who has lost the emotional and financial support of her legal guardians – indeed who is often subject to their abuse and neglect – but who nevertheless goes on to win her way in the world" (1978: 9). Baym continues by noting that such heroines' "own ways" are typically very humble by modern standards, generally involving only "domestic comfort" and a "social net-work" (p. 9). Correspondingly, the "overplot" formula of the central female character becoming a de facto orphan is given greater development in the *Ladies' Companion/* dime novel version of the Malaeska story (although Stephens did revise her *Ladies'* text for Beadle, the narrative remains largely the same in both editions). Also, once Malaeska arrives in Manhattan, her response to the environment underscores her role as a domestic-styled heroine: while she is walking the streets searching for the house of her husband's parents, passers-by gawk at her because of her Indian appearance. She is humiliated by the staring, but she bears it without complaint with the "delicacy and refinement of civilized life" she had learned "from her husband" (p. 39). The mark of her "good breeding," of her natural aristocratic mien and her lost inheritance, is that she suffers in silence.

Upon reaching the Danforth home, Malaeska is mistreated and emotionally abused by her father-in-law, who is so racist that he demands that she hide from her son the racial reality of his parentage; Malaeska is allowed to stay in the house only as a hired servant. Here again, however, she suffers quietly, even serenely. Furthermore, this sentimental narrative element is echoed in the very language Stephens employs to describe Malaeska's situation: "she was his mother; yet her very existence in that house was held as a reproach. . . . poor Malaeska! hers was a sad, sad life" (p. 48). We are thus invited to feel pity for Malaeska, but also to feel admiration for her strength. Like Ellen Montgomery in the style-defining domestic novel *The Wide, Wide World*, Malaeska suffers in silence, but that silence reveals inner strength.

It is thus revealing that this version was chosen for republication as the first dime novel. When the Beadle editors selected *Malaeska* to launch their new series, they were apparently counting on Stephens' reputation to help boost sales (Mott 1947: 49; Stern 1963: 45). The fact that Beadle & Adams would attempt to capitalize on Stephens' great popularity as a writer for women's magazines suggests that the early dime Westerns did not aim *only* at working-class men and boys, or, at least, that popularity in genteel women's magazines did not preclude popularity with a male working-class readership. Certainly, young Civil War soldiers and even younger teenage boys, as well as loggers and immigrant factory workers in the cities, read the dime novel edition of *Malaeska*; but middle-class women also read it, and, furthermore, they had been reading Stephens' Indian stories in the magazines for some time, apparently enjoying them considerably.

Only a few months after the success of *Malaeska*, Beadle published Edward S. Ellis' first book, *Seth Jones; or the Captives of the Frontier*, as number four in the "Dime Novel" collection. Twenty-year-old Ellis was the schoolteacher son of the famous hunter Sylvester Ellis, and his extensively marketed book launched him on a lucrative writing career lasting until his death in 1916 (Johannsen 1950: 93–6). In 1864 Ellis published *Indian Jim: A Tale of the Minnesota Massacre*. At the time, nothing distinguished it from the other dime Western novels about Indian captivity, except that it did not have the bestselling potential of some of his earlier efforts. However, by that time he had established himself "as the new novelist of the frontier" (Brown 1997: 165), and Minnesota was just another frontier he chose to tackle.

It isn't clear how Ellis became interested in the US–Dakota Conflict, the six-week war fought in 1862 pitting white settlers, the US military, and conciliatory Dakota Indians against groups of militant Dakotas in the recently established state of Minnesota. But the opening up of new territories acquired after the Mexican War, the discovery of gold in California, and the Dakota War itself helped to re-establish "frontier conflict with Native Americans as a central topic in the national imagination" (Brown 1997: 166). However Ellis came across his information, details in *Indian Jim* indicate that he used historical persons and events to authenticate his novel and to provide the appearance of novelty and currency.

Because *Indian Jim* is not well known today, a brief plot overview is necessary. The book opens in August 1862 (the date the Dakota Conflict actually began) with two cousins, Marian Allondale and Adolphus Halleck, traveling up the Minnesota River to stay with family friends, the Brainerds. Marian and Adolphus are engaged but behave more like friends than lovers. An artist, Adolphus possesses overly romantic notions about Native Americans, while Marian exhibits stereotypically negative views, though she admits that "'The *Christian* Indians are somewhat different'" (Ellis 1864: 15). Despite the fact that Halleck's romanticism blinds him, Ellis is careful to tell readers that deep down he is a gentleman (p. 10). This is to validate the amount of space devoted to him and to make his final transformation more credible. The Brainerd family consists of both parents as well as two unmarried children, twenty-one-year-old Will, a wounded Civil War veteran, and seventeen-year-old Maggie, a beautiful and religious young woman. Predictably, during the course of the story, Marian is attracted by the "modest and manly" Will (p. 19), and marries him at the end, while Maggie is attracted by the possibilities of converting the irreligious and irresponsible Adolphus. He, in turn, responds to a related but different sensibility from his own – the spiritual rather than the artistic.

As war breaks out, the family has to leave its homestead, but a friendly Christian Dakota, the Indian Jim of the title, aids them in their flight and serves as a physical and even moral guide. Adolphus' romanticism, indecisiveness, and inability to interpret events correctly is constantly challenged, especially when Dakotas capture Marian and Maggie. Finally, when Maggie dies at the hands of a vengeful Indian, Adolphus understands the error of his ways and prepares to enter the ministry. This rather abrupt and sentimental plot resolution is typical of dime Westerns. Most of them were one hundred pages long, so Ellis may have rushed his ending to meet the formula length requirement.

The two most important characters in the book are Adolphus Halleck and Indian Jim. Ellis draws on nineteenth-century stereotypes of the impractical, illusion-filled artist and the "good" Indian respectively, yet he also complicates both characters somewhat. Through these opposing characters Ellis continues a dialogue initiated by Fenimore Cooper on reading the landscape, reading human nature, and reading books. In the presence of so much fragmented information, the writers ask, what interpretive guide should be used? While Halleck is the most important character because he changes so fundamentally (perhaps unconvincingly), the text also invites readers to examine their own methods of constructing politics, people, religion, and region. However, ultimately, Ellis issues not so much an invitation as an imperative to use the Bible as the single guidebook in life.

At the beginning, Halleck views the Indians in idealized terms as figures in a wild landscape, and he privileges his role as artist and scholar; that is, he "sees" things artistically but turns a blind eye to whatever does not fit his predetermined views.

This is no White Hunter! He is removed from reality because he is too busy either reading about it or representing it in his art. For example, at several points he withholds or ignores crucial information because it would reinforce the negative characteristics of the Sioux that he refuses to acknowledge. Sometimes his bravado is completely misplaced; at other times, he sketches at morally inappropriate points. Finally, in two clear but heavy-handed tropes, Will lectures his friend on reality versus fancy – "'It's time, 'Dolph, you gave up those nonsensical ideas, and came to look upon the American Indian as he *is*, and not as your fancy has *painted* him!'" – and then, a little later, on plain sight and common sense regarding Indians versus romanticized views that are not self-evident: "'You'll have to provide yourself with a microscope, 'Dolph, if you wish to discover these phenomena; for, you see, they are not visible to the naked eye" (Ellis 1864: 72, 78; emphasis in original). A little earlier, Adolphus had trouble interpreting information viewed through a telescope; now Will tells him he needs a microscope. Although Ellis introduces Halleck as someone influenced by the nineteenth-century American Romantic painter Albert Bierstadt (pp. 9–10), he may have decided to make his main male character an artist primarily to underscore his flawed *vision*. In other words, Halleck's being an artist may be just an excuse for a kind of character pun on sight and insight. By the end of the book, Adolphus Halleck abandons one-dimensional artistic representation for deep spiritual truths.

Indian Jim performs a number of functions in the book. At one level, Ellis cannot move beyond stereotypical characteristics; for example, like the presentation of many nonwhites in popular fiction – Indians and African Americans alike – Jim is inarticulate. But two things differentiate Jim from other Sioux in the book: his ability to read signs and his Christianity. Late in the novel, in a remarkable authorial comment, Ellis writes that Adolphus and Will "were hourly in danger of attack and massacre; but under the good providence of God, the skill of Christian Jim saved them. *He detected 'signs' constantly*, and, by timely foresight and precaution, avoided discovery" (Ellis 1864: 76, emphasis added). At several points, the narrative conspicuously uses the word "signs" to describe Jim's and the settlers' as well as the Dakotas' attempts to read what is going on (see pp. 77, 80, 83). But Jim's success in negotiating danger is based not only on sound knowledge of the land but also on the bedrock of Christianity; it is typological and providential. Yet he has to disappear from the novel because, with Maggie's death, *she* becomes the major Christian sacrificial symbol. And in contrast to Jim, her last words to Adolphus are not just articulate but eloquent: "'Yes; seek me – meet me –'" (p. 98).

Two other aspects of this dime novel, its literary and historical allusions, suggest more technical skill than is evident in many other examples of the form. Sometimes Ellis is self-consciously literary, for example, when he describes Halleck as having admired the Indians ever since he read Cooper, or when he refers to Longfellow's *Hiawatha* or to the humorist Artemus Ward (1864: 10, 14, 30). Yet there are also subtler examples of intertextuality that may indicate Ellis' influences and reading. For instance, while Maggie's dying words fall into a nineteenth-century sentimental tradition of saintly characters' final prophetic utterances, they do seem to recall one of the most famous examples, little Eva St. Clare's transcendent death in *Uncle Tom's Cabin* (1852). Also, after dinner on the evening that Marian and Adolphus arrive at the Brainerd house, the moonlit atmosphere is described as "a fairy veil thrown over the rugged, disproportional outlines" (p. 25). The full passage is several pages long and is reminiscent of Hawthorne's famous definition of romance in the Custom House section of *The Scarlet Letter* (1850). Both earlier novels were bestselling romances that must have been familiar to the bookish Ellis. Perhaps he was trying to legitimate his own writing by such apparent allusions and by establishing *Indian Jim* within the same genre.

The historical references to the US–Dakota Conflict, however, help to place the novel in the dime Western and historical romance traditions. It is true that many of the references are fleeting, but Ellis inserts them fairly naturally and convincingly within the fabric of the narrative. For example, in discussing Christianized Dakotas, Marian refers to the real-life missionaries Dr. (Thomas) Williamson and Mr. (Stephen) Riggs. And in line with the dime Western's sensationalism as well as the actual reports of Indian atrocities during the war, Ellis describes several whites killed brutally (1864: 90–1). Such accounts, whether true or not, had been extensively reported in the local and national press and had reinforced the call for massive executions after the war was over, even though Abraham Lincoln reduced the number actually hanged to thirty-eight – something also mentioned in *Indian Jim* (p. 71).

In conclusion, what may have made *Malaeska*, *Indian Jim*, and the Western dime novels which followed so enormously popular was that they combined and transformed two very popular narrative types, the frontier tale and the "sentimental" tale. Such stories had great appeal across both gender and class barriers. Indeed, *Malaeska* and *Indian Jim* tend to suggest not only that the broad reading public was willing to read novels which combined the stock characters and narrative formulae of the frontier "Indian" story and the "sentimental" tale – either in women's magazines or as paperbound dimes – but that they particularly prized such genre transformations, if the popularity of these two novels is any indication. *Malaeska* specifically sold more copies than any other Beadle & Adams dime novel and stands as the only truly "bestselling" dime.

NOTE

The National Endowment for the Humanities partly funded the writing of this article through a Summer Stipend awarded to Kathryn Zabelle Derounian-Stodola.

REFERENCES

Baym, Nina (1978). *Woman's Fiction: A Guide to Novels by and about Women in America, 1820–1870*. Ithaca, NY: Cornell University Press.

Brown, Bill, ed. (1997). *Reading the West: An Anthology of Dime Westerns*. Boston and New York: Bedford.

Cox, J. Randolph (2000). *The Dime Novel Companion: A Source Book*. Westport, Conn.: Greenwood.

Denning, Michael (1998). *Mechanic Accents: Dime Novels and Working Class Culture in America*. New York and London: Verso. (First publ. 1987.)

Durham, Philip (1954–5). "Dime Novels: An American Heritage." *The Western Humanities Review* 11, 33–41.

Ellis, Edward (1864). *Indian Jim: A Tale of the Minnesota Massacre*. New York: Beadle.

Johannsen, Albert (1950). *The House of Beadle and Adams and its Dime and Nickel Novels: The Story of a Vanished Literature*, vol. 2. Norman: University of Oklahoma Press.

LeBlanc, Edward (1996). "A Brief History of Dime Novels: Formats and Contents." In Larry E. Sullivan and Lydia C. Schuman (eds.), *Pioneers, Passionate Ladies, and Private Eyes: Dime Novels and Series Books, and Paper Backs*. Binghamton, NY: Haworth.

McMurtry, Larry (2001). *Sacagawea's Nickname: Essays on the American West*. New York: New York Review of Books Press.

Mott, Frank L. (1947). *Golden Multitudes: The Story of Best Sellers in the United States*. New York: Macmillan.

Stephens, Ann S. (1836). "The Jockey Cap." *Portland Magazine*, 1 April, 193–208.

Stephens, Ann S. (1860). *Malaeska; the Indian Wife of the White Hunter*. New York: Beadle & Co.

Stern, Madeleine B. (1963). *We the Women: Career Firsts of Nineteenth-Century America*. New York: Schulte. Repr. Lincoln: University of Nebraska Press, 1994.

Tompkins, Jane (1992). *West of Everything: The Inner Life of Westerns*. New York: Oxford University Press.

24
Reform and Antebellum Fiction
Chris Castiglia

The seventy years between the ratification of the Constitution and the beginning of the Civil War brought profound change in the United States. With the incorporation of territories acquired in the 1803 Louisiana Purchase and the Mexican War (1846–8), the US grew from thirteen to thirty-four states, while the population increased from 3.9 million in 1790 to nearly 31.5 million in 1860. The statehood of territories with large populations of Spanish, French, and Native American inhabitants diversified the American population, as did unprecedented numbers of immigrants, who jumped from 5,000 annually at the start of the nineteenth century to 600,000 during the 1830s, 1.7 million in the 1840s, and 2.6 million in the 1850s (Mintz 1995: 7). Immigrants settled the western territories, but they also pioneered new ways of life in America's growing cities. By 1860 the United States had eight cities with populations greater than 150,000, and immigrants formed 40 percent of the populations of the nation's fifty largest cities (Mintz 1995: 7). Consequently, urban citizens experienced at first hand the varying mores and conventions of diverse cultures, making belief in a single "natural" way of life harder to maintain. At the same time, the anonymity, mobility, and new forms of association and leisure offered by city life made conventional forms of surveillance and moral authority more difficult to enforce. By 1835 there were nearly 3,000 licensed drinking places in New York, for instance – nearly one for every fifty persons over fifteen – and an estimated two hundred brothels (Mintz 1995: 4).

With conventional ideals of family and community life eroding in the face of urbanism, migration, and greater cultural diversity, how was social order to be maintained? Who was to determine the mores for a newly liberalized society, and oversee their implementation? Both the revolutionary rhetoric, which promised greater freedom to the American people, and the growth of free-market capitalism, which required less legislative involvement, called for a *laissez-faire* attitude on the part of government. What, then, would take the place of law in preserving the nation's civic and economic order? One answer would be that the burden of maintaining order shifted in the early nineteenth century from the civic to the civil sphere, as citizens were encouraged to keep order among and for themselves, rather than being legislated for and policed from without. It is in this context that we can understand the extraordinary popularity of reform movements that introduced new notions of proper character, self-restraint, and civil responsibility into public discourse, calling for voluntary self-control with a benevolence that an age of freedom and reason demanded.

In the three decades before the Civil War, movements emerged to reform almost every aspect of the nation's institutional life. Religious reform brought the "liberalization" of the churches and synagogues, resulting in the emergence of new faiths – Universalism, Unitarianism, Mormonism, African Methodist Episcopalianism, Shakers, Transcendentalism – that encouraged free will and self-improvement, while old faiths that refused to change – particularly Catholicism – were virulently attacked. Societies formed to send out bibles, religious tracts, and missionaries, both within the United States and abroad. Alongside these religious reforms, national associations formed to abolish slavery, to encourage temperance, to ease the condition of the urban poor, to renovate education, to establish the vote for women. Communities like Brook Farm, Oneida, and Fruitlands attempted to put into practice the principles of collective economic responsibility and healthful living espoused by the French socialist Charles Fourier. Conventional home life was challenged, both by "free love" reformers and by domestic reformers like Catharine Beecher, who attempted to make housework more productive and rewarding for women. These reformers saw structural inequalities within traditional American institutions, owing to the coercion of labor, the unequal distribution of profit and opportunity, the legal alienation of classes of citizens from civic participation, and the stultifying imaginative aridity of conventional domesticity. In response they called for the overthrow of economic, political, and social structures – of what Ralph Waldo Emerson decried in 1841 as "a system of distrust, of concealment, of superior keenness, not of giving but of taking advantage" – and sought to establish ways of life that the individual might consider with "joy and self-approval in his hour of love and aspiration" (Emerson 1982: 132–3).

Three years later, however, Emerson, addressing an audience of reformers in Boston's Amory Hall, declared that "society gains nothing whilst a man, not himself renovated, attempts to renovate things around him: he has become tediously good in some particular, but negligent and narrow in the rest; and hypocrisy and vanity are often the disgusting result" (Emerson 1967: 15). While Emerson earlier saw reform as generating the self-reliance he popularized throughout his career, by 1844 he blamed reformers for building the very institutions they purported to challenge. "I have failed, and you have failed," Emerson characterized reformers' logic,

> but perhaps together we shall not fail. Our housekeeping is not satisfactory to us, but perhaps a phalanx, a community, might be. Many of us have differed in opinion, and we could find no man who could make the truth plain, but possibly a college, or

ecclesiastical council might. I have not been able either to persuade my brother or to prevail on myself, to disuse the traffic or the potation of brandy, but perhaps a pledge of total abstinence might effectually restrain us. The candidate my party votes for is not to be trusted with a dollar, but he will be honest in the Senate, for we can bring public opinion to bear on him. Thus concert was the specific in all cases. But concert is neither better nor worse, neither more nor less potent than individual force. (Emerson 1967: 17)

The following week, in the same venue, Henry David Thoreau faulted reformers with the same lack of individualism, the same projection of private grievance on to all of society, that Emerson had found egregious, characterizing reform as "the death that presumes to give laws to life," and accusing reformers' gothic depictions of human depravity of "affirming essential disease and disorder to the child who has just begun to bathe his senses and his understanding in the perception of order and beauty" (Thoreau 1973: 192).

Emerson and Thoreau register some of the less beneficial outcomes of reform's establishment of a volunteeristic society. As both noted, reform societies were becoming institutions of their own – by 1836 there were 527 anti-slavery societies, by 1838 1,300 containing an estimated 109,000 members (Mintz 1995: 127); in 1835 an estimated 1.5 million Americans belonged to temperance societies (Mintz 1995: 73). As reform institutionalized, it relied more heavily on publication, producing hundreds of thousands of tracts, newspapers, pamphlets, and novels, all geared toward effecting social policy through public opinion. As a result, reformers often seemed more interested in producing rhetoric than in effecting material change. "We rarely see the Reformer who is fairly launched in his enterprise," Thoreau noted, "bringing about the right state of things with hearty and efficacious tugs, and not rather preparing and grading the way through the minds of the people" (1973: 185); the result is that the reformer asks for sympathy with *words*; "he really asks for no sympathy with deeds" (p. 186). Similar criticisms of reform novels such as *Uncle Tom's Cabin*, which invite readers to have feelings for characters in print – "they can see to it that *they feel right*" (Stowe 1994: 385) – rather than taking action to remedy the social wrongs those characters supposedly represent, persist to this day.

Not only the means and the organization, but the *object* of reform efforts changed during the 1840s. From a focus on structural injustices – slavery, traditional domesticity, wage inequality – reformers began to focus on *individual* vices, from drinking and gambling to masturbation to eating spicy foods to wearing tight corsets. Aided by a host of pseudosciences like phrenology (which measured bumps on the skull for signs of disposition toward vice), reform moved from its gothic depictions of human suffering to the benevolent encouragement of health and productive energy (masturbation was said to waste reproductive energy needed to generate children, for instance, while eating spicy foods overstimulated the nervous system, making one unfit for productive labor). The change individualized social dysfunctions, shifting attention from structural ills to flaws of individual character, and encouraging not collective action but greater individual self-scrutiny and self-restraint. The shift from structural to individual reform is mirrored in the increased focus on private, rather than public, life. Parents were encouraged to spy on their children and servants, spouses to inspect one another for signs of disloyalty, employers to watch for alcoholism in employees. It also widened reform's reach: while everyone was not a slave or a poor laborer, everyone was potentially a masturbator, a drinker, or a consumer of dangerous foods or apparel. From an instrument of institutional change focused on the socially abject, then, reform became a program of general self-discipline, designed to make everyone normatively and privately middle-class rather than to generate greater opportunity and justice in the public sphere.

The phrenologist O. S. Fowler's *Amativeness; or, Evils and remedies of excessive & perverted sexuality, including warning and advice for the married and single* is a case in point. "Human character was made to be read without mistake, and in spite of all attempted concealment," Fowler begins; " 'Satan never keeps secrets.' 'Murder will out.' And so will sexuality" (Fowler 1844: 50). To aid parents and spouses in uncovering hidden perversion, Fowler provides the body's gestural lexicon.

> Thus, as the gestures of a carpenter, when talking earnestly, will be back and forth, as if shaving the jack-plane, or with a striking motion, as if driving a nail – as those of the blacksmith will be as if swinging his hammer, those of the farmer, often circular, as if turning the grindstone; and all because they severally make these repetitive motions so often as to assume them involuntarily – so, and for a similar reason, those who indulge much with the opposite sex, when they laugh, or gesticulate earnestly, will carry their hips and their organs forward, because so much accustomed to this motion; *forward* while those who abuse themselves will have a similar motion, only that this apparatus is directed a little upward, as well as thrown forward, because they assume this position so often in self-pollution. (Fowler 1844: 51)

While this passage suggests that the inner desires that Fowler purports to bring out through his canny scrutiny in fact originate in practices that are more social (such as labor) than biological, his interiorization of perversion is necessary to his characterization, not of acts, but of types of people: Fowler teaches readers how to spot perverts, not how to prevent individual acts of perversion. The nature of such persons, more than their actions, is, for Fowler, dangerous, and can be corrected only by the reformer's careful – and benevolent – vigilance: "Let every sensualist, especially *private* libertine, remember, that he is marked and known, and read by all men who have eyes and know how to use them. This exposition is made, in part, to *shame* them out of degrading vice, into moral purity and virtue" (Fowler 1844: 53).

Just as Fowler makes sexuality into a category for classifying groups of people ("perverts") based on a presumably shared (and flawed) "nature," reform coined other words – "addict," "alcoholic," "psychopath," "con men," "hoodlums," pornographers" (Mintz 1995: 10) – that turn actions (drinking alcohol, making pornography) into identities that were, despite their emergence in reform contexts, believed to be unalterable ("incorrigible," "intransigent," "recalcitrant," and "irredeemable" were also reform coinages). In an age of increased economic speculation, the objects of reform were thought to lack a contractual frame of mind, being characterized in terms of ephemerality, immediate gratification, nostalgia, and wastefulness, judged incapable of evaluating consequences, and therefore of sexual, social, or economic reproduction. Unsurprisingly, those characterized as incorrigible addicts and irredeemable hoodlums were most often immigrants and African Americans, the *most* economically and biologically reproductive citizens. In the preface to his bestselling *The Quaker City*, George Lippard promises to reform "the social system" of Philadelphia. Despite this promise, Lippard isolates "the colossal vices and the terrible deformities" (Lippard 1970: 2) of the city within the bodies of a range of gothic "types" composed of the very people most in need of systematic reform: Mother Nancy, the aged alcoholic who supervises the seduction of innocent girls; Bess, the ruined, strong-willed prostitute; Peggy Gird, who fences stolen goods; the counterfeiting Jew Van Gelt; Mosquito and Glow-worm, murderous black house-servants; and, above all, Devil-Bug, mastermind of several of the novel's gruesome plots. All of these characters are, in some way, hideously deformed or comically ugly – Devil Bug's "soul was like his body, a mass of hideous and distorted energy" (Lippard 1970: 105) – exemplifying Fowler's assertion that hidden vices must become legible on the surface of the body. Beyond the gothic deformities of their bodies, however, these characters are as much betrayed by the ethnic and racial markers – heavy accents, dark hair, large lips, heavy weight – that marks them as "other."

"Other" to what? What is the norm generated by reform literature? Against its ethnically marked villains *The Quaker City* presents the virtues of the middle class, represented by Luke Harvey, who apparently has no desires of his own: although he begins humbly yet ends the richest character in the novel, he neither schemes for nor explicitly desires his advancement. Similarly, he engages in no seductions, but remains nostalgically attached to his youthful love, Dora Livingstone. Neither seductively handsome nor monstrously ugly, neither fastidiously fashionable nor slovenly, Luke occupies the central space of the middle class and, as its representative, is also the ideal reformer: Luke saves his beloved Dora from Devil Bug's ravages and promises to keep her scandalous affairs secret, telling her:

> "Dora, there is yet a glorious hope for you!" cried Luke, as his ghastly features warmed with an expression of enthusiasm that might almost have been called holy. "Promise me that you will renounce all unhallowed love, promise me that you will from this time forth, dissolve all connection with the poor creature who has dishonored you by a foul crime, promise me that you will ever be to Livingstone a true and faithful wife; and I swear before God, to sustain you in your course, to defend you from all harm!"

Dora promises, and immediately her "ambition, her recklessness of soul alike were gone; she felt the modesty of a wife once more" and "wondered to herself that idle toys like the world's ambition and the love which is born of guilt, should ever have lured her from the duty of a wife, and purity of a woman" (Lippard 1970: 364). Yet as

Lippard, who wrote a prurient novel warning people against the dangers of aroused desire, must have understood, the middle-class reform ideal of evacuated desire, life-without-excess, was impossible for most to achieve: Dora, hopelessly mired in her excessive ambitions, dies a violent death. While the novel finally endorses continual (failed) self-discipline for women, ethnics, and the poor, it assumes that the ambitions and desires of middle-class (male, Anglo-American) businessmen, like Luke, however excessive, are nevertheless different *in nature* from the sexualized, greedy, and violent wants of those who challenge Luke's way of life.

If Lippard renders the middle-class heroic by vilifying the poor, T. S. Arthur's temperance novel *Ten Nights in a Bar-Room, and What I Saw There* (1854) takes the opposite tack, making the middle-class desire for great wealth into the most danger-ous form of intemperance. The novel focuses on three men: Simon Slade, a prosperous miller who, seeing an opportunity for even greater wealth, quits the mill to open the bar-room where the actions of the novel take place; Joe Morgan, another miller, whose alcoholism ruins himself and his wife, kills his beloved daughter, and earns the scorn of the town; and Willy Hammond, a wealthy lawyer's son, endangered throughout the novel by his intemperate taste for liquor and his consequent vulnerability to a nefarious con man. The novel argues, like most temperance literature of its period, that excessive drinking arises from an inner force – "What appeared on the surface was but a milder form of the disease," Arthur warns, "compared with its hidden, more vital, and more dangerous advances" (1964: 153) – that characterizes a type of person, rather than a dangerous action (many men sit in Slade's bar drinking, perhaps to excess, without becoming *alcoholics*). Although Arthur's novel ends by calling for more so-called "Maine laws," which prohibited the sale of liquor, his novel shows that "law," which legislates on actions, will not solve the problem of intemperance within types of human nature. The law is doubly ineffective for Arthur, who seeks to cure not only alcoholism, but economic intemperance as well. The most vilified character in the novel is, in the end, Slade, not primarily because he makes alcohol available to his friends and neighbors, but because he is a social climber: "tired of being useful, and eager to get gain" (p. 227), Slade, whose desire for excessive wealth mirrors the alcoholic's drive to drink, turns from a respectable day-laborer into a "coarse, bloated, vulgar-looking man" (p. 203). The rich in the novel are treated with suspicion – if Judge Hammond were a more responsible father and citizen, Arthur implies, his son would not be on the brink of disaster. While Arthur presents the poor as vulgar and craven, his real villain is upward mobility. With money as with booze, one should know one's limits. Although Slade never learns this lesson and is therefore, although not a drinker himself, ruined, Joe Morgan is "reformed" into a diligent, conscientious, and content worker, able to afford a life of modest "taste and comfort" (p. 231). The mill that Slade abandoned is again opened for business, and the town returns, happily, to "the old order of things" (p. 231). In this wildly nostalgic ending, America is restored to its village past: the rich and the poor generated by early capitalism are removed, leaving an economy characterized only by tradesmen like Joe Morgan who work in a system devoid of either alienated labor or bourgeois ownership. In this

"Huzza for the Rummies ! That's the ticket !"—Page 160.
Ten Nights in a Bar-room.

Figure 24.1 "Huzza for the Rummies! That's the ticket!" From T. S. Arthur, *Ten Nights in a Bar-Room, and What I Saw There* (New York: A. L. Burt Co., n.d.). Collection of Shirley Samuels.

vision of happy mediums, the "law" has no place (judges and legislators have been villains throughout); rather, the heroes are doctors (the doctor is the only consistently temperate and compassionate figure whom we actually see working in the novel), who contribute to turning intemperance into a "health" predicated on self-restraint and self-denying labor.

Another temperance novel, Walt Whitman's *Franklin Evans; or, The Inebriate* (1842) is similarly concerned with the excesses of capital, but presents a different outcome. The orphaned Franklin leaves his rural home to seek fame and fortune in New York City, but is warned by a fellow traveler, Stephen Lee, that the city will offer nothing but wickedness and dissipation. Proving the wisdom of Lee's warning, Franklin soon falls under the influence of fast-living urbanites, and begins to frequent theaters and bars, thereby precipitating the novel's tragic events. He marries a young woman who soon dies owing to his drunken neglect. Despondent over her death, Franklin drinks more, loses his job, associates with criminals, and winds up in jail for robbery. A benefactor secures his freedom and persuades him to take the temperance pledge. Soon, however, Franklin backslides: he moves to Virginia, where, while drunk, he marries a Creole slave. Once sober, he ignores his devoted wife and takes a mistress, leading his wife to kill the mistress and then herself. Having failed to escape temptation in the country, Franklin returns to New York, where the dying Stephen Lee tells Franklin the sad tale of the death of his children as a result of his wife's drunkenness, prompting the young man to sign a pledge of total abstinence, and leaves Franklin all his money. As even this brief synopsis suggests, the seemingly incoherent plot of *Franklin Evans* repeats certain gestures in a meaningful pattern. Franklin initially takes a moralistic stance in relation to the city (a cesspool of sin), women (full of corrupting excess), foreigners (sources of effeminate luxuriousness), and above all liquor. Over time, however, Franklin experiences desire for increasingly rich men, causing moments of panic, usually manifested as a drinking spree. The panic is resolved when Franklin displaces his desire for men (always also a desire for capital) onto women, who become embodiments of whatever excess arouses both Franklin's panic and his desire. The women become more unruly as the novel progresses, and die in increasingly violent ways, while Franklin styles himself, in contrast to these criminal women, as rational and judicious in the manner of the male mentors who occasioned his panic in the first place. Desire is thus displaced, through disavowed identification with women, onto ambition, but in ways that show how capital operates by exciting the desire of young men who profit by reforming perversion into professionalism. Try as he might, however, Franklin, unlike Joe Morgan, never quashes his appetite in all its forms. His persistent desires call forth the need for more reform and, paradoxically, take him further from its self-restraint.

The Quaker City, *Ten Nights in a Bar-Room*, and *Franklin Evans* all, in different ways, attempt to reform excess, whether it be of drinking, greed, or sex. Among the "excesses" the novels disavow are those specific to fiction itself. Flights of fancy become another intemperance in these works, a sign of unproductive speculation and the tool of those who would lead innocent readers from the "realities" of a supposedly normal life. A libertine in *The Quaker City*, seeking to seduce an innocent virgin, reads to her from a romance of the American West. When the self-righteous narrator of *Ten Nights* finds an arch-villain hiding beneath his bed, he is reluctant to call for help because he realizes that whoever responds might leap to fanciful conclusions. He recognizes, in short, his participation in generating a narrative that might – indeed, did – become an intemperate (that is, imaginative) fiction. Reform-ers, often accused of exaggerating scenes of suffering and degradation, were eager to avoid the taint of excessive fancy, and the authors they employed shared that anxiety. At the same time, as the market for sensationalist and sentimental fiction grew in the nineteenth century, reform relied more heavily on fiction, while denying the literary status of such works through claims to their moral respectability and mimetic veracity (*Ten Nights*, its publisher's preface promises, contains "no exaggerations" [Arthur 1964: 3]). At the same time, fiction, which depicts institutional life through individuals who represent broader structures, reinforced reform's increased focus on individual "character" and its insistence on disciplining the "self" within the privacy of the bourgeois family.

Not all fiction served reform ends, of course. Following the outpouring of reform novels such as *The Quaker City* and *Franklin Evans* in the 1840s, the 1850s brought a new genre – the romance – that challenged reform literature by explicitly parodying its aims and methods, by insisting on the salutary influence of imagination, and by showing that the inner lives of citizens, which reformers claimed to read and organize into *types* of persons, remain opaque and mysterious. The best-known anti-reform romance is undoubtedly Hawthorne's *The Blithedale Romance* (1852), a fictionalized account of the author's three years at Brook Farm, in which the principal reformers come in for the most severe criticism and suffer the most tragic ends. Hollingsworth's plan to reform the prison system in order to make convicts useful members of society is characterized as "the cold, spectral monster which he had himself conjured up, and on which he was wasting all the warmth of his heart, and of which, at last – as these men of a mighty purpose so invariably do – he had grown to be the bond-slave" (Hawthorne 1978: 51). Broodingly obsessive, willing to sacrifice all who love him to accomplish his project, Hollingsworth apparently has "no heart, no sympathy, no reason, no conscience" (p. 65). While Hollingsworth's monomania frustrates his efforts at reform and ultimately ruins his health, he is better off than the feminist Zenobia who, despite her criticisms of conventional romance, falls hopelessly in love with Hollingsworth and, rejected by him, kills herself, her fists clenched in morbid parody of the defiance she embodied in life.

These characters represent, for *Blithedale's* narrator Miles Coverdale, the tragic tendencies of all reformers, who follow "an illusion, a masquerade, a pastoral, a counterfeit Arcadia" (Hawthorne 1978: 21); as Zenobia reluctantly acknowledges, "'Of all varieties of mock-life, we have surely blundered into the very emptiest mockery, in our effort to establish the one true system'" (p. 209). Sounding like Emerson and Thoreau, Coverdale insists that "reformers should make their efforts positive, instead of negative; they must do away with evil by substituting good" (p. 161), or else will end up, in relation to society, "in a position of new hostility, rather than new brotherhood" (p. 20). Coverdale especially resents reform's desire to bring into public scrutiny human emotions, a desire that "ruins, or is fearfully apt to ruin, the heart; the rich juices of which God never meant should be pressed violently out, and distilled into alcoholic liquor, by an unnatural process; but should render life sweet, bland, and gently beneficent, and insensibly influence other hearts and other lives to the same blessed end" (p. 224). Throughout *Blithedale*, Hawthorne represents reform as producing the mystifications necessary in modern capitalism. As Coverdale acknowledges, "we had pleased ourselves with delectable visions of the spiritualization of labor" (p. 61). Mrs. Silas, the farmer's wife who knits "a stocking out of the texture of a dream" (p. 30), contrasts with the reformers in *Blithedale*, who prefer to produce poetry about labor rather than actually digging in a field in order to know the lives of those they would reform.

Most of the criticisms cited above come from Miles Coverdale, whom Zenobia accuses of having "a monstrous skepticism" (Hawthorne 1978: 157). At other moments, however, Coverdale seems less skeptical, as when he claims, upon initially settling at Blithedale, "We had broke through many hindrances that are powerful enough to keep most people on the weary tread-mill of the established system, even while they feel its irksomeness almost as intolerable as we did" (p. 18). Coverdale criticizes the same economy he elsewhere mystifies:

> We sought our profit by mutual aid, instead of wrestling it by the strong hand from an enemy, or filching it craftily from those less shrewd than ourselves, . . . or winning it by selfish competition with a neighbor, in one or another of which fashions, every son of woman both perpetuates and suffers his share of the common evil, whether he choose it or not.

"I rejoice that I could once think better of the world's improvability than it deserved" (p. 19), Coverdale declares.

Like his narrator, Hawthorne was not quite the skeptic he might at first appear. True, he left Brook Farm fed up, as he relates in "The Custom House," with the airy utopianism of men like Bronson Alcott and Emerson. At the same time, Hawthorne appears to have recognized in reform an imaginative strain that he preserved and used in his romances. Whether it is Hester engaging in "speculations" in her lonely cottage in *The Scarlet Letter*, Clifford blowing soap bubbles from the upper windows of the House of the Seven Gables, or Zenobia arranging masques to cheer the laborers of Blithedale into a new brotherhood, the emotional centers of Hawthorne's romances are characters who maintain an optimism, an ability to imagine a more just and pleasurable world, in defiance of the harsh "realities" that would crush their hope, their inventiveness. Hawthorne writes, "real life never arranges itself exactly like a romance" (Hawthorne 1978: 97); but that did not mean that imagination, the force that enables at least some of his characters to survive and even prevail, played no role in reforming the harsher aspects of modern life. Perhaps Hawthorne carried this faith in imagination away from Brook Farm, where he associated with men and women who were not like Hollingsworth, but willing to risk their livelihoods and their lives in order to end slavery, distribute profit more equitably, enfranchise all citizens, and reduce the suffering of the poor and abject. Most importantly, they had the courage to imagine a public in which the pursuit of life, liberty, and happiness were more than the empty promise of a hypocritical government. If reformers often suggested that social ills could best be understood through the public confessions of private passions, if structural reform gave way to individual self-restraint and self-transformation (the roots of contemporary "makeover" culture), it also left a rich literary legacy, full not only of the gothic horrors and sentimental sufferings that would become characteristic of antebellum fiction, but of the *social* imagination, the world-transforming power to see, all evidence to the contrary, what *might be*, that links antebellum reform with the most powerful struggles for freedom and justice in the following century.

REFERENCES

Arthur, T. S. (1964). *Ten Nights in a Bar-Room, and What I Saw There*. Cambridge, Mass.: Harvard University Press. (First publ. 1854.)

Emerson, Ralph Waldo (1967). "New England Reformers" (first publ. 1844). In David Brion Davis (ed.), *Ante-bellum Reform*. New York: Harper & Row.

Emerson, Ralph Waldo (1982). "Man the Reformer" (first publ. 1841). In *Selected Essays*. New York: Viking.

Fowler, O. S. (1844). *Amativeness; or, Evils and remedies of excessive & perverted sexuality, including warning and advice for the married and single*. New York: Fowler & Wells.

Hawthorne, Nathaniel (1978). *The Blithedale Romance*. New York: Norton. (First publ. 1852.)

Lippard, George (1970). *The Quaker City; or, The Monks of Monk Hall. A Romance of Philadelphia Life, Mystery and Crime*. New York: Odyssey. (First publ. 1845.)

Mintz, Steven (1995). *Moralists and Modernizers: America's Pre-Civil War Reformers*. Baltimore: Johns Hopkins University Press.

Stowe, Harriet Beecher (1994). *Uncle Tom's Cabin; or, Life Among the Lowly*. New York: Norton. (First publ. 1852.)

Thoreau, Henry David (1973). "Reform and the Reformers" (1844). In Wendell Glick (ed.), *Reform Papers*. Princeton: Princeton University Press.

Whitman, Walt (1967). *Franklin Evans; or, The Inebriate*. New Haven, Conn.: College and University Press. (First publ. 1842.)

PART III
Authors, Locations, Purposes

25

The Problem of the City

Heather Roberts

Although Philip Fisher has credited Theodore Dreiser with first introducing the "cultural fact" of the city to the American popular imagination (Fisher 1985: 9), the statistical fact remains that the city never figured more prominently in the works of popular American writers than in the decades preceding the Civil War. Indeed, despite the massive westward exploration and relocation that took place during this same period, there were over three times as many urban novels published in the antebellum decades as there were novels set on the western frontier (Siegel 1981: 6). Whereas the more canonical literature of the American Renaissance – much of it centering on the escapist allures of elaborate "worlds elsewhere" – tended to envision America as a land of open wilderness and ocean vistas, the more popular fiction of the day explored the imaginative terrain of the country's new capitalist cities.

This proliferation of fictional efforts to represent the urban experience reflected, in part, the fact that the antebellum decades witnessed more people moving into cities than ever before. The unprecedented size and diversity of the new metropolises also made them experiential "frontiers" in their own right. Yet, in contrast to the western frontier, the new "urban wilderness" seemed to many contemporary observers to hold more peril than promise. For all the diversity of their approaches to the city, antebellum writers shared a sense of the city as a problem – whether representational, ideological, or spiritual – demanding resolution. This chapter surveys the manifold ways in which writers of the antebellum period interpreted the problem of the city, and the representational strategies that they adopted to address this problem.

Since the time of John Winthrop's first figuring of the English immigrants' Massachusetts Bay Colony as a "City on a Hill," a moral exemplar for a fallen world, American writers have concerned themselves with both the problem and the promise of the city as a model of human community. Yet while Puritan writers envisioned their founding colony as a model New Canaan or New Jerusalem, they also conceptualized the American continent as a pastoral refuge from the oppressive history of class stratification and urban corruption that they identified with the Old

World. In the centuries since, numerous novelists, social critics, and politicians have continued to figure America as what Perry Miller has termed "nature's nation," championing an American exceptionalism rooted in the nation's supposed pastoralism (Miller 1967; Marx 1964).

The predominantly agricultural tenor of life in eighteenth-century America reinforced such pastoralist national ideals, and the agrarian republicanism promoted by Thomas Jefferson profoundly influenced perspectives on urban development in the decades following the Revolutionary War. We see the impact of this nationalistic anti-urbanism on the popular literature of the post-revolutionary period in plays such as Royall Tyler's *The Contrast* (1787), which identifies cosmopolitan attitudes and aspirations as essentially European, and, as such, threats to the virtue of the new nation. Thus the national pride of Tyler's culture hero "Brother Jonathan" remains inseparable from his backwoods values and comic discomfort as a Yankee farmer in the foppish and artificial world of the city.

The country's historically conflicted attitude toward urbanization helps to explain the alarm with which many Americans witnessed, over the first half of the nineteenth century, what would prove to be the most dramatic period of urban growth in the nation's history (Machor 1987: 121). American cities grew, proliferated, and diversified at unprecedented rates, coming increasingly to dominate the country's cultural landscape (Brown and Glaab 1967: 23). Indeed, urban historian Sam Bass Warner, Jr. has claimed that "If the criterion of urbanity is the mixture of classes and ethnic groups," then "the cities of the United States in the years between 1820 and 1870 marked the zenith of our national urbanity" (Warner 1972: 84).

Many contemporary commentators hailed the nation's explosive urban development as a testament to its social progress and thriving mercantile capitalist economy. For others, however, the prospect that America was fast evolving into an urban nation seemed far more problematic. To a generation raised with the Jeffersonian ideal of America as a nation of yeomen farmers, the very idea of an "American city" seemed oxymoronic. The new cities' massing of humanity and increasing evidence of class stratification, recalling conditions in the Old World, seemed a dark fulfillment of Jefferson's prophecy that the nation's economic prosperity would prove "greater than our virtue can bear."

The phenomenon of what Thomas Bender has called "a new kind of city and city life" in America seemed to demand, in turn, new techniques for depicting the city and revealing the meaning of this new urban experience (Bender 1975: 7). Notably, the first popular genres of urban representation in the antebellum United States were more visual than verbal – from theatrical sound and light shows to sweeping "city panorama" paintings and bird's-eye-view lithographs. Many of the earliest urban painters and lithographers framed their cityscapes against a backdrop of open fields and hills, reassuringly depicting the seemingly "unnatural" city as an organic outgrowth of the landscape. Later, popular bird's-eye views offered spectators a more comprehensive urban vista, often presented from an aerial perspective that would, at the time, have been impossible to assume in real life (Bergmann 1995). Whereas the city's vast size, scope, and heterogeneity might seem overwhelming when experienced up close, the elevated vantage point of these bird's-eye panoramas enabled them to present viewers with an illusion of all-encompassing visual and epistemological control over the city's expanse.

Among the verbal genres of urban representation that attained popularity in the 1830s, the city guidebook was most obviously a product of the same cartographic impulse that had produced the earlier visual panoramas. Antebellum guides such as Asa Greene's *A Glance at New York* (1837), Joel Ross's *What I Saw in New-York; or A Bird's-eye View of City Life* (1852), and Cornelius Mathews' *A Pen-and-Ink Panorama of New York City* (1853) each offered its readers a "verbal panorama" of the city's representative sights. Like their visual antecedents, these verbal panoramas often present the city as perceived by observers perched upon distant hilltops or church towers. From such detached, elevated viewpoints, these would-be omniscient narrators delineate both the city's external boundaries and its internal divisions. Other guidebooks and collections of urban sketches, such as George Foster's *Fifteen Minutes around New York* (1853), offered a more mobile perspective on the city. In the manner of the European *flâneur*, their narrators stroll through the streets describing, in passing, the city's primary tourist attractions (Brand 1991). This latter genre of guides-on-the-go proposed to contain the city's sprawling excess by presenting it to middle-class readers in a consumable fashion, as a collection of commodified "sights" or "views."

Many of these antebellum urban guides also included sections offering to "map" the different social types that readers were likely to encounter on the city streets. Such an offer would have appealed not only to rural readers planning a visit to the city, but to urbanites who found themselves living in what seemed increasingly to be a world of strangers. Responding to the growing density, diversity, and anonymity of urban populations, contemporary advice manuals and etiquette books proposed to help their audiences read what historian John Kasson has termed the "semiotics of the city," and the street manners of its inhabitants (Kasson 1990). In the tradition of the French *physiologies*, guidebooks written by would-be urban anthropologists offered to help the reader manage the increasing heterogeneity and alienating immensity of the city's masses by indexing the social groups and individual types of which the urban crowd was composed.

If the panoramas and guidebooks of the 1830s offered cartographic solutions to the problem of how to read the city, the detective tales of Edgar Allan Poe represent his literary response to this same hermeneutic challenge. Poe's early story "The Man of the Crowd" (1840), centered wholly on the narrator's efforts to interpret the city and its crowds, forges a link between the urban tale of detection and the type of taxonomic guides mentioned above. The story begins on a sunny afternoon with the narrator comfortably seated in a coffeehouse, whence he peruses the city street from behind a pane of glass. Surveying the faces that pass before his window, he analyzes the crowd outside, confidently dividing its masses into social categories and hierarchies. As day shades into night, however, and the flickering gaslights cast a lurid glare over the faces he seeks to read, the city grows more threatening and illegible. The narrator also loses his affective detachment from the scene, pressing himself up against the glass as his interpretive effort takes on an air of increasing desperation. Once the narrator is drawn bodily into the street in feverish pursuit of a single, maddeningly unreadable face in the crowd, he loses all semblance of objectivity. The story ends with the collapse of the narrator's presumed interpretive authority in the face of the city's irreducible enigma; the interpretive challenge posed by the "absolute idiosyncrasy" of the elusive "man of the crowd" is, ultimately, that of the city itself.

Poe's "Man of the Crowd" illustrates how, as a genre, the detective story was born out of the novel experience of urbanization and the manner in which the anonymity and heterogeneity of city life made men mysteries to one another. Yet while this early story acknowledges the impossibility, for the ordinary individual, of reading the city when bodily immersed in its streets, the author went on to invent an urban superhero for whom the city and its mysteries proved wholly transparent. The paranormally rational Auguste Dupin of Poe's "The Mystery of Marie Roget" (1842), a tale based on the actual 1841 murder of a cigar vendor in Hoboken, New Jersey, is able to solve the bloodiest and most bewildering of urban crimes without ever leaving the safety of his armchair. Poe's Dupin tales offer a psychological equivalent to the bird's-eye view lithographs of the preceding decade, with Dupin coolly regarding the city from a perspective of analytical detachment – symbolized by his ever-present green-tinted glasses – that places him effectively above and apart from the city's threatened disorder.

Poe's use of urban settings to explore the human mind in its encounter with hermeneutic conundrums distinguished his own approach to the city, at least in his tales of ratiocination, from the expository aim of his more sensational contemporaries. Instrumental in the development of what David Anthony has termed the "sensational public sphere" in antebellum America, penny papers such as the *New York Sun*, *New York Herald*, *Evening Tatler*, and *Brother Jonathan* owed their wide circulations, which ballooned in the 1830s, to their low cost and their move away from dry news reporting into tabloid journalism (Anthony 1997). Overflowing with short, graphic accounts of local crimes and scandals, these papers offered a portrait of the city as the favored haunt of criminals, prostitutes, and corrupt politicians.

The publications of the journalist-turned-novelist George Foster exemplify the development of the sensational urban novel out of the newspaper exposé. Foster's collection of newspaper sketches entitled *New York by Gaslight* (1850) featured the "gaslight," with its lurid glare illuminating the dark underside of the city, as a potent trope for the sensationalists' perspective on urban life. Even as Foster promised to expose the "underground story" of life in New York – a phrase which connotes at once the city's subterranean recesses and its secret history – dozens of sensational urban novels such as Foster's own *New York Above Ground and Under Ground* (1853) and George Lippard's *New York: Its Upper Ten and Lower Million* (1853) represented the city as scandalously divided between the worlds of rich and poor, virtue and vice, sunlight and shadow.

The revelatory gaze of the sensational urban novel was at once disciplinary and pornographic; writers purported to be exposing the city's dens of vice and "orgies of pauperism" in order to facilitate the removal of such urban ills, yet also reveled unabashedly in the salacious details of their visits. Some sensational exposés even listed the names and locations of the brothels and gambling dens they ostensibly sought to close down, suggesting their potential appeal as guides to the illicit pleasures of the city. Written largely by and for men, these novels frequently narrated the inevitable sexual fall of young women who ventured to set foot in the city. Novels such as the anonymously authored *Emily, the Beautiful Seamstress; or, the Danger of the First Step. A Story of Life in New York* (1853); Charles Burdett's *Lilla Hart: A Tale of New York* (1846); and Osgood Bradbury's *Mysteries of Boston; or, The Woman's Temptation* (1855) and *Female Depravity; or, The House of Death* (1857) narrated such tales of womanly virtue lost in the city streets, and also popularized a new urban type: the shameless or "depraved" fallen woman, bent on avenging herself on men.

Of the period's sensational genres, the most successful by far was the "city mystery," which attained the height of its American popularity in the 1840s. Following in the tradition of the international bestseller *Les Mystères de Paris*, published by the French *feuilletonist* Eugène Sue in 1842–3, the city mystery also reflected the influence of two earlier English sub-genres: the 1830s "Newgate novel" of criminal life, and the "silver fork" novel of scandalous "high life." City mysteries presented the city, and its evident extremes of human experience, as social enigmas demanding investigation. These novels, exemplified by Ned Buntline's *Mysteries and Miseries of New York* (1848), enthusiastically detailed the "mysteries and miseries" of cities as diverse as Boston, San Francisco, New Orleans, Lowell – even Papermill Village. Indeed, no commercial center seemed too small or provincial to have sordid secrets in need of exposure.

One of the most provocative and original artists working in the genre, the labor activist George Lippard, appropriated the conventions of the city mystery in order to harness its affective power to his own politically radical ends. Lippard sought to make the city mystery into an instrument of socialist consciousness-raising, applying the genre's conventional tropes, plot patterns, and telos of revelation to uncover the false logic, injustices, and human costs of the capitalist system. He used the city mystery's hermeneutics of exposure to lay bare what he saw as the deepest "scandal" of the city: the oppressive social relations engendered by its economic system. To Lippard, the darkest secret of the industrial capitalist city was that, as he put it in *The Empire City* (1849), "its foundations [were] dyed in blood." He recognized the cities that had expanded at such an unprecedented rate throughout the 1830s and 1840s as the most concrete incarnations of capitalist enterprise blighting the American landscape. Because their growth had depended upon the exploitation of workers, Lippard insisted, the new cities stood as monuments to capitalist greed and inhumanity; they were tangible reminders of how the rich had "turned the sweat and blood of the poor into bricks and mortar."

Lippard's most famous novel, *The Quaker City; or, the Monks of Monk Hall* (1845), also represents his most original, extravagant and fantastical response to the emerging problems of the capitalist city. Lying at the heart of Lippard's Philadelphia, the archetypally gothic, labyrinthine structure of Monk Hall serves, as Michael Denning has noted, synecdochically for the city as a whole, with all its sin and excess (Denning 1987: 92). Specifying that Monk Hall "had been originally erected by a wealthy foreigner, some-time previous to the Revolution," and that it most likely functioned for some time as a monastery, Lippard links the vices showcased in the hall with those of Europe – specifically, the corrupt Old Europe portrayed by popular English gothic writers such as "Monk" Lewis, Ann Radcliffe, and Horace Walpole. Monk Hall thus stands for America's betrayal of her founding principles and perpetuation of the corrupt patterns of the Old World. Tellingly, however, the "Monks" of Lippard's Hall are neither the sadistic aristocrats of Radcliffe's novels nor the debauched Catholic monks imagined by Lewis; instead, they are the corrupt bankers, merchants, editors, and preachers of contemporary urban America.

By the 1850s the city had come to seem less "mysterious" to many American readers, though the economic and social problems associated with urban life were becoming all the more apparent. The decade witnessed the sensational city mystery wane in popularity, only to be succeeded by the sentimental domestic novel. Whereas most urban exposés appear to have been written by and for men – leading Leslie Fiedler to term the genre "the male novel" of the 1840s – domestic novels were predominantly written by, for, and about women (Fiedler 1970: 80). While valorizing the "woman's sphere" of home and family, many of the most popular midcentury sentimental novels are also, in important respects, urban fictions. In the numerous domestic novels set in metropolises such as Boston, New York, and Philadelphia – among them classics such as Susan Warner's *The Wide, Wide World* (1850) and Maria Cummins' *The Lamplighter* (1854) – we find sentimental writers approaching the social, psychological, and economic challenges of the antebellum city from the perspective of the middle-class woman. Even as Annette Kolodny has claimed that women writing about the western frontier effectively "project[ed] resonant symbolic contents onto otherwise unknown terrains" as a way of "ma[king] those terrains their own," so many antebellum women writers used the idioms of the sentimental novel to "domesticate" the city (Kolodny 1975: xii).

Thus, though Cummins opens *The Lamplighter* with the line "It was growing dark in the city," and proceeds to introduce her young heroine, Gerty Flint, literally poised on the boundary between home and street, girlhood and womanhood, the story Cummins goes on to tell is not one of virtue lost, but of community found. The novel opens with the seemingly orphaned Gerty having been left "the property of the city," yet the urban world proves "a good foster-mother" to her; she is adopted and mentored by strangers she encounters in the city's streets, who come, over time, to constitute her surrogate family. If the sensationalists represented the city as a world in which a woman on the streets was, as Mary Ryan has put it, "either endangered or dangerous," the sentimentalists countered with novels revolving around female prot- agonists who made the city their home (Ryan 1990: 86). In their focus on women surviving and ultimately thriving in the city, these novels reflected the contemporary reality of complex networks of urban women, with their own "economic relations and cultural forms," described by historian Christine Stansell (Stansell 1986). Yet these works were powerfully prescriptive as well as descriptive, critiquing the materialism, anonymity, and unpredictable market-driven economy governing antebellum urban life by imagining alternative cities in which social and economic relations are ruled by spiritual laws, and by the values of the home.

For many sentimental writers, no single urban type incarnated the city's potential threats to the values of home and family more effectively (and affectively) than the stereotypical "child of the streets." By using the figure of the street orphan – the hot-corn girl, street sweep, or newsboy – to represent the problem of urban poverty, sentimental urban writers were able to imagine its domestic solution: namely, the "cultural adoption" of such children into the homes and hearts of the middle classes (Bergmann 1995: 96–8). In the period from 1840 to 1870 over three dozen novels were published that centered on the neglected children of the city and the efforts of benevolent middle-class characters to come to their aid (Siegel 1981: 186). At once reflecting and promoting the shift in middle-class attitudes toward the urban poor that spawned many evangelical and secular reform programs in the same period, sentimental urban novels such as P. H. Skinner's *The Little Ragged Ten Thousand* (1853), Robert Greeley's *Violet: The Child of the City* (1854), and Elizabeth Oakes Smith's *The Newsboy* (1854) helped to bring the problem of street children "home" to their readers. In so doing, they both modeled and called into question various forms of cultural adoption by which the street child – and the working classes and immigrant groups represented by such children – could be assimilated into white, Protestant middle-class culture, and the social "family" made whole once again.

Of course, not all antebellum women writers chose to view the city through a sentimental lens. One who preferred satire to sentiment was the immensely popular *New York Ledger* columnist Fanny Fern (Sara Payson Willis Parton). To Fern, who was ahead of her time in her interrogation of gender roles, the real problem of the city was that it was dominated by men. As is evident throughout her *Ledger* sketches, Fern recognized that the public spaces of the city – whether geographical sites such as streets or discursive sites such as newspapers – were also sites of power. Men, she observed, exploited their own free access to such sites to reinforce their cultural domination of women. The cosmopolitan persona that Fern creates through her columns, however, aggressively asserts her right to inhabit these same spaces and sites. Although Fern was hardly the only woman writer of her time to write about urban life, she was one of the very few to assume the right to walk the streets and gaze at passersby with the freedom and authority of the male *flâneur*.

Whereas her contemporary, the author Elizabeth Oakes Smith, had opened her sentimental urban novel *The Newsboy* by proclaiming her intent to carry into the city streets "my eyes, and my heart also," Fern was concerned that, while remembering to take their "hearts" to the streets, women should not leave their "eyes" behind. As she liked to remind her readers, alluding to her botanical *nom de plume*, "Ferns have eyes – and they are not green, either." Thus renouncing the posture of the ingenuous

THE LITTLE PAUPER.

Figure 25.1   "The Little Pauper." Accompanies story of the same name in Fanny Fern, *Fern Leaves from Fanny's Port-folio* (Auburn: Derby & Miller, 1853). Collection of Shirley Samuels.

"greenhorn," Fern instead proclaimed her insider's knowledge of urban society, asserting the power and authority of her streetwise cosmopolitan gaze. Through her experienced eyes, the spatial city appears as a world of intrusive "quizzing glasses" against which she must defend herself. She does so by reversing their gaze in sketches such as "Peeps from under a Parasol," which lampoons the notion that a woman should be forced to "peep" from under a protective covering while on the city streets. Instead, Fern adopts the free and open perspective of the strolling *flâneuse* to describe, with much satire and even some sensuality, various male writers, editors, and public figures of the period as they promenade along Broadway.

The experience of urbanization was as much on the minds of the highbrow writers of the antebellum period as it was in the works of their more popular peers. To the Concord Transcendentalists, the problem represented by the city was less social and political than philosophical. The writing of leading Transcendentalists of the 1830s and 1840s reflected their rejection of what they saw as the convention, tradition, and artifice of urban life, all of which threatened to alienate human beings from nature and from their own more authentic selves. Morton and Lucia White have even read Ralph Waldo Emerson's *Nature* (1836) as, at least in part, a response to American urbanization – a philosophical manifesto through which Emerson sought to remind his contemporaries of what they risked losing in their rush to the city (White and White 1962). Certainly, Emerson distrusted the city for many of the same reasons that he distrusted society more generally; his essays question whether the assumed advantages of citified life in fact constitute "progress," and often imagine the self-reliant individual against a backdrop of undifferentiated urban masses. Yet Emerson also acknowledged that "cities give us collision," celebrating the city, and the dynamic and creative power of the "collisions" between different ideas and social types characterizing urban life, as a necessary means to the end of self-culture.

Often more adamant than his friend and mentor Emerson in his disdain for the hectic, cluttered superficiality of contemporary urban life, H. D. Thoreau famously insisted that the preservation of the world lay in "wildness" rather than in civilization. In his essay "Walking," Thoreau valorizes the spiritually restorative power of saunterings into nature, yet finds no equivalent value in the urban strolls that constituted the signature activity of the European *flâneur*: "what would become of us," he queries, "if we walked only in a garden or a mall?" Even as the bird's-eye lithographers could represent the city in its totality only by adopting a vantage point above and apart from it, Thoreau's removal to the woods in *Walden* (1854) is motivated by his conviction that it is only by temporarily withdrawing from civilization that he can remove the lens of convention from his eyes and become "an impartial and wise observer of human life." Yet, though the Whites have termed *Walden* "a bible of anti-urbanism" with some justification, given its portrait of the "lives of quiet desperation" led by citified men, it is essential to remember that Thoreau chose to situate himself within walking distance of the city's offerings. Likewise, his acknowledgment in the book's first paragraph that he is "at present...a sojourner in civilized life again" reminds us that the writer's civic participation only increased after his return from the woods.

Whereas Emerson and Thoreau turned to immersion in nature as a means to self-knowledge, the novelist, editor, and anti-slavery activist Lydia Maria Child explored the world of New York City through a Christian Transcendentalist lens in her remarkable collection of editorial columns, *Letters from New York* (1846). The city scenes so richly detailed in her public "letters" become occasions for the author's revelation of more abstract spiritual truths. If nature, for her fellow New England Transcendentalists, offered myriad analogies to the soul of the individual, so too, for Child, did New York City. Throughout her letters she works to decipher what she terms "the hieroglyphics of angels" within the text of the city itself. Child understood her urban walks, as Thoreau had understood his woodland saunterings, as journeys of the soul – daily pilgrimages whose end point was spiritual rather than geographical. Each moment of urban encounter becomes for Child an invitation to spiritual and moral reflection. Certainly, not all of Child's meditations are uplifting; on the contrary, she acknowledges the casual violence of urban life, and the manner in which such experiential assaults threaten to brutalize the soul. Ultimately, however, she reads the city as a moral testing ground affording opportunities for spiritual elevation unavailable to those who isolate themselves from its masses of humanity.

While Child's hopeful vision of the city depends upon her view of human nature as basically good and subject to reform, Nathaniel Hawthorne's dark, often Calvinistic view of human nature led him to view the city – a product of human ambition alone – with deep distrust. For Hawthorne, the problem of the city was but an extension and expression of the problem of humanity. In his 1843 story "The New Adam and Eve," for example – a post-apocalyptic tale in which "the unperverted couple" find them-selves wandering curiously through the empty streets of a deserted Boston – Hawthorne uses the vacant city to figure all the ways in which human culture, by the mid-nineteenth century, had fallen away from nature and from God. As seen through the innocent eyes of the new Adam and Eve, the city's structures and their contents, ranging from lavish mansions to tenements and prisons, prove perplexing mysteries. Even the piles of gold the pair find at the Merchants' Exchange, the city's former economic heart and "the very essence . . . of the system that had wrought itself into the vitals of mankind, and choked their original nature in its deadly gripe" mean nothing to them. The story leaves open the question of whether Adam and Eve will follow their better instincts out of the city and back to nature or return to Boston to pursue the answers to its tantalizing mysteries, thereby replicating humankind's fall into the knowledge of good and evil.

If Hawthorne frequently associates cities with protagonists' falls into social and historical knowledge, these falls are often also "fortunate" in that they make possible the characters' morally necessary participation in the wider human community. Thus the brutal knowledge of class conflict and democratic mob rule that Robin, the naïve country-bred hero of "My Kinsman, Major Molineux" (1850), gains through his venture to the city in quest of his kinsman will also enable his emergence as an individual historical and political agent, and, ultimately, an American citizen. Con-versely, Hawthorne condemns characters such as Richard Digby and Ethan Brand for the manner in which they voluntarily exile themselves from their communities, and thus also from the possibilities for redemption through human sympathy and charity contained therein. Even at the end of *The Scarlet Letter* (1850) Hawthorne presents the return of Hester Prynne and Arthur Dimmesdale from the forest to the town market-place as necessary – albeit tragically so – for their restoration to moral wholeness. As such examples demonstrate, Hawthorne routinely makes allegorical use of the polarity between city and country/wilderness to underscore themes, such as the fall into knowledge or the tension between society and self, that run throughout his work.

In the end, cities in Hawthorne's stories reveal less about the historically specific conditions of urbanization in the 1840s and 1850s than about the author's character-istic thematic preoccupations. Herman Melville's literary responses to the city, however, rank among his most experimental works, and, as Wyn Kelley has argued, show the author progressively struggling to find a literary form adequate to represent urban experience (Kelley 1996). Although his gothic representation of Liverpool in *Redburn* (1849) was very much in the style of urban sensationalism, Melville's genre-bending novel *Pierre; or, The Ambiguities* (1852) exploded the conventions of both the sentimental domestic novel and the sensational city mystery, subverting the trad-itional moral polarizing of country and city. Though Pierre's journey from his rural paternal estate to the horrors of an urban tenement replicates, on many levels, the traditional fall from innocence to vice, the dark knowledge of himself and others that Pierre gains through this experience forces him to acknowledge that his seemingly idyllic childhood in the country depended upon suppressed truths and repressed desires. Making a point upon which he would elaborate more fully in his diptych tale "The Paradise of Bachelors and the Tartarus of Maids" (1855), Melville shows that city and country are inextricably bound, both socially and economically, as interde-pendent parts of the same oppressive system.

In perhaps his best-known urban work, the short story "Bartleby, the Scrivener: A Tale of Wall Street" (1853), Melville explored the deeper social and psychological effects of urbanization. The tale's unprecedented exploration of the alienation and anomie of urban life resonates less with the work of Melville's contemporaries than with that of twentieth-century sociologists and existentialists. Although some critics have read the story as a meditation on the human condition more broadly, the experiences of the tale's protagonists arise from, and are tied inextricably to, their location in the heart of New York City. As Melville's subtitle indicates, it is a story as much about a place as a person, investigating the emerging phenomenon of what we might term "the urban condition." "Wall Street," newly identifiable as the heart of the nation's capitalist system, functions in Melville's tale synecdochically for both the city and its dehumanizing ethos. Similarly, the literal wall that stares back at Bartleby through his office window mirrors the figurative walls between characters – the unquestioned norms of social behavior in the city that alienate them from one another and from themselves.

Going beyond use of the city as a mere setting or backdrop, Melville's "Bartleby" reflects aspects of the new experiential reality of urban life. Read in this context, even his later novel *The Confidence-Man* (1857), though set on a steamship rather than in a city, can be understood as a meditation on the "culture of distrust" that, according to cultural historian Karen Halttunen, arose from conditions of life in the antebellum city (Halttunen 1982). In acknowledging the profound changes urbanization had wrought in the ways Americans viewed the world, each other, and themselves, Melville's works anticipate the realism and naturalism of turn-of-the-century authors.

Perhaps the most proto-naturalist of antebellum authors, however, was Rebecca Harding Davis. Both Davis' "Life in the Iron Mills" (1861) and her *Margret Howth:*

A Story of Today (1861) represent social worlds in which the interdependent forces of industrialization and urbanization have profoundly altered human life. In her probing of the seemingly ineluctable manner in which bodies and spirits are fragmented and regulated by "the vast machinery of system" ordering industrial capitalist society, Davis evokes the type of deterministic world-view that has since become associated with naturalism – the literary style, according to Philip Fisher, most organically suited to representing citified humanity. Her exposé of the dissolution of individual agency and creativity in the face of the massing and systematizing of human life adumbrates the ways in which the forces attending urbanization would, over time, come to transform human subjectivity itself.

An overview of antebellum writers and their approaches to representing urban life shows them expressing their ambivalence over the nation's rapid urbanization by posing the city as a problem – whether representational, ideological, philosophical, or spiritual – demanding a response. For many writers, their interpretation of the essential problem of the city invited the means of its solution: the city's vast expanse could be mapped, its mysteries could be solved, its criminal underworld exposed, its homeless children taken in, and its assaults on the spirit used to strengthen the soul. For others, however, the problem of the city was fundamentally insoluble – whether because, as for Hawthorne, the city's problems were but expressions of the fallen nature of humankind, or because, as for Melville and Harding Davis, the way of life emerging in the antebellum metropolises of the northeast heralded a new urban–industrial ordering of human life that would prove the unavoidable future of all Americans.

Coda

Yet there is one antebellum writer whose unconditional embrace of the city deserves a final mention. Virtually alone among his peers, Walt Whitman chose to extol the city's promise rather than lament its problems. Whitman's 1855 *Leaves of Grass* celebrated precisely those aspects of urban life, from the heterogeneity of the city's crowds to the erotic frisson between passing strangers on the street, that so many of his contemporaries greeted with alarm. Absorbing and translating into poetic form what he termed "the blab of the pave," Whitman's extravagantly inclusive "songs" incorporated the sights, sounds, scents, and novel vernacular of the city streets. Indeed, the poetic persona that he creates through "Song of Myself" is that of a street lounger, "of Manhattan the son" (l. 497) who stands reflectively apart from the crowd without standing above them – at once a reflective *flâneur* and "one of the roughs."

Not only did Whitman celebrate his participation in the New York of the 1850s, proudly asserting, "this is the city, and I am one of its citizens," he also envisioned a future, more radically democratic America in urban terms, as a utopian "city of comradely love." For Whitman, the city, with its "high growths of iron, slender, strong, light, splendidly uprising towards clear skies," was a trope for human aspiration rather than degradation. Indeed, his triumphant "City of Friends" represents a remarkable transfiguration of John Winthrop's original vision of the "Citty on the Hill." Whereas Winthrop's Citty was to be held together by the "ligaments" of sympathy binding those within the Puritan community to each other and to Christ, Whitman boldly envisioned diverse cities "with their arms around one another," inseparably united by a shared passion for democracy, charged with the homoerotic power of adhesive love. In an era in which American writers so persistently represented cities as what Janis Stout has called "Sodoms in Eden," Whitman worked to "discorrupt" his readers' perceptions of the city even as he strove to reclaim the native innocence of human sexuality and desire (Stout 1976).

REFERENCES AND FURTHER READING

Anthony, David (1997). "The Helen Jewett Panic: Tabloids, Men, and the Sensational Public Sphere in Antebellum New York." *American Literature* 69: 3, 487–514.

Bender, Thomas H. (1975). *Toward an Urban Vision: Ideas and Institutions in Nineteenth-Century America*. Lexington: University Press of Kentucky.

Bergmann, Hans (1995). *God in the Street: New York Writing from the Penny Press to Melville*. Philadelphia: Temple University Press.

Brand, Dana (1991). *The Spectator and the City in Nineteenth-Century American Literature*. Cambridge, UK: Cambridge University Press.

Brown, A. Theodore, and Glaab, Charles (1967). *A History of Urban America*. New York: Macmillan.

Denning, Michael (1987). *Mechanic Accents: Dime Novels and Working Class Culture in America*. New York and London: Verso.

Fiedler, Leslie (1970). "The Male Novel." *Partisan Review* 37, 74–89.

Fisher, Philip (1985). *Hard Facts: Setting and Form in the American Novel*. New York: Oxford University Press.

Halttunen, Karen (1982). *Confidence Men and Painted Women: A Study of Middle-Class Culture in America, 1830–1870*. New Haven: Yale University Press.

Kasson, John (1990). *Rudeness and Civility: Manners in Nineteenth-Century Urban America*. New York: Hill & Wang.

Kelley, Wyn (1996). *Melville's City: Literary and Urban Form in Nineteenth-Century New York*. Cambridge, UK: Cambridge University Press.

Kolodny, Annette (1975). *The Lay of the Land: Metaphor as Experience and History in American Life and Letters*. Chapel Hill: University of North Carolina Press.

Machor, James L. (1987). *Pastoral Cities: Urban Ideals and the Symbolic Landscape of America*. Madison: University of Wisconsin Press.

Marx, Leo (1964). *The Machine in the Garden: Technology and the Pastoral Ideal in America*. New York and Oxford: Oxford University Press.

Miller, Perry (1967). *Nature's Nation*. Cambridge, Mass.: Belknap/Harvard University Press.

Ryan, Mary P. (1990). *Women in Public: Between Banners and Ballots, 1825–1880*. Baltimore: Johns Hopkins University Press.

Sennett, Richard, and Thernstrom, Stephan, eds. (1969). *Nineteenth-Century Cities: Essays in the New Urban History*. New Haven: Yale University Press.

Siegel, Adrienne (1981). *The Image of the American City in Popular Literature, 1820–1870*. Port Washington: Kennikat.

Stansell, Christine (1986). *City of Women: Sex and Class in New York: 1789–1860*. New York: Knopf.

Stout, Janis P. (1976). *Sodoms in Eden: The City in American Fiction before 1860*. Westport, Conn.: Greenwood.

Tester, Keith, ed. (1994). *The Flâneur*. New York: Routledge.

Thomas, M. Wynn (1994). "Whitman's Tale of Two Cities." *American Literary History* 4: 6, 633–57.

Warner, Sam Bass, Jr. (1972). *The Urban Wilderness: A History of the American City*. New York: Harper & Row.

White, Morton, and White, Lucia (1962). *The Intellectual Versus the City*. Cambridge, Mass.: Harvard University Press.

Wilentz, Sean (1984). *Chants Democratic: New York City and the Rise of the American Working Class, 1788–1850*. New York: Oxford University Press.

26

New Landscapes

Timothy Sweet

Since its origin, the English novel has been associated with interiors. Indeed, scholars have argued that the novel participated in the simultaneous invention of the interior physical space of the domestic sphere and the psychological interiority of the modern individual who is at home in this space.[1] In England's American colonies, for so long as the population remained largely confined to the eastern seaboard the novel generally remained indoors, as in Samuel Richardson's *Pamela* (1740), the first novel printed in America and among the most popular during the colonial era. After the Revolution, the novel confronted American exteriors as Anglo-Americans began to colonize the new landscapes of the trans-Appalachian West.

We can think of the novel as conceptualizing space in terms of perceptual geography, as "social relations stretched out," particular places appearing as "articulated moments in networks of social relations and understanding."[2] The novel continued to be adept at the evaluation of interiors as manifestations of such "articulated moments," for example cordoning off the privileged space of home from the realms of vice, ignorance, poverty, unfeeling fashion, and so on. As the novel extended this evaluative process to exterior space, it engaged with several cultural schemata, two of which we will examine here. One, stadialist social theory, was relatively new. Another, the pastoral literary mode, was ancient, but took on a new form in America.

Stadialist social theory, developed by French and Scottish Enlightenment philosophers, posited that human society progressed historically through a series of stages correlated to economic modes. Antoine-Nicolas de Condorcet, for example, identified four such stages: a nomadic, savage state based on hunting; a migratory, patriarchal–tribal state based on herding; a sedentary, civilized state based on horticulture; and a sedentary–mobile, civilized state based on commerce. While the theory gained currency in America in more or less its European form, as illustrated for example by Thomas Cole's famous sequence of landscape paintings *The Course of Empire* (1834–6), it was also modified in its application to American space.[3]

Americans imagined that they could see the whole history of progress embodied on the North American continent. Thomas Jefferson, for example, described a hypothetical "philosophic observer" journeying from the Rocky Mountains to the Atlantic seaboard, encountering farthest west Native American hunter–savages; then a Hispanic herding culture; next, within the borders of the United States, "our own semi-barbarous citizens, the pioneers of the advance of civilization"; and so on through "the gradual shades of improving man," culminating in "the most improved state in our seaport towns."[4] Whether those "semi-barbarous" Western "pioneers" were the same farmers that Jefferson had earlier characterized as guardians of the republic's virtue in *Notes on the State of Virginia* (1785) remained unclear when the landscape was viewed at such an abstract level.

Other American stadialists gave a more situated sense of the transformation of environment and culture. The Philadelphia physician and educator Benjamin Rush, for example, saw the progress of American civilization exemplified in the settlement of western Pennsylvania by three successive classes of farmers. Rush correlated moral assessments of exteriors and interiors through a telling identification of detail from landscapes and domestic spaces, production patterns, and consumption patterns, arguing that in the permanent establishment of a class of market-oriented agrarians, "we behold civilization completed." Although Rush's narrative was soon satirized in Charles Brockden Brown's *Edgar Huntly* (1799), it expressed a prevalent understanding of westward settlement (Rush 1798: 221; and see Sweet 2002: 97–121).

The architect Andrew Jackson Downing's theory of design brought stadialism home to middle-class Americans. Linking spatial and psychological interiority, Downing asserted that "man's dwelling" was "the type of his whole private life." Thus in its design, construction, landscaping, furnishing, and domestic arrangements, a home ought to demonstrate that "it is intended not only for the physical wants of man, but for his moral, social, and intellectual existence" (Downing 1969: 22, 23). Carrying this evaluation of space outward, Downing told a story of cultural refinement:

> So long as men are forced to dwell in log huts and follow a hunter's life, we must not be surprised at lynch law and the use of the bowie knife. But, when smiling lawns and tasteful cottages begin to embellish a country, we know that order and culture are established.... it must follow that the interest manifested in the Rural Architecture of a country like this, has much to do with the progress of its civilization. (Downing 1969: xix)[5]

Like Rush, Downing linked discourses that were often divided along gender lines: men writing economic analyses and agricultural or architectural manuals, women writing treatises on domestic economy and conduct books. The novel, with its capacity to assimilate a variety of discourses, provided a similar threshold enabling communication between interiors and exteriors, while shaping those interiors and exteriors in terms of domestic ideals.[6]

Idealized images of rural life such as Downing developed have a long genealogy in the pastoral mode. Particularly in its differentiation from the georgic (the literature of rural labor), the pastoral sorts inhabitants and travelers in the rural landscape by class. Pertinent here are two related operations, both implicated in the construction and maintenance of class distinctions.[7] One is a spatial movement that identifies the rural setting as a site of retreat, restoration, and so on, which depends on the perspective of a certain class-based mobility (in English tradition, the movement of the gentry between town and country). The second operation is a screening process in which the rural scene of beauty or bounty is dissociated from the material activities that create and maintain it. Extending this logic to interiors, Downing's domestic–pastoral designs removed housework from sight, for example locating the kitchen as far as possible from the parlor and screening the vegetable garden (see Brown 1990: 76–7). However, while the esthetics of the screening process and the rural retreat often work to obscure any clear view of the social formation prevailing, we should remember that the *locus classicus* of pastoral, Virgil's first eclogue, opens with a dialogue about land redistribution in the aftermath of the Roman civil wars. A concern with social formation was there from the outset. Since the American class structure differed from the English – having not been embedded in the same way, over centuries, into the form of the American landscape – the pastoral mode's historic assumptions could potentially be complicated by its engagement with rural America.

William Hill Brown's *The Power of Sympathy* (1789), often considered to be the first American novel, sets up an abstract pastoral opposition between urban vice and rural virtue, although without particularly developing the implications of setting. Gilbert Imlay's *The Emigrants* (1793) explores this scheme more deeply, looking westward to lay out a set of issues that would preoccupy American novelists through the ante-bellum era.

The Emigrants imagines the establishment of a utopian republic in the trans-Appalachian West. Imlay posits the mountains as a moral and political divide: everything to the east is tainted by association with Europe, while the West offers the prospect of "begin[ning] the world afresh." The plot sorts the characters in two directions: the virtuous end up in the utopian community of Bellefont, while the vicious are returned to England. The Western American landscape is accordingly differentiated through the voice of the heroine, Caroline. Critical alike of English country "walks in shady groves," where one experiences "a continual sameness which insensibly produces *ennui*" and of "the promenades of London" which are invariably overcrowded, spoiling all pleasure and conversation, Caroline finds the mountain landscape near Pittsburgh to offer "a continual feast for the mind." Her picturesque sensibility contrasts with the more pragmatic view taken by her suitor, Capt. Arl—ton, who imposes regular order on the landscape, laying out the community in a tract of sixteen by sixteen square miles (a refinement even of the grid system of the Northwest Ordinance of 1787). As Caroline and Arl—ton are united in marriage, however, the two landscape esthetics harmonize at Bellefont: an "elevated prospect" reveals "the charms of cultivation contrasted by the beauties of wildness."

The political analogue of this "elevated prospect" is occupied by Capt. Arl—ton, who settles the republic with Revolutionary War veterans from whom he expects deference (no memory of Shays' Rebellion here) and by his former commander, General W—, who agrees to serve as first president.[8] The specifically agrarian base comments on emerging stadialist theories. At several points it is suggested that English corruption derives from "the aggrandisement of commerce," by which "every principle of the human heart seems to have been contaminated." Where European stadialists often posited the commercial state as the pinnacle of civilization, Imlay imagines the Western space of agrarian virtue as a temporal return, in which one might regain "the appearance of an Ancient Briton," with all its connotation of fundamental liberties – but without going through any intervening stages. The backwoods farmers at St. Vincent (Vincennes, Indiana), for example, are straight from the most artificial pastoral, their "*naiveté*" being said to embody the natural "sprightliness of the country" such that "you would believe you was [*sic*] living in those Arcadian days, when the tuneful shepherd used to compose sonnets to his mistress."

If Imlay parallels Jefferson in giving a rather abstract view of the Western land and colonists, James Fenimore Cooper parallels Rush in looking more minutely at a local manifestation. *The Pioneers* (1823) describes the settlement of a frontier community in extensive detail, and without utopian pretensions. However, the proprietorial perspective of Imlay's characters remains, given realistic subjectivity in the character of Judge Marmaduke Temple. Drawing on childhood recollections of Cooperstown as well as the pastoral tradition for his imagery, Cooper sets plots of romance, inheritance, and legal conflict against a backdrop of the repeated seasonal rhythms of rural life.[9] Chapters 1, 3, and 21 provide a stadialist frame for the main action (which takes place in 1793–4), depicting the same landscape in its wilderness state prior to the Revolution and again in the present of 1823, when "neat and comfortable farms, with every indication of wealth about them" surround "beautiful and thriving villages."

Interiors correspond to exteriors not only for Natty Bumppo, whose true home (to simplify matters) is the wilderness itself, but especially for Judge Temple: "Duke" as he is tellingly called throughout. Although architecturally awkward owing to frontier exigencies, Duke's great stone "castle" is distinctly antithetical to the "republican" spirit that A. J. Downing called for in rural architecture (see Downing 1969: 257–70). Christmas dinner is accordingly lavish, worthy of an English country-house poem, yet through want of a discerning woman's management (Elizabeth has not been present to direct the cook's efforts), it is not fully domestic: "the object seemed to be profusion, and it was obtained entirely at the expense of order and elegance." We do not see inside the cabins of the Judge's tenant farmers, nor do we see the landscape through their eyes. The tavern provides a composite interior space, however, admitting men of all classes and providing a venue for the public expression of democratic sentiments, albeit tempered by the Judge's presence. The proprietorial perspective is extended to the next generation through the resolution of the inheritance plot and Elizabeth's marriage to Oliver Effingham. Cooper would explore this perspective further in the *Littlepage* trilogy (1845–6), the last novel of which, *Redskins*, pits tenants against landlords during the anti-rent agitation of the 1840s in upstate New York.

The contrast in landscape esthetics that we have seen in *The Emigrants* is treated with greater complexity in *The Pioneers* and integrated into the plot, Natty's wilderness values posing a challenge to Temple's vision. The Judge and his cousin, Sheriff Richard Jones, are both pragmatists like Capt. Arl—ton, valuing the land as a repository of resources; but where Richard promotes projects only with an eye to short-term gain, Temple holds a more far-sighted view, hoping for example to preserve his maple trees by developing commercial sugar production rather than burning them for potash. A picturesque sensibility is similarly evident in moderate and extreme versions. Through Elizabeth's eyes we admire middle landscapes, such as a prospect of the "golden lustre" of Templeton illuminated by a clear winter sunrise.[10] This esthetic's compatibility with Temple's pragmatism is evident early on when Elizabeth sees the settlements "enlarging under her eye" as he directs her gaze. Natty, of course, despises the so-called "betterments and clearings." "None know how often the hand of God is seen in the wilderness, but them that rove it for a man's life," he reflects, recalling a scene that may have inspired Thomas Cole's painting *Falls of the Kaaterskill* (1826): "It is a spot to make a man solemnize." The economic and environmental implications of these respective positions are explored in many of the novel's scenic incidents, such as the pigeon shoot or the visit to the sugar-bush, as well as in the plot, the conflict over "rights" that eventually removes Natty westward.

In *The Prairie* (1827) Cooper undertakes a more formal exploration of stadialist theory by developing a set of characters who represent the second, herding stage, which had necessarily been omitted from *The Pioneers'* narrative of wilderness colonization.[11] Cooper's pastoralists, the Bush clan, are not classical Arcadians, but migratory, patriarchal tribesmen derived from Old Testament imagery. Their opposition to agrarian settlement is evident in the captivity plot, which (implausibly) takes all the characters out to the western Nebraska prairie, as well as in cultural details such as Ishmael Bush's views on landownership: "This is not nature, and I deny that it is law." Each stage articulates its own understanding of "nature" in accordance with its economic mode – Natty and the Pawnee Hard-Heart speaking for the wilderness, and Duncan Middleton and Paul Hover assuming our familiar sense of land as property.

The setting, so far beyond the region of white settlement in the novel's present of 1804 (or even Cooper's present of 1827), enables the conflicts among the representatives of the stages to unfold rather abstractly. Thus freeing the novel's primary landscapes from immediate economic signification, Cooper appropriates them for pure moral symbolism. For example, the "solitary," blighted willow tree that Ishmael chooses as a gallows for the execution of Abiram White "proclaimed the frailty of existence, and the fulfilment of time." In the longest perspective, this image evokes the cyclical stadialism of Cole's *Course of Empire*, rather than the teleological version of Jefferson or Rush. In the immediate moment, it suggests the barrenness of the Bush clan's values. Economic resonances remain nevertheless, connecting this passage to Natty's earlier observation on the nature of the Western environment: "these wastes have been spread, where a garden may have been created." The resolution of the captivity plot sends most of the characters back to the fertile settlements of Kentucky. Some of the Bush clan are thus "reclaimed from their lawless and semi-barbarous lives," but Ishmael continues to wander like his Old Testament namesake and is "never heard of more." Since Ellen "would be more like the flourishing flower in the sun of a clearing than in the winds of a prairie," she and Paul also return to Kentucky, where through Middleton's "patronage" Paul becomes "a prosperous cultivator of the soil" and politician.

Timothy Flint's *George Mason, the Young Backwoodsman* (1829) also returns its central characters eastward in the end, invoking domestic values to comment on pastoral and stadialist assumptions. The plot concerns the family of a New England clergyman who emigrate to Mississippi in 1816 under illusions of "pastoral enjoy-ments and pursuits" gathered from "the romances of Imlay and Chateaubriand" (see the latter's *Atala*, 1801). Although the clergy are said to "constitute the connecting link between the rich and the poor," the Masons find it difficult to adjust to the Western class structure. The planters are wealthy in land and slaves, but the Masons find their manners "outlandish." The locals in turn dislike the Revd. Mason's "college-learning preaching" and consider the family "mighty proud." As the Masons thus close themselves off from their neighbors' society, they open up to nature through "a private course of worship" – long walks in the woods, during which the Reverend finds "every object" to "furnish a theme for a lecture on natural history, or a warm and home-felt sermon on the goodness and wisdom of the Almighty." Although their nature esthetic is represented as preferable to that of their neighbors (who spend the Sabbath hunting and fishing), the Masons never establish a secure economic relation to the land. Nor do they become comfortable at rural amusements such as camp meetings and horse races, although these always take place in beautiful natural settings. Indeed, much of the plot concerns the family's resistance to integration into the local community, especially after the Revd. Mason dies and the marriage of young Elizabeth to a planter's son seems their only route to escape from poverty. George, however, initiates a trajectory that will return the family eastward, taking a position as steamboat clerk. Here the novel's rhetoric of landscape description shifts from spiritualized picturesque to technological sublime – as the technology of the steam-boat will enable the Masons' escape from the rural scene.[12] The long anti-pastoral interlude ends when George, now a captain, secures the family in "a handsome house, in a large and thriving village" near Louisville (that is, near the site of Imlay's Bellefont), which offers "a higher class, and respectable society." George's marriage to a Pennsylvania heiress confirms the family's Eastern cultural allegiance.

The Masons' inability to make themselves at home in the West suggests an important aspect of the cultural work of domesticity. Domesticity is commonly defined in opposition to the marketplace. In westering novels such as this, domesti-city particularly addresses the disruptions posed by Americans' unprecedented geographic as well as economic mobility (downward as well as upward). Mobility is a precondition of the pastoral perspective, as we have seen, yet here its threatening aspect is balanced by the stadialist narrative's promise of cultural refinement. A. J. Downing, for example, asserted that his designs created a "counterpoise to the great tendency toward constant changes" in American economic and social life.[13]

Hope for such a counterpoise animates Caroline Kirkland's narrative of the land boom in frontier Michigan, *A New Home, Who'll Follow?* (1839). Although Kirkland opens by dispelling pastoral illusions, the pastoral returns in another form through an implicit stadialist narrative very like Rush's. The narrator, Mrs. Mary Clavers, laments the lack of domesticity, "that *home*-feeling," among the first settlers: "the man who holds himself ready to accept the first advantageous offer, will not be very solicitous to provide those minor accommodations, which, though essential to domestic comfort, will not add to the moneyed value of his farm" (emphasis in original).[14] As the wife of a land speculator (as was Kirkland herself), Mrs. Clavers fails to acknowledge her own implication in this economy, which left little choice to farmers who possessed no liquid capital. Contrasting with these cash-poor first-wave settlers are the Beckworths, the Brents, and the Hastings, who come west with enough capital to buy an already improved farm, employ tenants to work it for them "on shares," and have it shaped according to Eastern patterns. This class embodies the domestic–pastoral ideal. The Beckworths' farm – its "noble, yankee" house and "inviting door-yard, filled to profusion with shrubs and flowers," surrounded by expansive "fields of grain, well fenced and stumpless" – presents a "scene . . . of *Eastern* enchantment" (emphasis in original). The story of Cora and Everard Hastings reverts to a pastoral romance of the sort earlier dispelled as illusory, but by now the work of refinement has progressed to the point where such narratives can be accommodated. Those of the most "vicious and degraded" class, such as the Newlands, have been forced westward. Log cabins "are becoming scarce" and "all the proper materials are at hand" for the "formation of a[n] . . . aristocracy," as Mrs. Clavers remarks with tongue only partly in cheek.

Such an "aristocracy" – a trans-local middle class, which identified itself with the East and maintained itself through a culture of gentility – became established in the Midwest by the late 1840s or early 1850s.[15] The transformation is evident in Alice Cary's *Clovernook* sketches (1852, 1853), which are often said to give the first realistic account of the West in American literature – and are, in any case, the first to delineate the suburban, border landscape that would come to be associated with the middle class (see Smith 1970: 230–8; Kolodny 1984: 178–89; Stilgoe 1988: 56–7). Many of the earlier sketches open on bountiful agricultural landscapes, and here Cary begins to explore the complexities involved in correlating exteriors with interiors. In "Peter Harris," for example, a harvest scene in which "every thing betokened plenty" ironically frames a tale of narrowness and meanness in the death of a little boy – an idea revisited in the second series in the more fully realized "Uncle Christopher's." By the end of the first series, suburban "cottages and villas have thickened" the landscape. Mr. Harmstead's new estate, Willowdale, "with its level meadows, nicely trimmed groves, picturesque gardens, winding walks and shrubberies, would not be recognised

Figure 26.1 Title-page from Mrs. C. M. Kirkland, *A Book for the Home Circle* (New York: Charles Scribner, 1853). Collection of Shirley Samuels.

by the proprietor, who, twelve or fourteen years ago, ploughed around blackened stumps, and through patches of briers and thistles." From the perspective developed here, the region appears in retrospect as "thinly settled and ill-cultivated." Harmstead's "predecessors of the same rank had lived in selfish isolation," like Mr. Middleton, a "descendant of one of the royalist families of the Revolution," who in "aristocratic" fashion keeps "deer in his orchard" and elicits "deference" from the neighbors. Thus Harmstead's estate would seem to betoken greater sociability, especially after the death of his wife ("never...much a favorite" among the neighbors). Yet the class barrier proves no easier to cross, as the schoolteacher Ellie hopes in vain for a proposal of marriage. Although Harmstead has acted as a "pioneer of elegance and refinement," encouraging friends from the East "to build houses and cultivate grounds," he himself moves into Cincinnati, finding no suitable second wife among the country girls. Class lines, as Cary remarks elsewhere, "are very sharply defined," and happy marriages across them are accordingly rare. "Two Visits," from the second series, narrates such a transformation on a more modest scale by contrasting the Knights, whose attachment to the old pioneering ways is evident in their slovenly farmstead and "comfortless" (although new) brick house, with their tenant Mrs. Lytle, who despite reduced circumstances has transformed the Knights' original log cabin into a cozy home with picturesque garden, which "contrasted well with the showy vulgarity of many more pretending houses."[16]

Other sketches in the second series reveal an increasing differentiation of the landscape. "Mrs. Wetherbe's Quilting Party" takes us from the rural hinterland through the "suburban gardens of this basin rimmed with hills," past smoky "candle and soap factories" and noisy "slaughter-houses," toward two destinations. One is a fashionable residential district in the city where Mrs. Wetherbe visits her niece: the Randalls residence lacks all signs of domestic virtue, for "the possession of wealth had...given scope to their natural meanness, without in the least diminishing their vulgarity." Some of the sketch's conflict concerns Mrs. Randalls' attempt to impose her fashionable ways on the usual arrangements of a quilting bee. The second destination, also contrasting with Mrs. Wetherbe's neat country home, is a "dingy," five-story tenement, where "dish-water, washing suds, and every thing else, from tea and coffee grounds to all manner of picked bones and other refuse, were washed down from these tiers of balconies to the ground below, so that a more filthy and in all ways unendurable spectacle can scarcely be imagined." Here live the family of Jenny, one of the Randalls servants. The romance plot brings Jenny out to the country to unite her with Helph, a blacksmith. Not tied by Helph's trade to a particular piece of ground, the couple live happily ever after in the suburban middle landscape between country and city, in a "very pretty" cottage of "cream-white walls" surrounded by "clematis and jasmine, and the clambering stalks of roses." Like Kirkland's, then, Cary's sketches of character and incident overlay a narrative of progressive refinement generally driven by Eastern capital, but that narrative is complicated by Cary's own position as a Western expatriate among the New York literati.

The consolidation of middle-class hegemony in the Midwest provided a frame for the "spate of women's novels set on western landscapes" that, as Annette Kolodny observes, "became so popular in the 1850s."[17] The protagonists of E. D. E. N. Southworth's *India: The Pearl of Pearl River* (1856) and Maria Cummins' *Mabel Vaughan* (1857), for example, do not witness a transformation, but rather emigrate to a West that is ready to receive them. Southworth uses the perspective of the new West to examine the culture of the South. Her protagonist, Mark Sutherland, emancipates his slaves and (after some knocking about) takes over a law practice established by a college friend in the West. The plot thus moves through three landscapes, each with corresponding interiors: "Cashmere," a richly verdant Mississippi cotton plantation described as "the Elysium of the sunny south"; a high valley plantation in Virginia's Blue Ridge, which "had not the luxurious beauty of the south, nor the fresh and vigorous life of the west"; and a Western river town evidently modeled on Prairie du Chien, Wisconsin, where Southworth lived for four years. In the latter setting, Mark and his new bride Rosalie try a "vigorous life" for one winter in a country cabin, then move to "Rose Cottage," a comfortable, two-story frame house with pleasant rose gardens "on the outskirts of town," where Rosalie's domestic arrangements are aided by two servants. Western pastoral displaces Southern in the end, as Mark revisits "Cashmere" to find failed crops, blighted orchards, "forests, and shrubberies, and grasses . . . and the very earth . . . *calcined* by the dry and burning heat" (emphasis in original). Despite a three-year drought, the banks of the once beautiful Pearl river are eroding, the "red and pulverized earth . . . sliding in and discolouring and thickening" its formerly "pellucid waters." Inside the mansion, "rust and must, mildew and canker, had crept over all." The human counterpart to these physical spaces is the dissipated St. Gerald Ashley, whom we first see "bloated and slothful . . . lazily reclining . . . with his right arm around the waist of a pretty, frightened quadroon girl." Sutherland thus wonders if his native Mississippi had "really ever been so beautiful. . . . Or had its beauty been only the glamour thrown over the scene by youth, and love, and hope?" For all the contrast is pressed, however, the opening descriptions of "Cashmere" remain more vivid and attractive than any subsequent scene in Virginia or the West. Moreover (in a novel that seems to want to comment on slavery) we see little of the substructure of labor that shapes the respective landscapes.

Domestic pastorals such as *India* and *Mabel Vaughan* further interiorize the signification of landscape by developing certain implications of the picturesque esthetic hinted at in earlier novels, as for example in Caroline's implicit identification with the landscape itself in *The Emigrants* (see Seelye 1991: 154–60). During the Blue Ridge interlude in *India*, Rosalie explicitly identifies a key to the development of her nature when she discovers "a new flower" that fails when transplanted to a conservatory, but thrives on a rocky mountain top, "exposed to all the snow, and wind, . . . and burning rays of summer." Drawing the analogy inward – "I am like that plant!" – Rosalie realizes that she has been overprotected by her mother in the luxurious South and is ready to emigrate westward with Mark Sutherland.

Cummins' *Mabel Vaughan* elaborates and spiritualizes this opening of self to, and through, external nature. Mabel's father has lost the family fortune through land speculation and is living on what remains of the investment in Illinois. At this trying time in Mabel's life (the New York mansion has been sold, she had been betrayed by Lincoln Dudley, her alcoholic brother's reformation is not yet assured), she must journey west to join her family. Stopping in Niagara to view the falls, she experiences a cathartic "natural outburst" of "uncontrolled weeping" that "relieved" her "strained nerves," freeing her to hear the voice of God and, under the tutelage of Mrs. Percival, to recognize his "providence" in these troubles. This episode prepares her to experience a similar, "strengthen[ing]" sense of divinity in the "boundless" landscapes of the West. However, only at the moment of Mabel's reconnection to the Percivals, which leads to her marriage to Bayard and thus to the restoration of her original class position, does the narrative open onto a fully realized landscape. The "expansive view" from the Percivals' Illinois estate, Lake Farm, and the "reflection" of this view "in Mabel's eyes" elicits a distinctive emotional response which – when affirmed by Mrs. Percival – signals that Mabel belongs here. She shares with Mrs. Percival not only a sensitivity to divinity in nature, to which the view from Lake Farm offers special access, but a counterbalancing appreciation of domestic space as well. The Percivals' mansion, furnished with "old family plate" and other "ancestral heirlooms" from their New York residence, offers respite from all that is "wear[ying]" in the "rough, new, and undeveloped character of . . . Western life," as well as replacing what has been lost to Mabel in the Vaughans' fall from fortune.

In the threshold thus presented by the Percival estate – opening inward to the Eastern continuity of family and class status, and outward to an encompassing view of the Western landscape – *Mabel Vaughan* reanimates the proprietorial esthetic that is variably configured in Imlay, Cooper, and Kirkland. Cooper had entertained an alternative in Natty's wilderness esthetic, which depends on the absence of any economic association in the landscape. By contrast, the domestication of the wilderness esthetic in the spiritualized picturesque of Flint or Cummins seems not to depend on any particular economic configuration – even though such an esthetic is available only to a narrative's privileged characters, never to the local rustics. This retreat from economics, which is enabled by economic privilege, marks a significant era in the history of American pastoral.

Notes

1 On the novel's involvement in the constitutive association of domesticity and interiority, see Tompkins 1985: 147–85; Armstrong 1987; Brown 1990.

2 For an introduction to perceptual geography, see Massey 1994; quotations are taken from pp. 2, 164.

3 On American adaptations of stadialism, including the influence of Condorcet, see Smith 1970: 211–50; Dekker 1987: 73–98. Wilton and Barringer (2002: 98–109) provide color reproductions of *The Course of Empire* series with explanatory narratives. Cole curiously omits the agrarian state,

which was particularly relevant to the American situation.

4 Thomas Jefferson, letter to William Ludlow, Sept. 6, 1824; quoted in Dekker 1987: 81–2. Discussion of Jefferson's discursive removal of Native Americans beyond US borders and related issues is beyond the scope of the present essay.

5 On Downing's influence, see Foster 1975: 51–131; Stilgoe 1988: passim.

6 Kaplan's concept of "Manifest Domesticity" is suggestive here: see 2002: 23–50.

7 This critique of pastoral draws on Williams 1973. On the distinction between pastoral and georgic, see Sweet 2002: esp. 2–6.

8 Watts (2002: 41–7) discusses the elitist subtext in this republican plan.

9 On Cooper's use of memory and history, see Taylor 1985.

10 On the esthetics of the "middle landscape," the cultivated space between wilderness and city, see Marx 1964.

11 On Cooper and stadialism, see Smith 1970: 218–22; Dekker 1987: 84–96.

12 On the technological sublime, see Marx 1964: 145–353.

13 Downing, *A Treatise on the Theory and Practice of Landscape Gardening* (1841), quoted in Brown 1990: 77.

14 On Kirkland's commitment to domesticity, particularly in the form of consumerism, see Merish 2000: 88–115. On the economics of pioneer farming, see Sweet 2002: 97–121.

15 See Mahoney 1999. Watts (2002) interprets this transformation as the effect of Yankee colonialism.

16 Stilgoe 1988: 69–77 documents antebellum-era complaints about farmers' disregard for landscape esthetics.

17 Kolodny 1984: 111. On *India*, see pp. 202–13; on *Mabel Vaughan*, pp. 213–23.

REFERENCES

Armstrong, N. (1987). *Desire and Domestic Fiction: A Political History of the Novel*. New York: Oxford University Press.

Brown, Gillian. (1990). *Domestic Individualism: Imagining Self in Nineteenth-Century America*. Berkeley: University of California Press.

Dekker, G. (1987). *The American Historical Romance*. Cambridge, UK: Cambridge University Press.

Downing, A. J. (1969). *The Architecture of Country Houses*. New York: Dover. (First publ. 1850.)

Foster, E. H. (1975). *The Civilized Wilderness: Backgrounds to American Romantic Literature, 1817–1860*. New York: Macmillan/Free Press.

Kaplan, Amy (2002). *The Anarchy of Empire in the Making of US Culture*. Cambridge, Mass.: Harvard University Press.

Kolodny, Annette (1984). *The Land before Her: Fantasy and Experience of the American Frontiers, 1630–1860*. Chapel Hill: University of North Carolina Press.

Mahoney, T. (1999). *Provincial Lives: Middle-Class Experience in the Antebellum Middle West*. Cambridge, UK: Cambridge University Press.

Marx, L. (1964). *The Machine in the Garden: Technology and the Pastoral Ideal in America*. New York and Oxford: Oxford University Press.

Massey, D. (1994). *Space, Place, and Gender*. Minneapolis: University of Minnesota Press.

Merish, L. (2000). *Sentimental Materialism: Gender, Commodity Culture, and Nineteenth-Century American Literature*. Durham, NC: Duke University Press.

Rush, B. (1798). *Essays Literary, Moral, and Philosophical*. Philadelphia: Thomas & Samuel F. Bradford.

Seelye, John (1991). *Beautiful Machine: Rivers and the Republican Plan, 1755–1825*. New York: Oxford University Press.

Smith, H. N. (1970). *Virgin Land: The American West as Symbol and Myth*. 2nd edn. Cambridge, Mass.: Harvard University Press.

Stilgoe, J. (1988). *Borderland: Origins of the American Suburb, 1820–1939*. New Haven: Yale University Press.

Sweet, T. (2002). *American Georgics: Economy and Environment in Early American Literature*. Philadelphia: University of Pennsylvania Press.

Taylor, A. (1985). *William Cooper's Town: Power and Persuasion on the Frontier of the Early American Republic*. New York: Knopf.

Tompkins, Jane (1985). *Sensational Designs: The Cultural Work of American Fiction, 1790–1860*. New York: Oxford University Press.

Watts, Edward (2002). *An American Colony: Regionalism and the Roots of Midwestern Culture*. Athens: Ohio University Press.

Williams, Raymond (1973). *The Country and the City*. New York: Oxford University Press.

Wilton, A., and Barringer, T. (2002). *American Sublime: Landscape Painting in the United States, 1820–1880*. London and Princeton: Tate Publishing/Princeton University Press.

27

The Gothic Meets Sensation: Charles Brockden Brown, Edgar Allan Poe, George Lippard, and E. D. E. N. Southworth

Dana Luciano

In the second volume of Louisa May Alcott's *Little Women*, Jo March has a brief, intense, and educational encounter with the excesses of sensation fiction. At a public lecture, she notices a "studious looking lad" who is absorbed in a copy of a luridly illustrated paper called the *Weekly Volcano*. Seeing Jo's interest, the lad offers her part of the paper, and she finds herself immersed in "the usual labyrinth of love, mystery, and murder," reading a tale which "belonged to that class of light literature in which the passions have a holiday" (Alcott 1983: 330). As Jo peers at the story's "thickly sprinkled exclamation points," the studious-looking lad tells her that its author, one Mrs. S.L.A.N.G. Northbury, is so successful because she "knows just what folks like" (p. 331). Jo resolves to try her hand at this type of writing, and begins publishing gothic-inflected stories such as "The Phantom Hand" and "The Curse of the Coventrys." After moving to New York, she is engaged by the *Weekly Volcano* but, though the work pays steadily, she is ashamed enough to keep it a secret from her family and friends. Suspecting the truth, her mentor, Professor Bhaer, lectures her on the poisonous nature of such writing, telling her, "I would more rather give my boys gunpowder to play with than this bad trash" (p. 437). Chastened, Jo burns all her stories and turns to writing didactic fiction, for which she can find no publisher.

Alcott's fictionalized reflection on her own career in the 1860s as a writer of gothic/ sensational literature reiterates the antebellum critique of the "literature of excess," but with a noteworthy alteration. Gothic and sensation fiction, while wildly popular, continued, in the first half of the nineteenth century, to receive the opprobrium directed in the late eighteenth century at all fiction; critics charged that it was unhealthy and dangerous, particularly to young, impressionable, and/or female readers. While *Little Women* echoes this view, however, it does not adhere to the antebellum indictment of excessive fiction for providing a "false picture of reality." Indeed, what is most troubling about Jo's involvement in sensationalism is, it seems, the truth it allows her to see. Although Jo, as an inexperienced writer charged with the task of "harrowing up the souls of the readers" on a regular basis, initially ransacks the European gothic, populating her tales with "banditti, counts, gypsies, nuns and duchesses" (Alcott 1983: 430), she increasingly turns, in her search for soul-harrowing material, to the world around her, scanning the newspapers for crime stories, ransacking libraries for works on poison, and peering into the faces of strangers on the street. Through her research she acquires, to her detriment, a "premature acquaintance with the darker side of life, which comes soon enough to all of us" (p. 431). The problem with her work, then, is that it involves too *much* reality, not too little. Though writing sensation fiction initially leads Jo away from her own American world, in the end it plunges her back into its unhappy heart.

Like Jo's (and Alcott's) sensation stories, the writing of Charles Brockden Brown, Edgar Allan Poe, George Lippard, and Emma Dorothy Elizabeth Nevitte (E. D. E. N.) Southworth issues from the intersection of the disturbingly alien and the painfully familiar. The fiction these prolific writers composed spans nearly a century – Brockden Brown began publishing in the 1790s; E. D. E. N. Southworth published until the 1880s. And although it is not always set in precisely the same world its authors inhabited, it consistently engages, using gothic tropes and sensational techniques, the agonizing realities of everyday American life – the harsh pressures of market capitalism and the melancholy failures of the democratic ideal – as they etch themselves into the vulnerable bodies caught in narrative webs of seduction, deception, and betrayal.

"Gothic" vs. "Sensation"

The adjectives "gothic" and "sensational" designate literary genres that, while not identical, refuse simplistic principles of distinction. This is partly an effect of the increasing conceptual mobility of both terms, resulting from the upsurge in critical attention these genres have received as American cultural criticism has begun to take seriously Walt Whitman's 1851 assertion that such literature is "a power in the land . . . very deserving of more careful consideration than has hitherto been accorded to it" (quoted in Reynolds 1988: 189). But the slipperiness of the boundary between the two genres has a much longer history. Gothic, which emerged in Britain in the late eighteenth century and was adapted by early American novelists like Brockden Brown and John Neal, seeks to produce unease and fear in its readers, and hence has always relied on sensational strategies. And the writing we understand as "sensation fiction" proper, which emerged, in the United States, in tandem with the lurid penny papers and crime sheets that became popular in the 1830s and 1840s, cannot be fully understood without reference to the gothic tradition that preceded and shaped it and which it revitalized. Walter C. Phillips' classic definition of sensation literature, which frames the genre as a "popular development in [nineteenth-century] fiction in which the [gothic] novel of mystery is crossed with that of fashionable life" (Phillips 1919: 34), could justly be applied to much of the American gothic tradition itself, beginning with the pioneering work of Charles Brockden Brown, who published most of his fiction before the nineteenth century had technically begun. Brown maintained that the American novel ought to depict the American scene, and insisted that it should be not the European past but the American present – not "gothic castles and chimeras," but "a series of adventures growing out of the condition of our country... the incidents of Indian hostility, and the perils of the Western wilderness" – that should form the basis of the American romance. Brown's reasoning was twofold: the American setting would, he believed, offer more accurate views to the "moral [psychological] painter"; and it would prove novel enough to capture the attention of the American reading public whose favor he hoped to win (Brown 1998: 641).

Brown's work was not especially popular during his lifetime, though critics praised him for his skill at creating sensational effects; as one anonymous reviewer of the first biography of Brown commented in 1819: "No reader would leave Wieland unfinished... nor Edgar Huntly... If we do not return to them, it is to avoid suffering, and not that they want fascination, and a terrible one, if we are willing to encounter it more than once" (Rosenthal 1981: 30). But if the American literary marketplace was not yet ready, at the turn of the nineteenth century, to have its attention ravished by the kind of thrills Brown's fiction delivered, by the 1830s the taste for sensationalism was a market force to be reckoned with. Inspired by (and often included in) the scandal sheets, trial reports, confessions, and criminal biographies that rose to popularity in the early 1830s, when the first American "penny papers" were founded, making daily doses of sensation available to working-class readers, sensation literature formed the base of what was increasingly understood as a three-tiered literary marketplace, with the middle tier occupied by sentimental writing, aimed at the middle-class reader, and "elite" literature defining itself against both popular currents (see Streeby 2002). Critics of sensational writing charged that it taught readers to contemplate, if not to perform, the kinds of acts it described; that it agitated the excitable constitutions of highly strung readers; and that it was addictive, habituating its readers to its excesses and spoiling them for more sober fare. Even Nathaniel Hawthorne's son described his father's penchant for sensational literature – he avidly consumed penny papers and criminal biographies – as a "pathetic craving" (quoted in Reynolds 1988: 171). Sensational writing created, as Michael Denning has pointed out, its own public sphere among the urban working-class readers who enthusiastically discussed the day's scandals and each weekly installment of the latest spine-tingling romance. But middle-class readers were also drawn to sensational literature, intrigued, no doubt, by the stinging editorial condemnations of the "scandalmongers" that appeared in their respectable journals. Sensational literature became, in a sense, the uncanny double of sentimental fiction, which attempted to produce the "fellow-feeling" necessary to a democratic nation by moving the reader to tears (see Samuels 1992); like the sentimental text, sensation stories also attempted to move the reader, but the embodied responses they sought emphasized a range of passions, insisting, against the putative disembodiment of the rational bourgeois public sphere, on the undeniable carnality of the readerly body.

Charles Brockden Brown (1771–1810)

Best remembered for his gothic work – four novels, two novel fragments, and a number of short stories – Charles Brockden Brown also published two sentimental novels, a dialogue on women's rights, and countless essays on political, moral, and esthetic questions. Born to a middle-class Quaker family in Philadelphia in 1771, Brown was given a solid literary and classical education, and as a young man fed his appetite for knowledge by participating in societies devoted to the exchange of ideas. At the behest of his family, he began reading law in 1789 in preparation for a legal career, but found the work stifling. Complaining to friends of the law's "endless tautologies, its impertinent circuities, its lying assertions and hateful artifices" (Warfel 1949: 29), he devoted as much time as possible to his literary pursuits. This period of his life was also marked by a number of attachments to both women and men. Brown began to court a series of young women, but his parents opposed each of these relationships because the women were not Quaker. He also developed passionate romantic friendships with several young men, including William Woods Wilkins, Joseph Bringhurst, Jr., and, later, Elihu Hubbard Smith, a physician and member of the Friendly Club, a New York-based society that debated moral, political, and scientific issues, which Brown attended whenever he was in the city. These attachments are paralleled in his novels, whose heterosexual relationships are often tense and abortive, frustrated by indecision or external obstacles, and which feature, as well, memorably intense homoerotic bonds.

In 1793, the year a yellow fever epidemic devastated Philadelphia, Brown abandoned the law and began writing seriously. For the first few years he met with little success; then, in 1798, he began to be published, releasing the first part of *Alcuin: A Dialogue*, an epistolary debate on women's rights, in April and *Wieland: Or, The Transformation* in September of that year. In July 1798 he moved to New York City, but left it after contracting a case of yellow fever during an outbreak that summer, interrupting the progress of his serialized novel *Memoirs of Stephen Calvert*, which remained unfinished. His friend Elihu Smith died of the fever during the same outbreak. After Smith's death Brown entered a period of intense productivity, composing and publishing the remaining three of his major novels within a three-year span. Traces of Brown's relationship with Smith surface in these novels: for example, the advice given by the rational and pragmatic physician Sarsefield to Edgar Huntly echoes many of Smith's statements to Brown; and the action of *Arthur Mervyn* is interrupted by a heartrending lament for a young man dead of yellow fever.

Like *Wieland*, these novels were in the gothic mode, though Brown eschewed the term because of its European associations and because he found most English gothic romances insupportably trite. He avoided both the supernatural and the Radcliffean gothic, which he parodied in an essay called "A Receipt for a Modern Romance":

> Take an old castle; pull down a part of it, and allow the grass to grow on the battle-ments . . . Pour a sufficiently heavy amount of rain upon the hinges and bolts of the gates, so that when they are attempted to be opened, they may creak most fearfully. Next take an old man and woman, and employ them to sleep in a part of this castle, and provide them with frightful stories . . . Convey to the castle a young lady; consign her to the care of the old man and woman, who must relate to her all they know, that is, all they do not know . . . (Brown 1992: 8)

Brown's gothic, rather, is one in which the ostensible openness of the American landscape and the transparency of the American democratic social arena are countered by an inescapable claustrophobia, which creates the conditions for the contagion of countless disorders – physical, psychological, and political – that develop out of unresolved social contradictions. His narratives explore the limits of the rational world, relying for their sensational effects on bizarre natural phenomena – ventrilo-quism and spontaneous combustion in *Wieland*, sleepwalking in *Edgar Huntly* (1799) – and on the medical and moral terrors of the plague- and conspiracy-ridden city in *Ormond* (1799) and *Arthur Mervyn* (1800). These phenomena, and, more importantly, the savage violence that they bring about (Wieland, believing that he hears the voice of God, murders his wife and children and pursues his sister Clara obsessively; Huntly, having sleepwalked into the woods at night, murders a series of Indians, initially in self-defense but eventually in sheer bloodlust; Arthur Mervyn is nearly buried alive by Philadelphians who think he has died of yellow fever and who want to get rid of his body) call into question the philosophical, political, and religious basis of the young republic. The religious fervor to which Wieland is heir (his father, a zealot, spontaneously combusted as a result of his intense faith) and the frontier violence to which Edgar so quickly becomes habituated suggest troublingly unre-solved aspects of America's history. The urban gothic novels, in turn, draw intricate pictures of the convolutions of the American social order, the false fronts and divided interiors that disable secure self-possession in the new nation. Business fraud and forgery feature prominently and the city is rife with political intrigue and conspiracy, including the shadowy presence of the Illuminati, a supposedly secret revolutionary order founded in Bavaria. These allusions to subversive foreigners, like the deranged Irish immigrant Clithero in *Edgar Huntly*, prefigure the concerns about the destabil-izing effects of foreign "influence" that would mark much of Brown's post-1800 political writing.

The instability of identity in Brown's gothic narratives confirms Eve Kosofsky Sedgwick's suggestion that in the gothic identities "are contagious metonymically, by touch" (Sedgwick 1986: 142). Characters in his fictions repeatedly become what they fear as a result of confronting that object. Constantia Dudley, after killing her tormentor, Ormond, begins to torment herself; Edgar Huntly becomes a sleepwalker after following one and a killer after seeking one. This tactile contagiousness operates not only within Brown's stories but also in the sensational narration of his novels. Brown's narrators generally insist that their readers must feel exactly what they have felt, and tell their tales as sensationally as possible in order to ensure that the reader will suffer along with them. Clara Wieland exclaims, "How will your wonder... be excited by my story! Every sentiment will yield to your amazement" (Brown 1998: 5). Edgar Huntly, more graphically, promises his fiancée, to whom his narrative is addressed, that "Thou wilt catch from my story every horror and every sympathy which it paints. Thou wilt shudder with my foreboding and dissolve with my tears... thou wilt share in all my tasks and all my dangers" (Brown 1998: 644). As Huntly's dual emphasis on horror and sympathy suggests, this transferential trauma echoes the sentimental circulation of benevolent fellow-feeling meant to support the self-regulating democracy.

After 1800, however, Brown consciously chose to tone down his writing, publishing two sentimental novels and promising, in the first edition of his *Literary Magazine and American Register*, that his prose would from now on be "free of voluptuousness or sensuality" and would "scrupulously aim at the promotion of public and private virtue" (Brown 1992: 128). In his later years he turned increasingly away from fiction, instead authoring historical and political tracts and works of geography. In February of 1810 he died of tuberculosis. Soon afterward, other writers began to develop an image of Brown as a figure of the melancholy, neglected American author, whose genius went unnoticed by the callous American marketplace. Richard Henry Dana, Sr., in an 1827 essay, lamented his appearance "in a new country, in which almost every individual was taken up in the eager pursuit of riches, or the hot and noisy contests of party politics" (repr. in Rosenthal 1981: 49). And George Lippard, in an 1848 essay dubbing him "the Broken-Hearted," lamented, "His books in any other civilized country but the United States, in any other enlightened city but Philadelphia, would have built a bridge over which the eloquent penster might have walked to Fame, and Wealth, and Honor; but here, in the United States, here in Philadelphia... Nobody knew him. Nobody cared for him" (Lippard 1986: 270–1). Brown, in this image, was a "martyr-author" who sacrificed himself for the good of a nascent American literary tradition, perpetually disappointed by the indifference of a public too busy with business to spare time for the work of the imagination.

Edgar Allan Poe (1809–1849)

By the 1830s, when Edgar Allan Poe began to publish his fiction, the American reading public's interest in sensational stories had grown prodigiously. Poe frequently commented on – and catered to – the public appetite for thrilling tales, acknowledging that he wrote primarily "with an eye to the paltry compensations, or the more paltry commendations, of mankind" (Reynolds 1998: 227). Poe's biography has itself become something of a sensational legend: his birth in Boston in 1809 to actor parents; his father's abandonment of the family and his mother's subsequent death in 1811; his rearing from 1811 by the merchant John Allan, who never officially adopted him and who left him, when he died in 1834, no share of the fortune into which he had come when Poe was in his teens; his court-martial and expulsion from West Point in 1831; his marriage to his thirteen-year-old cousin Virginia Clemm in 1836; the bouts of drunkenness and depression that lost him more than one job; and, especially, his mysterious death in Baltimore in 1849. The sensationalization of Poe's life and death illustrates the development of a "cult of the author" in popular fiction, from which Lippard and, especially, Southworth also benefited. In Poe's case, though, the amount of attention paid to the supposed resemblances between his "wild" life and his gothic writing reveals, as Sandra Tomc has argued, the nineteenth-century emergence of "a literary industry that embraced and cultivated dysfunction as a condition of authorial productivity and repute" (2002: 22).

Poe's stories of crime and confession drew heavily on the penny papers and scandal sheets that became, in the 1830s, steadily more lurid and more popular. His inclination, in adapting these stories, was to explore the gothic horrors of the human psyche, examining both the depths of human monstrosity and the "perverse" tendency toward self-annihilation. The narrators of tales like "The Cask of Amontillado" (1846), in which a man is lured into a wine cellar and walled up alive, and "The Tell-Tale Heart" (1843), in which an old man is tortured, smothered, dismembered, and buried under the floorboards, proudly recount their clever crimes, suspending moral judgment in favor of admiration of their formal and methodological brilliance. When retribution comes to Poe's criminals, it is powered not by external moral crusades, but by internal psychic division. Poe, like Brown, was fascinated by the alterity that lay within the human mind, and in stories like "The Imp of the Perverse" (1845), "The Black Cat" (1843), and "The Tell-Tale Heart" his narrators obey an apparently irresistible urge to undo themselves. The narrator of "The Imp of the Perverse" theorizes this tendency as an irrational, or rather anti-rational thirst for sensation, describing the way that: "a thought . . . which chills the very marrow of our bones with the fierceness of the delight of its horror" may become an uncontainable obsession (Poe 1981: 518). This impulse, he argues, operates not despite rationality but *because* of it; it is the other side of the utilitarian insistence on pragmatic productivity, which brings about a rebellious desire for experience for its own sake.

Poe's repeated portrayal of self-annihilating narrators can, in one sense, be read as commentary on the masochistic taste for sensation stories, which Poe savagely mocked in "The Psyche Zenobia" (later retitled "How to Write a Blackwood's Article," 1838). Zenobia's editor, Mr. Blackwood, informs her that if she wishes to write for his magazine, she will need to learn that "Sensations are the great things, after all"; as a model, he directs her to a recently published story, " 'The Dead Alive,' a capital thing! – the record of a gentleman's sensations when entombed before the breath was out of his body – full of tastes, terror, sentiment, metaphysics, and erudition. You would have sworn that the writer had been born and brought up in a coffin" (Poe 1981: 128). To oblige her editor, Zenobia goes out and gets her head slowly cut off.

The subject of self-undoing as a result both of repressed guilt and of gothic excitation also frames "The Fall of the House of Usher" (1839). The tale's narrator, on the final night of his stay with his nervous schoolfriend Roderick Usher, attempts to distract Usher from a fearsome lightning storm by reading a wild romance aloud to him; but the house, as if it were the impressionable reader that critics sought to protect from sensationalism, proceeds to act out each of the scenes described in the romance, culminating in the return of Madeline, the twin whom Roderick has buried alive. The narrator is amazed by this sequence of events, but Usher, who is himself a writer of "wild fantasias" (Poe 1981: 204), including a lyric called "The Haunted Palace" which uncannily prefigures the history of his house, is not at all surprised by these relays between sensational literature and the "real world." The difference in their responses can be read as charting the distance between a naïve reader of sensationalism, constantly astonished by each new spectacle, and an experienced habitué of the gothic, who eschews surprise for the deeper terrors of suspense – terrors which are no less intense for being anticipated.

Madeline Usher's reappearance also foregrounds another way in which Poe's preoccupation with the return of the repressed manifested itself: in a series of female characters, featured in tales like "Berenice" (1835), "Eleonora" (1842), and "Ligeia" (1838), who simply refuse to stay dead. Psycho-biographically inclined critics have linked this preoccupation with undead women (as well as with the beautiful female corpses who populate many of Poe's poems) to Poe's unresolved grief over the losses of his mother, his foster-mother Frances Allan, and, in 1846, his wife Virginia. But we can also connect this repeated motif to a broader cultural tendency to employ the bodies of dead women as a means of staving off (male) anxieties about impotence, decline, and decay; their return, in this sense, signals the horror of an incomplete repression, the insufficiency of this means of managing death anxiety – which leads to its iteration to the point of tedium, both in Poe's œuvre and in the male gothic tradition overall. (See Kennedy 1987; Bronfen 1992.)

Poe's gothic writing, unlike that of the other writers discussed in this essay, maintains an indistinct distance from the immediacy of the American scene; many of his tales are set in a vaguely European milieu, and even stories that start out in recognizably American surroundings, such as the *Narrative of Arthur Gordon Pym*, abandon these environs for the uncharted terrain of the romancer's imagination. Poe himself insisted that the physical and historical setting of his narratives was less important than the psychological terrain on which his horrors played themselves out. In the preface to his first collection of stories, *Tales of the Grotesque and Arabesque* (1839), Poe observed that many had accused his stories of " 'Germanism' and gloom," but insisted on the irrelevance of this national designation: "Tomorrow I may be anything but German, as yesterday I was everything else . . . I maintain that terror is not of Germany, but of the soul – that I have deduced this terror only from its legitimate sources, and urged it to its legitimate results" (Poe 1984: 129). This relocation of the gothic tradition away from Germany can also be read as a dislocation, a universalizing insistence on abstracting the mental processes that interested him from the specificities of period and culture. Much recent critical work on Poe has, however, succeeded in teasing out some of the traces of his own time and place that surface in his writing, highlighting such questions as the way Poe's consciousness of race relations, an issue that could not have escaped his notice in the antebellum South, shapes his gothic narratives (see esp. Kennedy and Weissberg 2001). Certainly his explorations of the problem of psychological self-possession – or, usually, of the lack thereof – cannot be separated from the way that the notion of self-possession marked antebellum debates about slavery, labor practices, and property rights. What Harold Bloom has called the "more-than-Freudian, oppressive and curiously original sense and sensation of overdetermination" that marks Poe's writing suggests a complex mutual imbrication of the psychic and the social that gestures obliquely but undeniably toward the hidden horrors of the contemporary American scene (Bloom 1987: 6).

George Lippard (1822–1854)

Despite their political and methodological differences, Poe's support proved beneficial in establishing the literary reputation of his fierier and more openly political compatriot, George Lippard, who, in addition to authoring numerous radical sensational novels, was deeply involved in labor struggles and local politics. Lippard's early acquaintance with hardship and loss may have shaped his penchant for gothic fiction, as his biographer, David S. Reynolds, speculates. Born on a Pennsylvania farm in 1822, the young Lippard, along with his sisters, was left under the care of his grandfather and two aunts when his parents, who were too sick to care for him, moved to Philadelphia. Bit by bit, his aunts were forced by financial need to sell off the family homestead in Germantown, finally giving up the house and moving to Philadelphia when George was nine years old. George's mother died of tuberculosis in 1831, and George remained with his aunts rather than moving in with his father, who remarried in 1833. He went briefly to Rhinebeck, New York to prepare for collegiate training as a Methodist minister, but, angered by the hypocrisy of the school's clergyman director, he abandoned his studies and returned to Philadelphia in time to witness the death of his father in October 1837. Left out of his father's will, Lippard was forced to take on work as a legal assistant, which paid so little that he was, for a time, homeless; this period gave him intimate acquaintance with the city that was to form the setting of much of his fiction. The depression that began in 1837 and lasted until 1844 made this a period of intense social misery, leading to Lippard's decision to enter the literary field. He began writing for, and later editing, penny papers, in which his sensational novels of American life were serialized, eventually founding his own, the *Quaker City Weekly*. Lippard insisted that literature ought to be devoted to the task of social change, declaring, in the pages of the *Quaker City Weekly*, that

> a literature which does not work practically, for the advancement of social reform, or
> which is too dignified or too good to picture the wrongs of the great mass of humanity,

is just good for nothing at all. . . . A national literature without a great Idea is plainly a splendid church without preacher or congregation, but with the coffin of humanity under its altar and the key of social progress in some rich publisher's pocket. (Lippard 1986: 281)

Lippard's primary means of using literature to work for the advancement of social reform was the sensationalized urban gothic novel, with its graphic, sensational description of the violence – physical, psychological, and sexual – that attended urban life in a market economy. Like Charles Brockden Brown, to whom he dedicated *The Quaker City; or, The Monks of Monk Hall* (1845), Lippard depicted the corruption that lay beneath Philadelphia's stolid exterior. The novel takes place over a period of three days at Monk-Hall, a pre-revolutionary relic transformed into a den of debauchery for the city's elite. Lippard's inference that the wealthy have hijacked the American revolutionary experiment for their own enjoyment is borne out through dozens of sub-plots detailing "the secret life of Philadelphia" (Lippard 1995: 4): bankers plot the fraudulent failures of their banks in order to bilk investors of their funds; wealthy men refuse coins to the starving poor, who are driven to crime and suicide; judges are revealed to be in the pay of businessmen; the clergy's hypocrisy is embodied in a temperance preacher who indulges in opium and who drugs and tries to rape a young woman he believes to be his daughter. Despite his insistence that "my motive in . . . composition was honest, was pure, was devoid of any idea of sensualism" (p. 2), Lippard's scenes of rape, murder, and torture are palpably sexual, enticing the reader with licentious thrills even as the narrator insists on the morality of the tales, a morality founded in "truth." Lippard's narrator breaks off repeatedly to heckle critics who can't handle this "truth": "Pass by delightful trifler . . . write syllabub forever, and pen blank verse until dotage shall make you more garrulous than now, but for the sake of Heaven, do not criticize this chapter! Our taste is different than yours. We like to look at nature and at the world, not only as they appear, but as they are!" (p. 305).

This insistence on the truth of his fiction also characterizes Lippard's other city novels, including the New York-based *Empire City* (1849) and *New York: Its Upper Ten and Lower Million* (1853), which, like *The Quaker City*, exploit the urban gothic model that became increasingly popular in the 1840s and 1850s as the reading public's fascination with the "mysteries of the city" grew. But while the debauched city provides the local frame for Lippard's social commentary, the novels insist that the networks of corruption they expose are not local but national, as suggested by the sub-plot in *The Empire City* that concerns a fugitive slave pursued across the North by a hired slave-catcher and his master, who is also his brother. Though he reluctantly grants that the North can have nothing to say to the "domestic institutions" of the South, the novel's narrator condemns at length the pursuit of fugitives:

what shall we say when . . . slavery sends its minions into the borders, and hunts out human flesh from our cities, and covers our free soil with scenes of riot, deeds of blood? . . . We cannot be silent when white slavery curses [our] soil: shall we be dumb when black slavery sends its ministers over the boundary line, and forces its most terrible features at once and in distinct hideousness upon our eyes[?] (Lippard 1969: 76)

Lippard's sensational exposés of the gothic underside of modern American life frequently skewered local and national political figures: the fugitive slave in *The Empire City* is hinted to be descended from Thomas Jefferson; and in the same novel a fictionalized version of Daniel Webster buys the fugitive's sister from her master for sexual purposes. Yet notwithstanding his critique of capitalist corruption, Lippard was deeply patriotic and nationalistic. His novels of the Mexican War, *Legends of Mexico* (1847) and *'Bel of Prairie Eden* (1848), sensationalized American exploits in the Southwest, while tales of the Revolution, such as *Blanche of Brandywine, or, September the Eleventh, 1777* (1846) and *Washington and His Generals: Or, Legends of the Revolution* (1847), lionized revolutionary heroes, depicting Washington and his followers as champions of the poor and oppressed. (Lippard mythologized Washington's concern for the workers to such an extent that the leadership post he held in The Brotherhood of the Union, a national workers' cooperative organization he founded in 1849, was "The Supreme Washington.") Characteristically, Lippard seeks, in these narratives, to eroticize the national body, and tales of sexual intrigue and personal vendettas are united with the historical material; *'Bel of Prairie Eden*, for example, concerns the exploits of a Texan colonist and a Mexican who, among other things, seduce one another's sisters and murder one another's fathers, while *Blanche of Brandywine* sets the stage for its revolutionary recollections with a mysterious and titillating flagellation scene. The violent agitation of the sensationalized and nationalized bodies in Lippard's fiction parallels both the invasive exploitation he saw as endemic to an economic system that permitted extremes of wealth and poverty, and the radical upheaval he sought in the American social order. Disdaining the "white-gloved" actions of sentimental middle-class moral reformers, Lippard's fiction insisted on a passionate politics of regeneration.

E. D. E. N. Southworth (1819–1899)

Unlike the other writers discussed in this essay, Emma Dorothy Elizabeth Nevitte Southworth is not generally considered part of the American gothic tradition. Rather, her gender and her typically domestic subject matter have caused her countless novels, short stories, and essays to be classed in the school of sentimental fiction (see Boyle 1939). Yet as Louisa May Alcott's allusion to her in *Little Women* makes clear, Southworth's work is far more sensational than sentimental. Like Lippard, Southworth used the sensational novel as a means of exposing the hidden networks of corruption that surrounded her; but because her focus on middle-class sexual politics located these exposes within the bourgeois household, the gothic rage that suffuses these domestic narratives has rarely been recognized.

One of Southworth's most successful tactics was the development of an authorial persona whose sufferings and triumphs, confided to the reader as if to a friend, appeared to bring her audience into her confidence. An "autobiographical preface" affixed to her collection of stories *The Haunted Homestead; and Other Nouvelettes* (1860) depicts her, even from her birth in 1819, as a "child of sorrow," lacking in beauty and outshone by her properly feminine younger sister (Southworth 1860: 30). She describes a profound melancholia resulting from her father's death when she was five, which caused her to lose interest in all spirituality except "old Uncle Biggs with his ghost stories" (p. 36). The narrative describes her successes in school as a young girl, but omits mention of the neglect she suffered after her mother's remarriage; it also insists on "pass[ing] over in silence the days of her marriage" and skipping directly to the point at which, "a widow in fate but not in fact," Southworth was forced to take up the pen in an effort to support her two children (p. 36). Emma Nevitte had been married to Frederick Hamilton Southworth of Utica, New York at twenty-one. She and her husband moved to Wisconsin, but in 1844 she returned to her family home, in the company of one child and pregnant with a second. Her stepfather refused to support her, so she began teaching in the Washington DC public schools and writing short pieces for various journals. Her first full-length novel, *Retribution*, was serialized in the anti-slavery journal *The National Era* in 1849 and then published by Harper & Brothers; it received positive reviews and launched her on her way to enormous success.

Southworth's concern for the fate of women in a patriarchal system is evident from simply glancing at some of her titles: works like *The Fatal Marriage*, *The Deserted Wife*, *The Discarded Daughter*, *The Changed Brides*, *Retribution*, *The Missing Bride, or, Miriam the Avenger*, and *Broken Pledges: A Story of Noir et Blanc* foreground women's exploitation within American structures of kinship. Her œuvre features a few often-repeated plot twists that highlight various aspects of this exploitation. One of these is the heartless father whose status consciousness leads him to forbid his daughter to marry her goodhearted but poor lover and instead forces her to wed some power- or wealth-seeking candidate of his choosing. These daughters occasionally run away or go mad, but most are simply crushed into meek submission, a tendency that emphasizes women's utter expendability as people to a system which treats them as objects of exchange. Another favored motif is the secret marriage, usually between a powerful and wealthy man and a poor but virtuous woman, which is nearly always followed by betrayal and abandonment, sometimes when the man (wrongly) suspects the woman of infidelity but more often as a result of his realization that the marriage conflicts with his class status and/or his worldly aspirations. The women, who are left pregnant or with infants to care for, cannot return to their families, emphasizing the irreversibility of their lives in contrast to those of the men, who go back to their own circles apparently unchanged. Some of Southworth's abandoned women, like Marah Rocke in *The Hidden Hand*, work themselves nearly to death in an effort to care for their children; others, like Harriette Newton in *Allworth Abbey* or Lionne Delaforet in *The Fatal Marriage*, become monomaniacal, obsessively pursuing and tormenting their spouses and others connected with their abandonment. Lionne fakes her own death and deprives her seducer and cousin, Orville Deville, of the title he thereby inherits and the child he bears with his legitimate wife; Harriette deceives her seducer's son into believing that his wife is her own daughter and thus his sister, wrecking their marriage, and then uses her real daughter to persecute the family of Lord Leaton, who had persuaded her husband, the Baron Elverton, to abandon her in order to preserve his social status. Their destructive fixations become the gothic shadows behind the structure of the bourgeois household, in which the wife is meant to center her entire being on her husband and children. Another version of this story is played out in plots in which the child of a cast-off comes to threaten the stability of the seducer's legitimate family, usually destroying him- or herself in the process. In these ways Southworth's sensational tales expose the gothic underside of domestic life, the horrors of domination, manipulation, and exclusion that the sentimental bonds of the "natural" family attempt to conceal.

Southworth's sensational fictions also challenge bourgeois domestic norms in their recurrent presentation of rebellious adolescent female heroines whose bravery and valor surpass those of most of the men in their spheres. The best-known of these, *The Hidden Hand*'s fiery Capitola Black, is even found living on the streets of New York disguised as a newsboy. When Capitola is taken in by the wealthy patriarch Old Hurricane, she refuses to settle down and behave as a wealthy young woman should; Old Hurricane complains that "Cap isn't sentimental ... [she] evidently thinks that the restriction of her liberty is too heavy a price to pay for protection and support!" (Southworth 1988: 175). Other gender-bending heroines include *The Fatal Marriage*'s Kate Kyte, who attempts to enlist in the army along with her six brothers and then, when they are all apparently lost in the French and Indian War, rides off to find them and ends up saving the life of the youngest; *The Mother-in-Law*'s Gertrude Lion, the Amazonian "Gerfalcon," who charges into a wedding to save the bride from a forced bigamous marriage; and *Allworth Abbey*'s Annella Wilder, who informs Malcolm Montrose, the fiancé of Eudora Leaton, imprisoned for a murder she did not commit, that she loves Eudora more than he does and is willing to give up her own life to effect Eudora's escape. These characters mount a pitched battle against women's subordinate social position; *The Hidden Hand*'s narrator informs us that, "when women have their rights, [Capitola] will be a lieutenant-colonel" (Southworth 1988: 348). Yet even these heroines are threatened by the webs of sexual violence that ensnare Southworth's female characters. Capitola, for instance, is sexually threatened by a number of men within *The Hidden Hand*'s two volumes, from the "bad boys" who menace her on the streets of New York and to protect herself from whom she dons boy's clothing, to Black Donald, the leader of a band of criminals, who breaks into her bedroom one evening in order to seduce her and carry her off, to the local dandy Craven LeNoir, who overtakes her as she is riding in the woods one evening and tries to force her to dismount and "have a cozy chat" with him (Southworth 1988: 117). Through a combination of exceptional courage, sharp wits, and extraordinary self-command, Capitola manages to evade these and other threats to her bodily autonomy – a freedom not shared by many of the passive, traditionally feminine characters in Southworth's fiction.

Southworth, a Southern woman, is often seen as an apologist for slavery because of the prevalence of the plantation setting in her fiction and of her repeated use of stereotyped slave characters, whose absurd superstitions and exaggerated dialects are meant to contrast comically with the white characters. Yet a number of Southworth's narratives also highlight the role the slave system played in the maintenance of a system of male domination based on economic exploitation and physical and sexual violence. In *Broken Pledges*, for example, the slave woman Phaedra, who has borne the child of her master, Colonel Waring, faints in shock when he returns from a sojourn in New Orleans with a new, white wife. Waring had asked a neighbor to inform Phaedra of his marriage, but, "for the sake of what he afterward called the joke," he neglects to do so (Southworth 1891: 55). Phaedra is permanently scarred by an injury she sustains in the faint, while the legal Mrs. Waring goes mad with jealousy and is eventually confined to an asylum. Waring's callousness ends up destroying his children as well: he fails to leave a will keeping his promise to Phaedra to free Valentine, their son, so that Oswald, his son by his legal wife, becomes his brother's master. Valentine, who has inherited a passionate temper – as a result, according to the narrator, of his mixture of black, white, and Native American blood – attempts to serve his increasingly tyrannical master faithfully but eventually is tried beyond his patience and strikes and accidentally kills him. Despite its editorializing about the "fatality" of blood mixture, *Broken Pledges* maintains sympathy for Valentine and for Governor, a slave on a neighboring plantation jailed for killing a white overseer who raped his wife. Governor's stubborn belief that he and Valentine cannot be executed because, as slaves, they are worth "at least twelve or fifteen hundred dollars" which the whites would be unwilling to lose reflects painfully on the trade in human flesh (Southworth 1891: 246). Valentine's story joins many of Southworth's other early novels, including *Retribution* and *India, the Pearl of Pearl-River*, in insisting that the violence inherent in the slave system will be passed down across generations. The repeated emphasis on the fear of ghosts felt by Southworth's stereotypical black characters is, in this sense, an insight into the historical dynamics that shape her sensational, melodramatic narratives. Although Southworth does not rely on the supernatural – in stories like *The Haunted Homestead*, the supposedly spectral occurrences turn out to be the combination of natural events and excited imaginations – her homesteads are indeed haunted by the legacy of the patriarchal violence on which they are founded.

*

Of these four writers, only Lippard would have endorsed the kind of "ruthless democracy" that Herman Melville described in an 1851 letter to Nathaniel Hawthorne. But their gothically inflected narratives emphasize another sense of the phrase: the relentless cruelty and brutality that infused the American social order. Illustrating the twisted minds and violated bodies of its citizens, these narratives perform what Michael Denning, describing the working-class novel, has termed the "dream-work of the social" (1987: 81), sensationalizing for popular consumption a vision that is part wild revolutionary fantasy and part nightmare.

REFERENCES AND FURTHER READING

Alcott, Louisa May (1983). *Little Women*. New York: Modern Library. (First publ. 1868–9.)

Ashwill, Gary (1994). "The Mysteries of Capitalism in George Lippard's City Novels." *ESQ: A Journal of the American Renaissance* 40: 4, 293–317.

Bloom, Harold, ed. (1987). *Modern Critical Interpretations: The Tales of Poe*. New York: Chelsea House.

Boyle, Regis Louise (1939). *Mrs. E. D. E. N. Southworth, Novelist*. Washington DC: Catholic University of America Press.

Bronfen, Elisabeth (1992). *Over her Dead Body: Death, Femininity, and the Aesthetic*. New York: Routledge.

Brown, Charles Brockden (1992). *Literary Essays and Reviews*, ed. Alfred Weber and Wolfgang Schäfer. Frankfurt: Peter Lang.

Brown, Charles Brockden (1998). *Three Gothic Novels*. New York: Library of America.

Brown, Charles Brockden (1999). *Ormond; Or, The Secret Witness.*, ed. Mary Chapman. Petersborough, Ont.: Broadview. (First publ. 1799.)

Denning, Michael (1987). *Mechanic Accents: Dime Novels and Working Class Culture in America*. New York and London: Verso.

Goddu, Theresa A. (1997). *Gothic America: Narrative, History and Nation*. New York: Columbia University Press.

Ingram, Ann (1999). "Melodrama and the Moral Economy of E. D. E. N. Southworth's *The Deserted Wife*." *American Transcendental Quarterly* 13: 4, 269–85.

Kennedy, J. Gerald (1987). *Poe, Death and the Life of Writing*. New Haven: Yale University Press.

Kennedy, J. Gerald, and Weissberg, Lilliane, eds. (2001). *Romancing the Shadow: Poe and Race*. New York: Oxford University Press.

Lippard, George (1969). *The Empire City, or, New York by Night and Day: Its Aristocracy and its Dollars*. Freeport, NY: Books for Libraries. (First publ. 1849.)

Lippard, George (1986). *Prophet of Protest: Writings of an American Radical, 1822–1854*, ed. David S. Reynolds. New York: Peter Lang.

Lippard, George (1995). *The Quaker City, or, The Monks of Monk-Hall. A Romance of Philadelphia Life, Mystery and Crime*, ed. David Reynolds.

Amherst: University of Massachusetts Press. (First publ. 1845.)

Luciano, Dana (1998). "'Perverse Nature': *Edgar Huntly* and the Novel's Reproductive Disorders." *American Literature* 70: 1, 1–27.

Martin, Robert K., and Savoy, Eric, eds. (1998). *American Gothic: New Interventions in a National Narrative*. Iowa City: University of Iowa Press.

Phillips, Walter Clarke (1919). *Dickens, Reade and Collins, Sensation Novelists: A Study in the Conditions and Theories of Novel Writing in Victorian England*. New York: Columbia University Press.

Poe, Edgar Allan (1981). *The Complete Tales*. New York: Chatham River.

Poe, Edgar Allan (1984). *Poetry and Tales*. New York: Library of America.

Reynolds, David S. (1982). *George Lippard*. Boston: Twayne.

Reynolds, David S. (1988). *Beneath the American Renaissance: The Subversive Imagination in the Age of Emerson and Melville*. New York: Knopf.

Ridgely, J. V. (1974). "George Lippard's *The Quaker City*; the World of the American Porno-Gothic." *Studies in the Literary Imagination* 7: 1, 77–94.

Rosenheim, Shawn, and Rachman, Stephen, eds. (1995). *The American Face of Edgar Allan Poe*. Baltimore: Johns Hopkins University Press.

Rosenthal, Bernard, ed. (1981). *Critical Essays on Charles Brockden Brown*. Boston: Hall.

Samuels, Shirley, ed. (1992). *The Culture of Sentiment: Race, Gender and Sentimentality in Nineteenth-Century America*. New York: Oxford University Press.

Sedgwick, Eve Kosofsky (1986). *The Coherence of Gothic Conventions*. New York: Methuen.

Southworth, E. D. E. N. (1860). *The Haunted Homestead; and Other Nouvellettes* Philadelphia: T. B. Peterson & Bros.

Southworth, E. D. E. N. (1863). *The Fatal Marriage*. Philadelphia: T. B. Peterson & Bros.

Southworth, E. D. E. N. (1865). *Allworth Abbey*. Philadelphia: T. B. Peterson & Bros.

Southworth, E. D. E. N. (1891). *Broken Pledges: A Story of Noir et Blanc*. Philadelphia: T. B. Peterson & Bros. (First publ. 1855.)

Southworth, E. D. E. N. (1988). *The Hidden Hand or Capitola the Madcap*, ed. Joanne Dobson. New Brunswick, NJ: Rutgers University Press. (First publ. 1859.)

Streeby, Shelley (2002). *American Sensations: Class, Empire, and the Production of Popular Culture.* Berkeley: University of California Press.

Tomc, Sandra (2002). "Poe and his Circle." In Kevin J. Hayes (ed.), *The Cambridge Companion to Edgar Allan Poe*, 21–41. New York: Cambridge University Press.

Warfel, Harry (1949). *Charles Brockden Brown: American Gothic Novelist.* Gainesville: University of Florida Press.

Watts, Steven (1994). *The Romance of Real Life: Charles Brockden Brown and the Origins of American Culture.* Baltimore: Johns Hopkins University Press.

28

Retold Legends: Washington Irving, James Kirke Paulding, and John Pendleton Kennedy

Philip Barnard

Washington Irving (1783–1859), James Kirke Paulding (1778–1860), and John Pendleton Kennedy (1795–1870) are closely related figures on every level. Examining them together brings out key aspects of all three figures and of the cultural–ideological landscape of their moment, which extends from the early national period before the War of 1812 through the Jacksonian and antebellum years to the Civil War. Theirs is a rapidly growing US society struggling with the large-scale social disruption and violence produced by industrialization, expansionism, and slavery, powerful class and ethnic tensions, and pervasive anxiety among the cultural–political elite concerning post-revolutionary democratization. Considered in more Atlanticist terms (Irving's is a notably Euro-American career), these three writers flourish during the post-Napoleonic era of legitimism and restoration, competing left and right nationalisms, struggles over industrialization and imperialism, and the specter of socialism and new revolutionary insurrections.

All three were born in the eighteenth-century revolutionary era. Crucial aspects of Irving's and Paulding's births and early childhood experiences are directly connected to the Revolution and its heroes, and all three wrote historical fiction and biographies that reflected on and mythologized the revolutionary moment in ways that became totemic for subsequent American culture. All three appeared in public life at the outset of the nineteenth century, emerging from financially unstable merchant-class family backgrounds to pursue careers that elevated them, by the ends of their lives, to the status of wealthy estate owners and elite civic figures: precisely the type of cultivated and paternalist landed gentry they idealized and mythologized in their writings. The first writings of Paulding and Irving appeared as part of the late Enlightenment print culture of the early republic (1788–1812), but all three became leading figures in the first generation to adapt to and flourish in the newly emerging conditions of the mass culture industry that shaped US society from the Jackson presidency onward. Their lives are significantly intertwined on the personal level. Irving and Paulding collaborated in 1807–8 on *Salmagundi*, which launched both their literary careers, and the somewhat younger Kennedy, who developed his fictional narrative style in imitation of Irving's successful formula in *The Sketch-book*, became (along with his in-laws) a family friend of Irving from the 1830s on. Despite doctrinal and partisan differences (Paulding became a famously Anglophobe Jacksonian, while Irving and Kennedy represent in different ways the acme of Whig Anglophilia and anti-Jacksonianism), these three lives trace out remarkably similar trajectories. All three pursued lengthy and highly successful dual literary and political careers that made them at once: prestigious writers and shapers of cultural tastes and norms; wealthy workers in and beneficiaries of the emerging mass culture industry; powerful state functionaries at the highest level of US political institutions; and, on perhaps the deepest level, widely influential ideologues of emergent US nationalism.

The literary styles, genres, and themes cultivated by Irving, Paulding, and Kennedy, beginning in the 1820s, are often seen as slightly musty, antiquated, or lesser achievements in relation to the perceived greatness of the better-known antebellum generation that was born after 1800 and flourished in the 1840s and 1850s (the "classics," such as Emerson, Hawthorne, Melville, Stowe). Irving, by far the most successful of the three, has been received as a (lesser) "classic" figure in US literary history since his heyday, and right up to the present remains a staple but relatively staid and unstylish subject in literary studies and university curricula. Paulding and Kennedy, on the other hand, were widely read and perceived as important literary figures at the height of their careers but by the ends of their lives had settled into the status of "minor" writers who were never, even in the later nineteenth century, understood as part of a canonical narrative of US literary history.

The contribution and significance of all three writers are distorted or misunderstood when viewed in terms of the traditional estheticist and continualist narratives of exclusively literary histories. All three were prolific writers and high-level political functionaries who excelled in a variety of genres and had some of their greatest impact on contemporaries as the authors of frankly didactic ideological histories, political biographies, polemics, and satires. Nevertheless, their popularity (such as it is) and legacy are generally linked to their "retold legends": that is, to story collections, sketches, and historical novels, the best known of which are Irving's *The Sketch-book* (1819–20), Paulding's *The Dutchman's Fireside* (1831), and Kennedy's *Swallow Barn* (1832). These narratives blend willful quaintness, antiquarian and nostalgic–sentimental tone, folktale-derived or historical-romance themes, and a certain patina of newly minted "oldness" into a mode of fiction that reflects the writers' carefully considered ideological positions and inflects the period's key struggles. These "retold legends" are artful and deeply nationalistic responses to the dilemmas of modernity seen from the perspective of elite US cultural and political actors in the decades between 1812 and 1860; an ensemble of generic and stylistic formulas whose key lies in the paradoxical necessity, in modernity (in capitalist market culture), of inventing tradition, of artificially constructing national–popular legends, of imagining cultural stability. The underlying anti-revolutionary, Burkean model of tradition, history, and social order that informs these narratives is an important early articulation of conservative ideas, myths, and cultural tendencies that will reappear as normative commonplaces in later US literature and culture through the twentieth century, even though no subsequent generation, movement, or school of writers or other cultural producers has ever regarded Irving, Paulding, or Kennedy as especially influential models. As befits figures whose long and successful careers were as political and professional–bureaucratic as they were literary in a narrow sense, the significance and influence of their writings becomes clear only when viewed as part of a socio-cultural and ideological narrative wider than an exclusively literary history of "major" figures, genres, and styles.

Irving, Paulding, and Kennedy were key purveyors and interpreters of American nationalism at the moment when ideologies of nationalism solidified as major forces in Jacksonian and antebellum America and, indeed, throughout the Atlantic and European worlds. Three general aspects of their lives and writings converge to make possible their contributions to and importance for US nationalist ideology: first, their status as part of the nation's cultural and political elite, and particularly as part of the subset of this elite who produced ideas using newly available technologies of mass culture; second, their dedication to an anachronistic vision of social order and historical time driven by their anxieties about modernity and democratization, and epitomized by their idealized conceptions of landed estate culture and ethno-racial "folk" essentialism; and third, their use of cultural forms and models that conveyed this vision effectively to a mass audience which received them as normative and dominant ideological tendencies. A review of these features of the lives and writings of these three figures can clarify the significance and historical impact of their "retold legends" as mediums for developing US nationalism.

Theories of nationalism emphasize several features of this crucial modern force that are important in this context. Our understanding of nationalism begins from the basic observation that, as an idea and a movement, it became a fundamental shaping force in Western societies after the American and French revolutions, filling the ideological void left by the decline of feudalism, religion, and monarchy as legitimating principles for the state. Nationalism provides an "imagined community," in Benedict Anderson's well-known phrase, a powerful ideology that produces both the collective imaginary and the repertoire of personal feelings necessary for the ideological unity and legitimacy of the modern state in all its forms, from liberal market societies to twentieth-century fascism (Anderson 1991; Gellner 1983). Nationalism rests on the notion of the sovereignty of the people, but left (Mazzinian) and right (Burkean) nationalisms in the nineteenth century interpret the possible expressions, implications, and limits of this idea of "the people" and their state in vastly different ways. In the classic modernization model of nationalism developed by Ernest Gellner, nineteenth-century and subsequent nationalisms are created and shaped "from above," generated and delivered by political and cultural–intellectual elites whose work organizes the assimilation and unification of socially diverse populations and communities through the institutions of mass culture and education (Gellner 1983). The imagined communities developed by these modern traditions entail political ideas, of course, but also far-reaching ideas and practices of social identity that impose ethno-racial, gender, and class-inflected notions of authority and commonality.

Thus the ideas, values, and effects of nationalism, as many historians have noted, are anything but natural, and are directly related to particular forms, genres, themes, and styles developed by early nineteenth-century cultural elites. As these ideas circulate in early Romantic and Napoleonic-era culture, new forms like the historical novel, the romantic folk-tale, and other literary invocations of "legends" real or imagined both reflect and help produce a new sense of historical time and a new historical consciousness of contemporary social order as a consequence of previous stages of development. The poems of Ossian, for example, are a notable hoax of the period that dramatically illustrates the power of these newly invented ideas and forms to convey a fantasy of the past. Composed in the 1760s by Scottish poet James Macpherson and published as translations of ancient, quasi-Homeric Celtic bards, these pseudo-primitive poems were repeatedly exposed as a fraud, yet continued to be received and revered as authentic expressions of the genius of a Celtic "folk" consciousness by political and cultural leaders from Napoleon (who kept a copy near his bed and commissioned paintings on Ossianic themes) to Emerson. More generally, scholars from Georg Lukács to the present have noted that this new sense of time and historical consciousness is basic to nationalism and constitutes the fundamental importance of the historical novel and historical fiction generally as they emerge in the early nineteenth century (Lukács 1983). Irving, Paulding, and Kennedy are precisely the types of politico-cultural figures who initiate and provide early cultural impetus for national consciousness through work that is not directly political, but primarily cultural, literary, and folkloric (Hroch 2000; Hobsbawm 1990).

In this light, the relations between the careers, nationalist visions of social order, and literary styles and achievements of Irving, Paulding, and Kennedy become clearer. Irving's career is the most cosmopolitan of the three, but Paulding and Kennedy are also impressive examples of the period's characteristic blend of Jacksonian populist meritocracy and patrician socio-cultural conservatism. James Kirke Paulding was born into a modest Anglo-Dutch family in Westchester County, New York in 1778. His father was a merchant army supplier who, during the Revolution, risked taking personal financial responsibility for supplies when the Continental Congress lacked sufficient funds, then went bankrupt and was humiliatingly confined in debtors' prison when the post-revolutionary Congress refused reimbursement for his patriotic efforts. Paulding entered literary life through his collaboration with Irving on a satirical periodical essay (*Salmagundi*, 1807–8), which he followed with a popular parody of Scott's folk historicism (*The Lay of the Scottish Fiddle*, 1813), widely read anti-British essays and pamphlets (*The Diverting History of John Bull and Brother Jonathan*, 1812; *The United States and England*, 1815), and patriotic journalism on American naval heroes and naval victories (in the Irving-edited *Analectic Magazine*, 1813–14). As a result of this writing and the political–cultural capital it provided,

Paulding was appointed Secretary of the Board of Navy Commissioners by President James Madison and held that position from 1815 to 1823. Just as his early writings led to his political appointment and economic security as a member of the cultured elite, his continuing work as part of the literary establishment, publishing a steady stream of novels, stories, biography, poetry, plays, and essays from the 1820s through the 1840s, led to his long personal association with Martin Van Buren before, during, and after Van Buren's terms as Vice-President and President, and to his appointment to a cabinet-level position as Secretary of the Navy under Van Buren from 1838 to 1841. Paulding accepted the cabinet position only after Irving and another nominee declined it, and Kennedy occupied the same cabinet post a decade later under Millard Fillmore.

Unlike Paulding and Irving, who understood themselves first as writers and second as government functionaries, Kennedy's literary career took second place to his development as a politician and civic leader, but the two sides of his career are similarly interdependent. James Pendleton Kennedy was born in 1795 to a mother from an established Maryland Anglo family and a Scots–Irish immigrant father whose mercantile speculations led to bankruptcy in 1809. After this setback, the mother's family connections provided the financial security and cultural prestige that allowed Kennedy to become part of the Maryland patrician class, pursuing an education at Baltimore College, becoming an attorney, and running for local and state political office before emerging into literary life as a follower of Irving with the novel *Swallow Barn* in 1832 (followed closely by *Horse-Shoe Robinson* in 1835 and *Rob of the Bowl* in 1838, both historical romances). As a prominent Baltimorean, Kennedy ran for US Congress several times and was elected in 1838, thereafter becoming Provost of the University of Maryland (1850–2), Secretary of the Navy under Millard Fillmore (1852–3), President of the Northern Central Railroad Company (1854–6), and President of the Peabody Institute (1860–70). Throughout this heady series of political and business engagements, and as an intrinsic part of it, Kennedy published novels, political satires (*Quodlibet*, targeting populist Jacksonianism, 1840), biographies (*The Life of William Wirt*, 1849), and journalism that publicized his Whig and nationalist positions, even to the point of opposing secession as a Southerner with a conservative nationalist rationale for preserving the Union (*The Border States, Their Power and Duty in the Present Disordered Condition of the Country*, 1860).

Washington Irving's social connections and literary success paved his way to an international career as a diplomat and cultural luminary with close ties to political, economic, and cultural power-brokers in the both the United States and Europe. Irving was born in New York in 1783 to a Scottish merchant father and English mother who had emigrated only twenty years earlier, and was named for national hero and iconic paterfamilias George Washington, who presided over the writer's life in an uncanny symbolic manner. In a famous chance encounter in 1789, Washington "blessed" Irving as a child, and a reverent, five-volume biography of the first president was to be Irving's final major work. The bankruptcy of Irving's family import business in 1818 was a painful personal ordeal that provided the immediate emotional backdrop and financial motivation for the composition of his landmark work *The Sketch-book of Geoffrey Crayon, Gent.* (1819–20). Biographical scholarship from Stanley Williams to Jeffrey Rubin-Dorsky provides detailed accounts of how Irving's early economic and personal anxieties led him from law training and a desultory relation to the family business to a long stay in western Europe during which he produced *The Sketch-book*, its sequel *Bracebridge Hall* (1822), and a series of other fictional, biographical, and historical works (Williams 1935; Rubin-Dorsky 1988). These writings established Irving as a international literary figure and led to his appointment as attaché to the American legation in Madrid with no diplomatic duties (1826), chargé d'affaires at the US Embassy in London (1831, while Van Buren was minister of the legation), and ambassador to Spain (1842–45) under President John Tyler. Irving participated in the negotiations for the Oregon territory and the settling of the forty-ninth parallel in London in 1846 and, in addition to his personal access to John Jacob Astor and every president from Madison to Tyler and Polk (including a long friendship and personal quarrels with Van Buren), he was on familiar terms with European notables from Walter Scott and Ludwig Tieck to Frederick Augustus I of Saxony, Louis Philippe, Napoleon III and his wife Eugenia de Montijo, and Isabella II of Spain. These diplomatic and personal connections provide the background for his production of further nationalist history (two accounts of Columbus in 1828 and 1831), writings promoting expansionism (*A Tour on the Prairies*, 1835; *Astoria*, 1836; *Adventures of Captain Bonneville*, 1827), and biography (notably the *Life of George Washington*, 1855–9, which replaced Paulding's 1835 biography of Washington as the standard work). Irving, Paulding, and Kennedy, then, were no isolated artistes. As part of the cultural–political elite of Jacksonian America, these writers were ideally positioned to play important roles in shaping the development of nationalist ideology in the United States.

The "retold legends" created by Irving, Paulding, and Kennedy provide a series of models for imagining US national community. Closer examination of a key example from each writer can show how these stories, sketches, and historical novels are driven by anxieties concerning democratization and modernity generally, and envision a world based on a nostalgic pastoral vision of paternalist social order that is summed up in their idealized representations of estate or plantation culture.

Irving wrote *The Sketch-book of Geoffrey Crayon, Gent.* during a long residence in England. It initially appeared in installments published by C. S. Van Winkle (the eponym of Rip) in New York from June 1819 to September 1820 before appearing as a book in London in the latter year. Although sometimes seen primarily as the source of two iconic tales set in America, "Rip Van Winkle" and "The Legend of Sleepy Hollow," the book is a genteel, lightly ironic, humorous, and sentimentalized account of English culture seen from the perspective of an American narrative persona, Geoffrey Crayon. To be adequately understood, the two famous tales need to be grasped in the context of the Anglo-sentimental setting that gives them their meanings in the book considered as a whole. It is through the narrator's self-consciously American perspective on and emotionalized response to the book's fantasy of British culture that *The Sketch-book* provides its powerfully paternalist and conserva-tive model for US national self-consciousness. Rather than representing actual features of English society in 1818, which Irving both recognizes and excludes with a wink to the reader conveyed in the narrator's perspective of self-deprecating irony and "poet-ical" sensibility, the book constructs an almost Disneyesque Britain of venerable cultural monuments and precedents (for America), and antiquarian, hierarchical, folkloric, and other non-threatening forms of stability and harmonious social rela-tions. In this manner Irving provides oblique observations on and responses to the real conditions of the early nineteenth century.

The book's central representation of cultural order and stability appears in the chapters describing Christmas rituals at Bracebridge Hall, a country estate main-tained by "The Squire," a figure who requires no name because he embodies the hierarchical institutions, traditions, and way of life connected with the estate. These chapters are central in terms of their importance in the larger book as well as in their formal placement in the middle of the narrative, linking its earlier and later sketches and providing what proved its most popular material for contemporaries. The success of this representation of Christmas and British country life led to the book's sequel, *Bracebridge Hall*, in which Geoffrey Crayon returns to reflect again on the virtues of English estate culture. Additionally, if one considers the popular afterlife of Irving's vision of culture, it is notable that these chapters almost single-handedly invent the modern Anglo-American sentimental cult of Christmas. The great popular success of these chapters led within a few years to New York writer Clement Moore's popular poem " 'Twas the Night before Christmas" (1824), to successful new literary products, the "giftbooks" designed for presentation as Christmas or New Year's gifts, and, finally, to the vogue for Christmas that spread back to Victorian England where it appears, for example, in Dickens and Thackeray (Hedges 1988).

Christmas on a British country estate provided Irving with two interdependent themes. First, the narrator presents estate culture as a tradition of stable, deferential, organic institutions and identities (identified with "ancient rural life") in which family dependants, villagers, "rustics," the "lower orders," the young, and all females have their subordinate places in a harmonious system presided over by the patriarchal gentry personified in "The Squire." This system is admittedly an ideal and a set of values rather than a reality, since, as a result of enclosure, the current denizens of the British countryside are less deferential peasants than "vagrants" and "beggars" who "did not know how to play their part in the scene of hospitality" (Irving 1988: 178). "The Squire" laments:

> "Our old games and local customs . . . had a great effect in making the peasant fond of his home, and the promotion of them by the gentry made him fond of his lord. . . . The nation . . . is altered; we have almost lost our simple, true-hearted peasantry. They have broken asunder from the higher classes and seem to think their interests are separate."
> (p. 178)

This vision is indeed an admirable expression of compassionate Burkean conservatism, as the narrator indicates by editorializing:

> There is something genuine and affectionate in the gayety of the lower orders, when it is excited by the bounty and familiarity of those above them; the warm glow of gratitude enters into their mirth, and a kind word, and a small pleasantry frankly uttered by a patron, gladdens the heart of the dependent more than oil and wine. (p. 179)

Second, underlying this vision of estate culture is a nostalgic, anti-modern model of traditional or "folk" time that is crystallized in the institution and rituals of Christmas itself. Christmas celebrations, for the narrator, offer a window into cyclical and ritual practices that realize the ideal of estate culture, presenting the reader with an ethno-racial British "folk" consciousness that is the necessary condition of the (national) model of unity idealized in the estate's hierarchical system of "tradition" (Warner 2000). This ritual and quasi-religious sense of time provides the narrator with an antidote to the anxiety-provoking dynamism of modernity and its progressive historical consciousness that is even more appealing than the overall charm of the manor life and venerable traditions described elsewhere in the larger book. Indeed, when the narrator notes that the observance of Christmas was interrupted by Cromwellian revolution "and that Christmas had been brought in again triumphantly with the merry court of King Charles at the restoration" (Irving 1988: 176), this "holyday" and sense of time is explicitly understood as anti-revolutionary, as embodying a "deep" sense of time and social order that transcends modern revolutionary antagonisms. Thus, when the narrator tells the reader that "nothing in England exercises a more delightful spell over my imagination than the lingerings of the holyday customs and rural games of former times" (p. 148), he uses this static and nostalgic vision of folk time to reject the model of secular and modern time exemplified in revolutionary mottoes like *novus ordo seclorum* ("new order of the ages": one of the legends on the Great Seal of the United States), or in the historically recent attempts of French revolutionaries to symbolize the beginning of a new historical era by abandoning the Gregorian calendar.

Kennedy published *Swallow Barn, or A Sojourn in the Old Dominion* in 1832. As the book developed, it moved from an initial plan for a collection of sketches and fiction that would imitate *The Sketch-book* to a final mode that hovers between novel and sketch collection, incorporating aspects of historical romance and travel writing. More directly and didactically than Irving, Kennedy presents a world organized around paternalistic, anti-modern social forms, rituals, and identities. The narrative uses the plot elements of a land dispute and a romantic intrigue, both presented in a satirical manner reminiscent of Fielding or Sterne, but these are balanced with the book's primary didactic concern, namely the illustration and justification of the plantation world as a model for organizing US social diversity. Narrator Mark Littleton leaves New York's modern market culture behind him to experience the world of his host

Frank Meriwether and other representatives of the landed gentry, creating the opportunity for them to convey their justifications for slavery and the frankly hierarchical, deferential social world they have built as Anglo-American gentry. In the chapter "Traces of the Feudal System," the narrator echoes the basic features of Irving's vision of harmonious British country life organized according to cyclical, ritual, anti-modern time, paternalism, and ethno-racial modes of identity:

> The gentlemen of Virginia . . . are surrounded by their bondsmen and their dependents; and the customary intercourse of society familiarizes their minds to the relation of high and low degree. They are scattered about like the chiefs of separate clans, and propagate opinions in seclusion, that have the tincture of baronial independence. They frequently meet in the interchange of a large and thriftless hospitality, in which the forms of society are foregone for its comforts, and the business of life thrown aside for the enjoyment of its pleasures. Their halls are large, and their boards ample; and surrounding the great family hearth, with its immense burthen casting a broad and merry glare over the congregated household and the numerous retainers, a social winter party in Virginia affords a tolerable picture of feudal munificence. (Kennedy 1832: vol. 1, 76)

The same ideal is invoked to resolve the dilemmas of slavery and slave insurrection in a system that Meriwether envisions as a "feudatory" that would "establish a class of privileged serfs" and "elevate our slave population to a more respectable footing" (vol. 2, 230).

The anti-modern, anti-democratic, and anti-revolutionary goals of this model are explicit in both *Swallow Barn* and Kennedy's historical romance of the Revolution, *Horse-Shoe Robinson*. In the latter novel, the narrator's reflections on the merits of primogeniture and other "feudal" institutions in eighteenth-century Virginia produces an editorial exclamation of frustration with Jacksonian America:

> Since that period, well-a-day! The hand of the reaper has put in his sickle on divided fields; crowded progenies have grown up under these paternal roof-trees; daughters have married and brought in strange names; the subsistence of one has been spread into the garner of ten. . . . and everywhere over this abode of ancient wealth, the hum of industry is heard in the carol of the ploughman, the echo of the wagoner's whip, the rude song of the boatman, and in the clatter of the mill. Such are the mischievous interpolations of the republican system! (Kennedy 1937: 15)

Here the Burkean vision of social order developed in Irving and Kennedy is starkly opposed to the republican ideology that legitimated revolutionary transformation.

A "republican system" of sorts is precisely what Paulding defends, on one level at least; and in this respect the energetic denunciation of the old regime and its institutions that drives his anti-British writings, histories, and historical fiction contrasts directly with the anti-revolutionary nostalgia of Irving and Kennedy. Despite his republican vocabulary of liberty, rights, and virtuous independence, however, the nationalistic vision of a social order compatible with republican virtue that appears in

Paulding's historical romances shares basic features with the models of Irving and Kennedy, emphasizing even more powerfully than they do an atavistic logic of racialist patriarchalism and legitimated violence.

Paulding's historical romance *The Dutchman's Fireside* is set in an imagined world of frontier primitivism during the 1750s ("somewhere about the time of the old French war"); the novel's vision of estate culture is thereby removed from the necessity of representing complex social relations or institutions. A romance of the "frontier," in other words, offers a fantasy of basic social forces and a literary form that can represent those forces without the entanglements and complications of society as it actually is. This novel tells the story of an iconic young Anglo-American, Sybrant Westbrook, as he proceeds from an initial state as the symbolically "orphaned" offspring of a British father and Dutch mother, through a series of romantic, comic, and adventurous trials, to a final happy resolution that unites him to his fully Dutch "cousin" Catalina Vancour so that he can become a paternalist landowner presiding over an estate presumably identical to the ancestral Vancour estate that figures as the center of the novel's "frontier" action.

Like his better-known contemporary James Fenimore Cooper, Paulding uses the frontier setting to develop essentialist racial and gender categories that envision prototypical Americanness as a virile manhood that defines itself by its violent rejection of all that it is not. An American, in *The Dutchman's Fireside*, is a man whose rightful violence and "natural" authority are expressions of "liberty" derived from his status as someone who is not European, not "colored," and not feminine. The underlying fantasy of domination that supports this vision of "national manhood" is obviously offensive when stated plainly, but commentators such as Richard Slotkin and Dana Nelson have persuasively clarified the ways it shapes American nationalism and expansionism from this period forward (Slotkin 1985; Nelson 1998). The powerful myth Paulding articulates here, in which the frontier is rightfully mastered by violent Anglo domination and Manifest Destiny, extends forward from romancers like Paulding and Cooper to the later "Western" as it appears in Owen Wister's key novel *The Virginian* (1902) and becomes a standard narrative type in the twentieth-century mass culture industry. Understanding Paulding's model of US nationhood in this manner also explains the larger ideological coherence of his writings, helping us understand, for example, how his "republican" political lexicon is compatible with his famously pro-slavery position in *Slavery in the United States* (1836).

Paulding's vision of republican "simplicity" in *The Dutchman's Fireside* is as incompatible with the market culture of capitalist modernity as it is with the "feudal" holdovers of Irving and Kennedy. The opening chapters emphasize the nostalgic culture of "simplicity" that characterizes the Vancour estate. Chapter 1 ("Rural Scenes and Rural Manners") describes the "Doric dignity and simplicity" of the mansion house and establishes a motif repeated throughout the narrative, in which the narrator contrasts the virtuous "simplicity" of the Vancour way of life to the "monkish bigotry" of feudalism on the one hand and to the corruption and "luxuries" of commerce and the city on the other (Paulding 1868: 6, 19). The narrator recalls "the manners, usages, and morals of the ancient patriarchs of Albany" to contrast this venerable order of "manly independence" to the "stormy puddle" of modern dynamism (pp. 29–30): "An age of simplicity is an age of morality; and hence it is that the wisest writers of antiquity have made simplicity of manners essential to the preservation of that liberty which cannot be sustained by a corrupt and luxurious people" (pp. 30). Sybrant Westbrook's realization of his "manly independence," however, proceeds not through republican theory but through the more violent process of assuming rightful authority over Africans like Aunt Nauntje, who are natural dependants, Indians like Hans Pipe, whose "natural cunning was quickened by the acquirement of some of the practices of the white man" (p. 154), and women like Catalina, whose kinship to Westbrook makes the book's resolution a fantasy projection of white racial purity into the national future. That his apprenticeship to this authority involves violence (providing many scenes of frontier warfare and intrigue) appears as a natural consequence of American ethno-racial diversity. As the narrator explains, the Vancours, who "cherished the primitive Dutch manners and, above, all the primitive Dutch language," "all found it necessary to mingle the arts of peace and war together; all had their arms at hand, and all knew how to use them" (pp. 10, 18). The novel's resolution brings Westbrook both back and forward to the primitive authority vested in his Anglo-Dutch origins when he marries his Vancour cousin and inherits the responsibilities of reproducing Vancour estate culture.

In their "retold legends," then, Irving, Paulding, and Kennedy present visions of American national identity through literary models of nostalgic, paternalist, racially atavistic *estate* culture. These nationalist visions are alternatives to the real complexity of the US *state* institutions and culture industry in which Irving, Paulding, and Kennedy flourished as highly influential functionaries and ideologues. Their fictions reveal basic cultural contradictions of the Jacksonian moment as they use the tools of the marketplace, the mass culture industry, and the bureaucratic state to publicize nostalgic myths that seem to deplore the very modernity that gives them form. From our vantage point at the beginning of the twenty-first century, they stand out as influential conservative rejections of the legacy of the radical Enlightenment and the nation's revolutionary political beginnings.

References and Further Reading

Aderman, Ralph M., and Kime, Wayne R. (2003). *Advocate for America: The Life of James Kirke Paulding*. London: Associated University Presses.

Anderson, Benedict (1991). *Imagined Communities: Reflections on the Origin and Spread of Nationalism*, rev. edn. New York and London: Verso.

Gellner, Ernest (1983). *Nations and Nationalism*. Ithaca, NY: Cornell University Press.

Gwathmey, Edward M. (1931). *John Pendleton Kennedy*. New York: Nelson.

Hedges, William L. (1988). "Introduction." In Washington Irving, *The Sketch Book of Geoffrey Crayon, Gent*. New York: Viking Penguin.

Hobsbawm, Eric J. (1990). *Nations and Nationalism since 1780*. Cambridge: Cambridge University Press.

Hroch, Miroslav (2000). *In the National Interest: Demands and Goals of European National Movements of the Nineteenth Century: A Comparative Perspective*, trans. Robin Cassling. Prague: Charles University.

Irving, Washington (1988). *The Sketch-book of Geoffrey Crayon, Gent.* New York: Viking Penguin. (First publ. 1819–20.)

Kennedy, John Pendleton (1832). *Swallow Barn, or A Sojourn in the Old Dominion*, 2 vols. Philadelphia: Carey & Lea.

Kennedy, John Pendleton (1937). *Horse-Shoe Robinson*. New York: American Book Co. (First publ. 1835.)

Lukács, Georg (1983). *The Historical Novel*, trans. Hannah Mitchell and Stanley Mitchell. Lincoln: University of Nebraska Press. (First publ. 1937.)

Nelson, Dana (1998). *National Manhood: Capitalist Citizenship and the Imagined Fraternity of White Men*. Durham, NC: Duke University Press.

Paulding, James Kirke (1868). *The Dutchman's Fireside*. New York: Scribner. (First publ. 1831.)

Rubin-Dorsky, Jeffrey (1988). *Adrift in the Old World: The Psychological Pilgrimage of Washington Irving*. Chicago: University of Chicago Press.

Slotkin, Richard (1985). *The Fatal Environment: The Myth of the Frontier in the Age of Industrialization, 1800–1890*. Middletown, Conn.: Wesleyan University Press.

Warner, Michael (2000). "Irving's Posterity." *English Literary History* 67: 3, 773–99.

Williams, Stanley T. (1935). *The Life of Washington Irving*, 2 vols. New York: Oxford University Press.

29

Captivity and Freedom: Ann Eliza Bleecker, Harriet Prescott Spofford, and Washington Irving's "Rip Van Winkle"

Eric Gary Anderson

By 1780 both captivity and freedom were longstanding American concerns. Fleeing religious persecution, resisting political tyranny, responding to the widespread actualities of slavery and Indian captivity, American colonists and citizens understood both issues as matters of burning local concern, familiar topics of both conversation and a broad variety of earlier American writing. Ostensibly nonfictional captivity narratives, for example, were tremendously popular from the earliest European explorations of America and on through the nineteenth century. At times these narratives may appear to popularize and thus simplify abstract concepts such as race, gender, and freedom, but more often than not, upon closer examination, they register and even dramatize a tantalizing range of complexities. They reflect and respond to complicated acts of cultural exchange and accommodation, with captives and captors alike negotiating both the linguistic and the social terms of their relations. And they also blur distinctions between nonfiction and fiction, freely embellishing historical actualities and making all sorts of things up. The narratives under discussion here – a brief true story about long-term captive of Indians Petrus Groot as well as fictions by Ann Eliza Bleecker, Harriet Prescott Spofford, and Washington Irving – speak powerfully to the ambiguities and ambivalences of both captivity and freedom while at the same time recording that both were real and present conditions for people of any race, culture, or nation living near, on, or beyond an American frontier.

On June 8, 1807, the *Albany* [New York] *Gazette* printed a remarkable announcement: "On Thursday, the 4th inst. about four miles from the city of Schenectady, aside of the Mohawk turnpike, sitting under a tree, I discovered Petrus Groot, who was supposed to have been slain in the Oriskena battle, under General Herkimer, on the 6th of August, in the year 1777" (Vail 1949: 60). The author of this news item, Judge John Sanders of Schenectady, had joined the general consensus in supposing his friend

Groot dead for nearly thirty years. Even in late eighteenth-century upstate New York, where the cities were not far removed from the wilderness and where local residents were well conditioned to the realities of Indian captivity, the resurfacing of a man so long lost and so generally consigned to death smacked of the marvelous and prompted Sanders to stake a claim: "I discovered Petrus Groot." Surrounding his claim with volleys of carefully recorded facts and locating it specifically in both time and space, the judge safeguards and legitimizes it while, in effect, enclosing and recapturing the man claimed.

For, as it turns out, Groot had been not a casualty of war but a prisoner of war, taken captive by Indians. These captors are shadowy figures, not specifically identified by nation or language: "he has been last a prisoner among the Indians north of Quebec," Sanders reports, after observing that Groot speaks "English, French, Dutch and Indian" (Vail 1949: 60). More important to this brief account than the identities of the captors is the confused identity of the captive:

> His mental faculties are much impaired, supposed to have been occasioned by a wound of a tomahawk near the fore part of his head, though he is at most times tolerably rational. His head is bald – the circle or sear of the scalping knife is plainly to be seen on it . . . [he] is a middle sized man, has blue eyes, a long countenance, and stoops much in the shoulder. (Vail 1949: 60)

Given Groot's impairment, the judge cannot reconstruct a conventional "before, during, and after" captivity narrative, and must dwell instead on the aftermath, the physical and psychological consequences of the captivity. For one thing,

> He refused to go home[;] as one of his former neighbors whom he saw would not recognize him, he was fearful his children and brothers would not. He said he would go to the Governor's. Being at times deranged, it is fearful he will stray too far away for his friends to find him. He is of a very respectable family and connexions. Any person who will take him up and bring him to the subscriber, at Schenectady, shall . . . be the means of relieving this poor unfortunate man from his distress, by restoring him to his family and friends. (Vail 1949: 60–1)

But Groot wanders off, unrestored, evidently preferring a homelessness more or less of his own choosing to the risk of a homelessness imposed upon him. His distress lies less in his being a man without a state – he opts, after all, to "go to the Governor's" – than in his being a man without a continuous and secure domestic sphere, a man who might not be reincorporated into the "very respectable family" that most powerfully defines, reinforces, and protects his identity.

For Groot, freedom from captivity is really just another form of captivity. He remains subjugated to the physical and psychological consequences of his long involuntary tenure with the Indians, and, at age sixty-three, he holds out little hope for a happy ending to his story. (In fact, the story as we know it does not have a resolution of any kind; Groot simply vanishes.) Perhaps his deeply ingrained skepticism about the likelihood of a happy ending helps explain his ambivalent response to being "discovered" and "taken" by Sanders, who writes: "I immediately recognized him, and on conversing with him he confessed himself to be the person I took him to be." Sanders' discovery works as another sort of capturing, or recapturing, and maybe Groot simply doesn't wish to be taken, even for himself, let alone "taken up" by those who would answer the judge's well-intentioned plea and return his reclaimed yet still straying friend to him. The discovered man seems, in any event, less confident than the discoverer and less than fully cooperative, hesitating when the time comes to name and claim himself, and then *confessing* that he is in fact who he appears to be. Perhaps Groot is once and for ever captive, once and for ever lost, himself and yet never again himself, whether or not Sanders intervenes.

Judge Sanders' brief captivity narrative has not received a great deal of critical attention. Yet the story of Petrus Groot intersects with its fuller and richer contemporaries in illuminating ways, bringing into clearer focus some of the complexities of captivity and freedom as they play out in late eighteenth- and early nineteenth-century American literature. It serves as a baseline or touchstone that helps foreground the blurry distinctions between fiction and nonfiction, subject and object, the knowable and the unknowable, as well as a host of other pressing concerns about gender, race, and transcultural engagements on complicated and contested colonial ground. Many of the most familiar captivity narratives are, like Sanders', presented as nonfictional; but during the 1780–1865 period fictional captivity narratives began to emerge with increasing frequency and to capture new generations of readers. At first, fictions such as "The History of Maria Kittle" (1793) by New York writer Ann Eliza Bleecker (1752–83) resemble their nonfictional counterparts in various ways: for example, her narrative, like Sanders', makes possible a critique of frontier masculinity. But as American fiction in both longer and shorter forms takes stronger hold, fictional treatments of captivity and freedom begin to diversify; short stories such as "Rip Van Winkle" (1819) by another New Yorker, Washington Irving (1783–1859), and "Circumstance" (1860) by Maine native Harriet Prescott Spofford (1835–1921) overlap but glancingly with older and more conventional captivity narratives. The captors in Irving's story are not even Indians, and the captor in Spofford's story is not even human – though, as an animal known as "the Indian Devil," it metaphorically represents the often demonized and dehumanized Indians. Thus Spofford both acknowledges and retools a popular and familiar racial representation even as she more searchingly rethinks the narrative form of captivity.

Certainly Groot's story as it is packaged by Sanders evinces a familiarity with captivity narratives as a popular genre, which is to say that it meets some (though not all) of its readers' genre-driven expectations: the white captive is the protagonist of the story, the Indian captors are paradoxically presumed to be culturally subordinate to their captive(s), the released captive is to some significant extent "impaired," and the narrative draws contrasts between the mundane and the exotic. Major critical issues raised by students of captivity narratives typically grow out of an acknowledgment that such questions of genre, entangled with questions of historical and cultural contexts, are inescapable. For example, stories of captivity and freedom typically involve more than one race and culture, yet writing, and by extension literary genre, are white Euro-American tools. James Levernier and Hennig Cohen emphasize that "Indian captivity was a massive historical reality" (for both Natives and non-Natives) that "helped to shape the [American if not, here, tribally specific] national character" (1977: xiii). But as Kathryn Zabelle Derounian-Stodola and Levernier observe, "by the latter half of the eighteenth century, the historicity of any narrative written in the first person becomes suspect because, in imitation of the novel, wholly fictional narratives were customarily expected to use various strategies to appear factual" (1993: 11). Seen in this light, Sanders may seem, prior to investigation, to be another fictive traveler–adventurer, another Gulliver or picaresque hero, while Indian captors may be viewed in a distorted or limited way because they do not use writing, let alone European literary conventions, to record and retell stories of captivity and freedom.

One of the principal problems with captivities, then, is "defining exactly what the term *Indian captivity narrative* means" (Derounian-Stodola and Levernier 1993: 9). Since roughly the 1970s, narratologists – theorists of narrative structure and function – have raised searching questions about the stability and reliability of the generic categories "fiction" and "nonfiction," enabling critics to embrace a broad spectrum of eligible captivity-related narratives. But such a flexible, expansive definition prompts many challenging questions. What, if anything, does a particular narrative reveal about its characters' and author's historical and cultural contexts, including both public and private understandings of personal, national, and cultural freedom? Do these narratives give voice to American Indians? Do they permit students of "the Indians north of Quebec," say, to draw on Sanders' brief narrative to help them understand Indian–white relations? Is "The History of Maria Kittle" "simply a captivity narrative turned novel of sensibility," as Roy Harvey Pearce claimed in 1947 (Derounian-Stodola and Levernier 1993: 186), or is it more complicated than that? Does it, as Allison Giffen contends, help readers recognize and measure "the racist conventions of Indian captivity narratives ... and ... the powerful rhetorical strategies of sentimentalism in the construction of a national identity" (Irving 2002: 1167)? And how do other fictional treatments of captivity, such as Charles Brockden Brown's *Edgar Huntly* (1799), Irving's "Rip Van Winkle," Catharine Maria Sedgwick's *Hope Leslie* (1827), and Spofford's "Circumstance," mobilize the gothic, the sublime, the folkloric, and other (often European-derived) literary modes in the service of a distinctly American yet demonstrably transcultural and even transnational Indian–white literary terrain? Such questions proliferate, underscoring the complexities of captivity and freedom and allowing readers to reconsider both the supposed truths of the older captivity narratives and the alleged fictionality of the newer.

In a similar post-structuralist vein, feminist critics have called intensified attention to the ways in which gender roles and relations are represented and critiqued in earlier American narratives that investigate (among other things) captivity and freedom. For example, while women were abducted more frequently than men (Castiglia 1996: 199 n. 14), husbands and fathers in captivity narratives are often and in one way or another absent. Many of these men (though not, so far as Judge Sanders lets on, Petrus Groot) err in some way when it comes to dealing with potential and actual attacks on their home places and loved ones. Each of the three fictional narratives under discussion here mobilizes the absent husband and father motif. In "The History of Maria Kittle," Maria's husband William (who has a positive genius for leaving home at the wrong time) most classically fits the mold, contributing in the process to Bleecker's larger critique of masculine agency. Although patriarchal defense of the home is far from infallible and at times hopelessly inept even when the men are there, absence nevertheless diminishes masculinity – in part because it does *not* cause or otherwise accommodate Indian violence. In "Rip Van Winkle," which like Bleecker's narrative is set in the upstate New York backyard of Petrus Groot and John Sanders, Rip escapes both his wife and his workload by vanishing for twenty years. From Dame Van Winkle's point of view, of course, her husband has been scandalously absent for many years prior to his physical disappearance, while their daughter rehearses the familiar suspicion that missing persons have been taken by local Indians: " 'his dog came home without him; but whether he shot himself, or was carried away by the Indians, nobody can tell' " (Irving 2002: 2090). The key narrative fact, however interpreted, is Rip's absence. Finally, in the Maine wilderness of "Circumstance," the unnamed husband appears, finally, at almost the last moment and liberates his wife, who has been traveling alone, from captivity.

Christopher Castiglia argues that while many early white American women writers wrote nonfictional captivity narratives, many others, such as Bleecker, also helped propel the genre into what he calls "the wilderness of fiction." Within this ambiguous and liberating space, the absent patriarch operates as a critique of "masculine heroics" and the "conventional rescue plots" that promote them (1996: 126, 125). More generally, questions about the identity of the captivity narrative intersect with questions about the identities of authors, captors, captives, and (sometimes) others: "Captivity narratives . . . have repeatedly transgressed boundaries between cultures and identities. As these historical narratives became fictionalized, they allowed white women authors to cross literary boundaries as well, combining conventional genres and challenging distinctions between fact and fiction" (p. 106). That is, the narratives describe or evoke ambiguous, multiple identities; and the narratives themselves often have ambiguous, multiple identities. And when Stephen Greenblatt, discussing an earlier period of European travel writing about the Americas, observes that "I catch myself constantly straining to read into the European traces an account of what the American natives were 'really' like" (1991: 7), he approaches a similar problem from a somewhat different angle. Such complexities are no strangers to American narratives of captivity and freedom. Identity, in the historical and transcultural contexts of colonial America, is subject to change, revision, stress, disintegration, and the motivated as well as the unsuspected vagaries of narration.

The fictional narratives by Bleecker, Irving, and Spofford, very much of their time, traffic in the identity politics of writing and reading captivity and freedom. Set primarily in the Albany area and in Montreal around the time of the French and Indian War, Ann Eliza Bleecker's "The History of Maria Kittle," written in 1779 and published posthumously in 1793, conflates biography, history, captivity narrative, and the novel. It is perhaps best described as a fictional captivity narrative that resembles its nonfictional counterparts in multiple ways while also drawing on various novelistic tropes and modes, including romance, sympathy, sensibility, and frontier/wilderness adventure. The text's epistolary opening directly addresses questions of genre: "However fond of novels and romances you may be, the unfortunate adventures of one of my neighbours, who died yesterday, will make you despise that fiction, in which, knowing the subject to be fabulous, we can never be so truly interested" (Bleecker 1793: 19). And the narrative ends with the reunion of Maria Kittle and her truant, lost husband: "he believed not for joy, he was conducted to her arms, and found his bliss wonderfully real" (Bleecker 1793: 69–70). Bleecker's decision to end the narrative with the word "real" operates as something of an inside joke, given that the narrative is in fact fictional – however well disguised in the (still primarily nonfictional) form of a captivity narrative. The seeming move away from romance and toward the real is of course belied by the narrative's "wonderfully" coincidental resolution as well as by the text's various excursions into the wilderness realms of the supernatural, the psychological, the violent, and the Indian.

Again and again, Bleecker, as well versed as her readers in the attractive conventions of nonfictional captivity narratives, gives those readers what they want. At the same time, she remaps the terrain by turning to "the wilderness of fiction" and by critiquing white husbands. Comelia Kittle's husband, for no clear reason, responds to an Indian attack on the Kittle house by unbarring the door and letting the Indians in. In short order, white people are tomahawked to death, corpses are mangled, infants are dashed to pieces in front of their mothers, houses are burned to the ground, captives – here, Maria Kittle and her brother Henry – are taken, and relatives are left to discover the violated remains while readers are granted a second look at scenes of graphic violence. Here and elsewhere Bleecker both respects generic conventions and reinvents the genre, not only by opening it up to fiction but also by identifying and arguing out questions of gender in relation to questions of captivity and freedom. In a captivity story told later in the narrative, for example, Mrs. Willis remarks that "Mr. Willis...all pale and astonished, neither understood nor had power to answer" the attacking Indians, who, in a parody of domestic repast, seated themselves around the table with him and "took a great pleasure in terrifying him, by flourishing their knives, and gashing the table with their hatchets. Alas! this sight shot icicles to my soul" (Bleecker 1793: 75). Speaking in her own narrative voice, Mrs. Willis links muteness to male disempowerment and male domesticity to phallocentric violence. Such unsettlings of both race and gender had been implicit in even some of the earliest nonfictional captivity narratives – when, for example, Indian women challenge white parenthood by suckling white infants – but Bleecker gives them explicit and even dramatic voice.

For example, when Maria Kittle is released from captivity in Montreal, she meets sympathetic French and English women who take in newly freed American captives such as herself and Mrs. Willis, tend them, and listen to their captivity narratives. Castiglia argues that these shared storytelling sessions produce "America's first literary consciousness-raising group" (1996: 127) – a group that, by extension, includes Bleecker's own female readers. More than most of her nonfiction-writing predecessors, Bleecker underscores the process of translating painful immediate experience into memory and narrative. But even more brilliantly, she explores the psychological dynamics of the transformative exchanges that take place among women who tell violent, painful stories to each other for pleasure. As one of the Frenchwomen exclaims, "'my ear is now sweetly tuned to melancholy. I love to indulge these divine sensibilities, which your affecting histories are so capable of inspiring'" (Bleecker 1793: 56). The emphasis on listening raises startling questions about how captivity narratives function transculturally: what does it mean, for example, to transform abject terror into esthetic pleasure, captive bodies into sweetly tuned hearts? Is captivity narrating, like captivity itself at times, sexually or homo-socially charged? The French, English, and American women hunger for each other's oral stories and transform captivity into something like freedom by way of tender ministrations and the construction of a flourishing community in which men are absent by design.

Rip Van Winkle, also absent by design, vanishes from his upstate New York home before the American Revolutionary War and returns "home" after the war's conclusion, to the astonishment of those who knew him many years ago. But the relationship between Irving's 1819 short story and conventional captivity narratives is oblique. It is possible to argue that Rip is deeply in thrall to his wife – whom the narrator repeatedly characterizes as a shrew and a tyrant – prior to his disappearance. But it is also possible to see Dame Van Winkle's complaints as well founded and justified, given her husband's laziness and apparent ineptitude when it comes to almost any work-related activities. In any event, Rip is not abducted by Indians, and it is an open question whether he is ever held captive at all; maybe he just nods off for twenty years, or maybe he enters some sort of liquorish supernatural time warp, a liminal space inhabited by early Dutch explorers who like to bowl. Maybe his sleeping through the Revolution is a way for Irving, a few years into what turned out to be a seventeen-year stint in England and Europe, to measure and articulate various anxieties of nation-formation. Old Peter Vanderdonk reports that he and his father have heard and even seen these substantive yet ghostly discoverers without vanishing for twenty years; it is another open question why Rip does when others do not. In various ways, Rip's experience is shrouded in mystery. Perhaps the longer title of the story, tucked inside the frame of "Rip Van Winkle," furnishes an important clue: "Rip Van Winkle: A Posthumous Writing of Diedrich Knickerbocker," raises the question of what exactly "A Posthumous Writing" might be, let alone what it might mean, especially in relation to captivity and freedom. Texts are published posthumously often enough rarely to raise eyebrows – but "A Posthumous *Writing*" suggests something rather more supernatural, something like ghost writing.

Certainly the story has much to do with ghosts, both tangible and intangible. The old Dutch bowlers appear to be solid and stolid, though at the same time spectral and reminiscent of "the figures in an old Flemish painting" (Irving 2002: 2086). Dame Van Winkle is dead and the old Van Winkle house is an early American ruin, "gone to decay – the roof fallen in, the windows shattered, and the doors off the hinges" (Irving 2002: 2088). The village as Rip once knew it is no more, and colonial America has been transformed into a new nation, a transition wittily registered by the portrait of King George III at the downtown inn, which, with a bit of retouching to alter the coat and hat, now portrays General Washington. In a sense the perfectly transparent image of the King and what he represents gazes out from the signboard portrait now captioned "General Washington" and retooled ostensibly to signify what *he* represents. As the nation wrenches itself out of the captivity of political tyranny and toward something like self-determined and self-representing freedom, citizens like the local innkeeper see no reason not to use essentially the same portrait to signify, in turn, loyalty, captivity, and freedom. In this same vein, the post-"captivity" Rip Van Winkle re-establishes himself in the village with, as is characteristic of him, little effort, finding himself "reverenced as one of the patriarchs of the village and a chronicle of the old times 'before the war'" (Irving 2002: 2091). Rip, who prior to his disappearance regaled village children with "long stories of ghosts, witches, and Indians" (Irving 2002: 2083), resurfaces as a village storyteller who is also a subject for one of his own stories, a sort of ghost or remnant of a freshly (and yet not so freshly) historical past. These peculiar kinds of hauntings, in which ghostly otherness doubles as an uncanny sameness, work as a sort of flexible loop or noose; Rip cannot entirely break free of it, but he can stretch it to some extent and find ways of making himself comfortable within it. At the same time, Irving's transatlantic vantage point and use of German folk-tales help to reposition American writing in transnational contexts – bearing in mind that many American narratives prior to Irving's are inescapably transnational – while at the same time almost entirely excising indigenous transnationalisms.

"Circumstance" was first published in *The Atlantic* in May 1860 when its author, Harriet Prescott Spofford, was in her mid-twenties and very near the beginning of her long literary career; it was then reprinted three years later in the collection *The Amber Gods and Other Stories* (1863). In this story Spofford imagines an ambiguous escape from an extraordinary captivity, wherein a woman uses wile and song to fend off the sexually threatening wild male panther that holds her in its grip. Although pinned down rather than carried off – a significant difference from conventional captivities, which frequently double as travel narratives – the immobilized captive finds herself in grave danger from her brute, Indianized captor. Finally liberated by her husband after a full night of captivity, she returns home with him and their child, only to find that home burned to the ground:

> There is no home there. The log-house, the barns, the neighboring farms, the fences, are all blotted out and mingled in one smoking ruin. Desolation and death were indeed there, and beneficence and life in the forest. Tomahawk and scalping-knife, descending during that night, had left behind them only this work of their accomplished hatred and one subtle foot-print in the snow. (Spofford 1989: 96)

The unnamed woman's abduction by a devilish panther both represents and averts abduction – and perhaps murder – by unnamed destroyers whose tomahawk and scalping-knife imply but do not absolutely confirm their Indianness. The horror of the scene lies in its combination of erasure and mixing, its translation of contemporary 1860s anxieties about miscegenation: everything is "all blotted out *and* mingled in one smoking ruin." But the horror also lies in the immediate subsequent turn to a flimsy binary opposition – "Desolation and death were indeed there, and beneficence and life in the forest" – which flies in the face of what has just happened to the woman in the forest. Perhaps the "beneficence and life" refer to her rescue and its crowding out short-term memories of all that preceded it; perhaps the woman's generally comfortable, sympathetic sense of the natural world (wild animal attacks notwithstanding) also takes precedence over her desperate but singular nocturnal troubles in the wilderness; perhaps the narrator reaches for a nearly unendurable irony here at the close of the story. But, as with each of the other narratives discussed in this essay, the loss of home, however "home" is constructed, links to the experience of captivity in complicated ways and renders freedom ambivalent at best. The condition of being left behind, in conjunction with Spofford's decision to leave all characters (including the animal) unnamed, oddly connects the principal players in this story: the animal captor's dead body is left behind, the captive's memories of her captivity are left behind, and the smoking ruins of home are left behind by destroyers whose shadowy traces produce an uncanny, unsettling, shadowy sense of the left-behind – unsettling not least because it is oddly artistic, "subtle" and "accomplished," yet eerily unknown or unknowable, like an artwork without a fully legible signature.

Like Bleecker's and Irving's narratives, Spofford's has a haunting, gothic quality and even behaves as a haunt, as Emily Dickinson perceptively remarked: "I read Miss Prescott's 'Circumstance,' but it followed me, in the Dark – so I avoided her" (Baym 1998: 2574). Dickinson underscores two important points: that the identities of the story and the storyteller merge, and that the captivity narrative is capable of enacting what it describes – capable of taking readers captive in ways that stretch well beyond sheer, or mere, entertainment. In various ways, all four narratives discussed here pose similar questions about what it means to transform experience into story, and all four think skeptically about the desirability of freedom. At times they intimate that neither pre- nor post-captivity experience is quite as energizing, quite as captivating, as life during. But the terrors and dangers of captivity must not be underestimated. Captivity and freedom in American fiction of this period have a great deal to do with Rip Van Winkle's anguished cry and his need to make it:

> I'm not myself – I'm somebody else – that's me yonder – no – that's somebody else, got into my shoes – I was myself last night, but I fell asleep on the mountain, and they've changed my gun, and every thing's changed, and I'm changed, and I can't tell what's my name, or who I am! (Irving 2002: 945)

Such confusion is often rampant for the captives, the captors, *and* the proliferating, multiplying narratives that worry and sometimes reproduce the conditions of captivity and freedom – the conditions, more broadly, of American cultural exchanges and transformations. Even as they are gradually transformed from nonfiction into "the wilderness of fiction," stories of captivity and freedom take their place as part of an American literary economy in which oral and written language defines, confirms, and produces – or befuddles, impairs, and obstructs – identities. In other words, captivity seems to generate narrative: Sanders is compelled to write down and circulate his account of Groot's reappearance, Maria Kittle and Ann Eliza Bleecker join a women's storytelling circle, Rip Van Winkle (whether taken captive or not) cannot help but retell his story, and the protagonist of "Circumstance" sings what amounts to her autobiography while in the heavy paws of a wilderness animal. Whether in the desperate immediacy of that woman's narrative or the leisurely recollections of Rip Van Winkle, the friendly concern of Judge Sanders or the pleasurable melancholies of oral stories exchanged by women in Bleecker's text, captivity itself is captive to narrative, word-locked and captivating in turn to the generations of readers who freely take up wildernesses of their own.

References and Further Reading

Baym, N., gen. ed. (1998). *The Norton Anthology of American Literature*, 5th edn., vol. 1. New York: Norton.

Bleecker, A. E. (1793). "The History of Maria Kittle." In *The Posthumous Works of Ann Eliza Bleecker, in Prose and Verse. To which is added, a Collection of Essays, Prose and Poetical, by Margaretta V. Faugeres*. New York: T. & J. Swords.

Burnham, M. (1997). *Captivity and Sentiment: Cultural Exchange in American Literature, 1682–1861*. Hanover, NH: University Press of New England.

Calloway, C. (1997). *New Worlds for All: Indians, Europeans, and the Remaking of Early America*. Baltimore: Johns Hopkins University Press.

Castiglia, C. (1996). *Bound and Determined: Captivity, Culture-Crossing, and White Womanhood from Mary Rowlandson to Patty Hearst*. Chicago: University of Chicago Press.

Derounian-Stodola, Kathryn Zabelle, and Levernier, James Arthur (1993). *The Indian Captivity Narrative, 1550–1900*. New York: Twayne.

Ellison, J. (1993). "Race and Sensibility in the Early Republic: Ann Eliza Bleecker and Sarah Wentworth Morton." *American Literature* 65: 3, 445–74.

Gaul, T. S. (2002). "Captivity, Childbirth, and the Civil War in Harriet Prescott Spofford's 'Circumstance.'" *Legacy* 19: 1, 35–43.

Giffen, Allison (2002). "Ann Eliza Bleecker." In P. Lauter (gen. ed.), *The Heath Anthology of American Literature*, 4th edn., vol. 1, 1166–8. Boston: Houghton Mifflin.

Greenblatt, S. (1991). *Marvellous Possessions: The Wonder of the New World*. Chicago: University of Chicago Press.

Irving, Washington (2002). "Rip Van Winkle." In P. Lauter (gen. ed.), *The Heath Anthology of American Literature*, 4th edn., vol. 1, 2081–93. Boston: Houghton Mifflin.

Levernier, J., and Cohen, H., eds. (1977). *The Indians and their Captives*. Westport, Conn.: Greenwood.

Spofford, H. P. (1989). "Circumstance." In *"The Amber Gods" and Other Stories*, ed. A. Bendixen. New Brunswick, NJ: Rutgers University Press. (First publ. 1863.)

Vail, R. W. G. (1949). *The Voice of the Old Frontier*. Philadelphia: University of Pennsylvania Press.

30

New England Tales: Catharine Sedgwick, Catherine Brown, and the Dislocations of Indian Land

Bethany Schneider

Catharine Sedgwick's first novel, *A New England Tale* (1822), begins with travelers arriving in an unnamed town. One of them, Mrs. Lloyd, is a "Quaker" interloper from Philadelphia, though her Quakerism is a stand-in for the scandalous Unitarianism to which Sedgwick herself had converted.[1] Dying from a wasting disease, Mrs. Lloyd has come in search of better air, and Sedgwick gives to her arrival in New England the same sanctity that would attend the arrival of a soul in heaven. Mrs. Lloyd says to her husband upon entry into the Housatonic valley: "It certainly matters little where our dust is laid, if it be consecrated by Him who is the 'resurrection and the life;' but I derive a pleasure which I could not have conceived of, from the expectation of having my body repose in this still valley, under the shadow of that beautiful hill" (Sedgwick 1995: 33). The view that God and "the world" are separate quickly gives way to an alternative understanding of faith located not only in the generic "earthly," but in a very particular place in the world, the area surrounding the town. The hills, Mrs. Lloyd continues, seem to "enclose a sanctuary, a temple, from which the brightness of His presence is never withdrawn." Knowing that she is dying, Mrs. Lloyd hopes that her daughter's "path [will] le[a]d along these still waters, far from the stormy waves of the rude world" (p. 33).

Something extraordinary has happened to the landscape through Mrs. Lloyd's description. The Housatonic has *become*, in Mrs. Lloyd's formulation, the "still waters" beside which the speaker of the Twenty-third Psalm is led. This formulation goes further than typology. In Mrs. Lloyd's eyes, the Housatonic is neither metaphoric nor metonymic of the heavenly. Rather, in its physical being, it is simultaneously sacred and this-worldly, a precept of Unitarian thought that came to be known later as Panentheism. Such thought posits that God exists in all things, but is also *more than* all things. But Sedgwick splits this theological hair even further. She does not argue that God sheds his extra-sacred grace on *all* of nature. Across the course of Mrs. Lloyd's description, the valley of the Housatonic becomes heavenly, if not heaven itself, while everywhere else remains "the rude world." The coincidence of heaven with this small section of western Massachusetts is repeated and saluted throughout *A New England Tale*. The novel proposes that belonging to and being of this particular land is the prize for those white people who can read its special sacred status. Thus even a foreign interloper like Mrs. Lloyd can become, in the blink of an eye, indigenous to New England. Belonging to New England soil thus parallels the anti-Calvinist theological argument that belief and faith *can* effect one's salvation and that predestination is false. Indigeneity in a sacred landscape, like salvation, is conferred in a moment of passionate recognition.

A New England Tale stages its bid for the sanctity of New England land as a contest between Calvinists who eschew the worldly and non-Calvinists who recognize the land's divinity. But this cultural and doctrinal duel, and the ability of white non-Calvinists to experience belonging as conversion, is itself dependent upon not only the physical absence of Native Americans, but the absence of any conception that the land was ever Indian land.[2] Many novels, including Sedgwick's own *Hope Leslie*, illustrate the abandoning of the land by Indians, whether by choice or force; indeed, white American authors of the first half of the nineteenth century fell over themselves to produce fiction about Indians and by extension Indian land, taking up Charles Brockden Brown's 1799 edict that declared both Indians and land to be "suited" to an American literary palette: "The incidents of Indian hostility, and the perils of the western wilderness, are far more suitable [to American writers]; and for a native of America to overlook these, would admit of no apology" (Brown 1988: 3). In *A New England Tale*, however, Sedgwick distills Brockden Brown's formula for American fiction, dispensing with Indians and wilderness and going straight for the underlying question of nativeness. The plot of *A New England Tale* turns on a contest over which group of whites can recognize the implicit sanctity of New England, with indigeneity as the prize; Sedgwick therefore goes out of her way to ignore Native American claims. In *A New England Tale*, neither voluntary disappearance nor forced removal nor slaughter of Indians will solve Sedgwick's problem of making whites indigenous to the land. Whether the practices are depicted in a "sympathetic" or an "Indian-hating" mode, the disappearance, removal, and slaughter of Indians nevertheless involve a narrative which acknowledges the passing of a baton of ownership and occupation.

In "Frontier Democracy and Representational Management," Dana Nelson shows how the Indians in frontier narratives of the early nineteenth century function to dismantle the potential of local, radical democracy among white Americans (Dana 2002: 215–29). Nelson traces how the debate over what is "the local" had profound implications for the way American democracy developed, although she is "skeptical about claims for the local *as place* given the ways communities can define themselves through majoritarian, exclusionary, anti-democratic practices" (pp. 220–1). But that potential for exclusion in the suturing of the local to place is exactly what Sedgwick wants, and it allows her to dispense with Indians altogether. Sedgwick's insistence on the instantaneous indigeneity of those who recognize the sanctity of New England soil, combined with her insistence that Indians *not* be a part of that narrative, takes the anti-political goal Nelson ascribes to frontier narrative one step further, and achieves the "domestication" of the anti-political move that frontier fiction makes.[3] The ability of white women, white children, and marginal white men to recognize the sanctity of New England land and become indigenous redescribes the property-making at the heart of frontier narratives as belonging, and thus it is Indian land but explicitly not Indian people that must be digested and reconfigured in the bowels of *A New England Tale*. Unlike frontier narratives that rely upon the counting of dead Indian bodies in order to disguise avarice for land as a desire for freedom, Sedgwick's version depends upon her whiting-out of Native American bodies altogether in order to disguise the spoils of avarice as sanctified land to which white people belong.

But the geographical blanks left by whited-out Indians are only imperfectly inhabited by brand-new white indigenes. Blank spaces pock the physiognomy of *A New England Tale* and are the means to reading this Indianless novel as an Indian novel. The setting, we are told, is the town of ——, though it is obvious now and was obvious then that the town of —— is a thin disguise for Sedgwick's home town of Stockbridge, Massachusetts. Literary convention of the day allows that blank space and the Stockbridge that lurks behind it to pass unremarked. But that blank space in the text allows Sedgwick to perform all sorts of sleights of hand regarding Stock-bridge's status as a place. The fact that the town of —— is and was recognizable as Stockbridge serves to make Stockbridge all the more specific and all the more sacred; it is there to be *recognized* in a moment of revelation that depends upon identifying landmarks and geographical features, just as we see Mrs. Lloyd *recognize* the sanctity of the Housatonic valley. But the blank serves an equal and opposite purpose. It makes the specificity of Stockbridge generic and repeatable, and therefore designates an entire region composed of several states, rather than one small town, as local. This is "A New England Tale," a title which argues that Stockbridge could be any of several hundred small towns from northern Maine to southern Connecticut. Stockbridge could be any town in New England; *and* Stockbridge is presented as the template for New England, and by extension the nation and even the world. The blank is an active lacuna in the text, one that both corrals the appeal of the local for region- and nation-building purposes and telescopes the regional, the national, and the global into the local in order to claim the primacy and sanctity of a specific place.

Very early on in *A New England Tale* Sedgwick describes Jane, a newly orphaned child in the town of ——, at the grave of her dead mother. Here white, non-Calvinist belonging occurs through burial in sacred New English soil: "As [the clods] fell heavily, poor Jane shrieked, 'oh, mother!' and springing forward, bent over the grave, which, to her, seemed to contain all the world" (Sedgwick 1995: 13). The grave "seems" to contain the world because Jane's mother is dear to her and Jane sprang from her. But by placing the globe itself in a gaping New England grave (and from Mrs. Lloyd we know that to be buried in a New England grave is to come to repose in heaven itself) Sedgwick is able to argue that the ground itself is precious. The hole of the grave – like the blank name of the town – contains everywhere within it and refracts everything through it. Jane's ability to recognize this fuels and is fueled by the fact that she will go on to become the paradigmatic good New England girl, but not a Calvinist New England girl. Her virtue is predicated on a heresy. Her graveside vision is a very different lesson from that espoused in *The New England Primer* (1777), which teaches the child that death marks the end of attachment to this world; "Come welcome death the end of fears, / I am prepar'd to die: / Those earthly flames will send my soul / up to the Lord on high. / Farewell my children to the world, / where you must yet remain" (Ford 1962: 35). Here the act of looking into a New England grave prepares children to leave the world behind: "I in the burying place may see, / Graves shorter there than I, / From death's arrest no age is free, / Young children too must die. / My God may such an awful sight, Awakening be to me! / Oh! that by early grace I might / For death prepared be" (Ford 1962: 22). Jane, looking into the grave, sees not a preparation for death and a life beyond the worldly, but the world itself. The narrative continues *not* to illustrate her progression towards a holy death, as so many children's narratives did at that time (Brown 2000), but to narrate her progression into a life as a white indigene in a sanctified New English place.

Having re-educated us on how to read the grave, Sedgwick immediately goes on to illustrate how traditional Calvinist doctrine dislocates the "world" and fails to recognize the sanctity of New England. After the funeral, three equally selfish Calvinist sisters argue over which will take responsibility for raising Jane. The eldest, Mrs. Daggett, makes this excuse for not adopting her orphaned niece:

> Mr. Daggett and herself *calculated* to do a great deal for the Foreign Missionary Society; that no longer ago than that morning, Mr. D. and she had agreed to pay the expense of one of the young Cherokees at the School at ——; that there was a great work going on in the world, and as long as they had the heart given them to help it, they could not feel it their duty to withdraw any aid for a mere worldly purpose! (Sedgwick 1995: 14)

Mrs. Daggett uses opposing references to "the world." Smugly imagining herself part of a global mission, a "great work going on the world," at the same time she self-righteously rejects local and familial action as "a mere worldly purpose." This contradiction neatly negates Mrs. Daggett's position, but Sedgwick hammers home Mrs. Daggett's failure to become a white indigene through her attachment to – of all people – Indians. The Cherokee school at —— sits as an eerie opposite to the town of ——; it is the only other place marked by a blank in a book that is otherwise happy to mention place-names. The blank space of Indian occupation is represented as distant, non-local, and distracting. Sedgwick thus ties Calvinist disdain for the world to Indian spaces, in a move that names Indians not as the original and dislocated inhabitants of New England, but as inadmissible outsiders to New England (unlike Mrs. Lloyd), and as the paradigmatic agent in distracting white New Englanders from the sanctity of New English land and their own revelatory indigeneity in it.

In 1822 Sedgwick had reason to be concerned about Indian missions and about Cherokee mission work in particular. Founded in 1810, the American Board of Commissioners for Foreign Missions grew out of the Second Great Awakening, and the "firm belief within the New England Congregationalists that their benevolence must extend beyond themselves, their cities, and their villages. Equipped with this belief, each missionary sought to follow the Bible's great command to 'Go ye into all the World and preach the gospel'" (Phillips and Phillips 1998: 2). Sedgwick's "young Cherokees at the School at ——" have a historical counterpart. In 1817 the Board founded Brainerd School in the Cherokee Nation, on the Tennessee–Georgia border. The school, which operated up until Cherokee removal in 1838, was funded almost entirely by donations from New Englanders who, in enormous numbers, adopted the cause of converting Indian children.

In his influential study *Playing Indian*, Philip Deloria examines instances since the Boston Tea Party of white Americans pretending to be Indians, and shows how the impulse to adopt buckskin and feathers comes from an ambivalence about belonging that lies at the heart of white American identity. "Whereas Euro-Americans had imprisoned themselves in the logical mind and the social order," he writes, "Indians represented instinct and freedom. They spoke for the 'spirit of the continent.'" Whites, he argues, tend to don Indian costume at crucial moments because "Whites desperately desired that spirit, yet they invariably failed to become aboriginal and thus 'finished'" (Deloria 1998: 3). Sedgwick recognizes that white people need to "become aboriginal," but she also recognizes that imitating Indian bodies will never fully divest Indians of their indigeneity and will therefore never fully make whites aboriginal. Sedgwick wants the "spirit of the continent" to be a white spirit. Therefore, far from wanting to imitate Indian bodies, she wants to strip Indian bodies of what it means to be indigenous. She goes straight for the land, bypassing Indian people altogether. But even landownership is not enough; Sedgwick wants to belong to the land, in addition to having land belong to her. Jane and the other non-Calvinists neither dress as Indians nor do they own land; rather, Jane and the others perform a transformative recognition of place as sacred that is imagined by Sedgwick as appropriate to and creative of indigeneity. Indians enter only in order to illustrate that which is fundamentally foreign and to distract whites from their own potential to recognize New England's sanctity and thereby become indigenous.

But if the town of —— is sacred and the Cherokee school at —— is its evil twin, their twinness remains. And if Quakers and Unitarians, Cherokees and Osages can become interchangeable in Sedgwick's text, then Sedgwick's Cherokees and Osages can re-enter the town of —— as "Housatonics" (by which Sedgwick means the mixture of Mahican, Housatonic, and Wappinger Indians who came together to become the "Stockbridge Indians," a tribal name they still carry) through that overlapping double blank in the text. Stockbridge was founded as a missionary town and until immediately before Sedgwick's birth in 1789 was largely Indian-owned. A few years before Sedgwick was born (but over a century *after* the date she sets for the disappearance of Native New Englanders from the region in her 1827 *Hope*

Leslie), Samson Occom led the Stockbridge Indians to New York State in a voluntary removal that emptied the town of the very people for whom it was incorporated (Calloway 1995: 85–107). Sedgwick makes reference to the town of ——'s missionary past only once in *A New England Tale*, when she describes a chair that had been "a present from Queen Anne to the first missionary to the Housatonic Indians" (Sedgwick 1995: 52). Other than that, the town of ——'s Indian past and its history of removal is a blank. In fact, it is two blanks. As a town founded for the purpose of educating Indians in both religion and civilization, Stockbridge was, in many ways, the Brainerd of the eighteenth century, and indeed, Brainerd School was named for David Brainerd, a missionary who worked near and had extensive dealings with the Stockbridge mission. It is all very well to say that the first blank is Stockbridge and the second blank is Brainerd, but the fact that both are blanks raises the specter that they are the same place, and that Stockbridge *is* merely generic – a repetition rather than a template.

If Brainerd School made money by appealing to New Englanders' pride of place even as the institution, according to Sedgwick, distracted New Englanders from that place, the Cherokee children at Brainerd were equally encouraged toward distraction from their own locale. As the threat of removal grew ever more tangible, and as more and more Cherokees left the southeast for land across the Mississippi river in "Indian country," the children at Brainerd were taught to think first of New England, then of heaven, as a sanctified space.

In 1825 a thin volume calling itself *The Memoir of Catherine Brown, A Christian Indian of the Cherokee Nation* was published in New England, where it was intended to garner support for the American Board of Commissioners for Foreign Missions. Hardly a memoir, it was a posthumous collection of heavily annotated letters, interspliced with the didactic commentary of the editor, missionary Rufus Anderson. At the time of her death in 1824, Catherine Brown was already a household name in New England. Along with her fellow students, Brown had spent most of her time writing personal letters of thanks to New Englanders who gave to the school. Brown's letters were especially coveted, solicited, and often republished in New England newspapers, and "Catherine Brown" quickly became the Brainerd poster child.

Although Brown never left the Cherokee Nation, the missionaries carefully educated her in geography. Late in the memoir, after Brown's death has been recounted, Rufus Anderson rehearses the particulars of her geography lessons:

> Her acquaintance with the *geographical features of the earth*, before her introduction to the missionaries at Brainerd, must have been exceedingly vague and limited, hardly reaching beyond the wilderness, that embosomed her father's house. Afterwards, that acquaintance was extended to the great natural divisions of the world, its physical aspect, and its civil departments. (Anderson 1825: 123)

Rufus Anderson's excitement about Brown's acquired geographical acumen goes beyond a teacherly thrill in the achievements of a star pupil. His critique of Brown's

Figure 30.1 "Indians Dream of Heaven." Frontispiece from M. J. Percival (ed.), *The Oasis: Or, Golden Leaves of Friendship* (Boston: Wentworth & Co., 1856). Collection of Shirley Samuels.

original understanding of geography as "vague and limited" leads us to expect that her schooling filled in the map with knowledge of capitals and continents. Instead, he tells us that she became acquainted with the concept of multiplicity and generic partition: "natural divisions" and "civil departments." What is at stake here is not Catherine Brown's geographical knowledge, but her belief in and her attachment to the Cherokee Nation as special.

If Catherine Brown bore any trace of a traditional Cherokee world-view, it would include the understanding that the Cherokee nation was located at the center of the world. Her geographical education radically reorients her from the "embosoming" of her home within that center to an understanding of the world as a catalogue of physical, social, and spiritual segments. Anderson sets up a seeming democracy of geographical divisions, but covertly relocates Brown's center to – in this case – New England and the outskirts to – in this case – her own "wilderness home." What is perhaps even more fundamental to the plate tectonics of Brown's geographical re-education, however, is the way in which she is trained to understand the world's physical aspect and its civil departments as themselves divided and non mutually constitutive. The passage celebrates the mission school's education of the Indian subject in doctrines that insist upon the physics and metaphysics of geographical abstraction. Such a reorganization and setting adrift of geography from the social is essential to the logic behind Indian removal, which claims that land is exchangeable and that a nation can be physically moved from one plot of ground to another and remain a "civil department" unflustered by its journey. And of course this logic supports a general imperialist divestiture of land into generic currency that benefits New England pecuniary interests across the continent.

Brown's improved knowledge of geography, Anderson elsewhere assures us, is due not just to her acquaintance with missionaries, but to the very place of Brainerd Mission itself, on the outskirts of the Cherokee Nation. Throughout the memoir Brainerd figures as a "consecrated place," and much of the drama of the memoir's scanty plot centers on whether or not Catherine Brown will move west with her family or stay with the missionaries at Brainerd. Her parents keep threatening to depart, and Catherine must beg them to leave her behind. At first the missionaries are powerless to stop the parents from taking Catherine, but after a series of struggles the parents give up. Rufus Anderson quotes the journal of the Brainerd Mission upon the occasion of one of Catherine's father's visits: "How very different the scene from that, which passed here not quite two years since, when her father required her to leave the society of Christians and to accompany him to the then dark shades of the Arkansas! Now, he does not ask for her without our consent; will not take her except by our advice" (1825: 52).

For Anderson, this is triumph indeed. Brown's parents are now subordinate to the mission, and at the same time, have taken the antagonistic place of the federal government in the scenario of removal. The missionaries play double surrogate, occupying the place of both family and cultural belonging: they have taken on the position of parent to the Indian child and they ventriloquize Cherokee resistance to removal, arguing for the importance of staying in the Cherokee Nation. But the mission's adoption of Brown has reorganized both national and filial ties in the Cherokee young person; removal from Brainerd is still bad, but not because it enacts the destruction of Cherokee belonging on Cherokee land. Catherine, we are told, resists removal because remaining at Brainerd is the way to go to heaven. Brainerd is thus a blank like the blank in Sedgwick's text, another active lacuna that manufactures a radical shift in Brown's understanding of what kind of removal she is facing, and which geographies are sacred.

Brainerd was built to emulate a New England village and boarding school and was intended as an architectural and social outpost of New England itself.[4] The goal was not only to evangelize the entire world, but, in a sense that extended beyond the cultural to the physical, to make the whole world New England. In the tradition of empire-building as a palliative to the threat of internal fracture, this global goal worked to distract attention and energies from the internecine struggles of Christian New England itself. In the face of the Congregationalist church's instability and the steady loss of Federalist power, New England's ruling classes needed a new engine of control, an engine that worked via geographic abstraction. The American Board of Commissioners for Foreign Missions rose to the occasion, providing the consolidation of religious discipline and social cohesion at home through the dissemination of a fundamentally New English Christianity and culture abroad.[5]

New England, of course, in its very "new"ness and "English"ness, is itself imagined to be a replicated landscape, one in a series of geographically located – and, importantly, geographically *dis*locatable or *trans*locatable – sites of earthly redemption on the road to the "New Jerusalem." New England's newness is a triple refraction from an original place of salvation – the biblical land of Israel, via England, to New England. New England was, for the Puritans, supposed to be the last in a series of geographically located promised lands, all experienced as progressing toward the kingdom of heaven. The kingdom of heaven is figured as a New Jerusalem, or a coming full circle to the place of origin, now transcendent and extra-worldly. Cotton Mather, in his *Magnalia Christi Americana* (1693–1702), expresses the geographically enacted drive of New Englanders toward New Jerusalem, if not best, then at least most outrageously: "*Geography* must now find work for a *Christiano-graphy*," he writes, calling his work "the HISTORY OF A NEW-ENGLISH ISRAEL," a "*history* of *some feeble attempts* made in the American hemisphere to anticipate the state of the New-Jerusalem" (Mather 1853: 5–7).

By 1800 it was clear that New England was not going to become the New Jerusalem. The region had become a hotbed of sin, religious diversity, and political unrest. The project of replicating an idealized New England – to anticipate the state of New Jerusalem as many times as necessary – became very attractive, and New England donors gave unprecedented amounts to aid the missionaries' disseminating activities. The creation of an evangelical empire of replica New Englands enabled the belief in a stable center, in a New England that was static enough to sit still for its portrait. The promulgation of that sense of stasis at home was an essential part of the ABCFM's dissemination of New English religion and culture all over the United States and the globe. An empire with a static center neatly anticipates the state of New Jerusalem where, we are told, there is no day or night and the nations of the earth "shall reign forever and ever" (Rev. 22: 3–5).

Thus Brainerd is telescoped, located within the Cherokee Nation and the state of Tennessee, designed as a mini New England, and part of the geographically enacted project of bringing about the New Jerusalem. It is a Cherokee location, a United States location, a New English location, and a heavenly location all at the same time, and thus can accommodate Catherine Brown's shift across the course of the memoir from an attachment to the Cherokee Nation, to an attachment to Brainerd mission as a "sanctified space," to a desire for and ultimate achievement of New Jerusalem. Catherine Brown's geographical re-education achieves the abstraction of the Indian from the land via the process of convincing the Indian that land is an abstraction.

A geography lesson at Brainerd is explicitly and purposely eschatological. Land and its abstractions, naïvely presumed by the New England missionaries to be a concept shared across divisions of language and culture, serves as the ready slate-book on which Brown's reorientation from earth to heaven is inscribed. The following passage mirrors the structure of the geography lesson segment almost exactly; only now Anderson traces Brown's abstraction from earthly geography and physical pleasures to heavenly geography and heavenly joy, celebrating the death of her body as the death of her attachment to a location on this earth:

> What a revolution was effected in her views of *this world.* An Indian's heaven, even when most distinctly apprehended, has fewer points of attraction than the earth. Catherine, on coming to Brainerd, evidently regarded it, when she thought of it at all, as an object remote, obscure, and undefined. Hence her imagination had contemplated whatever is lovely and attractive, as shining forth chiefly in this world. . . . But after her conversion, what a change! Her contemplations are elevated to a superior world of realities. She learns of a higher state of existence, designed for the good of the human race. . . . Now, her views of the world are changed. The contrast of earthly with heavenly things, and of the creature with God, hath spoiled the glories of the world. "How vain," she says, "does the world appear in my eyes. It is nothing but vanity and sin. Sweet and reviving is the thought, that I am not to continue long in this world, but hope soon to rest in the city of my God. How happy shall I feel, when I land on the shores of eternal felicity." (Anderson 1825: 129–30)

Brown's celebratory envisioning of her own death is represented as a celebratory envisioning of the removal of an Indian from the landed, spatial locations of this world. The removal of the Cherokee Nation from a homeland and a sovereignty grounded in right of possession to lands far to the west, lands owned, mapped, and provided by the United States, is made the mere correlative of conversion from the love of earthly to the love of heavenly things. The "memoir" triumphantly announces that the Indian child, before she died, had disconnected Cherokee sovereignty from land. It depicts Brown's hatred of the ways of the flesh increasing in inverse proportion to her loss of faith in her people's ability to survive outside of Christian conversion, until finally she is shown to view the kingdom of heaven as a more tangible and attainable location than the quickly dissolving land base of the Cherokee Nation.

NOTES

1 *A New England Tale* is, in part, an argument against what Cathy N. Davidson quotes Sedgwick as calling the "thraldom of [Calvinist] despotism," and promotes the precepts of Unitarianism, a "rapidly expanding movement toward a more humanized – to some, dangerously liberal – Christianity." But, Davidson points out, "the term 'Unitarian' never appears in the text, suggesting [Sedgwick] was profoundly aware of the ramifications of her decision to reject that theology that had held New England firmly in its grasp for more than two hundred years." Cathy N. Davidson, introduction to Sedgwick 1995: xii.

2 I do not mean to imply that other contemporary novels that do contain Indians have a conception that the land may have belonged to Native Americans in a way that dovetails with Native American understandings of their own sovereignty. William Cronon and Eric Cheyfitz point out that Euro-American and Native American conceptions of how Native American land was or continued to be "Indian" differed and differ to the point of incomprehension, given the multiplicity of Native American understandings of how land belongs to and claims belonging in a people. See Cheyfitz's critique of Cronon in Cheyfitz 1997: 45–6. Euro-Americans nevertheless had a patchwork of legal, literary, and street narratives about Indian tenure on North American soil, its provenance, tenure, and fate, narratives that enabled the two-fisted attack of romance and genocide.

3 I am indebted for the foundations of this reading to Amy Kaplan (2002).

4 Historian of the Cherokee Nation Althea Bass explains that the mission had "grown into something like a pioneer New England settlement transplanted to the outskirts of the Cherokee Nation. Here were houses for the mission families, a church and a school, with a farm and a garden and a flourishing young orchard to provide food. The newcomers [new missionaries] felt no sense of strangeness here; it was related to what they had known, and was what they had come to participate in and to help extend to the Cherokees. Indeed, when the American Board [of Commissioners for Foreign Missions] set out to carry salvation to the world, it had in mind the particular type of salvation that New England knew; and when missionaries went from the Missionary Rooms to the heathen, the salvation they took with them was inseparably bound up with that definite New England culture of which they were a product" (Bass 1936: 29).

5 For a useful discussion of the New England origins of Congregationalist missionary fervor across the period of the Second Great Awakening, see Andrew 1976.

REFERENCES

Anderson, Rufus (1825). *Memoir of Catharine Brown, a Christian Indian of the Cherokee Nation*. Boston: Crocker & Brewster.

Andrew, John A., III (1976). *Rebuilding the Christian Commonwealth*. Lexington: University Press of Kentucky.

Bass, Althea (1936). *Cherokee Messenger*. Norman: University of Oklahoma Press.

Brown, Charles Brockden (1988). *Edgar Huntly or, Memoirs of a Sleepwalker*. New York: Penguin.

Brown, Lois (2000). "Introduction." In Susan Ford, *Memoir of James Jackson, The Attentive and Obedient Scholar, Who Died in Boston, October 31, 1833, Aged Six Years and Eleven Months, By His Teacher*. Cambridge, Mass.: Harvard University Press.

Calloway, Colin (1995). *The American Revolution in Indian Country: Crisis and Diversity in Native American Communities*. Cambridge, UK: Cambridge University Press.

Cheyfitz, Eric (1997). *The Poetics of Imperialism.* Philadelphia: University of Pennsylvania Press.

Deloria, Philip J. (1998). *Playing Indian.* New Haven: Yale University Press.

Ford, Paul Leicester, ed. (1962). *The New England Primer.* New York: Columbia University Press.

Kaplan, Amy (2002). "Manifest Domesticity." In Robyn Wiegman and Donald Pease (eds.), *The Futures of American Studies.* Durham, NC: Duke University Press.

Mather, Cotton (1853). *Magnalia Christi Americana.* Hartford, Conn.: S. Andrus & Son.

Nelson, Dana (2002). "Frontier Democracy and Representational Management." *REAL: The Yearbook of Research in English and American Literature*, 215–29.

Phillips, Joyce B., and Phillips, Paul Gary, eds. (1998). *The Brainerd Journal: A Mission to the Cherokees, 1817–1823.* Lincoln: University of Nebraska Press.

Sedgwick, Catharine Maria (1995). *A New England Tale*, ed. Cathy N. Davidson. Oxford: Oxford University Press. (First publ. 1822.)

31

Harriet Beecher Stowe, Caroline Lee Hentz, Herman Melville, and American Racialist Exceptionalism

Katherine Adams

Captain Delano's nature was not only benign, but familiarly and humorously so. At home, he had often taken rare satisfaction in sitting in his door, watching some free man of color at his work or play. If on a voyage he chanced to have a black sailor, invariably he was on chatty, and half-gamesome terms with him. In fact, like most men of a good, blithe heart, Captain Delano took to negroes, not philanthropically, but genially, just as other men to Newfoundland dogs. (Melville 2002: 71)

This passage from Herman Melville's short 1855 novel "Benito Cereno" gives expression not only to the cardinal trait of Melville's protagonist and archetypal American, Captain Amasa Delano, but also to a founding structure of the United States national imaginary. Like Delano, whose happiness and self-concept are so closely tied to racial benevolence that he must incessantly seek out opportunities for exercising it, the US body politic has from the very outset drawn its form and identity from the legal, economic, and ideological subordination of blacks. This has never been more widely and explicitly acknowledged than during the era of American slavery from which Delano emerged.

To be sure, slavery was the source of much conflict within the white American polity. Besides contradicting the nation's ethos of democratic freedom, it promoted sectionalist tension between Northern and Southern interests, presented the terrifying potential of insurrection, and – as miscegenation became an increasingly apparent factor – threatened Anglo-Saxon purity. Yet, inasmuch as the presence of enslaved blacks endangered the coherence of white American political identity, it also provided an occasion for the "rare satisfaction" of *enacting* that identity and its utopian meaning. Indeed, many antebellum Americans found in slavery a divinely appointed opportunity by which their nation would become a model of spiritual and democratic righteousness to all other nations. By interpreting their race problem through the lens of American exceptionalism – the mythos of unique national destiny rooted in Puritan and revolutionary ideologies – they discovered fresh ground upon which to erect their New World city upon a hill.

This essay looks at how three American writers addressed the problem *and* opportunity of blackness, focusing on four novels from the 1850s: *Uncle Tom's Cabin* and *Dred* by Harriet Beecher Stowe, *The Planter's Northern Bride* by Caroline Lee Hentz, and Herman Melville's "Benito Cereno." In many ways, these novels represent contrary political impulses. Hentz wrote hers as a Southern rebuttal to Stowe's; and although Melville shared Stowe's anti-slavery stance, in "Benito Cereno" he skewers her brand of self-serving racialism. The three also differ markedly in how they have fared under the changing regimes of literary criticism. Stowe and Hentz, while phenomenally popular in their own century, would be dismissed in the next as sentimental propagandists. Today, following an explosion of work on women writers and on nineteenth-century American sentimentalism, Stowe is widely researched and taught while Hentz remains obscure – still unpalatable by virtue of her pro-slavery agenda. Melville suffered bitterly from hostile reception and neglect during his lifetime, but in the early twentieth century ascended to the literary canon, where he was posed as the disinterested, timeless, and masculine antithesis of writers such as Stowe and Hentz. It was not until scholars began historicizing Melville that his own literary responses to antebellum political issues were widely recognized (see Karcher 1980). Thanks in part to that work it is possible to demonstrate that, for all their differences in motivation and success, Stowe, Hentz, and Melville share fundamental qualities. All three wrote passionately about what they perceived (albeit variously) as the racial injustice of their day and believed that relationships between whites and blacks in America would determine the future not only for their own nation, but also for nations around the globe. Brought together here, they reveal how pervasive the discourse of racialist exceptionalism was on the eve of the Civil War, operating within disparate agendas and across hostile lines in the antebellum United States.

The discussion is divided into three sections, beginning with the relationship between slavery debates and sectional conflict in novels by Stowe and Hentz. Although the writers opposed each other on slavery, their more salient differences were over tensions within the political Union. The second part, therefore, begins by showing how these two writers imagined the resolution of such tensions in startlingly similar models of the US exceptionalist destiny, based on a symbiotic relationship between white benevolence and black dependence. This section concludes with Melville's scathing critique of such racialist narratives as self-deluding and potentially disastrous. The final section offers a brief consideration of all three novelists within the context of US expansionism. Even at their most sectionalist, the novels analyzed here are deeply informed by nationalist visions of expanding empire, and their conceptualization of the relation between black dependence and white benevolence was shaped by the racialized frontiers of American imperialism, continental and overseas. At every level, it will be seen, antebellum America required its newly emerging concepts of race and racial difference in order to articulate its national unity and identity, its exceptionalist destiny, and its imperialist projects.

Sectionalist and Racial Politics

Slavery was at the forefront of the sectional disputes that provoked Stowe and Hentz to write, but it was not necessarily at the core of those disputes. Nor had it been there in the preceding half-century of struggle between the North and South, which took place *over* slavery but *about* political and economic dominance. An early and important illustration of this distinction can be found in the infamous constitutional provision that each black would count as three-fifths of a person. Certainly this rule reflected the dehumanizing ethos and effects of slavery, but it was more immediately the result of Northern efforts to reduce population counts that determined Southern representation in Congress. Constitutionally, the enslaved black body stood not for itself but for the contending interests of whites. This would continue to be the case in the decades to come, as constant geographical expansion repeatedly forced the question of how far slavery and Southern political leverage would extend, generating a series of contentious legislative attempts to balance sectional interests and preserve union. Writing in the wake of the Compromise Bill of 1850 and the even more controversial 1854 Kansas–Nebraska Act, Stowe and Hentz echoed the priorities their political era. The one wrote against slavery, the other for it; but for both the central concern is the crisis of white national polity.

For Stowe, the immediate impetus to write came from the fugitive slave law, a part of the 1850 Compromise that enforced Northern compliance in the return of escaped slaves. Stowe was infuriated by this compulsion to act on behalf of what she believed to be immoral Southern interests. Moreover, as part of the famous Beecher family of ministers, educators, and reformers, she possessed a strong sense of public duty and election. The result was *Uncle Tom's Cabin*, published as a serial in the abolitionist *National Era* from June 1851 to April 1852 before coming out as a two-volume novel in 1852 (Hedrick 1994: 202–9). The novel follows the fortunes of three slaves who are sold to alleviate the financial woes of their otherwise kindly owners. Eliza Harris and her young son escape to Canada, passing through a series of adventures – including the famous dash on ice floes across the Ohio River – to be reunited with husband and father, George Harris. The family embarks at the novel's conclusion for a missionary career in Liberia. This northerly plotline clearly expresses Stowe's initial inspiration, for it features several encounters with whites who flout the fugitive slave law by assisting the Harris family, usually discussing the moral basis for civil disobedience all the while.

However, Stowe's sectionalist and anti-slavery sympathies are more confused in the other main plot of the novel, which follows the third character, Uncle Tom, into the deep South. Not only does Stowe tend to present Southern slaveholders in a positive light, she represents blacks as natural servants – docile, childlike, devoted to whites, and resigned to enslavement. "I wouldn't be the one to say no," declares Uncle Tom upon discovering he is to be sold, "Mas'r always found me on the spot – he always will. I never have broke trust" (Stowe 1981: 37). Indeed, the only black characters to display any capacity or desire for political freedom are those with a large admixture of white blood, and these Stowe dispatches to Liberia – much to the disgust of other anti-slavery activists like Frederick Douglass and William Lloyd Garrison who advocated black resistance and opposed colonization. Thus, even while *Uncle Tom's Cabin* brought the slavery question into high moral relief and promoted intense sectionalist identification (so that, if Abraham Lincoln really did greet Stowe as "the little woman who wrote the book that started this great war," he wasn't entirely wrong), it did so at the expense of advancing racial theories that would profoundly shape ideas about blacks well into the twentieth century and, many would argue, the twenty-first (see Baldwin 1997; Berlant 2998; Yarborough 1986).

Indeed, the immediate, immense, and lasting popularity of the novel indicates how deeply reassuring Stowe's black portraits were to her white audience. Selling 10,000 copies in its first week and 300,000 in its first year, *Uncle Tom's Cabin* ultimately outsold every other American novel in the century and made Stowe an international celebrity. It inspired innumerable adaptations to melodrama, minstrelsy, decorative art, advertising, and household commodities of staggering variety. If Stowe was torn between anti-slavery and racialist ideology, the spin-off industry made sure she was remembered for the latter. It fostered a nostalgia for the prewar era and a fantasy of black subordination with which the novel became increasingly identified, so that it was possible in 1881 for Joel Chandler Harris to compare his Uncle Remus series to "Mrs. Stowe's wonderful defense of slavery" (quoted in Railton 1998).

Among Stowe's other anti-slavery works, her 1856 novel *Dred* is the most interesting – largely because the ambivalent racial politics of her first novel had developed by then into outright self-contradiction. In many places, her critique of slavery is far more radical in *Dred*, suggesting, as Robert Levine has argued, that Stowe attended to the criticisms of Douglass and Garrison. Most remarkable is Stowe's titular character, whom she bases on the infamous insurrectionist Nat Turner *and* endows with unmistakable heroism. Dred dies before carrying out his spectacularly bloody plans – a death utterly predetermined in any world imaginable by Stowe – but not before presenting arguments for radical black action that are impossible to dismiss. And yet the novel's normative model of black consciousness is Aunt Milly, of whom the narrator approvingly remarks: "As far as her own rights were concerned, she would have made a willing surrender of them, remaining patiently in the condition wherein she was called, and bearing injustice and oppression as a means of spiritual improvement" (Stowe 2000: 521). In fact, Stowe's portrayals of racial injustice seem secondary to her sectionalist complaints against Southern political and economic aggression. Written while Free Soilers fought it out with pro-slavery advocates in bleeding Kansas, *Dred* focuses on violent white mobs who attack other whites, and courtroom dramas in which Big Cotton prevails over legal and democratic disinterest. As one character puts it, "These men are our masters; they are yours; they are mine; they are masters of everybody in these United States. They can crack their whips over the head of any statesman or clergyman, from Maine to New Orleans, that disputes their will" (p. 465). Ultimately, Stowe's concern in *Dred* is the metaphorical enslavement of white American democracy. Her critique of the actual enslavement of blacks is subordinated and, as we shall see below, comes to a troublingly ambiguous conclusion.

Southerners responded to Stowe's anti-slavery writing with a flood of outraged reviews, editorials, sermons, tracts, and as many as twenty-seven anti-Tom novels – the more successful of which included Mary Eastman's *Aunt Phillis's Cabin* (1852), William Gilmore Simms's *Woodcraft* (1854), and Caroline Lee Hentz's *Marcus Warland* (1852) and *The Planter's Northern Bride* (1854). In her two pro-slavery novels, Hentz deploys the usual anti-Tom tactics. She disparages Northern ignorance of slavery – Stowe's in particular – while emphasizing her own regionalist authority, and denounces the "intolerance" of anti-slavery "fanatics." Also typical is her representation of slavery as a pre-capitalist Eden, a "timeless natural order," as Jamie Stansea puts it, where labor relations are governed by paternal benevolence rather than profit motive (1992: 222). As the narrator of *Marcus Warland* remarks, "It is true, they were slaves, but their chains never clanked. Each separate link was kept moist and bright with the oil of kindness" (Hentz 1852: 59).

Yet Hentz stands out for her desire to avert sectionalist conflict rather than merely engage in it. Having grown up in the North (including a period during which she and Stowe both lived in Cincinnati and belonged to a writing group called the Semi-Colon Club), Hentz was divided in her sympathies. Her first novel, *Lovell's Folly* (1833), focuses on the danger of sectional biases and both pro-slavery works urge reconciliation. "It has been mine," announces Hentz in her preface to *The Planter's Northern Bride*, "to oppose the shield of defense to the sword of aggression, though I would gladly lay aside all belligerent weapons, and cultivate that friendly communion, which no sectional interest should disturb or destroy" (1970: 87). Further on, she imagines sectionalists as Siamese twins – "can you sever the interests of the North and the South without lifting a fratricidal hand?" – and portrays anti-slavery activity in apocalyptic images, as though to warn against the coming war (p. 238). The text's most pointed anti-sectionalist metaphor is the marriage to which its title refers, between the slave-holder Russell Moreland and Eulalia Hastings, the daughter of a New England abolitionist. In the course of the narrative, this happy couple convert a series of anti-slavery activists and ideologues, beginning with Eulalia herself. The marriage becomes, in the words of its presiding minister, "a golden link of union between the divided interests of humanity" (p. 136).

In her efforts to support the Union, Hentz strives to defend slavery without alienating the North. Where other anti-Tom writers accuse abolitionists of political ambition or prurient interest in female slaves, Hentz finds a kind of helpless fanaticism or a possessing evil that goes beyond sectionalist motive. At the climax of *The Planter's Northern Bride*, an imposter preacher attempts to incite a racial massacre among Moreland's slaves. Yet even the Revd. Brainard seems driven by motiveless malignity rather Northern animus. He is not so much a Northerner, nor even a man, as a snake who invades the South's Eden, "stealing and coiling himself secretly and insidiously into the heart of [Moreland's] household" (Hentz 1970: 457). In this way, Hentz recasts national history as millennial eschatology, positing a struggle in which North and South alike must resist satanic designs upon white American Union. For her, blacks appear to have little stake in this drama; indeed, the slavery debate concerns them only in that it imposes painful, self-destructive ideas. Like Stowe, Hentz portrays blacks as largely unimplicated in the question of their own freedom. Both writers place blacks at the foundation of white freedom.

National and Racial Politics

Even while nineteenth-century America sought juridical and geographical answers to its race problems, it was producing epistemological solutions through pseudoscientific confirmations of black inferiority. It was in this century, and in service to the US slave economy, that a theory of racial hierarchy first emerged. Building on racial classifications created by eighteenth-century naturalists (who had generally scorned the notion of ranking differences), American ethnologists such as John Van Evrie and Josiah Nott developed widely influential theories on the "natural" ordering of the races. Although they disagreed on many points, the fundamental aim of most American ethnographies was to confirm an absolute difference between blacks and whites, thereby justifying absolute separation in cultural status – hence Van Evrie's title: *Negroes and Negro Slavery: The First an Inferior Race: The Latter its Normal Condition*. Nor were such accounts exclusive to the South, for belief in absolute and hierarchically organized racial differences also dominated Northern, and even anti-slavery, opinion.

Many Northern ethnologists – including Alexander Kinmont, who shaped both Stowe's and Hentz's understandings of race – espoused a theory of polygenesis, positing that different racial groups had distinct origins and trajectories of development. These arguments, which historian George Frederickson describes as "romantic racialism," did not explicitly assert black inferiority. In fact, Kinmont and others found Africans superior to whites in a number of respects, including their supposed predisposition to Christianity. Romantic racialists viewed blacks as gentle children, unambitious for freedom, suited to menial labor, and – most important – in need of guidance from whites. Conversely, they found that Anglo-Saxons were racially inclined to independence, enterprise, and rationality, but also materialistic and aggressive in ways that made them poor Christians. For Kinmont, Theodore Parker, and others, evidence suggested that blacks were destined to eclipse whites: the rise of their mild and Christlike people would bring about the world closer to its millennial destiny. Hentz and Stowe reached a very different conclusion. By their logic, comparison of the two racial profiles indicated that black servitude was inevitable; more, dominance over blacks was essential to the development of the greatest political and spiritual expression of the Anglo Saxon race: American democracy.

For Hentz, America's racialist–exceptionalist mission began with the extension of slavery. In *The Planter's Northern Bride*, having aligned the Southern plantation with Eden and slavery with a prelapsarian state of grace, she logically proposes that slavery should help the North to regain Paradise in its labor relations as well (Hunt 1996: 26). Thus, even as her Northern middle-class characters convert to sympathy *with* slavery, their working-class counterparts convert to slavery itself. New England wage laborers envy the comforts of Southern enslavement; a free black volunteers herself in place of an escaped slave; and the escapee soon returns as beloved prodigal to Moreland's plantation. At every level, the action moves away from capitalist individualism and toward a great hierarchy of dependence that Hentz identifies with nothing less than the restoration of divine rule on earth. "There is a long chain," she writes,

> winding round the whole human race, and though its links be sometimes made of silver and gold, nay, even twined with flowers, it is still chain, and if the spirit struggle for liberation, it will feel the galling and the laceration, as much as if the fetters were of brass or iron. For six thousand years the cry for *freedom* has been going up from the goaded heart of humanity... And the answer has been, and now is, and ever will be – "Be still, and know that I am God." (Hentz 1970: 339)

The Great Chain of Being was a favorite among ethnologists, who resurrected it from pre-Enlightenment cosmology to validate racial hierarchy. Hentz adds her own riff on the chain metaphor to suggest an equalizing condition of universal thrall. She also makes gender a key component, taking enslaved blacks simultaneously as a figure *and* a foil for white womanhood. When Eulalia finally learns to embrace dominion over blacks, at the same point she also discovers bliss in her own "willing bondage" to husband Russell Moreland (p. 343). Unlike the nineteenth-century women's rights activists who deployed the same comparison, Hentz is describing her normative model: "I would reverence the master-spirit with the power to govern my own," breathes the too independent heroine of her *Robert Graham* (Hentz 1855: 59). Here, then, is Hentz's millennial plan: a Redeemer Nation of subjects nested in a long sequence of surrender and domination, structured by the natural organizations of race and gender, rooted in the bedrock of slavery.

It is already possible to find Stowe assembling her own great racial chain in *Uncle Tom's Cabin*, where she posits a moral regime based on white benevolence and equates blackness with need. However, it is not until *Dred* that Stowe fully develops black abjection into an active contribution to national millennial destiny. There, juxtaposed with Dred's forceful black liberationist sermons, we find Stowe imagining a central place for slavery in "the development of the national career." In her preface she writes, "If ever a nation was raised up by Divine Providence, and led forth upon a conspicuous stage, as if for the express purpose of solving a great moral problem in the sight of all mankind, it is this nation" (2000: 4). The direct reference here is to the crisis in

Kansas and Nebraska, but Stowe's rhetoric transports readers into the transhistorical drama of American exceptionalism, asking them to recognize that the "conspicuous stage" of slavery is the very same "Citty upon a hill" that John Winthrop invoked in 1630, which must again be fashioned into a model of righteousness for all nations.

To be sure, Stowe calls here for "*solving*" the "great moral problem," and *Dred* is an anti-slavery novel. But as the novel proceeds, it becomes clear that its exceptionalist plan requires the presence of slavery. Stowe's hero, strangely enough, is a Southern slaveholder named Edward Clayton who, although motivated by Christian benevolence, firmly believes that blacks must be guided by whites and aims to reform rather than abolish slavery. Hence, when Stowe's exceptionalist rhetoric resurfaces several times on behalf of Clayton's plan, it relies upon the continuing availability of enslaved blacks: "There isn't a sublimer power on earth than God has given to us masters," rhapsodizes Clayton in his first appearance. "A plantation such as a plantation might be would be a 'light to lighten the gentiles'" (Stowe 2000: 23). Later he adds: "The eyes of the world are fastened upon us ... Let us therefore show, by the spirit in which we administer our laws, by the impartiality with which we protect their rights, that the master of the helpless African is his best and truest friend" (p. 303). Here again is the conceit of America's conspicuous stage; but now it is a plantation-on-a-hill that must shine forth its light. Clayton, like Hentz, calls for a sustained symbiosis based on African dependence and Anglo-Saxon paternalism, through which the United States can achieve its national and racial destiny – the "sublime power" of spiritual and democratic transcendence.

Stowe never really amends Clayton's vision. Indeed, its actualization provides her with narrative closure. Having discovered that his "plantation as a plantation might be" *cannot* be within a corrupt US legal system that serves only capitalist self-interest, Clayton transports his slaves to Canada, where he resumes his supervisory role. The move emancipates the blacks, of course, but this fact is never addressed nor even acknowledged by the narrator, who simply states, "to this place he removed his slaves" (Stowe 2000: 543). Where Hentz strives to makes slavery a kind of freedom, Stowe manages to make freedom look like slavery. Finally, their racialist exceptionalisms come down to the same thing: belief in a nation whose very identity and future are driven by the providential plan of absolute and complementary black dependence and white benevolence.

In his short 1855 novel "Benito Cereno" Melville takes a satirical and portentous look at the sort of benevolent racialism espoused by Stowe and Hentz. Based on the actual events of an 1805 slave revolt, the story subverts and inverts the dominant reading of its historical source by using it to reveal the inherent violence of a white American identification that relies on incessant reaffirmations of black difference. Melville's story revolves around three principal figures: Benito Cereno, captain of a Spanish slaver; Babo, leader of the ship's African cargo; and Amasa Delano, a New England sea-captain who encounters the Spanish ship in distress off the shore of "Chili." Delano boards the *San Dominick* to offer assistance, meets Cereno – in ill-health and closely attended by Babo – and receives a "pale history" of how storms and sickness have disabled the ship and crew (Melville 2002: 46). Although Delano puzzles over the sinister and unruly atmosphere of the *San Dominick*, it is not until Cereno attempts to escape, closely followed by a dagger-wielding Babo, that Delano finally sees the truth: the Africans have held control all along, forcing Cereno and his crew to perform a charade of white mastery for his benefit. All comes to light, and the novel concludes in Lima where Delano, still cheerfully obtuse, visits the psychically devastated Spaniard. Our final image is Babo's head, "fixed on a pole in the Plaza," where it "met, unabashed, the gaze of the whites" (p. 102).

At the heart of "Benito Cereno" stands the problem of interpretation – the metanarration touches incessantly on difficulties of perception, judgement, skepticism, and trust – and at the heart of that problem stands American racial epistemology. During Delano's afternoon aboard the *San Dominick* he cycles between two moods, each based on racialist misinterpretation of evidence. From the start he is haunted by a sense of imminent threat, provoked by Cereno's strange manner and the ship's general disorder. Unable to imagine that the blacks might conspire against him, he suspects some treachery on the part of his Spanish host. Yet Delano is repeatedly distracted from his worries by pleasing images of African docility – such as the "slumbering negress" whom he compares to "a doe in the shade of a woodland rock" – that restore his sense of security. "These natural sights," the narrator blandly remarks, "somehow insensibly deepened his confidence and ease" (Melville 2002: 60–1). Most often, the soporific is some deliberate gesture of servitude from Babo that calls the American's attention "away from the spectacle of disorder to the more pleasing one before him" (p. 58). In Delano's motivated misinterpretations Melville paints a portrait of white American complacency and the way it constitutes itself against the backdrop of race caricature. He satirizes the illusion of white control – "I know no sadder sight," reflects Delano, "than a commander who has little of command but the name" (p. 47) – and savagely ridicules Americans who, like Delano, refuse to acknowledge what is plainly before them. As Delano watches Babo shave Cereno in the novel's famous barber scene, enjoying a fatuous internal monologue on the natural solicitude of blacks, he briefly entertains an "antic conceit" that "in the black he saw a headsman, and in the white, a man at the block," then hastily resumes his former thoughts (p. 72). The narrator's gloss on this pattern of denial – "All his old weakness for negroes returned" – is an apt *double entendre*, for Delano's racist fantasy is both a weakness in itself and a source of great vulnerability (p. 71). It is significant that "Benito Cereno" was published in the abolitionist periodical press, for Melville's primary targets are the readers he shares with Stowe. By limiting his tale to Delano's point of view, he forces them to read simultaneously with and against that Northerner's self-serving self-delusions and to confront their own epistemic vulnerability. Thus, the final image of Babo's head supplies a figure for the novel as a whole: it is a "hive of subtlety" that confounds its readers' racialist interpretation while leveling its gaze on them (p. 102).

Committed to an ideal of Melvillean ahistoricity, scholars long overlooked the writer's deep engagement with America's racial politics. It would be a shame to

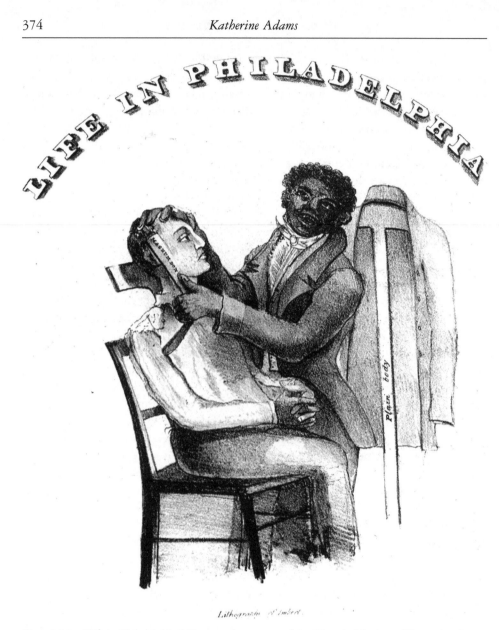

Figure 31.1   "Life in Philadelphia." Photograph courtesy of the Historical Society of Pennsylvania.

reintroduce Melville to history only to place him outside of ideology, granting him an Archimedean stance of insight denied the others. Arguably, his failure to invest Babo with the dimensionality he gives to Cereno and Delano is evidence enough against that. More important, like Delano, Stowe and Hentz are not merely deluded in their perceptions of US racial relations. Indeed, Hentz's analysis is often remarkably discerning, as when her Russell Moreland reflects, "[Negroes] are entwined with my affections as well as my interests. . . . I never dreamed, when a boy, that it was possible to separate my existence from theirs any more than I could flee from shadows of night" (1970: 225). Evidently Hentz understood the complications of white supremacist identity, driven as it is by the oppression, infantilization, and *fear* of blacks. The insight of her portrayal stands painfully at odds with her determination to make it a virtue. For her part, Stowe is capable of great clarity *and* courage as she writes through the voices of George Harris, Dred, and others like them; but, as we have seen, she cannot sustain the effort. Small wonder, perhaps, given the costs. Benito Cereno, who comes to understand his whiteness only when forced to parody it in a masquerade of racial dominance, seems in Delano's literalizing choice of metaphor "like one flayed alive" (Melville 2002: 80): to fully recognize the fiction of white superiority is to have it stripped from you.

Transnational and Racial Politics

The racial politics of American exceptionalism were not exclusively black–white. Nor, as Amy Kaplan, Shelley Streeby, Laura Wexler, and others have shown, is the domestic scene of black–white politics separable from the foreign contexts in which racialization of Native Americans, Mexicans, and Spanish underwrote the processes of conquest, incorporation, and expulsion by which US empire expanded. Even as it was used to bridge internal boundaries between Southern and Northern interests, the utopian narrative of interracial dependence also played a vital role at the nation's external borders, both continental and overseas. For the logic of racialist exceptionalism was easily imported to foreign populations of non-whites who, like American blacks, required white colonization to become freed from their own racial inferiority.

In *The Planter's Northern Bride*, Hentz puts it this way: "We would not depreciate the value of freedom. It is a glorious possession, but its glory depends upon the character of the nation or individual that owns it. Has it yet reflected glory or honour on the negro race?" In answer, she catalogs instances of black self-rule, moving from Haiti to Africa, to demonstrate that some races are, in essence, enslaved by freedom. God, Hentz reminds us, "has exhibited a gradually widening and ascending glory, through all the vast range of inanimate and animated nature" (1970: 294–300). We have seen her argument for divine racial hierarchy elsewhere in the novel. Here that argument "widen[s] and ascend[s]" outward from its initial, nationalist setting, to wrap the great chain around the entire globe. Stowe likewise demonstrates the inexorable expansion of racialist utopianism. There is her oft-noted deployment of mixed-race characters to disseminate Christian reform, *and* white blood in Liberia at the conclusion of *Uncle Tom's Cabin*. Also, as discussed above, *Dred* ends with an invasion of Canada, which is required for Clayton to establish his plantation colony. Given Stowe's heated condemnation of Southern expansion earlier in the novel – "They are going to annex Cuba and the Sandwich Islands, and the Lord knows what," predicts one character, "and have a great and splendid slaveholding empire" – it is interesting to find her plotting a moral counter-imperialism based on a racial arrangement nearly identical to slavery, as though she hopes to offset the immoral expansion below by mirroring it in ideal terms above. As Jane Tompkins famously says of Stowe's writing, "Its mission . . . is global and its interests identical with the interests of the race" (1985: 146).

Melville explores the continuity between racial domination within the United States and US imperialism abroad by mapping one over the other in the events that take place aboard the *San Dominick*. Through one lens, Delano, Cereno, and Babo are legible as figures for Northern and Southern interests in collusion over US slavery. Through another, their meeting forecasts the spread of US empire into Latin America and the Caribbean: here, the US interventionist confronts the dissipated Spanish imperialist to acquire power over the black population ("What the *San Dominick* wanted was . . . stern superior officers" [Melville 2002: 43]). As Allan Emery points out, Delano's impressions of the *San Dominick* echo descriptions of Cuba in the political press of the 1850s, which repeatedly called for US intervention into the "disorder" of that nation's slave population and ineffective Spanish government. Similarly, Eric Sundquist suggests that Delano's paranoia concerning Cereno alludes to rumors that the Spanish intended to "Africanize" Cuba by emancipating its slaves and turning the country over to their rule – rumors that fueled calls for American intervention. Thus "Benito Cereno" is a kind of double allegory, juxtaposing the suppressed reality of US slavery with the increasingly popular fantasy of US empire throughout the New World.

The effect of this juxtaposition is to present what Sundquist describes as the "wrenching paradox" of Manifest Destiny, whose utopian promise to spread democracy was haunted for its first half-century by the persisting question, "would it advance freedom or increase slavery?" (1994: 180). Indeed, as a figure for the convergence of romantic racialism and New World imperialism, Amasa Delano plays that paradox well. There is a great deal of menace in the generosity of this American who attempts to buy the African for himself and to "lightly arrange" the Spaniard's "fate" (Melville 2002: 57). Yet the image of Delano and Cereno shaking hands "across the black's body" suggests an irony that goes even deeper than the fact that, as Emery points out, American expansion into Cuba "would mean only a changing of the guard for Cuban slaves" (Melville 2002: 84; Emery 1984: 55). For, in the figure of Babo, the scene presents not just the contradictions of Manifest Destiny but also the instrument of their resolution – that is, the racial fact of the African's dependence on white colonization for freedom. Like the Northern and Southern delegates who formed political union in 1787 over the dismembered bodies of the three-fifths rule, the two whites aboard the *San Dominick* can consolidate interests only *because* the black body is there as the raw material for capitalist and Christian enterprise, the very mechanism of imperialism.

The Civil War put an end to plans for the great Southern empire, but not, of course, to Manifest Destiny or US exceptionalism. As the figure of the American city upon a hill has passed forward from Puritan and revolutionary ideology into the twenty-first century, it has continued to be co-articulated with racialist benevolence both within and outside of US borders. The portrayal of Amasa Delano, with his "blithe heart" and dogged resistance to memory – "The past is passed; why moralize upon it? Forget it. See, yon bright sun has forgotten it all, and the blue sea, and the blue sky; these have turned over new leaves" – has proved more prescient than even Melville may have realized (2002: 71, 101).

REFERENCES AND FURTHER READING

Berlant, Lauren (1998). "Poor Eliza." *American Literature* 70: 3, 635–68.

Bush, George W. "President Bush speaks at Goree Island in Senegal." http://www.whitehouse.gov/news/releases/2003/07/20030708–1.html. Accessed 23 July 2003.

Emery, Allan Moore (1984). "'Benito Cereno and Manifest Destiny." *Nineteenth-Century Fiction* 39: 1, 48–68.

Fredrickson, George M. (1987). *The Black Image in the White Mind: The Debate on Afro-American Character and Destiny, 1817–1914.* Hanover: Wesleyan University Press.

Gossett, Thomas F. (1985). Uncle Tom's Cabin *and American Culture.* Dallas: Southern Methodist University Press.

Hedrick, Joan D. (1994). *Harriet Beecher Stowe: A Life.* New York: Oxford University Press.

Hentz, Caroline Lee (1852). *Marcus Warland; or, The Long Moss Spring.* Philadelphia: T. B. Peterson & Bros.

Hentz, Caroline Lee (1855). *Robert Graham. A Sequel to Linda.* Philadelphia: T. B. Peterson.

Hentz, Caroline Lee (1970). *The Planter's Northern Bride.* Chapel Hill: University of North Carolina Press. (First publ. 1854.)

Hunt, Robert (1996). "A Domesticated Slavery: Political Economy in Caroline Hentz's Fiction." *Southern Quarterly* 34: 4, 25–35.

Kaplan, Amy (2002). *The Anarchy of Empire in the Making of US Culture.* Cambridge, Mass.: Harvard University Press.

Karcher, Carolyn (1980). *Shadow over the Promised Land: Slavery, Race and Violence in Melville's America.* Baton Rouge: Louisiana State University Press.

Levine, Robert (1996). "The African American Presence in Stowe's *Dred.*" In Henry Wonham (ed.), *Criticism and the Color Line: Desegregating American Literary Studies,* 171–92. New Brunswick, NJ: Rutgers University Press.

Melville, Herman (2002). "Benito Cereno." In *Melville's Short Novels,* ed. Dan McCall. New York: Norton.

Morrison, Toni (1993). *Playing in the Dark: Whiteness and the Literary Imagination.* New York: Vintage.

Omi, Michael, and Winant, Howard (1989). *Racial Formation in the United States.* New York: Routledge.

Railton, Stephen, dir. (1998). "Uncle Tom's Cabin and American Culture." University of Virginia. http://jefferson.village.virginia.edu/utc/sitemap.html.

Stansea, Jamie (1992). "Caroline Hentz's Rereading of Southern Paternalism; or, Pastoral Naturalism in *The Planter's Northern Bride.*" *Southern Studies* 3: 4, 221–51.

Stowe, Harriet Beecher (1981). *Uncle Tom's Cabin; or, Life among the Lowly.* New York: Bantam. (First publ. 1852.)

Stowe, Harriet Beecher (2000). *Dred, a Tale of the Great Dismal Swamp.* New York: Penguin.

Sundquist, Eric (1994). "'Benito Cereno' and New-World Slavery." In Myra Jehlen (ed.), *Herman Melville: A Collection of Critical Essays,* 174–86. Englewood Cliffs, NJ: Prentice-Hall.

Tompkins, Jane (1985). *Sensational Designs: The Cultural Work of American Fiction, 1790–1860.* New York: Oxford University Press.

Yarborough, Richard (1986). "Strategies of Black Characterization in Uncle Tom's Cabin and the Early Afro-American Novel." In Eric J. Sundquist (ed.), *New Essays on* Uncle Tom's Cabin, 45–84. Cambridge, UK: Cambridge University Press.

32

Fictions of the South: Southern Portraits of Slavery

Nancy Buffington

During the first half of the nineteenth century many American writers participated in the project of creating a national identity and a national literature. Some Southern writers took on the additional task of forging a specifically Southern cultural identity; as the century progressed this increasingly came to mean engaging with the practice of slavery. The fictions Southern writers created surrounding the "peculiar institution" required that slavery be portrayed as necessary and even beneficent. In some writers' hands, "freedom" and "slavery" became such abstract or relative terms that they ceased to mean anything at all. While Southern slavery was a touchy subject for a fiction writer to address, a look at its portrayal by several significant antebellum writers offers a telling glimpse at the power of a culture to create fictions of an institution already faltering under economic pressure from the industrial North and ethical challenges from the abolition movement.

From the early 1830s on, widespread abolitionist activity, public debate, and growing fears of slave insurrection threatened the institution of slavery. By 1830 more than fifty US newspapers carried anti-slavery columns, and in 1831 William Lloyd Garrison's famous *Liberator* began publication; the Virginia legislature held well-publicized debates over slavery in 1831–2, and fears of slave revolts gained strength after the Nat Turner rebellion of 1831. In the increasingly heated debate over slavery in the first half of the nineteenth century, the arguments of both abolitionists and apologists for slavery turned on discussions of natural law. Abolitionists insisted that slavery violated the doctrine of universal and inalienable rights; pro-slavery writers went so far as to reinterpret and appropriate the tradition of natural rights. They argued, for example, that the Declaration of Independence had been misunderstood; what the founding fathers had intended to establish was a government founded upon submission and inequality. Thus, novelist William Gilmore Simms claimed, the Declaration "not only recognized, but insisted upon inequalities – its laws declaring, not the fitness of all men for any place, but that all should be secured in the quiet possession of their individual right of place" (Simms

1968: 258). Simms redefined freedom and slavery in terms of social hierarchy, admitting as "free" anyone who occupies his "proper place" and a "slave" as anyone forced into a position below his capacity (p. 258). According to this view, Southern slavery was an ethically and politically legitimate institution, a keeper of public order and a preserver of liberty as framed by the founding fathers.

Simms (1806–70) offers a comparatively short and simple portrait of slavery in his best-known work, *The Yemassee* (1835). Simms was a South Carolinian, a novelist interested in law, politics, and journalism who acquired literary fame in the early 1830s with works including *Martin Faber* (1833), the border romance *Guy Rivers* (1834), and *The Partisan* (1835), a novel set during the American Revolution. Simms was interested in celebrating and developing all things American, from politics to literature. He preferred Southern settings and themes, though the bulk of his readership was Northern. A slave-owner himself, Simms saw Southern slavery as an absolute economic necessity and bitterly protested what he called "abolition mania" in the North. In 1852 he argued in the *Southern Quarterly Review* that "we hold slavery to be an especially and wisely devised institution of heaven, devised for the benefit, improvement, and safety, morally, socially, and physically, of a barbarous and inferior race" (quoted in Cowie 1962: xxx). Becoming strongly secessionist in the years before the Civil War, Simms eventually lost his Northern readers and abandoned his literary career.

While Simms confined most of his opinions on slavery to his nonfiction work, a glance at *The Yemassee* reveals the essentials of the ideal Southern notion of a master– slave relationship, replete with devotion, love, and an unrealistically complicated power dynamic. Here we have a loyal slave Hector, captured by Indians and delivered to an enemy ship. Gabriel Harrison, his master, vows to retrieve his property, vowing, "I'll not lose Hector, on any terms. He's the very prince of body servants, and loves me, I verily believe, as I do my mistress" (Simms 1962b: 109). Many adventures later, master and slave are reunited as Hector saves his master's life. In return, Harrison attempts to give Hector his freedom, offering him money and a house of his own in Charleston; this offer sets in motion a dizzying inversion of mastery and bondage. Hector is terrified at the prospect of freedom and protests that "I can't be free"; this prompts Harrison to reassert his power, as master, to free his own property: "Am I not your master? Can't I make you free, and don't I tell you that I do make you free?" (p. 392). Hector quizzes Harrison about the many services his master has provided him, and Harrison replies by now framing his position as one of servitude: "I have done for you all this – but I have done it because you were my slave, and because I was bound to do it." Hector counters with another inversion of who is being freed in this discussion: "Ah, you no want to be boun' no longer. Da's it!" – in other words, in offering to manumit Hector, Harrison is freeing himself and not his slave (p. 392). Hector refuses freedom to the last, citing a variety of terrible fates that would await him as a free black man, from drink to illness to death. Harrison, "deeply affected with this evidence of his attachment," accepts Hector's arguments with the great sentiment often attributed to the master by Southern apologists (p. 392).

Like Simms, Edgar Allan Poe tended to avoid direct treatment of Southern slavery in his fiction; when he does mention slavery explicitly, he offers a more complicated perspective than Simms's. Poe (1809–49) was born in Boston, but was orphaned at an early age and adopted by John Allan of Richmond, Virginia. He knew slavery intimately, as anyone raised in Virginia and living in Maryland in the early nineteenth century would. His adopted father John Allan owned slaves, and Poe himself served as agent in a slave sale. As editor of the *Southern Literary Messenger*, he would have been privy to even more slavery debates than most; numerous pieces on slavery were published during his tenure at the paper. Though its authorship is still a matter of debate, some argue that Poe wrote the "Paulding–Drayton Review" which appeared in the *Messenger* in 1836, and which waxed poetic on the sentimental, intimate connections between masters and slaves.[1] While he rarely addressed slavery in his fiction, most of his writing is built upon twisted power dynamics which have apocalyptic consequences, as in the bizarre return of the dead sister Madeline in "The Fall of the House of Usher," his horror story about an aristocratic family, or the criminal narrators exposed by their powerlessness in the face of their obsessions in "The Tell-Tale Heart" or "The Black Cat." In "The System of Doctor Tarr and Professor Fether" (1844) Poe offers the tale of an insurrection at an insane asylum; here the invalids overthrow their attendants, treating them as lunatics. More obviously, "The Man That Was Used Up" (1839) features a general's utter dependence on his black valet Pompey to reconstruct his body, which was mutilated in the Indian wars; here Poe dramatizes an extreme imbalance of power between master and slave, but in a characteristically fantastical context.

It is in "The Gold-Bug" (1843) that Poe explicitly develops a "conventional" Southern master–slave relationship, and while his other tales hint at more troubling facets and consequences of slavery, this portrayal falls in line with other Southern apologies for slavery. Poe's William Legrand comes from an old family but has been reduced to misfortune. He spends his time hunting and fishing on his island, accompanied by "an old Negro, called Jupiter, who had been manumitted before the reverses of the family, but who could not be induced ... to abandon what he considered his right of attendance upon the footsteps of his young 'Massa Will'" (Poe 1984a: 561). Jupiter asserts a certain degree of power in the relationship; one evening he plans to give his master a "d— good beating" when he arrives home late (p. 566). Legrand, the narrator, and Jupiter venture out one evening in search of treasure buried by Captain Kidd; while Jupiter uses dreams and superstitions to assert his authority in the search, his master Legrand is the one who takes charge as the servant becomes confused. Jupiter is tyrannical, but ultimately incompetent in this tale, and Poe's narrator credits the venture's success to Legrand. "The Gold-Bug" thus begins with a destabilized master–slave relationship but restores a conventional power dynamic by the end.

While Simms and Poe for the most part skirted the issue of slavery in their fiction, Robert Montgomery Bird (1805–54) visited the problem repeatedly, even obsessively, throughout his literary career. A playwright, novelist, and journalist whose tragedies and novels brought him considerable literary fame in the 1830s, Bird was at the center of Philadelphia culture and national politics. He was also a medical doctor and an amateur painter, musician, and inventor, and later in life became involved with politics, agriculture, and photographic experimentation. His wide range of interests put him in touch with prominent artists, doctors, and politicians of the day. Between 1830 and 1839 Bird completed four major dramas and eight lengthy novels, along with a number of other works; his most famous works are *The Gladiator* (1831), an early and popular tragedy about a Roman slave rebellion, and the frontier novel *Nick of the Woods* (1837). Bird shared a publisher (Carey, Lea, & Blanchard) with Cooper, Irving, Poe, Simms, and John P. Kennedy. Vernon Parrington has termed him the "most brilliant successor" of Charles Brockden Brown, and "probably the ablest man of letters that Philadelphia produced" (1927: 183). Born in Delaware, a state with divided sympathies on slavery, Bird grew up around slavery and in an environment that generally supported it. He traveled in the early 1830s and encountered the specific form slavery took in the deep South; while sympathetic to slaves enduring the more horrific conditions he witnessed, he identified with the masters as well, writing, "It is hard to enjoy freedom in a land of slaves. Slaveholders are said to be the freest men on the earth. They are, next to their own bondmen, the greatest slaves" (quoted in Anon. 1939–40: 80). Bird spent most of his literary career between Philadelphia and Delaware, and though the region became increasingly sympathetic to the abolitionist movement, he maintained his more conservative views to the end of his life.

Like many of his contemporaries, including Simms and Poe, Bird was consciously attempting to declare literary and political independence from England. His work represents a particularly clear intersection of political ideology and fiction, embodying the "cultural work," to use Jane Tompkins' term, often performed by literary texts. In a manner more blatant than most of his contemporaries, Bird was self-consciously fulfilling a patriotic mission, attempting to define and defend the nation's history, emergent identity, and political agenda. Because of his direct and lengthy literary treatment of slavery, Bird in particular illustrates the complexity of these discussions, using a rhetoric of freedom to develop a distinctively Southern philosophy of subjection and an apology for slavery.

It should not be surprising that these three authors, with similar agendas and interests, should have been intimately familiar with each other's work. Bird corresponded and exchanged work with both Simms and Poe. Simms initiated a correspondence with Bird in 1835; he had already read Bird's first two novels, *Calavar* (1834) and *The Infidel* (1835), and wanted to read more from the man to whom he was sometimes compared. Subsequent letters through 1839 suggest that Simms read all of Bird's later novels. While Simms often found fault with those works, the two writers shared literary and political interests, along with a sense that their literary works could – and should – serve political ends.

Poe asked Bird in June 1836 to submit an article to the *Southern Literary Messenger*, calling Bird "one of the first pens of the land" (quoted in Foust 1919: 101); while Bird was too busy to fulfill the commission, Poe's review of Bird's *Sheppard Lee* appeared in *The Messenger* only a few months later. Poe's description of one of the novel's episodes approves of the text's apologist message: "In his chapter of Nigger Tom, Mr. Lee gives us some very excellent chapters upon abolition and the exciting effects of incendiary pamphlets and pictures, among our slaves in the South" (Poe 1984b: 399). Poe's careful reading of this and other fiction by Bird may account for striking similarities in images and plot devices in stories such as "The Gold-Bug," "The Murders in the Rue Morgue," "Some Words with a Mummy," and "The System of Doctor Tarr and Professor Fether."

Sheppard Lee (1836), Bird's fourth novel, offers a lengthy treatment of Southern slavery. The episodic satire is held together largely by an extended meditation on the meaning of freedom and slavery, and in the end recommends a stable hierarchy that supports slavery. In his earlier works, *Calavar* (1834), *The Infidel* (1835), and *Hawks of Hawk-Hollow* (1835), Bird had treated similar themes but in the contexts of the Spanish conquest of Mexico and the American frontier just after the Revolutionary War. The objects of satire in *Sheppard Lee* are many, including American political campaigns, financial turmoil under Jackson and Van Buren, gambling, agriculture, philanthropy, and abolition. Bird published the work anonymously and with a new publisher, and it was such a departure in style and genre that some friends refused to believe Bird was the author. The book received good reviews but sales suffered from the poor economic conditions prevailing at the time (Foust 1919: 96).

While Poe dismissed Bird's intended message as "very doubtful" (1984b: 402), Bird wrote *Sheppard Lee* with a clear moral in mind: acceptance of one's fate. The title character is a lazy and dissatisfied New Jersey landowner who dies while searching for lost treasure, but discovers he is capable of spiritual transmigration, which allows him to revivify and inhabit the bodies of other recently deceased men. Endlessly seeking happiness in other men's bodies and lives, Sheppard Lee inhabits six different bodies in this text – those of an aged squire, a wealthy miser, a naïve Quaker, two impoverished dandies, and a slave – but finds only more misery and oppression each time (with one significant exception I will address below). At the end of his adventures Lee returns to his own body, vowing to become industrious, accept his social position, and "make the best of the lot to which Heaven has assigned me" (Bird 1836: vol. 2, 264).

A careful separation between a defensible institution and indefensible abuses of that institution surfaces in Bird's discussions of slavery in *Sheppard Lee*. Bird circles around the concepts of freedom and slavery, oppression and rebellion, frequently applying the terminology of slavery to conditions of white servitude and even mere dissatisfaction as the protagonist "becomes" a slave in repeated episodes. Bird consistently favors preserving the institution of slavery and the rights of the white man, condemning what he considers as threats to the republic: slave rebellion and the enslavement of a white man.

Bird's presentation of metaphorical and actual slavery draws on both traditional natural subjection theory and contemporary pro-slavery arguments. He works Simms's definitions of freedom and slavery into his scheme of submission and hierarchy, so that unhappy white characters are considered enslaved until they fulfill their potential, and African slaves are assumed to be happily occupying their proper places and thereby "free." Despite the satirical tone, the narrative clearly condemns the social disorder caused by individuals contesting their social position, and equally clearly supports the ideas of natural subjection and pro-slavery ideology.

Lee's entire adventure is framed as a movement from psychological slavery to independence; he begins as a "slave" to his own slave, shirking his duties as an owner of land and slaves, and gains freedom only when he becomes industrious and responsible at the novel's end. In attaining freedom through submission and duty, Lee embodies Simms's claim that *"our natural rights depend entirely upon the degree of obedience which we pay to the laws of our creation. All our rights, whether from nature or from society... result from the performance of our duties.* Unless we perform our duties, we have no rights; or they are alienable, in consequence of our lâchesse" (Simms 1968: 259–60, emphasis in original).

It is in the representation of Southern slavery that Bird's conservative adaptation of the natural law tradition, and in particular his pro-slavery stance despite his rhetoric of freedom, become unmistakable. Bird depicts an actual master–slave relationship early in *Sheppard Lee* to substitute his preferred definition of slavery as a metaphysical or psychological state for that of an absolute condition of enforced servitude. In other words, Lee turns his interaction with his own slave into a claim that he himself is the slave. This master–slave dynamic is typical of those depicted in Bird's work and apparent in Simms and Poe as well: the slave is more powerful than the master, takes unfair advantage of his master's good will, and is so contented with his condition that he is an adamant supporter of slavery. Lee describes his relationship with his slave, Jim Jumble, as strained; the latter is unmanageable and "would have all things his own way, in spite of me" (Bird 1836: vol. 1, 23). Lee refers to Jim as "a hard master" and a "tyrannical old rascal" who makes business decisions "as if he were the master and owner of all things" and sometimes even punishes Lee (vol. 1, 41, 25).[2] Later, as Lee returns to his house in the body of Squire Higginson, he is the object of Jim's aggression as the slave threatens him with a gun and throws a brick at his head. Despite his grumbling, we are to read Lee's criticisms as reflecting on both master and slave: Jim's misbehavior is largely attributable to Lee's insufficient job as a master which creates disorder in their relationship, as hinted at by the name "Jumble."

Because of his supposed power, Jim apparently prefers slavery to freedom. When Lee tries to free him, Jim "burst into a passion, swore he would *not* be free, and told me flatly I was his master, and I should take care of him; and the absurd old fool ended by declaring if I made him a free slave man he would have the law on me" (Bird 1836: vol. 1, 23).[3] In these arguments Bird draws directly on pro-slavery arguments. Lee attributes Jim's loyalty to mere laziness – what Thomas Dew called "the principle of idleness and dissipation" (1968: 430) – a preference for the comfortable life of a slave over the hard work and "precarious subsistence as a free man" (Bird 1836: vol. 1, 23). By positing the life of a slave as easier than that of the free laborer, Bird aligns himself with the likes of George Fitzhugh, who called the free laborer "a slave, without the rights of a slave," and Dew, who called the laborer "already a slave, or rather in a situation infinitely worse than slavery" (Fitzhugh 1981: 295; Dew 1968: 322).

Lee's next explanation for Jim Jumble's fear of freedom takes the form of another prevailing trope about slavery, the sentimental notion of affection. He asserts: "Some little affection for me, as I had grown up from a boy . . . under his own eye, was perhaps at the bottom of his resolution" (Bird 1836: vol. 1, 24). Here he echoes apologists such as Governor James Hammond, who opined, "there are few ties more heartfelt, or of more benignant influence, than those which mutually bind the master and the slave" (Hammond 1968: 161). Little affection is displayed between Lee and Jim at this stage; it is not until the novel's end, where Lee accepts his proper duties as master, that their relationship reflects order and mutual satisfaction. Bird's belief in social hierarchy as a desirable keeper of social order is evident when Lee becomes an industrious landowner and a responsible master; Jim is still "saucy" but is now faithful and industrious under the example of his master. Once Lee accepts his role, the master–slave relationship becomes a fruitful and happy one. The effective functioning of slavery is portrayed as dependent on both parties accepting their roles and fulfilling their duties.

The most extensive discussion of the institution of slavery as it impinges on an individual slave appears when Lee inhabits the body of the slave Tom; this plot twist allows for the closest thing to a first-person experience of chattel slavery in all Bird's work. The events leading up to this episode are themselves significant. Tom is among the slaves who climb a tree with a hanging rope, calling for the killing of a "cussed bobolitionist" (Bird 1836: vol. 2, 154). Slaves are presented here as enthusiastic participants in the lynching, and, like Jim Jumble, adamant opponents of abolition. Tom, "among the most active and zealous" of the group, falls out of the tree in his frenzy and dies. Lee passes into Tom's body, vowing, "It is better to be a slave than dead" (vol. 2, 156).

Lee's first reaction to his situation makes a gesture toward the dreadful realities of actual slavery. He is terrified, sure that after all his previous complaints, "*Now* I was at last to learn in reality what it was to be the victim of fortune, . . . the exemplar of wretchedness, the true repository of all . . . griefs" (Bird 1836: vol. 2, 159). But quickly Bird interjects a variety of apologist arguments to assure us that the slave life is easy, better than that of a fugitive or free black. As a slave woman tells Lee, "poor despise nigga wid no massa, jist as despise as any free nigga" (vol. 2, 160). Bird's characterization of the master and his family as "humane and gentle" reflects the apologist argument of a benign institution. The trope of affection (seen in a more cynical form in the Lee–Jim relationship) reappears here towards both Massa Jodge, whom Lee describes as "a great and powerful friend, whose protection and kindness I was bound to requite with a loyal affection," and to the entire family (vol. 2, 175; see also vol. 2, 163). For the first time Lee is perfectly content, with no desire to exchange his lot for another. Perhaps, he concludes, "there is nothing necessarily adverse to happiness in slavery itself" (vol. 2, 172).

Massa Jodge has a gentler temperament than Lee did as a master, but the two masters share some important faults: laziness and a lack of authority. The master's denial of his duties creates a power inversion like that seen in Lee and Jim; again we see a slave-owner called "in some respects, a greater slave than his bondmen," and all mistreatment is committed by the slaves unto the master, even as they are "great sticklers for their own rights and privileges" (vol. 2, 176).

In his persistent defense of institutionalized order, Bird apparently saw any portrait of Southern slavery as incomplete without some form of rebellion. In *Sheppard Lee* the slaves' happy, peaceful existence ceases not through any action of their master, but through their discovery of an abolitionist tract with graphic woodcuts illustrating the suffering of African slaves. Lee, drawing on remnants of his white man's education, deciphers the text's use of the principles of natural law and universal rights. Lee's fellow slaves at first resist the tract's ideas, but are finally persuaded by the pamphlet's appeal to the Declaration of Independence's "free and equal" clause, its "strange" notions of "natural freedom and equality," its description of them as "the victims of avarice, the play-things of cruelty, the foot-balls of oppression, the most injured peoples in the world" (vol. 2, 187–92). Lee himself begins to have "sentimental notions" regarding "liberty and equality, the dignity of man, the nobleness of freedom" (vol. 2, 192). An awareness of injustice leads quickly to the desire for vengeance. The slaves come to regard their master with fear and hatred, and they plan an insurrection despite Lee's concession that they have "no real cause" for their dissatisfaction. Lee repeatedly insists that slave life on this plantation was happy; that the slaves were "contented with their lot in life," that the master and his family did nothing to incite the rebellion, and that the abolitionist tract is an evil text which breeds discontent and violence where none rightfully exists. This view is clear from Bird's manuscript notes, including one which suggested that "when the reformers send their agents and publications to the South, they do not so much sound the cry of liberty among the slaves as raise the tocsin [*sic*] of revolt and the alarm of murder" (quoted in Williams 1939: lvii). As biographer Curtis Dahl observes, "for Bird the Negro slave of Virginia, though joyous and happy and good when a loyal servant to a good master, is a murderous savage when he strikes for his freedom" (1963: 59).

Bird had been concerned with Southern slavery throughout his literary career – his 1831 "Secret Records" contain extensive comments on the Nat Turner rebellion – yet it is probably no accident that he reserved a direct treatment of this issue for his satires. Here he can overtly mock various forms of slavery, finding humor in a range of dissatisfied and "enslaved" characters, before addressing the experiences of African slaves. By treating slavery as a metaphor and a source of satire amid extravagant transformations and unlikely disguises, Bird makes the concepts of freedom and slavery abstract, illusory, and even interchangeable; as apologist Governor Hammond would argue in 1845, "abstract liberty [is] the merest phantasy that ever amused the imagination" (Hammond 1968: 104). He can thus submit his own portrait of Southern slavery, one borrowing generously from natural subjection and pro-slavery rhetorics: one of a legitimate institution necessary to preserve social order and the public good, its only ills caused by misuse. In this extreme example of rhetoric divorced from reality, it seems that anything can happen. Here, almost lost among the elaborate inversions of virtually everything – life and death, dream and reality, and even black and white – freedom becomes slavery, slavery becomes freedom, abolition becomes treason, and the defense of slavery becomes a patriotic duty.

Thus did a peculiarly Southern version of natural rights, liberty, and civic duty inscribe itself across the foundational ideologies of the new nation. Eventually, of course, the chasm between the founding fathers' intentions and the circuitous reasoning of Southern apologists like Bird and Simms, and perhaps also Poe, became obvious. Bird himself, like many of this time, foresaw the conflict that tore the nation apart, though he died before it began. Typically, he named as the culprit in that war not the evils of slavery itself, but the instability and factionalism generated by the slavery debates. The fictions of the South were important for their contributions to a burgeoning national and regional identity, even as they pointed and indeed contributed to glaring flaws in the American experiment. As Simms put it, "It is by such artists, indeed, that nations live" (1962a: 36).

NOTES

1 See Dayan 1991 for an argument in favor of Poe's authorship of the "Paulding–Drayton Review."

2 Poe's "The Gold-Bug" features very similar interactions. Since Poe reviewed *Sheppard Lee* for the *Southern Literary Messenger*, these correspondences have led to critical speculation about Bird's influence on Poe's story. See Dayan 1995: 127; Dahl 1963: 110; Cowie 1948: 794 n. 116; Campbell 1962: 172 and nn. 2–3. In his biography of Poe, Arthur Hobson Quinn discusses the parallels between

the two texts but, citing minor differences, concludes that the connection "seems very uncertain" (1941: 394 n. 75).

3 Alexander Cowie and Cecil Williams have both noted the similarity between Jim's attitude and that of the slave Hector, whom Simms calls "the adhesive black" in *The Yemassee* (Simms 1962b: 391–2). See Cowie 1962: xxx; Williams 1939: lvi n. 132. Simms had sent Bird a copy of *The Yemassee* in October 1835, according to an arrangement for ongoing exchanges set up with a mutual friend.

REFERENCES

Anon. (1939–40). "Traveling with Robert Montgomery Bird." *University of Pennsylvania Chronicle* 7: 11–22, 34–50, 75–90; 8: 4–21.

Bird, Robert Montgomery (1836). *Sheppard Lee*, 2 vols. New York: Harper & Bros.

Campbell, Killis (1962). *The Mind of Poe and Other Studies*. New York: Russell & Russell.

Cowie, Alexander (1948). *The Rise of the American Novel*. New York: American Book Co.

Cowie, Alexander (1962). "Introduction." In William Gilmore Simms, *The Yemassee* (first publ. 1835). New York: Hafner, ix–xxxv.

Dahl, Curtis (1963). *Robert Montgomery Bird*. New York: Twayne.

Dayan, Joan (1991). "Romance and Race." In Emory Elliott (ed.), *The Columbia History of the American Novel*, 89–109. New York: Columbia University Press.

Dayan, Joan (1995). "Poe, Ladies and Slaves." In Michael Moon and Cathy N. Davidson (eds.), *Subjects and Citizens: Nation, Race, and Gender from Oroonoko to Anita Hill*, 109–43. Durham, NC: Duke University Press.

Dew, Thomas R. (1968). "Professor Dew on Slavery." In *The Pro-slavery Argument: As Maintained by the most Distinguished Writers of the Southern States*. New York: Negro University Press, 287–490. (First publ. 1852.)

Fitzhugh, George (1981). "Southern Thought." In Drew Gilpin Faust (ed.), *The Ideology of Slavery: Proslavery Thought in the Antebellum South, 1830–1860*, 272–99. Baton Rouge: Lousiana State University Press.

Foust, Clement (1919). *The Life and Dramatic Works of Robert Montgomery Bird*. New York: Knickerbocker.

Hammond, James (1968). "Hammond's Letters on Slavery." In *The Pro-slavery Argument: As Maintained by the most Distinguished Writers of the Southern States*. New York: Negro University Press, 99–174. (First publ. 1853.)

Parrington, Vernon (1927). *The Romantic Revolution in America: 1800–1860*, vol. 2 of *Main Currents in American Thought*. New York: Harcourt Brace Jovanovich.

Poe, Edgar Allan (1984a). "The Gold-Bug" (first publ. 1843). In *Edgar Allan Poe: Poetry and Tales*, 560–96. New York: Library of America.

Poe, Edgar Allan (1984b). "Sheppard Lee: Written by Himself." In *Edgar Allan Poe: Essays and Reviews*, 389–403. New York: Library of America.

Quinn, Arthur Hobson (1941). *Edgar Allan Poe: A Critical Biography*. New York: D. Appleton-Century Co.

Simms, William Gilmore (1962a). *Views and Reviews in American Literature*, ed. C. Hugh Holman. Cambridge, Mass.: Harvard University Press. (First publ. 1846.)

Simms, William Gilmore (1962b). *The Yemassee*. New York: Hafner. (First publ. 1835.)

Simms, William Gilmore (1968). "The Morals of Slavery." In *The Pro-slavery Argument: As Maintained by the Most Distinguished Writers of the Southern States*, 175–285. New York: Negro University Press. (First publ. 1853.)

Williams, Cecil B. (1939). "Introduction." In *Nick of the Woods, or the Jibbenainosay*. New York: American Book Co.

33
The West

Edward Watts

The conclusion, then, is that the familiarity of Western men with grand subjects of composition, breeds contempt therefor; that stranger and distant persons write about them better, their ignorance of the subject giving an originality to their statements, quite novel and pleasing; and finally, that the people of the West acquiesce in and encourage the state of things brought about by this faith, by neglecting Western literary enterprizes, and giving their money for the periodicals and papers of the east. Here is an evil which the Journal must rectify, before it can reign over the empire of the Western mind.

In 1836, when initiating the new *Western Literary Journal*, William Davis Gallagher recognized a pervasive interregional asymmetry in the trans-Appalachian book trade. Gallagher was fresh off the failure of *The Cincinnati Mirror* (1831–6) and would soon move on to the likewise doomed *Hesperian* (1838–9). Gallagher himself, best known as a poet, editor, and abolitionist, wrote only one traceable fiction: a novella, *The Dutchman's Daughter*, serialized in *The Hesperian*. Nonetheless, he was the first editor of George D. Prentice, Frederick Thomas, Phoebe and Alice Cary, Edward "Ned Buntline" Judson, Caroline Hentz, and a very young Harriet Beecher, all of whom would later support themselves through their fiction (Rusk 1926; Venable 1891). All, however, would need to publish (or republish) with Eastern publishing houses to do so. Others Gallagher published – such as Benjamin Drake, Alice Dumont, Thomas Shreve, and Maria Collins – either turned to other forms of writing or stopped. Their silence was the result of their exclusion from the dominant Eastern publishing centers of the antebellum period *and* the unwillingness of Westerners to buy locally published books, instead spending their money on writers from afar.

Gallagher's statement insightfully identifies the marginality of the "West" in the national literary scene as a two-edged sword. Despite the fact that the 1840 census revealed almost as many white Americans living west of the Appalachians as to their east, the series of bankruptcies through which Gallagher passed demonstrates the resistance of Western readers to local writing. Instead, the Western fiction market – in terms of both the invisibility of Western writers and the monopolization of Western subjects by Eastern writers such as James Fenimore Cooper, William Snelling, James Kirke Paulding, Caroline Kirkland, Eliza Farnham, and Robert Montgomery Bird – was nearly stillborn. Furthermore, the "ignorance" of non-Western fiction writers led them to misrepresent the region badly. In 1834 Daniel Drake noted that "No Western man can read these works with interest" because "no power of genius can supply the want of . . . personal observation." Western fiction needed to be written and, more importantly for Gallagher, *bought* by Westerners, or else important and difficult realities of Western life would be for ever lost.

This asymmetry might called "colonial," in that Westerners, although politically equal to Easterners, were held (and held themselves) in a position of cultural marginality, a sense of inferiority that discouraged and inhibited the development of a self-sustaining Western fiction (Donald and Palmer 1956). Nonetheless, Westerners slowly became aware of this exclusion, even as they excluded racial minorities in their own communities. Today, virtually no fiction by Western non-whites before 1860 is to be found in the archive. After the Civil War, this feeling of marginality – among the whites – fueled the Realist movement and produced Western writers like Garland, Howells, Cather, and Dreiser (Weber 1992). This essay will trace this sense of alienation – always a wellspring of literary expression – to antebellum Cincinnati, the Western publishing center between 1830 and 1860 (Glazer 1999). Not surprisingly, this feeling of fragmentation and dissociation was best shown in the region's short fiction: most novels written by Westerners – Timothy Flint, Caroline Hentz, and Frederick Thomas – are highly episodic (owing in most cases to their initial serialization) and are better described as loosely knit short-story cycles.

Indeed, the most important Western fiction came in the form of short stories: most of them appeared first in periodical form, then often being reprinted in the East, collected in an annual, and eventually perhaps in a collection of the author's work. That is, Western short stories, like the Western population itself, were mobile, shifty, energetic, and opportunistic. The antebellum West, then, might be most profitably discussed in the context of other communities formed by English-speaking whites around the world. Most literary historians of settlement colonies divide locally produced fiction into two categories: frontier adventure and domestic settlement, the former written by and produced for men, the latter by and for women. In Australia, this division might be represented by Henry Lawson and Rosa Praed; in South Africa, by Bertram Mitford and Olive Schreiner (New 1996; Van Herk 1996). However, in the work itself, the division into "separate spheres" is often revealed as mythical, and the boundaries imported from the metropolis get smudged, becoming just one more way in which settlement experience differed from metropolitan expectations.

Likewise in the antebellum West, as best exemplified in the work of James Hall and Alice Cary, there is an important and problematic intertextuality within the genre each employs. While the adventure story and the domestic fiction each served a nationalizing propagandistic purpose as practiced by metropolitan writers (Cooper and Kirkland, for example), colonial writers treat them simply as points of departure, and instead comment on the inadequacy of these standard narratives without forthrightly rejecting them. Their ambivalence toward the conventions of their genres reflects their more general ambivalence toward the marginality of their communities in the nation or empire in which they lived and wrote, a complicated articulation that represents the apex of Western fiction's achievement.

James Hall and Indian-hating

In *Facing West: The Metaphysics of Indian-Hating and Empire Building* Richard Drinnon represents James Hall as personifying a Western identity based on unmitigated greed, hatred, and racism. Drinnon based his reading on a veiled reference to Hall in Herman Melville's *The Confidence-Man* and the monumental series Hall co-wrote with Thomas McKenney, *A History of the Indian Tribes of North America* (1836–44). At times, Drinnon is right: Hall entered the collaboration on questionable grounds (to recover his losses from the Panic of 1836), and the *History* far too often repeats the racist cant that justified removal (i.e. ethnic cleansing and other forms of cultural and physical genocide). On the basis of this incomplete reading of Hall's writing on the subject, Drinnon obsessively and badly overstates and misrepresents Hall's link to what he considers to be the universal opinion of white Westerners – Indian-hating (Drinnon 1980: 196–215).

Indian-hating is a powerful and troubling theme both in Eastern writing about the West and in Western writing about itself. Bird, Flint, Snelling, Cooper, and others took up the theme of the white male reduced to savagery in response to some childhood crime committed by Indians against his family, usually arson accompanied by the slaughter of the parents (Slotkin 1973). The white male might then lead what appears to be a normal life, except when exposed to Indians, when an uncritical urge to kill is triggered. In this narrative, the murderous tendency is based in revenge, justified and not psychotic, though revelatory of the frontier's ability to deracinate otherwise civilized white men, reducing them to "new-made Indians," in the terms of Crèvecœur. Indeed, Hall is responsible for naming and writing about this phenomenon, starting in 1828. However, Hall's revision of the theme in a few stories written between 1828 and 1834 represents not only his own maturation as a fiction writer but also the arrival of Cincinnati as a place where "empire building" was not only practiced but also questioned, subverted, and rejected.

The crucial intervening event was the Black Hawk War of 1832. Prior to it, Hall had been living and writing in Shawneetown and then Vandalia, Illinois (Randall 1964). Although he had come to Illinois from Philadelphia as an adult, he sided with many of the older settlers and saw the conflict as the result of more aggressive and materialistic colonization following the War of 1812 and its safe delivery of the Mississippi valley. The Northwest Ordinance of 1787 had promised that "The utmost good faith shall always be observed toward the Indians, their lands and property shall never be taken from them without their consent." A former Federalist, Hall celebrated the interracialism of the Illinois frontier before 1820 and first wrote of Indian-hating as an aberration, a leftover of frontier atavism. To him, the coming of commercial farming and industrialism was a more pressing threat that corrupted the preferable village-based culture of the settlement period. In those days, local patriarchal order (both Native and white) had reined in the violence of the frontier and made biracial cohabitation possible. Hence, Indian-hating was the exception, rather than the rule (White 1991).

One exception to this was a real-life Indian-hater, Colonel John Moredock. Hall wrote both fictional and nonfictional accounts of Moredock. The nonfiction version – an obituary – he published twice, once in 1831 in Illinois and again in 1832 in Cincinnati; but it was in 1828 that Hall first fictionalized him as Samuel Monson in "The Indian Hater," a story included in *The Western Souvenir*, a Christmas collection of Western writing published in Cincinnati and Philadelphia. In it, although he was writing prior to the war, Hall shows how the leftover savagery of the frontier is managed as the region moves toward civility, yet how violence still haunted the region. Hall's narrator first encounters Monson as some Indians enter a store in a small Illinois town where both are passing the time. Monson is described reacting to the

THE STRUGGLE. Page 248.

Figure 33.1 "The Struggle." From Elijah Kellogg, *Sowed by the Wind; or, The Poor Boy's Fortune* (Boston: Lee & Shepard, 1874). Collection of Shirley Samuels.

Indians pathologically: "His eyes rolled wildly, as if he had been suddenly stung by madness, gleaming with a strange fierceness; a supernatural luster, like that which flashes from the eyeballs of a panther." However, his friends "led him off in one direction, while the Indians rode away in another." After this, the narrator is informed of Monson's long history of slaughtering Indians. Horrified, the narrator responds: "But is it possible, that in a civilized country, within the reach of our laws, a wretch is permitted to hunt down his fellow creatures like wild beasts; to murder a defenceless [*sic*] Indian, who comes into our territory in good faith, believing us a Christian people?"

The ensuing debate identifies the violent part of the frontier as anachronistic, and Monson is established as an unfortunate leftover of the contact period. Furthermore, the narrator's referring to Indians as "fellow creatures" and describing their entering the store to do business as an everyday occurrence corroborate historians such as Richard White, Marvin Mikesell, and John Mack Faragher in their common observation of the settlement period as one of intercultural cohabitation.

Following this, the narrator hires a Potawatomi guide for a tour of northwestern Illinois. For four pages they ride through the peaceful prairie as companions. Coming upon a remote farm long in ruins, they are ambushed, and the Indian is shot by a hidden gunman. Of course, Monson soon comes forward to explain, "with the malignity of gratified revenge." After disarming the petrified narrator, he relates a story of his entire family's supposedly unprovoked murder and his own eventual escape from a "gang of yelling savages." Following this, Monson fought in an "Indian War" and has since carried on a vigilante campaign against any and all Indians. In the 1831 essay, Hall added a twist that reveals a growing flexibility of thought, the start of an important transition in his self-identification: in the new account, the Mingoes – renegade Iroquois in the Ohio valley – are specifically identified as the "savages" responsible for the attack. That is, Hall distinguishes the peaceful Potawatami indigenous to the region from the Mingoes, Iroquois renegades from the East (White 1991). Hall, familiar with the intraracial and intertribal complexities of frontier life, was aware that tribal identity was often as important as race in determining the potential for cohabitation or confrontation. Moredock, by overlooking such intraracial distinctions, is typical of the racism of most American representations of Indians.

Unfortunately, Cooper, Snelling, Bird, and the others who appropriated this story for their own exploitative ends stopped reading Hall here. To a point, it is easy to put Hall in their camp (and in 1828, he may have belonged there): there is a certain ambiguity – why do the other whites not bring Monson to justice? Why does Hall give him space to justify his actions and create some sympathy for him as a victim as well as a victimizer? Lastly, Hall's tribal distinctions are generally Cooperian: good Indian/bad Indian. As such, the 1828 story exists as part of the "imperial archive" – the stage version of American history wherein the vanishing Native falls before the white man. The violence of the contact zone is a necessary catharsis in the achievement of Manifest Destiny. In any case, what his readers – from Melville to Drinnon – didn't read was a further rewriting of Moredock's story Hall published in 1835, after the Black Hawk War.

The Black Hawk War showed that Indian-hating was not idiosyncratic or individual, but rather systemic and collective, a revelation that horrified most writers in Cincinnati. In fact, Hall oversaw the later editions of the most devastating anti-war book – Benjamin Drake's *The Life and Adventures of Black Hawk* (from 1838) – after Drake's death. In 1832 he moved from Illinois to Cincinnati, appalled at the government's disregard for both the principles of the Northwest Ordinance and the rules of common decency. If his views on Indian-hating were ambivalent prior to the war, after the war they took firmer shape, and he viewed himself as clearly outside the official, "empire-building" racism implicit in the war's initiation, conduct, and settlement. The transition in Hall is best demonstrated in his final rewriting of the story of John Moredock in "The Pioneer," a very long short story first published in 1833.

Here, the Moredock/Monson character (hereafter "The Indian-hater") narrates the story entirely, and he is a changed man. Much of the story is an embellishment on the version told to the appalled narrator at the end of the 1828 "The Indian-hater." However, this time Hall adds a sister for the main character. The Indian-hater, believing his sister long dead, has used the image of her destruction to motivate his own pathological hatred for all Natives regardless of tribe. But in "The Pioneer" Hall takes his time arriving at this point, establishing the Old Northwest as far more complex than was usually imagined. First, his narrator, as a young man, lives in the woods outside of Kaskaskia with Peter, a Frenchman who was "Equally friendly with the whites and the Indians . . . [he] visited the villages and camps of both and was well received." From Peter, a lingering presence from the intercultural Middle Ground (White 1991), pre-1820, the narrator learns the arts of the woods. He also learns from the Frenchman that his family was killed, not by any tribe but by "a number of desperate individuals from different villages, led by a lawless chief, who still occasionally assembled the band for similar outrages" (p. 77): a band of renegades outside of tribal hegemony.

Again, the issue for Hall has more to do with the loss of patriarchal order in both white and Indian communities – only the deluded Indian-hater thinks race is the core issue. Hall's frontier is now a very complicated place, and, as he had in the nonfiction narrative of Moredock, Hall clearly exempts most Natives from the violence that triggered Indian-hating and most whites from hating Indians. Indian-hating is the exception rather than the rule, and the figure of Peter testifies to a functional intercultural cohabitation threatened by more aggressive white encroachments in the name of commercial agriculture and Indian removal.

To make a long story short, the narrator finds out where this renegade group is camping, gathers a posse to massacre them, and does. But he is not satisfied, and his rage becomes genocidal rather than specific. Importantly, though, while he goes off on his individual career of murdering those Indians not responsible for his family's death, the other white men go home. Opportunistically murdering even as he becomes a

farmer, he explains himself: "But you must remember that I had been raised on the
frontier; that I had been accustomed since infancy to hear the Indian spoken of as an
enemy – as a cowardly, malevolent, and cruel savage, who stole upon the unprotected,
in the hour of repose, and murdered without respect to age or sex" (p. 82).

Clearly blaming the rhetorical construct of the Indian in "white" discourse, Hall
carefully places this passage near the all-important incident where the narrator is about
to do precisely what he has just condemned. First, though, the narrator contemplates
the role of Indian-hating in the context of nationhood: "Filial piety sanctioned the
promptings of nature; and I believed that in killing a savage I performed my duty as a
man and served my country as a citizen" (p. 86). Hall's linkage of the Indian-hater's
pathology and the genocidal aspect of racist constructions of national citizenship is an
astonishingly perceptive and devastating observation. Importantly as well, the Indian-
hater has begun to feel its destructive tendencies. Slowly, he realizes that others around
him "forgave injuries and forgot bereavement" (p. 86). Despite these stirrings of a
conscience, however, he initiates one final act of savagery.

He comes upon an Indian family and stalks them with the intent to kill the
warrior, his squaw, and their two children. As they rest by a stream, he prepares the
massacre; however, the squaw turns around – and turns out, of course, to be his long-
lost sister. She had been taken captive, and like so many whites, acculturated into her
captors' tribe to the extent that she lost any memory of her "white" identity
(Derounian-Stodola and Levernier 1993). The Indian-hater walks into their camp
and is cautiously but graciously welcomed. Once the identities are confirmed, the
narrator offers to return her to the whites. Hall writes, "She received my proposition
coldly, and declined it with a slight smile of contempt" (p. 94). She's happy where she
is; a fact that seems acceptable – even commonplace – and reasonable to her and,
implicitly, to Hall – but not, at first, to the Indian-hater. Astonished, he leaves his
sister in her sylvan idyll and walks out of the woods.

Once he returns to his farm, the Indian-hater undergoes a cathartic deconstruction
of the images of Indians that dominated both his and the nation's representations of
them as subhuman impediments to Manifest Destiny. It ends with the question: "But
if they were murderers, what was I?" (p. 98). The story concludes with the Indian-
hater's transition to wandering defender of Native causes, "to endeavour to make some
atonement for my former guilty career of crime and passion" (p. 101). Writ large, the
story is about the violent frontiersman recognizing that he has become worse than the
savage he imagined. For Hall in 1833, however, Indian-hating had been the source of
the Black Hawk War, and Hall meant his story as a lesson for all whites not to become
what they feared. By the end, the Indian-hater, and all those like him, are wearing hair
shirts, seeking atonement and the re-establishment of that equilibrium of cohabitation without dominance, of cooperation rather than aggression.

Writing in 1835, Hall more directly and explicitly remembered the Black Hawk
War in an essay which he would reprint a number of times, including it finally as an
appendix to the eighth edition of Drake's book in 1848. Of the end of the war, he
writes: "I have seen in this region, evidences of persecution perpetrated by our people

upon this unhappy race, such as the American people would scarcely believe; and I am satisfied that if the events of the late war could be traced to their true source, every real philanthropist in the nation would blush for our country."

Likewise, in his response to Lyman Beecher's attack on Catholicism in the West in 1836, Hall refers to the eighteenth-century French settlement of the region, held up as a model of decadence and corruption in other American sources, as a better paradigm of racial interaction: "It shows that the Catholic appetite for cruelty is not so keen as is usually imagined, and that they exercised, of choice, an expensive benevolence, at a period when Protestants, similarly situated, were blood-thirsty and rapacious."

In regard to both Catholics and Indians, Hall crafts a narrative of a national or imperial culture running roughshod over a more inclusive, diverse, and improvised local culture. He rejects the East's insistence on a monolithic national identity and exposes how it both fought and wrote the more plural aspects of the region's entangled interculturalism out of existence (Gjerde 1997). In both cases, Hall takes a stand for diversity against uniformity.

After the Catholic controversy, Beecher and his acolyte David Brainerd, both Eastern immigrants, recognized Hall for what he was – an upstart colonial who disrupted the "universal Yankee nation" – and forced him out his editorship of *The Western Monthly Magazine*. Like many colonial writers, Hall's place as a writer in the colony was complicated by his resistance to the distant metropolitan culture (Watts 2002). However, again typically of colonials (think of Salman Rushdie in London), Hall was more welcome and popular in the East than in the West. Colonialism works best by making the colonials even more nationalistic than the metropolitans: the East was more open to criticism of the nation than the West, that is. After 1836, while Hall continued to write history and ethnography (not very well), he was finished as a fiction writer. Nonetheless, the damage had been done. Younger writers like Gallagher, Otway Curry, Amelia Welby, and others – most notably Alice Cary – took up Hall's call for a regional writing that was characterized by something more than the mere fact of geographical coincidence, even if they had to move to New York to do so.

Alice Cary and *Clovernook*

Alice Cary, along with her sister, the poet Phoebe, was first published by their kinsman William Gallagher in his various aforementioned journals. The sisters, however, soon realized the limitations placed on writers who stayed in the West while pursuing professional careers and, after publishing nationally with some success, moved to New York in 1851, to return only periodically to the family home outside Cincinnati. Alice's fiction – like that of Hentz, Collins, and other female writers in the Ohio valley – usually focused on the domestic aspects of settlement experience. As Annette Kolodny argued first and best, white women represented an ambiguous presence on the frontier. On the one hand, they were free from the shackling conventions of the "cult of true womanhood" created and monitored in

the Eastern cities and magazines; on the other hand, they often started the domesticating processes that "tamed" frontierswomen by measuring them by a metropolitan
standard of feminine legitimacy. Kirkland's *A New Home – Who'll Follow?* (1838) and
Farnham's *Life in Prairie Land* (1846) best articulate the metropolitan woman's
simultaneous celebration of the freedoms of the frontier and her role in ending them.

Kirkland and Farnham often refer to the little girls of the settlements as the best
hope for achieving that "home feeling" at the heart of women's role in taming the
frontier. The Cary sisters would have been the objects of such a gaze and, when they
began writing, they took up as a consistent theme a counter-narrative to Kirkland's
and Farnham's relatively sunny stories of white females having it both ways in the
West. Cary's women often resemble Hamlin Garland's later nineteenth-century farm
women who are worked to death. Nonetheless, like Hall's, Cary's fiction is more
reactionary than creative, colonial rather than post-colonial. Judith Fetterley has
suggested that "Cary's own writing, despite her technique, reinscribes class hierarchies as much as it calls them into question" (Fetterley and Pryse 1995: 112).

A specific illustration of this point can be seen in the story of Susan Tomkins in
"About the Tomkinses." This story first appeared in *The National Era*, a Washington-
based abolitionist journal with which Gallagher was connected, and then later in
Cary's own collection, *Clovernook; Or, Recollections of our Neighborhood in the West*,
published in 1851. Other, quite similar characters appear throughout *Clovernook*,
but this story stands out for its combination of a number of Old Northwestern
resistances to the Eastern hope that local divergences from the national story of
westward expansion could be written off as passing distractions and so removed as
threats to the East-based nation. For example, like Hall, Cary mines the French past of
the Ohio valley for an alternative to the commercial capitalism and social-climbing
obsessions of colonial Cincinnati by triangulating a settler family, a wealthy Eastern
family, and a French suitor as choices for Susan's future loyalty.

As the story opens, Susan is fighting with her pioneering parents. Thus far, they
have urged Susan to resist the incursion of middle-class culture represented by the
purchase by the more genteel Haywood family of the adjacent farm. Instead, they
treat her as little more than a servant and caregiver for her repellent younger brothers.
The Haywoods build a modern house and keep servants, setting up as the local gentry,
as is encouraged in the story as told by Kirkland. Following the model of the natural
aristocrat, Dr. Haywood even "accepts the office of trustee of the district school"
(Cary 1987: 40), but Cary does note that they had left Cincinnati because of their
waning economic status. Nonetheless, the Tomkinses view the Haywoods as snobbish
and elitist and instead insist on a simpler way of life. At the same time, Cary portrays
the Tomkinses as equally flawed: they are small-minded and miserly. When the
Haywoods plan a gala ball and invite Susan, her parents refuse to let her go.
Surreptitiously, she begins making her gown anyway, albeit out of her apron. When
her brothers tattle on her, she is forcibly kept at home. To this point, Cary has
presented two equally unacceptable choices: the foppish false gentility of the Haywoods and the brutish ignorance of the pioneers.

The third alternative arrives that night: one Maurice Doherty shows up and begins to work for Mr. Tomkins. Maurice is French and, although at the moment having "exhausted his means," is obviously schooled in the rudiments of society. He has traveled and is literate (unlike many of the less sophisticated denizens of Clovernook), both genteel and peasant. After a period working in the sugar mills on the Tomkins's land, he is allowed to build a cabin in the woods and "insisted on its being well-done . . . a carpenter must be had to make the door and windows, to lay the floor and put in a closet or two, and a mason to build the chimney and lay down the hearth . . . Maurice urged the propriety of its being comfortable and durable, and finally carried the point" (Cary 1987: 47).

Of course, he and Susan end up happily married and living in this house. For Cary, this is meant to represent a third alternative: the victimized young woman is freed both from her parents' fate and from her anxiety about not measuring up to the conventional standards of the Haywoods. But this resolution is still well within the conventions of sentimental fiction and its rhetoric of middle-class domesticity: Maurice is domesticated as much as Susan is liberated. But Susan is not a beautiful girl and Maurice does not whisk her off to a glamorous life. Instead, what Cary impresses upon her readers is a more realistic and hopeful view of white settlement through the abandonment of the standard characterizations of frontier experience.

In her preface to *Clovernook*, Cary wrote:

> in the interior of my native state, which was wilderness when my father first went to it, and is now crowned with a dense population, there is surely as much in the simple manners and the little histories every day revealed, to interest us in humanity, as there *can* be in those old empires where the press of tyrannous laws and the deadening influence of heredity acquiescence necessarily destroys the best life of society. (1987: 7)

Cary's fiction reflects a similar impulse to resist the old empires of unrealistic and decidedly un-local fictionalizations of American life. Moreover, she states these ideas in terms quite similar to those of her kinsman, Gallagher. Clearly the decolonization of the American West and the shedding of the older narratives that had made it a colony was, to both writers, of a piece: each development was necessary to make Westerners view themselves as equal contributors to the national culture alongside Easterners. While the Realist movement is more often associated with the postbellum period, Cary's decoupling of description from its imperial implications make her, and the other Cincinnati writers, important forerunners to Realism's more explicit social activism.

Conclusion

In 1841 Gallagher published *The Poetical Literature of the West*, which brought together the work of thirty-eight poets from every state in the Ohio valley and southern Great Lakes basin. He planned it as the first in a series of volumes to collect Western fiction, belles-lettres, and other subjects. It did not sell well, and Gallagher was soon swept up in agitation against the Mexican–American War as secretary to Senator Thomas Corwin. Nineteen years later, Gallagher's acolyte, William T. Coggeshall tried again, with the 860-page *Poets and Poetry of the West*, a more comprehensive and professional volume and, again, the first of an intended series. Unlike Gallagher, Coggeshall excluded poets from slave-holding states. While many of the Cincinnati writers wished to remain at peace with their Kentucky neighbors, they recognized that slavery polarized the discussion of place, limiting the options to nationalism or sectionalism. Each meant the absorption of the region – and all its defining paradoxes and ambiguities – into a nonrepresentative monoculture. As opposed to Southerners, the Western writers conceived of a far more sophisticated and functional voice that might be called "regionalist." This concept required the nation not to act like an empire and the region not to act like either a subservient colony or a reactionary section; a concept that combines the inevitable entanglement in the nation with place-specific historical, demographic, and racial distinctiveness.

In *Poets* and in an accompanying lecture, "The Protective Policy in Literature" (1859), Coggeshall strove to preserve regional difference within the nation without going so far as the destructive rhetoric of secession. Here, Coggeshall singles out three of the first histories of "American Literature" – ones edited by Rufus Griswold, Charles Dana, and Charles and Evert Duyckinck, all published in the East – and disputes their claim to "national legitimacy" because of their ignorance of Western writers: "nor can they be given credit for due respect to Western authorship, while they exhibit active diligence in 'making a good show' for all the giants and many of the dwarfs of eastern authordom" (Watts and Rachels 2002: 938). For Coggeshall, the nation was a multiregional construct in which no single region or population could rightly claim nationally representative authenticity. By calling for a decentralized national literary culture, Coggeshall continues the work of Hall and Cary and points out a path for decolonizing regional writing throughout the country, an ideal of balance between the local and the metropolitan that would be more fully realized only after the Civil War.

References and Further Reading

Cary, Alice (1987). *Clovernook Sketches and Other Stories*, ed. Judith Fetterley, 37–48. New Brunswick, NJ: Rutgers University Press.

Derounian-Stodola, Kathryn Zabelle, and Levernier, James Arthur (1993). *The Indian Captivity Narrative, 1550–1900*. New York: Twayne.

Dippie, Brian W. (1982). *The Vanishing American: White Attitudes and US Indian Policy*. Middleton, Conn.: Wesleyan University Press.

Donald, David, and Palmer, Frederick A. (1956). "Toward a Western Literature, 1820–1860." In David Donald (ed.), *Lincoln Reconsidered: Essays on the Civil War Era*, 2nd edn., 167–86. New York: Vintage.

Drinnon, Richard (1980). *Facing West: The Metaphysics of Indian-Hating and Empire Building*. Minneapolis: University of Minnesota Press.

Faragher, John Mack (1986). *Sugar Creek: Life on the Illinois Frontier*. New Haven: Yale University Press.

Fetterley, Judith, and Pryse, Marjorie, eds. (1995). *American Women Regionalists, 1850–1910*. New York: Norton.

Gjerde, Jon (1997). *The Minds of the West: Ethnocultural Evolution in the Rural Middle West, 1830–1917*. Chapel Hill: University of North Carolina Press, 1997.

Glazer, Walter Stix (1999). *Cincinnati in 1840: The Social and Functional Organization of an Urban Community During the Pre-Civil War Period*. Columbus: Ohio State University Press.

Kolodny, Annette (1975). *The Lay of the Land: Metaphor as Experience and History in American Life and Letters*. Chapel Hill: University of North Carolina Press.

Kolodny, Annette (1984). *The Land before Her: Fantasy and Experience of the American Frontier, 1630–1860*. Chapel Hill: University of North Carolina Press.

New, W. H. (1996). "Colonial Literatures." In Bruce King (ed.), *New National and Post-Colonial Literatures*, 102–19. New York: Oxford University Press.

Power, Richard Lyle (1953). *Planting Corn Belt Culture: The Impress of the Upland Southerner and Yankee in the Old Northwest*. Indianapolis: Indiana Historical Society.

Randall, Randolph C. (1964). *James Hall: Spokesman for the West*. Columbus: Ohio State University Press.

Rusk, Ralph Leslie (1926). *The Literature of the Middle Western Frontier*, 2 vols. New York: Columbia University Press.

Seelye, John (1991). *Beautiful Machine: Rivers and the Republican Plan, 1755–1825*. New York: Oxford University Press.

Slotkin, Richard (1973). *Regeneration through Violence: The Mythology of the American Frontier, 1600–1860*. Norman: University of Oklahoma Press.

Smith, Henry Nash (1950). *Virgin Land: The American West as Symbol and Myth*. Cambridge, Mass.: Harvard University Press.

Thacker, Robert (1991). *The Great Prairie Fact and Literary Imagination*. Albuquerque: New Mexico University Press.

Van Herk, Aritha (1996). "Pioneers and Settlers." In Bruce King (ed.), *New National and Post-Colonial Literatures*, 81–101. New York: Oxford University Press.

Venable, W. H. (1891). *Beginnings of Literary Culture in the Ohio Valley: Historical and Biographical Sketches*. Cincinnati: Clarke.

Watts, Edward (2002). *An American Colony: Regionalism and the Roots of Midwestern Culture*. Athens: Ohio University Press.

Watts, Edward, and Rachels, David, eds. (2002). *The First West: Writing from the American Frontier, 1776–1860*. New York: Oxford University Press.

Weber, Ronald (1992). *The Midwestern Ascendancy in American Writing*. Bloomington: Indiana University Press.

White, Richard (1991). *The Middle Ground: Indians, Empires, and Republics in the Great Lakes Region, 1650–1815*. New York: Cambridge University Press.

34

The Old Southwest: Mike Fink, Augustus Baldwin Longstreet, Johnson Jones Hooper, and George Washington Harris

David Rachels

Mike Fink and the Old Southwest

Like Daniel Boone and Davy Crockett, Mike Fink was a historical figure who became a legend of the American frontier. From his birth *c.*1770 to his death in 1823, Fink moved westward with the frontier. He was born in Fort Pitt, Pennsylvania, around which Pittsburgh grew. As a teenager, he began working as a scout on Pennsylvania's western frontier, delivering messages, gathering information, and fighting Native Americans, all the while earning a reputation for daring and fearlessness. After Native Americans had been driven from the area, Fink, in search of further adventure, moved into the Old Southwest. While historians define this region fairly narrowly, to include, roughly, Mississippi, Alabama, and the western half of Georgia, literary scholars draw it more broadly, sometimes stretching it all the way from Virginia to Texas. Mike Fink's tenure in the Old Southwest was spent on the Ohio and Mississippi rivers as a keelboatman. When keelboats, which the boatmen moved with long poles, began to disappear as the steamboats moved in, Fink moved west again, this time to the Missouri river and the Rocky Mountains, where he lived his final years as a trapper.

The first published Mike Fink story, Morgan Neville's "The Last of the Boatmen" (1828), appeared five years after Fink's death. Neville, a Pittsburgh native who knew Fink personally, gives this description of him:

> His stature was upwards of six feet, his proportions perfectly symmetrical, and exhibiting the evidence of Herculean powers. To a stranger, he would have seemed a complete mulatto. Long exposure to the sun and weather on the lower Ohio and Mississippi had

changed his skin; and, but for the fine European cast of his countenance, he might have passed for the principal warrior of some powerful tribe. Although at least fifty years of age, his hair was as black as the wing of the raven. (Blair and Meine 1956: 47–8)

Though descriptions of Fink vary – one writer says he was five feet nine and another gives him red hair! – comparisons to Hercules are common. Fink was nothing if not powerful.

"The Last of the Boatmen" includes the only extant tale of Fink's Pennsylvania years, which Neville claims to have heard from Fink himself. According to the story, Fink was working as a scout when he discovered signs of Indian activity: a moccasin footprint and drops of deer blood. He then lay low for several days, not even hunting lest his rifle attract the attention of the Indians. One morning, however, he spied a large buck and decided to risk a shot. Just as he was about to fire, however, Fink spotted an Indian aiming at the same target. Fink turned his rifle toward the Indian and fired at him at the same moment the Indian fired at the buck; both Indian and animal fell dead. Thus Fink was able to escape undetected with the buck (see Blair and Meine 1956: 53–4).

After "The Last of the Boatmen" appeared, other Mike Fink stories followed in a steady stream through the middle decades of the nineteenth century. Walter Blair and Franklin J. Meine, in their anthology *Half Horse, Half Alligator: The Growth of the Mike Fink Legend* (1956), tabulate the frequency with which Fink stories were published:

1828–40	10
1841–50	24
1851–60	23
1861–70	1
1871–80	4
1881–90	7
1891–1900	3

(Blair and Meine 1956: 19)

Many of the early Fink stories circulated orally before finding their way into print. For example, Joseph M. Field, author of the lengthy "Mike Fink: 'The Last of the Boatmen'" (1847), based his work on stories he had heard in Cincinnati (where his informant was Morgan Neville), Louisville, New Orleans, Natchez, and St. Louis. Though Field wished to make his narrative as accurate as possible, he recognized that his material left him stranded somewhere "between truth and fable" (in Blair and Meine 1956: 94–5). Field was among the last of Fink's biographers for whom truth was an issue. Fable was beginning to dominate.

Most Mike Fink stories – both the truthful and the fabulous – deal with his years in the Old Southwest as a keelboatman, though few are much concerned with his prowess as a river man. Rather, these tales immortalize Fink's mastery of skills more highly valued on the frontier: shooting, fighting, drinking, and bragging. In Emerson Bennett's "Mike Fink: A Legend of the Ohio" (1848), Fink assures his listeners that he can "lick five-times [his] own weight in wild-cats," "use up Injens by the cord," and "swallow niggers whole, raw or cooked." He can "out-run, out-dance, out-jump, out-dive, out-drink, out-holler, and out-lick, any white things in the shape o' human that's ever put foot within two thousand miles o' the big Massassip" (in Blair and Meine 1956: 170).

Fink's most famous demonstration of skill, apparently performed on multiple occasions, was to shoot a tin cup off the head of a volunteer. Unfortunately, this eventually resulted in two corpses: one of Fink's volunteers and Fink himself. The first written account of the incident appeared in the *Missouri Republican* on 16 July 1823:

> By a letter received in town from one of Gen. Ashley's expedition we are informed that a man by the name of Mike Fink well known in this quarter as a great marksman with the rifle . . . was engaged in his favorite amusement of shooting a tin cup from off the head of another man, when aiming too low or from some other cause shot his companion in the forehead and killed him. Another man of the expedition (whose name we have not heard) remonstrated against Fink's conduct, to which he, Fink, replied, that he would kill him likewise, upon which the other drew a pistol and shot Fink dead upon the spot. (Quoted in Blair and Meine 1956: 14)

Fink's biographers have offered various explanations for his errant shot. Neville heard that Fink was drunk at the time. According to the anonymous "Mike Fink: The Last of the Boatmen" (1829), the shot was intentional – an act of murder. A *Crockett Almanack* story, "Mike Fink: The Ohio Boatman" (1837), reported that Fink fired too quickly. William T. Porter, in his sporting newspaper *The Spirit of the Times* (1842), denied that Fink had killed his volunteer. In Porter's version of the story, Fink's volunteer moved as the shot was fired, which caused the bullet to graze the top of his head. This was enough to knock down and stun the man, leading bystanders – including the volunteer's brother – to think him dead. Before the brother discovered his mistake, he shot and killed Fink.

Whatever the explanation for Fink's errant shot, one thing is clear: His earliest biographers would not consider that he might simply have missed. For the legendary Mike Fink, that was impossible.

Augustus Baldwin Longstreet and *Georgia Scenes*

Augustus Baldwin Longstreet's *Georgia Scenes, Characters, Incidents, &c. in the First Half Century of the Republic* (1835) was the first major work of Old Southwest humor, the literary tradition that gave rise to Mark Twain and influenced such writers as William Faulkner and Flannery O'Connor. As well, Longstreet was a founder of American literary realism.

Longstreet was born on September 22, 1790, in Augusta, Georgia, to parents who had moved from New Jersey to the frontier in search of a better life. When Longstreet was nine or ten years old, his family moved to Edgefield District, South Carolina, a rough-and-tumble community known as "Bloody Edgefield" because of its high murder rate. During his two or three years in Edgefield, Longstreet thrilled to a freedom unknown to him in Augusta, and he made it his goal to "out-run, out-jump, out-shoot, throw down and whip, any man in the district" (quoted in Rachels 2001: 117). In other words, he wanted to be Mike Fink.

Longstreet claims that he was well on his way to fulfilling his goal when he received "the heart-sinking order" that his family was returning to Augusta (quoted in Rachels 2001: 117). Longstreet's mother, Hannah Randolph, had other ambitions for her son. Most importantly, she wanted Gus, as he was known, to have "a good education" (quoted in Rachels 2001: 116). In this she certainly succeeded. In 1811 Longstreet graduated from Moses Waddel's academy in Willington, South Carolina. In 1813 he graduated from Yale. And in 1815, after attending Litchfield Law School in Litchfield, Connecticut, he passed the Georgia bar exam.

Longstreet's career as a storyteller began at Yale, where he regaled his classmates and professors with stories of life on the Georgia frontier. Longstreet further honed his storytelling skills as a circuit-riding lawyer, trading tales with his colleagues as they traveled from town to town and roomed together in makeshift hotels. Life as a circuit-rider also exposed Longstreet to all classes of Georgians, thus providing him with additional material for his storytelling. (Only one of Longstreet's published stories – "The Debating Society," in which he appears as "Longworth" – is strictly autobiographical.)

Longstreet's first published story, "The Dance," appeared in the *Milledgeville Southern Recorder* on October 30, 1833, which continued to publish its successors until Longstreet founded his own newspaper, the *Augusta States' Rights Sentinel*, its first issue appearing on January 9, 1834. Longstreet's last story to appear in the *Sentinel*, "A Sage Conversation," was published on March 17, 1835. These stories would probably have been forgotten had Longstreet not collected them in a book. *Georgia Scenes* was published from the *Sentinel* office in September 1835 in an edition of 3,950 copies. In March 1836 Edgar Allan Poe published an enthusiastic review of it in the *Southern Literary Messenger*. In 1840 a second edition was published in New York by Harper & Brothers, who kept the book in print for the rest of the century.

Whereas the Mike Fink stories preserve the legendary life of a single man, *Georgia Scenes* preserves the more prosaic fabric of life as it was lived in the Old Southwest by ordinary people. Longstreet hoped, in his words, "to supply a chasm in history which has always been overlooked – the manners, customs, amusements, wit, dialect, as they appear in all grades of society to an ear and eye witness of them" (quoted in Rachels 2001: 113). Longstreet did more, however, than simply record life as he saw it around him. In order to increase the popularity of his work – and thereby increase the chances of its long-term survival – in some of his stories he took the liberty of "[combining] *real* incidents and characters; and throwing into those scenes, which would be otherwise dull and insipid, some personal incident or adventure of my own, real or imaginary, as it would best suit my purpose – usually *real*, but happening at different times and under different circumstances from those in which they are here represented" (Longstreet 1998: 3). In addition to these liberties, Longstreet introduced two fictitious narrators, Hall and Baldwin, in an effort to mask his identity, as fiction-writing was not the most reputable pastime for a newspaper editor with political ambitions. Every edition of *Georgia Scenes* published during Longstreet's lifetime was credited to "A Native Georgian."

Hall is the dominant voice of *Georgia Scenes*, narrating twelve sketches to Baldwin's six. (One other sketch, "The Militia Company Drill," was written by Longstreet's friend Oliver Hillhouse Prince and narrated by "Timothy Crabshaw.") Longstreet, by his own account, had Hall narrate those sketches dealing primarily with male characters and Baldwin narrate those dealing primarily with female characters. It might be more accurate, however, to say that Hall narrates sketches that Longstreet felt treated masculine subjects while Baldwin dealt with feminine subjects. This explains, for example, why Baldwin narrates "The Dance," even though as many men as women populate the sketch and the central character in the narrative is a man – Baldwin himself. The most anthologized Georgia Scenes – "The Horse Swap" and "The Fight" – are both narrated by Hall, whose more stereotypically masculine world better reflects conventional images of life on the frontier.

Like Longstreet, Hall and Baldwin are men of humble origins who have ascended to the upper classes. Over the course of *Georgia Scenes*, they both attempt to negotiate a comfortable position in the social hierarchy of the Old Southwest. The trajectories of these attempts are commonly taken as unifying elements of the book. Baldwin fails, ending the book socially adrift and alienated. Hall succeeds, ending the book at home among all people. But while Longstreet did arrange *Georgia Scenes'* sketches for artistic effect, he did not arrange them in chronological order. Critics who trace the "development" of Hall and Baldwin over the course of the book disregard this fact.

Of the other characters in *Georgia Scenes*, the most famous are Rancy Sniffle and Ned Brace. Five feet tall and 95 pounds, living on a diet of clay and blackberries, pale of complexion, long of limb, round of abdomen, Rancy Sniffle is the prototypical literary representation of white trash. He foments the main event in "The Fight," in which rough-and-tumble combat determines the "best man" in a frontier community. Ned Brace, an inveterate practical joker, appears in two sketches: "The Character of a Native Georgian" and "A Sage Conversation." While Ned Brace was the most popular character in *Georgia Scenes* among nineteenth-century readers, today his jokes show how much taste in humor has changed. On one occasion, Brace interrupts a funeral procession with a racist joke. On another, his insistence on drinking from water buckets disrupts efforts to extinguish a fire.

Longstreet had a varied working life after 1835, including a year as a Methodist minister and a more substantial career as the president of four colleges: Emory College (now Emory University), Centenary College of Louisiana, the University of Mississippi, and South Carolina College (now the University of South Carolina). He wrote several additional "Georgia Scenes" but never carried out his plan of publishing an expanded edition of his famous book. His only novel, the didactic *Master William Mitten: or, A Youth of Brilliant Talents Who Was Ruined by Bad Luck* (1859), is not highly regarded. Longstreet died on July 9, 1870, in Oxford, Mississippi.

Johnson Jones Hooper and Simon Suggs

In 1844 Johnson Jones Hooper created Captain Simon Suggs of the Tallapoosa Volunteers, perhaps the most famous character in the genre of Old Southwest humor. Suggs, the original American confidence man, lives by his famous aphorism, "It is good to be shifty in a new country." This means, Hooper explains, "that it is right and proper that one should live as merrily and as comfortably as possible at the expense of others" (Hooper 1993: 12). And Suggs does this very well.

The life of Johnson Jones Hooper was similar in many ways to that of Augustus Baldwin Longstreet, who was twenty-five years his senior. Hooper was born on June 9, 1815, in Wilmington, North Carolina, to a family with dwindling financial resources. Whereas Longstreet's parents managed to fund his time at Yale, however, there may have been no money left for Hooper's parents to send him to college, his older brothers having already attended the United States Military Academy and the University of North Carolina. Hooper's education would be limited to attending the Wilmington public school and working as an apprentice in the office of his father's newspaper, the *Cape Fear Recorder*.

It may have been more than money, however, that kept Hooper out of college. Like Longstreet, Hooper was, for a time, incorrigible, but while Longstreet's mother gained control of her son while he was still a boy, Hooper's delinquent phase lasted much longer. In a letter to Johnson's brother D.B. their mother, Charlotte deBerniere, lamented Johnson's "wild" behavior and admitted his "many and inexcusable" faults, including his tastes for disreputable company and Wilmington's night life. She denied, however, that he was the "unprincipled reprobate which some of his friends think" (quoted in Shields 1993: xvii).

In 1834, when Johnson, aged eighteen, announced his intention of joining his other brother, George, a lawyer on the Alabama frontier, his parents hoped that the change in environment would do him good. In the best-case scenario, Johnson would study law with George and gain admittance to the Alabama bar. Writing to D.B., George considered Johnson's prospects and described Johnson in terms that might be applied to Simon Suggs: "if he can be made steady he is just the fellow to advance in the practice of law in this part of the country where a fluent tongue & abundant assurance invariably succeed with any modicum of talent" (quoted in Shields 1993: xx).

In the short term, Hooper's parents were to be disappointed. He spent several years wandering the frontier, holding an occasional job, amassing debts, and perhaps engaging in some "shiftiness" of his own. In early 1840 Johnson accepted a job as assistant census marshal for Tallapoosa County, Alabama. By October he had gathered data on 6,444 residents. More importantly, though, his experiences as census taker would provide the material for "Taking the Census," the story that was to give him his first national recognition as a writer.

After his census experience Hooper finally did dabble in the law, entering into partnership first with a friend, Charles Stone, and then with his brother George. But in December 1842 Hooper, like Longstreet before him, set aside his legal career to become editor of a newspaper. When he accepted the helm of the Whig *East Alabamian*, the first newspaper published in Chambers County, Alabama, Hooper faced the weekly grind of finding enough material to fill its columns. In addition to gathering material from "exchanges" with other newspapers, Hooper wrote the expected political editorials, but he also began to show a flair for humorous writing as well. "Taking the Census" appeared in the *East Alabamian* in August 1843, and William T. Porter reprinted it in the national *Spirit of the Times* in September. Instantly, Hooper was a star.

Hooper would not seal his literary fame, however, until he created Simon Suggs. Eventually, the identities of author and character would become so intertwined that relatives, friends, acquaintances, and strangers would sometimes call Hooper by the name of Suggs. The first Suggs story appeared in the *East Alabamian* in December 1844. *Some Adventures of Simon Suggs, Late of the Tallapoosa Volunteers; Together with "Taking the Census," and Other Alabama Sketches* appeared in 1845.

When Hooper gathered material for *Some Adventures of Simon Suggs*, he faced an easier task in creating a coherent whole than did Longstreet with *Georgia Scenes*, as his stories focused on a single protagonist. (He appended "Taking the Census" and "Daddy Biggs' Scrape at Cockrell's Bend" to fatten the book.) *Some Adventures of Simon Suggs* is a burlesque campaign biography that traces the major events of Suggs's life in chronological order. We meet Suggs at the age of seventeen, just before he leaves his home on the Georgia frontier. An inveterate sinner, Simon is more than a disappointment to his father, who is a Baptist preacher. They part soon after Simon's father catches him playing cards and reminds him that card players always lose their money. "Who win's [*sic*] it all then, daddy?" Simon asks (Hooper 1993: 21). Before Simon leaves home, he swindles his father out of a pony.

Just as Suggs swindles his father, so he swindles everyone else he meets. Among other feats, he manages to speculate in land without having any capital, and, when his neighbors mistakenly believe that Indians are attacking, he convinces them to name him captain of the "Tallapoosy Vollantares" (Hooper 1993: 89). Throughout it all, Hooper does not condemn Suggs's behavior. Indeed, he praises the "genius" of a man who can buy and sell land without having any money (p. 35)! But he allows the irony of Suggs's behavior – he is, after all, a political candidate – to speak clearly. Hooper concludes by soliciting votes for Suggs:

> We have endeavoured to give the prominent events of his life with accuracy and impartiality. If you deem that he has "done the state some service," remember that he

seeks the Sheriffalty of your county. He waxes old. He needs an office, the emoluments of which shall be sufficient to enable him to relax his intellectual exertions. His military services; his numerous family; his long residence among you; his gray hairs – all plead for him! Remember him at the polls! (Hooper 1993: 148)

After *Some Adventures of Simon Suggs*, Hooper published one other collection of stories, *A Ride with Old Kit Kuncker, and Other Sketches, and Scenes of Alabama* (1849), which was republished in an expanded version as *The Widow Rugby's Husband, A Night at the Ugly Man's and Other Tales of Alabama* (1851). He also published a hunting book, *Dog and Gun: A Few Loose Chapters on Shooting* (1856). Hooper died in 1862, at the age of forty-seven, while working to publish the congressional proceedings and the constitution of the Confederate States of America.

George Washington Harris and Sut Lovingood

George Washington Harris's *Sut Lovingood: Yarns Spun by a "Nat'ral Born Durn'd Fool," Warped and Wove for Public Wear* (1867), the last major work of Old Southwest humor, stands as the genre's finest example. When *The Paris Review* asked William Faulkner to name his favorite literary characters, his list included Falstaff, Don Quixote, Huckleberry Finn, and Sut Lovingood. F. O. Matthiessen, in his seminal *American Renaissance: Art and Expression in the Age of Emerson and Whitman* (1941), wrote, "Harris possesses on the comic level something of what Melville does on the tragic, the rare kind of dramatic imagination that can get movement directly into words" (quoted in Caron and Inge 1996: 96).

Like Mike Fink, George Washington Harris was born in an area that would later become part of Pittsburgh. Harris, however, was born on March, 30, 1814 – roughly forty-four years after Fink – by which time the frontier had receded a fair distance from Pennsylvania. In 1819 Harris's newly married half-brother, Samuel Bell, moved to Knoxville, Tennessee, taking young George with him. Rather than attend school, George was apprenticed to Bell, who was a metalworker. Milton Rickels has speculated that George's training as a metalworker may have contributed to the meticulous craftsmanship that he would later show as a writer (1965: 20).

At nineteen, Harris became captain of the steamboat *Knoxville*. Rickels wonders whether the life of a boatman might have exposed Harris to the underbelly of the American frontier:

Whether he kept aloof from the temptations of the straggling river towns or whether he roistered in places like Waterloo, Alabama, described in a contemporary account as a "hamlet of doggeries & of brothels, got up to entertain the low and sensual tastes of the boatmen who navigate the rivers," is unrecorded. Probably a sense of social separation from the "lower orders," reinforced by strict Presbyterian upbringing, had already produced a reserved, sedate, rather formal character. (Rickels 1965: 21)

But the opposite seems equally likely. As we have seen, both Longstreet and Hooper had rebellious periods despite coming from good families, and their depictions of the frontier were genteel compared to the earthy anarchy that Harris would unleash in his Sut Lovingood stories. When Mark Twain reviewed *Sut Lovingood: Yarns*, he speculated that "the Eastern people will call it coarse and possibly taboo it" (in Caron and Inge 1996: 79). Edmund Wilson named *Sut Lovingood* "the most repellant book of any real literary merit in American literature" (in Caron and Inge 1996: 100). Surely this streak in Harris's character did not appear spontaneously in 1854, when, at the age of forty, he wrote the first Sut Lovingood yarn.

Around 1840 Harris began writing on politics for the *Knoxville Argus and Commercial Herald*. In 1843 he published four "sporting epistles" on the subjects of hunting, horse racing, log rolling, corn shucking, and the like in *The Spirit of the Times*. In the years following, Harris published in the *Spirit* only sporadically. In the issue of December 23, 1848, editor William T. Porter noted that "the communication of 'S——l' ['Sugartail,' a Harris pseudonym] has been long under consideration. It is too highly seasoned to be published as it is, but we will try to 'fix it'" (quoted in Caron and Inge 1996: 49). This is a remarkable comment coming from Porter, who was not a squeamish reader. The first Sut Lovingood story, "Sut Lovingood's Daddy, Acting Horse," appeared in the *Spirit* on November 4, 1854, but Harris sent nothing further to Porter after that. He realized, perhaps, that Sut's career would be "too highly seasoned" for Porter's taste.

No description can convey the experience of reading *Sut Lovingood Yarns*. Harris' use of dialect is perhaps his greatest artistic achievement, but this dialect is also an obstacle to an easy appreciation of the stories. Readers must learn to read the language well – at first, reading aloud may help – because mayhem is not best appreciated in slow motion. The sense of action in Harris' writing is created in part by his rapid-fire use of metaphors, as in this passage from "Sut Lovingood's Daddy, Acting Horse," in which Sut's father, who is pretending to be a horse, runs into a hornet's nest:

> 'Bout the time he wer beginin to break sweat, we cum to a sassafrack bush, an tu keep up his kar-acter es a hoss, he buljed squar intu an' thru hit, tarin down a ball ho'nets nes' ni ontu es big es a hoss's head, an' the hole tribe kiver'd 'im es quick es yu cud kiver a sick pup wif a saddil blanket. He lit ontu his hans agin, an kick'd strait up onst, then he rar'd, an' fotch a squeal wus nur ara stud hoss in the State, an' sot in tu strait runnin away jis as natral es yu ever seed any uther skeer'd hoss du. I let go the line an' holler'd, Wo! dad, wo! but yu mout jis' es well say Woa! tu a locomotum, ur Suke cow tu a gal. (Harris 1987: 24)

Sut Lovingood is Longstreet's Rancy Sniffle taken beyond the realm of realism. Paradoxically, his narratives celebrate the awfulness of life. Though his yarns teem with misery and vulgarity – the most famous example may be "Hen Bailey's Reformation," in which a mole travels the length of Hen's digestive tract, beginning at the end – Sut always survives, an enthusiastic narrator till the end. Often Sut foments the chaos himself. Roughly half his narratives describe practical jokes in which he delights in humiliating preachers, lawmen, and other symbols of power and propriety. Faulkner said he admired Sut because he "had no illusions about himself, did the best he could; at certain times he was a coward and knew it and wasn't ashamed; he never blamed his misfortunes on anyone and never cursed God for them" (quoted in Rickels 1965: 95).

Harris completed the manuscript of a second collection of stories, *High Times and Hard Times*, but the manuscript was lost at the time of his death. In late 1869 Harris traveled to Lynchburg, Virginia, where he sought a publisher for the manuscript. On his return trip to Chattanooga, he became unconscious on the train. While unconscious, he was transferred to another train in Bristol, Tennessee. Later, he was able to tell the conductor that he wanted to be removed from the train in Knoxville; he died there that night, December 10, 1869. His mysterious final word was "poisoned."

REFERENCES AND FURTHER READING

Baldwin, Joseph Glover (1987). *The Flush Times of Alabama and Mississippi*. Baton Rouge: Louisiana State University Press. (First publ. 1853.)

Blair, Walter, ed. (1937). *Native American Humor (1800–1900)*. New York: American Book Co.

Blair, Walter, and Meine, Franklin J., eds. (1933). *Mike Fink: King of the Mississippi Keelboatmen*. New York: Henry Holt.

Blair, Walter, and Meine, Franklin J., eds. (1956). *Half Horse, Half Alligator: The Growth of the Mike Fink Legend*. Chicago: University of Chicago Press.

Caron, James E., and Inge, M. Thomas, eds. (1996). *Sut Lovingood's Nat'ral Born Yarnspinner: Essays on George Washington Harris*. Tuscaloosa: University of Alabama Press.

Cash, W. J. (1941). *The Mind of the South*. New York: Knopf.

Clark, Thomas D., and Guice, John D. W. (1996). *The Old Southwest, 1795–1830: Frontiers in Conflict*. Norman: University of Oklahoma Press. (First publ. 1989 as *Frontiers in Conflict: The Old Southwest, 1795–1830*.)

Cohen, Hennig, and Dillingham, William B., eds. (1994). *Humor of the Old Southwest*, 3rd edn. Athens: University of Georgia Press.

Griffith, Nancy Snell (1989). *Humor of the Old Southwest: An Annotated Bibliography of Primary and Secondary Sources*. New York: Greenwood.

Harris, George Washington (1967). *High Times and Hard Times: Sketches and Tales by George Washington Harris*, ed. M. Thomas Inge. Kingsport, Tenn.: Vanderbilt University Press.

Harris, George Washington (1987). *Sut Lovingood Yarns*, ed. M. Thomas Inge. Memphis: St. Luke's. (First publ. 1867 as *Sut Lovingood: Yarns Spun by a "Nat'ral Born Durn'd Fool," Warped and Wove for Public Wear*.)

Hoole, William Stanley (1952). *Alias Simon Suggs: The Life and Times of Johnson Jones Hooper*. University, Ala.: University of Alabama Press.

Hooper, Johnson Jones (1993). *Adventures of Captain Simon Suggs*. Nashville: J. S. Sanders & Co. (First publ. 1845 as *Some Adventures of Captain Simon Suggs, Late of the Tallapoosa Volunteers; Together with "Taking the Census," and Other Alabama Sketches*.)

Inge, M. Thomas, ed. (1975). *The Frontier Humorists*. Hamden, Conn.: Archon.

Inge, M. Thomas, and Piacentino, Edward J., eds. (2001). *The Humor of the Old South*. Lexington: University Press of Kentucky.

Jones, Hamilton C. (1990). *Ham Jones, Ante-Bellum Southern Humorist: An Anthology*, ed. Willene Hendrick and George Hendrick. Hamden, Conn.: Archon.

Longstreet, Augustus Baldwin (1998). *Augustus Baldwin Longstreet's Georgia Scenes Completed*, ed. David Rachels. Athens: University of Georgia

David Rachels

Press. (*Georgia Scenes, Characters, Incidents, &c. in the First Half Century of the Republic.* (First publ. 1835.)

Meine, Franklin J., ed. (1930). *Tall Tales of the Southwest*. New York: Knopf.

Rachels, David (2001). "A Biographical Reading of A. B. Longstreet's *Georgia Scenes*." In M. Thomas Inge and Edward J. Piacentino (eds.), *The Humor of the Old South*, 113–29. Lexington: University Press of Kentucky.

Rickels, Milton (1965). *George Washington Harris*. New York: Twayne.

Rourke, Constance (1931). *American Humor: A Study of the National Character*. New York: Harcourt, Brace.

Shields, Johanna Nicol (1993). "Introduction." In Johnson Jones Hooper, *Adventures of Captain Simon Suggs*. Tuscaloosa: University of Alabama Press.

Thorpe, Thomas Bangs (1989). *A New Collection of Thomas Bangs Thorpe's Sketches of the Old Southwest*, ed. David C. Estes. Baton Rouge: Louisiana State University Press.

Wade, John Donald (1969). *Augustus Baldwin Longstreet: A Study of the Development of Culture in the South*, ed. M. Thomas Inge. Athens: University of Georgia Press. (First publ. 1924.)

Yates, Norris T. (1957). *William T. Porter and the BIG BEAR School of Humor*. Baton Rouge: Louisiana State University Press.

35

James Fenimore Cooper and the Invention of the American Novel

Wayne Franklin

Early in November 1827, a 77-year-old Revolutionary War veteran left his Hudson valley farm for a visit to New York City, where he was to testify in a lawsuit about conflicting claims to a tract of land near his home. Having passed most of his life in settled obscurity, Enoch Crosby had no reason to expect anything more from the trip than the break from routine that his time on the stand would afford. No sooner had Crosby entered the courtroom, however, than one of the witnesses, the well-known jurist, historian, and Revolutionary War spymaster Egbert Benson pointed him out to the assembled crowd. Benson, who had managed Crosby's covert activities for a time in the 1770s, knew this man well. He also knew that Crosby's espionage career had formed the basis of a celebrated novel published a few years earlier. Having secured the attention of the courtroom audience, Benson therefore introduced Crosby as "the original Harvey Birch of Mr. Cooper's *Spy*." Immediately the lawyers, other witnesses, newspapermen, court reporters, and spectators on hand before the start of the trial knew that Enoch Crosby was a figure to be reckoned with. They knew that not because they recognized Crosby or had even heard of him before. They knew it instead because, like so many other American readers in 1827, they were familiar with the common hero of Cooper's novel and his uncomplaining sacrifices for the cause of American freedom from Britain. Crosby must have been thunderstruck when the crowd proceeded to greet him with warm regard. Suddenly he was a celebrity.

Crosby's confusion may have derived from the fact that he was himself only vaguely familiar with James Fenimore Cooper's *The Spy: A Tale of the Neutral Ground* (1821). He knew of the book; indeed, he had been given his own copy of it early in 1827 by a writer who had sniffed out the spy's identity and showed up at his home in Putnam County. But he had not yet read it, and hence had no way of knowing how – or even that – he had been portrayed in it. Small wonder. Cooper's source of information had not been Crosby himself, after all, but the father of William Jay, the novelist's schoolmate in Albany and then New Haven years before. Statesman John Jay, a lifelong friend of Egbert Benson, had also overseen espionage efforts in the Hudson valley early in the Revolution. He it was, in fact, who had recruited Crosby when the militiaman on his own initiative happened to bring useful intelligence about Tory recruitment efforts to Jay and his colleagues at White Plains in 1776. Benson had later taken over management of Jay's "Commission for Detecting Conspiracies" and become the handler of Crosby and a few other agents. Since Benson and Jay both were close associates of the Cooper family, it is quite possible that Benson knew of Crosby's connection to Cooper's novel because Jay had explained it to him. But Benson, long the president of the New-York Historical Society, may have known enough to figure it out by himself. In 1827, in any case, he had no doubt about the question.

One of the individuals in attendance at the trial early in December was a reporter for the New York *American* by the name of Edward V. Sparhawk, who would later publish a pamphlet summarizing the proceedings. He also must have fed to his paper's editor, Charles King, details about the flurry of attention accorded to Crosby once his presence and identity were pointed out. King, a friend of Cooper's and an active member of the "Bread and Cheese" lunch prior to the novelist's departure for France a year-and-a-half before, in turn ran a brief item on Wednesday, November 15, noting that "the original Harvey Birch," still in town a week after the trial began, was planning to go to the Lafayette Theater that evening. The visit was no mere outing of a country resident stuck longer than expected in the city. Literate but no "natural" reader, Crosby knew that the fare for that evening, Charles P. Clinch's 1822 drama-tization of *The Spy*, would allow him to see why he had been so noisily received in the courtroom some days before. As it happened, though, his trip to the Lafayette would extend his notoriety rather than just explain it. The theater's proprietor, Charles W. Sandford, saw the notice of Crosby's impending visit in the paper and, when the veteran arrived, talked him into returning for another, better publicized performance hastily arranged for two nights later. Here, to Sandford's mind, was a chance to use Crosby's sudden celebrity as a means of boosting ticket sales. In a notice published on Friday morning in the *American*, he therefore promised the public that "This evening, Mr. CROSBY, whose extraordinary adventures form the subject of the novel and drama of THE SPY, will occupy the centre Box in the 1st Tier, when will be presented the national drama of THE SPY."

On both visits to the theater, Crosby must have been absorbed in contemplating what had been made of his experience over the course of its various transformations. His risky adventures, after all, had become a gentleman's anecdote, then a wildly successful novel, then a well-received dramatic representation, and now, with him there at the center of the large crowd that Sandford's come-on had produced on the seventeenth, a raucous public spectacle. Even as the audience cheered on the actors and showed its appreciation of the play, it kept turning to "the old soldier" to give him "several rounds of applause." All the attention probably pleased Crosby, but what riveted his eye was what was taking place on the stage. It struck him, he later said with characteristic understatement, "that some of the incidents resembled transactions in which he himself had been an actor in 'olden time,' on 'the Neutral Ground.'" There before him was his own life reborn as art. So moved was he by this experience that, early the next year, Crosby agreed to tell his personal story to that writer who had given him a copy of *The Spy* some months before. In due time H. L. Barnum would publish *The Spy Unmasked* (1828), sharing the details of Crosby's experience behind enemy lines with the American and soon English reading publics.

This anecdote is suggestive, I think, of the means by which the American novel, after several decades of struggling, straggling life, was transformed in the 1820s into a vital and important literary form. Fenimore Cooper's own career not only is indicative of the change: at the time it was in many ways responsible for it. In 1820 James Cooper (who did not add "Fenimore" to his name until six years later) self-published a novel that, by its perfect post-colonial mimicry of metropolitan modes, looked back over and summarized much that had been true of American fiction over earlier decades. *Precaution*, a marriage novel set in the English countryside, concealed its author's name and thereby cast doubt on his nationality and even gender. It chronicled the trials of a middle-class British family that had long been threatened with a fall from gentility by the mismanagement of its wealth, but that now at long last was regaining its old luster. Cooper, who had visited London twice during his brief career before the mast in 1806–7, knew English society very superficially at this time. In creating this book he relied on his wide reading, especially of fiction, and pulled off the imitation convincingly enough for *Precaution* to be viewed as an English work in some American circles, while in England itself it had a larger readership and longer life than in the United States. Even before Cooper had finished work on the hastily written manuscript, however, he became very much disappointed with it. His feelings sprang largely from the fact that he already had begun a second novel, one set in New York and deeply engaged with things about which Cooper and his American readers knew a great deal more than either did about the life of the English gentry. Although he would have greater difficulty finishing *The Spy* than *Precaution*, he recognized from the outset that its purchase on American life and therefore its claim on an American audience were substantially better. This was the sort of book he wanted to write. It also was the sort that Americans wanted to read.

The origins of Cooper's second novel were complex. The most obvious of them had to do with the book's unexampled subject. None of the hundred or so novels published before 1820 by Americans had taken up in any serious way the country's decisive post-colonial event – the political and military liberation from Britain. As Henri Petter declared thirty years ago, it therefore was left to Cooper to codify "the spirit of the War of Independence" in fiction (Petter 1971). Petter's point is proven by a brief review of Cooper's most important predecessors. Charles Brockden Brown, who wrote more novels in the early national period than any other figure except English immigrant Susannah Haswell Rowson, had been born early enough to experience the Revolution at first hand. Although Brown implicated the war in his works, he never addressed it frontally. Part of his avoidance probably derived from the very novelty and nearness of the topic. Dramatist William Dunlap, Brown's (and later Cooper's) friend, began a tragedy on the theme of Major André in the early 1790s, but its completion was delayed until 1798 by concerns that the familiarity of the subject put him at a double disadvantage. On the one hand, he feared that the audience would scorn his attempt to turn so recent an event into a work of fully tragic proportions; yet he also worried that the fresh memories most Americans had of the underlying historical events would make them hypercritical. Each member of the audience would expect such a play to contain all he or she recalled – and would condemn Dunlap for the least deviation. In either instance, history would trump imagination.

In Brockden Brown's case such considerations probably had similar force. Yet it is also important to recognize how constrained individual authors were in the early decades by the very personal legacy of the Revolution. The war had been productive of considerable suffering on all sides. Until it had been given some public literary shape by Cooper, it would remain a disorderly congeries of personal memories, often bitter and conflicted. For Brockden Brown the experience of his own father, one of eighteen prominent Quakers arrested by Pennsylvania's ruling radicals and sent into exile in Virginia in 1777, surely complicated his feelings. As a consequence, the subject lay beyond genuine exploration for him – certainly beyond the sort of naïve celebration that Dunlap, for one, sought to produce in *André*.

Susannah Rowson showed a similar avoidance for arguably similar reasons. Having come to the colonies as a girl of about six in 1768, she lived through the first years of the war before returning to England. That experience surely provided her with the same kinds of personal memories that Brown, though slightly younger, also possessed. Even though Rowson quickly showed herself an avid supporter of the new republic once she came back to America as an adult in the 1790s, like Brown she shunned the Revolution as a literary subject. Parental shadows intervened in her case as well. That her widowed father, a Royal Navy officer, had been assigned to the revenue service in Boston in the years leading up to the war helps explain her silence. So does the fact that because of Lieutenant Rowson's position the family was stripped of its property by the Whigs and interned among Massachusetts loyalists after the start of hostilities. In her fiction, allegory of the sort that may have made *Charlotte: A Tale of Truth* far more popular in America than in England was a happy – though inadvertent – solution. The result was that in her novel, as in all the others of the early decades, the war was only hinted at suggestively. Young Charlotte's seduction and abandonment by the British officer Montraville sufficed to vindicate the extra-narrative war for American readers and indicate its moral causes without a descent into political actualities over which the author and her newfound republican audience conceivably might have differed, even bickered. Not even Rowson's long residence in the United States over the decades following, though, could push her to explore the difficult subject. In *Charlotte's Daughter* (1828), published four years after Rowson's death, her retreat from the Revolution was even more pronounced. The story of the same troubled Anglo-American family was picked up again in England long after the messy transatlantic altercation had been settled, leaving the author's adopted homeland virtually offstage. In Brown's case, the Revolution fell, as it were, between the murderous episodes of the isolated Wieland family's saga in the 1760s and the wanderings of young Arthur Mervyn in disease-ridden Philadelphia in the 1790s. Not until Cooper broached the topic directly a decade after Brown's death, even including George Washington among the characters of *The Spy*, would it be apparent how absent the key national event always had been from so-called "American" literature. And Cooper at last set the recollective tone with which future writers would come to regard the war. In the process, I would argue, he invented the American novel as a literary form in which writers came to terms with the distinctive events of national emergence and differentiation. *The Spy* put an end to the post-colonial epoch in American literature.

Even Washington Irving, who made the most intriguing use of the Revolution in the pre-1821 period in "Rip Van Winkle," showed how much remained to be overcome. Irving let his hoary-locked, hen-pecked hunter "sleep" through the conflict, making the war literally an offstage event (as well as a comically shallow one to the sensibility of "author" Diedrich Knickerbocker). Irving's anti-hero thus was a figure of forgetting rather than memory, perhaps the one American of the revolutionary generation who claimed to know nothing whatever of the nation's bloody origins – nowhere bloodier, of course, than in his own Hudson valley. By implication, Irving may have been suggesting what all the rest of the survivors *might* divulge were they so inclined. But Irving did not help them speak what they knew. Part of the reason was personal, part cultural. Rip's creator himself had been born precisely in Rip's position: belatedly, in New York City in 1783, part of a "nation" that for him always had been there, regardless of how new it literally was. Irving, too, had just awakened to America. Yet there was more to the personal background of his most famous story than that. The evasions of "Rip Van Winkle" (and of "The Legend of Sleepy Hollow") stemmed more immediately from the fact that, unlike Cooper in *The Spy*, Irving hardly had engaged himself in a self-consciously American endeavor as he began *The Sketch-book*. In many ways, his volume is – like *Precaution* – a perfect post-colonial product. It is full of the displaced ex-colonial's sentiments of alienation ("I stepped upon the land of my forefathers," runs "The Voyage," " – but felt that I was a stranger in the land") even as it recites its pieties about the English capital and the rural countryside as if for all the world neither the Revolution nor the quite recently ended second conflict with Great Britain had occurred. In keeping with its post-colonial nature, "Rip Van Winkle" was written not in the shadow of the Catskills or the heart of New York City but rather in the English midlands, where the story came to Irving in a rush of American memories during a visit with old New York connections, his sister Sarah and her husband Henry Van Wart, then resident in Birmingham. In a very real sense, the tale's nostalgic aura had more to do with the recent failures of the Irving family business (in which Henry Van Wart also suffered embarrassments) and Irving's own exile than with the Revolution or the needs of American readers and citizens. As if rendered politically powerless by his own refusal to come to terms with the war, Irving only gestured toward it. He could not directly confront it as a literary topic.

Then there were the wider cultural reasons for Rip Van Winkle's amnesia. Especially in its long popularity as a sketch and a stage-piece, it marked the unsettled
political value of the war. For many Americans, even some who had supported the
war, the subject called up long-lasting post-colonial "regrets" about the destruction
visited on the old order of things. A similar impression is conveyed in "The Legend of
Sleepy Hollow." The vicinity of that tale's setting is said to have been "infested with
refugees" and "cow-boys" during the Revolution, an especially promising hint for the
future reader of Cooper. But it also was infested with what Irving terms "all kinds of
border chivalry," less an American figure than one suggesting the British borderlands
just then being explored by Walter Scott, whom Irving had visited even while he was
filling his notebooks with hints for other parts of *The Sketch-book* in 1817. Irving's
deference to Scott is telling, since it suggests how easily the setting of an apparently
"American" tale might suddenly transform itself into some dimly remembered Old
World terrain. For this New York descendant of Scots immigrants who was also the
namesake of America's national "savior," the memory of Old World borderlands
hardly was remote. Indeed, those regions were fresher to him during his composition
of "The Legend of Sleepy Hollow" in London than were the story's New World scenes,
which at that time lay years behind him in America. And if the "Legend" is full of
hints that might prove of use to later writers, Cooper among them, they are hints
Irving himself seemed not to hear, or certainly chose not to take up. For instance,
Ichabod Crane's comeuppance occurs at the spot, we read, where "the unfortunate
André was captured." Yet the true cause of the New England schoolmaster's fright is
his super-heated Yankee imagination rather than the resurgence of the revolutionary
past in the person – or rather ghost – of Major John André. It is "Cotton Mather's
History of Witchcraft" that has guided his response to the scene, not one of the many
contemporary accounts of André and his American partner in treason, Benedict
Arnold. The laughable old ghosts of the colonial era are to blame, not the more
ominous ones that had attended the recent birth of the post-colonial nation.

Cooper, who chose to confront those ghosts head-on, did not just sit down and
write *The Spy* as he *had* just sat down and written *Precaution*. Nor, for all his reliance
on Walter Scott's example as he abandoned domestic fiction for historical romance,
did he (as Irving did in "Rip Van Winkle") rely extensively on Old World literary
models or sources. Cooper's most important sources for his second novel were not
literary at all. And they were overwhelmingly American in provenance. Derived from
Revolutionary War memoirs, personal anecdotes gathered from a number of quarters,
and the political controversies of the years following the War of 1812, they were
multiform and multivalent. Yet all of them were essential to the effort to transform
post-colonial mimicry into national art. Cooper supplemented John Jay's crucial
anecdotes about Enoch Crosby by tapping oral lore he had encountered in many
venues over the first three decades of his life. At Yale, he may well have caught wind
of President Timothy Dwight's view that the "Neutral Ground" of Westchester, where
Dwight had served as a chaplain during the Revolution, had been morally devastated
by the long, difficult guerilla warfare typical of the region. Almost certainly he

learned similar, even darker lessons from the mentor to whom he was closest in New Haven, Professor Benjamin Silliman, whose father had been ruined by his selfless devotion to the patriot cause. But Cooper had arrived at Yale with his own complex view of the Revolution as a civil war, not just a rebellion from Britain, already formed. He had picked up a less-than-orthodox view of the war from his Quaker relatives, most of whom had avoided the fight by one means or another and knew the cost paid by pacifists such as Brockden Brown's father (one of the other Quakers exiled to Virginia with Elijah Brown was Henry Drinker, an early and important patron of Cooper's father). From other individuals settled around the Coopers near their frontier outpost in New York, where a great many Yankee veterans put down their roots after the peace, the future novelist had received various hints about the nature and cost of the armed combat, as I shall suggest later. From the loyalist family of his wife, the DeLanceys, he gained access to lore rich in lamentation but yielding, too, a sense of endurance and survival. Finally, once Cooper had decided to write the book, he went around among his neighbors in Westchester, where *The Spy* was both set and written, seeking out their memories of the grim, bloody business that had swept away so many people and left the rest, in Timothy Dwight's terms, blank-faced, apathetic, and fearful.

All this lore contributed to the dominant impression created by Cooper's novel, the sense that the war was to be recalled not as a Fourth of July pageant but rather as a tough passage through the "Neutral Ground" of history — the space between, that is, the colonial past and the national future. His "refugees" and "cow-boys" were not, as Irving's were in "The Legend of Sleepy Hollow," empty terms. Instead, they were intensely realized figures who rooted the novel in political truths Cooper insisted that his audience must confront. But in fact that audience was ready to confront such things in 1821, making the success of the book both timely and inevitable. Political issues in the partisan as well as the larger, institutional sense were central to Cooper's imagination of the tale and to its galvanizing effect on American readers and theater-goers. Cooper Americanized the novel as a form not simply by using American settings, events, and characters in ways no earlier writers had. He Americanized it by seeing such things in the light of political shifts only just occurring in the years after the end of the second war with Britain. The most important insight Cooper had derived from John Jay's anecdotes was not that individuals such as Enoch Crosby had existed or fought hard in the first war. It was that such ordinary soldiers (Cooper himself described Jay's spy as both "poor" and "ignorant") had been motivated by principles as deeply and consciously held as those that moved George Washington or indeed John Jay himself. While few would dispute such a point today, in Cooper's era it was an emergent view rather than a dominant one. The ruling assumption at the time was that, with very few exceptions, only the elite leaders of society could articulate and respond to abstract motivations. Ordinary men and women were moved instead by what were essentially "animal" urges — appetite, greed, fear, and the like. History therefore was to be written — or imagined — from the top down.

John Jay's contrary emphasis on the conscious patriotism he saw ordinary citizens exhibit during the war certainly was not widely shared among his fellow Federalists at the time he conveyed his tales to Cooper. He was moved to tell Cooper about Enoch Crosby in the first place because the spy had driven that very point home to his handler by means of a stinging rebuke. When Jay was appointed to the post of ambassador to the court of Spain in the later 1770s, as Cooper recalled the tale, he had requested a special appropriation from New York's provincial Congress in order to pay Crosby the gold he assumed the man expected for all the risk and exposure he had endured as a spy. Crosby had often infiltrated enemy lines in order to seek out information about Tory and loyalist operations. On several occasions, he had been arrested by patriot forces acting on tips that he himself had supplied. Those who arrested him, knowing nothing of his agency in their success, took him to be simply one more enemy among many. Only Jay and a few of Jay's confidants such as Egbert Benson knew the truth of the matter, and each time Crosby was seized they would secretly arrange for him to escape, often with American soldiers in potentially deadly pursuit. In addition to the dangers he ran among the British and their American sympathizers as a result, Crosby suffered the opprobrium of the very men and women whom he was so dangerously aiding. Worse yet, Jay could offer no guarantee that Crosby would ever be able to take open credit for what he had done. Many individuals had suffered from his operations, some of them now repatriated but unreconstructed. For his own good and the sake of the public peace, he might have to take their secrets as well as his own to the grave with him. For this reason, Jay assumed that the gold he secured for Crosby would be very important to the former spy. There was no question about Crosby's courage or commitment. However, there also was no question in Jay's mind about Crosby's motivation. Such a man would expect compensation. Why else would he have run such risks? When Jay arranged a lonely meeting with Crosby to transfer the money, however, he was stunned to learn that his spy, poor and ignorant as he might be, did not want it and would not accept it. Hence the scene late in *The Spy* in which "Harper" (George Washington himself) offers Harvey Birch gold, only to be refused and reminded that Birch has acted on the same principles as himself.

This collapsing of the moral stratification that had long ruled the empire, along with America itself for the past forty years, was very much the point of Cooper's narrative. Had he shared the old view at this point in his life, he would have produced a very different tale. Under that prior dispensation, a novel set in the Hudson valley and concerned with espionage ought to have taken Major John André as its central figure. André, after all, still lived on at the center of much of the valley's revolutionary lore, as Irving suggested. Cooper, to the contrary, opened his narrative a few days after André's execution, as if to suggest that America could come into being only with the death of that man and the corrupt system he represented. Cooper always thought little of André; he certainly did not share the weakness of many Americans of his class for the dead spy they almost ritualistically referred to as "the unfortunate André" (Irving's very phrase, one recalls, in "The Legend of Sleepy Hollow"). Ignoring the English adjutant who had bribed an American general, Cooper focused instead on an

American commoner who willingly sacrificed all he had, even his future reputation, in order to promote his seemingly ungrateful nation's cause – and who did so without thought of, indeed, with no wish for worldly compensation. Arnold and André were activated by greed; not so Enoch Crosby or Harvey Birch.

It was crucial to the literary experiment on which Cooper was engaged that he should reimagine revolutionary history from the bottom up. He thereby replaced the Tory sympathies evident in Walter Scott's historical romances with a Whig emphasis that suited his own political evolution away from the highly partisan Federalism of his father and older brothers. The ex-midshipman's conversion to Republicanism began during the War of 1812, when he broke with the Anglophile Federalists and cheered the early naval victories of the United States over the supposedly invincible British fleet. Except for those extraordinary victories and the post-treaty devastation visited on a British land force by Andrew Jackson at New Orleans, the war for the most part was a string of indecisive encounters. The United States endured rather than won. For Cooper, however, that outcome validated his own view that England had been frustrated in its attempt to reduce the nation to its old colonial status. Of completely English background personally, and with little sense that his family had fought for or even supported the colonies' opposition to the empire during the Revolution, Cooper grew up with a sentimental regard for England and things English. However, during his time at sea as a merchant sailor and then in the navy, and finally through the course of the War of 1812, he suffered a profound American-ization that turned him against England and English culture. He became a patriot not because he thought America perfect or right but rather because he understood the post-colonial mentality and its deleterious effects on communities and individuals, and chose to set himself against it at home and abroad. Soon he became active in partisan politics, working for Governor DeWitt Clinton's re-election early in 1820, the very year he also began his career as a novelist. Before long, moving well beyond Clintonian Republicanism, he would become a partisan of Andrew Jackson and the Democrats because of their championship of the common man. His interest in Jackson was keen enough that he would visit Washington in February 1825 to personally witness the run-off election for president in the House of Representatives that resulted in the loss of the Jeffersonian candidate to the Federalist John Quincy Adams. He knew Jackson's time would come, and he was right.

Cooper's more important political insight had to do with the fundamental values of democratic society rather than with parties. His emphasis on the ordinary citizen in *The Spy* marked his intent to rewrite the Revolution in the wake of his own radical conversion in the previous decade. That war had not simply been a difficult act of colonial defiance to the empire, nor a civil war during which Americans fought against and at times preyed upon each other. More crucially, it had been a time of ferment when the essential ideology of democratic patriotism was born. Harvey Birch's commitment to the as-yet-unrealized nation revealed Cooper's confidence in the ordinary citizen's capacity for selfless self-government in the future. In creating this figure, as in creating the uneducated but wise and forbearing frontiersman Natty

Figure 35.1   "The Expected Canoe." Painted by J. G. Chapman, and engraved by J. Andrews and C. Jewett. Frontispiece from S. G. Goodrich (ed.), *The Token and Atlantic Souvenir, A Christmas and New Year's Present* (Boston: American Stationers' Co., 1838). Collection of Shirley Samuels.

Bumppo in *The Pioneers* immediately afterwards, Cooper was drafting a cultural manifesto. And he was not doing so in a vacuum. His second novel, in fact, aligned him with a widespread effort then underway that was aimed at revising the popular memory of the Revolution.

For a complex of reasons, tales about similar figures were just then beginning to circulate with some frequency throughout the United States. Interest in the wartime sacrifices of the surviving revolutionary soldiers had been on the rise for several years. It had become especially intense as a result of a bitter debate in the House of Representatives early in 1817, a debate stimulated by a petition filed by one of Major André's three captors, an impoverished and ailing farmer named John Paulding. When Paulding's heretofore acclaimed role in arresting André and thereby saving the nation was called into serious question by Federalist Congressman Benjamin Tallmadge of Connecticut (who had been head of George Washington's secret service in 1780), a battle line in what Robert Cray has called the "revolutionary memory wars" was sharply drawn. Tallmadge, true to form, made the outrageous claim that Paulding and his fellows had been motivated only by greed. If André had been able to bribe them sufficiently on the spot, they never would have arrested him and led him to an American post in the expectation that some bigger reward might come their way. Although Tallmadge's attack was countered by Paulding's supporters in the House, they did not have enough votes to win him the enhanced pension he had been seeking. Especially in the Hudson valley, however, Paulding was vindicated and widely praised in public meetings, newspaper pieces, even a long pamphlet from the hand of Egbert Benson. One of Paulding's strongest supporters was Cooper's friend (as well as his militia commander and a fellow campaigner for DeWitt Clinton), General Pierre Van Cortlandt.

The debate initiated in Congress, which revealed the drawing of class as well as party lines in national memory, did not quickly fade. Indeed, it expanded well beyond the question of Paulding's service and sacrifices and Tallmadge's unfair assault. The summer following, James Monroe, the newly elected president and himself a revolutionary veteran sorely wounded in action, undertook a tour of the northeast. What was intended as a routine inspection of the country's forts in the wake of the War of 1812, however, soon was transformed into a nostalgic survey of neglected Revolutionary War sites. At many of those sites, as historian Jack Resch has noted, Monroe, clad in his old uniform, was greeted by ordinary Revolutionary War veterans who were given new recognition by him for their suffering not only during the war but, often enough, in the lean years since as well. By the end of 1817 Monroe had decided to aid these "suffering soldiers" by calling on Congress to create the first general pension program in the nation's history. Congress, which had refused Paulding's plea, soon agreed to do so. By late the following spring, aged revolutionary veterans therefore were coming forward in courtrooms all across the country to dictate the details of their service. Over the coming decades, as the program was dramatically expanded, more and more individuals followed suit until tens of thousands of pension files were created in the War department. The image of the old soldier adopting an anecdotal pose before the younger generation was a lasting reminder of the sea-change that had created the first entitlement program in US history.

Among the pension files accumulating in Washington would be that of James Cooper's uncle and namesake, who had served in various militia units in Pennsylvania in the 1770s and 1780s. In 1846 the younger Cooper submitted a deposition on the old veteran's behalf in which he recalled hearing various tales almost fifty years before, including "a humorous account which the said James Cooper gave to himself, of the manner in which his regiment retreated from the battle of Brandywine." The future Revolutionary War novelist heard similar tales from other adults in his community, including his schoolmaster, Oliver Cory, who as a boy had enlisted as a fifer in a Connecticut unit and went on to take part in the battles of White Plains and Trenton. Among other veterans who, like Cory, had immigrated to the Cooperstown vicinity were several men who had been present when Major André was executed at Tappan (as, incidentally, had Enoch Crosby). It is clear from the larger archive that such ordinary witnesses of the great events of the nation's past had been sharing their stories with neighbors for years prior to 1817. One of the men who provided a supporting deposition for Oliver Cory noted, for instance, that he had often heard the former schoolmaster tell stories about his services around New York City, and especially about the time George Washington personally appealed to Cory and his fellows to re-enlist, a call which Cory proudly declared he had heeded.

Cooper formalized such exchanges by modeling his first American tale on what we might well call the country's "narrative economy" – the process, that is, by which personal anecdotes with broader social meaning circulated from person to person, thereby building a sense of shared values and giving individual experience a richer context. Besides particular anecdotes, he drew from the veterans and their supporters two other things as well, more important than individual accounts: the sense of added meaning such stories assumed as they received wider public credit in the years following the War of 1812, and the accompanying implications about the worth of individual stories in a democratic culture. *The Spy* did not succeed by creating its audience, nor did the audience on its own make the book a success. Instead, the book expressed emergent public concerns by imagining the colonial and post-colonial past in such a way that it cleared the way for a national future. Cooper told Enoch Crosby's story in a form that Crosby himself could and did recognize. But Crosby played more than himself in the novel. He was the proxy for John Paulding and countless other ordinary heroes, as Natty Bumppo would be the proxy for Daniel Boone and the Otsego hunter Daniel Shipman and many other backwoods pioneers. In telling such stories, Cooper fashioned potent ideological myths. He also created a *modus operandi* for future American novelists. Storytelling, Cooper learned as he reflected on John Jay's anecdotes and then wrote *The Spy* on the basis of what he had heard, began first of all in the act of listening. From this time forward, American novelists would often seek out ways to make ordinary figures bear extraordinary meaning. In doing so, they were repeating a formula first tried and proven successful in New York in 1821.

REFERENCES AND FURTHER READING

Annals of Congress, 14th Congress, 2nd Session (1817), 473–5.

Barck, Dorothy C., ed. (1924–5). *Minutes of the Committee and First Commission for Detecting and Defeating Conspiracies in the State of New York.* New York: New-York Historical Society.

Barnum, H. L. (1828). *The Spy Unmasked; or, Memoirs of Enoch Crosby, alias Harvey Birch, the Hero of Mr. Cooper's Tale of the Neutral Ground.* New York: J. & J. Harper.

Benson, Egbert (1817). *Vindication of the Captors of Major Andre.* New York: Kirk & Mercein.

Brown, Chandos Michael (1989). *Benjamin Silliman: A Life in the Young Republic.* Princeton: Princeton University Press.

Buel, Joy Day, and Buel, Richard, Jr. (1984). *The Way of Duty: A Woman and her Family in Revolutionary America.* New York: Norton.

Coad, Oral Sumner (1917). *William Dunlap.* New York: William Dunlap Society.

Cooper, James Fenimore. Papers. American Antiquarian Society, Worcester, Mass.

Cooper, James Fenimore (1820). *Precaution: A Novel,* 2 vols. New York: Andrew T. Goodrich.

Cooper, James Fenimore (1839). *The History of the Navy of the United States of America,* 2 vols. Philadelphia: Lea & Blanchard.

Cooper, James Fenimore (1846). *Lives of the Distinguished American Naval Officers,* 2 vols. Philadelphia: Carey & Hart.

Cooper, James Fenimore (1960–8). *The Letters and Journals of James Fenimore Cooper,* ed. James Franklin Beard, 6 vols. Cambridge, Mass.: Harvard University Press.

Cooper, James Fenimore (1991). *Notions of the Americans: Picked up by a Travelling Bachelor,* ed. Gary Williams. Albany: State University of New York Press. (First publ. 1828.)

Cooper, James Fenimore (2002). *The Spy: A Tale of the Neutral Ground,* ed. James P. Elliott et al. New York: AMS Press. (First publ. 1821.)

Cooper, Susan Fenimore (1861). *Pages and Pictures, from the Writings of James Fenimore Cooper.* New York: W. A. Townsend & Co.

Cooper, Susan Fenimore (1922). "Small Family Memories" (written 1883). In *Correspondence of James Fenimore-Cooper,* ed. James Fenimore Cooper (1858–1938), 9–72. New Haven: Yale University Press.

Cooper, William. Papers. Paul Fenimore Cooper Archives, Hartwick College, Oneonta, NY.

Cray, Robert E., Jr. (1996). "The John André Memorial: The Politics of Memory in Gilded Age New York." *New York History* 77, 32.

Cray, Robert E., Jr. (1997). "Major John André and the Three Captors: Class Dynamics and Revolutionary Memory Wars in the Early Republic, 1780–1830." *Journal of the Early Republic* 17, 371–97.

Dann, John C., ed. (1980). *The Revolution Remembered: Eyewitness Accounts of the War for Independence.* Chicago: University of Chicago Press.

Drinker, Elizabeth (1991). *The Diary of Elizabeth Drinker,* ed. Elaine Forman Crane, 3 vols. Boston: Northeastern University Press. (Written 1758–1807.)

Dunlap, William (1798). *André; a Tragedy.* New York: T. & J. Swords.

Dunlap, William (1817). *The Glory of Columbia: Her Yeomanry.* New York: David Longworth.

Dunlap, William (1929–31). *Diary of William Dunlap (1766–1829),* ed. Dorothy C. Barck. New York: New-York Historical Society.

Dwight, Timothy (1969). *Travels in New England and New York,* ed. Barbara Miller Solomon, 4 vols. Cambridge, Mass.: Harvard University Press. (First published 1821–2.)

Fisher, George P. (1866). *Life of Benjamin Silliman,* 2 vols. New York: Scribner.

Franklin, Wayne (1997). "Introduction." In James Fenimore Cooper, *The Spy: A Tale of Neutral Ground.* New York: Penguin.

Franklin, Wayne (2001). "Fathering the Son: The Cultural Origins of James Fenimore Cooper." *Resources for American Literary Study* 27, 149–78.

Franklin, Wayne (2003). "Fenimore Cooper: A Writer's Life in the Early Republic." Biography in progress.

Gilpin, Thomas (1848). *Exiles in Virginia: With Observations on the Conduct of the Society of Friends during the Revolutionary War.* Philadelphia: C. Sherman.

Irving, Washington (1983). *History, Tales and Sketches*, ed. James W. Tuttleton. New York: Library of America. (First publ. 1802–21).

Judd, Jacob, ed. (1981). *Correspondence of the Van Cortlandt Family of Cortlandt Manor, 1815–1848*. Tarrytown, NY: Sleepy Hollow Restorations.

Nason, Elias (1870). *A Memoir of Mrs. Susanna Rowson*. Albany, NY: J . Munsell.

National Archives and Records Administration, Washington DC, Revolutionary War Pension and Bounty-Land Warrant Applications Files.

New York City, Common Council (1827). *Report of the Select Committee, on Erecting a Monument to the Memory of John Paulding, with an Address by the Mayor of the City of New-York*. New York: William A. Davis.

New York *Daily American*, 1827.

Oaks, Robert F. (1972). "Philadelphians in Exile: The Problem of Loyalty during the American Revolution." *Pennsylvania Magazine of History and Biography* 96, 298–325.

Petter, Henri (1971). *The Early American Novel*. Columbus: Ohio State University Press.

Pickering, James H. (1966). "Enoch Crosby, Secret Agent of the Neutral Ground: His Own Story." *New York History* 47, 61–73.

Pickering, James H. (1975). "Introduction." In *The Spy Unmasked*. Harrison, NY: Harbor Hill.

Resch, John (1999). *Suffering Soldiers: Revolutionary War Veterans, Moral Sentiment, and Political Culture in the Early Republic*. Amherst: University of Massachusetts Press.

Sparhawk, Edward Vernon (1827). *Report of the Trial, before Judges Thompson and Betts, in the Circuit Court of the US for the Southern District of New-York*. New York: Elam Bliss.

Tallmadge, Benjamin (1904). *Memoir of Colonel Benjamin Tallmadge*, ed. Henry Phelps Johnston. New York: Society of Sons of the Revolution in the State of New York. (First publ. 1858.)

Waldo, S. Putnam (1820). *The Tour of James Monroe, President of the United States, through the Northern and Eastern States, in 1817*, 2nd edn. Hartford, Conn.: Silas Andrus.

Williams, Stanley T. (1935). *The Life of Washington Irving*, 2 vols. New York: Oxford University Press.

Young, Alfred F. (1999). *The Shoemaker and the Tea Party: Memory and the American Revolution*. Boston: Beacon.

36

The Sea: Herman Melville and *Moby-Dick*

Stephanie A. Smith

"For God's sake, be economical with your lamps and candles!"

Wading into Herman Melville's titanic 1851 novel *Moby-Dick* (and also into the flood of commentary written since the nineteenth century about that novel) is daunting. A complete critical bibliography would be almost as large at the novel itself, depending on how inclusive or exhaustive a student, scholar, "late consumptive usher to a grammar school" (Melville 1978: 75), or "sub-sub-Librarian" (p. 77) chooses to be. For many, merely *reading* the novel is a challenge. Given the book's reputation as "the" American novel, and often simply because of its evident bulk, *Moby-Dick* casts a shadow across all of Melville's other writings, as well as across American culture. For despite the fact that "maritime experience informed virtually all of his writing" (Melville Society 1999), and even though other American authors like James Fenimore Cooper have tackled the sea, for most Americans – even those who haven't read it – *Moby-Dick* remains the quintessentially American sea-yarn.

Not bad for a book that sank like a stone soon after its publication, criticized for being mere babble, in the "run-amok style of Carlyle" (Howard 1951). It wasn't that American readers didn't like tales of the sea. Quite the opposite. *Typee*, for which Melville mined his youthful life-experiences as a seaman, was a bestseller. And if his readers were less thrilled by *Mardi*, they quite liked *Oomo*, *Redburn*, and *White-Jacket*. *Moby-Dick*, however, was a critical and, for Melville as well as his publisher, a financial disappointment. It didn't sell. Not only did it deal with an "unpoetical and disreputable" (Melville 1978: 203) industry – which the novel defends as noble – it wasn't much of an adventure. *Typee* had allowed the armchair traveler to get a peek at "exotic" Polynesia. But who wanted to read three volumes about low-class work like whaling, with pages of tedious philosophy in between?

For anyone alive before the Civil War battle between the ironclads, the *Merrimac* and the *Monitor*, wooden sailing ships upon the sea, whalers or otherwise, were a common feature of daily life. Americans imported and exported *all* goods at least partway by water, either upon the sea or up and down rivers. News, newspapers, books, letters, in fact any long-distance communication likewise traveled the waterways. In short, shipping by sea or river was as necessary, as ubiquitous, and as commonplace as, say, electricity is today. Imagine writing a 650-page novel about the work of an electrical line-man! Yet, in a sense, that is precisely what Melville did by writing a story told, at least nominally, by "a simple sailor, right before the mast, plumb down in the forecastle" (Melville 1978: 96). Neither a commodore nor a cook, and with no particular skill like that of a harpooneer, Ishmael is your ordinary "salt" (Melville 1978: 95), on the "lowest rung on the maritime ladder for a seaman" (Philbrick 2000: 25). He is your most basic working man, employed in an industry that required long hours, unreliable pay, and backbreaking, terrifying butchery. Sounds like fun. But *Moby-Dick* is fun: a profoundly funny, often joyous book, about one of the more degraded and fatal forms of labor imaginable outside of slavery (see chapter 21 in this volume); and work upon which most of the world relied, just as we now rely on electricity. Whale-oil kept lamps burning, and spermaceti candles gave off the purest, clearest light; and because of their prowess in hunting the sperm whale, Nantucketeers "once commanded the attention of the world" (Philbrick 2000: xvi). Or, as the Advocate chapter of *Moby-Dick* declares: "But though the world scouts at us whale hunters, yet does it unwittingly pay us the profoundest homage; yea an all-abounding adoration! for almost all the tapers, lamps and candles that burn around the globe, burn, as before so many shrines, to our glory!" (Melville 1978: 204).

So although there are many things to say about how the sea figures in Melville's work – given that only one or two of his major works do not address seafaring – what is most remarkable about *Moby-Dick* is how clearly Melville saw the sea as the internet superhighway of his time, and how he understood whaling as an unusually provocative, promising, and oftentimes frightening pre-industrial experiment in social, political, and erotic relations between men. If the sea itself had once provided the world's primary means of exchange, of both goods and information, whaling, as a global industry, was one that prefigured, in many ways, the soon-to-be-industrialized international commerce that would change Melville's world altogether, not long after the Civil War. For, as critic Cesare Cesarino points out, "the political economy of the sea under mercantile capitalism had anticipated two definitional and enabling features of industrial capitalism", these being "free and fully waged laborers who found work and worked among a large number of similarly situated men" and a "fully international, multiethnic, multilingual and also increasingly multiracial labor force" (Cesarino 2002: 4.5) – conditions that became necessary, particularly after the Civil War, to sustain industrial capitalism.

As Cesarino also explains, whaling was an unusual type of work. On the one hand, it was notoriously medieval in its pay-structure, offering laborers recompense not in wages but in shares or lays; on the other hand, it was "by far the most international, multiethnic, multilingual and especially multiracial labor force of any other sea practice" (Cesarino 2002: 4.5). Melville describes whaling as a global industry, and in so doing exposes how capitalism, as an economic system (whether mercantile or industrial), weds labor and life. That which is, or becomes, your life's work also takes your life. For example, Captain Ahab, a whaleman who, even before his encounter with Moby-Dick, was well known as one who had a distinct relish for the hunt, is finally consumed by his own life's pursuit of the whale, bound by the ropes of his passion to the creature he works to destroy. Or, as Cesarino notes, "Ahab is . . . an unwitting agent of [the] whale as well as of capital, and his monomaniac desire and fate is, after all, to become indistinguishable from and lose himself in both whale and capital" (Cesarino 2002: 116.6).

Of course, the crew of *any* whaler tempts death on every lowering, as they wrestle with a creature of immense muscle and power. As one Enoch Cloud, a young greenhorn aboard the doomed ship *Essex*, a true drama upon which *Moby-Dick* is based, wrote: "It is painful to witness the death of the smallest of God's created beings, much more, one in which life is so vigorously maintained as the Whale!" (Philbrick 2000: 54). Certainly, all the crew of the *Pequod* but one lose their lives. So it is no wonder that Ishmael passionately reminds readers, "For God's sake, be economical with your lamps and candles! Not a gallon you burn, but at least one drop of man's blood was spilled for it" (Melville 1978: 306). Capitalism not only identifies the laborer with the labor he or she performs, but, as Karl Marx pointed out, forces a disconnect between the process of production and the product (Marx 1967: 25) – a circuit of connection and disconnection that makes Ishmael cry out as he does, "For God's sake, be economical with your lamps and candles!"

The Gam

Furthermore, without the sea, and without those who traveled upon it, harvested from it, and risked their lives in so doing, folks at home would be left, as it were, in the dark – both figuratively, in terms of information exchange, and literally (at least with respect to whaling), because whale-oil provided light. Tellingly, Ishmael says of water, "There is magic in it" (Melville 1978: 94), and of course the contemporary "magic" of a steady, daily electrical flow to light the night is only possible through the use of water. Water; light: without these, daily life on the smallest scale, not to mention international commerce on a grand scale, grinds to a halt. Of course, for anyone living now, in the early twenty-first century, it is electricity and petroleum, not whale-oil, that illuminate the world; and today the word "surf" has far less to do with the sea, and far more to do with the internet. But even if the internet has speeded up the process of globalization, it is well worth remembering that the sea was the first means by which commercial globalization became possible, and whaling, as previously mentioned, one of the first truly global industries. The sea allowed those who sailed upon it to communicate between cultures, nation-states, families; it was a means by which many kept in touch over vast distances both geographic and geopolitical – a means of information exchange, as is the internet today.

As *Moby-Dick* tells us, should two American whalers, most of which originated from New Bedford or Nantucket, espy each other on the "illimitable Pine Barrens and

Salisbury Plains of the sea" (Melville 1978: 341), they would engage in a form of seaborne social intercourse Melville names the Gam.

> GAM. Noun – A social meeting of two (or more) Whaleships, generally on a cruising ground; when, after exchanging hails, they exchange visits by boats' crews; the captains remaining, for the time, on board one ship, and the chief mates on the other. (Melville 1978: 343)

Significantly, "gam" also means a head or school of whales, who engage in their own, whalish form of social intercourse (*OED*). Whalemen were tied to their "line" of work economically, literally (by the line of the harpoon-rope), and by their own language, making them truly "whale"-men: examples of a hybrid, working (capitalist) creature, whose life was determined by the form of work he did. Cesarino makes a similar point when he argues that Melville's use of the word "wild" ties the crew of the *Pequod* to their prey through parallel sentence constructions (Cesarino 2002: 116.6). The gam allowed Nantucketeers to keep in touch with loved ones, to receive and send news to and from home over the whole of the vast, ever-expanding cruising ground of the whale-fishery. In his chapter on the gam, Melville takes note that ships other than whalers don't tend to socialize in this manner: merchant ships cut each other on the high seas, "like a brace of dandies in Broadway" (Melville 1978: 342); military ships spend too much time bowing and scraping and sizing each other up; slavers are in a "prodigious hurry" (Melville 1978: 342); and pirates are "infernal villains on both sides, and don't like to see overmuch of each other's villainous likenesses" (Melville 1978: 342). "But look at the godly, honest, unostentatious, hospitable, sociable, free-and-easy whaler! What does the whaler do when she meets another whaler in any sort of decent weather? She has a *Gam*; a thing so utterly unknown to all other ships that they never heard of the name even" (Melville 1978: 343).

Of course, one of the major reasons why whalers "gammed" is that a whaling voyage, by the 1850s, could last two to four years. Nantucketeers had become so good at the job of whale-killing, and the demand for oil was so great, that by 1819 few islanders who weren't whalemen had ever seen a sperm whale. "It is estimated that the Nantucketeers and their Yankee whale-killing brethren harvested more than 225,000 sperm whales between 1804 and 1876 ... researchers believe that by 1860 whalemen may have reduced the world's sperm-whale population by as much as 75%" (Philbrick 2000: 223). Having fished out the waters close to home, whalemen ended up traveling further and further afield; what once was a nine-month voyage had stretched to a three-year-away, three-month-at-home cycle that took ships from Nantucket to Africa, around Cape Horn and out to the Marquesas. Thus, news from home was dear. And when whalers "spoke" to each other in the Gam, they exchanged news, letters, newspapers, stories, and warnings. Homesick men who did not receive a letter, recalled one whaleman, would follow those who had "around the decks and whilst we were reading our letters would seat themselves beside us, as though our letters could be of service to them" (Philbrick 2000: 66).

In *Moby-Dick*, the *Pequod* gams (or nearly gams) with nine other boats: the *Goney* (Albatross), *Town-Ho*, *Jeroboam*, *Virgin* (Jungfrau), *Rose Bud* (Bouton-de-Rose), *Samuel Enderby* of London, *Bachelor*, *Rachel*, and *Delight* – all these, despite the fact that Ahab never seeks out a gam; not only does his injury make it difficult for him to travel in the manner that captains do during a gam – aboard the small and seatless whale-boats – but he is also uninterested in social intercourse, since it interferes with his mission. However, he will stop in order to ask: "Have ye seen the White Whale?"; and during each encounter between the *Pequod* and another ship, Melville shows the reader how life aboard the *Pequod* is organized to be fatal. Not only does *Moby-Dick* challenge the idea that the whale is a "legitimate" prey, by suggesting that murdering God's creature in so foul a fashion might be blasphemous; one of the most compelling underlying questions this novel asks of its reader: What is, or ought to be, the appropriate state of relations between men? While this question, for a modern reader, invites answers about sexuality (as queer studies of the novel demonstrate), Melville never separates out questions about passion and eroticism from questions of labor, politics, religion, and philosophy, and of how they might function together; or, as critic Sam Otter writes, "as always in *Moby-Dick*, philosophy and theology are melded with flesh" (Otter 1999).

What is man's most proper relation to man? This is a fundamental question, one that speaks to flesh, to politics, to religion; and I would argue that the voyage of the *Pequod* is a rumination upon the certainties that subtend the politics, religion, culture, and economy of nineteenth-century America. For example, although every crew aboard a whaler must organize their mutual labor of the hunt, the kill, the trying-out and boiling down of their prey, according to a pyramid-like hierarchy with the captain as the pinnacle and the lines of command running through the mates to the rest of the crew, each ship the *Pequod* encounters handles this "pyramid" differently, and each ship responds to what it finds aboard the *Pequod* tellingly. "Surfing" the sea for information about the white whale, Ahab is repeatedly forced to face the fact that his rigid, paternalistic rule has made the *Pequod* into a (capitalist) killing machine. "Old Thunder" is an autocrat; his name means, in Hebrew, "father's brother," and the biblical King of Israel who bore this name seriously provoked God by his behavior (Melville 1978: 732), as Captain Ahab does. This capitalist patriarch has his "knights and squires": Starbuck, Stubb, and Flask, "who by universal prescription commanded three of the *Pequod*'s boats as headsman" (Melville 1978: 214). Each headsman, "like a Gothic Knight of old" (Melville 1978: 214), has his own harpooneer, Queequeg being Starbuck's, Tashtego – "an unmixed Indian from Gay Head" (Melville 1978: 215) – being Stubb's, and Daggoo – "a gigantic, coal-black negro-savage" (Melville 1978: 215) – being Flask's. This multiracial, multiethnic crew is managed by fear, cunning, superstition, and passion, as Ahab stirs up the crew's blood-lust to land the white whale, a lust that runs counter to any normal profit motive the crew ought to have: something Ahab knows he must keep in mind, not only because Starbuck is a staunch capitalist who believes in profit, but also because, as Ahab also knows, "of all tools used in the shadow of the moon, men are most apt to get out of order" (Melville 1978:

313). And so the *Pequod's* social organization is strict, full of rules and rumors, secrets, stories and lies – such as the fact that Ahab's headsman is a stowaway, Fedallah.

As the voyage lengthens, the *Pequod* becomes an increasingly paranoid ship on a paranoid mission that Ahab, despite his ability to rouse the crew to follow him, also disguises as part of a normal whaling voyage; for he "plainly saw that he must still in good degree continue to be true to the natural, nominal purpose of the *Pequod's* voyage" (Melville 1978: 314). In other words, he must forge, out of a capitalist industry, a killing machine, honed by capitalism, but turned to Ahab's purpose. Ishmael both fears and yet also joins in Father Ahab's madness, in part because he is there with his "bosom friend" Queequeg and in part because, as he says, "I gave myself up to the abandonment of the time and the place" (Melville 1978: 286). In fact, he understands Ahab's monomaniacal desire for revenge and finds himself in thrall to what he calls the symbolic "dumb blankness, full of meaning," of which "the Albino whale was the symbol." He then asks his readers: "Wonder ye then at the fiery hunt?" (Melville 1978: 296) as if no one could, in fact, resist.

Yet this fiery, symbolic hunt will be fatal; Ishmael knows it, not only because he alone survives it, but because, even as he gives himself up to it, he also "could see naught in that brute [Moby-Dick] but the deadliest ill" (Melville 1978: 286). For Ishmael knows, as does Starbuck, that the ship's mission should be a business venture. The crew and their captain, good capitalist workers, should be bent on profit, as is evidenced by the jolly, ornamented *Bachelor* the *Pequod* meets, "[a] full ship and homeward bound" (Melville 1978: 603), stuffed to the gills with sperm. The *Bachelor's* captain is in a good humor and, when asked about the white whale, replies, "No, only heard of him; but don't believe in him at all" (Melville 1978: 605) – a rational statement that renders the *Pequod's* infernal mission unreal. Ahab is, according to the jolly *Bachelor*, chasing air. Such a venture will yield no profit.

Indeed, as I suggested earlier, all the gams or near-gams are likewise comments on the *Pequod's* hunt. If the *Bachelor* is rich, full of sperm, unwasted, as it were, by the ship's labor, the *Pequod* – named after a New England Indian tribe known for their warrior spirit, a tribe who lost between 500 and 800 men in the 1637 Pequod massacre – is gloomy, fearful, and half-crazed. The crew looks "with grave, lingering glances towards the receding *Bachelor*" (Melville 1978: 605), as if only too aware that their captain will kill them. Of course, you might counter that their gam with the jolly *Bachelor* comes near the end of their voyage, after many a warning about Moby-Dick. However, even their very first near-gam is gloomy. The *Goney* (Albatross), named after an infamous white bird, is a forlorn ship, "bleached like a skeleton of a stranded walrus" and eerily reminiscent of the ship in the *Rime of the Ancient Mariner* (Melville 1978: 805). The dazed crew of the *Goney* do not respond to the men aloft in the *Pequod's* rigging, and the ship's captain drops his trumpet when he attempts to reply to Ahab's "Have ye seen the White Whale?" (Melville 1978: 339).

Indeed, every other ship the *Pequod* encounters comments negatively on the trust and sociability – or rather, the lack of it – Captain Ahab and his hunt have produced. The *Town-Ho* has suffered a mutiny, a fact Tashtego learns and unwittingly shares with his shipmates, but never with those in authority: they "kept the secret among themselves so that it never transpired abaft the *Pequod*'s main-mast" (Melville 1978: 346); the *Jeroboam* has a "malignant epidemic" (Melville 1978: 419) on board, as well as the archangel Gabriel, a "scaramouch" Shaker and a self-proclaimed prophet, of whom the crew is afraid. This prophet foretold the death of the *Jeroboam's* first mate Macey, who tried to kill Moby-Dick. Gabriel, claiming that the white whale is the Shakers' God incarnate, warns Ahab not to hunt the whale and, when Ahab persists, tells him he will soon follow Macey. He emphasizes his prophecy by returning a letter from the now-deceased Macey's wife that the *Pequod* tries to deliver: "as if by magic, the letter suddenly ranged along with Gabriel's eager hand. He clutched it an instant, seized the boat-knife, and impaling the letter on it, sent it thus loaded back into the ship. It fell at Ahab's feet" (Melville 1978: 424). Returned mail: no such address.

The Dutch, French, and English ships only sponsor nationalist competition, or outright cheating, while both the *Rachel* and the *Delight*, the very last two ships the *Pequod* encounters, have suffered losses inflicted by Moby-Dick: the *Rachel*'s Captain Gardiner has lost his youngest son, "a little lad, but twelve years old," when the harpooned Moby-Dick ran off with the whaleboat, "as often happens" (Melville 1978: 638). The *Rachel* is frantically searching for the lost whaleboat. Captain Gardiner beseeches Ahab, "Do to me as you would have me do to you in the like case. For you too have a boy, Captain Ahab – though but a child and nestling safely at home now" (Melville 1978: 640). As a father, both of his own crew and of a son, Ahab should join Gardiner; but he says: "I will not do it. Even now I lose time. Good bye, good bye. God bless ye, man, and may I forgive myself, but I must go" (Melville 1978: 640). This refusal is unthinkable to Gardiner and should be unthinkable among the close-knit Nantucketeers. Moreover, it is a refusal on Ahab's part to be the patriarch, a fatally symbolic refusal because it countermands his own sense of patriarchal order.

Finally, the *Pequod* encounters the truly misnamed *Delight*, with its hollow-cheeked captain, which is engaged in a burial at sea. Moby-Dick stove in a whale-boat. "I bury but one of five stout men," says the captain, " . . . only *that* one I bury; the rest were buried before they died; you sail upon their tomb" (Melville 1978: 648). But Ahab pushes on, eschewing the rules of civil society. By sponsoring a ruthless ship that refuses the ties of family, warmth, profit, compassion, understanding, and even the idea of mutual dependency; by throwing aside all that binds one man to another in nineteenth-century society and thus by eschewing the underlying certainties of the religion, politics, and culture of his time, Ahab has made his ship into an antisocial capitalist machine, inhuman and inhumane, bent *only* on the kill, until at last it is fastened to its fate, and taken down by Moby-Dick.

A Squeeze of the Hand

Yet despite what might be read as a despairing end, what Melville sinks is the machine/ship of capitalist despotism. An altered Ishmael is saved by the *Rachel*, as "she" weeps, searching for her lost son, only to find "another orphan" (Melville 1978: 687). And what has altered Ishmael? Not simply the ordeal of surviving the wreck of the *Pequod*, but the squeezing of case (sperm) that "has the rare virtue in allaying the heat of anger" (Melville 1978: 527). And he has met not simply wild Ahab, but also his bosom friend Queequeg, whose friendship "accorded him a socially designated place to stand on the boundary between civilized and savage" (Porter 1986). Ishmael finds not simply the bondage of the wild hunt, but also the bonding camaraderie of his shipmates, even if some of that international, multiracial bonding is for an infernal cause. In other words, Ishmael encounters a different form of sociability, alive inside the stifling forms of the *Pequod*'s productive and reproductive order; as Cesarino argues, "The secret, subterranean antagonism of Moby-Dick . . . is in that body that goes largely unacknowledged in this novel but whose 'rioting' presence is nonetheless felt throughout its pages" (Cesarino 2002: 116.6): the body of living labor, the being-in-common with other workers. Ishmael exclaims, "Oh! my dear fellow beings, why should we longer cherish any social acerbities, or know the slightest ill-humor or envy! Come; let us squeeze hands all around; nay, let us squeeze ourselves into each other; let us squeeze ourselves universally into the very milk and sperm of kindness" (Melville 1978: 527).

Famously, of course, the book begins with a "marriage" between Queequeg and Ishmael. This love-scene, and subsequent chapters and passages (including that about the squeezing of sperm quoted above), have inspired numerous claims about the not-so-subtextual homoeroticism in this novel. However, Ishmael's homoerotic ecstasies are not, as Cesarino aptly points out, overtly sexual. Indeed, the ecstasy Ishmael finds has more to do with his sense of boundary loss, as Porter argues, and his being in common with his fellow sailors who, after all, must work, sleep, eat, and be literally tied together (as in the monkey-rope chapter) in order both to labor and to live. Indeed, what Ishmael experiences in his ecstasy of squeezing case, which he claims he is ready to do eternally (Melville 1978: 527), is more akin to the transcendent/ Transcendental loss of the self that Ralph Waldo Emerson so famously called for when he wrote that in Nature "all mean egotism vanishes. I become a transparent eyeball" (Emerson 1960).

The loss of ego in which all men become as one is also, I would argue, part of the promise of pure democracy. Enlightenment statements such as "all men are created equal" put everyone in the same boat, as it were. And aboard the multiracial, multi-ethnic *Pequod*, the so-called melting(trying)-pot promise of American democracy gets a trial run. Ishmael's gestures, as Cesarino offers, are "gestures of pure possibility, that is, the urgent gestures of an abandon without reserve" (Cesarino 2002: 127.8). Yet Ishmael, working within capitalism, also knows that "in all cases man must eventually lower, or at least shift, his conceit of attainable felicity" (Melville 1978: 527); must give up the glimpsed and felt paradise of pure possibility located in the being-in-common that allows for the complete loss of self in others. Yet his glimpse leaves a trace, the ecstatic trace of the chapter's language, the power of ecstasy embedded in the novel, the rioting "body" of pure democracy.

Moby-Dick, of course, was published a good decade before the Civil War. A good decade, too, before the frenzy of industrialist expansion and invention to which the long, bloody conflict gave rise. Significantly, when Melville returned to the sea in *Billy Budd*, late in life and without hope of publication, he had replaced the rollicking fun of *Moby-Dick* with a tone of funereal exactitude. You might say, even, that before the war Melville had political hope that things in the fledgling democracy would turn out all right – as many saw, and some still see, the internet as a means to revive democracy. Even after the war, when Melville published his *Battle-Pieces and Aspects of the War*, he urged his fellow beings to forget and forgive because the future was at stake: "For the future of the freed slaves we may well be concerned; but the future of the whole country, involving the future of the blacks, urges a paramount claim on our anxiety" (Melville 1978). In what surely must be one of the most extraordinarily political epilogues to a collection of poetry, Melville dares to hope that blacks and whites, Northerners and Southerners, would alike favor democracy, would live together in peace as fellow, equal men. But by the 1870s, when Melville chose to sacrifice Baby Budd in order to guarantee good working order aboard the *Bellipotent*, that hope seems dead. Captain Vere himself argues there is no choice but to sacrifice the boy – the future, if you will – in favor of the system; and in that gesture one might just read an understanding on Melville's part that the juggernaut of industrial capitalism had overtaken the pure possibilities democracy once held. As a Customs Inspector Melville had to know full well the overweening importance of Cash (and Commodity) – an importance that would not only try, but in fact eclipse the Time, Strength, and Patience of any laboring man.

REFERENCES AND FURTHER READING

Cesarino, Cesar (2002). *Modernity at Sea.* Minneapolis: University of Minnesota Press.

Emerson, Ralph Waldo (1960). *Collected Essays of Ralph Waldo Emerson.* New York: Random House.

Gilmore, Michael T. (1985). *American Romanticism and the Marketplace.* Chicago: University of Chicago Press.

Herbert, Walter (1980). *Marquesan Encounters.* Cambridge, Mass.: Harvard University Press.

Howard, Leon (1951). *Herman Melville.* Berkeley: University of California Press.

Marx, Karl (1967). *Capital,* ed. Frederick Engels. New York: International Publishers.

Melville, Herman (1978). *Moby-Dick.* New York: Penguin.

Melville Society (1999). Melville Society website: http://people.hofstra.edu/faculty/ John_L_Bryant/Melville/soc.html.

Otter, Samuel (1999). *Melville's Anatomies.* Berkeley: University of California Press.

Philbrick, Nathaniel (2000). *In the Heart of the Sea.* New York: Penguin Putnam.

Porter, Carolyn (1986). "Call Me Ishmael, or How to Make Double-Talk Speak." In Richard Brodhead (ed.), *New Essays on Moby-Dick*, 73–108. New York and London: Cambridge University Press.

Rogin, Michael Paul (1983). *Subversive Genealogy: The Politics and Art of Herman Melville.* New York: Knopf.

Stone, Alluquere Rosanne (1996). *The War of Desire and Technology at the Close of the Mechanical Age.* Cambridge, Mass.: MIT Press.

Ziff, Larzer (1981). *Literary Democracy.* New York: Viking.

37

National Narrative and National History

Russ Castronovo

This essay opens with a quasi-scientific experiment in *national narrative*. This concept posits that literature does political and cultural work in enabling citizens to imagine the nation and its history in terms of a coherent storyline that promises a clear and unambiguous moral ending or destiny. Because it is both historical and fictive, national narrative can be difficult to pin down. For this reason, I propose a not altogether fanciful exercise to gauge, in a practical and verifiable way, the specific complexities that trouble the relationship of literature to national history.

HYPOTHESIS: Writing about national history presents a coherent, unified narrative of the nation.

MATERIALS NEEDED: A US one-dollar bill and a copy of Nathaniel
Hawthorne's *The Scarlet Letter*.

PROCEDURE:

1 Flip over the dollar bill so that the Great Seal of the United States shows face up.

2 Examine in detail the visual image of the federal eagle.

3 Open *The Scarlet Letter*, turning to the third paragraph of Hawthorne's preface, which describes "an enormous specimen of the American eagle" that ornaments the entrance to the Custom House, a federal building.

4 Compare the dollar bill's visual image of national authority with Hawthorne's textual rendition of this symbol.

OBSERVATIONS: Witness the critical discrepancies that emerge in the juxtapos-
ition of visual and literary images. According to Hawthorne, the American eagle holds "a bunch of intermingled thunderbolts and barbed arrows in each claw." But in turning to the dollar bill, it becomes clear that his description is inaccurate: no thunderbolts slash and zigzag across the seal. His mistake is doubly significant because not only does it endow "this unhappy fowl" with the symbolic penchant for dealing out swift and lethal punishment, it also erases from memory the olive branch that the eagle actually holds. Further

comparisons are useful in verifying whether Hawthorne's description of the eagle's ominous demeanor – its "fierceness," "truculency," and "vixenly" nature – are not also beset by inaccuracies, even willful misapprehension.

RESULTS: A volatile symbol emerges from this jumble of federal icon and Hawthorne's reinterpretation of that icon. Unstable and contradictory, this mixture has acidic properties, eating away at common assumptions that the government protects its citizens with tender regard. Instead, governmental authority seems quick to injure and stigmatize dissenters, much as the Puritan magistrates treat Hester Prynne in the story that follows.

CONCLUSION: The story of the nation is never simply told. Disproving our initial hypothesis, *The Scarlet Letter* experiment reveals that national narrative is not as clear or as unambiguous as first assumed. Rendered as literature, the nation's history, as in Hawthorne's faulty memory of the Custom House eagle, is always an exercise in memory, which is to say that it is also an exercise in amnesia. The nation can be casually misremembered or willfully misrepresented just as it can be faithfully remembered and dutifully represented. The literature that conceptualizes and imagines "America" as an exceptional political and social experiment also exposes deep rifts in the national fabric. Writing about the national past threatens the coherence of that past. The question remains how various authors deal with that threat as they return to the primal scenes of the storied past, including the Puritan settlement, Indian territory, and the American Revolution. Does the literary excavation of national history warrant caution lest literature's critical potential spill over and damage the symbols and myths that hold together the nation and its citizens? Or is this critical energy to be embraced as a tactic of counter-national dissent?

Union and Sex

Experiments in national narrative were conducted with unparalleled frequency in the decades leading up to the Civil War. Though often engineered to solidify faith in a national union that was scarcely a generation old, literary efforts to celebrate the country's past often ended up sending mixed messages. Walt Whitman tapped into this mission to estheticize "America" when he wrote in *Leaves of Grass* (1855) that "The United States themselves are essentially the greatest poem." Strangely enough, Whitman wrote this statement not in verse but in prose, as if to say that the great poem of the United States had not been realized. Yet despite the prospective nature of his declaration, Whitman certainly put his finger on the literary nationalism that had characterized writing in the new republic almost since its inception. Manifestos such as Ralph Waldo Emerson's "The American Scholar" and Herman Melville's "Hawthorne and his Mosses" stood at the forefront of this literary nationalism, taking American letters to task for what was perceived as their fawning imitation of European models.

After all, political independence from Great Britain had been declared in 1776; when would the American novel follow suit and break with the aristocratic tradition of European esthetics? When would literary independence come? That moment could not arrive soon enough for Melville and Emerson, as they sought to wrest fiction away from the putatively feudal associations of Old World stylistics and instead plant American writing on a democratic basis. Look away from the River Avon, Melville urged his countrymen in his call for a homegrown novelistic tradition, and instead turn to the "Shakespeares [that] are this day being born on the banks of the Ohio." Sounding a similar note, Emerson complained that English writers "have Shakespearized now for two hundred years" and that the time was ripe to Americanize literature.

But the plan to establish a national narrative was easier declared than implemented. Attempts to use literature as a means of imagining a national community raised a host of unintended but also unavoidable questions. If the United States were to be a poem, as Whitman suggested, what would be the status of decidedly unpoetic realities such as slavery and the removal and extermination of native peoples? If the New World were truly a novel experiment, could that production be imbued with a satisfying sense of closure? In short, what happens when the political character of the nation is given esthetic form? Whitman's pronouncement suggests that these rather difficult questions are best evaded through a focus on general patterns and not addressed specifically. The United States are indeed a great poem, but only "essentially" so; the particulars of class antagonism and racial injustice, for instance, have to be rendered as just that – particulars overshadowed by the more essential design of national narrative. Only then can fictional representations of national history steer clear of ambiguities and achieve closure. But the question remains: Can national narratives ever steer clear of the contradictions of their own history?

Although the skilled woodsman of James Fenimore Cooper's Leatherstocking saga avoids savages, panthers, and female seduction, the novels that encapsulate his exploits are tripped up by irresolvable national anxieties about citizenship and miscegenation. Three decades before Whitman called the nation a poem, Cooper's frontier fictions imparted esthetic form to early American history, lending an aura of romance to the Revolution and Indian wars. His hero, Natty Bumppo, a rough-and-ready woodsman, stands in vigorous opposition to the bumbling British colonials on the frontier. And although Hawkeye (as Natty is also called) easily maneuvers about the forest, he stumbles over the persistent ambiguities that mark the American ideological landscape. In *Last of the Mohicans* (1826), Natty attends the double funeral of Uncas, the last in a long line of Delaware chiefs, and Alice, the daughter of a British colonial officer. The maidens of the tribe intone a dirge for the slain lovers, hoping that the sexual union denied the couple on earth will transpire in heaven. But the frontiersman refuses to extract a sense of closure from this eulogy. Indeed, for Natty, this fantasy of interracial harmony proves disruptive and he dismisses it with a shake of his head. The closure that the tribe finds in its funeral ritual is unsuitable both to the white scout and to the novel as a whole. Reject this romantic vision he must, for it embellishes an affair that is politically and culturally abhorrent to Natty: the union of white womanhood and Native masculinity. Metaphors and similes abound in this passage as Alice is compared to various natural beauties; but in the overall cultural logic of *Last of the Mohicans* such images do not constitute poetry for the United States.

Despite the offensive nature of the maidens' free verse, Natty must remain outwardly unruffled. Were he to betray his inner disquiet, the other white men at the ceremony might pick up on his agitation and then Natty would have to translate the eulogy for them. Translation is not to be contemplated: Native meanings must not migrate into "American" consciousness. The uncomplicated line of national narrative – like the unsullied bloodline of Alice – must be maintained at all costs, even if that task withholds the promise of esthetic closure.

Quite simply, sex threatens the coherence of national imagining. In novels such as Lydia Maria Child's *Hobomok* (1824), Catharine Maria Sedgwick's *Hope Leslie* (1827), and Ann Stephens' *Malaeska; The Indian Wife of the White Hunter* (1860), miscegenation complicates the straightforward national history that these novels purport to tell. Set against plots of romantic attraction between whites and Native Americans, the history of early American settlement in these novels no longer reads as a quest for religious liberty that ends atop what John Winthrop famously called a "city upon a hill." Instead, in all these novels death and alienation are the result when the religious passion of Puritans and other dissenters gets reworked in the New World as sexual passion for an exotic Other. The return to national origins is always a dangerous affair. But this obstacle did not deter accomplished novelists from telling (or, at least, attempting to tell) the nation's story as a coherent narrative of union, progress, and equality.

By the time that Whitman imagined the United States taking poetic form, Cooper had already written national history as a novel of the American Revolution, *The Spy*. With this subject matter, the novelist's project was on uncontested and unambiguous ground. Surely any doubts about this conflict had been settled with George Washington's triumph over the British forces at Yorktown in 1781. The father of his country exerts a quasi-religious influence over the events in this 1821 novel, separating traitors and apostates from "true" American patriots. Just as easily, Washington's authority sets the stage for the happy resolution of marriage, in this case a conjugal match between families of Southern revolutionaries and Northern loyalists, which reflects a national union that transcends any divisive sectional feelings. Marriage as a trope thus heals many divided nineteenth-century fictions, from Caroline Lee Hentz's *The Planter's Northern Bride* (1854), in which the enmity between abolitionist and pro-slavery factions is buried in a sexual alliance between blooming New England maiden and genteel plantation owner, to the domestic alliances in Hawthorne's *The House of the Seven Gables* (1851) and Cooper's *The Pioneers* (1823), which happily settle outstanding claims that have festered since before the early days of the American republic.

The difference between sex and marriage is crucial. Sex disrupts national union by suggesting indelicate instances of interracial union; marriage, by contrast, as a form of contract backed by the state, promises lasting confederation and happiness. It is not surprising, then, that the conventional legal form of marriage proves consistent with literary conventions of closure and happy endings. In contrast to the destructive force of miscegenation that appears not only in Cooper's own work with *Last of the Mohicans* but also in the work of women novelists such as Child, Sedgwick, and Stephens, *The Spy*'s guarantee of domestic accord reconciles warring families and interests into a new federal whole. Narrative has no difficulty imagining the nation as a family when the family is racially and ethnically all the same. In *The Spy*, Washington proves adept in understanding the ideological work of marriage in binding citizens together into a compact that is at once personal and national.

Yet even the storied American past that had attained enough coherence and resolution to become safe literary subject matter was prone to disruption when brought within the domain of esthetic representation. The repetition of national history is always a critical reiteration. As that history becomes narrative, that is, as the United States becomes a poem, the gaps, inconsistencies, and loose ends that characterize literature reappear in the American fiction of a unified nation-state. Thus when Cooper returned to *The Spy*, updating his preface in 1849, he had to wonder if national narrative now lacked harmony and resolution. "There is no enemy to fear, but the one that resides within," he advised, alluding to the looming intensification of the sectional crisis over slavery. What had happened to the national narrative, so confidently expressed in the legendary authority of Washington, who symbolically had provided the grounds for national community? Perhaps that authority had never existed.

Doubts and Rumors

Or, if it did exist, perhaps that authority better served as the watchword for tyranny than for democracy. The befuddlement of that cagey snoozer of twenty years, Rip Van Winkle, only intensifies these doubts about national progress. When, in Washington Irving's disarming tale, Rip returns to one of his favorite haunts, the local tavern, he is comforted to see the familiar face of King George III swinging from the sign outside the door. But something is different: though the face remains recognizable, the king's red coat and scepter are replaced by a blue Revolutionary War uniform and a military sword. New letters adorn the sign with the legend of "General Washington." It is no coincidence, then, that this watering hole now advertises itself as the Union Hotel. The image of Washington cements the bonds that tie local communities – such as the Dutch ethnic enclave that formed the backdrop for much of Irving's *The Sketch-book* (1820) – to national forms of identification and belonging. Despite all these outward changes, however, the faces of kingship and democratic leadership remain indistinguishable. Rip's confusion suggests a series of troubling questions: Does the difference between George III and George Washington run deeper than their outward apparel? Wherein lies the difference between a tyrant and a president? Is national narrative really a story of progressive freedom? If citizens return to and reiterate national history, the distinct possibility exists that their memories might not strictly adhere to official historical forms. National narrative thus presents occasion for the exercise of critical memory, a mode of relating to the past that quite often stands in opposition to accepted historical "truths."

Challenges to such "truths" often appear in the form of gossip, innuendo, or, to take the case of Irving, rumor and legend. Specifically, in "The Legend of Sleepy Hollow" readers learn that the spectral sightings and "mournful cries and wailings" observed in that locale are often clustered around the tree where during the Revolution a British spy, Major John André, was captured. In the form of narrative, history is always haunted by the past. And the repressed but critical memory that returns in Irving's tale at this moment comes as a jab at Washington's legacy. Although many urged the leader of the American forces to stay the execution of this gallant British officer, the father of his country stood resolute. The Yankee schoolmaster in "Sleepy Hollow" is pursued by a headless horseman who receives his totemic power from the ghostly intimations emerging from the half-buried past that surrounds a gallows tree. As in "Rip Van Winkle," Washington appears as unnecessarily autocratic. The presumably stable referent of national narrative is irredeemably disfigured by some rather deep cleavages between democracy and tyranny as well as between benign paternalism and autocratic authority. All in all, then, when narrative returns to national foundations it just as readily upsets the pillars it is intended to preserve.

The elements and symbols that anchor this range of historical novels and tales from *The Scarlet Letter* to "Sleepy Hollow" as some mixture of nationalist and national commentary reappear in uncanny fashion in Herman Melville's *Moby-Dick* (1851). As with so many novels of the era, marriage is pivotal; but for Melville's narrator, Ishmael, the union is a homoerotic "bridegroom clasp" that identifies him as the "wife" of Queequeg, a native of the South Seas and a cannibal to boot. The father of his country appears in the novel, but in a comically distorted fashion as Ishmael muses in a way that reverses standard scientific assumptions about racial hierarchy of the day: "Queequeg was George Washington cannibalistically developed." So, too, the novel gravitates around a symbol: not a red letter, but a monstrous white whale that serves as a hideous allegory of the often unexamined and titanic force of whiteness in American psychic and political life. Melville's range in the novel is as expansive as the ocean that Ishmael and the crew sail, including critical references to slavery, Indian genocide (the naming of the boat the *Pequod* after a "now extinct" Indian tribe), and colonialism (the thorny questions about the annexation of Texas raised in the chapter "Fast Fish and Loose Fish"). Like Harriet Beecher Stowe's *Uncle Tom's Cabin* (1852) and other texts of the antebellum era, *Moby-Dick* places stress upon the "national" within national narrative. But the novel is remarkable for its ability to shift this stress to interrogate just how "narrative" works within national narrative.

Simply put, *Moby-Dick* interrogates the structure of narrative itself to ask whether stories of America and histories of the United States can come to some destined ending that would provide moral closure and political virtue. Ishmael wonders if stories, like nations, need move toward endings that resolve contradictions and put an end to the dynamic unfolding of his narrative. Beset by these doubts, Ishmael repeatedly delays the story of the *Pequod* and instead indulges in lengthy asides, character sketches, and other digressions that refuse to advance the book's plot. But the book is also driven forward by Ahab's imperious command. Clustered around the novel's struggle over narrative lie a host of questions, questions that are political in the most fundamental sense: Should the diverse voices of the sailors be subordinated to a single narrative voice? Or can the collective voices of the crew swallow up any individual perspective? What does democratic narration look like? *Moby-Dick* provides an answer – but, as with most answers that Ishmael gives us, it raises still more questions. Interpretations become multiple after Ahab nails the gold doubloon to the mast and the members of the crew successively comment on the fantastic markings on the coin. But only the cabin boy, Pip, narrates what occurs in ways that preserve this symbol as open-ended, muttering, "I look, you look, he looks; we look, ye look, they look." His conjugation of "to look" records all narrative positions without establishing a hierarchy among them. But lest a democratic national narrative appear realizable and straightforward, *Moby-Dick* reminds us that Pip is an imbecile. Is the citizen who strives to narrate national history in a democratic manner devoid of all sense? Must national history be told from a single and autocratic perspective, a perspective that eschews the ambiguities in Pip's narrative of looking?

Rebellion and Revolt

On no issue did the United States appear more autocratic and self-contradictory than on the crisis of slavery. For African American writers, this disjunction provided a treasure trove of protest and political dissent. The return to national foundations was a critical journey into the past – and, as ex-slaves discovered in autobiographical and fictional writings, that criticism could be turned against the laws, precepts, and assumptions that made bondage a fundamental part of the American poem. Unlike Cooper and others who were dismayed to learn that the repetition of national history is always a critical reiteration, black writers and orators such as William Wells Brown and Frederick Douglass were heartened by evidence of America's inconsistencies and contradictions. In an era of slavery, the story of American freedom quite simply no longer held together. Ex-slaves exploited these fractures, wedging their autobiographical accounts and stories into the space opened up in a supposedly once seamless national imaginary.

In short, slave narrative comes up against national narrative. Ex-slaves remember more than personal history when they juxtapose their sufferings under the lash against episodes from the revolutionary past – the signing of the Declaration of Independence, the pealing of the Liberty Bell, the carnage at Bunker Hill – that every schoolchild could rehearse. But they also override this juxtaposition by inscribing their personal stories *as* national history, much as Frederick Douglass sharply did by denominating himself "an American Slave" in the title of his 1845 autobiography. Family history resonated with patriotic tradition for two brothers in *Narratives of the Sufferings of Lewis and Milton Clarke* (1846), ex-slaves from Kentucky, who identified their father as a veteran of the Battle of Bunker Hill. For James Roberts, the connection to the origins of American liberty was that much closer, as his *Narrative of James Roberts, Soldier in the Revolutionary War and at the Battle of New Orleans* (1846) makes bitterly clear. Stripped of his regimentals, Roberts is forced to wear a "bare breechclout," the garb of bondage. It is as if Roberts' master confiscates this uniform because he realizes the danger of granting slaves access to potentially rebellious meanings lying in the materials of national history. After all, Nat Turner's slave revolt was originally planned for July Fourth.

While such material mementos can be impounded, the hallowed names and dates of the hallowed past are harder to control. Indeed, that legacy may be up for grabs. In one of the most sensational escapes from slavery, Ellen Craft disguised herself as a white man and fled with her husband across the Mason–Dixon line and eventually to England – to the chagrin of President James K. Polk, who urged that federal troops apprehend the couple. No less sensational was the account that William Craft published in the 1860 slave narrative, *Running a Thousand Miles for Freedom*, which freely cites passages about equality, liberty, and happiness from the Declaration of Independence. Craft's rhetorical strategy serves up escape and deception as ethical practices: "we felt perfectly justified in undertaking the dangerous and exciting task of 'running a thousand miles' in order to obtain these rights which are so vividly set forth in the Declaration." Even as the nation upholds the legality of slavery, its narrative legitimates the slave's resistance. In the same breath Craft invokes both American history and his own and his wife's personal history, purposefully confusing and tangling narratives in order to highlight the contradiction of slaves who speak about freedom.

These appeals hinge on an abiding belief that America's founding ideals remain uncompromised, that the bedrock of the country's foundation in liberty and equality is as solid as ever. If democracy can be realized, the story of America will achieve closure and the particulars – for example, the treatment and condition of black people – of the national poem, to recall Whitman's language, will not be at variance with the "essentially" broader claims about equality and liberty in the United States. For Roberts and the Crafts, adherence to the past can correct the injustices of the present. A more radical position, however, exhibits no such faith in the ultimate consistency or virtue of national origins. For William Wells Brown and Frederick Douglass, the central reference points in the founding mythos are as fractured as the "house divided" of the 1850s. Especially as they turned their hand to fiction rather than autobiographical narrative, Brown and Douglass stressed how the present *dis*articulation of national narrative is not something that occurs later down the road but is present from the outset, that is, from the birth of the American republic.

In two examples of the earliest African American fiction, Brown and Douglass revisit the legacies of Thomas Jefferson and George Washington to imply that the nation's history was split and incoherent from the start. The acutely critical nature of their literary enterprises can be imagined by returning to the experiment with the dollar bill and "The Custom House" with which we started. But in the case of fiction authored by ex-slaves the procedure is slightly different:

(1)   Turn the dollar bill so that the engraved portrait of Washington is face up.
(2)   Using both hands, pick up the dollar bill and slowly tear it in half.

The splintering of national narrative sets the plot of Brown's *Clotel; or, The President's Daughter* (1853) in motion by giving credence to rumors that Thomas Jefferson kept a slave mistress and fathered children by her. (A 1998 article from the scientific journal *Nature* presents DNA evidence in support of these allegations, which have been thrown around since the early nineteenth century. Despite these genetic findings, there remain those who are skeptical about the affair between Jefferson and Sally Hemings.) Like Irving's "Sleepy Hollow," which uses local legend and rumor to disrupt national "truths," Brown pivots off the scandalous private life of Jefferson to script a scenario that places the legally black daughter of the Declaration of Independence, as it were, on the slave auction block. Sexual history is national history: the story of America is every bit as tangled as are the bloodlines that result from miscegenation. How is it possible to narrate the history of such a nation? Coherent storytelling seems beyond possibility, and it is no coincidence that Brown's novel often reads as a fractured affair, full of disjointed chapters and a hodge-podge assortment of borrowings and citations.

What works better is a narrative strategy based on contradiction and paradox. The novel's climax finds Clotel in Washington DC, held as merchandise in a slave pen. In a daring move, she escapes and rushes across the Potomac, hoping to hide and find refuge "in the extensive forests and woodlands of the celebrated Arlington Place, occupied by the distinguished relative and descendant of the immortal Washington, Mr. George W. Custis. Thither the poor fugitive directed her flight." While Jefferson fathered slave children, Washington fathered a country but left no biological heirs, adopting Martha's children from a previous marriage and, by extension, the orphaned citizens of the new nation. Clotel intervenes at this collision of family and national history in a way that is bitterly ironic. As the blood descendant of Jefferson, Clotel is powerless to claim an inheritance of freedom; whereas Custis, only an adopted relation of Washington, has full use of the democratic past. Jefferson's legacy of independence, now embodied in the person of the quadroon slave, vainly searches for security in a false, indirect descendant of the national past. Just as the slave-catchers close in upon her, Clotel jumps to her death into the icy waters of the Potomac. The key signifiers of national narrative speak with forked tongues. "Jefferson" degenerates into a confused sign of freedom tinged with the blood of enslavement and "Washington," reduced to the single initial in Custis' name, forfeits any power to secure freedom for the hounded slave. As the first African American novel, *Clotel* inscribes national narrative as series of deathly paradoxes in which revolutionary inheritance circulates as interracial commodity and independence literally begets bondage.

While Brown pinpoints a single culprit – Jefferson – as the progenitor of narrative contradictions within the story of American freedom, Douglass levels a broader accusation in his 1853 novella "The Heroic Slave," generally regarded as the first work of African American fiction. The story begins with a dutifully patriotic reference to "the State of Virginia," often graced with the sobriquet "the mother of statesmen." But affirming reflections about Patrick Henry, George Washington, or James Madison are quickly scuttled by the more literal line of descent that originates with the slave mother. The lines of contradiction are drawn even tighter with the revelation of the hero's name: Madison Washington, the historical leader of a successful slave revolt aboard a slave brig in 1841. Even as the narrator pronounces this hero's name in all capital letters by the novella's end, Douglass never utters the name "George Washington," referencing him only through allusions to the Revolution. This rhetorical strategy leaves readers no choice but confusion in attempting to distinguish founding father from mutinous bastard. By simultaneously giving and withholding Washington's name, Douglass gives revolutionary history a dual significance, gesturing equally to statesman and to chattel. Indeed, the incendiary possibility exists that "true" American revolutionary history may, in fact, be the history of slave rebellion.

Within the novel itself, Madison Washington exploits this slippage to justify what was certainly one of the most alarming specters in the antebellum era: the spilling of white blood by black hands. He wraps himself in national narrative to legitimate revolutionary violence: "We have done that which you applaud your fathers for doing, and if we are murderers, so were they." Douglass forces the uncanny similarity between white patriot and black rebel to its logical conclusion when Madison Washington appeals to the principles of 1776 to underwrite black freedom as the slave ship is steered to the Bahamas and its "cargo" liberated. But this conclusion comes without closure, since freedom is found not in the United States but in the Caribbean. National narrative is radically estranged from its presumed geographical home; in short, American national narrative, in Douglass' hands, hardly seems national. As "The Heroic Slave" fictionalizes history, the contradictions within that history are replicated and, in Douglass' case, turned against the country whose institutions (such as slavery) purport to find legitimacy in the storied past.

In the years before the Civil War, such returns to the national past seemed both compulsive and obligatory. While patriotic historical consciousness no doubt worked to reaffirm the country's foundations, literary fictions of America and the United States also introduced an unpredictable amount of instability and doubt about that past. Literature surely imagines the nation. But we should remember that it also sets narrative against nation, placing fiction at the throat of the body politic.

REFERENCES AND FURTHER READING

Berlant, Lauren (1991). *The Anatomy of National Fantasy: Hawthorne, Utopia, and Everyday Life.* Chicago: University of Chicago Press.

Brown, William Wells (1969). *Clotel; or, The President's Daughter. A Narrative of Slave Life in the United States.* New York: Carol. (First publ. 1853.)

Castronovo, Russ (1995). *Fathering the Nation: American Genealogies of Slavery and Freedom.* Berkeley: University of California Press.

Child, Lydia Maria (1992). *Hobomok and other Writings of Indians.* New Brunswick, NJ: Rutgers University Press. (First publ. 1824.)

Clarke, Lewis, and Clarke, Milton (1846). *Narratives of the Sufferings of Lewis and Milton, Sons of a Soldier of the Revolution, During a Captivity of More Than Twenty Years among the Slaveholders of Kentucky, One of the So Called Christian States of North America.* Boston: Bela Marsh.

Cooper, James Fenimore (1958). *The Pioneers.* New York: Dodd, Mead. (First publ. 1823.)

Cooper, James Fenimore (1960). *The Spy: A Tale of Neutral Ground.* New York: Hafner. (First publ. 1821.)

Cooper, James Fenimore (1986). *The Last of the Mohicans.* New York: Viking Penguin. (First publ. 1826.)

Craft, William (1991). *Running a Thousand Miles for Freedom; or, The Escape of William and Ellen Craft from Slavery.* Salem, Mass.: Ayer. (First publ. 1860.)

Douglass, Frederick (1990). "The Heroic Slave" (first publ. 1853). In William L. Andrews (ed.), *Three Classic African-American Novels.* New York: Mentor.

Emerson, Ralph Waldo (1983). "The American Scholar" (first publ. 1837). In *Essays and Lectures,* ed. Joel Porte. New York: Library of America.

Hawthorne, Nathaniel (1980). *The Scarlet Letter.* New York: Signet. (First publ. 1850.)

Hawthorne, Nathaniel (1981). *The House of the Seven Gables.* New York: Viking. (First publ. 1851.)

Hentz, Caroline Lee Whiting (1970). *The Planter's Northern Bride.* Chapel Hill: University of North Carolina Press. (First publ. 1854.)

Irving, Washington (1989a). "The Legend of Sleepy Hollow." In Nina Baym et al. (eds.), *The Norton Anthology of American Literature,* 3rd edn., vol. 1, 822–42. New York: Norton.

Irving, Washington (1989b). "Rip Van Winkle." In Nina Baym et al. (eds.), *The Norton Anthology of American Literature,* 3rd edn., vol. 1, 810–21. New York: Norton.

Irving, Washington (1990). *The Sketch Book: The Legend of Sleepy Hollow and other Stories.* New York: Signet.

Melville, Herman (1956). *Moby-Dick or, The Whale.* Boston: Houghton Mifflin. (First publ. 1851.)

Melville, Herman (1984). "Hawthorne and his Mosses." In *Pierre, or the Ambiguities; Israel Potter, His Fifty Years of Exile; The Piazza Tales; The Confidence Man, His Masquerade; Uncollected Prose; Billy Budd, Sailor (An Inside Narrative).* New York: Library of America.

Pease, Donald E., Jr. (1987). *Visionary Compacts: American Renaissance Writings in Cultural Context.* Madison: University of Wisconsin Press.

Roberts, James (1945). *The Narrative of James Roberts, Soldier in the Revolutionary War and at the Battle of New Orleans.* Hattiesburg, Miss.: Book Farm. (First publ. 1846.)

Sedgwick, Catherine Maria (1987). *Hope Leslie; or, Early Times in the Massachusetts.* New Brunswick, NJ: Rutgers University Press. (First publ. 1827.)

Stephens, Ann S. (1929). *Malaeska; The Indian Wife of the White Hunter.* New York: John Day. (First publ. 1860.)

Stowe, Harriet Beecher (1984). *Uncle Tom's Cabin; or, Life among the Lowly.* New York: Penguin. (First publ. 1852.)

Sundquist, Eric J. (1993). *To Wake the Nations: Race in the Making of American Literature.* Cambridge, Mass.: Harvard University Press.

Whitman, Walt (1985). *Leaves of Grass.* New York: Penguin. (First publ. 1855.)

Index

Page numbers in italics refer to illustrations.

Abbott, Jacob 253, 254, 255–6, 259
abjection 170–5
"About the Tomkinses" (Cary) 396–7
Adams, Charles Hansford 228, 237
Adams, Henry 31–3
Adams, John 37
Adams, John Quincy 37, 419
Adams, William Taylor 256, 259
adoption, as theme 257–8, 293
The Adventures of Huckleberry Finn (Twain)
    Cooper's influence 34
    dialect writing 35
    folk-beliefs in 127
    male bonding 77
Africa, and slave identities 126–7
African Americans
    and American Revolution 441
    and children's fiction 251, 259
    and citizenship 57
    cultural influence 126–7
    education 98, 100, 104–5
    fictional portraits 138
    literary societies 104–5
    minstrel shows 180, 224–5
    perceived morality 278
    racial "science" 57, 370
    see also slaves and slavery
African Americans: novelists
    first extant fiction by 136, 443
    Jacobs, Harriet 45, 69, 106, 204, 237, 242
    Questy, Joanni 139–40

    Séjour, Victor 136
    Webb, Frank J. 60–1
    Wilson, Harriet 45, 69
    see also Brown, William Wells; Douglass,
        Frederick; slave narratives; slaves and slavery,
        as theme
African Free Schools 98, 104
Agamben, Giorgio 28
Agnes of Sorrento (Stowe) 57
Ahab (*Moby-Dick*) 35–6, 60
alcohol
    New York drinking places 274
    temperance movement and literature 255, 276,
        279–82
Alcott, Bronson 68, 95, 98, 254, 283
Alcott, Louisa May
    anti-slavery tales 188
    children's fiction 258, 259–60
    on motherhood 47
    sensational fiction 73, 187–8, 314–15
Alcott, William 43
Alcuin (C. B. Brown) 112–14, 317
Alencar, José de 140
Alger, Horatio 41, 70, 256, 259
The Algerine Captive (Tyler) 119–20, 155
Algerine captivity literature 119–20, 154–5
Allan, John 320, 380
allegorical stories 91
Allston, Washington 177
Allworth Abbey (Southworth) 325–6
Althusser, Louis 99

Amalia (Mármol) 140
Amativeness (Fowler) 277
"America" (Smith) 10
American Bible Society 88–9
American Board of Commissioners for Foreign
  Missions 357, 358, 361
American exceptionalism, and racial politics 57,
  170–5, 365–77, 394
American Medical Association 223
American Museum (Bennett) 159
American Register 149
American Renaissance (Matthiessen) 407
American Revolution
  and African Americans 441
  espionage during 411–12, 417–18, 421
  pacifism 417
  as theme 15, 324, 379, 411–24, 437–8
  veterans' pensions 421–2
"The American Scholar" (Emerson) 240, 435
American Shandyism (Dunlap) 162
American Temperance Union 255
American Tract Society 56–7, 88–9, 90, 91
"American way" *see* individualism
Analectic Magazine 333
anatomy 219
Les anciens Canadiens (Aubert de Gaspé) 142
Anderson, Benedict 8, 332
Anderson, Rufus 358–60, 362
André (Dunlap) 414
André, Maj. John 414, 416, 418–19, 421, 422,
  439
Andrews, William 208
Anthony, David 290
Antoinette de Mirecourt (Leprohon) 142
Anton in Amerika (Solger) 139
Apess, William 14–15
Appleby, Joyce 66
Appleton (publishing company) 133
Arnold, Benedict 416
Arnold, Clara 253
Arnold, David 222
Arthur, Timothy Shay 253, 255, 279–80, 281,
  282
Arthur Mervyn (C. B. Brown) 4, 55, 123, 217–18,
  317, 318
Asian religions, antebellum awareness of 95
Astor Place Riots (1849) 67, 183
Atlantic fiction 119–20, 154–5
Aubert de Gaspé, Philippe 142
Aubert de Gaspé, Philippe, *fils* 142

Augusta States' Rights Sentinel (newspaper) 403
Aunt Phillis's Cabin (Eastman) 369
Austin, Jane Goodwin 259
Australian fiction 389
Avellaneda, Gertrudis Gómez de 140
Averill, Charles 185
Awful Disclosures of the Hotel Dieu Nunnery
  (Monk) 57, 58, 93

Baker, Benjamin 73
Bakhtin, M. M. 35
Balibar, Etienne 28
Barde, Alexandre 136–7
Barnes, Elizabeth 160
Barnum, H. L. 413
"Bartleby the Scrivener" (Melville) 73, 297
Bass, Althea 363
Baudelaire, Charles 177
Bautée, Hypolite de ("D'Artlys") 137
"Bay Psalm Book" 87
Baym, Nina
  on Cooper 13
  on female independence 83
  on gender roles 45
  on growth in novel reading 22
  on male identity 41, 42
  on marriage 81–2
  on melodrama 193
  on women's fiction 267, 268
Beadle, Irwin 265
Beadle and Adams/Beadle Publishing
    Company 180, 181, 185, 256, 264–6
Beecher, Catherine 102, 275
Beecher, Lyman 57, 254, 395
"Behind a Mask" (Alcott) 187
Behind the Scenes (Keckley) 210
Behn, Aphra 149
'Bel of Prairie Eden (Lippard) 181, 186, 324
Bell, Samuel 407
Bellin, Joshua David 14
Beloved (Morrison) 234
Belton, John 191
Ben-Hur (Wallace) 92
Bender, Thomas 288
Beneath the American Renaissance (Reynolds) 179
Benedetti, Alessandro 225
"Benito Cereno" (Melville)
  Cuban allegories 376
  gothic aspects 168–9, 170–3, 175–6
  imagery 57

legal aspects 232–4
race 168–9, 170–3, 175–6, 365, 366, 372–5, 376–7
Benjamin, Walter 180
Bennett, Emerson 402
Bennett, Revd John 159
Benson, Egbert 411, 412, 421
Bercovitch, Sacvan 237
"Berenice" (Poe) 321
Bergland, Renee 174
Beulah (Evans) 47
Bhabha, Homi K. 11
Bhagavad-Gita 95
Bible
  Hebrew 94
  Higher Criticism 91–2
  importance to Protestants 87, 90
  publishing 89
Billy Budd (Melville) 232, 433
Bird, Robert Montgomery 14, 380–6, 392
"The Birth-mark" (Hawthorne) 218–19
"The Black Cat" (Poe) 320, 380
Black Hawk 15
Black Hawk War (1832) 390–1, 393, 394
Blackstone, William 110
Blair, Walter 401
Blake (Delany) 188
Blanche of Brandywine (Lippard) 324
Bleecker, Ann Eliza 344, 345, 346, 347–8
The Blithedale Romance (Hawthorne)
  labor in 241–2
  melodramatic elements 191, 193–4, 195–7
  reform aspects 282–3
  sources 68
Bloch, Edward 95
Bloom, Harold 322
Bloomfield, Maxwell 237
Blumin, Stuart 68
The Boarding School (Foster) 161
body
  anatomy 219
  body language 277
  contemporary attitudes 216
  literary analogies 217–25
  physiognomy and moral character 162–6, 220
Boelhower, William 55
Bolles, Albert S. 69
The Bondwoman's Narrative (Crafts) 81, 83, 84, 204–5, 208–15
Bonner, Robert 186, 198

A Book for the Home Circle (Kirkland) 308
bookselling *see* publishing and printing industry
The Border States (Kennedy) 334
Boston, as setting 291, 296
Botsford, Edmund 91
Bouis, M. Amédée 137
Bourdieu, Pierre 223
"Bowery b'hoy and g'hal" melodramas 73, 183
Bracebridge Hall (Irving) 335, 336
Brackenridge, Hugh Henry
  on class 65
  and dissimulation 162
  on female education 104
  as innovator 152–3
  on race 55
Bradbury, Osgood 291
Brainerd, David 358, 395
Brainerd School and Mission 357, 358, 360–1, 361–2
Braudel, Fernand 125
Brazilian fiction 140
Briggs, Charles Frederick 224–5
Bringhurst, Joseph, Jr. 317
Britain
  attitudes to and representations of 303–4, 333, 335–8
  literary influence on America 119–24, 148–9, 154–5, 250, 415–16, 435–6
Brodhead, Richard 194
Broken Pledges (Southworth) 327
Brook Farm community 68
  fictional portraits *see The Blithedale Romance*
Brooks, Peter 183, 192, 194, 196, 198, 201
Brotherhood of the Union 182, 324
Brown, Bill 264, 265, 266, 269–70
Brown, Catherine, memoir 358–60, 362
Brown, Charles Brockden
  and American Revolution 413, 414
  background and training 230
  British influence on 120–1
  on class 66
  contemporary popularity 122
  and the Enlightenment 230
  on fiction 149–50
  and the gothic/sensational 316, 317–19
  on government 176–7, 217–18
  and historiography 149–50, 153–4, 155
  importance 4
  as innovator 148–50, 151–2, 153–4
  and legal questions 228, 229–30

Brown, Charles Brockden (*Continued*)
  life 317, 319
  on marriage 112–15
  on Native Americans 4, 354
  publishing history 122–3
  on race 54–5
  reputation 319
  and science 218
  and sexuality 77
Brown, Charles Brockden: WORKS
  Alcuin 112–14, 317
  Arthur Mervyn 4, 55, 123, 217–18, 317, 318
  Clara Howard 120, 123
  Jane Talbot 120, 123
  "Memoirs of Carwin" 54
  Memoirs of Stephen Calvert 317
  Ormond 55, 114–15, 123, 166, 318
  "A Receipt for a Modern Romance" 318
  "A Sketch of American Literature for
    1807" 149–50
  "Sketches of the History of the Carrils and
    Ormes" 153
  see also Edgar Huntly; *Wieland*
Brown, Elijah 417
Brown, Gillian 166
Brown, William Hill *see The Power of Sympathy*
Brown, William Wells
  on class 69
  on marriage 84
  and national narratives 17–18
  on race 59–60
  see also Clotel
Brownson, Orestes 67, 93–4
Bryant, William Cullen 134
Buddhism, antebellum awareness of 95
Buffalo Bill, fictional portraits 182, 183, 266
Bullock, Stephen 160
Bulwer Lytton, Edward 122
Bumppo, Natty (Cooper character) 12, 13, 33–4,
  231, 304–6, 436–7
Bunkley, Josephine 57
Buntline, Ned (Edward Judson) 137, 181–3, 185,
  291, 388
Bunyan, John 20, 91, 249
Burdett, Charles 291
Burgett, Bruce 48
Burr, Aaron, fictional portraits 155
Burton, John 159, 160
Bushman, Richard 158
Bushnell, Horace 254

Butler, Judith 28, 171
Butler, Octavia 215

Calamity Jane (dime novel character) 266
Calavar (Bird) 382
Calisto (Testut) 137
Calvinism, Sedgwick on 352–6
The Canadian Brothers (Richardson) 141
Canadian fiction 141–2
Cannibals, All! (Fitzhugh) 194
Canonge, Louis Placide 136
capitalism
  children as wealth creators and consumers 260
  and class 66, 67
  early labor reform novels 72, 223–4, 297–8
  effect on labor 426–7
  as theme 240, 281, 291–2, 429–33
captivity narratives 269–72, 342–52
  Algerine 119–20, 154–5
Cardell, William 251
Carey, Mathew 122, 155
Caribbean, as setting 185
Caritat, Hocquet 122–4
Carl Scharnhorst (Strubburg) 139
Carleton, Cousin Mary 141
Carson, Kit 262–3
  fictional portraits 185, 263
Cary, Alice 307–9, 388, 389–90, 395–7
Cary, Phoebe 388, 395, 396
"The Cask of Amontillado" (Poe) 230, 320
Castiglia, Christopher 346, 348
Castlemon, Harry 259
Catholics and Catholicism
  anti-Catholic fiction 56–8, 93, 141
  Hall on 395
  Protestant attitudes to 275
  religious fiction 92–4
  as theme 57–8
Cawelti, John 201
Cecilia Valdés (Villaverde) 140
Cesarino, Cesare 426, 427, 428, 432
Channing, William Ellery 254
Chapman, Mary 48
"The Character of a Native Georgian"
  (Longstreet) 404
characters, fictional
  importance 33–5
  recurring charcters in dime novels 265–6
Charles Guérin (Chaveau) 142
Charlotte (Rowson) 414

Charlotte Temple (Rowson) 81, 103–4, 122, 155
Charlotte's Daughter (Rowson) 414
Chase, Richard 193
Chaveau, Pierre 142
Cherokee controversy (1829) 14
Cherokee Nation 356–64
Chesterfield, Lord, contemporary critiques
   of 158–67
Chevalier, Henri-Emile 142
Cheyfitz, Eric 363
Child, Lydia M.
  advice manuals 47, 253
  on American Revolution 15
  as children's author 251, 253–4, 257
  on cities 295–6
  on class 72
  on Edgeworth 250
  preface to Jacobs' *Incidents* 204
  on race 12–13, 14, 55, 84, 251, 437
Child, Lydia M.: WORKS
  Evenings in New England 253–4
  The First Settlers of New England 12, 14
  The Frugal Housewife 253
  The Girl's Own Book 253
  Hobomok 12–13, 55, 84, 251, 437
  Letters from New York 72, 295–6
  The Mother's Book 47, 250
  The Quadroons 207
  The Rebels 15
children
  advice books for 253–5
  advice on rearing 252–5, 259
  contemporary attitudes 252
  death statistics 258
  periodicals for 256–7
  as theme 255–6, 293
  welfare for poor 255
Children's Aid Society 255
children's fiction 249–61
Children's Magazine 257
Christmas, representations of 336–7
The Cincinnati Mirror (periodical) 388
Cincinnati oder Geheimnisse des Westens
   (Klauprecht) 139
Cincinnati writers 388–99
"Circumstance" (Spofford) 344, 346, 349
cities
  attitudes to 287–8, 302–3, 339–40
  guidebooks 289
  paintings 288

population 274
see also urban novels and themes
City Crimes (Thompson) 73
Civil War, as theme 258–9
civility, and dissimulation 158–67
Clara Howard (C. B. Brown) 120, 123
Clarissa (Richardson) 115
Clarke, Lewis and Milton 441
class
  and capitalism 66, 67
  civility and upward mobility 158–67
  contemporary definitions 64–5
  and culture 223, 224–5
  and democracy 66
  middle-class gentility as theme 307–9
  rise of middle 64, 66, 68
  and the rural landscape 303
  and social unrest 65, 67
  as theme 65–6, 69–74, 142, 185, 194
  see also labor
Clemens, Samuel Langhorne *see* Twain, Mark
Clinch, Charles P. 412
Clinton, DeWitt 419
Clotel (W. W. Brown)
  class 69
  conclusion 81
  as fictionalized slave narrative 204–15
  as national narrative 17–18, 442–3
  race 59–60
  sensational elements 188
Cloud, Enoch 427
Clovernook (Cary) 307–9, 395–7
Cody, Buffalo Bill *see* Buffalo Bill
Coffin, Charles Carleton 259
Coggeshall, William T. 398
Cohen, Hennig 345
Cole, Thomas 301, 305
Coleridge, Samuel Taylor 33
Collins, Maria 388
Columbus, Christopher 335
commodities *see* consumerism
The Communist Manifesto (Marx and Engels) 67
Compromise Bill (1850) 17, 57, 367
Condorcet, Antoine-Nicolas de 301
The Confidence-Man (Melville) 61–2, 297,
  390
The Conflict between Labor and Capital (Bolles) 69
Confucianism, antebellum awareness of 95
Conquest of Granada (Irving) 154
conservatism 332–40

consumerism
  children as wealth creators and consumers 260
  commodities as theme 128–9
  and Kirkland 312
  materialism in urban novels 293
  reactions against 331–40
  see also capitalism
The Contrast (Tyler) 155, 162, 288
The Convent's Doom (Frothingham) 57
Cooke, Rose Terry 76
Cooper, James 422
Cooper, James Fenimore
  on American Revolution 15
  as children's author 251
  and democracy 419–21
  democratic heroes 33–4
  influences on 392
  as inventor of American novel 411–24
  and the law 231, 236–7
  and male bonding 77
  on marriage 437–8
  and melodrama 193
  on miscegenation 84–5
  on moral values 418
  and national narratives 436–7, 437–8
  on nationhood 7
  and politics 38, 419
  on race 12, 13, 28, 55–6, 436–7
  and stadialist social theory 304–6
Cooper, James Fenimore: WORKS
  The Deerslayer 12
  The Last of the Mohicans 12, 13, 55, 77, 84–5,
    436–7
  Leatherstocking novels 12, 13, 33–4, 231,
    251, 436–7
  Lionel Lincoln 15, 109
  Littlepage trilogy 305
  The Pathfinder 12
  The Prairie 12, 55, 305–6
  Precaution 413
  Redskins 305
  The Spy 15, 411–24, 437–8
  see also The Pioneers
Copway, George 15
The Coquette (Foster) 42–3, 81, 110–11, 162–5
corporal punishment, for children 254
corruption, as theme *see* urban novels and themes
Corwin, Thomas 398
Cory, Oliver 422
Cott, Nancy 43, 82

Le Courrier de la Louisiane 136–7
The Course of Empire (paintings; Cole) 301, 305
Cowie, Alexander 386
Craft, Ellen 49–50, 207–8, 441
Craft, William 49–50, 207–8, 240, 441
Crafts, Hannah 81, 83, 84, 204–5, 208–15
Crane, Gregg 235, 237
Cray, Robert 421
Creole fiction 136–7, 139–40
Crèvecœur, J. Hector St. John de *see Letters from an
    American Farmer*
crime and punishment
  sex crimes 76
  see also law and legal questions
Cronon, William 363
Crosby, Enoch 411–13, 417, 418–19, 422
Cross-Examinations of Law and Literature
    (Thomas) 237
Cuba
  Cuban fiction 140
  literary allusions to 376
Cudjo's Cave (Trowbridge) 259
Cummins, Maria
  rural themes 310–11
  see also The Lamplighter
Cunningham, Noble E., Jr. 26
Curry, Orway 395
Cushing, Eliza 15
Cusick, David (Tuscarora) 14
"The Custom House" (Hawthorne) 283

"Daddy Biggs' Scrape at Cockrell's Bend"
    (Hooper) 406
Dahl, Curtis 385
Dall, Caroline 48
Dana, Charles 398
Dana, Henry, Sr. 177
Dana, Richard Henry, Sr. 319
"The Dance" (Longstreet) 403, 404
"D'Artlys" *see* Bautée, Hypolite de
Darwin, Charles, influence 259–60
Darwin, Erasmus 160
Davidson, Cathy N. 21, 38, 363
Davis, Rebecca Harding 72, 223–4, 297–8
Dayan, Joan 174, 177
Deadwood Dick novels 265–6
death
  Catherine Brown's envisaging of own 362
  Sedgwick on 355–6
"The Debating Society" (Longstreet) 403

deception, and civility 158–67
The Declaration of Independence 7, 8, 24
The Deerslayer (Cooper) 12
"Defence of Fort McHenry" (Scott) 10
Defoe, Daniel 20, 121, 149
Delano, Amasa 168
Delany, Martin 188
Deloria, Philip 357
democracy
  Adams on 37
  and class 66
  and Cooper 419–21
  definitions 37
  democratic heroes 33–5
  feared lack of discrimination in 21–8
  and fiction 20–39
  and Hawthorne 237
  history of 38
  Irving on 22, 438–9
  and the local 354
  Madison on 217
  Melville on 237, 327, 432–3, 439–40
  opening up of franchise 66
  representation's implications 23
  Stowe on 369
  as theme 31–3, 237
  vulnerability 175–7, 237
  Young America movement 38
Democracy (Adams) 31–3
Democracy (Didion) 38
Democracy in America (de Tocqueville) 82, 240
Democratic Party 33–4, 67
Denning, Michael 179, 181, 183, 292, 316, 327
Derounian-Stodola, Kathryn Zabelle 345
Derrida, Jacques 28
detective stories 289–90
  see also mysteries, urban
Dew, Thomas 383–4
dialect writing
  in Cooper 56
  in Harris 408
  in Melville 36
  in Stowe 35
  in Twain 35
Dickens, Charles 38
Dickinson, Emily 177, 350
dictionaries
  Webster's Dictionary 9, 55
Didion, Joan 38
dime novels 180, 181, 185, 256, 262–73

Dimock, Wai Chee 221, 237
dissimulation, and civility 158–67
*The Diverting History of John Bull and Brother
  Jonathan* (Paulding) 333
divorce 113–14, 116
doctors
  fictional portraits 216–25
  reputation 222–3, 225
  training 218
Dodge, Mary Mapes 257
Dog and Gun (Hooper) 407
Domestic Education (Humphrey) 254
domestic manuals 43, 47, 253
domesticity and domestic fiction
  attitudes to 306–7
  in captivity narratives 342–52
  and colonial writers 389–90
  on the frontier 395–7
  Southworth's gothic undercutting 325–7
  see also families
Dora Darling (Austin) 259
Dorsey, Anna 94
Douglas, Ann 47
Douglass, Frederick
  autobiography 16, 42, 48, 106, 212, 242, 440–1
  on class 69
  education 105–6
  on gender roles 42
  on nationalism 443
  rhetorical devices 48
  on Stowe 368
  and US–Mexican War 17
  see also "The Heroic Slave"
Downing, Andrew Jackson 302, 303,
  304, 307
Drake, Benjamin 388, 393
Drake, Daniel 389
Dred (Stowe) 234–6, 237, 366, 368–9, 371–2,
  375–6
Dred Scott decision (1857) 57
Dreiser, Theodore 287
Drinker, Henry 417
Drinnon, Richard 390
The Drummer Boy (Trowbridge) 259
duCille, Ann 205
Duganne, A. J. H. 183
Dumont, Alice 388
Dunlap, William 162, 413–14
Dupin tales (Poe) 290
The Dutchman's Daughter (Gallagher) 388

The Dutchman's Fireside (Paulding) 331–2,
      339–40
Duyckinck, Charles and Evert 398
Dwight, Timothy 89, 416, 417

East Alabamian (newspaper) 406
Eastman, Mary 369
economy 66
Edgar Huntly (C. B. Brown)
   on American virtue 55, 66
   as captivity story 345
   gothic/sensational aspects 318–19
   medical themes 317
   preface 120
   publishing history 123
   race 55
   as satire 4, 302
Edgeworth, Maria 250
education 97–107
   African Americans 98, 100, 104–5
   children's didactic literature 252
   within the family 252–5, 259
   Native Americans 357, 358–62
   slaves 104, 105–6
   as theme 48, 103–4
   women 98, 100–4
Edwards, Jonathan 250
Edwards, Justin 174
"Elegant Tom Dillar" (Briggs) 224–5
"Eleonora" (Poe) 321
Eliot, John 14
Ellis, Edward Sylvester 256, 269–72
Elster, Jon 68
Emerson, Ralph Waldo
   on cities 295
   on egotism 432
   and Hawthorne 2
   on labor 240
   and the law 237
   and nationalism 435–6
   and Ossian 333
   and reform 275–6, 283
   and religion 95
Emery, Allan 376
The Emigrants (Imlay) 303–4
Emily the Beautiful Seamstress (anon.) 291
empire *see* imperialism
The Empire City (Lippard) 291, 323–4
"Endicott and the Red Cross" (Hawthorne) 44
Engels, Friedrich 67

England *see* Britain
Enlightenment
   and C. B. Brown 230
   and the gothic 175
Eoline (Hentz) 240
Ernest Linwood (Hentz) 245
"Essay on Female Education" (Rowson) 104
*Essay on the Life of the Honourable Major-General
      Israel Putnam* (Humphreys) 150–1
ethnicity
   American ethnic composition 8, 55
   ethnic origins and nationhood 52–6, 57–63
   see also race
"Eulogy on King Philip" (Apess) 15
Evans, Augusta J. 46–7
Evans, Sara M. 101
Evenings in New England (Child) 253–4
Everett, Edward 88
The Executioner's Song (Mailer) 235

Facing West (Drinnon) 390
factories *see* labor
Fahs, Alice 259
"The Fall of the House of Usher" (Poe) 77, 321,
      380
Falls of the Kaaterskill (painting; Cole) 305
families, child-rearing 252–5, 259
families, as theme
   in sentimental novels 245–7, 257, 325–7
   in slave narratives 245
   urban novels 292
   see also domesticity and domestic fiction
"Fantômes" (Canonge) 136
Faragher, John Mack 392
Farnham, Eliza 389, 396
The Fatal Marriage (Southworth) 325–6
Faulkner, William 402, 407
Federalist Papers 102
Female Depravity (Bradbury) 291
The Female Quixote (Lennox) 152
Female Quixotism (Tenney) 152, 161–2
Ferguson, Robert 234, 237
Fern, Fanny (Sarah Payson Willis Parton)
   newspaper sketches 293–4
   see also Ruth Hall
Fern Leaves from Fanny's Port-Folio (Fern) 71,
      294
Ferraro, Thomas J. 53
Fetterley, Judith 396
feuilletons 133, 135–6

fiction
  C. B. Brown on 149–50
  as corrupting influence 80–1, 89–92, 102–3,
    160–2
  and democracy 20–39
  early experimentation 147–57
  as education 102–4
  feared lack of discrimination 21–3
  first extant African-American novel 136, 443
  first histories of American literature 398
  first novel published in America 301
  Franklin on 20–1
  growth in reading 119
  as guide to understanding life 160
  historiographical origins 147–8
  overseas influence on 119–30, 148–9, 154–5,
    250, 415–16, 435–6
  reformers on 281–2
Fiedler, Leslie 4, 77–80, 84–5, 174, 292
Field, Joseph M. 401
Fielding, Henry 121, 149
Fifteen Minutes around New York (Foster) 289
"The Fight" (Longstreet) 404
Fillmore, Millard 334
Fink, Mike, fictional portraits 400–2
The First Settlers of New England (Child) 12, 14
Fisher, Philip 287, 298
Fiske, Nathan 160–1
Fitzhugh, George 194, 383–4
Fleming, Mary Early 141
Fliegelman, Jay 108, 177, 230, 237
Flint, Timothy 306–7, 389, 390
folk-beliefs and folk-tales
  in fiction 127, 349
  folkloric themes 333–40
  and conservatism 333
Ford, John 262
Forrest, Edwin 192
Foster, Francis Smith 214
Foster, George 73, 289, 290
Foster, Hannah Webster 42–3, 81, 110–11, 161,
  162–5
  see also The Coquette
Foster, Henri 183
Foucault, Michel 76, 78, 79, 175, 176–7
Fourier, Charles 68, 241
Fowler, O. S. 277
franchise, opening up of 66
Franconia series (Abbott) 256
Frank on a Gunboat (Castlemon) 259

Frank's Campaign (Alger) 259
Franklin, Benjamin
  Autobiography 41, 69
  on fiction 20–1
  as publisher 88, 121
  "Sidi Mehemet Ibrahim" 155
  works for children 250
Franklin Evans (Whitman) 280–1
Fredrickson, George 60, 370
freedom, as theme
  captivity narratives 342–52
French-language fiction 136–7, 139–40, 142
Freud, Sigmund 84
Friendly Club 120, 317
Fries Rebellion 152
"Frontier Democracy and Representational
  Management" (Nelson) 354–5
frontier life, as theme 303–11, 339–40, 342–52,
  389–90
  see also Cooper, James Fenimore; Southwest, as
    setting; West, as setting
Frothingham, Charles 57
The Frugal Housewife (Child) 253
Fruitlands 68
Frye, Northrop 147

Gage, Francis 49
Galen 225
Gallagher, William Davis 388–9, 396, 397–8
Gardner, Jared 53, 173
The Garies and their Friends (Webb) 60–1
Garland, Hamlin 396
Garner, Margaret 234
Garrison, William Lloyd 368, 378
The Gay Girls of New York (Thompson) 184
Gayarré, Charles 137
Die Geheimnisse von New-Orleans
  (Reizenstein) 137–9
Gellner, Ernest 332–3
gender
  captivity narratives 345–6, 347–8
  children's literature 251, 253, 258–9
  dime novels 267–9
  in Fern 293–4
  and marriage 109–15
  melodrama 192–4, 195–7, 197–200
  in Paulding 339
  and race 49–50
  roles 40–51
  Rowson on 155

gender (*Continued*)
  sensational fiction 183, 184, 186, 187
  types of fiction for each gender 267, 292
"The Gentle Boy" (Hawthorne) 258
Gentle Measures in the Management and Training of the Young (Abbott) 259
George Balcombe (Tucker) 16
George Mason (Flint) 306–7
Georgia Scenes (Longstreet) 402–5
German-language fiction 137–9
Gerry, Elbridge 22
Gerstäcker, Friedrich 139
Giddens, Anthony 64
Giffen, Allison 345
Gilman, Caroline 16
Ginsberg, Lesley 174
Ginzberg, Lori 48
The Girl's Own Book (Child) 253
The Gladiator (Bird) 381
A Glance at New York (Greene) 289
A Glance at New York in 1848 (Baker) 73
Glazener, Nancy 226
Gliddon, George R. 57
Goddu, Teresa 173, 174, 217
Godey's Lady's Book 47
Godwin, William 112, 113, 114
"The Gold-Bug" (Poe) 380, 382
Gómez-Peña, Guillermo 131
Goodrich, Samuel G. 182, 250, 257, 420
gothic tropes 168–78, 314–29
  and counter-narratives 169–70
  distinction from sensational 315–17
  list of writers 177
  and sexuality 77–8
The Governess (Miles) 94
government
  American fears of democracy 21–8
  American hatred of monarchism 25–6
  C. B. Brown on 176–7, 217–18
  Madison on 217
  nation as body 217–18
  opening up of franchise 66
  see also democracy
Greeley, Robert 293
Greenblatt, Stephen 346
Greene, Asa 289
Grimes, William 16
Grimsted, David 191, 192–3, 203
Griswold, Rufus 398
Groot, Petrus 342–5, 346

Grossberg, Michael 108, 109
guidebooks, urban 289
Guy Rivers (Simms) 379

Hadley, Elaine 191, 192, 194, 201–2
Hagenbuchle, Roland 230
Haitian Revolution 128, 155
Hale, Sarah Josepha 47, 257
Half Horse, Half Alligator (Blair and Meine) 401
Hall, James 389–95
Halttunen, Karen 68, 158, 297
Hamilton, Dr Alexander 147
Hammond, Gov. James 384, 385
The Happy Family (Cardell) 251
Harper & Brothers 88, 122
Harris, George Washington 407–9
Harris, Joel Chandler 368
Harris, Sharon M. 43
Hart, Julia Beckwith 141
Hartog, Hendrik 116
The Haunted Homestead (Southworth) 325, 327
Hawks of Hawk-Hollow (Bird) 382
Hawthorne, Nathaniel
  and Catholicism 57
  on children 258
  on cities 296–7
  and democracy 237
  democratic heroes in 34
  and Emerson 2
  on labor 241–2
  and the law 230–1, 237
  on marriage 437
  and medicine 218–20
  and melodrama 191, 193–4, 195–7
  and Melville 327
  on national identity 174–5
  and national narratives 17–18, 434–5
  on Native Americans 11–12
  persistence of popularity 2–3
  on politics 28
  on race 59
  on reform 282–3
  and sensational literature 316
  and set-pieces 195
  on sexuality 78, 79
  on utopian socialism 68, 241
  and Young America movement 38
Hawthorne, Nathaniel: WORKS
  "The Birth-mark" 218–19
  "The Custom House" 283

"Endicott and the Red Cross" 44
"The Gentle Boy" 258
The Marble Faun 57, 174–5
"The May-Pole of Merry Mount" 79
"My Kinsman Major Molineux" 15, 411–24, 437–8
"The New Adam and Eve" 296
"Rappaccini's Daughter" 78, 219–20
"Roger Malvin's Burial" 11–12
see also The Blithedale Romance; The House of the Seven Gables; The Scarlet Letter
"Hawthorne and his Mosses" (Melville) 435
A Hazard of New Fortunes (Howells) 65
Heberton, Mahlon 184
Hedges, William L. 11
Hemings, Sally 206, 442
Hendler, Glenn 48
Hentz, Caroline Lee
  episodic nature of works 389
  family themes 245
  first editor 388
  on labor 240
  The Planter's Northern Bride 46, 366, 369–71, 374–5, 437
Heredia, José María 134
heroes, democratic 33–5
"The Heroic Slave" (Douglass) 16, 42, 48, 69, 443
The Hesperian (periodical) 388
Hiawatha (Longfellow) 271
Hickock, "Wild Bill", fictional portraits 266
The Hidden Hand (Southworth)
  legal aspects 228, 231–2
  melodramatic elements 191–2, 197, 198–200
  sensational aspects 187
  treatment of women 81, 325, 326
Higginson, Thomas Wentworth 169
High Times and Hard Times (Harris) 409
Hinduism, antebellum awareness of 95
An Historical and Geographical Account of Algiers (Stevens) 155
historical fiction
  Avencar 140
  Canadian 141–2
  for children 251
  and conservatism 333
  and historiography 151–3
  Jicoténcal 134–5
  Kennedy 334, 338
  Lippard 324

national narratives 7–19, 330–41, 434–44
  Paulding 339–40
  Simms 379
  Testut 137
  see also Child, Lydia Maria; Cooper, James Fenimore; *The Scarlet Letter*; Sedgwick, Catharine Maria; Stephens, Ann Sophia
historiography
  C. B. Brown on 149–50, 153–4, 155
  and fiction 147–57
"A History of the Indian Tribes of North America" (Hall and McKenney) 390
"The History of Maria Kittle" (Bleecker) 344, 345, 346, 347–8
History of New York (Irving) 154
History of Pennsylvania (Proud) 151–2
History of the Tuesday Club (Hamilton) 147
Hitchcock, Enos 22
Hobomok (Child) 12–13, 55, 84, 251, 437
Hobsbawm, Eric 9
Holmes, Mary Jane 245
Home (Sedgwick) 254
homosexuality
  contemporary views 76
  and minstrel shows 226
  as theme 77–9, 184, 281, 432, 439
Hood, Thomas 194
Hooker, Worthington 223
Hooper, Johnson Jones 405–7
Hope Leslie (Sedgwick)
  as captivity story 345
  as children's work 251
  marriage in 81, 83
  race 13–14, 55, 84–5, 437
Hopkinson, Francis 151
Horse-Shoe Robinson (Kennedy) 15, 334, 338
"The Horse Swap" (Longstreet) 404
Horwitz, Milton J. 109
"An Hour" (Alcott) 188
The House Breaker (Thompson) 184, 185
The House of the Seven Gables (Hawthorne)
  Clifford's character 283
  conclusion 81
  gothic and sensational elements 174, 188
  hero 34
  legal aspects 237
  on marriage 437
  melodramatic elements 193–4
  as national narrative 17–18
  race 59

How the Other Half Lives (Riis) 72
"How to Write a Blackwood's Article"
   (Poe) 320–1
Howells, William Dean 65
Huckleberry Finn (Twain) *see The Adventures of*
   Huckleberry Finn
Hughs, Mary 93–4
Humphrey, Heman 254
Humphreys, David 150–1
Huntington, Jedediah Vincent 94

identity
   and abjection 170–5
   in captivity narratives 346
   national *see* nationhood
   and self-narration 348, 351
   white identity and Native Americans 357
Imlay, Gilbert 303–4
immigrants, attitudes to 59, 278
"The Imp of the Perverse" (Poe) 320
imperialism
   imperial adventure fiction 185–6
   and racial politics 375–7
incest, as theme 23–9, 77, 255
Incidents in the Life of a Slave Girl (Jacobs) 45, 69,
   106, 204, 237, 242
Incidents of the Insurrection (Brackenridge) 153
India (Southworth) 310, 327
"The Indian Hater" (Hall) 391–2
Indian Jim (Ellis) 269–72
indigeneity, as theme 352–8
individualism
   and children's fiction 256
   and the law 231, 236–7
   and romantic love 81
   as theme 41–2, 69–71
industry *see* capitalism; labor
The Infidel (Bird) 382
L'influence d'un livre (Aubert de Gaspé *fils*) 142
Ingraham, Joseph Holt 92
insurgency, as theme 152
Iracema (Alencar) 140
Irish
   as influence 126, 127
   as theme 55, 60
Iroquois Confederacy 14
Irving, Washington
   and American Revolution 415–16,
   438–9
   British influence 415–16

on captivity and freedom 344, 346, 348–9,
   351
on class 69
conservatism 331–3, 335–7
as innovator 154
life 330–1, 334–5
on marriage 111
and nationalism 438–9
on popular politics 22, 438–9
on race 10–11
reputation 331
Irving, Washington: WORKS
   Bracebridge Hall 335, 336
   Conquest of Granada 154
   History of New York 154
   "The Legend of Sleepy Hollow" 10, 335–6,
     415–16, 439
   "Philip of Pokanoket" 10–11
   Salmagundi (with Paulding) 331, 333
   "Traits of Indian Character" 10–11
   "The Wife" 111
   see also "Rip Van Winkle"; *The Sketch-book of*
     Geoffrey Crayon
Isaacs, Jorge 140
Ishmael (Bible) 38–9
Ishmael (*Moby-Dick*) 35, 36
Ishmael (Southworth) 232, 237, 240
Islam, allusions to 95
Israel Potter (Melville) 72

Jack Halyard (Cardell) 251
Jackson, Andrew 14, 33, 382, 419
Jacobs, Harriet 45, 69, 106, 204, 237, 242
James, C. L. R. 36
James, Henry 260
Jane Talbot (C. B. Brown) 120, 123
Jay, John 23, 412, 417, 418
Jay, William 411–12
Jefferson, Thomas
   and agrarian republicanism 288
   on American virtue 66
   and C. B. Brown 120
   and crime and punishment 76
   and Declaration of Independence 7
   fictional portraits 60, 206, 324
   on human progress 302
   on labor 239
   on monarchical intermarriage 25–6
   on novel-reading 23
   and slaves 60, 206, 442

Jemison, Mary 14
Jesus Christ, fictional portraits 92
Jewish publishing 94–5
Jicoténcal (*Xicoténcatl*; anon.) 134–5
Jo's Boys (Alcott) 260
Joaquín Murieta (Ridge) 17–18, 185
"The Jockey Cap" (early version of *Malaeska*;
    Stephens) 267–8
Joy, T. M., paintings by *182*
Judson, Edward *see* Buntline, Ned
The Jungle (Sinclair) 65
The Juvenile Keepsake (ed. Arnold) *253*
The Juvenile Miscellany (ed. Child) 257

Kaestle, Carl 100, 104
Kansas–Nebraska Act (1854) 57
Kaplan, Amy 375
Karcher, Carolyn L. 12, 234, 366
Kasson, George 289
Kavanagh, James 233
Keckley, Elizabeth 210
Kelley, Mary 194
Kelley, Wyn 297
Kellogg, Elijah 391
Kennedy, John Pendleton 15–16, 330–5, 337–8
Kerber, Linda 110
Key, Frances Scott 9–10
The Key to Uncle Tom's Cabin (Stowe) 234
King, Charles 412
King Philip's war, as theme 12
Kinmont, Alexander 370
kinship, and democracy 25–8
The Kinsmen (Simms) 15
Kirkland, Caroline 307, 308, 396
Klauprecht, Emil 139
Know-Nothings 57
Kolodny, Annette 292, 310, 395
Kristeva, Julia 170–1
Kutzinski, Vera 132

labor
    early reform novels 72, 223–4, 297–8
    Lippard and labor reform 182, 278–9, 291
    rise of capitalism 66–7
    as theme 239–48, 429–33
    whaling industry 426–7
    and women 48, 101, 245
"The Laboring Classes" (Brownson) 67
Lacombe, Patrice 142
Ladies' Companion (periodical) 268

The Lamplighter (Cummins)
    class 70
    family in 245, 257–8, 292
    gender 48
    labor in 240
    race 59
    religious elements 48, 92
Lane, Charles 68
Lane, William 122, 123
Langdon, John 25
languages, attitudes to non-English 133
"Languages of What Is Now the United States"
    project 132
"The Last of the Boatmen" (Neville) 400–1, 402
The Last of the Mohicans (Cooper) 12, 13, 55, 77,
    84–5, 436–7
The Last of the Roman Tribunes (Bulwer
    Lytton) 122
Latin American fiction 140
Law and American Literature (Smith, McWilliams,
    and Bloomfield) 237
law and legal questions, as theme 228–38
Law and Letters in American Fiction
    (Ferguson) 234, 237
Law Miscellanies (Brackenridge) 153
Lawson, Henry 389
The Lay of the Scottish Fiddle (Paulding) 333
Leatherstocking novels (Cooper) 12, 13, 33–4,
    231, 251, 436–7
    see also individual novels by name
Leaves of Grass (Whitman) 298–9, 435, 436
Leeser, Isaac 94–5
Lefort, Claude 28
"The Legend of Sleepy Hollow" (Irving) 10,
    335–6, 415–16, 439
    see also The Sketch-book of Geoffrey Crayon
Legends of Mexico (Lippard) 181, 186, 324
'Lena Rivers (Holmes) 245
Lennox, Charlotte 152
Leprohon, Rosanna Mullins 142
Letters from an American Farmer (Crèvecœur)
    on American character and identity 42, 53–4,
    66
    innovatory aspects 147
    on labor 239–40
    on slavery 173
Letters from New York (Child) 72, 295–6
Letters to Mothers (Sigourney) 254
Levernier, James 345
Levine, Robert S. 9, 368

Lewis, Jan 108, 166
Liberator (periodical) 378
libraries
    circulating 119, 122
    society 21
The Life and Adventures of Black Hawk (Drake) 393
The Life and Adventures of Joaquín Murieta
        (Ridge) 17–18, 185
Life in Prairie Land (Farnham) 396
"Life in the Iron Mills" (Davis) 72, 223–4, 297–8
The Life of the Mind in America (Miller) 237
"Ligeia" (Poe) 78, 321
Lilla Hart (Burdett) 291
Lincoln, Abraham 46, 272, 368
The Linwoods (Sedgwick) 15, 111
Lionel Lincoln (Cooper) 15, 109
Lippard, George
    on C. B. Brown 319
    on fiction 281
    gothic/sensational aspects 322–4
    life and career 181, 182, 183, 322
    popularity 182, 183
    publishers of works 187
    and reform 182, 278–9, 291
    urban novels 290, 291–2, 323
    war novels 186
    *see also The Quaker City; or, The Monks of Monk
        Hall*
literacy
    in New England 119
    in seventeenth century 87
    slaves 105, 210, 244
    women 88
literary societies, African-American 104–5
The Little Drummer Boy (Trowbridge) 259
Little Men (Alcott) 259–60
"The Little Pauper" (Fern) *294*
A Little Pretty Pocket-Book 249–50
The Little Ragged Ten Thousand (Skinner) 293
Little Women (Alcott) 187, 258, 314–15
Littlepage trilogy (Cooper) 305
Locke, John 252
Lolita (Nabokov) 229
Longfellow, Henry Wadsworth 271
Longstreet, Augustus Baldwin 402–5
Lott, Eric 191, 226
L'Ouverture, Toussaint 105
Love and Death in the American Novel
        (Fiedler) 77–80, 84–5
Lovejoy, Elijah 234

Lovell's Folly (Hentz) 369
Lukács, Georg 148, 333

"M.L." (Alcott) 188
Mabel Vaughan (Cummins) 310–11
Macaria (Evans) 46–7
Macedo, Joaquim Manuel de 140
Machiavelli, Niccoló 154
McBride, Dwight 205
McConachie, Bruce 191
McDowell, James 169
McHenry, Elizabeth 104
McIntosh, Maria 240, 245
McKenney, Thomas 390
McKenzie, Clarence 259
Mackenzie, Henry 121
McMurtry, Larry 262
Macpherson, James 333
McWilliams, John P. 237
Madison, James 217
Magnalia Christi Americana (Mather) 361
Mailer, Norman 235
Malaeska (Stephens) 256, 263, 267–9, 272, 437
"Mama's Baby, Papa's Maybe" (Spillers) 84
"The Man of the Crowd" (Poe) 188, 289–90
"The Man That Was Used Up" (Poe) 129, 380
The Man Who Shot Liberty Valance (film) 262
Mann, Horace 99
The Marble Faun (Hawthorne) 57, 174–5
Marcus Warland (Hentz) 240, 369
Mardi (Melville) 237, 425
Margret Howth (Davis) 297–8
Maria (Isaacs) 140
"Maria Kittle" (Bleecker) 344, 345, 346, 347–8
Maria ou a menina rouhada (Sousa) 140
Mármol, José 140
Marr, Timothy 55
marriage
    contemporary attitudes 108–18
    and slavery 83–4
    as theme 4, 79–84, 110–15, 155, 437–8
Marshall, John 9
Martin, Robert K. 174, 221
Martin Faber (Simms) 379
Marvel, Ik 82
Marx, Karl 67, 427
"Mary Had a Little Lamb" (Hale) 257
mass media, origins 88–9
Master William Mitten (Longstreet) 405
materialism *see* consumerism

Mather, Cotton 361
Mathews, Cornelius 73, 289
Matthiessen, F. O. 38, 407
"The May-Pole of Merry Mount" (Hawthorne) 79
Mechanic Accents (Denning) 179, 181, 183
medicine 216, 218, 219, 220, 222–3
   medical analogies and portraits 216–25
   as theme 317
Meine, Franklin J. 401
melodrama 191–203
   "Bowery b'hoy and g'hal" melodramas 73, 183
   characteristics 192
   sensational fiction as form of 180
   see also sensational fiction
Melville, Herman
   on capitalism 429–33
   on Catholicism 57
   on cities 297
   on class 69, 72
   and democracy 237, 327, 432–3, 439–40
   and democratic representation 35–7
   on Hall 390
   and Hawthorne 327
   on human interaction 425–33
   Islam, knowledge of 95
   on labor 240, 241, 242, 429–33
   and the law 232–4, 237
   and male bonding 77
   and medicine 220–2
   and melodrama 193, 197
   narrators in 35–6
   and national narratives 17–18, 439–40
   and nationalism 435–6
   persistence of popularity 3
   on politics and incest 28, 77
   on race 52–3, 61–2, 168–9, 170–3, 175–6, 232–4, 365, 366, 372–5, 376–7
   on slavery 168–9, 170–3, 175–6
   on urban life 73
   and Young America movement 38
Melville, Herman: WORKS
   "Bartleby the Scrivener" 73, 297
   Billy Budd 232, 433
   The Confidence-Man 61–2, 297, 390
   "Hawthorne and his Mosses" 435
   Israel Potter 72
   Mardi 237, 425
   Oomo 425
   "The Paradise of Bachelors and Tartarus of Maids" 240, 299

Redburn 72, 297, 425
Typee 425
White-Jacket 220–2, 241, 425
   see also "Benito Cereno"; *Moby-Dick*; *Pierre*
"Memoirs of Carwin" (C. B. Brown) 54
Memoirs of Stephen Calvert (C. B. Brown) 317
Memoirs of the Bloomgrove Family (Hitchcock) 22
men
   and captivity narratives 345–6, 347–8
   male death anxiety and women 321
   and marriage 109–15
   models in melodrama 192–4, 198
   models in Paulding 339
   models in sensational fiction 184, 186
   roles and identity 41–2, 46, 49–50
   use of feminine rhetorical devices 48
   see also gender; male bonding (*under Adventures of Huckleberry Finn*; Cooper; Melville; *Moby-Dick*; Twain)
Mencken, H. L. 132
Mercer, Singleton 184
Mercier, Alfred 136
mesmerism 195
Metacomet *see* Philip, King
Mexican War (1846–8) *see* US–Mexican War
Mexico
   fictional portraits 134–5, 181–2, 186, 187
   publishing in 87, 135
"Mike Fink: A Legend of the Ohio" (Bennett) 402
"Mike Fink: The Last of the Boatmen" (anon.) 402
"Mike Fink: The Last of the Boatmen" (Field) 401
"Mike Fink: The Ohio Boatman" (anon.) 402
Mikesell, Marvin 392
Miles, George Henry 94
"The Militia Company Drill" (Prince) 404
Miller, Perry 10, 237, 288
Miller, Revd. Samuel 21, 161
Minerva Press 122, 123, 124
Minhag America (prayer books) 95
minstrel shows 180, 224–5
miscegenation, as theme 13–14, 84–5, 138, 251, 436–8
Miss Bunkley's Book: The Testimony of an Escaped Novice from the Sisterhood of Charity (Bunkley) 57
Missouri Compromise (1820) 9
Mitford, Bertram 389

Moby-Dick (Melville) 425–33
  class 69
  on democracy 237, 432–3
  Islam, allusions to 95
  labor in 241, 429–33
  male bonding 77, 425–33
  as national narrative 17–18, 439–40
  persistence of popularity 3
  politics of 128
  representation in 35–7
  sources 427
Modern Chivalry (Brackenridge) 55, 65, 152–3
monarchism, Jefferson on 25–6
Monk, Maria 57, 58, 93
The Monks of Monk Hall (Lippard) 57, 73, 181,
    182, 183, 184, 278–9, 281, 291–2
Monroe, James 421
"Monsieur Paul" (Quisty) 139–40
Montréal, publishing in 141, 142
Moore, Clement 336
Moral Tales (Edgeworth) 250
moral values
  and authorial persistence 2–3
  and children's fiction 249–60
  civility and dissimulation 158–67
  Cooper on 418
  corrupting influence of fiction 80–1, 89–92,
    102–3, 160–2
  early novels 23–9
  and melodrama 194–5, 200
  phrenology as proof of 276
  physiognomy as proof of 162–6, 220
  reform movements 274–84
  sexual discipline 76
  urbanism and migration's influence 274
  women and sex 76, 78, 81
Moredock, Col. John, fictional portraits 391–4
A moreninha (Macedo) 140
Moretti, Franco 150, 196
Morgan, John 223
The Morgesons (Stoddard) 81
Morrison, Paul 80
Morrison, Toni 173, 215, 234
The Mother's Book (Child) 47, 250
The Mother-in-Law (Southworth) 326
motherhood 254
  as theme 47
"Mrs. Wetherbe's Quilting Party" (Cary) 309
"Le Mulâtre" (Séjour) 136
Munro, George 265

"The Murders in the Rue Morgue" (Poe) 382
Murray, Judith Sargent 25, 101, 110, 166
My Days and Nights on the Battlefield (Coffin) 259
"My Kinsman Major Molineux" (Hawthorne) 28,
    296
"My Visitation" (Cooke) 76
Les Mystères de la Nouvelle-Orléans (Testut) 137
mysteries, urban 73, 137–9, 181, 183–5, 187,
    291–2
Mysteries and Miseries of New York (Buntline) 291
Mysteries of Boston (Bradbury) 291
The Mysteries of New Orleans (Reizenstein) 137–9
The Mysteries of Paris (Sue) 73, 183
Mysteries of Philadelphia (anon.) 139
"The Mystery of Marie Roget" (Poe) 290

Nabokov, Vladimir 229
Napoleon 333
Narrative of Arthur Gordon Pym (Poe) 321
Narrative of James Roberts 441
*Narratives of the Sufferings of Lewis and Milton
    Clarke* 441
The National Era (periodical) 396
national songs 9–10
nationalistic literature 7–19
nationhood
  and ethnic origins 52–6, 57–63
  melting-pot of national culture 124–30
  national narratives 7–19, 330–41, 434–44
  pastoral ideals 287–8
  and racial politics 57, 170–5, 365–77, 394
  and religion 56–8
  and slavery 57
  somatic analogies 217
Native Americans
  abjection of subjectivity 174
  Catherine Brown's memoir 358–60, 362
  Cherokee controversy (1829) 14
  Cherokee Nation 356–64
  and children's fiction 251
  conversion to Christianity 357, 358–62
  education 357, 358–62
  Iroquois Confederacy 14
  and white identity 357
Native Americans, as theme
  in de Bautée 137
  in Bird 14
  in C. B. Brown 4, 354
  captivity narratives 342–52
  in Child 12–13, 14, 55, 84, 251, 437

in Cooper 12, 13, 28, 55–6, 436–7
in Crèvecœur 54
dislocation 353–64
in Ellis 269–72
in Hall 390–5
in Hawthorne 11–12
imperial adventure fiction 185
in Irving 10–11
miscegenation 13–14, 84–5, 138, 251, 436–8
Native American memoirs and histories 14–15
in Richardson 141
in Sedgwick 13–14, 55, 354–8, 437
in Simms 14
in Stephens 256, 267–9, 437
nature
  attitudes to 287–8
  Sedgwick on 353–4
  Thoreau on 295
  see also rural life
Nature (Emerson) 295, 432
Neal, John 15, 230
"Nelly's Hospital" (Alcott) 259
Nelson, Dana 339, 354
Neville, Morgan 400–1, 402
"The New Adam and Eve" (Hawthorne) 296
New Criticism 132
New England
  attitudes to 352–64
  see also Puritans
The New England Primer 356
A New England Tale (Sedgwick) 352–8
New Harmony, Indiana 68
New Historicism 132
A New Home, Who'll Follow? (Kirkland) 307, 396
New Orleans
  publishing in 136
  as setting 137–9, 139–40
New York
  Child on 295–6
  Fern on 293–4
  Foster on 73, 290
  guidebooks 289
  Lippard on 73, 181, 188, 290, 323
  Whitman on 298–9
New York, as setting 290, 291, 297
  urban mysteries 182, 183–4, 187
New York: Its Upper Ten and Lower Million
    (Lippard) 73, 181, 188, 290, 323
New York Above Ground and Under Ground
    (Foster) 290

New York by Gaslight (Foster) 73, 290
New York in Slices (Foster) 73
New York Manumission Society 104
Newbery, John 250
The Newsboy (Smith) 293
newspapers
  non-English 133, 135–6
  penny papers 290, 316, 320
  see also individual newspapers by name
Newton, Sarah Emily 146
Nick of the Woods (Bird) 14
Noel, Mary 202–3
non-English-language fiction 131–43
The Non-Slaveholder (periodical) 208
Nord, David Paul 88
The North American Review 10
Northup, Solomon 242–5
Notes on the State of Virginia (Jefferson) 66, 239,
    302
Nott, Josiah C. 57, 370
novels *see* fiction
Noyes, John 246
Nussbaum, Martha 33

O Guarani (Alencar) 140
The Oasis (ed. Percival) 359
*Observations on the Principles and Methods of Infant
    Instruction* (Alcott) 254
Occom, Samson 358
O'Connor, Flannery 402
O'Hara, Daniel 67
"On the Equality of the Sexes" (Murray) 110
Oneida 275
Oomo (Melville) 425
Optic, Oliver 256, 259
Ormond (C. B. Brown) 55, 114–15, 123, 166, 318
Ossian 333
O'Sullivan, John L. 17, 38
Other
  and identity 170–1
  and miscegenation 437
  as theme 4, 54–5
  see also race
Otter, Sam 429
Our Nig (Wilson) 45, 69
Owen, Robert 68

Pablos, Juan 87
Padua, medicine at 219
Paine, Thomas 102, 123

Pamela (Richardson) 21, 33, 121, 301
pamphlet novels 264
Panentheism 353
paper production 121
"The Paradise of Bachelors and Tartarus of Maids"
     (Melville) 240, 299
The Parent's Assistant (Edgeworth) 250
Parker, Theodore 95, 370
Parley's Magazine 257
Parrington, Vernon 381
The Partisan (Simms) 15, 379
Parton, Sarah Payson Willis *see* Fern, Fanny
pastoral themes 301–12, 335–40
Pateman, Carole 111, 112
The Pathfinder (Cooper) 12
Paulding, James Kirke 10, 330–5, 338–40
Paulding, John 421
"Pauline's Passion and Punishment"
     (Alcott) 187–8
Paxton Riots (1763–4) 151–2
Peabody, Sophia 241
Pearce, Roy Harvey 345
Der Pedlar (Rupius) 139
"Peeps from under a Parasol" (Fern) 294
A Pen-and-Ink Panorama of New-York City
     (Mathews) 73, 289
Pequod War 251
Percival, M. J. 359
periodicals
   abolitionist 47, 255, 378, 396
   for children 256–7
   see also individual periodicals by name; newspapers
persistence of authors, reasons for 2–4
"Peter Harris" (Cary) 307–9
Peter Parley (Goodrich) 250
Peterson, T. B. 187
Petter, Henri 413
Phelps, Elizabeth Stuart 72
Philip, King (Metacomet; Indian chief) 15
"Philip of Pokanoket" (Irving) 10–11
Phillips, Walter C. 315
Philosophy in the Bedroom (de Sade) 25
phrenology 276
physiognomy, and moral character 162–6, 220
Pierre (Melville)
   on cities 299
   genealogical motifs 52, 53
   legal aspects 237
   politics and incest 28, 77
   sensational elements 188

The Pilgrim's Progress (Bunyan) 20, 91, 249
"The Pioneer" (Hall) 393–4
The Pioneers (Cooper)
   conclusion 81
   legal aspects 231, 236–7
   on marriage 437
   as national narrative 12
   race 12, 55–6
   rural themes 304–5
Pise, Charles Constantine 93–4
"The Pit and the Pendulum" (Poe) 57
plantation novels 15–16, 46–7, 366, 369–71,
     374–5, 437
The Planter's Northern Bride (Hentz) 46, 366,
     369–71, 374–5, 437
Playing in the Dark (Morrison) 173
Playing Indian (Deloria) 357
Plea for the West (Beecher) 57
Poe, Edgar Allan
   on American arrogance 17
   and Bird 381–2
   on Catholicism 57
   gothic/sensational aspects 177, 319–22
   on influences on American nationhood and
     culture 129
   and the law 230
   life 319–20, 386
   on literary nationalism 9
   on Longstreet 403
   sensational elements 188
   and sexuality 77, 78
   and slavery 322, 380
Poe, Edgar Allan: WORKS
   "Berenice" 321
   "The Black Cat" 320, 380
   "The Cask of Amontillado" 230, 320
   detective tales 289–90
   Dupin tales 290
   "Eleonora" 321
   "The Fall of the House of Usher" 77, 321, 380
   "The Gold-Bug" 380, 382
   "How to Write a Blackwood's Article" 320–1
   "The Imp of the Perverse" 320
   "Ligeia" 78, 321
   "The Man of the Crowd" 188, 289–90
   "The Man That Was Used Up" 129, 380
   "The Murders in the Rue Morgue" 382
   "The Mystery of Marie Roget" 290
   Narrative of Arthur Gordon Pym 321
   "The Pit and the Pendulum" 57

"The Psyche Zenobia" 320–1
"Some Words with a Mummy" 17, 382
"The System of Doctor Tarr and Professor
    Fether" 380, 382
"The Tell-Tale Heart" 230, 320, 380
The Poetical Literature of the West
    (collection) 397–8
Poets and Poetry of the West (collection) 398
politics
    American hatred of monarchism 25–6
    Democratic Party 33–4, 67
    early American fears of democracy 21–8
    literary influence 128
    Paulding's writings 333–4
    as theme 23–9, 31–3
    and women 45–7
    Young America movement 38
    see also democracy
Polk, James K. 17, 441
Poovey, Mary 192
population 274
Porter, Carolyn 432
Porter, Roy 220
Porter, William T. 402, 406, 408
Portland Magazine 267
Postl, Karl 139
The Power of Sympathy (W. H. Brown)
    on deception 109, 162
    on female education 104
    pastoral themes 303
    political aspects 23–9
    sources 81
Praed, Rosa 389
The Prairie (Cooper) 12, 55, 305–6
Precaution (Cooper) 413
Prentice, George D. 388
Prince, Oliver Hillhouse 404
The Prince of the House of David (Ingraham) 92
printing industry *see* publishing and printing
    industry
prize competitions, for stories 181
Prodigals and Pilgrims (Fliegelman) 237
Protestants and Protestantism
    anti-Catholic fiction 56–8, 93, 141
    Catholics, attitude to 275
    and children 249–50
    fiction, attitude to 89–92
    reform movements 275
    religious fiction 56–8, 92
    religious publishing 87–9

Sunday School movement publishing 252
    see also Calvinism; Puritans; Unitarianism
Proud, Robert 151–2
"The Psyche Zenobia" (Poe) 320–1
publishing and printing industry
    development 87, 88–9, 119–24, 180
    dime novels 264–6
    East's predominance over West 388–9, 397–8
    importation of British books 121–2
Puritans
    and children 249–50
    and fiction 89
    on New England 361
    and pastoralism 287–8
    and publishing 87
Puritans, as theme
    in Child 12–13
    in Hawthorne 258
    in Sedgwick 13–14, 251
    see also The Scarlet Letter
Putnam, Israel, biography 150–1
Putnam's (literary magazine) 224

The Quadroons (Child) 207
The Quaker City; or, The Monks of Monk Hall
    (Lippard)
    on corruption and vice 73, 278–9, 281, 291–2
    gender and sex 184
    gothic/sensational aspects 323
    imagery 57
    popularity 182, 183
Quaker City Weekly 322
Quakers
    schools 104
    as theme 258, 352
Québec, as setting 141, 142
Questy, Joanni 139–40
Quigley, Hugh 93–4
Quodlibet (Kennedy) 334

race
    American exceptionalism and racial
        politics 57, 170–5, 365–77, 394
    and gender 49–50
    and nationhood 52–6, 57–63
    and Poe 322
    racial "science" 57, 370
race, as theme
    American racial superiority 10–15
    in Brackenridge 55

race, as theme (*Continued*)
  in Brazilian fiction 140
  in Brown (C. B.) 54–5
  in Brown (W. W.) 59–60
  in Child 12–13, 14, 55, 84, 251, 437
  in Cooper 12, 13, 28, 55–6, 436–7
  in Crèvecœur 53–4
  in Hawthorne 59
  in Irving 10–11
  in melodrama 197–200, 201
  in Melville 52–3, 61–2, 168–9, 170–3, 175–6,
    232–4, 365, 366, 372–5, 376–7
  miscegenation 13–14, 84–5, 138, 251, 436–8
  in Paulding 339–40
  in Sedgwick 13–14, 55, 84–5, 354–8, 437
  in Séjour 136
  in sensational fiction 185–6, 187–8
  in Stephens 256, 267–9, 437
  in Stowe 59–60, 366, 367–9, 370–1, 371–2,
    375–6
  in Webb 60–1
  see also African Americans; Native Americans;
    slaves and slavery
Rachel Dyer (Neal) 230
Rachman, Stephen 177
Radway, Janice 132
Ragged Dick (Alger) 41, 70, 255
"Rappacini's Daughter" (Hawthorne) 78, 219–20
Raven, James 121
Realist movement 389, 397
The Rebels (Child) 15
"A Receipt for a Modern Romance" (C. B.
  Brown) 318
Recollections of a Southern Matron (Gilman) 16, 17
"Recovering the US Hispanic Literacy Heritage"
  project 132
Redburn (Melville) 72, 297, 425
Redskins (Cooper) 305
Reed, Rebecca Theresa 57
reform movements and literature 274–84
Reizenstein, Ludwig von 137–9
religion 87–96
  anti-Catholic fiction 56–8, 93, 141
  Asian religions, antebellum awareness of 95
  conversion of Native Americans to
    Christianity 357, 358–62
  Jewish publishing 94–5
  and nationhood 56–8
  Panentheism 353
  Protestant attitude to fiction 89–92

reform movements 275
religious fiction 56–8, 92–4
religious publishing 87–9
Sunday School movement publishing 252
and women 47–8
see also Catholics and Catholicism; Protestants
  and Protestantism; Puritans
Renan, Ernest 8
representation see democracy
Resch, Jack 421
Residues of Justice (Dimock) 237
Retribution (Southworth) 325, 327
Reveries of a Bachelor (Marvel) 82
Reynolds, David S. 73, 179, 322
Richardson, John 141
Richardson, Samuel
  C. B. Brown on 149
  Clarissa 115
  Franklin on 20
  heroines 33
  Pamela 21, 33, 121, 301
  published in America 21, 121
Rickels, Milton 407
A Ride with Old Kit Kuncker (Hooper) 407
Ridge, John Rollin 17–18, 180, 185
Riggs, Stephen, fictional portraits 272
Riis, Jacob 72
"Rip Van Winkle" (Irving)
  and American Revolution 415–16
  British influence 335–6
  as captivity tale 344, 346, 348–9, 351
  on nationhood 10
  on popular politics 22, 438–9
  see also The Sketch-book of Geoffrey Crayon
The Rites of Assent (Bercovitch) 237
river life, as theme 400–2
Roach, Joseph 196
Rob of the Bowl (Kennedy) 334
Robert Graham (Hentz) 371
Robert Merry's Museum (periodical) 257
Roberts, James 441
Roberts, Jennifer Tolbert 38
"Roger Malvin's Burial" (Hawthorne) 11–12
Rogin, Michael Paul 233
Rollo tales (Abbott) 255–6
Roosevelt, Theodore 259
Roper, Moses 16
Rosenheim, Shawn 177
Rosenthal, Bernard 316
Ross, Joel 289

Rousseau, Jean Jacques 252
Rowan, Steven 137
Rowson, Susanna Haswell 81, 103–4, 122, 155, 414
Ruíz de Burton, María Amparo 136
Running a Thousand Miles for Freedom (Craft) 49–50, 207–8, 240, 441
Rupius, Otto 139
rural life
    attitudes to 287–8
    as theme 302–12, 335–40
Rush, Benjamin 223, 302
Ruth Hall (Fern)
    class 59, 71
    conclusion 81
    labor in 245
    melodramatic elements 194
    on women's roles 43–5
Ryan, Mary 292

Sab (de Avellaneda) 140
Sade, Marquis de 25
"A Sage Conversation" (Longstreet) 403, 404
sailing *see* sea and sailing
The Sailor Boy (Optic) 259
Saint-Denis (Testut) 137
St. Nicholas Magazine 257
St. Ursula's Convent (Hart) 141
Saldívar, José David 132
Salem witchcraft trials, fictional portraits 230
Salmagundi (Irving and Paulding) 331, 333
Samuels, Shirley 15
Sánchez-Eppler, Karen 255
Sanders, Judge John 342–5, 346
Sandford, Charles W. 412
Sansay, Leonora 155
satire
    Bird 382
    Kennedy 334
    Poe 129
    sensational fiction as 73
The Scarlet Letter (Hawthorne)
    on cities 296
    on democracy 237
    Hester's character 283
    labor in 241
    legal process in 230–1
    literary allusions to 272
    as national narrative 17–18, 434–5
    Pearl's character 258

persistence of popularity 2
    set-pieces 195
Scheckel, Susan 11
schools *see* education
Schreiner, Olive 389
Scott, Sir Walter 122, 149, 416
sea, importance to Americans 425–6, 427
sea and sailing, as theme
    in children's fiction 259
    in Melville 220–2
    see also Moby-Dick
Sealsfield, Charles 139
Seaver, James 14
Secret History (Sansay) 155
Sedgwick, Catharine Maria
    on American Revolution 15
    as children's author 251, 254
    on indigeneity 353–8
    on marriage 81, 83, 111
    on race 13–14, 55, 84–5, 354–8, 437
    see also Hope Leslie
Sedgwick, Eve Kosofsky 318
seduction, fiction's encouragement thereof 160–2
seduction novels 80–1, 161–5
    Brown (C. B.) 114–15
    Brown (W. H.) 23–9, 104, 109
    Lippard 184
    and melodrama 192–7, 198–200
    Rowson 103–4
Séjour, Victor 136
Sekula, Allan 164
Self-Raised (Southworth) 240
sensational fiction 73, 179–90, 290–2, 314–29
    distinction from gothic 315–17
    see also melodrama
sensational psychology 184
sentimentality
    as diffuser of social conflict 71
    dime novels 267–9, 272
    sentimental fiction 179–80, 245–7, 257, 325–7
    urban novels 292–3
    see also Hentz, Caroline Lee; *The Lamplighter*; *Little Women*; *Ruth Hall*; Southworth, E. D. E. N.; *Uncle Tom's Cabin*; *The Wide, Wide World*
serial fiction 181, 198, 263–4
sermons 87–8
Seth Jones (Ellis) 256, 269
sexuality
    miscegenation 13–14, 84–5, 138, 251, 436–8

sexuality (*Continued*)
  and reform movements 276–7
  sexual discipline 76
  and slavery 83–4
  as theme 75–85
  and urban mysteries 183, 184
The Shame of the Cities (Steffens) 72
Shaw, Lemuel 233
Shell, Marc 133
Sheppard Lee (Bird) 381–6
A Short Account of Algiers (Carey) 155
Shreve, Thomas 388
"Sidi Mehemet Ibrahim" (Franklin) 155
Sigourney, Lydia 254, 257
The Silent Partner (Phelps) 72
Silliman, Benjamin 417
Simms, William Gilmore 14, 15, 16, 369,
  378–9, 381, 386
Simpson, David 120
Simpson, Lewis 21
Sinclair, Upton 65
Six Months in a Convent (Reed) 57
"A Sketch of American Literature for 1807" (C. B.
  Brown) 149–50
The Sketch-book of Geoffrey Crayon (Irving)
  British influence 10–11, 154, 335–7
  class 69
  conservatism 331–2
  on popular politics 438–9
  Scott's influence 416
  see also "The Legend of Sleepy Hollow"; "Rip
    Van Winkle"
Sketches of Ancient History of the Six Nations
  (Cusick) 14
"Sketches of the History of the Carrils and Ormes"
  (C. B. Brown) 153
Skinner, P. H. 293
slave narratives
  Clarke 441
  Craft 49–50, 207–8, 240, 441
  Douglass 16, 42, 48, 106, 212, 242
  familial dispossession in 245
  Grimes 16
  Jacobs 45, 69, 106, 204, 237, 242
  labor in 240, 242–5
  Northup 242–5
  overview 16, 106
  Roberts 441
  Roper 16
  vs. national narratives 440–3

slave narratives, fictionalized 204–15
  Crafts 81, 83, 84, 204–5, 208–15
slave revolts 16, 168–70, 378
slave revolts, as theme
  Bird 385
  in Delany 188
  Douglass 16, 42, 48, 69, 443
  in Melville 3, 57, 168–9, 170–3, 175–6
The Slave's Friend (periodical) 47, 255
slaves and slavery
  abolitionist movement 378–9
  abolitionist periodicals 47, 255, 378, 396
  and American nationhood 440–3
  anti-slavery societies 276
  and build-up to Civil War 367, 368
  Compromise Bill (1850) 17, 57, 367
  Dred Scott decision (1857) 57
  education 104, 105–6
  and identity 126–7
  Kansas–Nebraska Act (1854) 57
  legal texts about 234–6
  literacy 105, 210, 244
  as living death 177
  and marriage 83–4
  Missouri Compromise (1820) 9
  and nationhood 57, 170–5, 365–77, 394
  and Paulding 339
  racial "science" 57, 370
slaves and slavery, as theme
  abolition literature for children 255
  in Alcott 188
  in Bird 380–6
  in Crèvecœur 54
  in Cuban fiction 140
  in *Dred* (Stowe) 234–6, 237, 366, 368–9,
    371–2, 375–6
  in Hentz 366, 369–70, 370–1, 374–5
  in Kennedy 338
  in Klauprecht 139
  in Lippard 323–4
  in Melville 52–3, 61–2, 168–9, 170–3, 175–6,
    232–4, 365, 366, 372–5, 376–7
  memoirs and autobiographies 16
  passing 204–15
  plantation novels 15–16, 46–7, 366, 369–71,
    374–5, 437
  in Poe 322, 380
  in Reizenstein 138–9
  sensational elements in anti-slavery novels 188
  sexuality 83–4

in Simms 379
in Southworth 310, 327
in Stowe 59–60, 366, 367–9, 370–1, 371–2, 375–6
in Strubburg 139
in Testut 137
see also *Clotel*; race; *Uncle Tom's Cabin*
"Slaves in Algiers" (Rowson) 155
Slotkin, Richard 339
Smith, Adam 38
Smith, Anthony D. 8
Smith, Carl S. 237
Smith, Elihu Hubbard 317
Smith, Elizabeth Oakes 293
Smith, Samuel Francis 10
Smith, Sydney 10
Smith-Rosenberg, Carroll 43
Smollett, Tobias 121
Snelling, William 389, 390, 392
social order 274–5
    conservative defenses of 332–40
    social regulation, and the gothic 175–8
    social unrest 65, 67
social theory, stadialist 301–4
social welfare, and women 47–8
socialism, utopian 67–8, 275
    fictional portraits of communities see *The Blithedale Romance*
society, works about 69
The Soldier Boy (Optic) 259
Solger, Reinhold 139
Sollors, Werner 53, 139
Some Adventures of Simon Suggs (Hooper) 406–7
Some Thoughts Concerning Education (Locke) 252
"Some Words with a Mummy" (Poe) 17, 382
Sommer, Doris 140
A Son of the Forest (Apess) 15
"Song of Myself" (Whitman) 18, 298
songs, patriotic 9–10
Soulier rouge (de Bautée) 137
Sousa, Antonio Teixeira e 140
South, as theme
    in Kennedy 338
    plantation novels 15–16, 46–7, 366, 369–71, 374–5, 437
    in Southworth 310
    see also New Orleans; slave narratives; slaves and slavery, as theme
South African fiction 389
Southern Literary Messenger (periodical) 380, 381

Southwest, as setting 181–2, 186, 187, 324, 400–10
    Old Southwest humor 402–9
Southworth, E. D. E. N.
    gothic/sensational aspects 186–7, 324–7
    and the law 228, 231–2, 237
    life 325
    and melodrama 191–2, 197, 198–200
    publisher 187
    rural themes 310
    on slavery 310, 327
    treatment of women 81, 325–7
Sowed by the Wind (Kellogg) 391
Spanish-language literature 134–6, 140
Sparhawk, Edward V. 412
Sparks, Jared 9
Spengemann, William 131–2
Spillers, Hortense 84, 132
The Spirit of the Times (newspaper) 402, 406, 408
The Spiritual Voyage (Botsford) 91
Spofford, Harriet Prescott 344, 346, 349
The Spy (Cooper) 15, 411–24, 437–8
The Spy Unmasked (Barnum) 413
stadialist social theory 301–4
Stanley, Amy Dru 110
Stansea, Jamie 369
Stansell, Christine 293
Steffens, Lincoln 72
Stephens, Ann Sophia 185
    Malaeska 256, 263, 267–9, 272, 437
stereotyping (printing process) 88
Stern, Julia 24
Sterne, Laurence 121
Stevens, John 155
Stockbridge, MA 355, 357–8
Stoddard, Elizabeth 81
Stone, Lucy 102
The Story of Jack Halyard (Cardell) 251
The Story of Margaretta (Murray) 166
The Story of the Whistle (Franklin) 250
story papers 181, 263–4
Stout, Harry 87–8
Stout, Janis 299
Stowe, Harriet Beecher
    and Catholicism 57
    and class 69
    on democracy 369
    and democratic heroes 34–5
    first editor 388
    and the law 228, 234–6, 237

Stowe, Harriet Beecher (*Continued*)
  and melodrama 191–2, 194, 197–8
  and national narratives 17–18
  and race 59–60, 366, 367–9, 370–1, 371–2,
    375–6
  on theater 194
  on women's role 46
Stowe, Harriet Beecher: WORKS
  Agnes of Sorrento 57
  Dred 234–6, 237, 366, 368–9, 371–2, 375–6
  The Key to Uncle Tom's Cabin 234
  see also *Uncle Tom's Cabin*
Streeby, Shelley 375
Strubburg, Friedrich 139
Sue, Eugène 73, 183
suffrage movement 102
Suggs, Simon (Hooper character) 405–7
Sunday School movement 252
Sundquist, Eric 376
Sut Lovingood (Harris) 407–9
Swallow Barn (Kennedy) 15–16, 331–2, 334,
  337–8
"The System of Doctor Tarr and Professor Fether"
  (Poe) 380, 382

"Taking the Census" (Hooper) 406
The Tales of Peter Parley (Goodrich) 250
Tallmadge, Benjamin 421
"The Tell-Tale Heart" (Poe) 230, 320, 380
temperance movement and literature 255, 276,
  279–82
Ten Nights in a Bar-Room (Arthur) 255, 279–80,
  280, 281, 282
Tenney, Tabitha 104, 152, 161–2
La Terre paternelle (Lacombe) 142
Testut, Charles 137
Thomas, Brook 233, 237
Thomas, Frederick 388, 389
Thompson, E. P. 194
Thompson, George 73, 183–4, 185
Thoreau, Henry David
  on labor 239, 240, 242
  and Mexican War 17
  and national narratives 17–18, 126
  on reform movements 276
  and religion 95
  on self-made men 41
  see also *Walden*
Ticonderoga (Cushing) 15
Tocqueville, Alexis de 37, 82, 240

The Token and Atlantic Souvenir (ed.
  Goodrich) *182*, *420*
Tomc, Sandra 320
Tompkins, Jane 2, 91, 197, 235, 246, 267, 381
Tonnewonte (Hart) 141
tradition, as theme 331–40
"Traits of Indian Character" (Irving) 10–11
Transcendentalism 95, 241, 254, 295
Treadwell, Daniel 88
trials, legal, fictional use 229–33
trickster theme 214
Trollope, Frances 38
Trowbridge, John Townsend 259
Troy Female Academy 98, 101–2
Truth, Sojourner 49, 50, 106
Tucker, Beverley 16
The Turn of the Screw (James) 260
Turner, Nat 105, 169, 378
  fictional portraits 368
Tuscarora see Cusick, David
Twain, Mark (Samuel Langhorne Clemens)
  and dialect writing 35
  on Harris 408
  influences on 34, 402
  and male bonding 77
  see also *The Adventures of Huckleberry Finn*
"'Twas the Night before Christmas" (Moore) 336
Twelve Years a Slave (Northup) 242–5
Two Pictures (McIntosh) 240, 245
"Two Visits" (Cary) 309
Tyler, Royall 119–20, 155, 162, 288
Typee (Melville) 425
Types of Mankind (Nott and Gliddon) 57

Uncle Remus series (Chandler) 368
Uncle Tom's Cabin (Stowe)
  children in 258
  class 69
  conclusion 236
  critiques of 276
  gender 46
  heroes 34–5
  imagery 57
  The Key to Uncle Tom's Cabin 234
  legal aspects 228, 235, 237
  literary allusions to 272
  literary reactions to 369
  melodramatic elements 191–2, 194, 197–8
  as national narrative 17–18
  race 59–60, 366, 367–8, 371, 375

religious elements 92
sales statistics 368
sentimental and sensational elements 188
sexuality 84
Unitarianism 95, 353
The United States and England (Paulding) 333
urban novels and themes 287–300
  early industrial novels 72–3
  Lippard 290, 291–2, 323
  urban gothic 318
  urban mysteries 73, 137–9, 181, 183–5, 187,
    291–2
  see also The Quaker City; or, The Monks of Monk
    Hall
US–Dakota Conflict, as theme 269–72
US–Mexican War (1846–8)
  as theme 181–2, 186, 187, 324
  writers' attitude to 17

Van Buren, Martin 334, 335, 382
Van Cortlandt, Gen. Pierre 421
Van Evrie, John 370
Van Wart, Henry and Sarah 415
Van Winkle, C. S. 335
Varela, Félix 134
Venus in Boston (Thompson) 73, 184
Vesalius, Andreas 219
Vicinus, Martha 191, 201, 202
Victor, Metta 179, 185
Le Vieux Salomon (Testut) 137
Views of Christian Nurture (Bushnell) 254
Views of Manners and Society in America
  (Wright) 69
Villaverde, Cirilo 140
Violet (Greeley) 293
The Virginian (Wister) 339
voice, Melville's use 35–6

WACOUSTA (Richardson) 141
Wald, Priscilla 174
Walden (Thoreau)
  on gender roles 41–2
  Irish influence 126
  on labor 239, 240, 242
  as national narrative 17–18, 126
  and urbanism 295
Walker, Cheryl 15
Walker, David 106
"Walking" (Thoreau) 295
Wall Street 297

Wallace, Lew 92
war fiction
  Civil War 258–9
  King Philip's war 12
  Pequod War 251
  US–Mexican War 181–2, 186, 187, 324
  War of 1812 15
War of 1812 141, 419
  as theme 15
Ward, Artemus 271
Warhol, Robyn 197
Warner, Sam Bass, Jr. 288
Warner, Susan B. *see The Wide, Wide World*
Warren, Mercy Otis 159
Washington, George
  and American Revolution 422
  biographies 9, 334, 335
  fictional portraits 15, 32, 150–1, 324, 415,
    418, 437–9
  and Irving 334, 335
  as national symbol 438, 442–3
  rhetorical devices 48
Washington, Madison 16, 48
Washington and His Generals (Lippard) 324
Watt, Ian 38
Watts, Edward 120
Watts, John 88
wealth, children as creators and consumers 260
Webb, Frank J. 60–1
Webster, Daniel 60, 324
Webster, Noah 9, 22, 47
Webster's Dictionary 9, 55
Weems, Mason Locke 9
Weinauer, Ellen 49
Welby, Amelia 395
Welter, Barbara 43
Wenska, Walter 42–3
West
  cultural marginality 388–9, 397–8
  local writers 388–99
West, as setting 180, 182, 185, 303–11, 339–40,
    388–99
  dime Westerns 262, 266, 267–72
West of Everything (Tompkins) 267
Western Literary Journal 388
The Western Monthly Magazine 395
Wexler, Laura 375
whaling industry 426–7, 427–8
  as theme 425–33
What I Saw in New-York (Ross) 289

Wheeler, Edward 266
Le Whip-Poor-Will (Bouis) 137
Whiskey Rebellion (1794), as theme 65, 153
The Whistle (Franklin) 250
White, Lucia 295
White, Morton 295
White, Richard 392
White-Jacket (Melville) 220–2, 241, 425
Whitefield, George 88
Whitman, Walt
  on cities 298–9
  on gothic/sensational fiction 315
  and nationalism 18, 435, 436
  and temperance 280–1
  and Young America movement 38
The Whole Booke of Psalmes 87
The Wide, Wide World (Warner)
  drop in popularity 2–3
  family in 245, 246–7, 257
  heroine 269
  melodramatic elements 194
  religious elements 92
  treatment of women 47, 81
Widmer, Edward L. 38
The Widow Rugby's Husband (Hooper) 407
"The Widow's Hope" (painting; Joy) *182*
Wiegman, Robyn 221
Wieland (C. B. Brown)
  deception in 166
  on democracy 4, 176–7
  gothic/sensational aspects 176–7, 318–19
  and Jefferson 120
  legal aspects 228, 229–30
  publishing history 123
  race 54, 66
  sexuality in 77
  as work of historiography 151–2
"The Wife" (Irving) 111
Wilkins, William Woods 317
Willard, Emma 98, 101–2
Williams, Cecil 386
Williams, Linda 191, 198
Williamson, Dr. Thomas, fictional portraits 272
Wilson, Edmund 408
Wilson, Harriet 45, 69
Wimsatt, Mary Ann 16
Winans, Robert 21, 119
Winthrop, John 14, 287, 299
Wirt, William, biographies 334
Wise, Isaac Meyer 95

Wister, Owen 339
Wollstonecraft, Mary 112, 114, 115
women
  advice manuals 43, 47, 253
  and captivity narratives 345–6, 347–8
  cities' threat to virtue 291
  education 98, 100–4
  and frontier life 395–6
  and labor 48, 101, 245
  literacy 88
  magazines 267–9
  and male death anxiety 321
  and male identity 42
  and marriage 79–83, 109–15
  motherhood 47, 252
  and politics 45–7
  and religion 47–8
  and sensational psychology 184
  and sexuality 76, 78, 81
  and social welfare 47–8
  suffrage movement 102
  symbolism in sensational fiction 183, 184, 186
women, as theme
  in C. B. Brown 112–14, 317
  in dime novels 267–9
  in melodrama 192–3, 195–7, 197–200
  roles 42–50, 71, 101
  in Sedgwick 14, 251
  in Southworth 81, 325–7
  in urban novels 292–3
  see also gender; marriage; seduction; seduction novels
"Women's Right to Labor" (Dall) 48
Wood, Gordon S. 23, 65
Woodcraft (Simms) 16, 369
Wordsworth, William 33
Wright, Frances 38, 69, 246

Xicoténcatl see Jicoténcal

The Yemassee (Simms) 14, 379, 386
Young America movement 38
The Young Christian (Abbott) 254
The Young Wife (Alcott) 43
The Youth's Companion (periodical) 257
The Youth's Emancipator (periodical) 255
Youth's News Paper 257
The Youth's Temperance Advocate (periodical) 255

Zamora, Lois Parkinson 132